RAINCOAST
CHRONICLES

FIFTH FIVE

RAINCOAST CHRONICLES

FIFTH FIVE

With contributions by
Jean Barman, Rick James, Peter Robson,
David Conn and Judith Williams

HARBOUR
PUBLISHING

Harbour Publishing Co. Ltd.
P.O. Box 219, Madeira Park, BC, V0N 2H0
www.harbourpublishing.com

Dust jacket illustration by Gordon Miller
Printed and bound in Canada
Printed on 100% recycled and FSC®-certified paper

Harbour acknowledges the support of the Canada Council for the Arts, the Government of Canada, and the Province of British Columbia through the BC Arts Council.

Library and Archives Canada Cataloguing in Publication
Title: Raincoast chronicles fifth five / with contributions by Jean Barman, Rick James, Peter Robson, David Conn and Judith Williams.
Names: Barman, Jean, 1939- contributor
Description: Includes index.
Identifiers: Canadiana (print) 20240407385 | Canadiana (ebook) 20240407431 | ISBN 9781990776939 (hardcover) | ISBN 9781990776946 (EPUB)
Subjects: LCSH: Pacific Coast (B.C.)—History. | LCSH: Pacific Coast (B.C.)—Social life and customs.
Classification: LCC FC3803 .R34955 2024 | DDC 971.1/1—dc23

Dust jacket: *Gastown, 1885* was meticulously created by maritime artist Gordon Miller based on his research of insurance plans and other documents of the era. In 1885, the little town of Granville, affectionately known as "Gastown" after its first saloon owner "Gassy Jack" Deighton, was a collection of wooden buildings along Water Street on the south shore of Burrard Inlet. In the foreground is Sullivan's store, and between it and the Granville Hotel are a Chinese store, a laundry and Blair's Terminus Saloon. Beyond is the telegraph office, the jail, two dwellings and the Deighton Hotel. Black's Butchers, George Black's store and the new and original Sunnyside Hotel are opposite, with Maple Tree Square at the end of the street. *Senator* is moored at Sunnyside Hotel's wharf, *Robert Kerr* is anchored offshore, and a steel barque is loading lumber at Hastings Mill.

Table of Contents

HOW TO ADD A NEW WORD TO THE BC LEXICON

Howard White

The idea to start a magazine devoted to coastal BC history came to me some time in the early 1970s. My partner, Mary, and I were publishing a community newspaper in Pender Harbour, where I had spent the latter part of my childhood, and I had been filling in some of the spaces left vacant by cancelled ads by doing historical features based on interviews with elderly neighbours. These stories proved to be much more popular than the usual weddings and funerals we covered, and I had a lot more fun writing them— but there was only so much space it was decent to give to woolgathering about the past in a publication supposedly dedicated to news. This planted the seed for a magazine that would have more space for pipe-dreaming and more relaxed deadlines. When the government of Trudeau *père* came up with a scheme to keep young people off the streets by giving them grants to pursue their dreams, we applied for one to start a BC history magazine. To our amazement, we received $12,000 from the Local Initiatives Program—which had to be spent entirely on wages of not more than $400 a month, all within the next year. No allowance for printing bills.

We were gobsmacked. Our newspapering was entirely self-taught and we had no idea how to go about putting together a magazine. By sheer chance, on the way back from collecting the LIP cheque I picked up a fast-talking hitchhiker who quickly determined I had $12,000 burning a hole in my pocket and announced he was an experienced magazine designer. The crazy thing is that he actually was. His name was Clayton "Cal" Bailey and he would go on to a distinguished career as a photographer and filmmaker, but at that moment he was sowing wild oats on the BC coast. He not only took charge of the magazine's production, he originated the flamboyantly visual, sepia-toned look that became the magazine's trademark. Cal was also a good encourager, not to say butt-kicker, and I wonder if that first issue would ever have got to press if not for his constant prodding.

With Cal taking care of production, I was left to ponder the contents of this new wonder. I really hadn't given the matter much thought, beyond doing verbatim transcriptions of stories from some colourful local old-timers. But I had bounced around from Garibaldi to Palmer Bay to Nanaimo to Nelson Island to Pender Harbour since I was born, following my parents from one small resource community to another, and the coast was in my bones. I knew the stories, and I knew that most of them had never been told. And that was what interested me—the stories of the place. It bugged me that BC didn't have much of a literature, and when people thought about Canada, they thought about the Arctic and the Prairies and the Maritimes but never about my part of the country—or at least not in any way that the people who lived there recognized. In setting out our credo in the first editorial, I wrote, "If BC has any real identity problem, it is like that of the Canadian nation. It stems more from the diversity than the lack of character among its people…What we hope to do by starting ths [sic] magazine is to put just some of that character on display."

I had no grounding in history—I had studied writing and literature at college—and I was more interested in capturing the spark of coastal experience than in documenting dull facts. From the first I was convinced that a big part of the story was Indigenous, and the cover story of the first issue was about traditional West Coast whaling, as it was originally conducted in dugout canoes with bone-tipped spears. That first issue covered the waterfront, from coastal steamer stops like Pender Harbour to well-adapted Métis pioneers, from the glory days of rum-running to prehistoric petroglyphs.

It was an instant hit. We had printed 3,000 copies, against expert advice, and sold them all almost overnight. By the end of 1972 we had another issue with more of the same and sold 5,000 of it. Issue three, a special issue on early logging, ran to 10,000. By the time we reached issue five, those copies were all gone, so we decided to take a page from *Foxfire Magazine* and reprint all five in a single bound volume. Their collection was a *New York Times* bestseller and ours didn't quite do that well, but it went through 11 printings and counting. Fast-forward 52 years and here we are publishing our fifth quintuplet—*Raincoast Chronicles Fifth Five*. In it, award-winning historian Jean Barman details the life of a pioneer whaler and saloon keeper, "Portuguese Joe" Silvey. Maritime writer Rick James explores shipwreck mysteries and the courage of old towboaters. *Raincoast Chronicles 22*, edited by David Conn, records the contributions of doctors, deckhands and conservationists who have devoted their lives to the betterment of the coastal community. Judith Williams's *Raincoast Chronicles 24* traces the Schnarr family's pioneering life in isolated Bute Inlet—complete with pet cougars. Collectively, these works celebrate the adventurous spirit of BC's coast and demonstrate that we're nowhere close to running out of stories.

So how did we do with that brash vow that we were going to catch the elusive butterfly of BC coast identity, and place it on display? Some of the answer is contained in that word: Raincoast. We invented that word. I well remember the final throes of putting the first issue to bed and still grappling with the problem of what to call it. Scott Lawrence—a Roberts Creek poet I had persuaded to try his hand at prose—had once volunteered on a co-op radio project in Vancouver called RadioFreeRainforest and suggested we somehow work "rainforest" into the title. That appealed to me as a counterfoil to the tourism monicker for our area—"Sunshine Coast"— which I considered false advertising. We got as far that night as "Rainforest Chronicles," but I was unhappy projecting such a land-based image, since so much of the story I hoped to tell would be on and of the sea. We turned out the lights late that night still without a consensus title, but when I woke up the next morning there it was shimmering before me: RAINCOAST CHRONICLES. I suppose it's possible somewhere somebody put those two words together— "rain" and "coast"—before we did, but if so, they kept quiet about it and we never heard of it. But after we did it, a lot of people heard of it. It struck a note for the kind of authentic image of coastal life that people were hungering for, and the kind of down-to-earth stories and visuals in the magazine filled in the picture. Before long there were Raincoast theatres, boats named Raincoast this and that, at least one other publishing venture called Raincoast, Raincoast Custom Canned Salmon and even a popular snack called Raincoast Crackers. The name became so ubiquitous most people assume *Raincoast Chronicles* just tuned in on the fad and refuse to believe we actually originated the term. I guess that proves something.

The Remarkable Adventures of
"Portuguese Joe" Silvey

JEAN BARMAN

H A R B O U R   P U B L I S H I N G

Dedicated to Portuguese Joe's great-great-great-grandsons Kyle and Cole Silvey for asking me to tell the story, and to Portuguese Joe and his family for making the story possible in the first place:

Joseph Silvey, 1828–1902

Khaltinaht/Mary Ann, c. 1845–c. 1872

Kwahama Kwatleematt/Lucy, c. 1857–1934

Elizabeth, c. 1867–1945

Josephine, c. 1872–1930

Domingo, 1874–1941

Mary, 1877–1941

Joseph, 1879–1940

John, 1882–1907

Tony, 1884–1967

Manuel, 1886–1916

Clara, 1889–1893

Andrew Henry, 1890–1966

Lena, 1895–1957

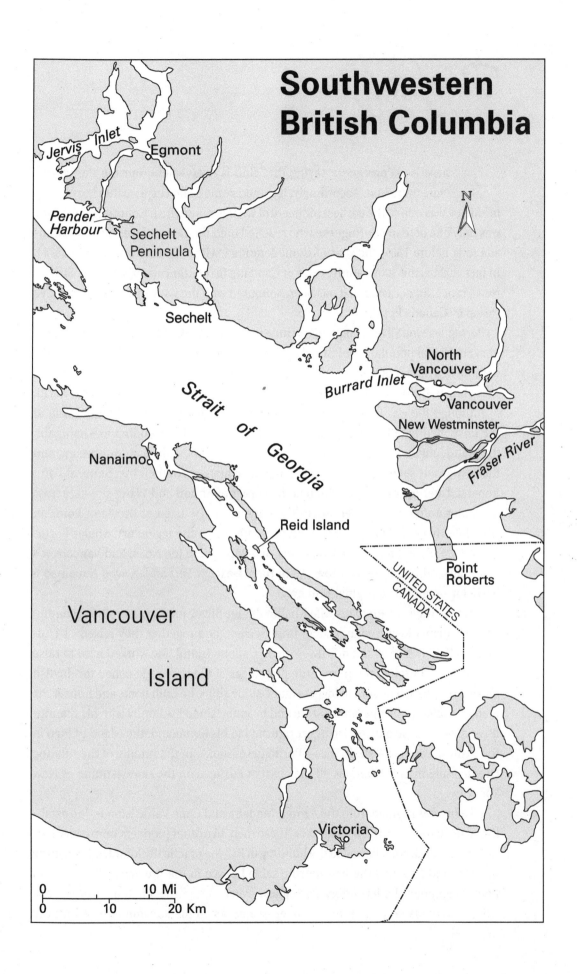

Southwestern British Columbia

Jervis Inlet

Egmont

Pender Harbour

Sechelt Peninsula

Sechelt

North Vancouver

Burrard Inlet

Vancouver

New Westminster

Strait of Georgia

Fraser River

Nanaimo

Reid Island

UNITED STATES
CANADA

Point Roberts

Vancouver

Island

Victoria

0   10 Mi
0   10   20 Km

Preface

There is a Portuguese saying that God is everywhere, but the Portuguese were there first. Accordingly, it should come as no surprise that Portuguese Joe Silvey was one of the earliest pioneers of what is now British Columbia. Joe Silvey was only one of many Portuguese who reached both the east and west coasts of Canada long before 1867, the year of Confederation (British Columbia joined in 1871). In fact, 2004 is the 300th anniversary of Canada's first letter carrier, Pedro da Silva of New France, an occasion that has been honoured with the issue of a commemorative stamp by Canada Post.

Portuguese Joe Silvey sought his fortune in the gold rush of 1858 at a time when the non-aboriginal population of British Columbia exploded from about 1,000 to 20,000 or more in a matter of months. Victoria, a sleepy town of about 400 people, became a sprawling tent city overnight, filled with gold seekers from every corner of the world.

Although Joe was unlucky in his search for gold, he did find a beautiful wife in the unspoiled paradise that would become Vancouver. His wedding to Khaltinaht, the granddaughter of the legendary Chief Kiapilano, took place at Musqueam, and the newlyweds set off in a canoe piled high with blankets to their first home at Point Roberts. Later Joe opened a saloon at the corner of Abbott and Water streets, across the street from Gregorio Fernandez's general store. He lived at Brockton Point, in what later became Stanley Park, with other pioneers: the legendary whaler Portuguese Pete (Peter Smith); Joe Gonsalves, aka Portuguese Joe No. 3; and Vancouver's first police officer, Tomkins Brew. All of them—except Fernandez, who remained a bachelor—married aboriginal women.

After the tragic death of his wife Khaltinaht, Joe Silvey found yet another beautiful wife, Kwahama Kwatleematt (Lucy) from Sechelt, and together they raised 11 children on Reid Island off the northwest tip of Galiano Island. Joe worked hard to raise his family and protect them from the prejudices of the times. He fished for dogfish and herring, which he sold to loggers and visiting ships, he built boats and houses, he planted orchards, he operated a store and he entertained his family with his mandolin and Portuguese dances. He never returned to his homeland, the island of Pico in the Azores, aka the Westerly Isles—Portuguese islands in the middle of the Atlantic Ocean, more than 1,000 miles off the coast of Portugal on the same latitude as New York City.

Like his countrymen from the Azores, Madeira and Cape Verde islands, Joe established deep roots in British Columbia. These men, like other pioneers from every corner of the world, contributed to the building of BC. Joe practically founded the fishing industry and obtained the first herring seine licence in the province. His Brockton Point neighbour, the legendary Portuguese Pete, started the whaling industry; Joe Gonsalves of Madeira built the first deep-sea docks on the Sunshine Coast with the help of the "black" Azorean, Joe Perry; John Silva of Cape Verde, later of Gabriola Island, planted what may have been the province's first apple orchard on Mayne Island; John Enos (Ignacio) of the island of Santa Maria in the Azores, the first European settler at Nanoose Bay, helped build the bridges of Nanaimo. In Victoria, Joseph Morais owned and operated a hotel, restaurant and miners' exchange in 1861. The Bittancourt and Norton brothers, from Sao Miguel and Flores islands (Azores), respectively, developed dairies, coal mines and quarries on Salt Spring Island.

Now, for the first time, the respected historian and professor Jean Barman gives us a very human glimpse of the life of one of these pioneer builders of British Columbia, Portuguese Joe Silvey. She traces his adventures, his fortunes and misfortunes through the stories told by his children and their descendants. In this very personal, heartwarming monograph, she brings one family to life, thereby providing us with a better understanding of the untold lives of hundreds of other early pioneers whose contributions and sacrifices made British Columbia what it is today.

—Manuel A. Azevedo
Vancouver

Introduction

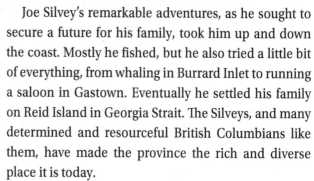

Portuguese Joe Silvey was born in the Azores, a Portuguese possession in the middle of the Atlantic Ocean. In the 1850s he came to British Columbia and decided to stay. At that time the gold rush attracted many thousands of men hoping to get rich quick. Most of them left in disgust almost as soon as they came, but not Joe. He fell in love with Khaltinaht, a Musqueam and Squamish woman, but she died just as they were starting their family. Joe then married a Sechelt woman named Kwahama, with whom he raised 10 children to adulthood.

Joe Silvey's remarkable adventures, as he sought to secure a future for his family, took him up and down the coast. Mostly he fished, but he also tried a little bit of everything, from whaling in Burrard Inlet to running a saloon in Gastown. Eventually he settled his family on Reid Island in Georgia Strait. The Silveys, and many determined and resourceful British Columbians like them, have made the province the rich and diverse place it is today.

The Portuguese Joes of the past are not easy to know. Most of us remember our grandparents, or at least something about them: we can picture them in our minds and we may have tucked away some letters they wrote. We are far less likely to know much about our grandparents' grandparents. They may have been illiterate, as Joseph Silvey was, or found reading and writing uncomfortable. Their lives survive mainly as stories that have passed down through the generations.

Family stories are about belonging. Each one is unique, but all of them are also parts of larger stories. Portuguese Joe has hundreds of descendants across British Columbia and beyond, each of whom is fortunate enough to have "genes" or inherited characteristics that come from him. He is part of them every day of their lives, and so are the stories that have been passed down to them. It is through the stories they have to tell, and are willing to share with others, that we can glimpse Portuguese Joe's extraordinary adventures. By doing so, we come to understand a bit better who we are as British Columbians and Canadians.

In the Azores

For as long as he could remember, young Joseph Silvey had heard stories about places far away from his island home in the middle of the Atlantic Ocean. Joe lived on Pico, one of nine islands that together are known as the Azores.

More than 400 years before Joe was born, ships from Portugal landed on the Azores and the islands were claimed for Portugal. The men and women who settled in the Azores made their living mostly by farming and fishing. They brought their way of life from the "mainland," as Portugal came to be known. All of them adhered to the precepts of the Catholic Church, and they took large families for granted. Men were responsible for supporting their wives and children with their labour, while women held sway in the home. Women were to respect their menfolk, and children their parents and all others older than themselves. Azoreans maintained such a traditional peasant lifestyle despite growing contact with outsiders, mainly explorers and merchants of many different countries who sailed between Europe and North America and stopped over in the Azores to get supplies. The stories these visitors told about the places whence they came and where they were heading were part of the folklore of Joe's childhood.

It was not easy for Joe's parents to make a living for their family. Pico Island is just 42 kilometres long and 15 kilometres wide, and has at its centre a huge volcano (Pico means "point" in Portuguese). The volcano, known as Pico Alto, or "high peak," towers 2,330 metres above the water. The only arable land on the island is a small rocky strip along the shore, at the foot of Pico Alto. Long before Joe was born, Pico Islanders

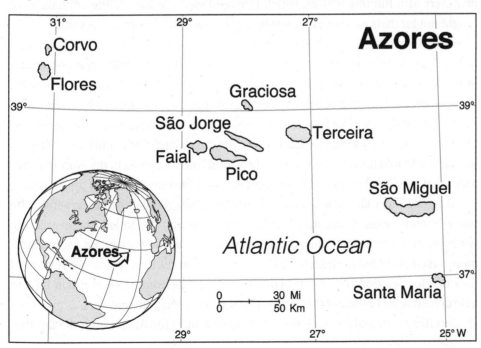

In the late 1830s, Pico Islanders began hunting the whales that migrated past their island. © Copyright New Bedford Whaling Museum

gathered the loose stones and made fences to mark out the boundaries between their hard-worked plots. Most families grew potatoes as a subsistence crop, ensuring that they would have something to eat during the winter. Some pastured cattle on the slopes of the volcano. Lower down, others grew figs to be sold or grapes for wine, but many more depended on the sea.

Pico Island families had fished for generations. When Joe was a child in the 1830s, they were also hunting whales, which migrated past the island. The animals were caught not for their meat but for their blubber, which was boiled for its valuable oil.

Ships in search of whales had begun to arrive in the Azores from the northeastern United States years earlier, when Joe's father was a boy. World whaling was dominated by the Americans, who had their principal home port at New Bedford, Massachusetts, about 80 kilometres south of Boston. The ships stopped to pick up supplies at Horta on nearby Faial Island, and took on crew as needed. Men wanting jobs came from all over the Azores, especially from the poorly endowed Pico Island. Joe's father, or perhaps it was his uncle, told him about sailing all the way to North America in the *Morning Star*, a ship that regularly hired young men from Pico and the other islands of the Azores.

Young Joe Silvey also heard stories about a Scottish grandfather. In one version he was a seaman named Simmons who owned his own ship and sailed wherever in the world profit was to be had. Indeed, records show that a whaling captain named Simmons sailed out of Massachusetts during the mid-19th century. In another version of the story, Joe descended from one of the soldiers sent by Britain to Portugal in 1808 to help drive out the French after they invaded during the Napoleonic wars. Some of the soldiers liked Portugal so much they settled there or in the Azores after the fighting was over. Joe once told his daughter that his mother's, or possibly his father's, Scottish ancestry was the reason why he was lighter-complexioned than most Portuguese. Elizabeth remembered her father as being "fair haired, with rosy cheeks." According to another descendant, "When Silvey men grow a beard, it's red." In family lore, Portuguese Joe has blue eyes and his son Henry has "greeny blue" ones. This inheritance may explain why Joe used the name Joseph Silvia Seamens when taking up land in British Columbia.

Going to Sea

Joe Silvey was 12 years old when he began to have his own adventures. His father decided the time had come for Joe and his older brother João, or John, to learn to make a living, and the next time he went whaling, he took the boys with him. Joe left Pico Island and his mother behind forever. They likely never even wrote to each other. Joe had not gone to school and never learned to read and write. These activities were not considered necessary in a society where the land and the water gave people a livelihood. For Joe, the sea provided a means of survival time and time again.

Young Joe soon found out that whaling was no easy job. A typical ship's crew consisted of 25 to 30 men: the shipmaster and his mates; a cook; artisans including a carpenter, cooper and blacksmith; several boatsteers; and seamen. Many of the recruits taken on in the Azores worked as boatsteers. They were the men responsible for navigating the small double-ended open whaleboats, about eight metres long, from which whales were harpooned.

Once whales were sighted—"there she blows!"—the ship manoeuvred to within a kilometre or two of the pod and the men launched the three or four whaleboats, which were slung on the sides of the ship. Each boat had five oarsmen, one of whom was the boatsteer. Once one of the boats got close enough, its boatsteer harpooned the whale. The harpoon was attached to the whaleboat by a line, which was played out as the hooked animal thrashed about in the water. The oars were brought into

Countless men from Pico left behind their island to better their prospects aboard American whaling ships that stopped in the Azores to pick up supplies. © Copyright New Bedford Whaling Museum

Whaling was a dangerous business, especially for the boatsteers, who were responsible for navigating the small double-ended whaleboats and harpooning the giant animals.
© Copyright New Bedford Whaling Museum

the whaleboat and the boatsteer took charge as the boat was pulled through the water behind the whale, sometimes for hours on end. When the hooked whale grew tired enough that it could be approached by the whaleboat, the men stabbed the animal to death with spears or lances. The harpoon was then reeled in, and the line was used to tow the carcass to the ship.

Killing the whale was only the first step. Now the crew had to boil the carcass in order to release the oil from the blubber just beneath the skin. The carcass was tied up on the side of the ship and the blubber was stripped off, cut in pieces and melted in huge iron cauldrons. This was hazardous work that required several days of intense labour by all aboard. As soon as more whales were sighted, the process began all over again.

Capturing whales was dangerous, so perhaps it is not surprising that Joe's father died of heart trouble while on board ship. According to the story Joe told his children, his father called his two sons to come to his side. He "was sitting in a big chair, and he told the boys to be good boys when they grew up, and then he just sunk down in the chair and was dead, while they were with him." Shortly thereafter, Joe's brother drowned.

Joe Silvey was left all alone in a tough occupation in which men were sometimes valued less for their hard work than for their willingness to endure poor working conditions and low wages. Azoreans were seen as men who would put up with such hardships. Two-thirds of the ship's profits went to the businessmen who had furnished the money for the trip, and one-third went to the workers on board. Each man received a predetermined portion of the net profit. Workers were only paid at the end of a voyage, which might last two or three years or even longer. By the 1840s, the average crew member's cut was considerably less than what he could earn in a Massachusetts factory. Whaling entrepreneurs believed that foreigners, particularly those who were illiterate and unskilled, as were most young Azoreans, were less likely to desert when another opportunity beckoned at some port of call.

Such prejudice made men like Joe restless. The whaling historian Elmo Hohman has described how, during the years when Joe was young, "more and more the intelligent and ambitious young American refused to go to sea,…least of all on a whaler." According to Hohman, "as the better types of Americans forsook the forecastles, their bunks were filled by criminal or lascivious adventurers, by a motley collection of South Sea Islanders known as Kanakas, by cross-breed negroes and Portuguese from the Azores and the Cape Verdes, and by the outcasts and renegades from all the merchant services of both the Old World and the New." He blamed the decline of whaling on the "ignorance, incompetence, and general inefficiency" of such men. In fact, the decline resulted from the discovery in 1859 in Pennsylvania of ground oil, which was a good substitute for whale oil and much more economical to harvest and process.

No wonder many recruits from the Azores and elsewhere who manned the hundreds of whaling vessels roaming the world's oceans each year began to seek other employment. Young men like Joe Silvey did not think of going home: Pico Island was unable to provide a good living for all of its population, and crop failures made conditions even worse during the mid-19th century. The island's main food crop was hit by potato blight, and a grape disease severely reduced wine production. Joe did not have much incentive to return home.

Whaling was not a good living, but it did offer opportunities to begin anew. When an American vessel returned to its home port, usually in Massachusetts, the employees were paid off and discharged. Members of Joe's family, including a sister, are said to have settled there. As well, some crew members jumped ship. By the time gold was discovered in 1849 in California, ships were travelling long distances in search of whales and men were dropping off without permission in ever greater numbers. On the way to whaling grounds in the Arctic waters of the Pacific Ocean, ships stopped for supplies at San Francisco and other west coast ports, and men slipped away—so many of them, both officers and crew, that the practice became almost commonplace.

Joe was one of these men. He decided the time had come to explore the opportunities these faraway places might hold. By now he knew some English and was confident about fending for himself in a strange land. On one of his trips, as the story has come down through Joe's family, the ship on which he was working got in a serious accident off the Pacific coast and had to put into port to make repairs. Joe and five other crew members, all Portuguese, seized the opportunity to slip away.

Once a whale was killed, its carcass was lashed to the side of the ship and its blubber stripped off for processing.
© Copyright New Bedford Whaling Museum

British Columbia-Bound

Just as it is not possible to know Joe Silvey's precise name or his birth year, we cannot know how or when he got to British Columbia. What repeats itself time and time again in the stories that have passed down through the generations is that he "jumped ship" with "five other Portuguese men" and did so from "a whaler." In one version of the story he landed in 1849 in California; in another, in 1852 at the fur-trade post of Fort Victoria in the British colony of Vancouver Island. In the 1901 census Joe Silvey gave the date as 1860, which seems most plausible: not only did it come from him, but in all versions of the story, Joe and his fellow deserters began searching for gold almost immediately. They might have done so first in California, where a gold rush was in full force from 1848. It is more likely they headed up the Fraser River to take advantage of the gold rush that began there in 1858 and gradually moved north to the Cariboo. As to the location at which the men slipped away, it might have been Victoria, but it might also have been, as one story suggests, Point Roberts, a tip of land on the British Columbia mainland that lies within the boundaries of the United States.

Wherever the Portuguese men came ashore, it is very likely that the first news they heard was about the fabulous riches to be had from gold. Perhaps they deserted because they had already heard the news. Ever since gold was discovered in California, stories had spread about how easy it was to get rich quick. In the spring of 1858, news got out about discoveries on the Fraser River. Later that year the mainland became a separate British colony named British Columbia. Men came from California and from all over the world in search of their fortunes. Now, very likely, Joe and his friends were among them.

In one version of the stories in Joe Silvey's family, the Portuguese newcomers got a hold of a dugout canoe and headed up the Fraser River. They paddled past the rough mainland capital of New Westminster, past the long-time fur-trading post of Fort Langley, and on they went. They might have gotten as far as Yale at the entrance to the Fraser Canyon. Perhaps they were already gold mining when they were warned that the local Natives wanted to get rid of newcomers, whom they considered to be trespassing on their land. The young Portuguese men became convinced that they

In one version of Portuguese Joe's story, he jumped ship with five other men at Point Roberts, acquired a dugout canoe and paddled up the Fraser River to join the gold rush. Later, he returned here with his bride.
BC Archives PDP02617

The walled fortress of Fort Langley would have been one of the few European settlements Portuguese Joe encountered after his arrival in the colony of British Columbia. BC Archives PDP 1891

were about to be attacked, and they did not want to be killed. So they took their canoe back down river as fast as they could, back to where they had jumped ship.

When the men were almost back at Point Roberts, as one story goes, some Musqueam appeared on the bank of the Fraser River. Joe and the others were convinced that their time had come: they would not be able to escape twice with their lives. Then they realized the Musqueam were not hostile. Indeed, they were beckoning the newcomers toward them. Grand Chief Kiapilano of the Squamish, who lived farther north on the north shore of Burrard Inlet, was visiting his mother's people at Musqueam. He stood in the middle of the crowd to welcome the men ashore. They were tired and in desperate need of something to eat, and they decided to take a chance. Much to their relief, the Musqueam treated them kindly, gave them food and invited them to stay the night.

The next morning, as the men continued on in their canoe across the Georgia Strait to the gold-rush boomtown of Victoria, Joe kept thinking about the friendship extended by the Musqueam people. After he had earned a bit of money and gotten some supplies together, he returned to Point Roberts. He built himself a cabin and opened a little store for passing miners such as he himself had been, not so long before. Intent on becoming self-sufficient, Joe also farmed, fished and hunted.

Compared with the austere living conditions of Pico Island, Point Roberts must have seemed a paradise.

It may have been at about this point in time that Joe Silvey began to be known as "Portuguese Joe." Perhaps it was his accent but it was also very likely his pride in his ethnic origins. Throughout his life, Joe remained very proud of being Portuguese.

Finding a Wife

Joe Silvey settled in Point Roberts and found himself a wife. In fact, that may have been his reason for returning. The granddaughter of Chief Kiapilano and of his wife Homulchesun from Musqueam had caught Joe's eye. Khaltinaht was the child of Kiapilano's son Kwileetrock and a woman named Sukwaht, whose brother Sam Kweeahkult was chief at the Squamish village of Whoi Whoi on the south shore of Burrard Inlet in what would become Stanley Park. Khaltinaht lived at Musqueam with her grandmother's people. Joe later told his eldest daughter that "she was a pretty girl with dark eyes, and hair down to her middle; large deep soft eyes." He soon discovered that she felt as kindly toward him as he did toward her.

Joe's eldest daughter Elizabeth shared her father's story about how he asked his prospective grandfather-in-law for Khaltinaht's hand in marriage. "Mother and Father were out in a canoe, and then afterwards Father said by signs, to the old chief, Chief Kiapilano, that he wanted my mother for his wife, and could he have her; all by signs. Then the old chief said, by signs, that he could; waved his hand and arm with a motion signifying to 'take her.' He motioned with his right arm and waved, quickly, upward and outward."

In a landscape dominated by thick vegetation and towering trees, Europeans like Portuguese Joe Silvey quickly adopted the canoe as a means of transportation. For Joe, a canoe ride with the lovely Khaltinaht sparked the romance that led to their marriage. Vancouver Public Library Special Collections VPL 12706

The marriage ceremony respected aboriginal practice. "In those days they were married under Indian law...The old Chief, Chief Kiapilano, took my father, and the chief of the Musqueams took my mother, and the two chiefs put them together...They had canoes and canoes and canoes, all drawn up on the beach, and a great crowd of Indians, and they had a great time. They had a lot of stuff for the festivities, Indian blankets and all sorts of things, and threw it all away; they had a great big potlatch. And, then, they put my mother and father in a great big canoe with a lot of blankets, made them sit on top of the blankets, and then brought them over to home at Point Roberts."

Joe Silvey and Khaltinaht may have been the young couple that a passing gold miner encountered at "Point Roberts, just within the boundary line of American territory," in the fall of 1862. It was commonplace for men of Portuguese descent to be called "Portuguese Joe." There were several such men around Burrard Inlet, so it's impossible to know for sure whether or not this was our Joe Silvey. "Here we met a retired sailor named Portugee Joe, who had gone in for a comfortable existence upon a very small farm, supplemented by the proceeds of his gun and fishing-boat. Joe had taken unto himself a maid of the forest, and had built himself a large snug log-house... There was plenty of room for all of us, whiskey galore, and any amount of

Portuguese Joe and Khaltinaht settled in Burrard Inlet, where he fished for dogfish to support them and she was close to members of her Musqueam and Squamish families. BC Archives A-00978

game and fish to be had for the killing…We had milk and butter too, for Joe managed to keep a couple of cows on his little paddock." The men undertook various hunting adventures together over the next two weeks. "One part of the elk we kept for Joe's household, and his wife set to work to cure the hams."

Going Fishing

Joe wanted more than just a bare living. It was time for another adventure.

More and more newcomers were settling around Victoria and New Westminster. A lumber mill began operating on the north shore of Burrard Inlet in 1863, bringing new opportunities. Not only did settlers have to eat, sawmills needed oil to keep in good condition the saws and other machinery used to cut lumber into wood. Joe thought back to the means of earning a living his father had taught him in the faraway Azores, and he knew exactly how to get both oil and food from the sea. Portuguese Joe went fishing.

On March 4, 1866, a strong tide forced a schooner heading north in Georgia Strait to anchor in Active Pass between Mayne and Galiano islands. There the crew encountered "some Fisher men," one of whom "generally known by the generic name of 'Portugee Joe' visited us." A long conversation ensued, which one of the men on board described in some detail. "Joe had just caught lb 500 of fish—enough for the Westminster & Victoria markets—he sent them up by the [boat] 'Enterprise.' He caught them with double hooked lines but the Dog fish (*anarchias suckleyi*) were very troublesome to him, biting off the hooks." A relative of sturgeon, dogfish were caught not for food but for their oil.

A natural salesman, Portuguese Joe sold dogfish oil to companies such as the Moodyville sawmill, on the north shore of Burrard Inlet, as lubricant for their machinery and skid trails. City of Vancouver Archives, CVA MJ P43

"Portugee Joe," as his name was pronounced by those who knew him, retailed his adventures of the past year. "He told me at first that he had lost $150 by his salmon fishing & on enquiry found that if he had kept them three weeks longer he might have made that sum in addition—a rather amusing way of putting it!" Joe was becoming an astute businessman. "Joe made by his own Confession last summer by salting & smoking salmon more than $2,000. He had caught a shark from the liver of which he had extracted 20 gals of oil."

Settling Down

By 1866 the gold excitement was over. To save money, the two British colonies of Vancouver Island and British Columbia were amalgamated into a single colony named British Columbia. It was men like Joe Silvey, able to do work other than mining, who decided to stay. Portuguese Joe's new life offered him more than he could have found back in the Azores. His success with fishing gave him confidence about what he could achieve with the help of Khaltinaht, who by now also went by the English name of Mary Ann.

Portuguese Joe began to think of settling down. On March 23, 1867, the *British Colonist*, a Victoria newspaper, reported: "Joseph Silva, a native of Portugal, took the oaths…and became a naturalized British subject." According to the story passed down to his grandson, he "was the first Portuguese in Canada to receive British citizenship and was called 'Portugee Joe No. 1' for that reason." It seems likely that this man was indeed our Portuguese Joe. What the declaration meant was that he could now vote and exercise the civil rights available to all other British subjects in this British colony of British Columbia. Very importantly, he could acquire land. Indeed, on the very same

Joe Silvey's resolve to remain in British Columbia became clear the day he chose to become a British subject. His naturalization was reported in *The Colonist*, on March 23, 1867.
BC Archives

Having grown up on an island where land was limited, Portuguese Joe quickly saw the advantages of living in a scarcely populated corner of the world where he could acquire property for little or no money. At left is his request for land at Mary Ann Point, Galiano Island.
BC Archives GR766

day, "Joseph Silva" signed with his *X* a request to preempt 100 acres at "Maryanns Point—Galiano Isl[an]d." Joe named the land—located off Active Pass, where he had anchored a year earlier—after his wife.

One of the reasons Portuguese Joe became proprietorial was his upcoming, or recent, fatherhood. His and Khaltinaht's eldest daughter Elizabeth claimed she was born in 1867, but it may have been a year earlier. There is no question as to the month and day of Elizabeth's birth. "Father told me that I was born on the Fourth of July. It was an American Day, and they were having a celebration at New Westminster." Portuguese Joe was as proud as any new father could be. "Father had a big time that day; treated his friends with brandy, because he had a baby girl, and that was the day I was born." Joe later told his eldest daughter how he had got "a bottle of brandy, a big barrel of beer, and invited the hand loggers." These were the men who cut down trees by hand for the sawmills that now operated on both sides of Burrard Inlet.

Precisely where Portuguese Joe and Khaltinaht were living at the time of Elizabeth's birth is unclear. Not until October 3, 1878, was the Galiano preemption "cancelled for cessation of occupation," but it seems unlikely the family lived there very long, if at all. Joe probably camped there while fishing in Georgia Strait.

The family chose to live on Burrard Inlet. A contemporary who worked at Hastings Mill on the south shore of the inlet described Portuguese Joe as "a fisherman" who had his own house on the beach but not his own landing. Joe used a flat-bottomed sailboat to fish "out in the body of the Inlet, and in English Bay." He landed his catch "just on the shore," "simply on the shore, the best part of the shore he could find." Joe "was a dog fisher, he fished dog fish for oil." A fellow fisherman explained that Joe caught dogfish on a sand bank off of Point Grey. These he took to Deadman's Island just south of Brockton Point. He put them in a "great big kettle" to boil the oil out of them. The oil he sold to a sawmill for "25¢—that was the price—per gallon for the dog fish oil for use on their machinery, or logging skid roads."

Portuguese Joe was ambitious for his young family. He wanted to expand his fishing activities. As a British subject he could acquire land, but that did not mean it would be granted to him. On May 15, 1868, "Joseph Silvy" signed with his mark a letter that began: "Being desirous of starting a fishery at Burrard Inlet I respectfully request that a lease of 20 acres on the Government Reserve inside the first narrows may be granted me (at a small rental) having a water frontage of 20 chains as shewn in the annexed sketch. I shall be prepared to leave at the shortest notice whenever the Government may require the land." The accompanying map indicated that the location was the southern shore of Brockton Point, whose sandy beach was ideal for hauling up fishing boats. Joe was not successful in his request. Officials responded that "it is not considered advisable at present to grant a lease to any portion of this Reserve." The "government reserve" designation for what would become Stanley Park harked back to the first years of the gold rush. The land was set aside so that its heights could be fortified should the mainland colonial capital of New Westminster be attacked by the expansionist United States.

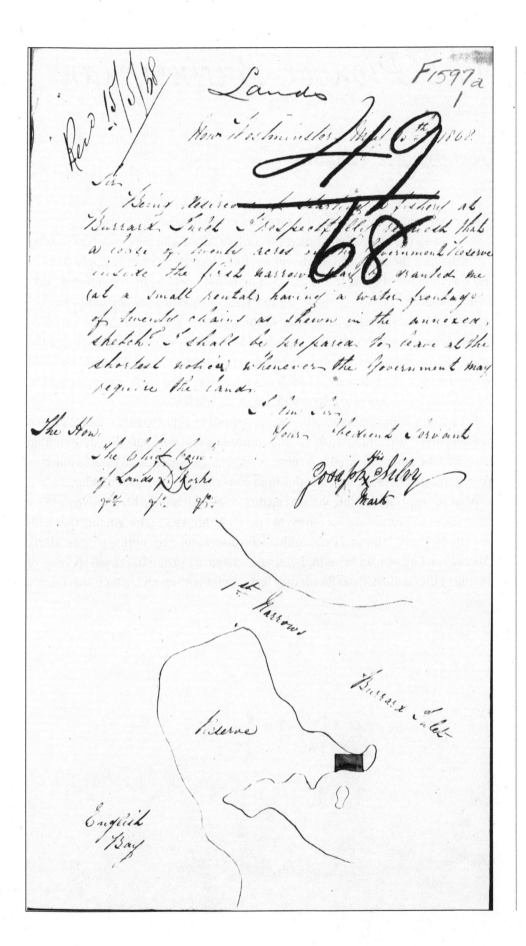

Joe's application to lease fishing grounds on the southern shore of Brockton Point, in what is now Stanley Park, was rejected by government officials who wrote that it was "considered inadvisable" to grant a lease for any part of their government preserve.
BC Archives GR1372

The Pioneer Businessman

Returning to Whaling

Joe was not easily deterred. He set off on a new adventure.

In March 1886, when Portuguese Joe had talked with the crew of the passing schooner about his fishing adventures, he mused about what he might do next. "He was thinking of going into whale fishing in the inlet—as they abounded," said a crew member. "He was going to use rockets." This passing remark indicates Portuguese Joe's considerable knowledge of the industry. The rocket-driven harpoon, sometimes known as the "rocket," contained an explosive device intended to kill the whale, unlike traditional harpoons, which hooked the animal until it could be killed by other means. The technology, which was never very successful, was only then being tried out by a handful of British and American whalers.

It is not surprising that Portuguese Joe was thinking about whaling. Native people had long been harpooning whales as they moved up and down the British Columbia coast, and the profit appeared to be enormous. A single whale could yield as much as a thousand gallons of oil, which at this time was selling for up to 50¢ a gallon.

Whaling was a far tougher job than catching dogfish. It was too big an adventure for one man, even Portuguese Joe Silvey, to take on by himself. So Joe got together with two others, Harry Trim and Peter Smith, who also wanted to capture whales. Harry Trim was an Englishman in his mid-20s, just arrived in Burrard Inlet from six years of mining in the Cariboo. Peter Smith may have been friends with Joe for much longer.

Portuguese Joe and his friends persuaded the legendary Abel Douglas to join them in starting up a small whaling camp on Pasley Island. They used his schooner, possibly the *Kate*, shown here, to tow their catch back to camp.
BC Archives H-02689

Peter was also born in the Azores and, like Joe, was in his mid-30s. They may have jumped ship together and been part of the group frightened off from the goldfields. Considerable trouble was taken during these years to track down and punish deserters, to make them examples and discourage others. It was likely Peter's fear of being caught that caused him to change his Portuguese name to just plain "Peter Smith." Sometimes he was known as Peter the Whaler or Portuguese Pete. Both Harry and Peter married Squamish women.

The three men had a plan. They had seen bleached whale bones lying on the eastern beaches of tiny Pasley Island, located to the west of larger Bowen Island, which was off the north shore of Burrard Inlet. The men knew that Native whalers towed their catch to the nearest shore, so the pods of whales that went up and down Georgia Strait must be passing by Pasley Island. That was where they decided to establish their camp.

Joe, Harry and Peter needed a vessel big enough for whaling, and they had their eye on a schooner captained by Abel Douglas, a Scot from Maine via California. Douglas had been in his late 20s in 1868 when he was enticed north from San Francisco by businessmen wanting to develop coastal whaling out of Victoria. He and his crew whaled quite successfully from Saanich Inlet, not far from Victoria, and the next year he went as far north as a site known as Whaletown on Cortes Island. Abel was ready for a new challenge, and the adventure began.

Abel Douglas's wife Maria Mahoi, whom Joe's daughter Elizabeth recalled as being "half Indian and half Hawaiian," was one of the women who lived at the whaling camp on Pasley Island. Salt Spring Archives

Whaling was a family affair at the Pasley "whaling camp," as recalled by Elizabeth Silvey. "Harry Trim's wife was an Indian; Peter Smith's wife was an Indian; and my father's wife was an Indian; all had little houses, nice little houses, and they built the wharf for the schooner to land. It was a nice bay...they got a lot of oil out of the whales." Abel Douglas's wife Maria Mahoi was, Portuguese Joe's daughter recalled, "half Indian and half Hawaiian." She was also part of the adventure.

Whaling imprinted itself in Elizabeth Silvey's mind. Her description from her memories as a small child makes it clear that the process was very like what it had been a generation earlier, except that the blubber was boiled on land rather than on the ship itself.

> I can remember Capt Douglas's big schooner coming in...I saw them bring one whale in. They were towing it. And all the people looked out and said, "Here they come." And they were towing it. We saw the schooner coming full sail, and they were towing something white. They were coming fast with all the sails. And they were towing this big thing behind the schooner. Yes. And when they turned it over it was black, and when they turned it back again it was white. They had a little wharf, and the schooner docked there; it was piles, small piles, and a pretty good little wharf. And then they had a great big cable as big as my arm; the cable was rope. They lowered the

Opposite top: On Pasley Island the whalers reduced the blubber by boiling it in large vats. The same technique was used by whaling ships at sea. © Copyright New Bedford Whaling Museum

Opposite bottom: Gastown was named after "Gassy Jack" Deighton, a contemporary of Joe's who opened the first saloon on Carrall Street for thirsty millworkers. BC Archives D-07873

Below: Portuguese Joe's daughter Elizabeth vividly remembered how the men used a windlass to haul the whale onto the beach and a "great big knife" to butcher it. As this photograph taken at Kyuquot in 1916 shows, similar methods were still in use 30 years later. BC Archives A-09221

whaleboat; they always packed the whaleboat on the schooner, and when they saw a whale they lowered the whaleboat. And then had a big line, like a cable, and a harpoon. And then, finally, they had a big shed where they had the iron pots, you know, where they boil the blubber, the fat, and they had the harpoon on the whale's head. And then they hauled it up to the shed…They had a big thing (a windlass) right on the shore; edge of the water, and two men kept going around and around, walking around the big thing. And the rope was coming in, and bringing the whale up; it was a slow job. And then they cut the whale up with a great big knife, ready to boil; all the fat. It was all chopped up in squares, and the fat *that* thick [gesticulating to show a thickness of about 12 inches]; it was all fat; just excepting the ribs, very fat.

At the time Joe and Khaltinaht's second child was born, likely in the spring of 1871, everyone was busy whaling. "My father, Peter Smith and Harry Trim, and a Captain Douglas were whaling. Captain Douglas had a schooner and there were some more men." Young Elizabeth never forgot her sister's birth. "When she was born I was taken out of the house by Mrs. Peter Smith and Mrs. Harry Trim. They took me out that night to stay in their house on Pasley Island, and when I came back in the morning there was a baby on the bed; a little baby, and it was Josephine. And I tried to pull it off so as to have it walk with me like a doll, and they told me I could not do that; that it could not walk yet."

The whaling boom was too good to last. The industry collapsed at about the time Josephine was born. Not only were fewer whales turning up, but the price of oil fell—for some 12 years, ground oil had been extracted from sites in the Unites States. Some whaling continued on a smaller scale, but it was no longer the profitable business it had once been.

Keeping a Saloon

Perhaps because whaling was seasonal, or because Portuguese Joe was by nature active and ambitious, he embarked on yet another adventure even before he had stopped whaling. He became a businessman.

Burrard Inlet was a hive of activity, with booming sawmills and a brisk shipping business. The need for a variety of goods and services was growing, and small businesses were springing up all along the south shore of the inlet, near where Portuguese Joe and his family lived. The community was called Gastown, after a saloon owned and operated by John "Gassy Jack" Deighton, a colourful Yorkshire seaman who like so many others had been enticed to British Columbia by the gold rush. He arrived at Burrard Inlet in September 1867, and a contemporary, Thomas Fisher, recalled how "I helped him build the first saloon, which was a little shack of a place [that] stood right on Carrall Street."

Like many other European men, Gassy Jack had a Native wife, and the story goes that on her death he purchased "for a larger price" her 12-year-old niece Whahalia. Perhaps because the exchange did not fit the image he wished to project in the community, he secreted Madeleine, as he called her, "in a little cabin back in the forest, to which he retreated for peace and quietness." Joe's daughter Elizabeth once mused, "I remember her when I was about five years old; gee, she was a pretty lady."

Among the other Gastown businesses was a general store that served both millworkers and local Natives, who could land their canoes on the long float jutting out from the store and trade furs for other goods. The store's owner was another Portuguese man, Gregorio Fernandez, who had come from the island of Madeira. A former

Portuguese Joe opened his saloon, Hole-in-the-Wall (visible at the end of the block), at the corner of Water and Abbott streets. Near the big maple tree was Deighton's bar, while across the street was Gregorio Fernandez's store. City of Vancouver Archives, CVA Dist. P11.1

Cariboo miner, he may have been one of the men with whom Joe Silvey jumped ship. Joe's daughter Elizabeth referred affectionately to Fernandez, who also went by the nickname "Portuguese Joe," as her uncle, although he was not a blood relative. Another of Joe Silvey's children recalled that Fernandez "had gold earrings; I saw them myself; it was an old custom with sailor men."

With Fernandez's encouragement, Portuguese Joe opened a saloon that, like Gassy Jack's down the street, catered to millworkers. The exact periods during which it operated are unclear. Joe got a new licence in January 1870, only to shut his doors in midyear, "owing to the mill being closed." On December 15, 1870, he requested permission to reopen, pointing out to the government official in charge of licensing: "I pay my rent and all government dues. I have built a saloon and paid for the ground and I should like to have my licence the same as before and the property is no account to me without the licence." Although one of his competitors was allowed to reopen, Joe's request was refused because of the "opposition of the agent of the Hastings Mill Company." The new mill manager, who was staunchly religious, considered such activity suspect and did not want any more saloons in operation than absolutely necessary.

At about this time Portuguese Joe got an opportunity to purchase the land on which his saloon stood. The area extending from Hastings Street north to Burrard Inlet and from Carrall east to Cambie Street—officially named Granville, although still informally known as Gastown—was surveyed and the survey was registered on March 1, 1870. Colonial regulations stated that town land, once surveyed, had to be offered for sale at auction. A land sale was held on April 11. Gassy Jack bought his property and Gregorio Fernandez purchased the land at the northwest corner of Water and Abbott streets on which his general store stood. Portuguese Joe did not follow suit. Perhaps he was out whaling; more likely the business climate was stagnant. Not until a year later, on May 9, 1871, did Joe buy Lot 7 of Block 2, located at the southeast corner of Water and Abbott streets, for $100. By then he must have reopened his saloon, which he called the Hole-in-the-Wall.

Two Worlds of Childhood

Joseph Silvey's ability to move between the fishing traditions he had absorbed from his childhood and the entrepreneurial ethos of Burrard Inlet was impressive. Equally so was the capacity of his eldest daughter Elizabeth to manoeuvre between the very different worlds of her parents. Even as an elder she retained vivid memories of both the raw frontier society of her father and the centuries-old aboriginal culture of her mother.

The Silveys lived in a house that Joe built near the saloon, so his business became a part of young Elizabeth's everyday life. "Father always had gold and silver. I've seen it in a little sack; no bills. That was when he had that little saloon in 'Gastown.' I saw it on the counter. And no one would ever touch it. He was putting out the rum; reaching up to the shelf for a bottle, and the men were all standing drinking in his saloon, and the money—he was making change. Them days they had gold and silver, no bills." She remembered all the bottles on the shelf, "and there was a counter. It was on the Gastown beach, and the street was just planked over." Her adopted uncle was a favourite. "I remember running over to Joe [i.e. Gregorio] Fernandez's store across from our place—just a few steps—nearly every day. The men who came into the bar room used to give me 10¢, or 50¢, and I used to run over to Joe's store and get candy. Joe Fernandez had a great big cordwood stove in the store; I used to stand by it when I went over to get candy from Joe."

Elizabeth described the special events that took place in that tiny community hugging the south shore of Burrard Inlet. "They used to have lots of fun at Christmas and Halloween in Gastown. The men used to dress up and put on long white whiskers, and at Halloween put on masks. Oh, yes, I remember it; it used to be delightful for the children." There were dances or at least musical evenings, at which "Father played the violin, guitar, and the mandolin."

When the Silveys lived in Gastown, they counted among their many friends Joe Thomas, "a full-blood Indian" who married Khaltinaht's sister Lumtinaht. City of Vancouver Archives, CVA Port P392

Elizabeth's mother Khaltinaht was especially close to her sister Lumtinaht, also known as Louise, whom she resembled closely. Lumtinaht married Joe Thomas, recalled as a "full-blood Indian," whereas their half-sister Rowia wed "Navvy Jack" Thomas. John Thomas was another Englishman lured to British Columbia by the gold rush. Having made some money from mining he headed to Burrard Inlet. In 1866, with lumber mills now operating on both sides of the inlet, Navvy Jack started ferrying passengers and their goods between them.

Portuguese Joe's wife Khaltinaht is said to have closely resembled her sister Lumtinaht, whose noble position in her tribe afforded her an honoured role during potlatches at Musqueam and at Whoi Whoi. City of Vancouver Archives, CVA Port P392

Navvy Jack settled his family in a small cottage on the north shore, perhaps to be closer to Rowia's grandfather, Chief Kiapilano. According to his eldest daughter Christine, "he was very fond of gardening and grew tobacco and sugar cane in his garden." For a long time Navvy Jack and his family were the only newcomers in what is today West Vancouver. At the same time, he remained an adventurer, and from time to time he returned to the Cariboo to try his luck once more. Christine told about her father's "good family," who begged him repeatedly to return home, or at least send his children to England to be educated, but he would never forgive his mother for the quarrel that caused him to leave in the first place. Like his brother-in-law Portuguese Joe, Navvy Jack did not look back but rather forward to the possibilities that British Columbia had to offer.

Khaltinaht's aboriginal world became an integral part of Elizabeth's own. Khaltinaht, her sister Lumtinaht and the young child spent much time together. One of the events recalled most vividly by Elizabeth in her old age was a large potlatch that was held in 1870 at Whoi Whoi, the Squamish village of which her great-uncle was chief. Whoi Whoi was located at what is now Lumberman's Arch in Stanley Park. An early Methodist minister described Whoi Whoi during these years: "As a side trip I frequently took a rowboat or canoe to the First Narrows to visit a small band living in Stanley Park where the Lumberman's Arch now stands... The biggest community house there was probably 100 feet long by 40 feet wide. The Indians did not live in separate homes, but in one long community house."

Because Lumtinaht was related to the chief, she played a special role at potlatches. "Lumtinaht was the 'princess' or 'queen' that they had at the potlatches, all over; sometimes at Musqueam, sometimes at Whoi Whoi." Lumtinaht's role was carefully circumscribed. "Before the potlatch started they had a great pile of blankets, and they got a [girl of] 'high' station to sit on it. That was part of the ceremony. To show that they had the blankets, I suppose. She, the princess, was my aunt; my mother's sister... It would be improper to have a common girl sit on the blankets; they had a great pile of them, and a princess sitting on top... The blankets were all in a pile, and the seat on top of them was the seat of honour."

"I was little, but I can remember [that potlatch] clearly," Elizabeth said.

My mother took me to it on her back; she "packed" me to it, and when we got near there were "thousands" of Indians…and I was frightened. I didn't know who gave the potlatch, but I think my grandmother's brother…They held the potlatch in a great big shed, a huge place; the Indians built it themselves long ago…There was no floor; just earth, and the fires were all burning…The platforms were high up, inside, of course, and the chiefs were away up on the platform, and throwing blankets and money down, and those below scrambling for it. Mother took me, on her back, but when they began to dance and throw money about, I got frightened, and ran. I darted through under their legs, in and out in the crowd, and dashed out of the building; I didn't wait for anyone; not even mother; she came after me, and had to take me home; she could not stop at the potlatch because I was so frightened.

Elizabeth was also taken to visit Khaltinaht's grandparents. Chief Kiapilano lived on the north shore of Burrard Inlet at the village of Homulcheson. "He was kind, and nice. I was a little girl then," she remembered. "When I was about three years old…my mother took me over to the Indian houses at Capilano Creek, and there I saw old chief Kiapilano; a great big old man with big legs, and loud voice…and long white hair hanging down over his shoulders; down to his shoulder blades, and the ends used to curl upwards; he was short-sighted." All her life Elizabeth retained fond memories of her great-grandfather.

Turned Upside Down

Portuguese Joe Silvey had worked hard since coming to British Columbia. By 1871, when the colony of British Columbia became a province of the new Dominion of Canada, he could take very real satisfaction in his accomplishments. Joe had a growing family and more than one way of making a living. He was still whaling, he fished, and he owned the property on which his saloon stood. Everything seemed to be turning out right.

Then Portuguese Joe's world turned upside down. His wife Khaltinaht grew ill and died. "She caught cold in her back, I gathered from remarks my father dropped, when my little sister was born," Elizabeth remembered, "and my little sister was less than a year old when Mother died…I must have been about four years old." Khaltinaht told Joe that in death she wanted to be returned to her people, and so it was. "She wanted to be buried at Musqueam, so she was buried there…I remember my mother dying in Gastown, and how her people at Musqueam came for her body, and took it in a canoe for burial at Musqueam."

Joe was devastated. "My father was left with two young children, one unable to walk," Elizabeth said. He could no longer bear to live in Gastown, so "he sold the saloon to some hand loggers."

Starting Over

Now in middle age, Portuguese Joe Silvey started all over again. He retreated to the site at Brockton Point that he had tried, unsuccessfully, to lease for a fishing camp. It is likely that the family already lived there from time to time, perhaps on a seasonal basis, but now they moved permanently. "Father sold out and went to live at Brockton Point," Elizabeth explained. "He put up a house there, near Deadman's Island, facing east." To make a living for his family, Joe returned, at least for a time, to the business he knew best and got a licence to run a saloon at Brockton Point.

The Silveys' new house was not far from Whoi Whoi, where Khaltinaht's people had their longhouse and where Elizabeth had been taken to the big potlatch from which she ran away. Joe maintained a close relationship with his wife's family, and Elizabeth recalled how "Great-grandfather Chief Kiapilano used to come and camp at Brockton Point; in a tent in front of our house, and I used to see him resting on his bed in the tent." From her perspective as a small child: "He was a great big man with a voice like a microphone on a loudspeaker; he spoke loud. Anyway, that's how it seemed to me; I was little. And he had long white hair; it was bobbed, and white, and he always had a smile. He beckoned to me to come to him, and I would not go, but afterwards I did, and he took me up in one arm, and held me to his breast. Oh, he was a nice man; everyone liked him." According to Elizabeth, "Chief Kiapilano had lots of wives…used to visit them every month." On his visits to Brockton Point, "he had a hunchback slave wife to look after him; I used to visit him constantly in that old tent."

Elizabeth found a friend near her own age at Brockton Point. "Tomkins Brew was living at Brockton Point when we went there; he had quite a nice little cottage; it was about 20 feet or so…on that little bit of clearing right on that little point." He was an Irishman in his mid-30s and worked as the constable and customs collector at Burrard Inlet. Tomkins Brew and his Native wife were the parents of Arthur, who was a little older than Elizabeth.

Devastated by the loss of his beloved Khaltinaht, Portuguese Joe left Gastown and moved with his two young daughters to the small community at Brockton Point, where he built a house just across the water from Deadman's Island.
BC Archives D-04722

Among the Silveys' friends was Ada Guinne, whose French-Canadian father farmed at Marpole and whose mother was Khaltinaht's aunt. Wed to Peter Plant, a French Canadian man, in 1866 at Moodyville, she was recorded as "Burrard Inlet's first bride."
City of Vancouver Archives CVA Port P714

Several other families lived nearby. Peter Smith had settled down in a ménage that included, next door to him, his wife Kenick's father Shwutchalton. According to Portuguese Pete's eldest daughter Mary, he built a house of "old split cedar," put a fence around it and constructed a float that extended out into the water. Johnny Baker was an Englishman who had likely also jumped ship. He and his Squamish wife Tsiyaliya had two sons, Johnny and Willie, and four daughters. Some indigenous Hawaiians, or Kanakas as they were called in the fur trade, lived south of Brockton Point at what was called Coal Harbour. Eihu, Nahanee and the others went by canoe to their jobs at Hastings Mill.

Life on Brockton Point had some practical disadvantages for young Elizabeth. Whereas Arthur Brew attended the small school at Hastings Sawmill, to the east of Brockton Point, Elizabeth was too little to do so. "I never went to the Hastings Sawmill school…but I remember Arthur Brew, son of Tomkins Brew; he was a big boy going to school." All the same, Elizabeth learned a lot of practical skills from her father, including boat building. Thinking back to his early years in the Azores, Portuguese Joe decided that he wanted his own *Morning Star*. "Father built a sloop; I helped him; he built it at Brockton Point. I was only a little girl but I could hold the boards and I could hand him the nails, and could hold something against the other side of the board when he was hammering; put a little pressure on."

With the *Morning Star*, Portuguese Joe could venture farther afield along the British Columbia coast. He must have gone north from Burrard Inlet and even considered settling there, for on May 28, 1872, "Joseph Silvia Seamens" preempted 160 acres on Howe Sound.

Rebuilding a Family

Portuguese Joe's first task in rebuilding his family was to find a wife and mother for his two daughters. "Josephine wasn't a year old; that's why Father got married again," Elizabeth said. "Two little girls and no one to look after them." It is likely that Joe was sailing on the *Morning Star* up Georgia Strait along the Sechelt Peninsula when he met Kwahama Kwatleematt, whose Christian name was Lucy. They were married in Sechelt.

Times had changed since Joe Silvey wed Khaltinaht in the traditions of her people. Missionaries had spent years convincing the Natives that they should be married in the "white" style. Lucy may have been educated by the Oblates, who had ministered at Sechelt since the early 1860s, for she knew how to read and write—unusual skills for a young Native woman at the time.

Lucy was just 15 and Portuguese Joe almost three times her age when, on September 20, 1872, Father Paul Durieu of the Oblate order married them in the Catholic mission church at Sechelt. They were both very properly dressed, Joe in a suit, vest and tie, his handlebar moustache neatly trimmed for the occasion, and Lucy in an elegant dress with her hair demurely pulled back. Lucy's parents, Andrew Kwakoil and Agatha, likely looked on. Elizabeth, who was about five at the time, recalled: "We went up in the *Morning Star*. I wasn't at the wedding; I was too young and small for that, but I was there and saw what was going on, and so was Josephine. Josephine was just a little thing."

Joe's new family returned to Brockton Point for at least part of each year. When he got married, Joe described himself as a fisherman, and he spent much of the time on the *Morning Star*. "He always used to go around fishing," Elizabeth recalled, "and we stayed at home in the house he built; he built a little house." Other times the family went with him. They travelled north up the Georgia Strait to Pender Harbour on the Sechelt Peninsula, across to Vancouver Island and the coal-mining town of Nanaimo and to nearby Newcastle Island, and spent time in "a bay by the lighthouse on Gabriola Island." Joe was coming to know the coast very well.

It was during these years, according to Elizabeth, that Joe Silvey pioneered seine fishing in British Columbia, building on practices he had learned as a young man. "Father taught the Indian women how to knit nets at Brockton Point; taught them how to make seine nets, and then he used to stain the nets in vats, and then they

Unlike Joe's first wedding, which was celebrated with a traditional Native ceremony, his second marriage was recognized by government officials in New Westminster.
BC Archives, Vital Statistics

Joe's second wife was
Kwahama Kwatleematt,
or Lucy, a Sechelt woman
a third his age. They celebrated
their marriage by having their
photograph taken.
Courtesy Jessica Casey

went out on the little bit of sandy beach, facing this way from Brockton Point, and used to catch herrings. One would go away out in the boat with one end, and one away out with the other end, and then they would circle around, and two men on one rope end and two men on the other end would pull the net slowly, slowly, into the sandy beach, and they would get—well, I heard them say there was a ton of herrings in the net, you could see the net coming in with the herring all splashing in it; drawing it up on the beach." Elizabeth remembered that her father was the first man in British Columbia "to have a seine licence to fish," or at least to have "the first herring seine licence." A younger sister recalled, perhaps referring to a later point in time, how "my father Portuguese Joe Silvey used to have gill nets and rent them out to the Indians and every Indian on the coast knew him."

It was important not only to catch the fish, but to make a living by doing so. "They used to put the herrings in barrels, and they used to salt it; they used to sell them to the schooners [which were in port to load spars and lumber]. The schooners used to come in, and get 100 barrels each, and go away; sometimes as much as 150 barrels." Joe used some of the herring for bait to catch dogfish up the coast. One of his grandsons said that Joe went as far north as Cowichan Gap, later renamed Porlier Pass, between Galiano and Valdes islands. Elizabeth recalled his going to "Pender Harbour, where they were fishing for dogfish, and Capt Douglas was there, too, fishing for dogfish.

Portuguese Joe is credited with pioneering seine fishing in British Columbia. His daughter Elizabeth recalled him teaching Native women how to knit nets at Brockton Point. Vancouver Public Library, Special Collections, VPL 54781

And they sold their oil to Nanaimo and Departure Bay [coal mines]." The early Vancouver historian Alan Morley termed Silvey "a prosperous manufacturer of dog-fish oil for the mills and logging camps."

Portuguese Joe worked as a fisherman for wages during part of each year, taking Lucy and the children with him. Two Englishmen, Alexander Ewen and James Wise, were among the first entrepreneurs to use the new tin can technology to export salmon. They opened their first cannery on the Fraser River in 1870. "Ewen and Wise, at Westminster used to call my father the 'net boss' during the summer fishing season; we used to live in the boathouse by Mr. Wise's store in New Westminster," Elizabeth recalled. "Mr. Ewen, the canneryman" once sent for her father, and the family went to New Westminster by rowboat, with a stop along the way at the farm of Quebecer Supplien Guinne to "get some butter and eggs." Guinne's wife was Chief Kiapilano's sister, hence young Elizabeth's great aunt.

Other men living at Brockton Point also fished, including some of the Hawaiians. "You know, there were a lot of Kanakas about, not just one or two, and they would talk in their language; it was queer to hear them, and they would go out where the lighthouse is at Brockton Point and fish with a line." Lucy, Elizabeth's stepmother, took her along to buy vegetables from Eihu's Squamish wife Mary See-em-ia, who "lived down at the little ranch at Coal Harbour," a short canoe ride from Brockton Point. Kanaka Ranch, as it was called, was at the foot of today's Denman Street.

"It was quite a profitable undertaking—fishing," Elizabeth recalled much later. "I remember some of the 'Gastown' men joking about going to give up store keeping and lumbering, and go fishing; there was money in fishing; lots of money in it." Joe Silvey helped to make fishing a viable and attractive occupation in British Columbia.

Whenever the work was over, Joe would return home to his new family at Brockton Point. Joe's first son Domingo was born on August 10, 1874. His daughter Mary was, according to her own recollection, "born in Stanley Park, just across from Deadman's Island, May 24th 1877." She explained how "they used to call me 'the Queen' because I was born on the 24th May, the Queen[Victoria]'s birthday."

All of the children retained special memories of Brockton Point. Mary "used to climb up in the boughs of the Maple tree, and drop little pebbles on people I did not like who passed underneath; used to climb up there, and stay up in the branches all day when they were looking for me to give me a hiding; used to take a pocket of pebbles up there with me." She remembered "Tomkins Brew, and the little Customs office; he had a long beard, and used to nurse me; I did not like him very well." Elizabeth recalled: "Tomkins Brew had an Indian wife; big fine beautiful woman, and he was fond of her. But she got sick, and I can see him yet, with his arm around her neck as she was lying there in her bed; but she did not get better, and she died."

It was not just the families at Brockton Point who visited back and forth. A number of families around Burrard Inlet besides the Silveys consisted of newcomer white men and Native women. For immigrants of British or white Canadian descent who arrived later and saw themselves at the centre of the emerging dominant society,

Portuguese Joe often stopped in Nanaimo to sell some of his dogfish oil to the local coal mines. BC Archives A-04429

In the summers, Joe and his family sometimes lived in a boathouse at the Ewen and Wise cannery on the Fraser River at New Westminster.
Vancouver Public Library, VPL 1788

racial hybridity was inherently suspect, as was anyone of an ethnic background different from their own. Thomas Bryant, the son of an early Methodist minister, replied to a request for information in the 1930s that "I did not know Gregorio Fernandez nor any of their kind—or any of the Portuguese gents."

Likely in part for that reason, a lively social life joined Portuguese Joe and his family with others like themselves spread across Burrard Inlet and on the islands that dotted the strait between the inlet and Vancouver Island. Thanks to Joe's fishing and whaling expeditions, he was so familiar with the coast that it was almost like his hometown, the water its main street. Khaltinaht's sister Rowia and her husband Navvy Jack Thomas lived in what later became West Vancouver. On the property east of Navvy Jack's was William Bridge, described by an early settler of North Vancouver as "an English sailor who had left his ship." Bridge was already living there with his Native wife in 1869 when he preempted 160 acres at the foot of today's Chesterfield Avenue. As well as a "cottage of board and batten with cedar shake roof," Bridge "planted orchard, made little garden, created a pasture for cows, made splendid little farm, and sold milk." Elizabeth Silvey recalled, "I used to play with his children at the north shore, when we went over there."

John Silva had been born at about the same time as Portuguese Joe. According to Silva's descendants, the two men jumped ship together. Silva worked for a time on coastal steamers, and by 1863 was operating a fruit and vegetable store in Victoria. He wanted more, and in 1873 he took up land on Mayne Island. Shortly thereafter he married Louisa, the 15-year-old daughter of a Cowichan chief. The story that has been passed down in the family has John Silva giving his future in-laws "two horses hitched and ready for working—two horses and about three sacks of spuds." This arrangement, like other cross-cultural unions, was difficult at first, as described by Louisa's granddaughter Margaret. "She was really frightened of marriage, you know, how it would be, so she was given part of the boat and she was crying away and my grandfather was kind and gentle and he took her to his log cabin on Mayne Island and Mother said that it was a dirt floor—a log cabin—and Mother said that Grandpa said, 'well, the first thing you have to do, Louisa, is to make a batch of bread because we do not have any bread,' so he got the fire going [and when] she was making that bread she was crying into the dough."

John Silva fished and Louisa bore the children, 10 of them. Like his friend Portuguese Joe, John Silva soon decided that there was no turning back. On June 27, 1876, he took his oath as a British subject, which entitled him to own outright the land on which they lived. A few years later, in the early 1880s, the Silva family moved from Mayne to Gabriola Island because of persistent Native raiding parties on their sheep. According to their granddaughter Margaret, "The Haida Indians kept coming through the passageway and they'd hoot and they'd holler and away they would come and they were a pretty fearful bunch and my grandfather kept sheep and he had goats and he had geese and stuff and these Indians would come through and they'd take about half of his stuff to feed their families—I guess they didn't like to live on fish all the time!—and anyway my grandmother decided, 'I am not living here,' so she said to my grandfather, 'I want to get out of here,' and so she talked him into moving to Gabriola Island."

Among the other Portuguese people who settled nearby were the Bittancourt brothers, John Norton and John Enos. Estalon and Manuel Bittancourt came from the Azores via the Australian gold rush of the early 1850s. Sometime thereafter they persuaded their fellow Azorean John Norton to join them on Salt Spring Island, located west of Galiano where Portuguese Joe had once held land. João Inacio, who simplified his name to John Enos, also came from the Azores. Like the others, he had gone to sea in his early teens. He jumped ship at Boston in 1852 and worked his way west to California, hoping to get rich from gold. He found all the good claims staked, and he made his way north to British Columbia as soon as he got news of the gold rush there. He tells a story of being scared away by Native people at Yale that is so similar to Portuguese Joe's account, it's very possible that they made the trip together. John Enos got work near Nanaimo, took up land a bit farther north at Nanoose Bay in 1863, and married a Songhees woman whom he named Teresa Elisia. Just as the Bittancourts and Norton had done, Enos acquired a reputation as a successful farmer. When Portuguese Joe and his family travelled on the *Morning Star*, they very likely stopped in to visit their countrymen.

One More Adventure

Perhaps it was the visits the Silveys made to families who lived on their own island or bay that inspired one more adventure. Having fished up and down the coast on the *Morning Star*, Portuguese Joe wondered whether a location other than Brockton Point might offer a better life to his growing family. More and more newcomers were settling on Burrard Inlet, bringing with them racist attitudes that were generally accepted whence they had come. Natives were scorned and persons of mixed race denigrated as "half-breeds." Portuguese Joe could recall the "old days" at Point Roberts and Gastown, when everyone was accepted on their merits as opposed to the accident of birth.

Joe's home in what is today Stanley Park was no longer the safe haven it had once been. Even though he was refused permission to lease the land on which his family lived, he and the others had been mostly left alone. But times were changing. During the mid-1870s the federal government, which had taken responsibility for Native people when British Columbia became a province of Canada in 1871, made a big

In 1913 a large wooden "Lumberman's Arch," built for a royal visit to Vancouver, was erected where the village of Whoi Whoi had stood for centuries. City of Vancouver Archives, CVA Arch P40

effort to confine them to reserves. Officials visited the long-time Squamish village of Whoi Whoi, which they preferred to believe had followed rather than preceded the newcomers' arrival. "These Indians have squatted on the Govt. Reserve between Coal Harbor and the First Narrows," wrote the British Columbia Reserve Commission in November 1876. "They have several small cottages but have made little improvement otherwise."

At this point the authorities had no interest in the other families living nearby, but Joe and his neighbours might well have wondered what would happen next. Once again Portuguese Joe Silvey pulled up stakes. He sold his Gastown property, and passed their Brockton Point home on to Gregorio Fernandez's nephew Joe Gonsalves. "I tried to find out if my father sold it to Gonsalves," recalled Elizabeth, "but from what I could learn he did not; he just left it." Fernandez brought his nephew out from Madeira in 1874 to become his heir, for he was ill, and a year later he died. "There was a drunken brawl, or fight, and Fernandez got mixed up in it, somehow, and got a cut on the leg, and gangrene set in; he died. I was a little girl, but I can just remember it. I think he was put in jail at [New] Westminster, and died there." Joe Gonsalves went on to make his living as a fisherman at Brockton Point until 1904. In that year he bought out the general store at Irvines Landing, at Pender Harbour on the Sechelt Peninsula, where some of his descendants still live.

Reid Island

J oe Silvey's destination when he left Brockton Point was Reid Island, located northwest of Galiano Island, where he had once taken up land. About 240 acres in size, Reid Island lies at a crossroads. Immediately to the east is Porlier Pass, which runs between the much larger Galiano and Valdes islands. Thetis and Kuper islands are due west, the Vancouver Island sawmill community of Chemainus is just beyond them, Nanaimo lies to the north and Salt Spring Island lies south-southwest. Reid Island is shaped like an egg with a smaller overlapping egg at its southern end. High tide almost cuts the island in half. A dike was eventually built on the east side where the two "eggs" intersect, the diked area between the overlapping eggs being known as Mud Bay.

Joseph Silvey preempted 160 acres of Reid Island on September 19, 1881. A decade later, on May 13, 1891, his eldest son Domingo applied for "the rest of the Island more or less." Domingo's portion was designated Lots 34 and 36, Portuguese Joe's Lot 35. Father and son each wrote an *X* on the signature line.

Joe was well into middle age when he arrived on Reid Island, but he essentially started over. He built his family a house, around whose windows he ran a grapevine said to have come from Portugal—in spirit, if not literally. The house, set back from the water on the east side of the small egg, was soon complemented by an apple or-chard. On Reid Island the Silvey family continued to expand. To Elizabeth, Josephine, Domingo and Mary were added seven more children, all but one of whom survived into adulthood.

The record of the Silvey children's baptisms, mostly at the Catholic mission to the Penelakut people on Kuper Island, chronicle their arrival. This record also indicates the various ways in which Portuguese Joe's surname was recorded by others as they heard him say it. Joseph was born on October 22, 1879, at Nanaimo, the son of Joseph Silvey and Lucia Cluett from Co-wichan Gap. On April 30, 1882, John was born to Jo-seph Silvy and Lucie of Reid Island. Antonio, known as Tony, was described at his baptism on May 4, 1884, as born 15 days earlier on Reid Island to Joseph Silva and Lucia. Manuel was baptized at the age of two months on November 10, 1886, the son of Joseph Silver and Lucia. Clara Rosa Isabella, aged seven months and the daughter of Joseph Silvey and Lucia, was baptized on October 16, 1889, at home. She died in 1893 on Reid

A map of Reid Island showing how it was developed in the early 20th century.

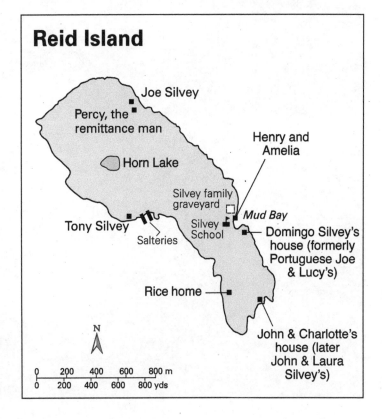

Reid Island

- Joe Silvey
- Percy, the remittance man
- Horn Lake
- Henry and Amelia
- Silvey family graveyard
- *Mud Bay*
- Tony Silvey
- Salteries
- Silvey School
- Domingo Silvey's house (formerly Portuguese Joe & Lucy's)
- Rice home
- John & Charlotte's house (later John & Laura Silvey's)

N

| 0 | 200 | 400 | 600 | 800 m |
| 0 | 200 | 400 | 600 | 800 yds |

Opposite: We owe much of our understanding of Joe's life to his eldest daughter Elizabeth, who shared her recollections with Major J.S. Matthews, Vancouver's first archivist. City of Vancouver Archives, CVA 371-2397

Below: Portuguese Joe's eldest son Domingo, his wife Josephine, and their children Clara, Laura and James. Courtesy Chris Thompson

Island. Andrew Trinidardi, known as Henry, was born on February 13, 1890, on Reid Island. Portuguese Joe's last child, Lena Rose, came along on April 9, 1895, on Reid Island. By then Joe was in his early 60s, Lucy in her late 30s. Portuguese Joe took great pride in his family. According to his daughter Mary, "Father had all our pictures taken; they were in tintypes; he sent them back to Portugal."

Even as children were being born, the eldest left home. Elizabeth wed not long after Portuguese Joe settled his family on Reid Island. She later claimed the marriage had occurred against her father's and her own wishes. Her 19-year-old husband James Walker was, like herself, the product of a cross-cultural union: his father was an American gold miner, his mother a Cowichan woman named Mary Sitkwa Whilemot. Shortly after James's birth, Mary married William Curran, another American enticed to British Columbia by gold. They and their growing family, which eventually totalled seven children, settled down on Thetis Island, where her family lived.

According to Elizabeth: "Mr. Walker kidnapped me; I did not know I was going to be married until I was in the little rowboat; nor did my father. James Walker asked my father if he could have me for his wife, and my father was furious about it; said 'no' that I could not be married until I was 20, and I heard him telling my stepmother that

he did not want me to marry James Walker." All the same, the couple courted. "James Walker, my husband, used to come over and visit me; what they call a boyfriend now; and he asked my stepmother if he could take me out for a boat ride. So I went. I stepped into his boat and he rowed away from Reid Island; his home was on Thetis Island; he kept on rowing, and rowed over to Kuper Island, and we were married by the Rev. Mr. Roberts." Roberts ran an Anglican mission that competed with a Catholic counterpart for Penelakut souls.

Elizabeth explained how "they have it down on this marriage paper that I was 20 years old when I was married, July 15th 1883, at Kuper Island Anglican Church, but they cheated on my age, I was only 16." She described what happened. "The minister said, 'She's not 20; she's just a child,' when we went to be married, but James Walker's stepfather, he said to the minister, 'Yes she is 20,' and the minister said he did not think I was that old, and I was too young, but Curran, that's James Walker's stepfather, he said he had known me since I was a baby, which was a lie because he knew of me only since I went to Reid Island." In old age, Elizabeth bitterly regretted what happened, reflecting that "I had four children, two girls and two boys, before I was 20," her supposed age upon her marriage.

At first Elizabeth lived with her Curran in-laws on Thetis Island. Her husband did odd jobs, sometimes for the Reverend Roberts, whose diary gives a good sense of the life of an itinerant labourer, one of whom was "Jimmy Walker ($1/2$ Breed)." Roberts considered him a kind of superior servant. On October 22, 1883, Roberts "told Jimmy Walker to come to assist in taking off a part of our freight." Three weeks later "Jimmy Walker and his wife" Elizabeth went with Roberts to Chemainus on Vancouver Island, likely to give assistance of some kind. On January 1, 1884, "my workman, Jimmy Walker, is away [having gone with his wife to see Joe Silvey]." Walker acted as interpreter into the local Cowichan language and Roberts noted on the following Sunday: "As Jimmy Walker was not there I addressed the Congregation in Chinook." Chinook was the jargon used across the Pacific Northwest since the fur trade as a means of communication between Natives and newcomers. At the service a week later, "Jimmy

Elizabeth's husband James Walker with their two oldest sons, William and Frank. James Walker "kidnapped" Elizabeth while out on a date and forced her to marry him. City of Vancouver Archives, CVA 371-2394

interpreted a short address on Luke 2:46 and then I spoke (without interpreter) for some length...The Currans & Walkers had dinner Chez nous, & went away in the evening. Before they went we had the Melodeon brought up for Singing of Hymns—& Again tonight I paid Jimmy Walker Balance due to him $5.50." Three days later, "[young Willie] Curran & Jimmy Walker came here at Noon. C. has contracted to saw 200 blocks @ 10¢ a block. They began work this P.M. and boarded Chez nous—sleeping on their sloop." By Friday, January 25: "Jimmy Walker this A.M. finished the Contract of cutting 200 blocks of wood. I paid Jimmy for his share $13.50 & also gave him for Mr Curran 2 fowl & 2 dozen eggs." At the time of the 1891 census James Walker was employed near Nanaimo as a general labourer and his wife Elizabeth worked as a servant.

Back on Reid Island, Joe Silvey continued to make a living from the sea, doing "all kinds of fishing according to the seasons—perch fishing with a small net, cod fishing with hook and line, trolling for spring and blueback salmon, clam digging night and day with low tide." According to one account, Portuguese Joe was "granted a fishing concession from Nanaimo to Sansum Narrows [between Salt Spring and Vancouver islands] to take dog and coho salmon. The dog salmon were sold to Todd's [cannery] for $2^{1/2}$ cents each, but the coho were thrown out—the cannery wouldn't take them because they were considered too dry." In the 1901 census, Joe Silvey described himself as a fisherman who had earned $600 over the past year, a fair income for the time.

Portuguese Joe combined occupations, much as he had done earlier at Brockton Point. "Father had a little store on Reid Island, alongside of the house." The store was convenient to Porlier Pass, much used by sailing vessels along the coast. Reverend Roberts' diary entry of October 7, 1883, makes it clear that family members sometimes ran the store. "Halfway between Joe Silvia's Island & Cowichan Gap [Porlier Pass] we saw Joe. S. and [John] Norton of Ganges Harbour [on Salt Spring] hauling dog-fish from their lines...Running back to Joe's Island there was a strong wind & heavy sea. We reefed mainsail—ran into a very small cove at Joe's place. Got some provisions at his store. It was wet & stormy as we went home [to Kuper Island]."

Reverend Roberts' diary testifies to Portuguese Joe's entrepreneurial bent. Roberts wrote on April 2, 1882: "Soon after the [Sunday] Service Charlie Quiem & a white man named Silvy came to the house to get me to write out a paper (a Promissory Note). Quiem was about to lend Silvy $100 at 12 per Cent per Annum for 12 months. Geo.

Sunday March 4th 1866   8

Anchored this forenoon off Maynes Islands
be calmed & becalmed — Landed & travelled over
part of the Island — Mr [Muir] ... Deer & [two] ... I & saw
Crossed over — & saw a settler in a canoe with
his squaw. Gathered some Lichens & mosses —
& in mid passing sailed for "Active pass"
always known as "Plumper pass" formed by
a passage between Maynes & Galeano Islands
& passed through by all vessels going to Fraser River
but tide being too strong anchored in Miners Bay

March 5th 1866 (Monday)

Tried to get out this morning but the
tide rip off "Georgina Point" too strong
& had again to run into the Pass & anchored
at our old place — in Miners bay by a
settler called McGready in partner-
-ship with Myers. who of course had
the inevitable squaw. There are
some Fishermen & one or two other
settlers here — One of the former generally
known by the generic name of "Portugee
Joe" visited us. Joe had just caught
6500 of fish — enough for the Westminster
& Victoria markets — He sent them up by
the "Enterprise" — He caught them with
double hooked lines but the Dog fish
(Anarchicas Scanleri) were very troublesome
them biting off the hooks — Joe never
by his own ...

Reverend Roberts's journal gives insight into the lives of Portuguese Joe and others living in the Reid Island area. Here he describes how Joe caught enough fish "for the Westminster and Victoria markets." BC Archives MS794

Whenwhutston & Charlie Seeyakahail witnessed the note." Three years later, on April 16, 1885, Roberts described how he went with "Indian Joe & Tom to Penelakut to see Charlie Quiem who appears to be dying. I wrote Some letters for him about monies due to him [by] Joe Silvia & Geo. Whenwhutston witnessed 'his mark.' Silvia gave him a dose of Castor oil." Quiem's widow pursued the debt. Roberts wrote on May 7, 1887: "Mrs. Quiem & her 2 daughters (Sarah & the one married to the Comox Indian) & son in law came to see me about monies due to her by Curran & Portuguese Joe Silvia."

As Reverend Roberts' diaries attest, Portuguese Joe was always out to make the best deal, which was not necessarily in others' interests. A family member has reflected that "he was a bit of a rascal with the Indians," and "it was Lucy who kept him alive." She was the connection with Native people who secured the family's well-being. "Granny saved his hide. Except for Granny, they would have shot and ate him."

Joe Silvey acquired a certain stature along the coast. On December 8, 1882, as Reverend Roberts was sailing from Nanaimo to Kuper: "We met Portuguese Joe going in his sloop to Nanaimo. He told us that the wind was strong below the Narrows." Joe got himself on the voters' list as soon as the South Nanaimo District was organized in the early 1890s. In the next enumeration he was joined on the list by his sons Domingo and Joseph, who, like their father, gave their occupation as "fisherman." Portuguese Joe participated in civic life in other ways as well. In the fall of 1888 he served on the jury of a coroner's inquest into the death of a Native named Solesum on Thetis Island. Indicative of the ways in which the coast was bound together, the interpreter at the inquest was the stepmother-in-law of Joe's eldest daughter Elizabeth.

Joe gave back to those around him, usually in ways that reflected his familiarity with the sea. Sometimes his generosity was informal. Roberts noted on November 14, 1886: "We went as far as Reid Island & anchored in front of Portuguese Joe's (Joe Silvia). Joe Came Aboard for an hour or so—he gave us a Codfish & some salt herrings—the latter were bad & we threw them overboard next day." Other times Portuguese Joe's largesse was more intentional. Joe's granddaughter Irene has described how he operated a food fishery for the Penelakuts of Kuper Island, who did not have their own seine boat and could only spear fish. "Portuguese Joe had a permit that only he could fish in the mouth of the river with a beach seine. Every year Grandfather had a seine boat and would go fish dog salmon in the fall; he got a permit to get food fish for Indians, and would get them for them. He would take them over and then they would smoke them for the winter." As to the reason: "Portugee [her pronunciation] Joe liked helping people and they helped him. When they killed a deer they would bring some meat over. A lot of Kuper Island people had trouble getting fish and Portugee Joe took it on himself."

People who depend on water for their transportation and livelihood tend to socialize together, and Joe's community was no exception. Fishing boats would tie up for the winter at Mud Bay. The first one to arrive set down next to the wharf and stuck poles in the mud. The next boat tied up next to the poles and planted more poles, another boat did the same and so on. The men "would winter there talking with Grandpa Joe." Among the winter sojourners and also throughout the year, there were "lots of Portuguese people who came around Reid." According to Irene, "Grandpa used to be the leader of them."

Visits from long-time friends such as Peter Smith of the old whaling days must have confirmed for Portuguese Joe the wisdom of having got his own island. He likely reflected on the freedom it gave his family to make their lives on their own terms. In 1887 the new city of Vancouver, brought into being by the completion of the transcontinental railroad, successfully lobbied the Dominion government for access to the government reserve, including Brockton Point. Stanley Park, as it was named, became the recreational preserve of newcomers from Canada and Britain who wanted it to reflect their mix of values and priorities. It was almost inevitable that long-time residents, including members of the Smith, Gonsalves and Baker families, would eventually be forced out of their homes. The simmering dispute, which reached its climax in the mid-1920s, reminded the Silvey family how right they had been to leave Brockton Point, although they likely did not realize the full extent to which persons like themselves were being marginalized in the new British Columbia.

On Reid Island, the Silveys were left far more to their own devices. They lived closer to the frontier according to both aboriginal and newcomer ways. In many respects Joe Silvey remained a Portuguese peasant all his life. Just as his father had done for him on Pico Island, Portuguese Joe was determined to imbue his children with traditional values along with the ability to make a living. They learned an appreciation of their Portuguese identity, which they would carry with them proudly through their own and their descendants' lifetimes. Khaltinaht had instilled aboriginal values in her children, and Lucy attempted to do much the same with hers. The family was multilingual. As a matter of course they spoke Portuguese, the trading jargon of Chinook, the local Cowichan language, and English.

Formal education was another matter. It had not been part of Joe's upbringing and did not acquire much value. Elizabeth, who had not attended school as a child, recalled how "Father had a man at Reid Island, he boarded with us for six months, and that is all the education I got; I can read a little." At the time of the 1891 census, the two oldest children still at home, Domingo and Mary, were recorded

Reverend Robert James Roberts and his wife on Kuper Island. Despite his initial misgivings, Roberts married Elizabeth and James Walker.
BC Archives D05957

as able to read but not to write, whereas Joe, age 12, John, who was nine, and Antonio, age seven, could do neither. In 1901 Tony was described as literate, but not so Manuel, age 15, Henry, age 11, or Lena, who was six. Schooling was not a high priority.

Joe Silvey's sons in particular received an education in the life of the sea. From their early teens they went fishing with him. Elizabeth recalled a herring seine licence "made out to Silvey & sons." A grandson who knew Portuguese Joe as a young child and who had been named for him took pride all his life in how "they fished as they had fished in Portugal; making their own nets in the winter and, during the fishing season, taking the nets out into deep water surrounding the fish and then dragging the net ashore." A dozen men were needed to do so. Even though Portuguese Joe had retreated, so he thought, from "civilization," it eventually caught up with him, according to a grandson. "Around the close of the century, beach seine licence fees of $10 were imposed. Old Joe Silvey refused to pay. The next season his net was seized and burned at Nanaimo."

Joe taught his sons not only how to make a living, but to take care while doing so. Sealing schooners were among the vessels that tied up for the winter at Reid Island,

Above: Manuel Silvey with a group of fishermen and sealers in front of the Commercial Hotel, Steveston, 1890s. Left to right: unknown man with bicycle, Manuel Silvey, Fred Corkill, Jesse Plant, the hotel-keeper, Frank Davis; Alexander King and Arthur Willie Palua (both lost in the *Triumph* in 1903), and Bill Shepard. Courtesy the Fisherman Publishing Society, UBC Special Collections

Opposite top: Portuguese Joe's daughter Josephine had eight children by the time she was 30. Courtesy Rocky Sampson

Opposite bottom: Joe's oldest son Domingo and his wife Josephine standing in front of the house Joe built on Reid Island. Courtesy Chris Thompson

and it may have been this proximity that encouraged Tony, when he was just 15, to sign up with the *Triumph*, reputed to be the largest and fastest sailing ship in the Victoria sealing fleet. Sealing was a lucrative activity that required trips north to the Bering Sea of six or more months' duration. His father considered Tony "far too young" and bought out his contract. "Dad went to sign up on a sealer and Grandfather got him off." He may have saved Tony's life—the *Triumph* sank four years later, in 1903, with all 35 men lost.

As time passed, Portuguese Joe's older daughters went their own ways. Joe's goal for them was very much that which had befallen Elizabeth. He wanted them to become good wives and mothers within a long tradition of peasant families. Josephine, Joe's second child by Khaltinaht, was a mother at age 16. By the time she was 30, she had eight children with her husband, a Ladysmith storekeeper. Following his death, Josephine found another husband, a Chemainus logger of Scottish descent, born in rural Ontario. Steve Anderson was 10 years her senior, and in 1901 he earned a very respectable $900.

Portuguese Joe's third daughter Mary, born at Brockton Point about six years after Josephine's birth on nearby Pasley Island, followed a similar path. Mary was still in her teens when she married David Roberts, a Welsh widower more than twice her age. Roberts had four motherless sons and a farm that needed tending on nearby Gabriola Island. Whatever happened to the relationship, by 1901 Mary, age 24, had four children and, like her sister Josephine, she was living with a rural Ontarian of Scots descent 10 years older than she was—a logger named Richard Brown. Joe Silvey's three eldest daughters were caught in a timeless pattern of female domesticity.

There was much less pressure on Joe Silvey's sons to settle down young. As males they possessed far more freedom of action than did their sisters. When they married, they were expected to be able to support both themselves and their families. It took time to acquire the means, hence the acceptability of a significant age difference within a marriage. According to grandchildren, with their "big long handlebars" and gleaming black hair, the Silvey sons were considered "catches." They had little difficulty finding mates as soon as they were in a position to do so.

Joe's eldest son Domingo had his first child by Josephine Crocker, five years his junior, when he was 23 years old. Her family lived just across the water at Chemainus. Her father Simeon Crocker, who like so many others combined logging and fishing, had come from Maine. Her mother Pakaltinatt, or Lucy, was from Kuper Island. Joseph was born in 1897 on Reid Island. John, known as Jack, followed two years later. Whereas Joseph's birth went unrecorded, Domingo had the Catholic priest on nearby Kuper register John for him on the grounds that he "cannot write." Like his father, Domingo preferred the life of a fisherman. He also did whatever was necessary to support his young family, which included working as a logger from time to time.

Domingo stayed close to home, as was expected of the eldest son, but his brother Joseph struck out on his own. In 1901 young Joe was working in Chemainus as a longshoreman, loading vessels come to pick up lumber. It was hard work, for which he earned an impressive $900 in a year. On June 2, 1900, the Catholic priest went over to Chemainus from Kuper Island to marry Joseph to Maria King. She was the daughter of an early Greek settler on Salt Spring Island, who had anglicized his name and married a Saanich woman named Mary Tegurviei. Like young Joe, Maria had grown up in a fishing family, but one that was star-crossed—two of her three brothers perished in the *Triumph* disaster.

The second generation of Silveys was fast finding its way. By the turn of the century Portuguese Joe's two daughters by Khaltinaht, Elizabeth and Josephine, had produced well over a dozen children between them. Lucy's two oldest, Domingo and Mary, were the parents of another six. Young Joe was newly married. Joe and Lucy's five other children, John, Tony, Manuel, Henry and Lena, ranged in age from five to 16.

No More Adventures

Portuguese Joe took special pleasure in his acquisition of Reid Island as a secure home for his family. As a young man, his son Tony drove oxen used for logging on Vancouver Island, and when he came home for the weekend, he told his father excitedly about an opportunity to buy much of the area around Saltair north of Chemainus. Joe advised him against doing so, for "we have the island, we don't need it." The island was a haven for the family, especially in view of the many changes that occurred during his lifetime. Joe's namesake grandson, born in 1897, recalled being taken across to Chemainus in a rowboat: "I remember my grandfather when I was just a young boy, my grandfather calling in great excitement, 'Come and look, there is a boat going

Portuguese Joe's son Tony
stayed on Reid Island.
Courtesy Jessica Casey

by with no sails and no oars,' and that was the very first gas boat I ever saw." One of Portuguese Joe's favourite expressions was: "Well, I'll be damned," and this time he expressed a very loud, "Well, I'll be damned, what's that?!"

Portuguese Joe was a tough man who was never sick. But in the fall of 1900 he caught a chill while "fishing for salmon with a net." According to his eldest daughter Elizabeth, he was "living in an old shack at Chemainus" and "had some men working with him, but he went home to Reid Island." Elizabeth, who lived not far away, decided that she wanted to see him, although she had not been told he was sick. "I was living at Ladysmith; three miles toward Nanaimo; right on the highway; on a little farm; that was where all my [10] children were raised." She shared her premonition with her sons. "I don't know what's the matter with me. I want to go see Grandpa. I've been thinking about him all night. I can't sleep." Elizabeth and one of her sons set out. "We got a little rowboat. It is only 10 miles from Ladysmith to Reid Island, and we rowed over. And then when we got there, there was my father still sick. He was sitting up in a chair and looked so ill. He said to me, 'My dear Elizabeth; Papa's so sick, I'll tell you later.' Later he told me he could not make water." The next morning Joe was put "in one of the sailboats he had just built." His daughter got hold of her husband "working right on the bay getting out some timber," and they took him to a doctor.

Joe recovered, but a year later he suffered a second attack, and this time it was fatal. On his death on January 17, 1902, on Reid Island, likely in his mid-70s, he was described as a fisherman. "Father is buried on Reid Island; that was his wish. He is buried on his own property."

Portuguese Joe's most precious asset was Reid Island, but whatever wishes he might have had for its future, he left no will. Domingo's status

Portuguese Joe and Lucy were laid to rest in the small family cemetery on Reid Island.
Courtesy Rocky Sampson

as the eldest son determined that he would take charge, but the situation soon grew messy. Portuguese Joe had not turned Lot 35 into a Crown grant. It could not be distributed among his widow and 10 children until outright ownership was secured, for which $400 in costs and taxes had to be paid. Domingo managed to get Crown grants for the smaller Lots 34 and 36 he had preempted, but not for Lot 35, which was sold for unpaid taxes at the end of 1919. Domingo used the opportunity to purchase it outright and on that basis secure a mortgage to cover the cost, thereby saving his father's legacy of Reid Island, but to the advantage of his own family.

Portuguese Joe's widow Lucy was in her mid-40s at the time of his death. Her youngest child Lena was just seven. Lucy continued to live in the family house and during the summer brought in a bit of money by making nets on the Fraser River. As she sought to make a new life for herself, she found companionship with an Irishman named Joe Watson, whom she met when he was cooking on a seine boat for her son Tony. A granddaughter remembered Lucy as "an old granny, just like grannies used to be, sitting in a rocking chair, teaching us how to shell peas, peel an apple, make bread." Lucy died on Reid Island on August 13, 1934. A measure of the self-sufficiency that characterized Reid Islanders can be seen on her death certificate. Under the category "Undertaker" is written: "By relatives."

Dozens of family members and friends turned out for Lucy Kwahama Kwatleematt's funeral. In the front row (from left to right) are Elizabeth Silvey, Clara Silvey Bell, Edith Beale holding hands with her mother Lena Silvey Beale, Lucy's second husband Joe Watson, Henry Silvey, Tony Silvey and Alice Aleck Silvey.
Courtesy Jessica Casey

Lucy outlived Joe by more than 30 years, and saw how their family expanded both on and off Reid Island.
Courtesy Jessica Casey

Continuing Portuguese Joe's Story

The remarkable adventures of Portuguese Joe Silvey did not end with his death in 1902, or even that of his second wife Lucy a third of a century later. He instilled in each of his 10 children ways of seeing and doing that they carried with them through their lifetimes. The means by which the Silvey sons and daughters dealt with the legacy their parents bequeathed them are part of Portuguese Joe's story.

The young Silveys continued to follow in their father's footsteps in their choice of occupation, and they looked to the example of their parents' neighbours and acquaintances when it came time to start a family. The sons fished and logged, much as Portuguese Joe had done. They chose wives whose priority was home and hearth, just as it was for their sisters. Through the First World War, British Columbia's newcomer population consisted of two to three times as many men as women. A daughter of mixed heritage could choose between a newcomer of modest means, as had Josephine and Mary, and another person of mixed race, as had happened to Elizabeth. Either way, women were expected to submerge their identities into those of their husbands, making a hybrid daughter-in-law just tolerable. In sharp contrast, no newcomer family wanted, under any circumstances, a mixed-race son-in-law. A son's choice was between another hybrid person like himself, as Domingo and Joe had done, or an aboriginal woman. All of Portuguese Joe's children believed that they were exercising free will when they settled down, but their decisions also reflected both their father's desires for them and the larger social pressures at work in British Columbia.

Khaltinaht's Daughters

Upon Portuguese Joe's death, his two families divided. His daughters by Khaltinaht went their own ways, and Elizabeth never returned to live on Reid Island. At about the end of the First World War, she left the husband she had married so reluctantly and by whom she had had 10 children in rapid succession. "I was just his 'slave,'" Elizabeth asserted two decades later. Jimmy Walker lived for a time with family members in a coastal logging camp, where, his great-granddaughter Marie recalled, he used to "tease us with the old Native words." As for Elizabeth, whom she saw from time to time, "she always wore long black skirts and was stately and stern." In 1938 Elizabeth was living on relief in "an old dilapidated rooming house" at 721 Cambie Street in Vancouver. Vancouver City Archivist Major J.S. Matthews visited Elizabeth in what he described as "her solitary room, at the back, about 10 by 12 feet square, and containing a poor bed, two chairs, a gas cooking plate and a small tan heating stove."

Elizabeth continued to take pride in her mother Khaltinaht's family and, in her later years, attempted to renew relationships with the Musqueam and Squamish people. By this time aboriginal people had internalized their forced separation from the dominant society in profound ways. "I did apply once to be allowed to share in the distribution of Indian monies," Elizabeth said, "and there was a meeting over at Capilano Creek, and I might have got my share, but Old Mary Capilano, [Chief] Capilano Joe's wife, objected, and said something sneering about the women who went off and became white, and gave themselves airs."

In 1939 Elizabeth took a chance and attended a potlatch on the Musqueam Reserve south of Vancouver, reminiscent of the one she had attended with her mother at Whoi Whoi two-thirds of a century earlier. No sooner had she sat down than the son of her mother's cousin recognized her and invited her to the head table. Informally he gave her much the same message as she had got on the Capilano Reserve. "If I had not become a white woman I would have had a home and land. I would have had a home and land, if I had stayed Indian, and I did not know how high up in [status in] Indian life I was." At the same time he publicly defended Elizabeth's presence. "John [Guerin] got up to make a speech, and he spoke in Indian, but I knew what he was saying. I don't think he knew I did. He told all those Indians there not to insult me, that I was a great-granddaughter of Old Chief Kiapilano."

Elizabeth remained close to her cousin Christine, daughter of her mother's sister Rowia and Navvy Jack Thomas. After she was informally recognized at Musqueam, Elizabeth accepted an invitation via Christine to visit Gassy Jack Deighton's widow Madeleine, a basket maker on the Mission Reserve in North Vancouver. "She says she remembers me when I was a little girl, and Father lived at one end of the Gastown beach and Gassy Jack at the other." The visit was a success. Elizabeth discovered, to her great pleasure, that "she knew my father, Joe Silvey, 'Portuguese Joe,' and she knew me when I was little." Joe Silvey's eldest daughter died in Vancouver on July 14, 1945, at the age of 78.

Elizabeth's sister Josephine spent most of her adult life along the coast. She cooked in logging camps, near where her husband Steve Anderson logged and fished. Josephine "had never gone to school and couldn't read," her great-grandchild Florence explained, "so she had to do all her cooking from memory." As soon as the children grew up, they mostly headed off to "the big city," but Josephine and her husband liked the outdoor life and held on as long as they could. Eventually age and poor health caught up with them. Josephine died in Vancouver on March 27, 1930.

Perhaps because Josephine did not have the opportunity to know her mother, she identified herself as Portuguese—so strongly that her daughter, who gave the information on Josephine's death registration, recorded only that part of her mother's heritage. She was so convinced of it that she reported Josephine's mother Khaltinaht, as well as her father Portuguese Joe, had been born in Portugal.

Sons on Reid Island

In accordance with Portuguese tradition, Joe Silvey's eldest son Domingo took seriously his responsibility as the keeper of Reid Island. On December 20, 1905, he formally wed the mother of his children, Josephine Crocker, after being prodded to do so by the priest on nearby Kuper Island. In the story passed down through their children, the priest admonished them: "You get married or else." Families of similar background were closely linked: Josephine's brother Abraham married Louisa Silva, a daughter of Portuguese Joe's countryman, and they settled down near the Silva clan on Gabriola Island.

Domingo, Josephine and their seven children lived at the eastern edge of the small "egg" on Mud Bay. Everyday life was self-sustaining, as far as possible. Domingo's

Domingo formally married Josephine Crocker after being coerced by a Catholic priest on nearby Kuper Island. The two had previously "eloped" and were married in a Native ceremony on the banks of the Chemainus River.

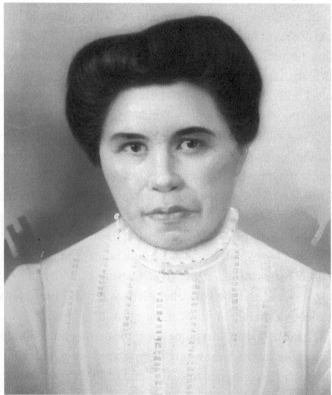

oldest son Joe, born in 1897, recalled: "When I was young we had fish, vegetables were grown on north Galiano, we would trade fish for vegetables. The only things we needed cash for were tobacco, salt, sugar and gasoline." Josephine played a major role. "Mother could do things," Joe said. "She would see the recipe and it would stick in her mind." She crocheted, which had the practical benefit of keeping "her fingers nimble, and it helped her to mend nets." Domingo likely made her large net-mending needles. The family served as a centre for community on Reid Island. "We were really at-home people, and if someone didn't have a place we would put them on the verandah or where-have-you. I think in those days people were more considerate."

According to a niece who grew up on Reid Island, Domingo was "into everything"—troller, seiner, logger, drag seiner. He also acquired a reputation as "a very good boat builder." Young Joe once mused how, "in those early days, times were hard and men were tough; they had to be to survive." The family possessed at least one visible reminder of tradition, a big black pot "the size of a dining table and as high." Portuguese Joe had used it, and Domingo after him. "You put dogfish livers in it to get out the oil, you could smell it, it smelled like 'heaven,' we said, by which we meant 'hell.'" One of Domingo's daughters recalled how "we went to Vancouver and you could smell us, we went to the theatre in Vancouver and people moved away from us."

Domingo followed his father's example in mentoring his sons in the life of the sea at an early age. His eldest son Joe recalled: "I went fishing with him. At this time I was between nine and 10 years old. I was big enough to pull some of the fish in and I did what I could. I didn't make the nets at this age but I made them after I got about 15 or 16 years of age. I could make any kind of net." Domingo and his sons fished and logged on much of the Gulf Islands and part of Vancouver Island. "We would camp on Galiano, we moved off of Reid to the gulf side of Galiano." Silvey's Cove, as the site on the northeastern shore of Galiano became known, is still considered a prime location for landing boats. Domingo used horses and a steam donkey to bring out logs to be sold to the coal mines around Nanaimo and for wood-burning tugboats.

The one activity that did not much tempt second-generation Silveys was whaling. A spurt of new interest in the industry rose briefly in the early 20th century. Domingo's

Dressing up and going to town was an exciting but sometimes difficult experience for the Silveys, who were used to a more frontier-style existence. Pictured here is Nellie Francis (Anderson) MacDonald, one of Portuguese Joe's granddaughters, and her friend Barbara May Kimball. Courtesy Rocky Sampson

son Joe described how, when he was a boy, "we would sit there and watch the whalers" chase down "whales in front of our house on Reid Island." Young Joe did not quite understand what was happening until, travelling the north shore of Valdes Island with his father, they came upon "a whale lying on its back with 13 to 14 Japanese working on it." Joe was perplexed. "I asked the old man and he said, 'That is a whale, don't you know? You see them in front of the house all the time.' I said, 'I've never seen them like that.'" Domingo explained to young Joe that his grandfather, Portuguese Joe, had been a whaler, making $1.25 to $1.50 per four-gallon can of oil for use in coal miners' pit lights.

A neighbour was determined to get in on the action and, convinced that by definition "a Silvey is a whaler," he persuaded Domingo's younger brothers Tony and Manuel to accompany him. According to Domingo's son Joe, the trip was a disaster. "The whale was sleeping in the water and they got too close to the whale and the whale tipped the boat." Tony was scared off, but Manuel talked their older brother Joe into having a try. "Joe went out as brave as could be, so they harpooned a whale, they managed to get the harpoon on him and he took off for Dodds Narrows. They got the rope and tied her down and they all laid down in the bottom of the boat and every once in a while, they would peek over the side. The boat was making one mile an hour and the whale was doing 15. Every once in a while he would pop up and get his wind and then down he would go again." Finally, in desperation, they "cut the rope and away went the whale." To save face on returning home, the story goes, they "said the whale bit the line off." There were no more whaling adventures.

Theirs was a demanding but satisfying way of life, which was disrupted by World War I. As far as everyone knew, Domingo's two oldest sons Joe and Jack were "working on Galiano logging." According to a younger sister, "Joe went to town and came back in a uniform— we all got sick with it." Jack did the same. "Because Joe joined up, Jack had

Right: One of Domingo's boats. Domingo developed a reputation as "a very good boat builder."
Courtesy Eunice Weatherell

Opposite top: In 1917, Domingo's oldest son Joe sneaked off and joined the armed forces.
Courtesy Chris Thompson

Opposite bottom: Like his older brother, Jack signed up to join the war effort, but his father refused to let him go overseas and he was discharged—a humiliating experience he never forgot.
Courtesy Chris Thompson

to, he would do whatever Joe did." Their official applications to join the Canadian Over-Seas Expeditionary Force are both dated June 8, 1917. Twenty-year-old Joe and 18-year-old Jack gave their occupations as loggers. Joe described himself as 5'9" with black hair, brown eyes and "dark" complexion, Jack as 5'6" with black hair, brown eyes and "red" complexion. Both boys were conscious that they were not "fair," the usual response to the last question.

Domingo, who was ill at the time, could not bear to lose both his sons. He openly opposed them to try to get at least one of them out. Jack's application bears the notation: "Discharged, 23-6-17. D.S." Domingo's second son was humiliated. "I don't think he ever forgave Pa," his siblings recalled. Joe spent two years in military service: "I was overseas 18 or 19 months." He spent time in the trenches and got gassed. "We did a lot of praying in those days," a sister remembered. The prayers had the desired effect. Joe returned and, after a stint longshoring in Chemainus for 80¢ an hour plus board, he settled down on the northern tip of the big egg. His younger brother Jack lived on the southern tip of the small egg.

Both Joe and Jack married women from among coastal and island mixed-race fishing families. Joe's wife Amelia Wilson was part of a formidable Fraser River clan that, on being forced off the Coquitlam Indian Reserve, settled at Canoe Pass near present-day Ladner. They met on the Skeena River, where both Joe and Amelia's family were fishing. Jack's wife Laura was a granddaughter of James McFadden, a Hudson's Bay fur trader, and of a Bella Bella woman, and of Edwin Rosman, a Cornishman come with the gold rush, and his Tlingit wife. Laura grew up at Fernwood on northeast Salt Spring Island, where her father, like so many others of similar mixed background, made a living as a sealer. The story goes that the couple met when Jack rowed over to see the medical doctor on Salt Spring. Laura was about to go on a mail run and offered to give him a ride from the Fernwood dock in her horse and buggy.

Portugueses Joe's son John, eight years Domingo's junior, also used Reid Island as a base. Like the other Silvey men, Jack married a woman from the neighbourhood. Charlotte Peterson was born on Gabriola to a Danish farmer and a Native woman named Jane, recalled as "strong and strict." Jack and a partner had a logging and log-salvaging business at Yellow Point north of Chemainus. On October 8, 1907, Jack was murdered while on his way home to Reid Island by rowboat. According to one version of events passed down through time, "John was shot while on the boat; he was buying clams and it was known he had a lot of money, so he was shot and robbed." A variation of the story, also told in the family, has him heading to Reid with $50 he had received in

Right: John Laurence Silvey married Laura Georgina McFadden on February 26th, 1922, at Saint Mark's church, Salt Spring Island.
Courtesy Eunice Weatherell

Opposite top: Jack's daughter Eunice Silvey relaxing on Reid Island. One of the salteries is visible behind her.
Courtesy Eunice Weatherell

Opposite bottom: Although he was disinherited for the actions of his older brother Domingo, Portuguese Joe's fourth son Tony remained on Reid Island out of affection for his mother Lucy Kwatleematt.
Courtesy Rocky Sampson

Nanaimo for "a big raft of logs." Everyone had their suspicions as to who was responsible, but no one ever knew for sure.

Portuguese Joe's fourth son Tony, who was born in 1884, two years after John, also stayed on Reid Island. He settled on its western edge despite his very deep unhappiness over being disinherited. In 1923 he, his mother and seven siblings initiated legal proceedings on the grounds that Lot 35 could not have legally been sold for taxes when "the title was still in the name of the Crown." Land records in the British Columbia Archives indicate provincial authorities were aware of a lack of due process, but at the same time unwilling to reverse the sale. Domingo retained ownership of Lot 35, much to his siblings' dismay. Tony is said to have remained on Reid out of affection for his mother.

On September 29, 1904, Tony wed Philomena Beale, the 18-year-old daughter of an American farmer on Galiano and a Penelakut woman whose father was a chief on Kuper Island, but the marriage did not last. In one version of the story, Minnie asked her husband to let her go home for a visit. Tony asked her to wait a day while he went fishing. "He came home and she was gone, he couldn't write and couldn't look for her." Not only had Minnie gone back to her family, she took their infant son Thomas with her. In another telling of the same event, "Philomena ran off with Jimmy Crocker from Gabriola." Indicative of the ties that bound together coastal families of mixed race, Jimmy was Domingo Silvey's brother-in-law.

After his wife's bunk, Tony turned to a Kuper Island woman, Alice Aleck, or Swealt. According to their daughter Irene, Alice's Cowichan name, which means "little tiny thing," was given to her because she was only "four feet and a bit" tall. Alice's parents had drowned when she was just eight months old and her brother Dave, or Thaamalt, was a couple of years older. Their maternal aunt took them in and, when they reached school age, sent them to the Kuper Island residential school run by the Oblates, where they remained into young adulthood.

Alice was aged six when she entered the Kuper Island school on November 20, 1898, just over a year after her brother David had arrived there. The school's 60-some pupils were closely monitored, being allowed just two visits home a year: three weeks in June or July and a few days over Christmas.

As was the usual practice in residential schools, pupils were taught a combination of basic literacy and practical skills. According to records held in the British Columbia Archives, the term after Alice arrived, the 28 girls made 27 dresses, 23 aprons,

Tony's great love Alice Aleck entered the Kuper Island residential school when she was just six.
BC Archives PDP 05505

16 napkins, 10 yards of lace, 2 pairs of pants, 2 chemises, 1 big curtain and 2 mattress ticks. Alice gradually advanced from "sewing & darning" to "machine sewing" by 1906. While no conduct book survives for the girls, it does for the boys. Their punishments for misbehaviour during the years Alice was enrolled ranged from "confinement, writing lines, bread and water" to private or public "reprimands." Throughout her life, Alice appreciated the lessons in everyday living she learned at Kuper Island. Her daughter Rose said that Alice "could sew just like a seamstress."

Tony Silvey and Alice Aleck may have met through Domingo's wife Josephine. Her brothers Abe and Jimmy—who was implicated in the departure of Tony's wife—both attended the Kuper Island school at the same time as Alice. The sanctions that the Catholic Church put on human relations had their effect on the couple: however great their commitment to each other, Antonio Silvey remained in the eyes of the church bigamously married to the errant Philomena. The church did not permit divorce, regardless of the circumstances. Tony's former wife clearly suffered as well. In 1917, using her maiden name and describing herself as a spinster, Minnie Beale married James Crocker in Anglican Christ Church Cathedral in Victoria. They described themselves as living in Crofton, where Jimmy was a logger.

In 1935 Alice died of tuberculosis, leaving Tony with a houseful of children, the youngest only five months old. "The fine way in which he raised his young family by himself won the admiration of all who knew him," Tony's obituary stated. He brought them up much as he himself was raised. "I didn't know how to speak English for a long time. I got the Chinook mixed up with the Portuguese. Dad spoke Portuguese. He threw Chinook at us. All of the old people knew the Cowichan language, even some of the white fishermen. So, for a long time we didn't know there were different nationalities. We thought everyone was the same." Tony's daughter Irene astutely reflected that "they were a smart bunch of people, they could speak all those languages."

Although life at the residential school was restrictive, Alice (front row, far left) always appreciated the practical skills she developed there.
Courtesy Rocky Sampson

Reid Island also had a couple of tenants. A well-connected Englishman recalled only as Percy "needed a place to stay." When he and young Joe were in the trenches together, he told Joe that his wife had left him and he wanted to escape "to the colonies." Joe invited George Percy Blizard home with him. He explained how he helped Percy build a small cabin on the edge of his holding, and there this self-described "distant relative of Winston Churchill" settled down. Percy's family sent him regular remittances, perhaps to ensure that he stayed away.

Percy's elite education at Westminster Public School in London seemed a lifetime away. He brought his wife's clothes with him from England and sometimes wore them. His eccentricities were for the most part accommodated. Grandchildren raised on Reid Island remember how "he wore his wife's clothes all the time," that is, unless he was around his own place, where he "never wore clothes and so we had to whistle that we were coming." Sometimes he decorated his nude body with a sash. Once, when he was going to Ladysmith with the Silveys in their boat, "he came down wearing his wife's silk stockings, skirt, white blouse, high heels, little hat." That was too much. "Cousin Jack made him go back and put on jeans." Gradually Percy became more peculiar. "He was out of his head by the time he left, the police came to get him, he said he had to go back, he dug up a box of old remittance cheques, none of them had been cashed." Portuguese Joe's grandchildren emphasized that Percy was

George Percy Blizard, an English friend of Joe's from the war, settled in this cabin on Reid Island, where his eccentricities were largely accepted. Courtesy Rocky Sampson

not unique but typical of a whole number of individuals who during these years were able to make a life on their own terms on an island.

On the west side of Reid, near where Tony lived, two Japanese families had got permission to erect wharves and construct herring salteries. They went into operation in about 1908, and soon numerous others sprang up on nearby islands, including Valdes and Galiano. The Tanakas and the Kashos lived all year-round in houses just above the Reid Island salteries. Tony's daughter Irene recalled them as elderly couples without children of their own. "They started in October/November to seine the herring," she explained. Two boats with a net between them would purse it tight as soon as it filled with herring. The seiners would unload the herring onto scows, from which the fish would go on a conveyer to the salteries, which was set on piles at the edge of the water. The herring was put into vats in layers, which Irene remembered as being five feet deep, 30 feet wide, and 16 feet (1.5 x 9 x 5 metres) long. The fish was not heated, just salted—"layer of salt, layer of herring, layer of salt, and so forth." Portuguese Joe used a similar process at Brockton Point.

The two salteries required much labour on short notice. Domingo's son Joe described upwards of a hundred Japanese float homes in the area. Each saltery required about 150 workers during the height of the season. "When the herring was coming, they would start a fire and the Indians would paddle over." Tony Silvey worked as net boss, in charge of making nets. Perhaps for that reason, his daughter Rose explained, the Japanese "watchmen used to bring us cake and cookies and canned pineapple."

Tony's daughter Irene washed dishes at the salteries when she was 12 and 13 years old. There were separate cookhouses for the different groups of workers. "The old Japanese women would ring the bell," she recalled, "and I would run down the little trail from our house and wash the dishes, there were only bowls and chopsticks at the Japanese cookhouse, so I liked it much more than the white cookhouse, where there were cups and saucers and everything else." The salted herring was shipped to Japan. The annual round continued until the Second World War, when the two families were evacuated, along with others of Japanese descent living on the coast, and the salteries perforce abandoned.

Through the recollections of Domingo's and Tony's children, it is possible to glimpse everyday life on Reid Island during their childhoods in the 1930s, when the Great Depression raged. Third-generation Silveys contributed to the family economy in many ways, including washing dishes at the salteries and digging clams. "We gave all our money to our dad," said Irene, and sometimes "Dad would buy us a chocolate bar and we would divide it into pieces."

Men on relief got $29 per month. "Father worked on the road to get it. We were so ashamed that we had to say Father was away, not that we were on relief and he was working on the road." Tony's daughter Irene recalled "eating cabbage and stuff when times were tough in the winter." Their father would tell them that this was food "fit for a king." They thought he was referring to the king of England but it was to himself, since he was known as the "king of the cod fishermen" and had the nickname "King." Sometimes it was outsiders who came to the rescue. According to Irene, a good sa-

Two Japanese families—the Tanakas and the Kashos—built herring salteries on the west side of Reid Island. At their peak, the salteries employed about 150 workers each. *Courtesy Eunice Weatherell*

maritan of sorts went "up and down the coast in a boat, he would steal from the various logging camps and then repaint the boat." One side would be painted white and the other green, so that when he went back down the coast no one would realize it was the same boat. "He would give poor people what he stole…He unloaded at the rock [a flat rock on Reid Island]—three cases of bully beef, canned goods—he left it for us."

Everyone banded together. "It was a good life—we helped each other." Food was got where and when it could be had. "When potatoes were for sale, we would get enough for all the family." Barter was the rule. "We wouldn't sell anything, we would pick crabapples, everything was traded. We had mush, eggs, our own bacon and ham. We made our own lard and soap. We had our own blueberry patch, we had our own little horn lake (so named because there was a horn on a tree near it), we had our own playing field, we had everything on that island, it was a happy time."

"We were like one big family on the island." The isolation of Reid Island allowed the Silveys and others to maintain a Portuguese lifestyle that in retrospect acquired an idyllic quality. Third- and fourth-generation Silveys who grew up there have similar memories of their childhoods. "We were happy, we were content, we had love. There was togetherness in those days that there's not now." Children were taught deference and respect. "No kids were allowed around when adults were talking." "We were all trying to help the older people." "They were quite a nice bunch, you never heard any swearing." "Being Portuguese, there was not much drinking in the family." Church services were obligatory on Sundays. "The priest either came to Reid or we went to Kuper." Every once in a while there would be a shopping trip to Mouat's store in the market town of Ganges on Salt Spring Island, where the Silveys were allowed to charge their goods if they didn't have the cash. "We would go by boat to Fernwood on the east side of Salt Spring and a friend would take us to the store in a horse and buggy."

Through the hard years, there were plenty of sociable times as well. "We used to go on picnics and make everything on the beach—we would take flour, baking powder,

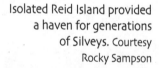
Isolated Reid Island provided a haven for generations of Silveys. Courtesy Rocky Sampson

The Remarkable Adventures of "Portuguese Joe" Silvey

The Silveys shopped at Mouat's store on Salt Spring Island, where they could get credit when they were short on cash.
Salt Spring Archives

etc.—we would catch the fish." Dances were held on weekends. Domingo and Tony both "played the button accordion" and Tony also "played the violin, guitar, mouth organ and Jew's harp." As for young Irene, "I got a kerchief and learned a dance, each person held an end of a kerchief, I put it around and over the head, we did this Portuguese dance."

Traditional protocols held. "We had our brothers as chaperones at dances. We couldn't sit together and hold hands, we were told if we held hands or looked at each other we'd get pregnant." Another of Portuguese Joe's granddaughters recalled: "Mother said babies are under cabbage leaves, it was my older sister who had to tell us things." The prohibitions served their purpose. "For a large family, no one came home pregnant and no boys made girls pregnant."

Portuguese Joe's grandchildren and great-grandchildren were brought up by example, very much as their parents had been. "My aunt would say, 'get up, Irene, & watch me.'" "They taught the boys very well to log, fish, hunt, repair boats." The women "taught the young children cooking, bread making, canning, knitting, sewing, they took time out for us." Domingo's daughters Laura and Gloria recalled how "we learned how to cook, to make bread, to iron clothes." It was not just the girls who acquired such skills. Even "the men can cook whole meals." "We were taught how to wash clothes, we learned how to chop kindling, haul water, wash dishes, we all had something to do." The "men made their own bacon and ham," and this skill was also passed down. "We were taught very young how to accomplish every job, we had to do it over and over again until we got it."

When neither the residential school on Kuper Island nor the "white school" on Galiano would accept children of mixed race, the Silveys started up their own school on Reid Island, welcoming other families who found themselves in a similar bind.
Courtesy Art More and Laurie Williams

Some of the students at Silvey School commuted to school by boat.
Courtesy Art More and Laurie Williams

For all the lessons that were learned at home, formal schooling was also an essential part of all children's lives by this time, wherever they might live in British Columbia. Schooling became a family affair during the interwar years. Tony's two eldest children followed their mother to the Kuper Island residential school, but then the family was told that "it was not accepting half-breeds any more." Students "had to be full-blood Indians." This recollection coming down through the family is consistent with the general policy of the Department of Indian Affairs whereby only persons with status, which descended paternally and thereby excluded Tony's children, were permitted to live on reserves or attend residential school.

The nearest public school was on north Galiano. It was a log structure, which, according to family recollections, Domingo helped to build. Some of his older children attended, but "half the time we could not get to school on Galiano for bad weather." Not only that, increasingly "the white people didn't want us there, they said, 'we don't want you.'" One of Portuguese Joe's granddaughters explained that the children "weren't allowed to go to the white school." She summed up the dilemma in which the Silvey clan found themselves: "The Indians wouldn't accept us and neither would the whites. We might as well put it the way it was."

Like other British Columbia families in similar circumstances, the Silveys took matters into their own hands. On Gabriola Island, Josephine Silvey's brother Abe Crocker wangled a school near Silva Bay, where the extended family lived. On Reid Island the leadership came from Josephine's husband Domingo, their son Jack and his brother Tony. They named themselves school trustees and, in 1936, requested from the provincial Department of Education their own school on the island. More than 700 small rural elementary schools dotted the province, so officials in Victoria probably did not think twice about adding one more, or even about its name—Silvey School. At first, classes were held in the net shed located by the Mud Bay dike. When the shed became too dilapidated, the parents constructed a proper school.

"The parents got together and built the school and imported a couple of half-breed families to get enough children—the Crockers and the Rices." Domingo's wife Josephine was a Crocker, and the school-age members of her extended family lived during the school year in Portuguese Joe's old house, which was vacant after Lucy's death in 1934. "The Rices lived on their own island, Norway Island. When school started, nine of them had to paddle across. Then the Silveys built them a house across on the southern side of Reid Island." The Rice family originated with an American from Port Townsend in Washington and an Indigenous woman from Galiano Island. It was their son Charles's widow, a local Native woman, who took the initiative to ensure that their children were educated. To these were added Domingo's youngest child Gloria and the children of his son Jack and brother Tony. Tony's daughter Irene recalled with pride how, at the start of each year, "my father would buy us new pencils—we could choose our colours."

The published annual reports of the Department of Education indicate that Silvey School enrolled 15 to 18 children, mostly in the lower grades. The teacher's salary of $780 came primarily from the provincial government, with the "school district," in effect the parents, contributing another $20 to $100 a year to keep Silvey School in operation. It was not always possible to do so, because of falling average daily attendance. At least twice Silvey School was closed partway through the year.

Each year up to 18 children attended the one-room Silvey School at Mud Bay. Courtesy Art More and Laurie Williams

Portuguese Joe's son John with his sister Laura Silvey Thompson and his wife Laura McFadden Silvey behind him.
Courtesy Chris Thompson

Learning was not necessarily an easy matter for these island children. "These were tough lessons—we would help each other." One of Tony's sons limped, "so we would pack his books." The self-selected trustees did the best they could, Tony's daughter Irene recalled. "At the school if any child was bad, trustees would take the child out and have a good talk to them and get them on the right track again. They always had time for the kids."

Tony's children moved most easily of their generation between their Portuguese and aboriginal inheritances. As Irene explained, "We had the best of two cultures." As well as living on Reid, "we were also raised with our adopted grandmother on Kuper." Irene had "lots of fun" as a child on Kuper. "We would go in a canoe and everyone got a paddle according to their size." Multilingualism continued to prevail, for her "adopted grandparents on Kuper Island always spoke Indian to us."

Whatever else Tony might do to make a living for his family, he remained a fisherman. "Fishing was his life, and he always returned to the industry after his excursions into other fields." He made his own spoons and lead lines when cod fishing or trolling on his boat, the *Last Chance*. As well as supporting his family, Tony took on the food fishery for Kuper Island from his father. Tony's three sons, who lived in the Ladysmith and Saltair districts, followed him into fishing. One of them took over the Penelakut food fishery.

Domingo Silvey, the patriarch of Reid Island, died in 1941. When he became seriously ill and could no longer support his family, the story in the family goes, everyone lent a hand. "Aunt Josie would go into town and, when the men would shake hands with her when she got off the boat, each one would give her $5 to go shopping. There was no welfare in those days." In death as in life, Portuguese Joe's oldest son successfully maintained the heritage his father held so dear. He was described on his death registration as "Portuguese" by racial origin.

The confirmation of Jack and Laura Silvey's daughters Patricia, Silvia, Della, Bernice and Eunice (dressed in white from left to right), on May 20, 1944, was a cause for celebration.

Students at the Silvey School in June, 1937. Back row: Henry Crocker, Irene and Stan Silvey, Francis Crocker, Bernice Silvey and Joe Rice. Front row: Mary Crocker, Della Silvey, Rice child, Sylvia Silvey, Helen Rice, Gloria Silvey, Annie and Alex Rice, Ray, Jackie and Leonard Silvey. *Courtesy Art More and Laurie Williams*

Domingo's widow Josephine coped with his death by spending the summers at Steveston on the Fraser River or at one of the other coastal canneries. "She made a living making and mending nets. There were about five Indian ladies and mother mending nets." Her daughters sometimes went with her, for there was good money to be made. "$250 to make a net, $2.75 an hour to mend, you had to make a net in 10 hours or less." Josephine died in 1945.

Portuguese Joe's son Tony, who never owned any of the island, moved to nearby Ladysmith in about 1965 and died two years later. On his death certificate his daugh-

Sylvia, Sanford, Darlene, Sam and John Silvey on a family outing in Pendrell Sound, north of Powell River. *Courtesy Eunice Weatherell*

ter Edith recorded her bicultural family. She identified her paternal grandmother as Lucy Kwatleematt, thereby acknowledging Native descent, and her father as Portuguese.

After Domingo's death, Reid Island was divided among his children, and the entire island was eventually sold off—Domingo's eldest son Joe sold the last of it in 1974. Today there are about 30 holdings, most of them belonging to "summer people." Only the family cemetery, containing several generations of Silveys, gives a reminder of the important role Reid Island played for this coastal family.

Sons Away from Reid Island

Other Silvey children left Reid Island to embark on their own adventures. Portuguese Joe's second son Joseph, born in 1879, initiated a migration to Egmont, at the mouth of Jervis Inlet on the northeast edge of the Sechelt Peninsula. Some members of the Silvey family still live in the area: "Uncle Joe went in and found it a nice place and decided to settle there." According to Betty Keller and Rosella Leslie's history of the area, it was Portuguese Joe who first came across the spot. "Sometime during the late 1880s, he spent several years living in one of the bays near Egmont Point and fishing in Jervis Inlet."

Young Joe, together with his wife Maria King and two children, purchased 40 acres on the water at Egmont in 1904. Joe owned his own boat, and he seined, trolled and fished for lingcod. Five more children were born before Maria died in 1919. In the family tradition Joe mentored his sons into fishing. Over the next decade three of his children died in young adulthood, two from tuberculosis and the third by drowning after being swept overboard from a gillnetter. According to his grandson Leonard, the deaths devastated Joe. "I would sit with him for hours and he wouldn't say a word, he would just whittle and carve all these little boats. It was like he had died inside." At the time of his death in early 1940, Joe was living in Egmont. As with his older brother Domingo, his racial origin was shown on his death certificate as Portuguese. The identity was so entrenched that his son Ernie claimed both of Joe's parents—Portuguese Joe and Lucy—had been born in Portugal.

Portuguese Joe's second son Joseph initiated a small family migration to the village of Egmont near the mouth of the Sechelt Inlet.

Like his father before him, "young Joe" took to the sea and taught his own sons how to fish. Courtesy Jessica Casey

Above: Frank Silvey (young Joe's son), Alfie Jeffries, Tom Wright, Harry Baines and young Joe Silvey.
Courtesy Jessica Casey

Opposite top: In keeping with tradition, Portuguese Joe's youngest son Henry became a fisherman who proudly named his boat the *Silvey*.
Courtesy Jessica Casey

Opposite bottom: Henry Silvey's wife Amelia Andrew.
Courtesy Jessica Casey

The two youngest Silvey sons, Manuel, born in 1886, and Henry, born in 1890, became fishermen almost as a matter of course. They took such pride in their work as a family endeavour that Henry named his boat the *Silvey*. His sometime partner in trawling and seining was Nick Stevens, a Salt Spring Islander linked by family and proximity. Nick's mother was the older sister of Maria King, married to Henry's brother Joe. Nick recalled that at the end of the season Henry Silvey "went to North Vancouver to visit." The reason he did so was decidedly romantic. Both Henry and his brother Manuel married sisters from North Vancouver. Charlotte and Amelia were the daughters of a Chilean man, who, according to family tradition, jumped ship at Vancouver in the early 1880s, when he was just 17.

Afraid of being caught, Balinto Fidele Sanhueza sought refuge from Chief Squamish Jim of the Mission Reserve in North Vancouver. He was soon living on a small farm with the chief's daughter, Kwaxtelut or Katherine. Charlotte was only four and Amelia Henriette just six months old when their mother died in 1890, at the age of 20. Sanhueza, who restyled himself Manuel Andrew, took as his new wife a local woman named Cecilia, who already had two children, including a daughter named Madeleine or Maggie, and who would herself die in 1909. One of the consequences of this upheaval was that all three girls—Charlotte, Amelia and Maggie—were sent to the Catholic residential school located on the Mission Reserve. On leaving school, Charlotte married a Chilean named Avaleno Savedra, by whom she had a son Frederick, born in February 1903.

Two years later Savedra was killed in a dynamite explosion while clearing land in North Vancouver, whereupon his widow married Manuel Silvey. Two years later, Charlotte's younger sister Amelia wed Manuel's younger brother Henry.

By virtue of marrying the Andrew sisters, Manuel and Henry Silvey acquired a large extended family. Manuel Andrew, who lived until 1945, encouraged visits to North Vancouver. His great-granddaughter Grace recalled the exhilarating experience, when she was a child, of walking across the newly opened Lion's Gate Bridge and then "up this huge hill" to reach his house. Charlotte and Amelia's maternal aunt had in 1894 married Willie Baker, son of the Silvey family's long-ago neighbour at Brockton Point. Charlotte's son Frederick Savedra had a family by the granddaughter of a Hawaiian, George Kamano, who was long settled on Harbledown Island off of northern Vancouver Island with his wife Claheara, or Pauline, from Fort Rupert. Charlotte and Amelia's stepsister Maggie lived at Chemainus with a Mexican known as Joe Rae, or Joshua Renosha. Grace remembered going there on the family fish boat and having Joe "teaching me Spanish, I was eight or nine, Grandmother said, 'Where did you learn those words?'...they were all swear words, and that was the end of my Spanish."

In about 1920, Henry and his family followed his older brother Joe from Reid Island to Egmont. The impetus was Henry's great discontent over Domingo's handling of Reid Island, their father's legacy. "I can see his boat piled high with stuff, he went to Jervis Inlet, and did not come back for three years." Henry skippered vessels for BC Packers, which operated canneries along the coast, and also seined, trolled and fished for cod with his own boat, the *Rose Silvey*. He had a saltery at Egmont, much like those operating on Reid and Galiano islands.

As always, the hard work was mixed with pleasure. Dances were held in the schoolhouse, and Henry sometimes played the guitar. These events gave Egmont's youthful enthusiasts an opportunity to dream. "When the floor manager said, 'Allemande left,' I would allemande left until he blew the whistle. I would then dance with the person I was facing. I tried my best to get close to the person I really liked." Henry and Amelia had six children and almost 60 years together before she died in 1966. He followed her two weeks later—dying of a broken heart, according to family legend.

Mano, as he was sometimes known within the family, was a "tugboat skipper who had his own boat and towed booms." Manuel and Charlotte had five children before he was drowned

One of the Silvey boats, the *Argent*, heading up Jervis Inlet.
Courtesy Eunice Weatherell

in 1916 at Brockton Point, when his launch full of fish was run down by a tugboat. On board was his sister Mary's eldest son, who also perished. Charlotte Silvey was a housekeeper living at 786 East Hastings in Vancouver when she died on July 6, 1943. Her death certificate stated that she had been in the occupation for 35 years, or since her husband was killed. Her son proudly described her as Chilean by racial origin.

Both Manuel's and Henry's families preferred their Portuguese and Chilean identities over their aboriginality. Their neighbour Florence West, who moved to Egmont as a child, had no doubts that the families were, as she put it, "of Portuguese and Indian descent." Amelia in particular had good reason to downplay her family's aboriginal heritage. She used to tell about how, on being sent to residential school at age five, she had a needle pushed through her tongue for not being able to speak English.

She knew first-hand the racism that prevailed across mainstream British Columbia toward persons perceived as Indians or "half-breeds," and did not want her children and grandchildren to suffer its consequences.

Amelia would tell her children, "You can't be Native!" She emphasized to them: "We Silveys were only Portuguese, Chilean and a little bit of Greek from Maria King." A granddaughter reflected: "My grandmother was determined to protect us as well as she could. She was taking care of us in her own way. As long as Amelia was alive, we could not be Indian." Physical appearance counted. Charlotte in particular was remembered as "Hispanic."

The strategy of subordinating aboriginal to Portuguese identity did not always have the desired end. Manuel's son Tony, who lost his father in 1916 when he was only seven years old, lost touch with his Portuguese heritage. His daughter identified him solely as a "Native Indian" on his death in 1972.

Lucy's Daughters

Portuguese Joe and Lucy's two daughters, Mary and Lena, divided their loyalties between the men in their lives. Initially Mary followed the marital path taken by her older half-sisters, but although she did her best to sustain her children, she could not always manage the feat. Her married daughter Laura Roberts was living with her in Vancouver when, at age 21, she fell out of a window and died of a fractured skull. In the same year, 1914, Mary's eldest daughter from her second marriage, Mina, married into the Wilson family, the same Fraser River fishing clan that her cousin Joe would shortly join.

Joe and Lucy's daughter Mary (left) was a very talented basket weaver. Beside her is Laura G. Silvey.
Courtesy Eunice Weatherell

Portuguese Joe's youngest daughter Lena was a rebel whose great love for her family did not stop her from living an unconventional life.
Courtesy Chris Thompson

Over time, Mary turned more and more to her birth family. She lived on her brother Henry's property at Egmont and then got her own place nearby. Their neighbour Florence West recalled Mary and her then husband Harry Buss as "colourful characters." Mary had what might be termed personality. "She used to cause a lot of trouble with her gossiping but if anyone got sick she would be the first to help. She lived in Egmont and she raised her grandson Arthur."

In 1936 Vancouver celebrated the 50th anniversary of its incorporation, and the city encouraged early residents to participate in Jubilee events. Mary was determined to do so, which speaks to her toughness of character and also to her integration of her paternal and maternal inheritances. Wanting to ensure that her father's contribution to city building was acknowledged, she paid a visit to the Vancouver archivist, Major Matthews. He did not know quite what to make of Joe Silvey's daughter. "She has come to Vancouver to witness the Golden Jubilee festivities of her native home, but has come without money, and is trying to sell Indian basketry, of her own make, to raise the small sum sufficient for her humble needs." Mary was, by Matthews's description, "a stout woman with the characteristics of an Indian, and in this respect takes after her mother, who was a full-blooded Sechelt Indian, she cannot read or write, but is very clever in making Indian basketry." Mary was by then becoming somewhat hazy about the events in her life and died in1941 at Essondale Mental Hospital near Vancouver. Her husband gave the information and described her, unlike any of the other Silvey children, as an "Indian."

The youngest Silvey was Lena. She was just six when her father died and, perhaps for that reason, was much more her own person than his other daughters. According to her nieces, "Lena was a free spirit." Her mother was repeatedly frustrated by Lena's antics. She lived for a time in Chemainus, where Lucy's partner Joe Watson worked as a longshoreman, and when she came home would "la-di-dah." Sometimes she had a man in tow. "Aunt Lena was always introducing her new husband, 'This is your new uncle, my dear.'"

Lena's resourcefulness in life made her the one her brothers leaned on when something went wrong. When Domingo built his son Jack his first fishing boat in 1918, he named it *Lena* after his youngest sister. "It was Lena who they used for advice. They called her in when there was a problem in the family. Auntie Lena was like a matriarch on Reid Island." Lena, her five children and an American husband lived for a time near the saltery in the Silvey compound at Egmont. Then she bought property and built a house of her own. Lena's husband went off to the Second World War and, the story goes, "when he came back she had another man there." Lena was described as a widow on her death in 1957.

Portuguese Joe's Legacy

Portuguese Joe Silvey was a determined, resourceful, hardworking man who left an important trace on British Columbia. He was one of the earliest entrepreneurs in today's Vancouver. He contributed in diverse and significant ways to the development of the province's fishing industry. He understood the importance of community to family survival in difficult times, and he laid the foundation for a largely self-sustaining way of life.

The Silvey legacy is considerable. Portuguese Joe had six sons and four daughters who survived into adulthood. Through their marriages, they consolidated a hybrid coastal society that originated with the gold rush and continues to contribute to the making of British Columbia. At least 70 grandchildren were born, well over half of them bearing the Silvey surname, and many more great-grandchildren, and so on into the present day.

Portuguese Joe inculcated into his children the traditional Portuguese values of his childhood, and these they sought to pass down to the next generation. Sometimes the values have transferred at a personal cost, such as what transpired when Henry and Amelia's daughter Violet became pregnant at age 16 at Christmas 1927, by her cousin Ernie, son of Joseph and Maria. Violet was promptly married off to a much older man who had been a friend of her grandfather, Portuguese Joe. However much in love the young couple might be, Portuguese tradition dictated that cousins did not wed. "Her father was very old-fashioned and Portuguese— that was a no-no, they were cousins." Violet was not to be deterred. She ran off on her wedding night to her Aunt Lena, then living in Vancouver. There she stayed until her daughter Grace was born the next August, in the hospital after which she was named. Violet then took off alone, up the coast in search of her beloved Ernie, who was out fishing for the season. For a time it seemed that the only option was to have baby Grace adopted out—that is, until Aunt Lena stepped in and persuaded her sister-in-law Amelia to come and get the infant.

Grace was raised mostly at Egmont by her grandparents, Henry and Amelia, and she found herself subject to much the same restrictions as her mother had been.

Henry and Amelia Silvey's children Bill, Violet and Ky.
Courtesy Jessica Casey

Amelia Silvey with her
daughter Rose and
granddaughter Grace.
Courtesy Jessica Casey

She recalled being carefully chaperoned to dances and on other social occasions. "Portuguese descent, you're old fashioned, you know. You were chaperoned all the time." Grace's solace came from her beloved Aunt Lena. Now living at Egmont, Lena taught embroidery and fancywork to the niece she had rescued from adoption. Like her mother, Grace was pushed in traditional Portuguese style toward an arranged marriage, to a man who fished with her father. But before the actual wedding, she was able to escape to her biological parents, who were by now settled with a family.

The Silveys' strong sense of Portuguese identity was reinforced by countrymen living nearby and also by visits from relatives. Portuguese Joe's oldest daughter Elizabeth used to receive letters from "cousins in Massachusetts," whom she recalled as children of her father's sister. Portuguese Joe's nephew "came twice to see them at Reid Island to make certain his uncle was receiving merchandise sent from the family at New Bedford, Massachusetts, USA." Tony's daughter Irene described how, in about 1945, "a cousin in the states that had a vineyard, a big vineyard in California, came to see dad in a yellow Cadillac." Antonio Christian de Silvia got as far as Ladysmith, but could not find the family because he was looking for them by his own surname. Eventually the "fisheries officer came and told Pa that somebody was looking for him in Ladysmith." Irene and her siblings were taken to meet him. "Out of respect we called him uncle, but he was a first cousin." The children were sent back home to Reid Island, while their father Tony stayed on to visit with this new-found relative who "took over the Europe Hotel and stayed a week there."

However much family members might conceive of themselves as Portuguese, they had to negotiate their aboriginality and, even more, their hybridity. All her life, Portuguese Joe's eldest daughter Elizabeth valued the understandings her mother Khaltinaht had given her about her Squamish and Musqueam ancestry. For her younger half-brother Tony, it was his wife Alice Aleck who played that role. Other Silvey children and grandchildren were ambivalent about their maternal inheritance, and they had pragmatic reasons for these feelings. Domingo's eldest son Joe considered World War I an important learning experience in terms of his racial inheritance. He trained in England, which was a revelation: "The British saw us as soldiers, they treated us as soldiers." The sense of equality Joe experienced there was in sharp distinction to Canada, where he was scorned and treated as an inferior.

For a long time in British Columbia, almost no one who had a choice wanted to be an Indian or a "half-breed." As Tony's daughter Irene recalled, "Auntie Josie [Domingo's wife] and Grandma [Silvey] and Grandma on Kuper would send the children out and speak Indian to each other, they didn't want the children to know that they spoke Indian." Asked when the racism stopped, a granddaughter responded, "maybe it stopped in the late '40s or '50s," and, on reflection, "no, it isn't really stopped." Referring to a Silvey grandson, a Chemainus businessman claimed in the 1970s that "the

Domingo and Josephine Silvey's son Jack.
Courtesy Art More and Laurie Williams

The "Reid Island Beauties" (Laura, Pat, Della, Sylvia and Eunice) going for a dip at Starvation Bay, Valdes Island.
Courtesy Chris Thompson

Most of the Silvey men, including Jack Silvey (in foreground), worked as fishermen or loggers.
Courtesy Eunice Weatherell

old Indian owes me money." Descendants were caught. Outsiders equated the Silvey family's near-subsistence lifestyle with their stereotypical perceptions of aboriginal ways. Whatever the measure, "everyone wanted to be white people," to quote Irene, but the Silveys were not.

In the second generation and to a considerable extent subsequently, the Silveys coped by relying on each other and marrying within familiar settings. They were resourceful and strategic. As descendant after descendant has explained, "it seems like everyone knows everyone else among the old families." The water linked coastal and island families. Their children, particularly those who had aboriginal mothers, were given every encouragement to intermarry, and all six of Portuguese Joe's sons and his eldest daughter did so. Proximity of and adherence to Catholicism encouraged relationships, but so did the racial antipathies of the day. "Families of mixed race stuck together, they had to." Joe Silvey's other three daughters looked to newcomer men, who turned to mixed-heritage women when newcomer females were in short supply. Whether or not the tensions inherent in such situations played a role, none of Portuguese Joe's daughters had relationships as outwardly stable as those of their brothers.

Some descendants, by choice or circumstance, came to see themselves over time as principally Native, others as primarily Portuguese. "There's a definite divide in the

family between Portuguese and Indian Silveys." Due to the demographic imbalance and the expectation that a woman would in any case adopt her husband's identity, descendants through the female line have found it easier to shed their aboriginality, should they so choose. It is only in the present generation that negative attitudes toward aboriginality and mixed race have moderated in the larger society. Family members now take pride in reclaiming their Native heritage, as Joe's oldest daughter Elizabeth attempted to do with middling success in her last years.

The self-confidence that families like the Silveys could realize by working in the resource sector has been a powerful counterpoint to issues of racial identity. Economic survival was never easy—it required hard physical labour to make a living. The Silveys have made that commitment for a century and a half in British Columbia. Portuguese Joe's granddaughter Irene has characterized the Silveys as "seine boat skippers, cod fishermen, so many things, they could do anything to do with logging and fishing." Their way of life gave them self-confidence and a strong sense of self. "If there was no sea and no fishing, there would be no me," as Portuguese Joe's great-grandson Leonard put it.

A newspaper obituary of young Joe and Maria's son Frank, born in Chemainus in 1901, says that with his wife Violet at his side, "he died last month as he had lived, fishing the Strait of Georgia waters from which he had wrested a living over the past six decades." This description from 1972 applies to any number of Portuguese Joe's descendants: "Silvey was skipper of a seine boat at the age of 16 and spent many years trolling, packing, longlining, gillnetting, and cod fishing...The industry veteran began fishing with his father as a boy and was skipping a seiner before he was out of his teens. During his long career, he worked in virtually all sections of the industry, as a seiner, troller, longliner, tenderman, gillnetter and cod fisherman." The strength that marked Silvey women as well as men is evident in the story, for it was Violet who on her own "brought their 31-foot *Francis Point* back to Deep Bay." In the space for "racial origin" on Frank Silvey's death certificate, his son proudly put down "Portuguese."

The ethos of hard work that has guided and sustained the Silvey family from the time of Portuguese Joe into the present day is captured in the lines of a poem written by his great-great-granddaughter Jessica Silvey Casey, in honour of her father:

A fisherman
Is all I will ever be
I was born to a family
That lived to sail the sea.
The tides of change
May flow
In and out
But this
I will never doubt
Wherever there are salmon
I will surely go
It is the only way
Of life
I know.

Or, to put the matter another way, "I will not forget who I am, here I am, I'm a Silvey, and I'm proud of it."

Opposite top: Ken Silvey near Domingo's old home.
Courtesy Eunice Weatherell

Opposite bottom: Della Silvey, Domingo's first grandchild born with the Silvey name.
Courtesy Eunice Weatherell

Below left: Jack Silvey's packer *Great Northern 9*.
Courtesy Eunice Weatherell

Afterword

by Rocky Sampson, great-great-grandson of Portuguese Joe Silvey

What a delight it was to read *The Remarkable Adventures of Portuguese Joe Silvey.* Dr. Barman, I was very impressed by the way in which you handled the large and overwhelming family I call mine. I find there are so many named Josephine, Joseph, Amelia and many other names that can be confusing, but you kept the right person and the right "Joe" in line. Your book is my book, is our book, and this book shows that in a world where strangers come and go it is great to have a sense of belonging and family. Family is not always perfect by any means but it is all we have at the end of the day. We overcome challenges and obstacles with family. We pull together in good times and sad, with family. We forgive as family and we love as family.

I remember as a boy when I first went to my mom's home, "Reid Island." I was still a small child and my Great Uncle Joe and Aunt Amelia picked us up at Chemainus in his small wooden green boat. The boat was so tiny I thought we would sink, but it took me, my two brothers, parents and Uncle Joe and Aunt Amelia the distance to Reid Island. The journey was magical as we slowly motored our way through the islands, tides and sun. Time stood still and time did not matter. I recall coming ashore at Reid Island and setting foot on land that was somehow familiar. The dry grasses of summer, the scent of arbutus leaves and sea air were all familiar to my soul. Reid Island was a special place for us kids to explore. "Qulus," Reid Island's Hul'qumi'num name, means "quiet and peaceful place" and I think it lives up to its real name. We had grown up on islands but I felt a connection to Reid. I can recall finding a lizard in the cemetery by the sea; I followed his whipping tail to his hiding place in the middle of the cemetery. Then I realized where I was. I stood in silence listening to the tide in the channel and the waves splash on the rocks...the magic was simply knowing I was part of all around me, part of family.

On that same first trip I recall nightfall too. It must have been the first night on our visit as the coal oil lamps were out and candles burned to make light for family stories. I recall all went fine until great Uncle Joe began telling family ghost stories. Suddenly my hair stood on end and fear filled me. My fears took me away and I was scared beyond belief! But the trip was far too short and far too soon we were heading home.

What strikes my memory most was the trunk Uncle Joe had, filled with family memorabilia and photographs, some yellow with age and others printed on tin. I recall placing it all together: the pictures, ghost stories, the smell of the sea, the smell of the wild grasses in the cemetery and the feeling of family and love. Reid Island wasn't my home Island but it was my connection to my people.

They say we don't remember days but rather we recall moments in our lives; I tend to think we recall it all. When I go to Reid Island today I taste the apples, grapes and berries, I smell the honeysuckle wild roses and mosses. I smell the blackened earth, dry like summer. I hear the distant rip of tide at Porlier Pass. My hands feel the sun-baked sandstone. I see how the sun glints a million sparkles on the sea, I remember it all, not just a moment.

Sources

Portuguese Joe Silvey's story was written at the request of his great-great-great-grandsons, Kyle and Cole Silvey. They and their teacher Pauline Falck at Quadra Elementary School at Quathiaski Cove, British Columbia, heard me talk about Portuguese Joe on Mark Forsythe's show *Almanac* on CBC Radio in the fall of 1998. They wanted to know more about this man who shared their surname and who, they speculated, might be related to them. I took "The Remarkable Adventures," written for them, to a Silvey family reunion at Ladysmith the following spring. Since then, numerous copies have been shared with descendants and others. Manuel Azevedo, a historian of the Portuguese community in British Columbia who is from Pico Island in the Azores, as was Joe Silvey, introduced the story to the Portuguese community in Vancouver and Toronto.

Many persons have added their voices to this expanded text. Among those sharing memories, photographs or other materials are Marilyn Baines, Gloria Blomley, Barrie Bradshaw, Jessica Casey, Mackie Chase, Margaret Hall Corbett, Gordon de Frane, Florence West Dubois, Grace Faulds, Marie Gabara, Irene Griffith, Brenda Hammond, Maria Lima, Marie Malbon, Jane Marston, Art More, Rose Peddie, Phyllis Roberts, Sylvia Sampson, Leonard Silvey, Rose Silvey, Marlene Smith, Chris Thompson, Laura Thompson and Eunice Weatherell. I owe a special thank you to Rocky Sampson for his contributions to the book. I am grateful to Howard White for suggesting Portuguese Joe's story merited publication, and to Shyla Seller, Mary Schendlinger, Vici Johnstone, and Alicia Miller for guiding it there. I have received much useful advice as to what I got wrong and what is right. Sometimes I have had to make choices as to which sources appear most reliable and consistent with other information. I take full responsibility for any misunderstandings and errors that may have resulted. Joe Silvey's story is just that, a story.

The most vivid stories about Portuguese Joe come from his eldest daughter Elizabeth, who shared her memories with Major J.S. Matthews, Vancouver City Archivist. The two had more than a dozen conversations between October 1938 and October 1943, about a year and a half before her death. Matthews would type up his notes, either as they were talking or afterwards. He would read the text back to her for any changes or additions, and she would then sign the transcript with a shaky hand. It is important to keep in mind that Elizabeth's stories are only her recollections and some parts of them may have become exaggerated over time. On the other hand, they remained remarkably consistent over the five years she talked with Major Matthews.

I have also drawn from Major Matthews's conversations and correspondence with Thomas Bryant, Alice Crakanthorp, Thomas Fisher, Jim Franks, W.A. Grafton, Christine Thomas Jack, Jennie Beale Jeffries (in Silvey file), Tom MacInnes, William Mackie, Mr. and Mrs. Joseph Silvey, Calvert Simson, Charles Tate and Madeline Williams (widow of John "Gassy Jack" Deighton). Elizabeth Silvey's sister Mary Buss talked with Major Matthews twice in June 1936. Transcripts of all his conversations and related materials are in City of Vancouver Archives [CVA], Add. Ms. 54, excepting Bryant, which is in Matthews, *Early Vancouver*, Vol. 4, typescript CVA, Add. Ms. 97. Leo and Gaylia Nelson talked about the Silva family on March 7, 1975. The transcript is held in the British Columbia Archives [BCA], Ms. 242.

Just as with each of our stories, some parts of Portuguese Joe's remarkable adventures are easier to disentangle than others. Silvey family photos, correspondence and other papers going back in time a century and more were kept on Reid Island following its sale out of the family and, sadly, lost in a house fire there in 1978.

Basic information we take for granted about ourselves sometimes remains a bit of a mystery. Because Joseph Silvey could not do so, others wrote his name for him. When necessary, he wrote an *X* to confirm the accuracy of what he "signed" his name to. Among spellings put down on paper were Silva, Silvey, Silvia, Silver and Silvia Seamens. At his marriage, he described himself to the Catholic priest who performed the ceremony as Joseph Silvy, born in about 1834 to John Silvy and Francesca Hyacintha on Piopiko Island, Portugal. Brenda Hammond and Manuel Azevedo have separately initiated searches through records of Catholic baptisms on Pico Island. The single plausible record names the parents as João Joze, or John Joseph, de Simas and Francisca Jacinta, not that different from the names Joe used. Their son José, or Joseph, was born on April 23, 1828, six years before the birth year Portuguese Joe gave for himself. It is very likely but not certain that they were the same person.

Written sources include vital statistics kept by churches and the provincial government, preemption records, wills and probates, and the manuscript censuses for 1881, 1891 and 1901, all in BCA, excepting St. Ann's baptisms and marriages, held at St. Edward's Church, Duncan. Other information can be found in Robert James Roberts, Diary, BCA, A/E/R54/R54A; Kuper Island Indian Industrial School records, BCA, Ms. 1267; "Chief Squamish Jim, Sikemain, 1850–1924," CVA, Add. Ms. 5; Crown Lands records, BCA, GR 1088, box 1, files 1, 33; Soldiers of the First World War, National Archives of Canada web site; Joseph Domingo Silvey, "The Silvey Family," in Lillian Gustafson, comp., *Memories of the Chemainus Valley: A History of People* (Victoria: Chemainus Valley Historical Society, 1978); Florence Dubois, *William Jeffries and Other Pioneers of the Sunshine Coast* (privately published, 1996); Florence Tickner, *Fish Hooks & Caulk Boots, Raincoast Chronicles 14* (Madeira Park: Harbour, 1992); and Betty C. Keller and Rosella M. Leslie, *Bright Seas, Pioneer Spirits: The Sunshine Coast* (Victoria: Horsdal & Schubart, 1996).

I have also drawn from general sources. The Azores are introduced in Jerry Williams, *And Yet They Come: Portuguese Immigration from the Azores to the United States* (New York: Center for Migration Studies, 1982); whaling and its relationship to the Azores in Elmo P. Hohman, *The American Whaleman: A Study of Life and Labor in the Whaling Industry* (New York: Longmans, Green & Co., 1928); Briton Cooper Busch, *"Whaling Will Never Do for Me": The American Whaleman in the Nineteenth Century* (Lexington: University Press of Kentucky, 1994); and E. Davis, Robert E. Gallman, and Karin Gleiter, *In Pursuit of Leviathan: Technology, Institutions, Productivity, and Profits in American Whaling, 1816–1906* (Chicago: University of Chicago Press, 1997). Portuguese Joe's cabin at Point Roberts is described in R. Byron Johnson, *Very Far West Indeed: A Few Rough Experiences on the North-West Pacific Coast* (London: Sampson Low, Marston, Low, & Searle, 1872). Descriptions of Joe Silvey as a fisherman come from Major Matthews's sconversations noted above and also from Robert Brown, "The Land of the Hydahs, a spring journey north," in BCA, ms. 794, Vol. 2, file 10; and testimony of Joseph Mannion, in the appeal of Attorney General vs. Canadian Pacific Railway, Victoria, January 4, 1905, CVA. His activities in Gastown are described in Joseph Silvy to Chief Commissioner of Lands and Works, New Westminster, May 15, 1868; Joseph Silvy to A.T. Bushby, Burrard Inlet, December 15, 1870; A.T. Bushby to Colonial Secretary, Burrard Inlet, December 28, 1870; and E. Brown to A.T. Bushby, New Westminster, December 28, 1870, in BCA, GR1372, files F159a and F245. The activities of the British Columbia Reserve Commission are detailed in Department of Indian Affairs, RG10, Vol. 3645, file 7936, microfilm reel C-10113.

Information on William Bridge comes from John Rodger Burnes, *Saga of a Municipality In Its Formative Days 1891–1907* (North Vancouver: n.p., 1972?), and J.S. Matthews, *Early Vancouver*, Vol. 1 (Vancouver: City of Vancouver Archives, 1932), 160E. Navvy Jack Thomas is mentioned in William Scott, "The Early Story of North Vancouver," *Museum and Art Notes* (Art, Historical and Scientific Association of Vancouver), 2nd ser., Vol. 1, No. 2 (March 1950), 14; note with "Daughter of West Van Pioneer Dies," unidentified newspaper, March 25, 1960, CVA; and Charles W. Cates, *Tidal Action in British Columbia Waters* (North Vancouver: n.p., 1952). Nick Stevens recalled fishing with Henry Silvey in Nick Stevens, "Ice on the Fraser," 1949, typescript in Delta Archives, DE-48.

Newspaper stories quoted from are "Naturalized," *British Colonist*, March 25, 1867; "Gassy Jack," *Vancouver News*, September 14, 1886; Whyawhy, "Poor Jack's End," *Vancouver News*, September 15, 1886; Alan Morley, "Romance of Vancouver," *Sun*, May 21, 1940; "Portuguese Joe," *Province*, July 31, 1945; Nick Stevens, "Old Picture Stirs Memories," *Fisherman*, December 18, 1961; "Old Picture Prompts Story," *Fisherman*, January 19, 1962; "Death of Tony Silvey Snaps Link with Past," *Fisherman*, February 10, 1967; "Veteran Frank Silvey Stricken on Grounds," *Fisherman*, July 7, 1972; "Fisherman Passes Away," *Nanaimo Daily Free Press*, June 26, 1972; and Helen Plester, "History Comes Alive," *Daily Colonist*, June 26, 1977.

Raincoast Chronicles 21

West Coast Wrecks & Other Maritime Tales

Rick James

HARBOUR PUBLISHING

To my mentor and in-house editor, Paula Wild,
who remained always patient and understanding
while going over innumerable drafts with a critical eye
over the past twenty years.

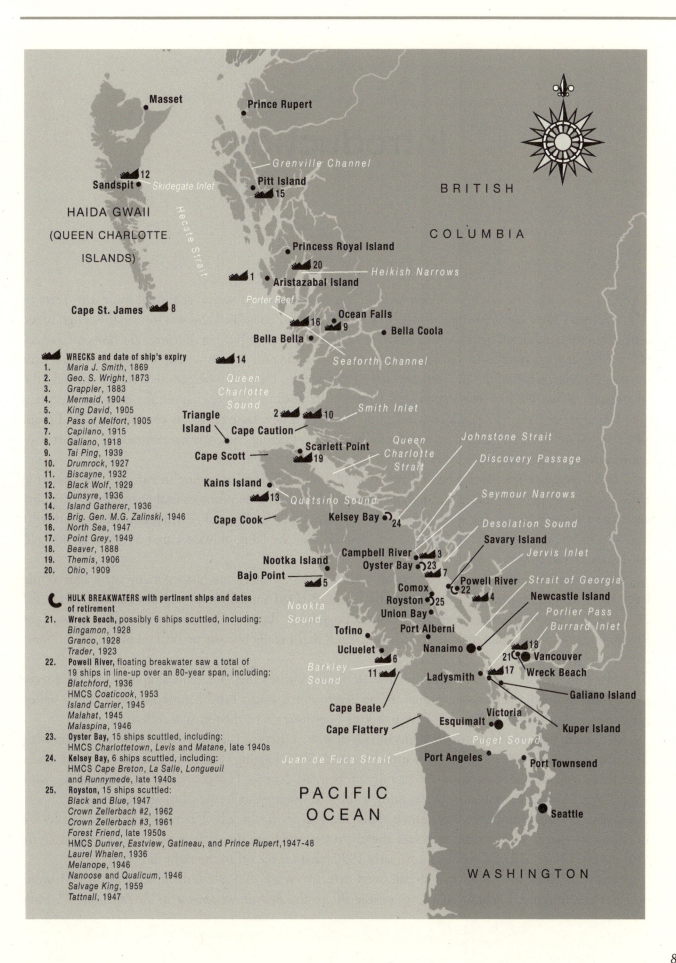

Masset

Prince Rupert

Grenville Channel

BRITISH

Sandspit ◤12   *Skidegate Inlet*

Pitt Island
◤15

HAIDA GWAII
(QUEEN CHARLOTTE
ISLANDS)

Hecate Strait

COLUMBIA

Princess Royal Island
◤20
1◤ ●Aristazabal Island   *Heikish Narrows*

Porter Reef

Cape St. James ◤8

Ocean Falls
16◤ ◤9   ●Bella Coola
Bella Bella ●

Seaforth Channel

◤14

◤ **WRECKS and date of ship's expiry**
1. *Maria J. Smith,* 1869
2. *Geo. S. Wright,* 1873
3. *Grappler,* 1883
4. *Mermaid,* 1904
5. *King David,* 1905
6. *Pass of Melfort,* 1905
7. *Capilano,* 1915
8. *Galiano,* 1918
9. *Tai Ping,* 1939
10. *Drumrock,* 1927
11. *Biscayne,* 1932
12. *Black Wolf,* 1929
13. *Dunsyre,* 1936
14. *Island Gatherer,* 1936
15. *Brig. Gen. M.G. Zalinski,* 1946
16. *North Sea,* 1947
17. *Point Grey,* 1949
18. *Beaver,* 1888
19. *Themis,* 1906
20. *Ohio,* 1909

☾ **HULK BREAKWATERS with pertinent ships and dates**
of retirement
21. **Wreck Beach,** possibly 6 ships scuttled, including:
    Bingamon, 1928
    Granco, 1928
    Trader, 1923
22. **Powell River,** floating breakwater saw a total of
    19 ships in line-up over an 80-year span, including:
    Blatchford, 1936
    HMCS *Coaticook,* 1953
    Island Carrier, 1945
    Malahat, 1945
    Malaspina, 1946
23. **Oyster Bay,** 15 ships scuttled, including:
    HMCS *Charlottetown, Levis* and *Matane,* late 1940s
24. **Kelsey Bay,** 6 ships scuttled, including:
    HMCS *Cape Breton, La Salle, Longueuil*
    and *Runnymede,* late 1940s
25. **Royston,** 15 ships scuttled:
    Black and Blue, 1947
    Crown Zellerbach #2, 1962
    Crown Zellerbach #3, 1961
    Forest Friend, late 1950s
    HMCS *Dunver, Eastview, Gatineau,* and *Prince Rupert,*1947-48
    Laurel Whalen, 1936
    Melanope, 1946
    Nanoose and *Qualicum,* 1946
    Salvage King, 1959
    Tattnall, 1947

*Queen
Charlotte
Sound*

Smith Inlet

Triangle
Island
Cape Caution

2◤ ◤10

*Queen
Charlotte
Strait*

Scarlett Point
Cape Scott ●   ◤19

Johnstone Strait

Discovery Passage

Kains Island ●
◤13

Seymour Narrows

Quatsino Sound

Kelsey Bay ●☾
24

Desolation Sound

Cape Cook ●

Savary Island

Campbell River ●◤3
Oyster Bay ●☾23

Jervis Inlet

Nootka Island
Bajo Point ◤5

7◤

Powell River ●◤4
22

Strait of Georgia

Comox ●☾
Royston ●☾25
Union Bay ●

Newcastle Island

Porlier Pass

*Nootka
Sound*

Port Alberni

Burrard Inlet

Tofino ●

18

Nanaimo ●

Ucluelet ●

11◤ ◤6

21☾ Vancouver ●
17☾ Wreck Beach

*Barkley
Sound*

Ladysmith ●

Galiano Island

Cape Beale

Cape Flattery

Victoria ●
Esquimalt ●

Kuper Island

Port Angeles ●

Puget Sound

Juan de Fuca Strait

**PACIFIC
OCEAN**

Port Townsend ●

Seattle ●

WASHINGTON

87

Introduction

West Coast Wrecks and Other Maritime Tales is a compilation of stories spanning some 140 years of British Columbia's maritime history, which I researched, assembled and was fortunate enough to see featured in such publications as the Victoria *Times Colonist Monitor, Western Mariner, The Beaver: Canada's History Magazine*, as well as in various Underwater Archaeological Society of BC shipwreck reports over the past 20 years. Most of the chapters are tales of shipwrecks, but the book goes beyond just relating the circumstances that led to many a good ship going to the bottom. In one chapter, for instance, I explain how a number of retired Cape Horn windjammers gained a new lease on life as coastal barges and then, when they were worn out, ended up scuttled as hulks for a logging company breakwater. In another I set out to solve a 60-year-old mystery: How did Wreck Beach earn its name?

I also investigate the history behind the most famous early marine engine in British Columbia, the Easthope, but more importantly, throughout the book I allow some unique coastal characters to step forward and tell their stories. There are old towboaters such as Joe Quilty and Alan Heater, who risked their lives as a matter of course, along with a short biography of the King of West Coast Shipwrecks himself, retired diver Fred Rogers.

So what set off this interest and obsession with West Coast maritime history many years ago? While I did come from a family with a seafaring background (Dad served in the Royal Canadian Navy for 21 years), it wasn't until I began exploring Comox Logging & Railway Company's old hulk breakwater at Royston, just south of Courtenay on Vancouver Island, that I really became hooked on old ships and their fascinating stories.

I first explored the Royston site in the early 1970s, back when the 15 derelict ships scuttled there were still reasonably solid and standing proud off the beach, but it wasn't until I moved to the Comox Valley permanently, in the mid-1980s, that I began asking questions about the unusual collection.

Since there were obviously the remains of two or three nineteenth-century windjammers, along with a number of steam tugs and warships, scuttled seaward of the logging company's booming ground, I was confident that someone must know the identity of them all. Not so, I soon discovered. After talking with a number of long-time residents and making a diligent attempt to locate old company records, I was shocked to find that very little was known about the graveyard. Luckily, I came across some articles by BC history writer T.W. Paterson, who had already investigated the site, that appeared in Victoria's *Daily Colonist* and *Crown Zellerbach News* in the early 1970s that set me off in the right direction.

Finally, in 1992, after a lot of old-fashioned detective work that allowed me to confirm and build on Paterson's findings, I submitted a story on the site to the *Resolution: Journal of the Maritime Museum of British Columbia*. Once it was published, it was full steam ahead tackling other facets of our coastal maritime history.

My next serious undertaking was working up the story behind all the retired sailing ships that had been cut down into barges by BC towboat companies in the 1920s and 1930s to transport logs, sawdust and hog fuel along the West Coast. Of course, I was ecstatic when my story was featured in the Victoria *Times Colonist* (see Chapter 14) but then, a few days later, a letter arrived in the mail. The first line read: "As one writer to another I have taken the liberty of amending the odd phrase or construction in your article." I was crestfallen; I had put so much into the story, and yet had still gotten a couple of details wrong. Of course, the letter was written by someone who knew his stuff; Bent Sivertz had sailed on one of the ships, the five-masted barquentine *Forest Friend*, as a teenage deckhand back in 1922–23.

Looking back, I recall that incident with fondness as it introduced me to a fascinating old salt whom I would otherwise never have met. It was the start of a great friendship, one I learned a lot from, and in the end that short letter was far more rewarding than the cheque I received from the newspaper.

Inspired, I went on to write other stories and eventually connected with the Underwater Archaeological Society of BC in the mid-1990s. At that time, then president Jacques Marc encouraged me to join the association even though I wasn't—and have yet to become—a diver. The UASBC is perhaps the most active and dedicated group of volunteer underwater archaeologists in North America and it has made an enormous contribution to the documentation and recording of shipwrecks along Canada's West Coast.

Still, the most rewarding aspect of exploring maritime history for me has been the opportunity to meet and interview countless individuals who lived and worked BC's challenging West Coast waters. Whether they were deepwater sailors who travelled the sea lanes of the world or those who spent most of their lives on inside waters towing booms from upcoast camps to south coast lumber mills, all have fascinating stories and adventures to relate.

Inevitably, *West Coast Wrecks and Other Maritime Tales* includes some stories of disaster at sea in which lives were lost. I hope this book, therefore, will serve as a written memorial to all whose bones lie on the bottom along one of the most treacherous stretches of coastline anywhere on the planet.

Acknowledgements

I won't attempt to list all those who provided support with all my research and writing endeavours and were there to answer my never-ending stream of phone calls and emails with research queries, but some stand out from the rest; people such as Leonard McCann, Curator Emeritus at Vancouver Maritime Museum, and Eric Lawson, who informed me back in the early 1990s that my first big project, setting out to document the historic ships of Royston's hulk breakwater, was indeed a very important undertaking. As it happens, Eric knows his stuff, having spent time in the Falkland Islands, the graveyard of ships wrecked rounding Cape Horn and whose beaches are littered with windjammers and steamers dating as far back as the early nineteenth century.

Of course, whenever I started on a shipwreck story, the first person I'd get on the phone to would be none other than Mr. West Coast Shipwrecks himself, Fred Rogers. Frank Clapp, too, who maintains impeccable records on the innumerable vessels that worked our coast, deserves special mention for always being there to answer a tough question; and then there was Captain Harold D. Huycke Jr. on whom I relied as the expert on Cape Horn windjammers on the Coast.

I still don't think I could really have made a go of it if were it not for some great editors such as Ross Smith, editor of the Maritime Museum of BC's journal *Resolution*, and Peter Salmon, editor of the Victoria

Times Colonist Monitor back in the 1990s. Also, I can't say enough about Rob Morris and publisher David Rahn, of *Western Mariner*, with whom I have maintained a great relationship for some 20 years now. Then, of course, there are Jacques Marc and David Stone, who always made sure I got things right once I was hooked up with the Underwater Archaeological Society of BC.

The diligent staff and volunteers of the excellent archives and museums we're fortunate enough to have here on our coast also deserve special mention. Particularly hard-working and knowledgeable are those with the Maritime Museum of BC and British Columbia Records and Archives Service in Victoria, CFB Esquimalt Naval and Military Museum, the Vancouver Maritime Museum, the Puget Sound Maritime Historical Society in Seattle and the J. Porter Shaw Library in San Francisco, along with the National Archives and Records Administration in both San Francisco and Seattle. For any records I needed access to in Ottawa, there was No. 1 researcher Ken McLeod, ever willing to lend a hand.

Still, were it not for my partner and in-house editor, author Paula Wild, I don't know if I would have even set out on this voyage in the first place. Her key to becoming a successful writer? "Don't keep talking about it, just do it!"

Bow of the *Riversdale* at Royston, BC. RICK JAMES PHOTO

Chapter 1

Maria J. Smith: The *Flying Dutchman* of the West Coast, 1869

On November 14, 1869, Victoria's *Daily British Colonist* reported that "the schooner *Surprise*, Captain Francis, arrived from the West Coast Vancouver Island yesterday morning having on board Captain David Smith of American bark *Maria J. Smith*, his wife and children and officers and crew. The bark was wrecked on Tuesday morning last near Barkley Sound. All hands escaped to the shore and the second was left in charge of the wreck."

Only some seven years old at the time of her loss, the three-masted barque *Maria J. Smith* (named for his wife) was the ship of Captain Smith's dreams. Smith's father was claimed to be the richest man in Chatham, Massachusetts, and the family invested their money in shipping and maritime interests. Although David Smith was a carpenter and a schoolteacher through the 1850s, he also owned a business that canned and hermetically sealed seafood provisions. He made a whaling voyage to the Pacific and Arctic Oceans and, by 1859, was captain of the trading schooner *Mary E. Smith* running commercial freight between Philadelphia, Pennsylvania, and Mobile, Alabama.

In 1862, master mariner Smith signed a contract for $21,000 with Toby & Littlefield, shipbuilders located in Portsmouth, New Hampshire, for the construction of *Maria J. Smith*, a 475-ton wood vessel built out of eastern oak. She was to measure 113 feet long and 28 feet in breadth. Noted in Smith's logbook were instructions for the forward cabin to be painted, the after cabin to be finished in hardwood, and ". . . a house for the accommodation of crew and galley" to be built upon the main deck. While Smith was the majority shareholder, Toby & Littlefield agreed to take a one-quarter interest, with a number of other individuals retaining smaller shares in the barque. By the time the vessel was equipped and ready for sea, $34,000 had been invested by the shareholders.

Maria J. Smith's maiden voyage in the fall of 1862 was from New York to Montevideo, Uruguay, carrying assorted cargo and passengers along with Smith's wife and their three young daughters. A year later, records from the Shipping Master's Office in New South Wales, Australia, indicate that *Maria J. Smith* ". . . of Boston, David Smith, Master, Burthen 494 tons . . ." arrived in Sydney in distress from Newcastle on November 14, 1863. Along with the ten crew members aboard (two had died at sea) there were three passengers—Smith's wife, one of his daughters and a Miss Armstrong. The following year, Mrs. Smith succumbed to cholera on a voyage to Burma.

Over the next seven years, the barque made long voyages to ports all over the globe, reportedly with excellent returns. In two years alone during the Civil War, Captain Smith was said to have earned $70,000 as his share with *Maria J. Smith*. In 1865, the *Smith* made a voyage from New York to Europe the long way around—via Australia, China and the East Indies. The barque returned to the West Coast in 1868 with a cargo bound for Seattle but while being towed into port a violent storm sprang up. The tug was forced to cut the towline and the *Maria J. Smith* consequently ended up on the rocks. Unfortunately, the insurance on the vessel had been allowed to lapse. Upset with the disaster, Smith refused to return home until he repaid the loss to family and friends who were the vessel's shareholders. It would take him nine years to fulfil his promise.

Once repaired, the ship received a charter for a voyage from San Francisco to the Chincha Islands. Located 10 nautical miles off the coast of Peru, these dry and desolate islands were a major centre of a nineteenth-century shipping boom. It was the discovery of massive deposits of accumulated seabird feces—in hills over 100 feet high—that led to a guano rush. The bird droppings' particular balance of nitrates, phosphates and potassium made this the ideal fertilizer for replenishing the depleted soils of Europe and the United States.

An entry in the Captain's account book, dated September 4, 1869, noted that although the vessel was still in debt, this voyage to the Chinchas proved particularly lucrative and helped put Smith back on the road to solvency. Unfortunately, in early November 1869, *Maria J. Smith* was to find herself in distress once again.

The lumber-laden barque sailed from Port Townsend, Washington Territory, on the evening of Saturday November 6, 1869, passed Cape Flattery light at 2:00 p.m. on November 8, and by 6:00 p.m. was fighting a strong gale with a high sea running from the south-southeast when the deck load of lumber began to work itself loose. Soon afterward the vessel started to leak and then, with the wind steadily increasing, some of her sails were carried away. Once the blow began to ease up, topsails were hoisted in an effort to get away from land sighted close by, but this effort proved futile.

Captain Smith, who arrived in Victoria with his family and crew aboard the schooner *Surprise* on November 13, 1869, after being rescued, gave a report to the *British Colonist* as to what happened next. "(We) got the best boat out, and when nearly in the surf, got all hands into her safely and left the ship to her fate . . . Not knowing on what part of the coast we were, we laid by our boat waiting for daylight, which came at last and revealed to our sight one of the most terrific views imaginable: the sea was running mountains high and breaking over the reefs with irresistible fury . . . With much difficulty and no little damage we found our way among the rocks and breakers . . .

"At this time we were visited by a white man, Peter Francis, a trader, and found we were ashore at the extreme entrance of Barkley Sound, Vancouver Island. He informed us he had a house nearby and invited us all to take provisions and make ourselves as comfortable as possible. We accepted his invitation with many thanks and were heartily glad to find a warm fire and lunch awaiting. On Tuesday, Wednesday and Thursday we employed our time in saving what we could from the wreck and trying to get her afloat again, but the Indians were very numerous and troublesome, stealing everything that came to hand . . . On Friday there was a very high tide and the wreck floated off which we succeeded in getting to anchor in a small harbour where Mr. Francis' trading post is, since which time the Indians have ceased to steal, and by threats of sending a man-of-war to punish them have got some of the stolen goods back again . . ."

This anonymous Chinese painting of the *Maria J. Smith* in a typhoon is from George Francis Dow's *The Sailing Ships of New England*, Series Three (1922), plate #687.

According to *Lewis & Dryden's Marine History of the Pacific Northwest*, the *Maria J. Smith* was apparently written off as a wreck, since she was sold to "Broderick" for $950, her lumber for $750 and the sails for $300. (This was probably Richard Broderick, a coal and shipping agent and wharf manager in Victoria.) On December 21, 1869, the *British Colonist* reported that the American steamer *Politkofsky*, Captain Guindon, had left for the scene of the loss to retrieve and then tow *Maria J. Smith* to Meigs Mill, Port Madison, Washington Territory. Here she was to be discharged, docked and repaired. ". . . Her damages are slight."

Although *Politkofsky* managed to tow the wrecked barque clear of Barkley Sound, they encountered a severe gale once they were out in the open Pacific and were forced to cast *Maria J. Smith* free. According to the *British Colonist* of January 5, 1870, ". . . after the blow the steamer lost sight of her. *Maria J. Smith* had a crew on board, and there is just the remotest room for the indulgence of the hope that she will reach San Francisco." Captain Smith and his crew were on the barque at the time, while his wife (probably his second) and children remained safely behind in Victoria.

Five days later, an unidentified (probably Washington Territory) newspaper went into more detail on the failed salvage attempt. "At 9 o'clock on the morning of Dec. 31st, steamer started with the bark— weather moderate—but found, on arriving . . . a heavy southwest sea running. At 2 p.m., parted the hawser; ran up the bark's lee; passed out another hawser, and bent it on the other, started ahead again. At 8 o'clock, it began to blow fresh from the eastward, increased until 11 o'clock, making a nasty cross sea; found it impossible to steer the steamer with the bark in tow, and was obliged to let her go for our own

The steamer *Politkofsky* was built in New Archangel (today's Sitka, Alaska) in 1863 by the Russian-American Company. She was never a "gunboat" as some accounts suggest but was employed as a harbour tug and used primarily for towing sailing vessels in and out of Sitka Sound. BAINBRIDGE ISLAND HISTORICAL MUSEUM, IMAGE #336

safety. She was heading south by east when last seen, and behaved as well as any vessel loaded with lumber that leaves the Sound, answering her wheel with charm . . . We are informed that the bark *Maria J. Smith* was in good sailing condition, with plenty of sails and provisions and five men on board, and there is not the . . . danger of her going ashore or making a harbour short of S.F . . ." Still, the *Port Townsend Weekly Message* of January 7 did note that, ". . . the vessel was in a very critical condition when left being full of water, having knocked a large hole in her bottom while lying on the rocks . . ."

Then, on the 14th of the month, the steamer *Politkofsky* arrived in Victoria with a Mr. G.A. Meigs (owner of Meigs Mill, Port Madison, as well as of the steamer *Politkofsky*) and Captain Smith of *Maria J. Smith* aboard. In giving his account of what had transpired after they were cut free from the steamer, Smith reported that they beat about for 12 days trying to enter the Straits but, owing to the waterlogged state of the barque, were unable to do so. Thinking they were close to a lee shore, the Vancouver Island coast once again, Captain and crew abandoned the vessel for the second time and boarded a passing ship, the barque *Sampson*, on January 11. Then the wind changed direction. Once Smith learned from *Sampson*'s captain that they were actually off Cape Flattery they took off in pursuit of the abandoned vessel. Unfortunately they were unable to overhaul her as she was some 10 miles to windward—with all sails set.

When it reported on the high seas drama, the *British Colonist* noted, "She is certainly a remarkable ship, and her adventures may yet fill a volume." Captain Smith remained hopeful since he

The *Politkofsky* was later purchased by joint American and Canadian interests in 1868 and rebuilt in San Francisco. A year later, the "Polly," as she became known, was bought by George Meigs and William Gawley and was put to work towing log rafts and lumber vessels for their Port Madison, Washington Territory, lumber mill.
BAINBRIDGE ISLAND HISTORICAL MUSEUM, IMAGE #420

was of the opinion that his ship was still afloat and could be rescued by a powerful tugboat. Still, it would be another two months before news was received of what had actually become of the phantom barque.

When the mail steamer on the run between Port Townsend and Alaska, the *Constantine*, arrived in Victoria from Sitka in mid-March 1870, the *British Colonist* reported that with her came news that the ". . . derelict bark *Maria J. Smith* has been found by Indians near Bella Bella and is now in the possession of Mr. Moss. [Probably Morris Moss, a well-known Jewish fur trader on the Central Coast.] The waif has sailed without aid of helmsman or compass nearly 500 miles from the point where she was abandoned, threading her way through intricate channels and dangerous tide rips to her present harbour of refuge. Twice this remarkable bark was abandoned and twice she has saved herself."

The *Olympia Washington Standard* reported that, "Capt. Small, of the steamer *Constantine*, informs us that on the 24th of February on the voyage from hence to Sitka, the steamer anchored at Fort Rupert near the north end of Vancouver Island and shortly after, a canoe arrived with Mr. Morse, the H.B.Co.'s Agent, who reported that the *Maria J. Smith* had drifted ashore on the west side of Aristazable [*sic*] Island just north of Milbanke Sound, and was hard and fast on a reef of rocks. Her cargo being of lumber will keep her from breaking up as fast as would have done if she had been empty or had been loaded with coal. She is a total loss. When last reported here, the bark had been seen off Cape Flattery. Since, she has drifted north some two hundred miles. The place where she lies is in Lat. 51 deg. 40 min. north, Long. 129 deg. 10 min. west."

The actual distance, as the crow flies, from Cape Flattery to Aristazabal Island, is about 375 miles—a remarkable feat indeed.

In 2003, while harvesting sea urchins, divers Pat Olsen and Rod Taylor located some anchor chain and other bits and pieces of wreckage off the west coast of Aristazabal Island. This information was passed on to the Underwater Archaeological Society of BC, a volunteer group of divers and underwater archaeologists, which was intrigued by the discovery since the society was in the midst of compiling its next report, the *Historic Shipwrecks of the Central Coast*. On June 8, 2005, some UASBC divers made a trip to the outer coast of Aristazabal Island to search for the wreckage. Unfortunately, after swimming more than a mile of coastline around the reported coordinates, nothing was found. The UASBC plans to return to the area sometime in the future and hopefully locate the remains of the ship of Captain David Smith's dreams, the barque *Maria J. Smith*.

Chapter 2

Steamship into Oblivion: The *Geo. S. Wright*, 1873

Weeks after the remains of a ship washed up on beaches near Cape Caution, Queen Charlotte Sound, in January 1873, disturbing stories began to circulate in US newspapers. Rumours had it that survivors from the missing American steamer *Geo. S. Wright* had been massacred by a fierce tribe of Canadian Indians. Worse yet, according to the wildly speculative reports, some of the female passengers had been captured and were being held as slaves. So much controversy arose in the newspapers of the day that the shipwreck soon took on the stature of an international incident.

At the time of the tragedy, *Geo. S. Wright* was operating under the flag of the Oregon Steamship Company and was on a return voyage to Portland after transporting mail, troops and supplies to Alaska. Twenty-one officers and crew along with about a dozen passengers were aboard when the *Wright* disappeared in late January 1873.

The screw steamer or "propeller" *Geo. S. Wright* was built for John T. Wright Jr., who named it in honour of his brother, and was launched in Port Ludlow, Washington Territory, on September 1, 1863. The wood steamer was schooner rigged with two masts and measured 118 feet long, with its steam machinery consisting of a single-cylinder engine that produced 125 nominal horsepower.

After *Geo. S. Wright* was launched for the Wrights' steamship fleet, she was soon making runs between Portland and Puget Sound with stops in at Victoria and New Westminster. Then, early in 1865, the propeller was bought by the Western Union Telegraph Company and spent the next two years involved with the company's enterprising Collins Overland Telegraph project. Western Union's goal was to extend a telegraph line north through the interior of British Columbia into the Yukon and then across Russian America (Alaska) and the shallow Bering Strait to link up with a telegraph line in Siberia. When completed, the ambitious project would connect the capitals of Europe with North America by telegraph. Unfortunately, the successful completion of Cyrus Field's underwater telegraph cable across the Atlantic in 1866 brought an abrupt end to the venture and it was officially suspended in February 1867.

Two years later, *Geo. S. Wright* was purchased by Oregonian Joseph Kamm and put back on the Portland, Puget Sound and Victoria run until the fall of 1869 when the ship was sold to the North Pacific Transportation Company. When Ben Holladay, President of the North Pacific Transportation Company of Portland, Oregon, purchased the *Wright* he was already recognized as the "Vanderbilt of the Pacific." Holladay managed to accumulate some 25 deep-sea steamers and, as maritime historian Norman Hacking noted, all except for one ". . . were purchased second-hand and were badly maintained . . . the lifesaving

Peter Rindlisbacher created this rendering of a possible scenario of the loss of the *Geo. S. Wright* off Cape Caution. PETER RINDLISBACHER

equipment was inadequate, and the navigational abilities of the officers were open to question." Between the years 1868 and 1870, four steamers from the Holladay fleet were lost to marine mishaps between Mexico and southern British Columbia.

Five steamers, one being *Geo. S. Wright,* in the North Pacific Transportation fleet were sold to the Oregon Steamship Company in August 1870. (The new steamship company was created by Ben Holladay in an attempt to avert a financial crisis.) At the time, several of the company's ships were employed transporting mail, troops and supplies to Alaska, which the United States had purchased from Russia only some three years earlier.

In early January 1873, *Geo. S. Wright* sailed from Portland, loaded coal at Nanaimo and headed north to Alaska on her final voyage. The steamer was commanded by Captain Thomas J. Ainsley, ". . . brother of a Mrs. Mouat of this city, an experienced pilot," according to Victoria's *Daily British Colonist.*

The paper also reported that on about the 13th of January the steamer stopped in at Fort Tongas where she took on freight, mail and passengers including John Williams. "Mr. Williams had $15,000 in gold dust in his possession." The *Wright* arrived in Sitka on the 19th and, after taking on more passengers and freight, departed two days later. In her final stop—at Kluvok—the steamer loaded a particularly heavy load of freight that was reported to be some 800 barrels of salmon and 100 barrels of oil, along with some skins and furs. In addition to her 21 officers and crew, it was estimated that *Geo. S. Wright* now had 11 or 12 passengers on board. On January 25, Captain Ainsley—possibly in a hurry to be home for his wedding to a Victoria woman—put to sea into a particularly bad snowstorm.

On February 27, 1873, Victoria's rival newspaper, *The Daily Standard,* broke the bad news with the headline: "Wreck of the Steamer *Geo. S. Wright*—probably Foundered at Sea." It was reported that when the steamers *Emma* and *Sir James Douglas* had arrived in Nanaimo the previous day with five Nuxalk (Bella Coola) canoes in tow, the natives had given a first-hand account of what they had come across two weeks earlier close to Cape Caution in Queen Charlotte Sound. The group reported that, while camping near the Cape, they discovered a large quantity of wreckage along the beach.

Among the items found were the deck of a steamer, the pilot or wheel house, parts of a mast, boxes, blankets, clothing and "the board bearing the name of the unfortunate vessel upon it . . ." and "having prosecuted a strict search for five days, gave up the hope for finding anybody, dead or alive, and hastened down to Nanaimo." As it happened, below the story on the wreck published in *The Daily Standard* was a letter from Alden Westly Huson, storekeeper in Alert Bay, who informed the paper that he had received news of the *Wright*'s loss; somewhere near Cape Caution sometime earlier. Huson concluded with "I have no doubt but that all are past and gone."

In this engraving of the Western Union Telegraph Company Fleet, the square-rigged ship at centre is *Nightingale,* with the schooner-rigged steamer *Geo. S. Wright* directly off her bow. The engineer-in-chief of the project, Charles S. Bulkley, noted in a February 4, 1866, *New York Times* story that "...the steamer *George S. Wright* proved a valuable vessel, both economical and serviceable." Seven years later it was to be a different story. THE BANCROFT LIBRARY, UNIVERSITY OF CALIFORNIA, BERKELEY, BAN PIC 1950:004: 28.2

As it happened, a *British Colonist* reporter was able to learn more about the loss from his interview of the Central Coast Indians. He reported that they also came across "... a plank tied to a box as if some unfortunate on board a sinking vessel tried to make a raft ..." and said that, not far from the beach in deep water, two masts were sticking out and that "... they could stand on the beach and toss a stone to the wreck."

When it reported the latest news on the marine tragedy the *Colonist* was quick to acknowledge "... that this brave little steamer has been lost, with all on board ... and the cause may never be known." It continued, "... the steamer was very poorly provided with canvas, and that in the case of her machinery breaking down she would have much difficulty in sailing. When at Nanaimo the chief engineer wanted to have the ship beached to repair the discharge pipe; but for some reason this was not done. It is said, too, that he complained of his assistant (a new man) being incompetent. Other hands are said to have stated that the vessel was in very bad condition. Fierce gales prevailed on the coast during the month of January and it is thought that the disaster occurred on the downward trip, either by an explosion of the boiler (as in the case of the *Emily Harris*) or by the breakdown of the machinery." The *Victoria Standard* agreed, noting that the *Wright* had a broken escape pipe and that the "unfortunate" chief engineer, Mr. Sutton, had severe reservations about the voyage ahead. Overall, the *Geo. S. Wright* was "... in a very pitiable state to make any resistance to heavy gales, or to combat the terrific seas which are known to have prevailed in the locality of the disaster ..."

It wasn't until early March that any kind of search vessel was able to steam north to the scene of the disaster. In Victoria, the United States consul pressured local authorities to dispatch the Royal Navy steam sloop HMS *Peterel* to search Queen Charlotte Sound. Across the border, concerned American citizens and distressed family members demanded that the USRC (United States Revenue Cutter) *Lincoln* be dispatched to the scene immediately. Unfortunately, USRC *Lincoln* met a heavy westerly swell entering Queen Charlotte Sound and turned back. According to the Collector of the Marine Revenue Service, M.S. Drew, the revenue cutter's boiler was defective and the ship was in no state to face the storm-tossed waters of Queen Charlotte Sound. Meanwhile, the *Wright*'s owners in Portland ordered North Pacific Transportation Company's sister ship on the Alaska run, *Gussie Telfair*, to leave immediately for the north.

HMS *Peterel* left Nanaimo around March 7 and on board were Captain Spaulding of the BC Provincial Police and James F. McGrath, owner of the Alert Bay store located on Cormorant Island, a small island off the northeast coast of Vancouver Island. McGrath was returning to the island to relieve his storekeeper, "Wes" Huson. By doing so, McGrath hoped Huson could join the warship as pilot and interpreter. He was very familiar with "... the habits of the Indians of Cape Caution," as well as being "intimately connected with the Captain and officers."

When *Peterel* rounded the corner into Alert Bay on its way north, British officers and crew were greeted with a disturbing scene; the Stars and Stripes was flying at the trading post. An offended Commander Cecil George Sloane Stanley RN was quick to bring McGrath, owner of the post, to task and reprimand him. In a letter to the *British Colonist* later that month, titled "That American Flag at Alert Bay," McGrath took great care to explain the background behind the perceived insult to Her Majesty's Government.

Apparently, Huson had raised the American flag at half mast hoping to draw the attention of the American steamer *Gussie Telfair* to have her stop in so he could convey news of the missing *Geo. S. Wright*. (As it happened, nailed farther down on the flagstaff, but not noticed until pointed out by McGrath, was the name board of the lost Oregon steamer retrieved at Cape Caution.) Still, Captain Stanley was not in the least impressed, especially since he may have been well aware that Wes Huson was an ex-Yankee from New York State. As a result, no invitation was forthcoming to the local trader to come aboard the warship and lend his assistance to the search.

This was a particularly unfortunate development. As one of the few whites in the District, Huson was probably more up on news of *Geo. S. Wright* than anyone else. Since there were only two trading posts in the area (the other was the Hudson's Bay Company's Fort Rupert), Alert Bay was a focal point for trade and supplies as well as a gathering place for the many tribes in the area. Indeed, when the steamer *California* stopped there three years later, it noted there were around ". . . some 400 Indians and one white man, Mr. West [sic] Huson."

On March 17 both HMS *Peterel* and Ben Holladay's steamer *Gussie Telfair* returned to Victoria with the sad news that neither a wreck nor any survivors from *Geo. S. Wright* were to be found.

The loss of *Geo. S. Wright* was reported in January 1873 but it was early March before any kind of search vessel was able to steam north to the scene of the disaster. The United States' consul in Victoria pressured local authorities to dispatch the Royal Navy steam sloop HMS *Peterel*, seen here, to search Queen Charlotte Sound. IMAGE FROM A LATE 19TH CENTURY EDITION OF *THE NAVY & ARMY ILLUSTRATED*

On instructions from the government, *Peterel* prosecuted a strict search along the coast. The Royal Navy sloop attempted to explore every cove and point, and fired guns and rockets day and night to alert survivors, while officers and crew in boats scoured beaches and reefs for clues. Still, *Peterel* was unable to land a search party anywhere near Cape Caution where most of the wreckage had been found. According to the *San Francisco Daily Evening Telegram* of March 19, 1873, ". . . Captain Stanley describes the coast as the roughest and wildest he in the whole course of his experience witnessed, and also pictures the neighbourhood of Cape Caution as a perfect pyramid of surf and waves."

Ben Holladay's *Gussie Telfair* sailed all the way to Alaska and back but, like the *Peterel*, was unable to land at Cape Caution. On its way down the coast, the steamer stopped at a number of villages to make inquiries. At Bella Bella, a trader named Lowden produced a barrel of oil he had purchased from some Indians, retrieved 200 miles north of Cape Caution. The trader bought the barrel along with an iron band torn from the mast as it lay on a beach. Natives also reported that on the beach near Cape Caution were signs of someone having built a house ". . . after the fashion of the white man." Regrettably, no one seemed to have any direct knowledge of the wreck or possible survivors.

In the end, according to the officers of the *Telfair*, *Geo. S. Wright* had probably struck the low sunken rocks of the Sea Otter Group a few miles outside Cape Caution. In response to this report on the loss, an "Old Salt" wrote the *British Colonist* to point out that after he learned how much freight the steamer had taken on in Kluvok alone, he'd come to the conclusion that the *Wright* was terribly overloaded. "May she not have been too deeply laden for any emergency likely to arise in the winter season . . . had her decks been swept by a heavy sea, filled and gone down?"

Writing to the *Colonist* on March 23, James McGarth noted that he had it on good account, that the Aurkeno (probably Oweekeno, who occupy the head of Rivers Inlet) Indians were the first on site at the wreck of *Geo. S. Wright*, ". . . on their way down to the Fanaughtas [?] to a feast." They picked up valuable furs by the bale. "One Indian is said to have picked up 100 sea otter skins. The Indians are *mum* about anyone getting ashore." McGrath reported that, the week before, he had been told that two white men actually got ashore where the skins were found. Still, "The Indians are laughing how they fooled the man-of-war again. It is a pity the Awikenos [*sic*] were not visited. It is too late now."

In a letter to Wes Huson on March 22, McGrath was somewhat more forthcoming with details than he was in his letter to the *Colonist*. "The *Telfair* did not call or did anyone see her; Ben Holladay had better look sharp. Some of those pilots might cause the Cooper dodge on him [probably James Cooper, Dominion Agent for Department of Marine and Fisheries]. It is strange too she might not have called at Nanaimo. Now I don't know if she will proceed to the wreck. It will be forgotten now as the first ex-

Alden Westly ("Wes") Huson, a storekeeper in Alert Bay and one of the few whites in the district, informed Victoria's *Daily British Colonist* in late January of 1873 that he had received news of the *Geo. S. Wright*'s loss somewhere near Cape Caution. "I have no doubt but that all are past and gone." HARBOUR PUBLISHING COLLECTION

citement was frustrated. I am of the opinion that it was done intentionally to turn the *Lincoln* back for fear she would proceed to Owikeno and get a loop hole on those Indians. The matter ought not to be dropped in the District. Old Spaulding [Captain, BC Provincial Police Force] is smart . . ."

When someone with the pen name "Suwanee" wrote to the *Puget Sound Daily Courier* in late March claiming they'd heard two men and a woman reached the shore from the wreck of the *Wright* and were seized by the natives, the men eaten, and ". . . the woman kept for vile purposes," readers of the *British Colonist* were incensed. What was particularly galling was that the "brute" charged that these horrific deeds were a direct result of "the teachings and advice of the British authorities" who taught natives to abhor Boston Men (i.e. Americans; the British were called King George Men.) "We really think that the alacrity with which the Canadian government sent a British war-ship in the vicinity of the wreck, and the zeal with which the officers of the ship prosecuted their search, should have protected our people from the publication of charges which only a vile mind could conceive . . ."

Residents of Victoria had good reason to be annoyed. While the *Geo. S. Wright* was indeed flying under the Stars and Stripes and was registered in San Francisco, many aboard on the fateful voyage had close ties to Vancouver Island. Along with Captain Ainsley, who had a sister living in Victoria and was engaged to a young lady there, the chief engineer, John Sutton, had a large family in Victoria, as did his second engineer, James Minor. Purser Frank Weidler's brother was a steamship agent in the capital city, cook Jewell Michel's father lived in Esquimalt and passenger John Williams was formerly of the Victoria firm, Evans & Williams. (The paper didn't bother to report what village the three native crewmen hailed from.)

Ironically, the editor of the *Courier* claimed that the Suwanee letters actually originated from an un-named source in Alert Bay. (He pointed out that they were handed to him by a gentleman who ". . . is of the highest respectability" and who assured him that the writer was ". . . perfectly reliable and trustworthy.") Three days later, another letter to the editor appeared, this time from someone in Port Townsend who felt compelled to respond to the sensational story. "The letter in the COURIER of the 26th inst., from Alert Bay, signed 'Suwanee,' is all a fabrication. The same report was made to Capt. Stanley, of H.M. Steamship Petrel [*sic*], and he proceeded to the Indian mission [probably Harbledown Island] and interviewed the priest [probably Oblate Father Leon Fouquet], from whom the rumour was said to have started, and the whole thing is pronounced false. There is no ground for the report. It is a falsehood, cut from whole cloth, and should be denounced immediately."

With the return of HMS *Peterel* and *Gussie Telfair* to port later in March, reports of wreckage and bodies found slowly drifted in from up coast. On March 27, the steamer *Otter* returned to Victoria with a boy's copper-tipped shoe and a life preserver. The Indians from whom Captain Lewis retrieved these items also related that they had found the body of a boy, ". . . a *sitkum* or half-breed and aged about eight years . . . the body had been frightfully mangled by dogfish. Even the little shoe bears marks of the voracity of these fish." The body was discovered in Hykin (Hiekish) Narrows, Finlayson Canal, and it was believed to be that of Charles Waldron's son. The fact that the small body was wearing a life jacket indicated that those aboard had had enough time to prepare themselves for whatever had befallen the ship. (It was suggested at first that the boiler might have exploded, which would never have allowed those aboard the opportunity to escape, let alone don a life jacket.) The *Otter* also learned that Captain Ainsley probably changed his mind and chose to come down through exposed outside waters rather than staying within the sheltered Inside Passage. Ainsley was to blow the steamer's whistle when passing Bella Bella, signalling to residents there that he was safely on his way south. No one ever heard it.

By April, Ben Holladay had promised to spend $150,000 to launch a search for relics from *Geo. S. Wright* and her crew and passengers since he felt some might still be alive. Earlier that month, two Tsimshian canoes that had stopped at Alert Bay had reported that the body of a man, which the group buried, had been found in Indian Cove at Cape Caution. They were also fortunate enough to recover several packages of skins.

When the sloop *Yellow Lane* returned to Victoria from Skeenamouth on April 26, it reported that they had put in at Indian Cove (a safe anchorage at Cape Caution) on the way south where wreckage of *Geo. S. Wright* lay on the beach. The party on board found the foremast, bowsprit, part of the wheel and some cabin planking. While the mast was intact with no damage, ". . . the bowsprit was shivered [splintered] as if it had struck a rock." Those on the sloop also learned that another body was discovered some distance north at Aristazabal Island. The partial remains were those of a man lashed to two chairs with a wool comforter and wearing a life jacket while some cabin furniture and planking were found washed ashore. Another month was to pass before any more relics surfaced.

In late May, the gunboat HMS *Boxer* left Esquimalt with the Superintendent of Indian Affairs, Dr. Powell, aboard to interview tribes of the north. On stopping in at Bella Bella, a keg, a lantern, a candle, a fragment of a newspaper and some biscuit were obtained, supposedly off *Geo. S. Wright*. On the way south *Boxer* stopped in at Takush Harbour, Smith Sound, where the natives were found ". . . to be both well disposed and quite in contradistinction [*sic*] to the letters written by 'Suwanee.'" They also

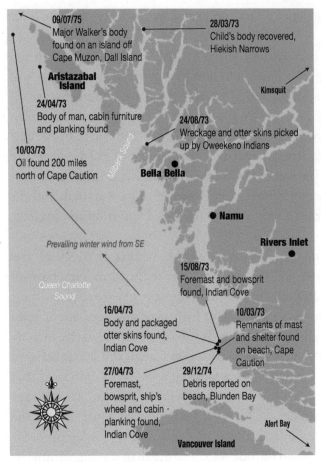

09/07/75
Major Walker's body
found on an island off
Cape Muzon, Dall Island

Aristazabal Island

24/04/73
Body of man, cabin furniture
and planking found

10/03/73
Oil found 200 miles
north of Cape Caution

Milbank Sound

28/03/73
Child's body recovered,
Hiekish Narrows

Kimsquit

24/08/73
Wreckage and otter skins picked
up by Oweekeno Indians

Bella Bella

Namu

Rivers Inlet

Prevailing winter wind from SE

Queen Charlotte Sound

15/08/73
Foremast and bowsprit
found, Indian Cove

16/04/73
Body and packaged
otter skins found,
Indian Cove

10/03/73
Remnants of mast
and shelter found
on beach, Cape
Caution

27/04/73
Foremast,
bowsprit, ship's
wheel and cabin
planking found,
Indian Cove

29/12/74
Debris reported on
beach, Blunden Bay

Alert Bay

Vancouver Island

A wreckage chart showing the locations of artifacts and bodies recovered from the lost American steamer *Geo. S. Wright*. The actual location of the wreck site or who was behind the massacre of survivors—if there indeed was one—remain shrouded in mystery. BASED ON A MAP CREATED BY JACQUES MARC

reported that they had no tidings of the wreck. When the sloop *Duncan* arrived in Victoria on June 23 Captain Collins produced more relics—a cigar holder, a meerschaum pipe and part of an account book—which he said he had purchased from Indians some 175 miles north of Cape Caution.

On August 2 the Portland *Oregonian* reported that, ". . . earnest efforts have been made at Portland to elicit interest enough to induce the dispatch of a vessel . . ." to try to determine what became of the 32 people aboard the lost *Geo. S. Wright*. Among those who were "unremitting and indefatigable" in their requests to have a steamer sent out on a search were Mrs. A.B. Sutton, wife of the engineer John Sutton. On April 19, 1873, Mrs. Sutton forwarded to the Secretary of the Treasury a petition signed by a number of prominent Oregon citizens appealing to the government to send out a vessel at once to look for the *Wright*. Letters were also written to the President of the United States, Ulysses S. Grant. (Oregon descendants of the *Wright's* engineer, John Sutton, state that family lore has it Sutton attended West Point with Ulysses S. Grant.)

However, it wasn't until early August 1873 that an American government vessel, USRC *Lincoln*, arrived on the scene in Queen Charlotte Sound. Since the lifeboats from *Geo. S. Wright* were yet to be found (in the end, they never were) it was speculated that survivors might be living on the beach somewhere along the coast. Captain A.B. Davis stressed that no pains were spared by the cutter's crew and officers in their attempts to locate anyone still alive. After an intensive search throughout Queen Charlotte and Milbanke Sounds, all that was found were some skins and a copper plate from the *Wright's* gangway, which was obtained from Nuxalk natives when the *Lincoln* stopped in at Bella Coola.

"These Indians were found to be peaceable and quiet, and according to the Hudson's Bay Company living among them . . . all stories of foul play are utterly without foundation," noted Captain Davis. He finished his report to US government authorities by noting that the ". . . the rumors and reports of foul play being done to any of the passengers and crew of the 'Wright' were instigated by a few unreliable and unprincipled white men, whose reputation in British Columbia is very bad."

The missing *Geo. S. Wright* was slowly fading into memory as just another one of a number of shipwrecks along the North West Coast in the mid-nineteenth century, when, two years later, natives reported seeing a makeshift European-style shelter on a rocky coast. Then, in July 1875, the body of John Stevens Walker, Major, United States Army, who had boarded the *Wright* in Sitka, was found on the beach at Bazan Bay, Dall Island, off Prince of Wales Island, Alaska. Part of his skeleton was found in the remains of his dark blue Army of the Union uniform and greatcoat, all held together by a lifejacket. The discovery was destined to be the final chapter in the tragic tale of *Geo. S. Wright*; that is, until a year and half later.

In early 1877, Bella Bella Chief Charley Hemsett related a peculiar and disturbing story to Alfred Dudower, a high-ranking Tsimshian and captain of the trading schooner *Ringleader*. Hemsett said he met a native named Billy Coma, living in Nanaimo, who claimed to be the coal passer on *Geo. S. Wright* when she wrecked. According to Coma, after the steamer was swamped by mountainous seas in January 1873, he, along with 14 other survivors, struggled onto two small islands somewhere off Cape Caution. That night, their fires attracted some Oweekeno canoes whose occupants landed and set upon the hapless group, robbing them and slitting their throats. Fortunately for Coma, who was a Nimpkish (a 'Namgis native, one of the many Kwakwaka'wakw Nations), he was able to claim an Oweekeno blood connection that saved him from certain death.

When these startling new revelations were brought before the authorities, Lieutenant Charles Reynold Harris, in command of the gun vessel HMS *Rocket*, was ordered to steam north from Esquimalt in March 1877. Also aboard the warship were Sergeant Bloomfield of the Victoria police, representing the civil authority, and George Hunt, an interpreter, who was picked up in Fort Rupert. Once in Central Coast waters, landing parties were sent ashore at various villages to perform interrogations and obtain scraps of information from various First Nations.

On March 30, 1877, HMS *Rocket* arrived off the Nuxalk village of Kimsquit in Dean Channel. Here a series of events led to a terrible outcome. Sergeant Bloomfield of the BC Police was sent ashore with a small party to demand that the Kimsquit chiefs hand over four individuals implicated in the massacre. Only two suspects were delivered up and, after a fight broke out on the beach when one of the chiefs refused to cooperate, the chiefs were warned that the village would be destroyed if the other two suspects were not brought to the ship.

When the pair weren't forthcoming, Harris put the ship in a position where the *Rocket*'s guns could be levelled on the village. He then ordered the villagers to stand clear as the settlement was fired on and set ablaze in reprisal. The residents could only watch as their homes and possessions were destroyed.

"The settlement, which had probably numbered one hundred or more before the shelling, was uninhabitable and was abandoned, and its population dispersed to other settlements," wrote maritime historian Barry Gough in *Gunboat Frontier: British*

Last Voyage of *George S. Wright*

21 Officers and crew:
Captain Thomas J. Ainsley; B.F. "Frank" Weidler, purser; and John Sutton, chief engineer—all of Portland;
James Minor, second engineer;
Daniel Noonan, first officer;
William Price, second officer;
P. Clawson, Owen McGough, firemen;
Edward Johnson, Archibald Dunn, James Irwin, Gus Proffe, J. Jensen, seamen;
Chris Adams, steward;
Pedro Salvo, Jewell Michels, cooks;
C. Hevendehl, waiter;
Moses Baptiste, pantryman;
Indian James, messboy;
Indian Jack and Jim, coal-passers.

11 or 12 Passengers (sources are contradictory):
Major John Stevens Walker, Paymaster, US Army, and his wife;
Lieutenant Henry C. Dodge;
Charles Waldron;
Charles Kincaid;
Mr. Sincheimer; a former cooper from the Kluvok fish saltery;
John Williams;
a "Frenchman" returning from the Omineca gold fields;
a miner on the Stikine River;
Mr. Hogan and son.

Maritime Authority and Northwest Coast Indians, 1846–1890. Gough went on to say that the unfortunate incident was ". . . among one of the last cases of sanctioned use of violence by the Royal Navy . . . to teach recalcitrant natives that crimes against Whites and property would be repaid in kind."

Four native people—two Oweekeno and two Nuxalmc (Nuxalk people) from the village of Kimsquit—were arrested, taken to Victoria and charged, but later that year, when the matter came up in court, it became clear that a grave mistake had been made. Referring to the Crown's star witness, the *British Colonist* reported on October 20, 1877, that "the Indian reported as being saved from the wreck is said to be one who served a long term in the Victoria jail." In his final statement before His Honour, H.C. Courtney, the Superintendent of Police told the court that the lone witness to testify against the four accused was ". . . an Indian named Coma . . . bearing so bad a character that it is almost impossible to believe him." The Superintendent stressed that the Attorney General had done all he possibly could but was still unable to come up with any evidence at all to corroborate Coma's statements. Consequently, all charges

In March 1877, the gun vessel HMS *Rocket* arrived off the Nuxalk village of Kimsquit in Dean Channel with Lieutenant Charles Reynold Harris (centre, sitting on a chair) in command. Sergeant Bloomfield of the BC Police (at left, leaning on the rail) was sent ashore with a small party to demand that the Kimsquit chiefs hand over four individuals implicated in a massacre, setting off a series of events that led to a terrible outcome. COURTESY OF ROYAL BC MUSEUM, BC ARCHIVES A-00255

were dropped and the prisoners discharged from custody. On hearing the outcome, a Captain Thomas Laughton told a reporter that he wasn't at all surprised, adding that he was certain Coma was not on board *Geo. S. Wright* at the time and ". . . that if anyone ought to be punished it certainly should be Coma."

Today, over 130 years later, the actual details of the loss of the *Geo. S. Wright*, the location of the wreck site or who was behind the massacre of survivors—if indeed there was one—remain shrouded in mystery. As noted in *Lewis & Dryden's Marine History of the Pacific Northwest*, ". . . all that can be said is that she sailed away and no message ever came to quiet the heartaches of those whose friends and relatives perished with her."

Final footnote:

Even before the trial was over, Ben Holladay's European bondholders had already caught up with him. He lost his fleet of steamships early in 1876, his over-extended transportation empire collapsed and the "Vanderbilt of the Pacific" died in Portland in July 1877. In July 2009, the Underwater Archaeological Society of BC, as part of its survey of Central Coast shipwrecks, anchored off Indian Cove at Cape Caution and did an underwater as well as a beach survey of Indian Cove and Blunden Bay hoping to locate remains of the lost steamer. The group came up empty-handed.

Chapter 3

Gunboat Grief:
The Loss of the *Grappler*, 1883

Twenty-four-year-old Lieutenant Edmund Hope Verney arrived in Esquimalt from England in May 1862 to assume command of his new ship, HMS *Grappler*, a combination sail and steam gunboat. The young Verney soon discovered that the three-masted, 108-foot-long, shallow-draft vessel (the gunboat only displaced 6.5 feet) was a pleasure to handle under sail. Two years later it was a different story. After rigorous service along the Northwest Pacific coast, Verney began to complain that *Grappler* had become defective, steamed badly and that her bottom was "all knocked about."

The Commander-in-Chief of the Pacific Squadron eventually paid heed to these dismal reports and the gunboat was put on the market in the fall of 1867. It was while going about her business as a commercial freighter after passing into private hands that the *Grappler* was involved in one of the worst marine disasters on the West Coast.

Lieutenant Verney's predecessor, A.H.P. Helby, had left HMS *Grappler* in excellent condition and in the hands of a well-disciplined crew with a positive attitude back in the spring of 1862. Crew and officers deserved to be proud: their warship was one of a new design to join the Royal Navy (RN) fleet. The idea of the gunboat as a purpose-built ship for the RN had come about as a result of the need for a revised naval strategy during the Crimean War (1854–56.) The reluctance of the Imperial Russian forces to battle the British and French navies confined allied operations to blockading and attacking enemy coastlines, and this new reality soon highlighted the value of steam over sail.

Nearly 100 of the Albacore class, like *Grappler*, were built, but haste in constructing them resulted in the use of unseasoned timber and many of the vessels later fell to pieces. As is happened, not one was completed in time for active service in the Crimean War, but both HMS *Grappler* and her sister ship HMS *Forward* did take part in the St. George's Day naval review held by Queen Victoria at Spithead to celebrate the end of that war.

Following the Fraser River gold strike in 1858, the Admiralty dispatched a number of warships to the colonies of Vancouver Island and British Columbia to secure British sovereignty and maintain law and order. HMS *Grappler* and HMS *Forward* sailed from England in August 1859 after being specially fitted out for their new role. While the United States government would use its army to quell disturbances throughout its frontier West, Great Britain had its own answer for unruliness along the fringes of its vast empire: send in a gunboat.

In the fall of 1862 *Grappler* transported a number of settlers to Comox, BC, pioneers of what was soon to be a thriving agricultural community. BILL MAXIMICK PAINTING

It was hoped that the mobile, shallow-draught vessels would not only offer the means to counter Indigenous threats but, more importantly, would act as a presence to forestall any American territorial ambitions imported with the hordes of American forty-niners flooding the Fraser River gold bars. Once the gunboats reached Esquimalt in July 1860, they were quickly discovered to be ideally suited for the treacherous and restricted coastal waters of the Northwest coast.

Although *Grappler* was often preoccupied with more mundane activities—laying navigation buoys in the Fraser River, serving as a lighthouse tender, aiding ships in distress—the ship did take part in some noteworthy historic events. During the summer and fall of 1862, the *Grappler* transported a number of white settlers to both the Cowichan and Comox valleys on Vancouver Island, pioneers who subsequently founded these areas' first agricultural communities.

The sister ships HMS *Forward* and *Grappler* also played central roles in the Lemalchi incident in the spring of 1863, when the gunboats were used to hunt down the Indigenous murderers of some Gulf Island settlers. In the attempt to bring the perpetrators to justice, the Kuper Island village of the Lemalchi people was levelled by the guns of *Forward*.

After another two years of hard service, and Lieut. Verney's growing concern over her condition, the overworked *Grappler* was paid off on May 13, 1865. A Captain Frain purchased her for $2,400 in 1868 and, soon after passing into private hands, the clean-hulled profile of the Royal Navy gunboat

In May 1862, 24-year-old Lieutenant Edmund Hope Verney arrived in Esquimalt from England to assume command of his new ship, HMS *Grappler*, a combination sail and steam gunboat. He soon discovered the vessel to be a pleasure to handle under sail. COURTESY OF ROYAL BC MUSEUM, BC ARCHIVES I-51693

was altered by the addition of an ungainly midship house. The silhouette of the warship-steamer conversion was to remain a familiar figure in coastal waters for 15 years—up until the night of her loss on April 29, 1883.

An April 1883 advertisement in the *Victoria Daily British Colonist* announced that the steamer was to depart for Fort Wrangel (today's Wrangell, Alaska), Skeena and Rivers Inlet from the Dickson, Campbell & Co. wharf at 6:00 p.m. on April 28. The coaster left that evening headed up the coast with a cargo of cannery supplies and around 100 passengers, most of whom were Chinese cannery workers. The following day *Grappler* stopped at Nanaimo for 40 tons of coal, discharged 50 kegs of powder and immediately left. The steam schooner *Grace* was hailed that afternoon and a pilot was taken on board.

At 9:55 p.m. on the night of April 29, when the *Grappler* was in Discovery Passage and about four miles south of Seymour Narrows, a fire was discovered behind her boiler by engineer William Steele. The donkey engine was immediately started and a hose connected, but once it was realized how serious the blaze was, the crew and passengers ran for the boats to abandon ship. The inquiry that followed learned that Captain John Jagers ordered the pilot to head the ship for the Vancouver (probably Vancouver Island) shore.

Unfortunately, the steamer became unmanageable once the fire had burned through the hemp ropes connecting the wheel to the rudder. To complicate matters, due to the heat, no one could get near the engine room to slow the vessel down, so the ship was still travelling at full speed. The *Grappler* continued to run out of control for some time, constantly changing course from one side of the channel to the other.

The vessel came equipped with only two lifeboats but cannery owner John McAllister had shipped four fishing skiffs of his own. He went to clear the boats but found it next to impossible to lower them properly. Both the smoke from the blaze forward and McAllister's inability to communicate with his panicking Chinese employees complicated any attempt to get the boats into the water in an orderly fashion. One turned bottom up but at least one was successfully launched. Of the steamer's two lifeboats, one of them made it into the water right side up and picked up several survivors from the water.

A few of the many who jumped overboard found themselves immersed in the frigid waters of Discovery Passage clinging to bits of flotsam tossed overboard by crew and passengers.

John McAllister, who pulled himself into one of his skiffs after jumping over the side, told the *Daily British Colonist* that those who had abandoned the inferno helplessly watched the steamer ". . . going backwards and forwards . . . the passengers shrieking and yelling for assistance" as the flames spread.

The newspapers of the day provided the names of the 21 white survivors while noting that "two Indians" and "13 Chinamen" were also saved. Captain Jagers, who stayed with his ship as long as possible before being driven off by the flames, was among those found alive. Estimates of those who perished that night varied from 70 to as high as 90. The exact number of lives lost remains unknown since the purser's records were lost with the ship.

On May 5, 1883, the *Daily British Colonist* reported that on the morning following the catastrophe the ill-fated steamer was last seen drifting down from Seymour Narrows with the tide and that she finally ". . . sank beneath the waves in 30 fathoms of water at the same spot she became unmanageable." The sleek gunboat of which Lieut. Verney had assumed command in the spring of 1862 had met a tragic end as a fiery wreck 21 years later.

Grappler is in the foreground in this photograph of the Royal Navy Fleet at Esquimalt, BC. The mobile and shallow-draft gunboat was ideally suited to her new role in Pacific Northwest waters. VANCOUVER MARITIME MUSEUM #2772

An inquest was held in Victoria into the death of Donald McPhail, passenger on the *Grappler*, and on May 15 the jurors found that the SS *Grappler* was not licensed to carry passengers on leaving the port of Victoria on April 28 and did so without making provisions for their safety. They also declared the owners (Warren and Saunders of Victoria) and officers of culpable negligence.

Captain Jagers' reputation appears to have survived the consequences of the inquiry. Once he had recovered from his horrendous experience that fateful night, he was given charge of the steamer *Beaver*. He was later employed by the Canadian Pacific Navigation Company where he commanded a variety of well-known coastal steamers.

Steele, one of the most prominent marine engineers in British Columbia in the nineteenth century, also survived the disaster. The ill-fated *Grappler*'s chief engineer went on to take charge of the government dredge employed in Victoria Harbour and on the Fraser River and remained with that service as superintendent until his death in 1893.

In 1868 the former Royal Navy gunboat *Grappler* passed into private hands and her sleek lines were marred by the addition of a square midship house, seen in this photograph taken in Victoria, BC. COURTESY OF ROYAL BC MUSEUM, BC ARCHIVES G-06346

Chapter 4

On the Bottom of Jervis Inlet: The Paddlewheeler *Mermaid,* 1904

The enthusiastic crowd that gathered at Rock Bay in Victoria's Inner Harbour on May 31, 1884, never imagined that the freshly built steamer they watched slip down the ways that spring evening would one day be lying on the bottom of Jervis Inlet—or that rumours of sabotage would cling to the disaster.

A Victoria *Daily Colonist* reporter, who witnessed the launching, reported that the new side-paddle wheeler *Mermaid,* ". . . was gaily decorated with English, American and other flags, and the launch was achieved in a perfectly successful manner." The reporter then went on say that *Mermaid,* ". . . was intended for towing purposes and her model and build are highly creditable to her experienced builder."

The wooden steamer—74 feet in length, 18 feet wide, 5.25 feet in depth and fitted with two high-pressure steam engines producing 26 combined horsepower—was built to order by H.B. Bolton of Victoria for a partnership of four individuals with connections to Hastings Mill in Burrard Inlet. Partners Richard H. Alexander (sawmill manager), Mary G. Raymur (wife of former manager Captain R.A. Raymur), Ainslie J. Mouat (accountant) and Charles A. Coldwell (sawmill foreman) intended to use the *Mermaid* as a towboat and general workboat.

Hastings Mill was built in 1865 on the southern shore of Burrard Inlet where the National Harbour Board is now located in the Port of Vancouver. It was one of the first major lumber export mills established in British Columbia. Historic photographs of the site taken in the late nineteenth century often feature large sailing ships tied alongside the sawmill's dock loading lumber while others lay anchored out in the stream waiting their turn. Steam tugs were required for towing the windjammers into and out of the harbour and berthing them, as well as for other general sawmill duties. By 1896 Hastings Mill was operating a fleet of around eight towboats.

Mermaid worked—apparently uneventfully—for Hastings Mills for around nine years, and was then sold to the Northern Shipping Company Ltd. of Vancouver on March 14, 1893. The new owners replaced the paddlewheels with twin screws and her high pressure engines with two new steeple compound steam engines.

It was only a matter of months before the steamer was in trouble. Northern Shipping was attempting to run *Mermaid* as a coasting steamer serving the ports of Victoria and Nanaimo with stops throughout the Gulf Islands when she lost a propeller in Ganges Harbour on December 22, 1893.

Captain John W. Gisholm managed to return the steamer to Nanaimo on one engine but her troubles weren't over, as Northern Shipping Company was already undergoing financial difficulties. The company had been in the hands of a liquidator since October and, on June 2, 1894, he ordered Northern Shipping's business affairs wound up. *Mermaid* was consequently sold to the New Vancouver Coal Mining & Land Company, Limited (NVCM&L).

NVCM&L was a British firm that had taken over the original Hudson's Bay Company land grant and coal interests in and around what is today's town of Nanaimo, BC. One of their mines, the Protection Mine, was under Protection Island, a small island off the Nanaimo waterfront. The coal mining company was soon using *Mermaid* both as a tug for towing barges and a ferry to carry miners across the water from their Nanaimo homes to Protection Island.

Mermaid went on the rocks in Kanaka Bay, Newcastle Island, on March 12, 1902, and NVCM&L decided to sell the stranded steamer as is, where is. Charles Wardill, a steam engineer, purchased the vessel, made temporary patches to her bottom and had her towed to Victoria for repairs.

Wardill was originally hired by the NVCM&L soon after his arrival in Canada from England. He worked in the shops of the coal mining operation and acted as a steam engineer for the company's locomotives and tug. Judge Stanley Wardill (Charles' grandson in Nanaimo) recalled that after his grandfather bought *Mermaid* he attempted to run the vessel as a steam packet to carry loggers and supplies from Vancouver into Jervis Inlet. Stan Wardill heard from other family members that his grandfather sank everything he had into the venture and probably didn't bother with insurance on the steamer, which was valued at $22,000 in turn-of-the-century dollars.

In the early morning darkness of March 25, 1904, *Mermaid* was running at full speed in Jervis Inlet with Mate Roberts at the wheel and a crew of six and three passengers aboard. Charles Wardill, who was acting as chief engineer, had brought three of his children along: Stan's father Mike, who later ran a bicycle shop in Nanaimo; Oz, who went on to become a Nanaimo schoolteacher; and Kate, who eventually married and moved to California.

The *Mermaid* had just dropped off some loggers in Vancouver Bay when, at 5:00 a.m., she turned the corner too soon, struck the rocks of Moorsam Bluffs and stove in her bows. Captain Walters attempted to run his sinking ship across Jervis Inlet to beach it on the Brittain River flats several miles away but the rising water flooded the boiler room forcing Chief Engineer Wardill to abandon his post, and the vessel consequently lost steam and came to a stop. The lifeboat was launched while the captain and engineer stayed aboard for as long as possible in an attempt to save the holed vessel.

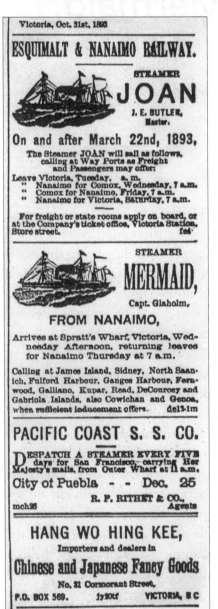

This advertisement for the Victoria-Nanaimo passage of the steamer *Mermaid* appeared in the *British Colonist* newspaper in 1893.

UNDERWATER ARCHAEOLOGICAL SOCIETY OF BRITISH COLUMBIA COLLECTION

The *Mermaid* was employed towing barges and ferrying miners from Nanaimo, BC, to a mine on nearby Protection Island when she stranded on the rocks at Kanaka Bay, Newcastle Island, in March 1902. NANAIMO MUSEUM COLLECTION Q3.89

Although it was only a short distance to shore, *Mermaid* sank in 60 to 100 fathoms of water. The crew and passengers spent the next two days rowing the lifeboat out to Pender Harbour where they were able to catch Union Steamship's *Comox* for Vancouver, where the press was informed of the disaster.

To this day the tale persists among the Wardill family that someone had been intentionally put aboard *Mermaid* to sabotage her and put an end to Charles Wardill's challenge to Union Steamship's monopoly of the run. Some even say he had been warned in particular to watch out for her captain.

The Underwater Archaeological Society of BC tried using side-scan sonar in May 2001 to locate the remains of *Mermaid*, but the attempt was unsuccessful. The deep, craggy bottom of Jervis Inlet keeps *Mermaid's* final resting place a secret to this day.

Chapter 5

The *King David*: Did Lost Crew Join Doomed Ship? 1905

On April 5, 1973, Comox Valley residents witnessed a peculiar sight: a Canadian Forces Labrador helicopter passing overhead with a large anchor dangling beneath it. The unusual artifact was once an essential part of the ground tackle of *King David*, a three-masted steel sailing ship wrecked on Bajo Reef off the west coast of Vancouver Island in December 1905.

The three-masted British ship *King David* (pictured here in about 1900) was in ballast and in-bound for Royal Roads, Vancouver Island, when—in the midst of a southwesterly gale—she drove ashore on Bajo Reef, Nootka Island. STATE LIBRARY OF SOUTH AUSTRALIA PRG1373/15/57

Someone had happened to notice the anchor in the intertidal area of Santa Gertrudis cove in Nootka Sound and had convinced the 442 Transport and Rescue squadron at Canadian Forces Base Comox it was worth recovering for the Courtenay and District Museum. Its heart-shaped palms and square shank indicated that it was a nineteenth-century Admiralty pattern anchor, probably forged in the 1840s in Great Britain for a sailing ship. What wasn't known at the time was that the owner of a log salvage business, who was also a diver, had deposited the anchor and a capstan from the *King David* wreck site at the convenient location after recovering them from Bajo Reef.

The 2,240-gross-ton, 279-foot-long British ship *King David*, owned by the Glasgow Shipping Company, left Salinas Cruz, Mexico, in ballast for Royal Roads, Vancouver Island, on September 30, 1905. According to the January 20, 1906, edition of the *Victoria Daily Colonist* the vessel was 74 days out and on the overdue list when she finally drove ashore on Bajo Reef. Although the survivors reported it a slow voyage, the trip had gone reasonably well until *King David* approached Vancouver Island. There a series of southwesterly gales and snow squalls carried the vessel to the north.

She arrived off Nootka Sound on December 10 in calm conditions only to face another gale that night. The anchors were let go to hold the big windjammer off the beach but they dragged bottom three days later and huge seas drove *King David* onto the submerged rocks of Bajo Reef. (The *Colonist* reporter located Bajo Reef by noting that it stretched seaward south of Bajo Point two miles north of Maquinna Point "where the great whale totem and the weather-broken sewing machines and rusted rifles mark the grave of Chief Maquinna.")

JANUARY 20, 1906.

King David Is a Wreck

Eighteen Survivors Are Rescued From Bajo Point by Queen City.

Chief Officer and Six Men Who Went for Assistance Believed Drowned.

Shipwrecked Men on the Beach for Over a Month—Sailmaker Dead.

In the *Victoria Daily Colonist*, dated January 20, 1906, a crewmember of the *King David* reported that the doomed voyage "went along fairly well until we got off the Vancouver Island coast, and then we struck a series of southerly and southwesterly hail and snow squalls." UNDERWATER ARCHAEOLOGICAL SOCIETY OF BRITISH COLUMBIA COLLECTION

After the Cape Horn windjammer struck ". . . with a shock which shook her every plate," Captain Davidson ordered the boats provisioned and lowered. Experiencing the massive steel hull breaking up on the rocks apparently unhinged the old sailmaker, Donald McLeod, who became deranged and had to be forcibly restrained in one of the boats. The ship's company landed at Bajo Point, the rugged and inhospitable southwest corner of Nootka Island, to encounter rocky cliffs open to the Pacific and then dense forests and impenetrable salal undergrowth inland. The shipwrecked sailors spent 33 wintry days in this hostile environment.

The stranded seamen had only limited knowledge of the local area and were unaware that they were only about eight miles away from Friendly Cove. The village had a number of Indigenous lodges and also a well-stocked general store that contained more than enough provisions to feed 25 shipwreck survivors. The captain sent two men out to reconnoitre and, within two days, they met a wandering prospector, but unfortunately his knowledge of the area was as vague as their own. He told them—incorrectly as it happened—that a steamer wouldn't be by until March.

Oblivious to the fact that they were so close to rescue, Captain Davidson sent his ship's boat off with his chief officer, A. Wallstron, and six men to Cape Beale, a lighthouse some distance to the south. As

The *King David*'s Chief Officer, A. Wallstron, and the six men who were sent out in a ship's boat to find help at the Cape Beale lighthouse may have been picked up by the in-bound, four-masted steel barque *Pass of Melfort* (pictured here around 1898). Unfortunately, the barque herself wrecked off Ucluelet, BC, with loss of all life. STATE LIBRARY OF SOUTH AUSTRALIA PRG1373/17/36

Davidson explained later, when he first made landfall he was disoriented because he had old charts and had mistaken a new light at Clayoquot for Cape Beale. Wallstron and the other six seamen and the boat were never seen again.

The *Daily Colonist* suggested that the small boat's course probably crossed that of the ill-fated *Pass of Melfort* inbound in ballast from Panama for Port Townsend, Washington. The four-masted barque was itself caught in a southeast gale and wrecked on Amphitrite Point at the entrance to Ucluelet Harbour. There were no survivors to say whether their ship had indeed picked up the seven *King David* sailors.

The 18 men who remained huddled under tarpaulins and canvas at their barren campsite on Nootka Island were ultimately more fortunate. When they had spent more than a month on the inhospitable shore, the vessel *Queen City* noticed their fire and rescued them. The ordeal was too much for the old sailmaker, however, and he died aboard *Queen City*.

Today, the big anchor in the Comox Marina parking lot sits unrecognized as once belonging to *King David*, a stately Cape Horn windjammer that met its end off the West Coast with the loss of eight lives. To many who pass by the anchor, it's just another of the numerous bits and pieces recovered from the ocean floor that are often found decorating parks and the yards of sport divers.

A final note

Underwater archaeologists suggest that interesting artifacts found on the ocean floor are better off left where they are. Most objects submerged in salt water reach an equilibrium point where deterioration stops due to a lack of oxygen, but once out of the water, the artifacts often quickly turn into an unrecognizable pile of rust. Another point to remember is that the British Columbia Heritage Conservation Act clearly states that it is against the law "to damage or alter a heritage wreck or remove any heritage object from a heritage wreck" without an authorized permit.

Passersby can't help but notice the massive early 19th century Admiralty pattern anchor on display in the Comox Marina parking lot but most are unaware that it once belonged to the *King David*, which met its end off the West Coast in 1905 with the loss of eight lives. RICK JAMES PHOTO

Chapter 6

Melanope:
Witch of the Waves, 1905

Launched from the shipyard of W.H. Potter & Company in Liverpool, England, in 1876, the iron three-masted *Melanope* was the subject of curious tales in her day. For most of her life she was considered a cursed ship, while others who sailed the vessel actually found her a pleasure to sail and a "witch of the waves." One of her last masters, Leighton Robinson, recalled in later life how it had been to handle *Melanope*. "She was very fine aft with a clean run and fine entry forward, never lost steerage way during my experience with her, and an able vessel in heavy weather."

While nearly all of the hulks at Comox Logging & Railway Company's abandoned breakwater at Royston on Vancouver Island have long since collapsed into the estuary mud, there is one whose bow section was still holding up in the spring of 2011—the old Cape Horn windjammer *Melanope*.

In 1966, Bruce Watson recounted to *Vancouver Sun* marine writer Charles Defieux his impressions of rowing around the breakwater hulks as a boy. Particularly fascinated with *Melanope*, he would peer through a hole in the waterline. "I could lean inside and view in the musty interior the changing patterns of light produced by sun-rays poking through the rotting planking and open mid-section. The exposed ribs were webbed with strings of seaweed beaded with water droplets and the light glistened from these, the rusty spikes, the rippling water of the flooded area, and the dripping water from the fallen beams. It was an eerie and haunting sight."

Melanope was one of the thousands of square-rigged iron and steel windjammers that flourished across the oceans of the world in the late nineteenth century. Although these massive, slab-sided, flat-bottomed vessels lacked the fine lines and elegance of their forebear, the wooden clipper, they were often almost as swift. Still, many considered them no less attractive than their wood ancestor since the ornamentation of the hull and deck fittings, often teak, was just as lavish.

In essence, these tall ships symbolized the last gallant attempt of the age of sail to challenge the arrival of the steamship. They earned the name "windjammers" because their crews were required to "jam" or brace their yards all the way around in order to get the monsters to sail into the wind. Still, whereas a clipper ship often required a crew of 35 to 40 men, the new windjammers were usually managed with about 30. However, the iron ships did suffer from some shortcomings, especially since owners and builders were reluctant to reduce the top hamper—the overall weight of the rigging—and had a tendency to over-mast the ships.

As a three-masted ship 258 feet long and of 1,686 gross tons, *Melanope* was rigged with a standard rig of the day and carried double top-gallant and royal sails above her upper and lower topsails and mainsails.

Before leaving San Francisco for Australia in 1900, *Melanope* (pictured here riding at anchor off Sydney, Australia) was "rigged as a barque and poorly rigged in the way of running gear at that," according to her new captain, Leighton Robinson. PUGET SOUND MARITIME HISTORICAL SOCIETY #1587

The huge mainsails of a typical windjammer often weighed a ton dry and considerably more when wet. The iron yards (the spars from which the sails are set), sometimes 90 feet in length and 2 feet in diameter at the centre, were in themselves extremely heavy. When the miles of wire rope, chain and manila line needed to support this collection of masts, sails and yards were added, the weight aloft became terrific. Even though wire backstays were doubled, the strain on the rigging was still enormous. *Melanope* herself suffered the consequences from an overly generous sail plan on her first voyage.

The ship was constructed for a prominent rice milling and trading firm—Heap & Sons of Liverpool, England, and Rangoon, Burma. They maintained a fleet of six or seven ships carrying cargo and emigrants from Great Britain outward to Australia and bringing goods from Southeast Asia to European ports on the return trip.

Marine writer Basil Lubbock once told a curious tale concerning *Melanope*'s maiden voyage, and almost every writer since has made a point of including the story in their own account of the ship's exploits. It appears that as *Melanope* was being towed out of the Mersey River to open water, an elderly woman selling apples was discovered on board. The ship's master, Walter Watson, was quick to act and had his potential stowaway deposited onto the towboat headed back to port. The indignant lady left in a huff, cursing both the ship and all aboard as she went. Of course, every mishap that was to befall *Melanope* from that day onward was attributed to this unpleasant incident.

The premonitions of an already superstitious crew appeared vindicated when their new ship got into trouble only a few days out from Liverpool. On October 7, 1876, *Lloyd's List* reported that *Melanope* had returned to Canning Dock, Liverpool, after being dismasted some 200 miles northwest of Cape Finisterre in a gale. The underwriters who inspected the vessel tried to convince the crew that the mishap was directly attributable to the shipbuilders having over-masted the iron ship by nine feet.

After repairs were made, *Melanope* set sail for Melbourne, Australia, and over the next few years the ship carried new immigrants out to Australia and then loaded rice or jute in Southeast Asia for her return voyage to Great Britain. In 1882 the Heap & Sons fleet was sold to William Gracie and Edwin Beazley of Gracie, Beazley & Co., who subsequently formed the Australasian Shipping Company that same year.

Sailing ships continued to earn good dividends for their owners by transporting three great bulk cargoes throughout the 1880s. The Calcutta, Rangoon and Chittagong jute and rice trades, the San Francisco and Puget Sound grain trade and the Australian wool trade were all booming at this time. In essence, the huge iron and steel square-riggers were the forerunners of today's container ships; floating storage bins used to transport the raw materials in high demand by Europe's new industrial age. For outbound voyages, the windjammers loaded cotton, heavy machinery, rails, coal or salt. As a result, the Australasian Shipping Company was able to keep *Melanope* fully engaged as a merchant ship throughout the 1880s and 1890s.

As the 1890s progressed, *Melanope* became more involved with charter work along the Pacific coast of the Americas. By December 1898, *Melanope* was found sitting at a dock at Antwerp, Belgium, and it was here that Basil Lubbock picked up his "cursed ship" tale once again. This time the supposedly ill-fated ship was bought by a disreputable master. Captain J.R. Craigen was apparently a ". . . very thirsty master mariner, who had run off with the equally thirsty and very rich daughter of a wealthy Indian officer." When the ship arrived in Panama in February 1900 and his bride succumbed to a fatal combination of drink and fever, it is said a broken-hearted Craigen put an end to his pain by jumping overboard. Fo'c'sle gossip had it that the mate assumed command, brought the vessel into San Francisco that summer and then quietly absconded with the dead captain's gold, leaving the crew "d.s." (distressed seamen).

Melanope was seized and sold by a United States Marshal on November 27, 1900, for $53,900 to an American citizen. The new owner offered young Leighton Robinson the command and he accepted on the condition that he could take his new bride with him. Writing in 1930, Robinson remarked, "I took charge of her here in 'Frisco in the later part of 1900 leaving the *Coptic* and took Kate with me on voyage to Sydney, Australia. She was then rigged as a barque and poorly rigged in the way of running gear at that. Pope and Talbot owned her . . . they wanted a man with British licence to take command. She had come up from Panama with scrap iron, part of the old French Canal stuff. J.J. Moore of the Australian Dispatch Line were agents [a San Francisco lumber exporting firm]."

Unlike the earlier honeymoon trip, the Robinsons' passage to Sydney, Australia, with a cargo of lumber aboard was trouble free and completed in a record time of 45 days. Captain Robinson considered Lubbock's story of *Melanope* in *Last of the Windjammers* as "a lot of bunk . . . particularly that pertaining to the purchase at Antwerp etc." Before taking on his charge, Robinson made a point of questioning one of the crew about the incident. "The story I got from Green, who was mate, was that the captain Creighton [*sic*] and his wife, who was a Miss Emma Taylor, had purchased the vessel at Antwerp, intending to cruise around the world. On reaching Panama she died of fever, and he didn't care whether he lived or not, and contracted fever of which he died en route to S.F. There were a lot of newspaper write-ups etc. and all sorts of weird yarns about his having other wives and running away with the lady who purchased the vessel for him, but I don't put much stock in any of that."

The iron square-rigger set a record in 1903 that probably has yet to be equalled by a vessel under sail. During August and September, the iron ship shifted between the lumber mill towns of Port Townsend, Port Ludlow and Port Blakely, Washington State. On September 10 *Melanope* was finally under sail and passing out past Tatoosh Island. Known as a "witch of the waves," the iron ship raced from Puget Sound, Washington, to Table Bay, Cape Town, South Africa, in an incredible 72 days. This record is doubly amazing because it was done short-handed after 18 of the 30-man crew mutinied.

Captain Wills was dissatisfied with the way the helmsman had allowed the ship to drift off course and, after the crewman denied it, put him in irons for insolence. When some of the crew protested the severity of this punishment, Wills—armed with a revolver and his mates with clubs—called them one by one up to the poop. Each member who refused duty was then put in irons as well. Unfortunately, *Melanope* was still some 3,000 miles from Cape Town, and now short-handed.

N.K. Wills, who retired in Vancouver, BC, told a reporter for the city's *Province* newspaper in 1942, "Oh, she could pass anything under sail . . . . We handled her alright. We had fair winds and we all knew our business." When they reached South Africa on November 23, 1903, the mutineers were tried and sentenced to work in a rock quarry for six weeks until the ship cleared for Newcastle, Australia, on January 8, 1904. Although there was no trouble from the malcontents on this voyage, they were dismissed in Australia and signed off with no reason given on their papers. This action by the captain was tantamount to beaching them.

After filling her holds with coal in Union Bay on Vancouver Island in early 1906, *Melanope* sailed for Unalaska in the Aleutian Islands in the spring. Upon returning to the Pacific Northwest, she then set sail from Bellingham, Washington, to Manzanillo with a cargo of railroad ties aboard and, before she reached there, was caught in a hurricane off the Mexican coast. Once she was in safely at the port and had delivered her cargo, *Melanope* left Manzanillo on November 1 on what was to be her last voyage.

Charles Wills, son of Captain Wills and nine years old at the time, recalled the details of the loss of *Melanope* to maritime historian Norman Hacking in 1975. She was sailing north on her way to Tacoma, Washington, with sand ballast in her holds when she ran into a violent storm off Cape Blanco. The ballast shifted, the mainmast was dislodged, and the ship went over on her beam ends. In an attempt to save her, the fore and main topmasts were cut away, with the main topmast and royal yards toppling through the main topgallant stays and rigging before they crashed through the deck. Captain Wills, his wife, son and daughter and the crew of 22 were forced to spend a harrowing night in the rigging and it was not until morning that they were able to clear a lifeboat from the half-submerged deck.

Fortunately, they were found and picked up by the steam schooner *William H. Smith* and taken to Port Townsend, Washington. *Melanope* herself was discovered later as a drifting derelict with a severe starboard list off the Oregon coast. The steam

The wrecked barque *Melanope* was towed into Astoria by the steam schooner *Northland* in December 1906. After encountering a violent storm off Cape Blanco, Oregon, the ballast in the *Melanope* had shifted and she had gone over on her beam ends, forcing crew and passengers to seek refuge in the rigging. SAN FRANCISCO MARITIME NHP, E3,2.304

schooner *Northland* put a line aboard and towed her into Astoria on December 14, 1906. Three days later, the Wills family were reunited with their dog, Queenie, who had been left behind on the wreck.

As *Melanope* was damaged beyond repair, J.J. Moore & Company sold the 30-year-old windjammer. She was bought by James Griffiths, an entrepreneur in Puget Sound marine transportation, who had made a good part of his fortune by purchasing retired sailing ships and turning them into barges. The tall ships were shorn of rigging and had their hatchways enlarged, while some also had their main deck torn out.

James Griffiths & Sons also owned and operated a Canadian subsidiary, the Coastwise Steamship and Barge Company of Vancouver, BC, with eight vessels, all registered as barges and all built between 1872 and 1885. The stripped-down three-master was put into service between Puget Sound, Northern British Columbia and Alaska for Griffiths' Coastwise Steamship and Barge fleet. Among other jobs, *Melanope* probably barged rock from Waldron Island, in the San Juan Islands, to Grays Harbor where a jetty was being constructed.

On May 25, 1911, James Griffiths sold *Melanope* to the Canadian Pacific Railway (CPR) who bought her to replace their old collier, *Robert Kerr*, which had wrecked in the Gulf Islands that March. *Melanope* remained a familiar sight around the West Coast for decades, but still it was distressing to see what was once a majestic tall ship now weather-beaten and looking forlorn at the end of a towline as a coal hulk. "It was like discovering the armless and legless trunk of a once-beautiful statue," William McFee, a former mate on a tramp steamer and author of *The Watch Below*, reflected while bunkering his ship from another

square-rigger turned collier. "The ship's bowsprit had been sawn off flush with the stem, her masts were cut down . . . . She was black with coal dust and crusted with grimy sea salt."

The collier *Melanope* worked on a regular run from the Union Bay and Ladysmith loading facilities on Vancouver Island to the CPR docks in Burrard Inlet for some 30 years. Although now only a weather-beaten coal barge, *Melanope* remained a source of peculiar tales. R.E. Griffin recalled striking up a conversation with an old sailor while looking over the hulk. The sailor enlarged on the story of the curse and told Griffin that when the mizzen mast was removed, 32 pounds of opium were found stashed inside it.

The blackened collier was seen regularly in Burrard Inlet waiting to bunker the graceful white ocean liners *Empress of Russia* and *Empress of Asia*. The big liners were requisitioned as troop transports during the Second World War and, unfortunately, both were lost. The *Asia* was turned into a fiery wreck off Sumatra by Japanese bombers in February 1942 while the *Russia* was destroyed by fire during an overhaul at Barrow-in-Furness, England, in September 1945. This effectively brought

In her reincarnation as a collier, *Melanope* is seen here rafted next to the CPR's trans-Pacific liner *Empress of Asia* in Burrard Inlet, BC, discharging coal. CHARLES BRADBURY PHOTO, 1916, COURTESY OF ROYAL BC MUSEUM, BC ARCHIVES A-07162

While the hulls of the ships surrounding her have all collapsed into the estuary mud, the bow and stern section of the *Melanope* still remain standing at Royston. The steel hull plates of the CPR tug *Qualicum* and HMCS *Dunver* are now only piles of rusted wreckage, while the wrought iron construction of *Melanope* still maintains the structural integrity of her remaining elements—a proud testament to British shipbuilding at the height of the Victorian age. RICK JAMES PHOTO, 2011

Melanope's career as a coal hulk to an end. Although she also supplied some coal to the CPR's tugs and galley coal to the "*Princesses*" of the company's British Columbia Coast Service, the CPR deemed her no longer essential in 1946.

"Old *Melanope* To End Days As a Breakwater," the *Vancouver News Herald* announced on April 12, 1946. The *Vancouver Province* of the same day stated: "Proudest, fastest full-rigged sailing ship afloat in her heyday, *Melanope* will be sunk in shallow water off the Comox Logging & Railway Co. wharf at Royston." Retired Captain N.K. Wills came down to have a last look at his old command before she left Burrard Inlet on the towline. He was very interested to discover that the bird's-eye maple was still intact on the bulkheads of his quarters, while his bath—close to four feet deep—could still hold water.

Melanope's registry was finally closed with the note, "Vessel beached & broken up . . ." and she was left to the mercy of the weather and sea at Royston. By the early 1950s, the southeasterlies had collapsed her bulwarks, leaving only her bow and stern sections intact. Local residents were happy to discover that the old collier still had some cargo in her hold and that preparing for the cool winter months was only a matter of picking up coal washed up on the beach.

At the time of writing, although the hulls of the other 13 vessels that were scuttled at Royston have nearly all completely disintegrated, the wrought iron plates of *Melanope* still hold her bow high—some 135 years after her launching at the height of the Victorian Age when Britannia still ruled the waves.

Chapter 7

Loss of the Union Steamship
Capilano, 1915

On October 4, 1915, a small news item appeared in the *Vancouver Sun* titled, "Crew Brings News of Disaster." The paper reported that, "according to the word brought by the crew of the Union Steamship company's steamer, *Capilano*, which sank on Friday night at a point midway between Savary Island and Cape Mudge, the vessel struck . . . some obstruction some eight hours before disaster and

The single screw steamer *Capilano* was the second of three steel ships built in Scotland for the Union Steamship Company of British Columbia Ltd., which was formed to transport passengers and cargo around the BC coast.
VANCOUVER MARITIME MUSEUM PHOTO NEG 2618

although an examination was made of the hull when the boat put into Van Anda [on Texada Island] . . . she sank shortly after leaving that port."

The single screw steamer *Capilano* was the second of three steel ships (the other two were *Comox* and *Coquitlam*) ordered to be built in Scotland in the early 1890s for the Union Steamship Company of British Columbia Ltd. While the three steel vessels were fabricated by J. McArthur & Co., Glasgow, they weren't completed there. Instead the vessels were shipped in sections around Cape Horn to arrive in Vancouver where they were assembled.

Founded in November 1889, the Union Steamship Company was formed, "to supply the increasing demands for passengers and cargo to the outlying new settlements, sawmills, logging camps, stone quarries, agricultural and mining districts," according to Company historian Gerald Rushton. The company began operations with a small fleet operating in Burrard Inlet and consisting of the 57-foot paddle steamer SS *Leonora*, the 51-foot SS *Senator* and the 76-foot tug *Skidegate*, along with several scows. These vessels were primarily engaged in harbour towing and on the Moodyville-Hastings Mill ferry run. Then, in order to exploit the growing opportunities along the coast, capital was raised in the United Kingdom and three new steel ships were ordered.

The second of the trio completed was *Capilano*, which slid down the recently cleared shipway on Coal Harbour on December 5, 1891. She was 120 feet in length with a breadth of 22.2 feet, a depth of 9.6 feet and a gross tonnage listed as 231.1. Although *Capilano* was primarily intended for freight carriage (the builder guaranteed the vessel for 350 tons of deadweight cargo), she was also licensed, and had the deck space to berth 25 passengers.

Powered by a pair of compound steam engines built by Bow McLachlan & Co., Paisley, Scotland,

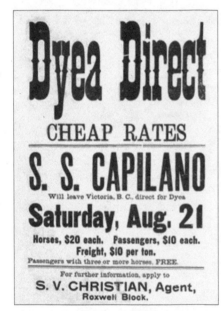

The SS *Capilano* advertised cheap rates for passage from Victoria, BC, to Dyea, Alaska: "Passengers with three or more horses, FREE." This advertisement is probably from 1897. UNDERWATER ARCHAEOLOGICAL SOCIETY OF BRITISH COLUMBIA COLLECTION

Capilano was, according to Gerald Rushton in his book *Whistle Up the Inlet*, "powerfully engined, with large steel boilers for economic consumption." The estimated speed of the new steamer was 8 to 9 knots loaded, and 10 knots travelling light.

After running her trials in Burrard Inlet, on February 4, 1892, *Capilano* left for Victoria to fetch new boilers for the Moodyville Mill in Burrard Inlet. Her next job was carrying coal from Nanaimo. In 1894 both *Capilano* and *Coquitlam* were chartered to the New England Fish Company and participated in the development of the British Columbia halibut industry. During this time *Capilano* was also involved in transporting stone from quarries on Nelson Island and elsewhere to Victoria for the building of the new Parliament Buildings.

Three years later, when news of the rich gold strikes in the Klondike reached the outside world, hordes of miners arrived in British Columbia seeking transportation to Dyea and Skagway at the head of the Lynn Canal in Alaska. Gerald Rushton claimed that *Capilano* was the first Canadian steamer to leave a British Columbia port for the main gateway to the gold fields when she departed Vancouver July 22, 1897, with a full load of passengers, 69 head of cattle and 20 horses. *Capilano*, along with *Cutch* and *Coquitlam*, were to remain occupied with scheduled Skagway service from Victoria

When she departed from Vancouver in 1897, *Capilano* became the first Canadian steamer to leave a British Columbia port heading for the Klondike gold fields. In this photograph she is seen towing the paddlewheeler *Lightning* into the harbour at St. Michaels, Alaska, in 1899. VANCOUVER MARITIME MUSEUM NEG 1927

and Vancouver for two years. By 1900, as runs to southeast Alaska became more linked to the port of Seattle, there was a slackening in demand for service from a BC port.

As a result, *Capilano* was withdrawn and redirected to serve the expanding trade in British Columbia's northern waters where a mail contract had been approved for the Nass River. By the early 1900s, *Capilano* was making scheduled runs to northern connections while stopping at various fish canneries along the way. Once Union Steamship began constructing modern passenger vessels, both *Capilano* and *Coquitlam* were assigned entirely to cannery and freighting demands.

It was while operating in this service that *Capilano* left Vancouver early in the morning of September 29, 1915, carrying general cargo and with a crew of 16 aboard but without any passengers. She called in at two or three ports and by the evening of September 30 was proceeding to Van Anda on Texada Island to discharge some freight. The night was particularly dark with a considerable amount of smoke in the atmosphere, which was quite common at that time of the year as many logging companies were burning slash.

After rounding Scotch Fir Point (the northern point at the junction of Jervis Inlet with Malaspina Strait) Samuel Nelson, the ship's master, retired to his cabin for a short rest leaving the acting second mate, Fletcher Hemmonds, in charge. (Nelson was fatigued after spending a considerable amount of time on deck, making several landings and struggling to navigate through the smoky haze.)

Around 9:25 p.m., and about two miles from Van Anda, *Capilano* struck a submerged object. Most of the witnesses examined by the subsequent investigation into the ship's loss stated that they thought that the vessel had struck a log. The wreck commissioner and his assessors disagreed and pointed out that due to the dark and smoky conditions *Capilano* was probably further off coming round Scotch Fir Point than estimated, thus bringing her close in to the Texada shore where she may have struck a submerged rock, not a log. In making this observation, they noted that the master had been awakened by the sound of the whistle, and a short five-second echo bouncing off land. It brought him running into the wheelhouse to yell at the helmsman, "Haul her to the westward . . . Port!!"

Although it was suspected that *Capilano* had received serious damage, no leak was found and the coastal freighter continued on to Van Anda. She left there at about 11:00 p.m. and then, at about 1:30 a.m. on the morning of October 1, while steering east by north, she began listing heavily to port into a southeasterly blowing hard with rain and haze. Water two feet deep was now discovered in the lower hold.

Captain Nelson was hopeful that his ship could still make Campbell River but the hull was badly punctured and, as the water rose, the ship's condition became more perilous. Also, a number of drums of gasoline in the hold began washing back and forth with the movement of the ship, and fears that the drums would eventually open her seams convinced the crew to take to a large lifeboat at 3:00 a.m.

Capilano sank at 5:30 a.m. on October 1, 1915, five miles WSW of Harwood Island according to her Wreck Register entry. The crew rowed easterly in search of land and eventually reached Indian Point on the west end of Savary Island—but not before they had watched their ship slip beneath the waves. They gave vivid descriptions of the steamship's demise; of how her lights remained ablaze as she sank and how, just before she went to the bottom, the steam whistle gave a final, solitary blast.

A newspaper account of the day stated that *Capilano*, valued at $30,000, "had a cargo worth an additional $8,000 or $10,000, consisting chiefly of cannery supplies, gasoline and lumber." The Union Steamship Company had the vessel itself insured for 5,000 pounds sterling at the time of the loss.

In its attempt to unravel what caused the sinking, the court investigating the circumstances leading up to the loss was of the opinion that the submerged object *Capilano* struck the night before was a rock, some of which may have been carried away with her. The rock, along with coal in the hold, probably plugged the hole punched in the vessel initially, allowing little water to penetrate. However, once the ship left Van Anda and encountered increasing wind and rough water, it was suggested, whatever was blocking the hole worked itself loose and allowed the vessel to fill with water.

Since there was only speculation, and no evidence, as to what the submerged object indeed was, Samuel Nelson was given the benefit of the doubt and his master's certificate was returned to him. The court did censure Nelson though, "for retiring to his cabin under the conditions of the weather then prevailing, and leaving an uncertified man . . . in charge of the ship." The acting second mate, Fletcher Hemmonds, was criticized for not calling the master under the existing circumstances and nearing the next port of call, Van Anda.

Since he didn't possess a certificate, the court warned him that once he obtained a certificate he certainly would be held responsible for similar, future incidents.

The final resting place of the old Union Steamship Company freighter is on the bottom in some 120 feet of water on the south side of Grant Reefs located between Savary and Harwood Islands in the Strait of Georgia. Apparently, once the investigation into the loss was completed, no known commercial salvage was ever attempted on *Capilano*, probably because she was in deep water and was transporting goods considered of no great value. She would remain undisturbed on the bottom by Grant Reefs for some 57 years.

In 1972, a Lund fisherman, Neil Gustafson, pulled up a piece of metal railing from an unknown wreck on Grant Reefs. He subsequently reported the find to diver Rick McIntosh, and McIntosh and his diving buddy, Courtenay Powell, became the first to dive the wreck. Later, McIntosh returned to the wreck site with fellow diver Bob Briggs of Powell River in an attempt to identify the mystery ship. In the course of some 15 dives they retrieved a number of items, including 16 portholes, the ship's compass, bottles, china and a marble sink, but what they were most excited about was finding the ship's strong box. Once ashore they broke it open, only to discover that their hoped-for treasure consisted of bills of lading and four pennies dated 1907, 1911, 1912 and 1914.

While McIntosh and Powell were successful in keeping the location a secret for a while, by the mid-1970s a number of others had learned where the wreck was and began diving it. Now that it was well known, especially after being written up in *Diver Magazine* in December 1981, the secret was out: *Capilano* was considered the best wreck dive on the BC coast.

Finally, with the increasing traffic to the site, the Underwater Archaeological Society of BC was contacted and on June 9, 1984, an information/education plaque was placed on the stern to encourage divers to respect the heritage site. On November 6, 1985, the *Capilano* officially became a Designated Provincial Heritage Site through a Provincial Order-in-Council.

Nonetheless, despite the fact that the *Capilano* is a designated historic site—and it is illegal to remove anything—it was reported some years ago that a group of divers had made off with the ship's wheel, a destructive act that is entirely unacceptable by today's diving standards. Hopefully, as more dive groups continue to visit the fascinating and beautiful wreck site of *Capilano* (the entire hull is festooned with white plumose anemones) they will have the decency to "remove nothing, leave only bubbles."

Colin Stares, a diver with the Underwater Archaeological Society of BC, explores the wreck *Capilano*, resting at a point midway between Savary Island and Cape Mudge. JACQUES MARC PHOTO, 2007

Chapter 8

Wooden Ships: Wartime Shipbuilding that Fuelled Victoria's Economy, 1917–1918

Streetcar passengers returning from an evening in Gorge Park witnessed "a vast fairyland of lights" from the Point Ellice Bridge during the summer of 1918. The source of this spectacle was the night shift of wartime shipbuilding underway in Victoria Harbour. Beneath powerful searchlights the huge gantry derricks of the Foundation Company lifted their loads over a number of wooden ships in various stages of production.

The American company, a specialist in constructing bridge piers, industrial foundations and mine shafts, was in the midst of finishing a contract for five wooden cargo steamships for Canada's Imperial Munitions Board (IMB). The names of the new vessels on the stocks—*War Songhee*, *War Babine*, *War Camchin*, *War Masset* and *War Nanoose*—left no doubt as to their intended purpose.

The year before, the *Daily Colonist* had forewarned that the old Songhees reserve was about to undergo a transformation "in the relentless march of industrial progress." As the city entered a new era of shipbuilding, old landmarks were to make room for newer monuments, with the *Colonist* reporter prophesying that "never again will the curling smoke wreaths from the Indian campfires be seen floating through the treetops."

The Imperial Munitions Board saw the West Coast as an untapped source of shipbuilding potential after war losses incurred in the North Atlantic had begun to reach crisis proportions. Between May 1916 and January 1917, more than 1,150 ships were sunk. When Germany declared unrestricted U-boat warfare in February 1917, the rate of these losses more than doubled and another 2,566 ships went to the bottom by year's end.

Shipping experts from England, Canada and the United States arrived in British Columbia looking for a solution to an impending disaster. While some steel shipbuilding was already underway on the West Coast, steel plate was imported at great cost. As a result, the international group proceeded to inspect some five-masted wooden auxiliary schooners already under construction in Victoria's Upper Harbour.

The Cameron brothers, owners of a large Victoria sawmill, had leased the foreshore next to the Point Ellice Bridge in July 1916 and had built a shipyard. The deepwater sailers now under construction were a desperate attempt to deliver their wood products to overseas markets. The group was visibly impressed with

The building of wooden ships, such as these on the ways at the Foundation Company Shipyard in Victoria Harbour, created a demand for enormous quantities of timbers and planking, keeping local sawmills humming and thousands of loggers employed in British Columbia forests. COURTESY OF ROYAL BC MUSEUM, BC ARCHIVES C-05376

the efforts of Cameron-Genoa Mills Shipbuilders Ltd., declaring the motor-sailers on the ways ". . . the very best . . . turned out anywhere in the world."

After hearing these glowing testimonials, the IMB wasted no time in awarding contracts for the construction of both steel and wooden cargo steamers. The 27 wooden ships were to be three-island single deck vessels of 2,800 deadweight tons with dimensions of 250 x 43.5 x 23 feet. Before it had completed the sixth and last of its own auxiliary schooners, *Beatrice Castle*, Cameron-Genoa Mills Shipbuilders Ltd. had an order on hand for four of the new vessels. *War Haida*, *War Skeena*, *War Stikine* and *War Yukon*, all standard Canadian wooden cargo steamers, were to be built out of Douglas fir and powered by triple expansion engines.

With this development it appeared that Cameron-Genoa Mills was firmly established in the shipbuilding business, but in reality their success was to be short lived. Jaime Cameron, a son of one of the founding fathers, attributed this to a change in the provincial government, which subsequently cut off their financing. Another factor that may have played a part in the Cameron brothers' change of fortune was a serious fire that gutted their sawmill in June 1917.

After receiving a 60-ship contract from the French government in 1918 the Foundation Company's British Columbia operation took over the Camerons' shipyard. Their vast operations now included all the

The launchings of large wood cargo ships in Victoria Harbour in the later years of World War I were celebratory affairs attended by large audiences. The *Victoria Daily Colonist* of August 30, 1918, noted that the entry of the *War Nanoose* into the water on September 9 was to be a particularly noteworthy event since ". . . the Foundation Company has decided to combine the launching of the last vessel of the old Imperial Munitions Board programme with the laying of the two keels of the first two of the twenty ships under contract for the French Government." COURTESY OF ROYAL BC MUSEUM, BC ARCHIVES F-04535

harbour foreshore from Point Ellice Bridge to what is the site of today's Songhees development. While the company also built yards in Tacoma and Portland for the construction of 20 auxiliary schooners each, the Victoria operation received the wooden steamship portion of the order. These 20 ships, with approximate dimensions of 260 x 46 x 22 feet and a deadweight tonnage of 3,000, were somewhat larger than their IMB counterparts and were fitted with twin screws driven by triple expansion engines.

Although the vessels' stated loaded speed was 10 knots, they usually averaged between 12 and 13 knots in their trial runs. One worker recalled that the resilience and strength of the wooden hulls were put to the test at the Ogden Point outfitting plant when a cable holding aloft a 5-ton boiler being prepared for installation broke. When the hull was checked for damage, there wasn't any.

Since the Point Ellice yard was allowed to retain its supervisory staff and yard crew, a rivalry developed with the Point Hope yard, stimulating production in the process. If keels happened to be laid at the same time, the race was on to see which yard would be the first to launch. The local community was kept apprised of this friendly competition and other company news via a weekly newspaper—*Shipyard Shavings*—published every Saturday and available at some newsstands. When a magnificent clubhouse was erected (close to where the Princess Mary restaurant stood for years) the paper professed that it was "symbolic of the wonderful spirit which animates [sic] from the Foundation activities."

This industrial *esprit de corps* was further cultivated by sporting activities and entertainment programs. The company formed baseball and football teams and, it was rumoured, even went as far as hiring local sport stars as ringers to boost morale in Tacoma and Portland. Archie Wills, a *Colonist* reporter, later recalled that the Foundation Company sponsored a lacrosse team that returned from Winnipeg with the Mann Cup. The company also had a band that entertained employees during lunch hour and performed in the community after hours. When one of the sleek grey hulls was finally ready for launching, the band, under the baton of Lou Turner, played a rousing rendition of the *Marseillaise*.

The employees gladly participated in the festive atmosphere and by early 1919 the fortnightly payroll was $230,000. By the time the last of the ships, *Nouvelle Ecosse*, had been launched, on October 9, 1919, the entire French contract had paid out over $5.5 million in wages. Archie Wills (along with war weary soldiers returning from the Western Front in France) was surprised to find the city prospering and shipyard employees "rolling in money, even to the use of . . . motorcars!"

The unprecedented prosperity was all too brief and with the last of the ships on its way to Le Havre, France, the once bustling Inner Harbour began to look like an industrial wasteland, but the most notable change was the loss of a large payroll to Victoria's economy. Chris Cholberg, a recent Norwegian immigrant to British Columbia, attempted to revive shipbuilding in 1919 as a government-supported project to relieve unemployment, which was rampant among demobilized servicemen, but after the fourth sailing

Workers at the Foundation Company Shipyard in Victoria, BC, look contented as they pose in front of a wooden ship under construction. The city and its shipyards were experiencing a period of great prosperity. COURTESY OF ROYAL BC MUSEUM, BC ARCHIVES F-02253

ship, *S.F. Tolmie*, was completed in 1920, it was realized that commercial sailing was no longer financially viable. The launching of the four-masted barquentine only served to signal the end of large wooden ship-building in Victoria.

Even the Imperial Munitions Board's wood cargo steamer program proved to be a disappointment: the 27 ships were built of unseasoned softwood and most were either scrapped or lost to fire or marine perils by 1925. (The lone exception was the *War Yukon*, which managed to survive as a barge up until 1937.)

While the ships were somewhat of a commercial failure, the high wages earned during their construction attracted thousands to shipyards throughout the Lower Mainland and Victoria. Supplying the enormous quantities of timbers and planking needed for the ships—around 50 million board feet annually—also kept local sawmills humming and thousands of loggers employed in British Columbia forests. Wood ships kept Victoria's economy alive through the Great War and the province's vast first-growth forests were somewhat reduced in the process.

Chapter 9

From Lumber Freighter to Floating Cannery to Beach Hulk: The *Laurel Whalen*, 1917

Other than a hawse pipe sticking out of the mud at the end of the breakwater, there's nothing left to be seen of *Laurel Whalen* at the old Comox Logging & Railway Company booming grounds at Royston. The five-masted auxiliary schooner was originally one of six built at the Cameron-Genoa Mills Shipbuilders Ltd. Victoria shipyard during the Great War. The other five that slipped down the Point Ellice ways in 1917 were *Margaret Haney*, *Esquimalt*, *Jean Steedman*, *Beatrice Castle* and the infamous *Malahat*, which went on to gain notoriety as a mother ship to the rum-running fleet off California and Mexico.

These unusual wood sailers, with their two Swedish Bolinder semi-diesel engines and twin screws, were built in response to a wartime tonnage shortage. When the heavy losses to U-boats during the First World War drained steamships away from the Pacific and disrupted commercial shipping in the process, British Columbia's lumber industry was already suffering from overproduction and poor demand. (A little known fact is that while there may have been more tonnage lost to U-boats in World War II, more actual vessels were lost during the First World War.) By 1915, with virtually no shipping available for the offshore cargo trade, British Columbia sawmill owners found themselves in a desperate situation. In 1895 BC mills accounted for 35 percent of west coast North America lumber exports to Australia; through 1912 to 1914 this average was down to less than 5 percent, and as the war progressed the situation only worsened.

While British Columbia sawmills struggled to stay alive, US sawmills throughout Washington and Oregon were busy filling orders for foreign buyers. What kept American mills busy trying to meet the demand was the fact their owners had had the foresight to build up their own fleet of lumber carriers to transport their product across the Pacific. As a consequence, lumbermen such as the Cameron brothers, who owned a large sawmill in Victoria's Inner Harbour, quickly came to the conclusion that they needed to build their own fleet of freighters in order to save their languishing enterprises. (James Oscar and Donald Officer Cameron, who were originally from Tennessee as it happened, had no prior experience in shipbuilding, let alone lumbering, when they immigrated to British Columbia.)

In early 1916 the Camerons, along with shipping interests, the Manufacturer's Association and other worried sawmill owners, began lobbying the provincial government for financial assistance to build a Canadian-owned commercial sailing fleet. With the passage of the Shipbuilding Assistance

Upon the launch of the *Laurel Whalen* into Victoria harbour, Victoria's *Daily Colonist* reported the following on March 25, 1917: "Amidst the hoarse blasts of whistles and the cheering of thousands of spectators, the gaily bedecked hull of the auxiliary schooner *Laurel Whalen* glided speedily down the ways." RONALD GREENE COLLECTION

Act in May of that year, the Cameron Lumber Company, in conjunction with the Genoa Bay Lumber Company (also owned by the Camerons), utilized government promises of loans and bonus provisions to create its own shipbuilding arm, Cameron-Genoa Mills Shipbuilders Ltd. Unfortunately the two brothers encountered financial difficulties and their shipbuilding venture on the southwest side of the Point Ellice Bridge was short lived. The shipyard was turned over to the Foundation Company in September 1918, but not before the Camerons' operation had completed its own six schooners as well as four wooden cargo steamers.

Ship plans reveal that these *Mabel Brown* class schooners didn't stint on wood and used massive timbers and planks in their construction. To start with, the new ships measured some 240 to 245 feet in length and 1,350 to 1,550 gross tons (the *Laurel Whalen* was 240.5 feet and displaced 1,357 tons.) The keel and nine keelsons used for structural strength were made of 20-inch square timbers. Frames of 12 inches square were doubled and spaced at 32 inches. Hanging knees were cut from naturally grown crooks of Douglas fir. The outside planking varied in size from 4 inches square on the bulwarks to 7 x 11 inches near the waterline, with ceiling planking as large as 14 x 16 inches. Planks were fastened with hardwood treenails, while driftbolts of 1–1.5 inches in diameter studded the hull.

These were "bald-headed" schooners since they were lacking in topsails. *Laurel Whalen* was rigged with fore, main, mizzen, jigger and spanker sails, a fore staysail, and inner, outer and flying jibs. Art Jones, writing in 1954, recalled that the *Mabel Brown* class vessels were ". . . good sea-boats, and had good lines . . . . After being in the Australian square-rigger grain ships, these five-masted schooners seemed like a sailor's

With masts and rigging raised, the *Laurel Whalen* is pictured here in 1917, across Victoria harbour from the Cameron–Genoa Mills Shipbuilders Ltd. yard located off the southwest corner of the Point Ellice Bridge. COURTESY OF ROYAL BC MUSEUM, BC ARCHIVES G-3571

dream of heaven. A wheelhouse, electric light, steam to hoist the anchor, compressed air winches to hoist sail. No brass and no varnish work to look after. No chipping hammer. One yard (swung from the foremast) instead of ten or fifteen, and only two persons on the ship who knew what it was for. One was the skipper, the other myself. There were no gaff topsails so the boys didn't need to go any higher aloft after dark than the top bunks."

Hugh "Red" Garling, who sailed on *Laurel Whalen*'s sister ship, *Malahat*, was struck by the great expanse of deck—some 200 feet from fo'c'sle to poop—and the enormous flexing in her hull; the hogging and sagging as well as twisting, especially in a quartering sea. "In the fo'c'sle, or below, all about you was the dissonance of sounds her timbers made as they worked and resisted the flexing."

Unfortunately the Armistice of November 1918 was followed by a post-war economic depression, and an oversupply of steamships that were no longer required for the war effort flooded the commercial market. The subsequent drop in freight rates soon brought an end to viable commercial sail. As a consequence, the six Cameron-Genoa Mills auxiliary schooners built for the Canada West Coast Navigation Company ended up seeing little active service in the deep-sea lumber trade.

On her first lumber voyage, in June 1917, *Laurel Whalen* sailed for Port Adelaide, Australia, with a cargo of over 1.5 million board feet aboard. On her second, and last, lumber voyage out to Australia in the spring of 1918, she experienced a plague of labour problems amongst the crew while mechanical breakdowns bedevilled the schooner. Finally, on her return voyage back to the West Coast, *Laurel Whalen* ran into heavy seas and her rigging was torn away. Since her Bolinder auxiliaries had already broken down in

Australia, she was effectively disabled by the time she was able to limp into Tahiti. A survey there revealed that teredo worms (burrowing, wood-digesting molluscs) were well established in her hull.

After sitting derelict in the tropics for a few months, the troubled vessel was retrieved early in 1919 by the powerful steam tug *Hercules*, dispatched from San Francisco. When the tug arrived in Vancouver Harbour with the *Whalen* on the towline, the *Vancouver Daily World* proclaimed, "The tug established a record for towing on the Pacific and brought the vessel to her native coast without a mishap of any kind." However, according to the *Vancouver Province*, within days of tying up, the schooner was embroiled in a "great mass of insurance claims," the ship was "in a pretty spongy state below the waterline," and ". . . has had five different crews and been delayed for months by weather and repairs . . . "

In a perilous state, *Laurel Whalen* seemed fated to join the scores of retired sailing vessels sitting on their anchor chains in quiet backwaters all along the west coast of North America. Instead, in December 1920, R.P. Butchart bought the ship and converted her into a cement barge. Butchart owned the BC Cement Company, the operators of a large plant on the Malahat side of Saanich Inlet, Vancouver Island. (His Tod Inlet quarry is the site of today's Butchart Gardens.)

However, the local industrialist only held onto the retired schooner for a short time, and in November 1923, *Harbour & Shipping* magazine noted that ". . . the *Laurel Whalen* underwent repairs at Victoria Machinery Depot, and has been purchased by the Somerville Cannery interests in Vancouver, to be used as a cannery tender." At this time, she was probably shorn of what was left of her masts, rigging and engines, if the Butchart interests hadn't already done so. The new owner, canneryman Francis Millerd of Vancouver, apparently had no intention of using the schooner as a tender. He instead obtained a cannery licence in the normal manner for the vessel. But it was to stay in the same location for the whole season.

Still, not one to miss an opportunity, Millerd decided he would rather take advantage of his floating operation and tow it around the coast to wherever migrating salmon were returning. As a result, his land-bound competitors weren't all that amused and the Fisheries Department subsequently charged him with operating a cannery without a licence. Since they couldn't make the charge stick in the courts, it ended up before the Privy Council who finally ruled that licensing canneries was a provincial responsibility and not a federal one.

A young Frederick Corneille got a job as a tally man on *Laurel Whalen* one summer in the early 1920s when the hulk was anchored in Ferguson Bay in the Queen Charlotte Islands (Haida Gwaii). Completely self-contained, the cannery had a steam plant with two canning lines and began the season with 10,000 cases of empty cans aboard. Every 10 days the Canadian National steamer *Prince John* came alongside to load the full cans and drop off a supply of empties. Corneille recalled that the crew packed some 40,000 cases in 25 days of operation that August. He claimed that the $600 he earned that summer was the most money he was to make until sometime after the Second World War. (Frederick Corneille, or "Cornie" as he was called, became a deckhand on Union Steamships in 1926 and eventually went on to become a Chief Officer. He also served in a corvette during the war and retired from the navy as a Lieutenant RCN(R).)

When *Laurel Whalen*'s licence finally expired in 1929, Corneille thought the schooner-cannery was laid up in fresh water, either at Lake Washington or up the Fraser River. (Fresh water deters most marine wood borers, such as teredo worms, which thrive in salt water.) As it happened, former Langley resident Glen Olson was a boy when *Laurel Whalen* and the Victoria-built four-master *S.F. Tolmie* were laid up for the winter at Ewans Cannery, near Lion Island in the Fraser River. Glen's father, Sig Olson, was a watchman for BC Packers, which apparently chartered the old hulls as pilchard scows. Around 1936, Sig was at the wheel when the *Whalen* was towed out of the river to Vancouver.

Canneryman Francis Millerd, after purchasing the *Laurel Whalen* hulk in November 1923, took advantage of an obscure Fisheries Department clause to convert the retired lumber schooner into a floating salmon cannery. Here, the converted *Laurel Whalen* is operating in this capacity at Ferguson Bay, Queen Charlotte Islands. FRANCIS MILLERD COLLECTION

The ship's 1924 registry document reveals that *Laurel Whalen* remained in Millerd's hands until he sold the floating cannery to Alfred Robie Bissett in March 1936. This may explain why marine writer Norman Hacking said he remembered seeing the hulk in Coal Harbour in the late 1930s. Bissett was manager of BC Wharf and Machinery Co. Ltd. located at 1901 West Georgia, a block east of Stanley Park. The Bissetts also owned the Britannia Sand & Gravel Co. Ltd., located at the same address. If they didn't have plans for converting the hulk into a barge, they may have been involved in conversion work for a new floating venture.

On May 11, 1936, an article in a Vancouver newspaper reported that the *Laurel Whalen* was being fitted out as a cabaret. "Permission to anchor the craft in English Bay has been granted by the port authority, and the old *Laurel Whalen* will soon resound to the saws and hammers of the carpenters who fit her up with dance floor and other accommodations. The boat will be anchored a few feet outside the half mile line, just beyond the boundary which the city police have authority."

Later, the *Comox Argus* named the man behind the scheme as none other than Tommy Burns, a Canadian who was the heavyweight boxing champion of the world between 1906 and 1908. Burns invested his prize money in business ventures, including British pubs, a New York speakeasy and, apparently, the floating cabaret. Unfortunately for the local party crowd, the authorities were opposed to the venture. As the *Argus* reported: "But somehow or other, no licence could be procured; and so after two nights of revelry she was deserted."

With their ambitious plan now dead in the water, the owners put the hulk up for sale but were also considering wrecking her on a beach for scrap metal and the firewood in her hull. Instead, on August 12, 1936, *Laurel Whalen* was sold to the Comox Logging & Railway Company for $452.63. After her varied career, she was destined to become the first in a collection of retired ships used as a breakwater at the company's Royston log dump and booming grounds.

By the 1990s there was not much left to identify the *Laurel Whalen* at Royston other than a tangled litter of drift bolts and two hawse pipes (where the anchor chains pass through the hull) sticking out of the mud next to the rusted hull of the CPR steam tug *Nanoose*. RICK JAMES PHOTO, 1992

The lumber schooner's steering quadrant identifies what would have been the stern section of the *Laurel Whalen*. Sometime around 2000, Primex Forest Products, who were still using the site to store logs destined for their sawmill on the Courtenay River, extended the rock ballast breakwater out over the remains of the *Laurel Whalen*.
RICK JAMES PHOTO, 1992

On August 20, 1936, the *Comox Argus* reported on the tow across the Strait of Georgia from Vancouver to Comox Harbour by the big outside tug *Gleeful*, owned by Comox Logging's sister company, the Canadian Tugboat Company. "She was turned over to the tug *Gleeful* to tow to Royston. A west wind sprang up and the old hulk, swinging sluggishly in the sea, pulled hard against her fate and the *Gleeful* had a tussle with her in the storm during which her only remaining mast snapped off and went through the cabin." Tug and tow finally made into the protected waters behind Goose Spit where the hulk was tied up to the company's log booms. There, the small (40 feet registered length) harbour tug *Joyful* put the towline on to take her across Comox harbour to Royston.

Once *Laurel Whalen* was secured to pilings, Royston's boom camp foreman set to work scuttling her. "Mr. Hugh Cliffe and his gang bored four-inch holes in her hull last night, and she gradually settled down on the beach where she will be a feature of the landscape for years to come."

Charles Nordin, whose father was skipper of the *Joyful*, went along for the excitement of watching the sinking of the old auxiliary schooner that day. He recalls that it took a major amount of doing and "there was a lot of ki-yiing and bad language coming from Hughie Cliffe during the process to get her to lay exactly upon her resting place."

Nordin also has fond memories of rowing out to the hulk with a buddy while it was still anchored off Comox Spit and remembers, in particular, the vessel's beautiful hardwood dance floors. The two lads crawled around inside the ship while fantasizing that they were taking part in an episode from *Tom Sawyer*.

The lumber schooner's bones have lain off the small community of Royston on Vancouver Island for over 60 years now and the weather and sea have long since taken their due. While she was still afloat, and even after she was scuttled at Royston, she was able to find useful service in a variety of roles along the West Coast. Still, the purpose for which she was originally intended—a life under sail, deepwater lumber trading—was short lived.

Nonetheless, while the *Mabel Brown* class motor sailers, such as *Laurel Whalen*, were never commercially successful in the offshore lumber trade, they did prove effective in rescuing British Columbia's languishing coastal sawmills from impending disaster. The 50 million board feet of lumber required annually during the First World War for a crash shipbuilding program of auxiliary schooners and wooden steamships helped pull a young British Columbia lumber industry through to better times. In 1946 the Cameron brothers were able to sell their successful sawmilling operation in Victoria to Toronto promoter E.P. Taylor, who was busy buying up West Coast mills and timber. Taylor eventually combined all his acquisitions into the timber giant BC Forest Products Ltd.

Chapter 10

West Coast Gale Claims
HMCS *Galiano*, 1918

A brief signal—"Holds full of water; send help"—was picked up by the wireless operator at Triangle Island off the northwest end of Vancouver Island near Cape Scott on October 30, 1918. The distress call was from the Royal Canadian Navy's (RCN) 393-ton, 162-foot patrol steamer HMCS *Galiano*. The vessel was caught in open water as the first serious fall storm hit the West Coast.

The RCN had come into existence only seven years earlier with the passing of the Naval Service Act on May 4, 1910. Other than two submarines secretly purchased from the Americans by British Columbia's provincial government in 1914, there were just two outdated cruisers, *Niobe* and the *Rainbow*, that served as the only offensive warships during the Great War. The bulk of the Naval Service was made up of a motley assortment of vessels acquired when the RCN incorporated the fishery patrol, hydrographic, tidal survey and wireless telegraphic services of the Department of Marine and Fisheries with the passage of the

The brief signal "Holds full of water; send help" was picked up by the wireless operator at Triangle Island off the northwest end of Vancouver Island near Cape Scott on October 30, 1918. The distress call was from the Royal Canadian Navy's 393-ton, 162-foot patrol steamer HMCS *Galiano*. CFB ESQUIMALT NAVAL & MILITARY MUSEUM

Act. Although they maintained their regular peacetime duties, the primary role of these ships during the First World War was to serve as patrol craft, minesweepers and examination vessels.

Galiano and her sister ship *Malaspina* were originally built in Dublin Dockyard, Ireland, in 1913 as fishery patrol craft for Canada's Dominion Government. The ships were named for Don Alejandro Malaspina and Don Dionisio Alcala Galiano, both officers in the Spanish navy who commanded exploratory expeditions to the northwest coast of the Americas in the 1790s. *Galiano* maintained her role as a fishery patrol ship until the First World War began and was then assigned to Esquimalt as a naval patrol vessel, but it was while performing a task as a lighthouse tender late in 1918 that the ship came to a tragic end.

An order was received in October to proceed to Triangle Island with supplies as the wireless station there was nearly out of the fuel needed to run its power plant. *Malaspina* was scheduled to leave with stores and supplies for the wireless stations and lighthouses on the West Coast but the morning the ship was to begin the voyage her bow was crumpled in an accident at the jetty. The supplies were quickly transferred to *Galiano* even though the ship had just returned from the Queen Charlotte Islands to Esquimalt and needed boiler work and repairs to her tail shaft.

Able Seaman James Aird (like a number of his fellow shipmates on what was to be their ship's last voyage) had misgivings about the voyage. A letter Aird posted at Alert Bay hinted at nagging fears of impending disaster. Addressed to Mrs. Ranns, "mother" of the Sailor's Club at Esquimalt where the Able Seaman from Calgary bunked while ashore, the missive noted that the *Galiano* had run into foul weather after leaving Vancouver. Aird went on to state that they had already heard that the Canadian Pacific Railway boat *Princess Sophia* was experiencing difficulties as a result of a bad storm.

(As it happened, these "difficulties" were to result in one of the worst marine disasters ever in the Pacific Northwest. On October 24 the CPR's coastal steamer ran aground on Vanderbilt Reef in Lynn Canal and during a gale the next day slid off into the depths taking all 343 souls aboard with her.)

Aird added that he was dreading the trip across to Triangle Island, as it meant crossing one of the most dangerous stretches of water along the West Coast—Queen Charlotte Sound—in foul weather. Adding to his worries was the fact that many of the ship's complement were absent, as the worst epidemic of the twentieth century, the Spanish flu, had just arrived on the West Coast. A.B. Aird added "I am not worried for myself, but I hate a green crew . . ."

Knowing that any of *Galiano*'s regular crew that could get down to the ship were going to be desperately needed, Aird had walked aboard still wearing several plasters applied by Mrs. Ranns. Others who were well enough to sail included the ship's commander Lieutenant Robert Mayes Pope, Royal Naval Canadian Volunteer Reserve (RNCVR), the bo'sun, Chief Petty Officer James Vinnecombe, chief artificer engineer Frank Greenshields and the wireless telegraph operator, Michael Neary. (In an unusual twist of fate, Neary's brother Jack happened to be one of the wireless operators stationed at Triangle Island when *Galiano*'s distress call was received. Contrary to what many later writers claimed, it was Arthur Ashdown Green who actually copied the doomed ship's message, not Jack Neary, who was asleep at the time.)

Lieutenant Pope had commanded *Galiano* since its arrival on the West Coast in 1913. An able and experienced mariner, Pope had established an impressive career before joining the RCN. He had served on sailing ships, East India Company steamers and a Royal Navy cruiser, and had also made several voyages as third officer on the Canadian Pacific Railway's oceanic liner *Empress of India*.

So many of the ship's complement were sick that the navy was forced to borrow crew from *Malaspina* and assign men from the Esquimalt Navy Yard to serve. Joseph Gilbert arrived off HMCS *Rainbow* and

This portrait shows the crew of the ill-fated HMCS *Galiano*. The lucky ones missed the voyage. Many of the ship's complement were overcome with the Spanish flu, the worst epidemic of the 20th century, and stayed ashore recuperating. CFB ESQUIMALT NAVAL & MILITARY MUSEUM VR 999.684.1

replaced the ship's regular chief officer, Ernest Alcock, who had been taken ill. Leading Seaman Alex Munroe, who had served on *Galiano* earlier but had since been working in the dockyard and on *Malaspina*, replaced *Galiano*'s sick quartermaster. Able Seaman William King, who was in the dockyard armoury at the time, signed on along with 16-year-old Roderick McLeod who joined the ship as captain's boy. Young McLeod wrote home that he feared he was about to leave on a dangerous trip.

When *Galiano* arrived at Triangle Island, the ship was to pick up the housekeeper, Miss Emily Brunton, and Sydney Eliott, one of the operators. It was while she was performing these duties that a gale began to rise. At the last moment, Eliott discovered his leave was cancelled and he returned to the station. The last of the supplies were unloaded in a hurry and Miss Brunton was taken on board *Galiano*'s work boat, which returned to the ship. *Galiano* then pointed its bow northward to its next stop, Ikeda Head on the Queen Charlotte Islands.

The *Daily Colonist* of Thursday, October 31, reported that the patrol boat left Triangle Island at 5:00 p.m. on Tuesday with a fierce southwest gale building. The paper noted that naval officials estimated that when her distress signal was received, at 3:00 a.m. on Wednesday morning, the ship should have been within visual range of the light on Cape St. James on the far southern end of the Queen Charlotte Islands, 95 miles from Triangle Island.

In an attempt to explain why no further signals were received, it was suggested that her aerials may have been carried away or the set of dynamos in the engine room powering the wireless equipment might have been put out of commission. The *Colonist* also spoke with local mariners who agreed that the stretch of water *Galiano* was in was the worst anywhere along the Pacific coast.

Among the vessels that responded to the SOS and raced to the scene were the American tug *Tatoosh*, the Grand Trunk Pacific tug *Lorne*, trawler *G.E. Foster* and three whalers from the Rose Harbour whaling station. Anxious relatives spent a long four days waiting to hear news of the lost vessel. Then on Sunday, November 3, the *Daily Colonist* ran a full-page article featuring short biographies of those aboard *Galiano* along with some photographs of crew and officers. The article opened by saying the only traces of *Galiano* found were a lifebelt, a skylight with a ditty bag containing a few articles of clothing owned by stoker George Musty hanging from it, and three bodies. The body of Leading Seaman Wilfred Ebbs was recovered by *G.E. Foster* 28 miles south of Cape St. James and the bodies of Stoker Arthur Hume and Able Seaman James Aird were found about 15 miles east of Danger Rocks by the whaler *Brown*.

When *G.E. Foster* arrived in Prince Rupert, her captain gave his account of what he thought had happened. He felt the vessel had probably foundered in heavy seas and he stressed the fact that, "the whole of the Hecate Straits is just one mass of foam . . . with a tremendous sea running." He went on to suggest that *Galiano* probably shipped a large wave and the weight of the water rolling around inside had caused her bulkheads to give way, causing the ship to roll and ship more seas. It appeared that *Galiano* had gone down fast; the lifebelts and clothing of the men they picked up looked as if they had been put on in a hurry as the belts were not fastened properly.

Today, Canadians can view a memorial to this maritime disaster in the far southeast corner of Ross Bay cemetery along Victoria's waterfront. The large block of granite overlooking Juan de Fuca Strait has chiselled into it the names of 36 crew and officers serving in HMCS *Galiano* whose bodies were never found. The memorial also happens to commemorate the only warship lost by the Royal Canadian Navy in the First World War. Sadly, HMCS *Galiano* disappeared only a few days before the signing of the Armistice on November 11, 1918, which signalled the end of the Great War and four years of slaughter in the trenches of France.

A memorial to all those whose bodies were never found following the loss of HMCS *Galiano* was erected in the far southeast corner of Victoria's historic Ross Bay cemetery overlooking the Juan de Fuca Strait. RICK JAMES PHOTO

Footnote:

In September 2007, Jim Hume, columnist with the Victoria *Times Colonist,* attempted to verify whether there was indeed a Miss Emma Mary "Emily" Brunton who boarded HMCS *Galiano* at Triangle Light.

After some assistance from his readership, it was discovered that, according to the 1917 Victoria directory, in 1916 an Emma Brunton, dressmaker, was living at 1124 Fort St., Victoria, where she was possibly a housekeeper for one Charles Long, manager of the New Brunswick Cigar Shop. That same year, at the age of 35, she was hired as a housekeeper by bachelor radio operators at Triangle Island, who were probably tired of their own cooking and cleaning.

Thanks to Frank Statham, who maintains a wealth of information on early coastal radio stations, Miss Brunton was reported to be "rather plumpish" in appearance and that, "to the chagrin" of the bachelor operators on the island who pooled their money to hire her, ". . . she soon had them organized. They had to dress for dinner with clean shirts, ties and jackets, and their shoes had to be polished. As compensation she was an excellent cook and their dwelling was kept spotless."

On October 29, 1918, after being relieved of her duties as a housekeeper, Brunton was seen boarding HMCS *Galiano*. She was never seen alive again. Records of the Supreme Court of BC reveal that after the court authorized that Emma Mary Brunton be presumed dead, her $716.69 in bank savings was ordered to be shared equally between her mother, two sisters and a brother in Glossop, England.

Chapter 11

Chinese Junks Make Landfall on the BC Coast: 1922 and 1939

There's always been talk drifting about the docks about how it would have been entirely possible, sometime in the past, for an Oriental vessel to sail or drift across the North Pacific to make landfall somewhere along our West Coast. When two actually completed this remarkable feat—one sailing into Victoria's busy harbour in 1922 and the other ending its arduous voyage in the remote Central Coast mill town of Ocean Falls in 1939—they caused quite a sensation.

The *Amoy*

In the article "Crowds Throng to see Chinese Junk," the *Victoria Daily Colonist* of September 21, 1922, reported that ". . . skipper and ship were well nigh swamped by the incessant questioning of the hundreds who went over the junk." Of course, members of the city's considerable Chinese population were particularly excited and ". . . flocked in great numbers to see the *Amoy*, this link with home making a strong impression on them." The *Colonist* also noted that Captain George Waard's wife, Chang Lee, ". . . garbed in the traditional trousers of her native China, officiated as gatekeeper, [and was] taking toll in the sum of 25 cents of all who passed her."

Long-time *Colonist* contributor Archie Wills, in a story to the paper's weekend supplement, the *Islander*, in May 1970, recalled being on hand for the momentous occasion and meeting Waard, his wife and son, Bobbie, in person. Wills noted that Waard was a rugged seaman who sailed out of Victoria with the sealing fleet in its heyday and then fished on the Fraser River for years. It was there he met Chang Lee, whom he married in Steveston in 1913. That same year the Waards sailed to China where Waard worked for seven years on the Yangtze River as a pilot, followed by a job in the port of Amoy supervising construction of a government dock. Eventually he got homesick for British Columbia and late in 1921 talked his wife into helping him build a junk to sail across the Pacific.

Chinese labour was cheap and plentiful so Waard was able to make good progress getting the vessel ready prior to the April 1922 typhoon season. Still, the three Chinese seamen who signed on as crew—Chan Tai and the brothers Loo and Wong Fook—were quite dismayed when they arrived at the boat to discover it had no eyes and therefore wouldn't be able to "see" on a long voyage. After Waard had fashioned a pair of eyes, 16 inches in diameter, out of camphor wood, a "jossman" (probably Buddhist monk) performed a ceremony and prayed to the appropriate spirits before the eyes were nailed to the *Amoy*, 15 feet back from the bow.

When Captain Waard of the *Amoy* suggested to Percy Shadforth, captain of the pilot boat that came out to meet them, that he might as well tie up at the Outer Harbour, Shadforth said, "No, let's give them a show, we'll sail her right into the Inner Harbour and tie up at The Empress' steps." Note the CPR coastal steamers in the background. VANCOUVER MARITIME MUSEUM PRS10

The junk with seven aboard (a Shanghai River policeman, George Kavalchuck, also joined the crew) cast off on May 17, 1922, for their first port of call, Shanghai. Early one morning, while they were travelling on the river, a python slithered aboard to be quickly dispatched by Captain Waard's revolver. The Chinese crew dined on its meat, and the skin of the python, ". . . which was eleven feet long and as thick as a man's calf," later proved to be of great interest to visitors upon the *Amoy*'s arrival in Victoria Harbour.

The junk spent 10 days in Shanghai and then set off to cross the Sea of Japan where the small craft encountered water spouts and a typhoon and had her rudder fouled by a large fishing net. Arriving in Hakodate, Japan, on July 12, water tanks were filled and charts for the Aleutians secured. Waard's intention was to work the *Amoy* up to the 42nd or 43rd north parallel and hold a course for 30 days for the Juan de Fuca Strait.

The *Amoy* crossed the 180th meridian on August 6 but, after running into a bad southwester with a cross sea, lost her rudder. Captain Waard jury-rigged a replacement and, despite lacking a chart of the area, chanced a run into Nazan Bay in the Aleutian Islands where he had a new rudder installed. Upon leaving, another bad storm was encountered and the replacement rudder gave out under the strain. Not to be deterred, Captain Waard hauled the remains aboard and re-rigged the tiller using tackles from each quarter.

This arrangement held up for the remainder of the voyage and Waard was relieved when Cape Beale light was finally spotted on the west coast of Vancouver Island. After berthing in front of The Empress

The junk *Amoy* garnered a tremendous amount of attention when she moored in front of Victoria's Empress Hotel in September, 1922. The BC Parliament buildings can be seen in the background. MARITIME MUSEUM OF BRITISH COLUMBIA 999.043.0001

Hotel, the final entry in the logbook read, "Arrived Victoria, B.C., noon September 19th 1922, one hundred and twenty-four days from Amoy, China. All's well."

Once in Victoria the Chinese crew of *Amoy* returned to China on the *Empress of Australia*. The Waards, hopeful that stopping at various ports and hosting tours would continue to prove profitable, had the *Amoy* call in at Vancouver, Seattle and Portland on her way to California. After a long stay in San Francisco the junk then continued on to Los Angeles, the West Indies and South America. Captain Waard finally took the *Amoy* up the US eastern seaboard to Bridgeport, Connecticut, where he sold her to a crewman he'd picked up in San Francisco and who in turn sailed her for 20 more years. The last report of the junk *Amoy* has it that she sank in North Carolina's Pimlico Sound in the 1960s.

Captain Waard and Chang Lee returned to BC but unfortunately they drowned in a boating accident off Galiano Island in 1950. Their son, Robert, was living in Vancouver at the time.

The *Tai Ping*

The *Amoy* wasn't the only oriental vessel to sail across the Pacific in the first half of the last century—there were at least 10, if not more, that arrived in American and Canadian ports up and down the coast. Even though he was only a young boy at the time, Campbell River resident Bob Logan can still vividly recall the day in October 1939 when a Chinese junk appeared in the harbour of his hometown of Ocean Falls. Of

The *Tai Ping* was towed off the rocks at Princess Royal Island by the Balmer Brothers' (managers of the marine shop for Pacific Mills Ltd., Ocean Falls) old cruiser *Charles Todd* and taken into Ocean Falls, but while being lifted onto a scow she slipped off and sank. This photo shows the junk just after being raised from the bottom. BOB LOGAN COLLECTION

course, the arrival of an exotic boat from the far side of the Pacific caused a lot of excitement among the population of the isolated pulp- and paper-mill town, located far up Dean Channel on British Columbia's Central Coast.

The strange and ungainly looking sailing vessel (at least to western eyes) was the small, 50-foot-long *Tai Ping* (Great Peace), which had just completed a 113-day voyage of 5,000 miles across the Pacific from China. Much to Logan's delight and amazement, the stranded American captain and his beautiful wife—who appeared to have stepped right out of a 1930s Hollywood movie—were invited to stay with his grandparents.

Captain John Anderson was working as a Yangtze River pilot based in Shanghai when he realized he and his wife, Nellie, ". . . a White Russian educated in a French convent, who spoke English fluently with an attractive accent . . ." desperately needed to escape from the belligerent Japanese forces that had overrun China. Well familiar with the sailing capabilities of the versatile junks that plied the Yangtze River, he purchased one from its Chinese owner and prepared for a perilous voyage across the Pacific to San Francisco.

However, *Tai Ping* was beset by difficulties and delays right from the start. As soon as they departed, the semi-diesel engine gave out and they were forced to rely on their sails. Then, when the junk stopped in Kobe, Japan, for repairs, her Chinese crew, overcome with seasickness, deserted the vessel. Fortunately

Anderson was able to replace the crew with four European sailors—Hans Liblow, Bergen Larson, Harry Olsen and Charles Kraigh. Unfortunately he was forced to sell his sextant to complete the engine repairs and top up the lockers with fresh provisions.

Finally, on June 14, 1939, *Tai Ping* set sail from Japan only to encounter foul weather and adverse winds for the remainder of the voyage across the Pacific. Some of Danish crewman Charles Kraigh's description of the voyage would later appear in an article in the *Victoria Daily Colonist* on February 11, 1951: ". . . [conditions] did prove the toughest in his 14 years of sailing. Adverse winds, and strong, from east and southeast instead of the westerlies which generally prevail in the latitude the skipper of the junk selected as the course (the route followed by trans-Pacific steamers to and from Japan) helped to upset all calculations. For three weeks after the junk left Kobe gale after gale buffeted *Tai Ping*. Then came a break of 17 days when winds held fair, but bad weather set in again and for 87 days of the 113 days it took to raise the northwest end of Vancouver Island, the junk was constantly battered by stiff winds . . ."

One hundred days later, when they were down to their last drop of water and nearly out of provisions and cigarettes, they sighted the Queen Charlotte Islands, but their troubles weren't over yet. As it happened, the United States survey vessel *Discoverer* came upon the *Tai Ping* flying distress signals off Cape Cook on the exposed northwest coast of Vancouver Island and took her under tow, but the rough seas sprang the foremast and Anderson was forced to cut the junk loose. Then the tiller was carried away, requiring the crew to jury-rig an anchor stock as a replacement. Fortunately the fishing vessel *Flying Cloud* encountered the junk and took her under tow into Quatsino Sound, northern Vancouver Island. After the stranded crew were supplied with fresh provisions and the damaged craft was repaired, Anderson attempted to make sail for Seattle, but barely 20 miles past Cape Cook *Tai Ping* ran into a howling gale that drove her steadily northwards until she ran up on rocks in Hecate Straits near Princess Royal Island.

The survivors made it to the beach where they were picked up a few days later by a passing fish packer that took them into Ocean Falls. Arrangements were made to tow the *Tai Ping* into the mill town but once there, and while being loaded onto a scow for transportation south, she slipped off the scow and sank in 125 feet of water. When raised, the junk was found to be in such a poor state she was abandoned on a local beach where her remains probably lie to this day.

Captain John Anderson and Nellie were eventually able to make it to Seattle. During the war Anderson got a job as a foreman and assistant to the superintendent at Todd-Seattle Drydocks while he and his wife raised a family. In October 1949 their 12-year-old daughter Angelina (who had been left behind in China at the age of two and had lived

A rather gaunt Captain John Anderson and his wife, Nellie, are seen here on an Ocean Falls boardwalk in October 1939, following their harrowing voyage across the North Pacific. BOB LOGAN COLLECTION

with her maternal grandparents until taken by the Japanese and imprisoned in the Lunghua prison camp in Shanghai for two years) was finally reunited with her parents and two younger sisters.

This is probably Nellie Anderson, wife of Captain John Anderson, trying on a hard hat dive suit, much to the amusement of onlookers aboard the harbour tug *Kwatna*. BOB LOGAN COLLECTION

Captain John Anderson is shown here with the well-known Vancouver hard hat diver Charles Anstee, who worked on raising *Tai Ping* from the bottom at Ocean Falls. Fred Rogers, the retired shipwreck expert, was told by some old mariners that Charles Anstee lost his life later at Prince Rupert while working on anti-submarine nets protecting the harbour. BOB LOGAN COLLECTION

Chapter 12

Drumrock: Mighty Log Barge was Cape Horn Windjammer, 1927

On February 8, 1927, Pacific (Coyle) Navigation Company contacted the Commissioner of Wrecks in Victoria, BC, to inform them that, "Our barge *Drumrock*, in tow of tug *Pacific Monarch*, became a total loss through stranding in Takush Harbour, Smith Inlet on February 1."

The big steam tug *Pacific Monarch* (ex-*Dreadful*) had headed out from Buckley Bay in Masset Inlet, Queen Charlotte Islands, on January 29 making its way south to Squirrel Cove at Cortez Island with the log barge *Drumrock* on the towline loaded with some 950,000 board feet of hemlock and spruce logs. Tug and tow never made it intact across Queen Charlotte Sound.

Pacific Monarch was bucking into a southeast gale with 40-knot winds as she attempted to cross the Sound and, at 10:30 a.m. on February 1, the long-time Pacific (Coyle) skipper, Captain Hugh Stanley McLellan, apparently decided he'd had enough, turned around and headed for shelter. At 3:45 p.m., with tug and barge safely in Takush Harbour, Captain McLellan was attempting to anchor his tow when the deeply laden barge hung up on an uncharted rock and stranded. On board the log barge at the time were the barge master, John P. Johnson, and 10 bargees.

The massive Pacific (Coyle) Navigation log carrier, originally launched as the steel Cape Horn windjammer *Drumrock*, was 329 feet in length and 3,182 gross tonnage. She was built as a four-masted barque in 1891 in Leith, Scotland, by Ramage & Ferguson for the Liverpool shipping interests, Gillison & Chadwick. *Drumrock* sailed under the British merchant fleet's "red duster" until 1899 and was then sold to Reederai F. Laeisz of Hamburg, Germany. The massive square-rigger was renamed *Persimmon* and joined that company's famous Flying "P" line of sailing ships, which were heavily involved in the nitrate trade from Chile around Cape Horn. Nitrates mined in the high desert of Chile were valued as a necessary ingredient for both fertilizer and gunpowder in Europe.

Sometime around 1913 *Persimmon* was sold to another German shipping firm, F.A. Vinnen & Company of Bremen, and renamed *Helwig Vinnen*. In the spring of 1914 she was on her way down the Elbe River with her holds filled with German coke destined for a copper smelter at Santa Rosalia, Baja, California. *Helwig Vinnen* arrived in the Mexican port on the last day of August only to find herself interned for the remainder of the First World War, which had broken out in Europe earlier that month.

The German master and crew of *Helwig Vinnen* had plenty of company since 11 other full-rigged ships and four-masted barques from their country were also trapped in Santa Rosalia, where their decks blistered in the desert-like heat for seven years. Finally, in 1923, San Francisco lumberman Robert Dollar bought all

The majestic four-masted steel barque *Drumrock* is pictured here, probably riding at anchor, at Semaphore Anchorage, Port Adelaide, Australia. COURTESY OF STATE LIBRARY OF SOUTH AUSTRALIA PRG1273/6/49

12 Cape Horn windjammers from the various Allied countries that had been awarded them by the Allied Reparations Commission. Dollar was hoping to regain his position in the trans-Pacific trade to the Orient by utilizing sailing ships to transport his lumber products. He had had a sizable fleet of steamships prior to the war but had sold all to aid the war effort.

When *Helwig Vinnen* was found to be unsuitable, Dollar put her up for sale and the derelict square-rigger was subsequently bought by Hecate Straits Towing Company of Vancouver, BC, and was towed out of San Francisco Bay in early January 1925. Four other of Dollar's German windjammers were also destined to end up in British Columbia where they were cut down into barges: *Harvestehude* (ex-*Riversdale*); *Adolph Vinnen*; *Orotava* (ex-*Comet*); and *Walküre*.

In October 1925 the *BC Lumberman* ran a feature story on the new log-carrying barge *Drumrock*. It reported that the managing owners of Hecate Straits Towing Company, Messrs. Johnson, Walton & Company of Vancouver, had completed the conversion of the former four-masted steel barque *Helwig Vinnen*. Only the year before, British Pacific Transport Co. Ltd., also of Vancouver, had had the very first self-loading and unloading log barge built by using the undocumented wooden hull of the American-built Ferris freighter *Bingamon*. After a bad experience in January 1925, in which the barge was almost lost on her first voyage to the Queen Charlotte Islands, it was decided steel or iron hulls would probably prove more durable.

In 1925, the *Drumrock* was converted to a self-loading and unloading log barge. The massive 329-foot, Scottish-built, riveted steel hull proved ideal for hauling logs across the treacherous waters of Hecate Straits and Queen Charlotte Sound. VANCOUVER MARITIME MUSEUM

Each of *Drumrock*'s three hatches had five winches that were controlled by one operator stationed 10 feet above the main deck. "All the control gear is very conveniently assembled and easy to operate. A powerful brake is attached to each winch, while all the steelwork has been built with a test of 30 tons and a guaranteed faction of eight tons."—*BC Lumberman*. VANCOUVER MARITIME MUSEUM, 5629

Concerned with possible hold-ups and problems with the established shipyards, Barney Johnson leased the Terminal City Dock, hired his own workforce and assembled the necessary riveting, cutting and other required equipment. During the conversion, the barque's lower yards were turned into 60-ton (capacity) derricks, and five winches (tapping, loading and yarding winches and two swinging winches) were installed alongside each of the three 58-foot x 36-foot hatches. With her original name reinstated, *BC Lumberman* concluded, "The *Drumrock* will carry 1,000,000 board feet of logs each trip . . . from the Queen Charlotte Islands to Vancouver in four days in place of the 15 days required for boom-towing. The crew will consist of 13 or 14 men, including loaders, winch-men and drivers. A unique feature of the equipment of the *Drumrock* is a low-tower (power) radiophone, which is installed in the pilothouse to enable the ship to keep in constant communication with tug ahead."

After a sizable financial outlay for the innovative design, the log barge *Drumrock* saw barely a year's service before she was lost to this marine mishap in Smith Inlet. When she stranded in February 1927, *Drumrock* was drawing some 22 feet of water with her massive load. The tide was falling and at low water, at 7:00 p.m. that evening, *Drumrock* broke in two. The "Return for Wreck Register," the official record of the stranding, noted, "Accident could not have been avoided. Barge total loss, cargo intact." In his final report to the Commissioner of Wrecks in Ottawa the Deputy to the Commissioner concluded that those on board both the log carrier and tug *Pacific Monarch* ". . . can be in no sense held to blame."

Longtime UASBC member David Stone explores the former Cape Horn windjammer *Drumrock*—a very attractive shallow water dive in Takush Harbour, Smith Inlet. The sheer size of the ship with her classic sailing ship prow and bowsprit make this one of the most attractive underwater heritage sites anywhere on BC's Central Coast.
JACQUES MARC PHOTO

Chapter 13

The Wrecks of Wreck Beach, 1928

While Wreck Beach near Point Grey continues to be a popular recreation spot for Vancouver residents—especially since the wearing of clothing remains optional—few who frequent it have any idea how the site may have earned its name. There was indeed a shipwreck off the beach in the early 1920s, but it was only a small vessel that left too little in the way of wreckage for it to garner much attention, let alone have a piece of geography named for the incident. What may have been the wrecks of Wreck Beach didn't arrive until sometime in the late 1920s and they actually weren't wrecks at all. Instead they were some old hulks that were intentionally sunk there for use as a breakwater.

The remains of one of the many Ferris hull wood cargo steamers built in the US during World War I is scuttled at Wreck Beach. D.M. THOMSON COLLECTION, VANCOUVER MARITIME MUSEUM

The only recorded loss of a vessel was that of the coastal freighter *Trader* (101 feet in length and 172 tons gross) off the North Arm jetty in the spring of 1923. The small steamer's first owner was the Gulf Steamship and Trading Company Ltd. of Victoria, who used her on a freight run to and from Puget Sound. While in that service, carrying a cargo of canned salmon, she happened to collide with the sternwheeler *Capital City* near Tacoma in 1902. *Trader* was transferred to the Trader Steamship Company Ltd., also of Victoria, around 1919, and the rest of her career was devoted to the workaday role of carrying freight and passengers throughout the Strait of Georgia as well as to remote northern logging camps.

On March 16, 1923, *Trader* was headed into Vancouver with a cargo of cement from Vancouver Island when she ran into heavy weather as she tried to round Point Grey. In an attempt to run for cover, Captain Fred Anderson pointed her bow for the safety of the Fraser River. Unfortunately, the gale drove her up onto a sandbar just 200 yards from the North Arm jetty.

The crew could do nothing for her in the falling tide so they took the lifeboat to shore. By the time the storm abated, *Trader* had taken a pounding. The hull was holed and her upperworks were smashed, and as a result she was written off as a complete loss.

Trader's boiler and engines were later salvaged and the hull was moved to a beach across the river. There she was abandoned, and for many years *Trader*'s half-buried wooden skeleton, filled with sacks of solidified cement, could be seen along Wreck Beach. Today the wreck is no longer visible but the shifting sands may uncover her remains sometime in the future.

The other "wrecks" of Wreck Beach were far more substantial than *Trader* and it was these vessels that probably provided the inspiration for the name. In January 1950, Vancouver City archivist Major J.S. Matthews placed a query in local newspapers asking if anyone knew how Wreck Beach got its name. Two months later Matthews published an article titled "Mystery Name Solved" detailing what he'd learned. According to replies to his query, three wood log barges (the Ferris hulls *Biscayne*, *Bingamon* and *Black Wolf*) and a floating grain elevator (*Blatchford*) were towed around the North Arm in 1928 to act as a breakwater for the log storage grounds. A steel ore carrier, *Granco*, was also supposedly added to the collection.

While Major Matthews' sources were correct about *Bingamon* and *Granco* being part of the breakwater site, the other names suggested are probably wrong. *Biscayne* foundered as a Pacific (Coyle) log barge off Cape Beale in 1932; *Black Wolf*, a log barge in the same fleet, stranded in 1929 in Skidegate Inlet, Queen Charlotte Islands, where she lies on the bottom to this day; and the former floating grain elevator *Blatchford* joined a collection of floating breakwater hulks at Powell River around 1936.

When he was researching his detailed history of British Columbia's early log barges, which was published in *Sea Chest: The Journal of the Puget Sound Maritime Historical Society* in 2001, maritime historian Frank Clapp interviewed Captain Joseph S. Marston of Victoria and Ernest Taylor of Ladner, both of whom, as boys, had lived near today's Wreck Beach. Both of them seemed quite certain four hulks were laid to rest there. The most likely Ferris hulls to have accompanied *Bingamon* are *Chalcis* and *Abydos*, originally owned by the British Pacific Transport Company but never put into service as barges. Another possibility is the Pacific (Coyle) Navigation Company log barge *Abnoba*, which sank in Nootka Sound in 1929 and was later raised and towed to Vancouver.

In the late 1920s, Pacific (Coyle) Navigation was leasing booming grounds along the North Arm of the Fraser River and federal records indicate that the firm's subsidiary, Burrard Boom Company, submitted plans to the Department of Public Works for the construction of a close-pile wall to shelter the grounds. Once they realized how expensive this undertaking was going to be, they resorted to scuttling old hulks as breakwaters instead.

Here, *Bingamon* is pictured with her massive loading crane on rails. On *Bingamon*'s maiden voyage as a log barge in January 1925, while under tow of the tug *Masset* crossing Queen Charlotte Sound in a howling gale, it was this crane that wreaked havoc when it broke loose. VANCOUVER PUBLIC LIBRARY, SPECIAL COLLECTIONS VPL 21910

On October 24, 1928, the *Victoria Daily Colonist* reported that the self-loading log barge *Bingamon* was to be towed to the North Arm of the Fraser River and sunk as a breakwater. Six days later, Pacific (Coyle) Navigation's tug *Cape Scott* performed the task. Another hulk, *Granco,* apparently followed shortly afterward, since Pacific (Coyle) finally registered the hulk on January 17, 1930, possibly to ensure that it was recognized as private property and not an abandoned derelict on the beach.

Bingamon was a unique vessel with a very interesting history. She began life as one of some 161 Ferris-type wooden freighters built in Washington and Oregon state shipyards for the United States Shipping Board during the First World War. These 265- to 268-foot-long steamships of some 2,200 to 2,500 gross tons were a single deck with a "three-island" superstructure design. The *Bingamon*, United States Emergency Fleet Corporation (EFC) Contract 94, was launched from the Sanderson & Porter shipyard in Raymond, Washington, on January 14, 1919. However, *Bingamon*, like many of the American-built freighters built late during the Great War, never served in her intended role since the war was over before she could be completed.

By the end of 1918 (the Armistice was signed on November 11, 1918) the EFC had taken delivery of only 118 of 589 wood freighters built in various shipyards throughout the United States. Only 87 of these saw more than a month of service while the rest saw none whatsoever. A post-war depression accompanied a peacetime oversupply of shipping and the resulting depressed freight rates saw the bulk of the US ship-building program rafted together in backwaters such as Lake Union, Washington, where a derelict fleet of some 40 hulls became known as "Wilson's Woodrow" (Woodrow Wilson was US President during the First World War). *Bingamon* happened to be one of 10 unused Washington-built Ferris-type hulls that ended up being purchased in the early 1920s for use in British Columbia waters as log barges. (*Abnoba, Abydos, Bingamon, Blatchford, Biscayne, Black Wolf* and *Chalcis* were all examples of the Ferris design.)

In December 1924, the British Pacific Log Transport Company, Ltd. bought *Bingamon* from Washington Tug & Barge, who had purchased 23 Ferris-type hulls from the United States Shipping Board. British Pacific then set to work converting her into the West Coast's first self-loading log barge. Up until this time the Davis raft was the preferred choice for transporting logs from coastal logging operations to lumber mills, but the loss of logs while towing them in rafts, especially across open waters such as the treacherous Hecate Straits, was heavy, resulting in costly insurance rates. It was hoped that by using derelict ships for barges, logs would be delivered safely, quickly and at less cost, and that the wood would also be less susceptible to marine borers.

Unfortunately, the innovative vessel was almost lost on her first voyage, to the Queen Charlotte Islands in early January 1925. Norman Hacking, who wrote the column "Ship and Shore" for the *Vancouver Province* in the 1960s, recalled talking with Bill Ballantyne, who was engineer on the big steam tug *Masset* for *Bingamon's* trial run. *Bingamon*, while under tow of *Masset*, was halfway across Queen Charlotte Sound in a big blow when the six bargees (barge crew) sent up a distress signal. The massive crane had broken loose and was careering out of control up and down the rails, creating chaos aboard the vessel. The tug managed to get the barge in her lee, allowing the crane to be secured, but it wasn't over yet.

On the way across Hecate Straits, in the midst of the raging gale, *Masset's* 50-ton water tank burst, flooding the engine room. Coal, water and ashes rose to within two inches of the boiler furnaces. With no option but to run before the wind, tug and tow were driven toward Prince Rupert. Finally, off Triple Island, the towline parted and *Bingamon* disappeared with her six bargees aboard. Fortunately she drifted into a rocky bay where they were able to anchor their vessel safely in sheltered waters. Once a new towline could be attached, tug and barge headed across to the Queen Charlotte Islands once again and when they reached Cumshewa Inlet nearly a million board feet of prime spruce logs were loaded aboard *Bingamon*. As Hacking has it, as the last log was put in place the crane collapsed in pieces.

The British Pacific Transport Company's hulks mothballed at Bedwell Bay, located up Indian Arm in Burrard Inlet, in November 1928, are identified as (left to right) *Addison, Abydos, Endymion, Chalcis, Abnoba* and *Oelwein*, along with Pacific (Coyle) Navigation's steel-hulled *Granco*. VANCOUVER MARITIME MUSEUM

Regardless of this unfortunate start, *Bingamon* soon proved a success and, with the need for more log barges by the forest industry, the British Pacific Log Transport Company (the name was changed to British Pacific Barge Company, Ltd. in August 1925) had nine more Ferris hulls towed up from Lake Union to Vancouver that summer and moored them in Bedwell Bay, Indian Arm, in readiness for conversion.

Bingamon herself had only seen about three and a half years of barge service when, on July 7, 1928, she caught fire while anchored in Plumper Harbour, Nootka Sound. Some 90 feet of her stern were burned to the water's edge and her hoisting machinery was ruined. *Bingamon* was towed to Esquimalt where she subsequently sank in the harbour. Once refloated, she was written off as a total loss. The *Victoria Daily Colonist* of October 26 reported, "The log carrier *Bingamon*, now merely a shell with part of her stern levelled off, is being patched with canvas in the drydock for towing to the Fraser River . . ." Soon afterward, she was finally laid to rest on the mud flats off Wreck Beach.

Like *Bingamon*, the hulk *Granco* had had a varied and unusual past. She was originally launched as the 275-foot-long, 2,114-net-ton steamship *Barracouta* from the shipyard of J. & G. Thompson in Glasgow, Scotland, in 1883. She was first owned by the Barracouta S.S. Co. and was registered in London. *The Record of American and Foreign Shipping* noted that she was regularly surveyed in New York from 1883 through to 1888, implying she probably served on a trans-Atlantic steamship run. In 1893 she was surveyed in San Francisco and four years later was acquired by the Pacific Mail Steamship Company. *Barracouta* operated as part of their Panama fleet out of the port of San Francisco up until 1915 when Pacific Mail terminated service and sold off their steamship fleet.

Sometime between 1915 and 1917, the out-of-service steamer *Barracouta* was purchased by Griffiths & Sons, a major Puget Sound towing company, for conversion into a barge. She was then transferred over to the company's Canadian subsidiary, Coastwise Steamship & Barge Co., and assigned to their regular run transporting ore from northern British Columbia to a smelter in Tacoma, Washington. In early December 1917, the huge barge, encrusted with some six to eight inches of ice, was swept from her

In 1897, the *Barracouta* was acquired by the Pacific Mail Steamship Company and operated as part of their fleet out of San Francisco until the service was terminated in 1915. Since it is dated 1915, this photo may have been taken following her last voyage with the company. SAN FRANCISCO MARITIME NATIONAL HISTORICAL PARK, B7.1,902PL

anchorage in Seward, Alaska, and carried away by a gale. Since she didn't look very different from an iceberg, the *San Francisco Chronicle* reported, ". . . searchers passed her by many times." Eventually the huge barge was located with the three crew members still safe aboard.

Apparently *Barracouta* underwent a name change while with Coastwise Steamship & Barge, since the 1920–21 Lloyd's Register lists her as "*Granco*, steel barge, former S.S. *Baracouta* [*sic*]" for the first time. In February 1927, Coastwise Steamship Company sold off their ore carrier to Albert & McCaffery Ltd., a Prince Rupert building supply company who, a month later, turned around and sold *Granco* to Pacific (Coyle) Navigation Company, who brought her to join *Bingamon* on Wreck Beach.

One of Major Matthews' informants told him in 1950 that, while there were originally four hulks at Wreck Beach, only the remains of two were left. He went on to say that the wood vessel (probably *Bingamon*) was set afire back in the "Hungry '30s" in order to salvage scrap metal for sale.

According to a 1943 file on the *Granco* in the National Archives in Ottawa, Wartime Salvage Ltd. intended to have her broken up on site for some 1,000 to 1,500 tons of much needed steel for the war effort in late 1942. However, the plan to remove the hulk met with heavy opposition from the North Fraser Harbour Commission since ". . . the barge, plus a wooden hulk, forms an indispensable part of the protection southward from Point Grey behind which log booming areas have been constructed." The file doesn't indicate what became of *Granco* but what is certain is that her remains haven't been visible for decades.

This is probably the remains of the *Granco* at Wreck Beach. The steel barge was originally launched as the trans-Atlantic steamship *Barracouta*. Griffiths & Sons, a major Puget Sound towing company, transferred her to their Canadian subsidiary, Coastwise Steamship & Barge Company, sometime around 1915 to 1917 for use as a barge transporting ore from northern BC mines to a Tacoma smelter. D.M. THOMSON COLLECTION, VANCOUVER MARITIME MUSEUM

Chapter 14

Island Tug & Barge Gave Old Sailers Second Wind, 1937

"Better to be taken care of and wind up their affairs in gainful occupation than be transformed into scrap before their days of usefulness are done," Harold Elworthy, manager of Island Tug & Barge Ltd., remarked to a Victoria *Times Colonist* reporter in April of 1937.

Victoria's Inner Harbour towing firm had just bought the five-masted barquentine *Forest Friend*, which had been lying idle up the Fraser River since 1929, to cut down into a barge. *Forest Friend*, launched in Aberdeen, Washington, in 1919, became part of a fleet that eventually included 13 retired sailing vessels that Island Tug & Barge purchased for their cheap bottoms to haul wood chips, hog fuel (scrap wood waste from sawmills used to fire boilers in pulp and paper mills) and, following the Second World War, logs.

Advances in the mechanics of steam propulsion in the late nineteenth century foreshadowed the demise of the wind-driven vessel. By the 1930s a large sailing vessel seen off the Victoria waterfront was a special occasion as few were left in active service, although old-timers could recall when it was a daily occurrence to see ships powered by billowing white canvas entering Juan de Fuca Strait looking for a tow to a Puget Sound or British Columbia port. A few of these tall-masted ships, however, gained a reprieve from the wreckers. Shorn of their tall spars, with hatchways opened up and some of their main and 'tween decks ripped out, once graceful wooden lumber schooners and barquentines, along with massive Cape Horn square-riggers, were converted into utilitarian barges.

Harold Elworthy's Island Tug & Barge started operations in 1925 by towing a boom of logs with the small tug *Island Planet* for the grand sum of $125. From this modest start, the company went on to develop a substantial fleet of towboats and barges that hauled forest products throughout British Columbia and Washington state, but the local Victoria company wasn't the first on the West Coast to introduce the practice of converting retired ships into barges. An earlier entrepreneur in northwest Pacific coast towing, James Griffiths & Sons based in Puget Sound, began the practice around the turn of the twentieth century. Deepwater square-riggers bought at low prices and transformed into barges helped build Griffiths' fortune. *Melanope* (see Chapter 6) was one of these ships.

Gordon Gibson, of early west coast Vancouver Island logging fame, claimed the distinction of developing the first self-powered, self-loading and unloading log barge. In 1934 the rough and tumble Gibson Brothers outfit purchased the 1,550-ton wood-hulled *Malahat* and fitted her with two steam donkeys for loading logs.

Harold Elworthy restricted Island Tug & Barge Company's wood-hulled sailing ship barges to carrying hog fuel and wood chips and had them avoid open waters as much as possible. The *Betsey Ross* (shown here loading hog fuel), *Drumwall*, *Sir Thomas J. Lipton* and *Forest Friend* plied between lumber mills on Vancouver Island and pulp and paper mills in Washington State. HAROLD ELWORTHY COLLECTION

A sister ship of *Laurel Whalen*, built by Cameron-Genoa Mills Shipbuilders Ltd. of Victoria in 1917, *Malahat* was originally launched as a deepwater lumber freighter, but the five-masted auxiliary schooner was retired from the trade in 1922. *Malahat* then became involved in a profitable trade as a floating warehouse and mother ship to the rum-running fleet off the coast of California and Mexico. After the end of Prohibition in the United States in 1933, *Malahat* was picked up by the Gibsons who didn't bother to re-register her as a freight ship. Under load, the auxiliary power of the two old Swedish Bolinder semi-diesel engines could barely manage in rough weather in the confined waters of BC's coast, and after courting disaster once too often *Malahat* was relegated to the towline.

Art Elworthy, one of Harold's sons, recalled that the company restricted their old wood-hulled sailing vessels to carrying wood chips and hog fuel and had them avoid open water as much as possible. The former barquentines *Forest Friend* and *Drumwall* (ex-*Puako*), along with the schooners *Sir Thomas J. Lipton* and *Betsey Ross*, plied between the BC lumber mills in Port Alberni and Chemainus and the ports of Port Townsend and Port Angeles in Washington state.

Many of these ex-sailing vessels were given new names more suited to their drab roles as barges (see below). The four-masted barquentine *Puako*, for example, whose Hawaiian name meant "flower of the sugar cane," was renamed *Drumwall* by Hecate Straits Towing Co. who purchased her in 1925 and cut her down into a barge. She was subsequently sold to Island Tug & Barge.

Melanope is pictured here as a cut-down CPR collier passing through Vancouver's First Narrows with a full load aboard. Note the crane amidships for discharging coal into CPR Empress liners. H. BROWN PHOTO, JULY 1925, COURTESY ROYAL BC MUSEUM, BC ARCHIVES A-07611

Names and Origins

Island Tug & Barge Company's Sailing Ship Barges	Barge Launched As
Homeward Bound	steel ship *Zemindar*, Belfast, Ireland, 1885
Lord Templetown	steel barque *Lord Templetown*, Belfast, 1886
Dunsyre	steel ship *Dunsyre*, Port Glasgow, Scotland, 1891
Island Forester	steel barque *Comet*, Port Glasgow, 1901
Fibreboard	steel barque *Robert Duncan*, Port Glasgow, 1891
Island Carrier	steel barque *Somali*, Port Glasgow, 1892
Island Star	steel ship *Blairmore*, Dumbarton, Scotland, 1893
Riversdale	steel ship *Riversdale*, Port Glasgow, 1894
Drumwall	wood, four-masted barquentine *Puako*, Oakland, Ca., 1902
Island Gatherer	steel barque *Alsterberg*, Dumbarton, 1902
Betsey Ross	wood five-masted schooner *Betsy Ross*, Tacoma, Wa., 1917 (*"Betsey"* was probably an I.T.& B. Co. misspelling)
Forest Friend	wood five-masted barquentine *Forest Friend*, Aberdeen, Wa., 1919
Sir Thomas J. Lipton	wood four-masted schooner *Sir Thomas J. Lipton* Brunswick, Georgia, 1919

The log barge *Island Forester*, riding light and high out of the water with the tug *Island Navigator* alongside, dominates Victoria's Upper Harbour. The photo was probably taken soon after the end of the Second World War since the log barge is still in reasonable shape and has yet to have her loading cranes installed. (*Island Navigator* was one of a number of Mikimiki tugs built in the US during the war and then sold off with the return of peace.)
MARITIME MUSEUM OF BRITISH COLUMBIA P 1181.06

The four-masted steel barque *Comet* served her barge years with Island Tug & Barge under the utilitarian name *Island Forester*. *Somali*, at one time one of the largest commercial sailing ships afloat under the British flag at 3,410 gross tons and 330 feet in length, became *Island Carrier*.

The steel three-masted ship *Riversdale*, the schooner *Thomas J. Lipton*, the steel ship *Dunsyre* and the stately barque *Lord Templetown* all retained their original names while in service with the Elworthy fleet. When the old windjammers *Somali*, *Comet*, *Riversdale* and *Blairmore* were sold by Island Tug & Barge Co. to Crown Zellerbach in the mid-1950s their new names gave no clue as to their former, more dignified careers, their only identification being *Crown Zellerbach #1, #2, #3* and *#4* painted on their counters.

Most of the coast's old sailing ships whose lives were extended by barge conversion have long since disappeared. Of those who worked under the Island Tug & Barge Co. flag *Lord Templetown*, *Blairmore* (barge *Island Star*) and *Zemindar* (barge *Homeward Bound*) went to the Capital Iron Co. breaker yard in Victoria Harbour. In the winter gales of 1936 both *Dunsyre* (while still under canvas, the first sailing ship through the Panama Canal) and *Island Gatherer* were lost in marine mishaps (see Chapter 15). Fortunately, in both instances, the "bargees" (the barge crew of usually three men responsible for steering the ship, slipping the lines, picking up tow, etc.) managed to escape with their lives. A few hulks did manage to escape the cutting torch and avoid disaster along the coast, and the remains of five exist as part of the old hulk breakwater at Royston, a little south of Courtenay on Vancouver Island (see Chapter 17). The prominent

After the Second World War, three large steam cranes were installed on the *Island Forester* for self-loading and unloading logs. Here the size of the logs, probably spruce butt ends, suggests the barge is probably loading in the Queen Charlotte Islands. HAROLD ELWORTHY COLLECTION

bow of *Riversdale* is lodged in the rock ballast with the bow of the *Comet* fallen over to seaward. There, too, rest *Forest Friend* and *Laurel Whalen*, as well as the collier *Melanope*. Disappearing into the mud nearby are two of her old towboats, the CPR's steam tugs *Nanoose* and *Qualicum*. Ships bells, wheels, figureheads, and brass fittings salvaged from these vessels are scattered throughout museums and private homes along the West Coast. The large wooden wheel of *Melanope* is displayed in the Maritime Museum of British Columbia in Victoria, while her brass bell hangs in the Comox Legion. Several tons of gear were rescued from *Lord Templetown* before she was scrapped in Portland, Oregon, and sent to the San Francisco Maritime Museum.

In 1970, to aid in the restoration of another Cape Horn windjammer, *Wavertree*, Capital Iron sent a crew to Royston and stripped *Riversdale* of its bollards, fairleads, windlass and capstan. Some enterprising and historically minded Americans had retrieved *Wavertree* from South America and the vessel is now open to public viewing at the South Street Seaport Museum in Manhattan, New York.

In British Columbia, although a few of the former steel square-riggers were still afloat as barges as late as the 1960s, none was saved to remind us of the varied roles they served in our maritime heritage. All that remains is a few broken and collapsed hulks now resting at Royston, slowly succumbing to the elements and disappearing into the Courtenay River's estuary mud.

Chapter 15

Adrift in a West Coast Gale: The *Dunsyre* and *Island Gatherer*, 1936

The winter of 1936 was a hard one for Victoria's Island Tug & Barge Company. On November 17, the company barge *Dunsyre* went adrift in a raging gale off the west coast of Vancouver Island and was dashed to pieces the next day on Kains Island at the entrance to Quatsino Sound.

A month later, the *Victoria Daily Times* of December 15 reported that another barge, *Island Gatherer*, had also lost its towline during a southeaster. This time, the disaster occurred in the treacherous waters of Queen Charlotte Sound, and after the barge crew was rescued, the hapless vessel was never seen again.

These massive hulks were two of the collection of retired sailing ships that Harold Elworthy, owner of Island Tug & Barge Company, had bought during the Depression for hauling wood chips and hog fuel along the West Coast. Old iron and steel windjammers were ideally suited for this role once they were shorn of their tall spars, their hatchways had been opened and some decking was cut away. When they were stripped down, the after cabin—the captain's inner sanctum—was always left intact. It was here that the barge's captain (possibly a former windjammer master fallen on hard times) lived. As master of the barge he looked after such chores as handling lines and firing up the steam donkey, and he was generally responsible for taking care of the owner's interests while lying in port. He was usually joined by two seamen while under tow.

Island Gatherer was one of three already stripped-down hulls that the Victoria towboating entrepreneur bought from Pacific (Coyle) Navigation Company in 1936. Pacific (Coyle) had named her *Pacific Gatherer*, but she started her deep-sea sailing career as *Alsterberg*, a 330-foot, 3,239-ton, steel four-masted barque launched from Dumbarton, Scotland, in 1902. Island Tug had purchased their other recently cut-down windjammer, *Dunsyre*, in 1935 in San Francisco, where she had been laid up since the early 1920s. She had been originally launched in 1891 in Port Glasgow, Scotland, as the *Dunsyre*, a steel three-masted ship of 2,056 tons and 279 feet in length.

Alan Heater, crewing on the tug *Anyox* in November 1936, found himself assigned to the barge *Dunsyre* that ill-fated winter. Still in his teens, Heater had landed a job that fall with Island Tug & Barge after mentioning that he had just spent a summer with his grandfather, Bill Heater, whaling in the North Pacific. Elworthy hired him on the spot.

The three-masted steel ship *Dunsyre*, built in Port Glasgow in 1891, was said to be the first sailing ship to pass through the Panama Canal when it opened in 1914. She is pictured here riding at anchor at an unidentified port.
VANCOUVER MARITIME MUSEUM

Anyox was returning with the empty *Dunsyre* from the paper mill in Port Alice when the tow was caught in a West Coast gale. The over-stressed hawser parted between the two vessels and *Anyox* frantically tried to rocket a line across to the wallowing hulk in order to rescue Captain W. Billington, Ray Larkin and Heater. After two unsuccessful attempts, the third succeeded, but as *Anyox*'s crew was preparing to send across a heavy line and breeches buoy to the barge, the sound of the booming surf informed them that they were dangerously close to the rocky shoreline. As the barge drifted closer to the breakers, Captain F.H. Cole, skipper of *Anyox*, took the decision to abandon the rescue rather than sacrifice his wooden-hull tug with some 15 men aboard.

Left drifting and alone, the three bargees were reluctant to share their thoughts on the inevitable; that when the helpless craft finally hit the rocks they wouldn't stand a chance. "We saw the last of *Anyox* about an hour after dark on Tuesday night, and from that time on were alone with the breaking seas, which did everything possible with the barge except stand her on end. It's a good thing she was riding light and not handicapped with a load . . ." Captain Billington later told a reporter.

To keep their spirits up, Alan Heater drew his mouth organ out of his pocket and played *Home Sweet Home*. Then, around 1:30 in the morning, a large object loomed out of the dark, which Captain Billington identified as Solander Island. Incredibly, *Dunsyre*, drifting stern first in the storm, rather than going up on the island or onto the rocks scattered throughout the water between it and Cape Cook, passed through the passage unscathed.

In September 1930, *Island Gatherer*, as Pacific (Coyle) Navigation Company's *Pacific Gatherer*, was involved in a bizarre accident. In tow of the tug *Lorne*, the barge was caught in an eddy and swept into the Second Narrows Bridge, lifting a span off with the rising tide. Stories have it that the captain of the *Lorne* committed suicide soon after. VANCOUVER PUBLIC LIBRARY, SPECIAL COLLECTIONS VPL 3115

Billington recalled that, "All through the night, from minute to minute, we just expected to hit bottom. *Dunsyre* rolled heavily from crest to trough and to crest again with monotonous regularity, shipping heavy spray continually as we carried on. We had the lifeboat in slings all ready to swing out on the lee side of the ship, but I'm certain it wouldn't have been of much use if we had gone ashore in the sea that was running."

At dawn's break, the three men decided their only chance of survival was to get away in the lifeboat. The six-foot-tall Heater volunteered to go over the stern in the boat since they all knew he was probably the only one strong enough to hold it off from the crushing force of the rolling barge's counter. The bargees successfully cleared the doomed ship and Heater managed the large tiller while his two mates manned the oars. At first the thick weather and high waves made it impossible to gauge whether the boat was being blown farther out to sea or landward. Then, after three hours of scanning the horizon, they picked out the flashing beacon of Kains Island lighthouse. Their problems weren't over yet, however. The island was surrounded by rocks and reefs that made it a formidable place to land at the best of times.

Here Heater proved his worth as a seaman by threading a safe a passage through the reefs as Captain Billington and Ray Larkin leaned into the oars. Once they were in behind the island they rode in on a big swell, jumped to shore and turned to see the next swell smash the lifeboat into staves. Three hours later the lightkeeper, his wife, the wireless operator and the three survivors all watched as the gale-blown *Dunsyre* was driven broadside onto the rocky island. In less than half an hour only the top of her housework remained to identify the wreck as a once stately square-rigger.

Another teenager, Joe Quilty, was just out of school in the Depression year of 1935 when he approached Harold Elworthy and offered to work for his board to gain some experience. Elworthy told him to be at the company dock at eight the next morning when *Salvage Queen* (the retired CPR coastal steamer *Tees*) was pulling out. December 1936 found the young seaman on the big tug taking the loaded *Island Carrier* to Ocean Falls, to return with the empty *Island Gatherer* through the inside waters of Johnstone Straits.

Quilty was aboard *Island Gatherer* when the tow entered the open waters of the notorious Queen Charlotte Sound. With Bull Harbour station reporting winds of 92 knots that night, the tug and barge found themselves in the midst of a full-blown North Pacific hurricane.

"The crew on the *Salvage Queen* had to turn on the steam winch to hold the towline because the brake was slipping and the line was gradually working off the drum," Quilty recalled. "Then the crank disks on the towing winch snapped in half from the strain . . . the brake wouldn't hold and all the line ran off the drum. *We were adrift!* . . . but with all that towline draggin' more or less kept head into the wind . . . but if we'd been broadside, don't think would have got us off."

Quilty was off watch at the time and when he came on deck to discover *Salvage Queen* gone he feared the worst. He still considers it miraculous that the tug eventually found them. The tug captain, Frederick

The *Salvage Queen* was the converted CPR coastal steamer *Tees,* purchased by the Canadian Pacific Navigation Company in 1893 and registered in the name of the CPR in March 1903. She was renamed *Salvage Queen* after being sold to the Pacific Salvage Company in 1925. She is shown here in First Narrows in about 1930, a few years before Island Tug & Barge acquired her. VANCOUVER MARITIME MUSEUM

MacFarlane, had always told his bargees that if they ever went adrift he would get them all off or the tow-boat would go to the bottom trying. As it was, when MacFarlane brought *Salvage Queen* in close to the massive hulk towering over his wheelhouse, the tug sustained a major amount of damage. As Joe Quilty described it, the wallowing *Island Gatherer* "... smashed the foremast out ... bust the wheelhouse, smashed the davits in on starboard side, bust lifeboat starboard side and pushed starboard anchor right through the bow ... so she was takin' a lot of water!"

One crewman was able to jump off on his own but Joe Quilty and Captain Poulsen remained behind. Quilty assisted the desperately seasick Mrs. Poulsen while Captain Poulsen struggled with the barge. (Mrs. Poulsen later told local papers that she considered Joe Quilty an "angel" for his actions throughout the ordeal.)

With *Salvage Queen* finally in position, Quilty and Poulsen helped Mrs. Poulsen along the side of the barge where they sat on a handrail and waited for the right wave. When it arrived, they picked up the elderly woman and unceremoniously tossed her toward the foredeck of the tug, where the waiting crew caught her in a canvas tarp.

Captain Poulsen and Quilty then jumped to safety. While Captain MacFarlane had performed a daring rescue with no loss of life, *Salvage Queen* was wrecked beyond repair by the wallowing *Island Gatherer* in the high seas drama.

Looking back, both Joe Quilty and Alan Heater dismissed any thought of the idea during their 1996 interviews that they were heroes 60 years earlier. Instead, the two former Island Tug & Barge hands

In this mid-1930s photo of the crew of the *Salvage Queen*, Joe Quilty is the boy to the right of the life ring and Captain Fred Cole—master of the *Anyox* at the time of the *Dunsyre* loss—is directly behind the life ring. JOE QUILTY COLLECTION

attributed their courage to that casual disregard for danger held by most teenage boys. When Harold Elworthy congratulated them and then asked his new hands if they were now through with the seafaring life, they both replied, no, they were ready for their next voyage.

Postscript

In January 1942, Island Tug & Barge lost another sailing ship barge conversion off the west coast of Vancouver Island—*Fibreboard*, which was originally the four-masted steel barque *Robert Duncan* built in Port Glasgow, Scotland, in 1891. Once again, all the bargees managed to get off safely. In my research into old sailing ships used for barge service in British Columbia, I've discovered that while a number of them succumbed to marine hazard, apparently no lives were ever lost.

"... not knowing where they were or when they would go ashore . . . their wind-driven ship passed through perilous waters; and after they had abandoned her in the lifeboat . . . they watched their late home destroyed in the surf right below Kains Island light-house." —November 21, 1936, Victoria *Daily Colonist.*
RICK JAMES COLLECTION

VICTORIA **BRITISH COLUMBIA**, SATURDAY, NOVEMBER 21, 1936

Played Mouth Organ While Waiting Doom On Rolling Dunsyre

Capt. W. Billington, Roy Larkin and Allan Heater Return to Victoria After Harrowing Experience on Drifting Barge; Expected to Be Dashed Ashore in Darkness; Rowed Five Miles Through Big Seas to Safety of Lighthouse

"A Miracle—"

"Home, Sweet Home" Was Tune Played

"The worst part of it was just sitting there waiting for her to hit," said Allan Heater, nineteen-year-old member of the crew of the ill-fated barge Dunsyre, who returned to Victoria this morning aboard the Ss. Salvage King with Capt. W. Billington and Roy Larkin, who also spent all Tuesday night, in a howling gale, aboard the helpless craft off the West Coast of Vancouver Island.

The three men thought they would never see land again. For eighteen hours they were aboard the Dunsyre, with lifebelts strapped to them. They were soaking wet, for spray dashed over the decks. They could hardly stand as the vessel was rolling and plunging so heavily. Yet throughout the night they kept their nerve and only felt shaky when they reached safety at Kains Island lighthouse on Wednesday morning.

"The wind was howling so badly we had to shout at each other," young Heater said. "It was raining so hrad we couldn't see half a mile. We had to crawl along the deck on our hands and knees, it was blowing so hard."

ALLAN HEATER
who said it was "a miracle" that the three men of the barge Dunsyre ever saw land again.

"For eighteen hours they were aboard the *Dunsyre*, with lifebelts strapped to them . . . They could hardly stand as the vessel was rolling and plunging so heavily. Yet throughout the night they kept their nerve . . ."
—November 21, 1936, Victoria *Daily Colonist*. RICK JAMES COLLECTION

Chapter 16

From Heroes to Hulks: The 1940s

A few months after the end of the Second World War, the War Assets Corporation, the government disposal agency, ran a nationwide advertisement announcing that "39 frigate-type ships declared surplus to Canadian Naval requirements . . ." were to be sold off "as is, where is." With the return of peace, Canada's federal government realized it could ill afford to maintain what had evolved during the war into one of the largest naval forces in the world, and put most of it on the block.

In the early years of the war Canada's fledgling navy, the Royal Canadian Navy (RCN) had found itself hard pressed to assist a beleaguered Great Britain. Lean Depression years' budgets had allowed for only a bare bones fleet of six destroyers, four minesweepers, a trawler and two small training vessels. In an attempt to curb the ever-increasing shipping losses to U-boats in the North Atlantic and the impending economic strangulation of Britain, Canadian industry undertook a massive shipbuilding program. Shipyards on both the west and east coasts, as well as in the Great Lakes, were soon actively immersed in building a substantial small-ship fighting force for the RCN.

With the return of peace, the federal government decided that the bulk of this wartime shipbuilding program (more than 350 fighting ships) was to be disposed of. Most, like the corvettes, were simply broken up if they weren't sold to a mercantile venture or to a Central or South American navy. Here on the West Coast, however, a number of the larger vessels—the minesweepers, corvettes and frigates—managed to find local peacetime employment.

The Union Steamship Company bought three Castle-class corvettes—HMCS *Leaside,* HMCS *St. Thomas* and HMCS *Hespeler*—for the bargain price of $75,000 each. After expensive conversions and the repainting of their drab wartime grey with bright white, the 1,060-ton-displacement, 252-foot corvettes were transformed into the SS *Coquitlam II,* SS *Camosun III* and SS *Chilcotin* and were soon recognized along the coast as the Union Steamship Company's White Boats.

Union Steamships also purchased four Bangor minesweepers—HMCS *Bellechasse, Miramichi, Courtenay* and *Chignecto.* The company hoped to convert and operate the 672-ton, 180-foot ships as a passenger express service but the plan was shelved. Although it was rumoured that a San Francisco firm had made an offer on them, no record apparently exists as to what actually became of the four minesweepers.

Victoria's Island Tug & Barge Company also bought one of the RCN veterans—the Flower-class corvette HMCS *Sudbury.* The towboat company equipped the 950-ton, 205-foot-long vessel for salvage work and the investment soon paid off; the corvettes were noted for their seakeeping abilities in the North Atlantic and *Sudbury* made an excellent deep-sea tug. The dramatic sea rescues performed by *Sudbury* soon

Lieutenant Commander R.W. "Bob" Draney, DSC RCNR ret., surveys his old wartime command, *K324*, at Royston. He happened to be mate on the tug *Florence Filberg* when they picked up the gutted hull of HMCS *Prince Rupert* to tow her to her final resting place. BOB DRANEY COLLECTION

earned Island Tug & Barge a high profile along the coast even though the company was primarily occupied with the more mundane job of towing logs, chips and hog fuel for their forest company clients.

When *Sudbury* arrived under Lions Gate Bridge in December 1955 with the Greek ship *Makedonia* under tow, thousands of local residents lined the shore cheering. The tug had just performed an incredible rescue. The freighter was picked up adrift with a damaged drive shaft off the Kamchatka peninsula and was then towed 3,500 miles through "gale lashed seas and stubborn currents," according to the *Vancouver Province*.

Along with a number of minesweepers and corvettes disposed of on the West Coast were 14 frigates. The frigate building program didn't start until well into the war and therefore the first of the "twin-screw corvettes," as the new design was originally called, didn't arrive for the Battle of the Atlantic until late in 1943. These efficient U-boat hunter-killers were soon discovered to be the ideal convoy escort vessel: they had twice the range of the smaller corvette and were better armed as well as being far more pleasant to be aboard. Around two-thirds of the 70 River-class frigates built for the RCN were paid off at the end of the war, even though most had experienced only a year, or two at most, of active war service since their launch.

Local Victoria scrap dealer Morris Greene of Capital Iron & Metals Ltd. was quick to notice the War Assets Corporation advertisement and he convinced his two partners, Izzy Stein and Harry

After 1945, the federal government disposed of all but a handful of the Royal Canadian Navy's wartime fleet. Here on the West Coast, the decommissioned vessels sat mothballed in Bedwell Bay, Indian Arm, waiting to be sold off by the War Assets Corporation. Circa 1946 photo. MARITIME MUSEUM OF BRITISH COLUMBIA P 3570 C

Wagner, that there was money to be made scrapping warships. Greene bought all 14 frigates that were put up for sale on the West Coast, as well as the Algerine-class minesweeper *Border Cities*. The firm of Wagner, Stein and Greene was established and a breaker's yard was set up at Ogden Point next to the grain elevator.

The first RCN ship to pass under the wrecker's torch, in January 1948, was *K324*, HMCS *Prince Rupert*, launched only five years earlier at the Yarrows Ltd. shipyard in Esquimalt. Once the ship had been stripped, the gutted hull was destined to be towed to Royston, BC, where she became part of a hulk breakwater to protect Comox Logging & Railway Company's log dump and booming ground. Through a strange quirk of fate, the tug sent to pick up the *K324* was *Florence Filberg*, which just happened to have on board as first mate retired Lieutenant Commander Robert Draney DSC, RCNR, from New Westminster. He had been the *Prince Rupert*'s commander during the Second World War.

After the *Prince Rupert* was dismantled and disposed of, efficiency rose to the point where the Ogden Point yard could completely scrap a ship in six weeks. Eleven more frigates were stripped and their hulls sold to logging companies who used them all for hulk breakwaters. HMCS *Dunver* and *Eastview* joined the *Prince Rupert* at Royston, while HMCS *Matane*, *Levis* and *Charlottetown* went to Iron River Logging's operation at Oyster Bay near Campbell River. Forest company giant Macmillan Bloedel purchased HMCS *Cape Breton*, *La Salle*, *Longueuil* and *Runnymede* for their Kelsey Bay Division and HMCS *Coaticook* for the floating hulk breakwater surrounding their big pulp and paper mill operation in Powell River. Two frigates that managed to escape the cutter's torch were HMCS *Kokanee* and HMCS *Waskesiu*, which were resold to the Indian government for conversion to Hooghly River pilot boats. (Two hulls that remain unaccounted

HMCS *Sudbury*, which served in the Battle of the Atlantic, was one of over a hundred corvettes built for the Royal Canadian Navy during the Second World War. Unlike the frigates, nearly all the corvettes were disposed of at war's end. Most were scrapped but some were sold off, and the *Sudbury* ended up working as a towboat and salvage tug with Island Tug & Barge of Victoria. CFB ESQUIMALT NAVAL & MILITARY MUSEUM, NEG. F-3365

The dramatic sea rescues performed by the deep-sea salvage tug *Sudbury* soon earned Island Tug & Barge a high profile along the coast, even though the company was primarily occupied with the more mundane job of towing logs, chips and hog fuel for their forest company clients. VANCOUVER MARITIME MUSEUM #12557

for, and which were probably cut for scrap metal, are the frigate HMCS *Grou* and the minesweeper *Border Cities*.)

Wagner, Stein and Greene later scrapped the war-weary destroyer *H61*, HMCS *Gatineau*, which had already seen strenuous service as the Royal Navy's HMS *Express* before being turned over to the RCN early in 1943. The E-class destroyer was part of the Dunkirk rescue mission in the summer of 1940. *H61* made six trips to the besieged beach and after rescuing some 3,500 troops was reported to be the second-to-last ship to leave the area. While serving in the Far East as escort to the battle cruiser HMS *Repulse* and the battleship HMS *Prince of Wales* in December 1941, *Express* was on hand to take off nearly 1,000 officers and crew from the slowly capsizing *Prince of Wales* when both warships were sunk by Japanese planes off Malaya. Declared surplus in 1947, HMCS *Gatineau* was later broken up at Ogden Point and her stripped hull joined the three frigates at Royston.

Residents of Canada's East Coast are fortunate that they can visit two restored examples of the RCN's contribution to victory in the Battle of the Atlantic. The Flower-class corvette HMCS *Sackville* is open to the public in Halifax Harbour, while the Tribal-class destroyer HMCS *Haida* is berthed in Hamilton, Ontario. Here on the West Coast, even though a number of RCN warships that served in the Second World War were granted a reprieve and saw some active peacetime service, none remains afloat.

The destroyer *H61*, HMCS *Gatineau*, was scrapped at the Ogden Point ship-scrapping yard in Victoria's Outer Harbour in about 1948. The shipyard was organized by the firm of Wagner, Stein & Greene to deal with decommissioned RCN warships following the end of the Second World War. MARITIME MUSEUM OF BRITISH COLUMBIA P 4046 B

Wagner, Stein and Greene

The Ogden Point ship-scrapping yard in Victoria's Outer Harbour was organized by the firm of Wagner, Stein & Greene primarily to deal with RCN warships bought from the War Assets Corporation. Morris Greene, originator of the project, owned the Capital Iron store on Store Street. Today, Capital Iron still serves as a popular hardware, clothing and recreational supplies outlet, as well as a surplus goods establishment, next to Victoria's Chinatown.

Greene got his start in the scrap business with a brother-in-law who owned Atlas Iron & Metals in Vancouver. They collected scrap, sorted it and sold the segregated material to dealers. In 1934 Greene went into partnership with Izzy Stein and Harry Wagner, forming Capital Iron & Metals Limited soon afterward. Wagner, Stein & Greene handled the Ogden Point ship-scrapping operation while Capital Iron & Metals Limited dealt with all non-ferrous metal.

In 1964, when it became too expensive to run two separate yards, the Ogden Point facility was closed. Ship dismantling at the dock behind Capital Iron continued to draw the nostalgic and the curious to the Store Street business until the early 1970s. While rusted hulls no longer clutter the dock, photographs of the scrapped ships adorn walls and pillars throughout the store, and bits of salvaged wood and brass ship paraphernalia still attract customers to the surplus department in the basement.

Chapter 17

Royston's Ship Graveyard, 1940s–1960s

Scattered just off the beach along the inside waters of British Columbia's southern coast are several collections of badly deteriorated and rusted remains of ships' hulls. While forest companies normally chose protected bays, coves and inlets to dump their logs and sort them into booms, on occasion they had to operate in areas exposed to strong tides, currents and foul weather. As a result, timber companies working out of Kelsey Bay near Sayward, Royston near Courtenay and Oyster River near Campbell River,

The bow of the three-masted ship *Riversdale* still stands proud off the beach of the small east Vancouver Island community of Royston. The bow of what was once the massive four-masted barque *Comet*, standing to seaward in the fog, has long since fallen over. RICK JAMES PHOTO, 1982

along with the pulp and paper mill at Powell River, have used the stripped hulls of retired ships to build protective breakwaters.

At Royston, directly across the bay from the town of Comox, there is one of the largest and most unusual of these hulk collections. It consists of the remains of four Royal Canadian Navy warships, one United States Navy destroyer, two whalers, two Canadian Pacific Railway steam tugs, a deep-sea rescue tug and, from the vanished days of commercial sailing, a wood-hulled barquentine and an auxiliary schooner, along with three massive Cape Horn windjammers.

The first hulk to arrive and be sunk at the site was the five-masted lumber schooner *Laurel Whalen* (see Chapter 9) in 1936. Once Comox Logging & Railway Company realized how effective the old lumber freighter's hull was in protecting their log dump, they began accumulating more retired vessels to scuttle on the weather side of their booming grounds. Together, in their varying states of deterioration, the grounded fleet of 14 vessels soon came to represent a fascinating cross-section of West Coast maritime history.

After *Laurel Whalen* was beached in 1936, it was to be another 10 years before more hulks arrived at Royston. On April 12, 1946, referring to the Canadian Pacific Railway Company's collier, the *Vancouver News Herald* announced, "Old *Melanope* to End Days as a Breakwater" (see Chapter 6.) Once they, too, were deemed no longer essential to the CPR's requirements, two steam-powered workhorses, the 305-gross-ton,

Some 135 years after her launching in Liverpool in 1876, the proud bow of the *Melanope* still remains upright at Royston. Just in front of her, the rusted remains of a two-cylinder compound engine and Scotch marine boiler mark the last of the steam tug *Qualicum*. The *Melanope* may well have ended up on the towline behind the *Qualicum* at one time or another while serving as a collier in the CPR fleet. RICK JAMES PHOTO

116-foot-long tug *Nanoose* and the 200-ton, 96-foot *Qualicum*, were also turned over to Comox Logging & Railway. Part of either tug's working routine may have included towing the blackened collier *Melanope* from Ladysmith or Union Bay, the West Coast's principal coaling stations, to Burrard Inlet, where she would often be seen loading the bunkers of a graceful trans-Pacific Empress liner.

Courtenay resident Rolf Bruhn figures it was early in 1947 when the gutted hull of the American destroyer *Tattnall* was towed up from Puget Sound to Royston. At the time, Bruhn was a deckhand on the tug that undertook the job, the *Florence Filberg*, owned by Canadian Tug Boat, a sister company to Comox Logging & Railway.

The *Tattnall* is one of the many fleet destroyers mass produced in the United States during and just after the First World War. Commissioned on June 26, 1919, the 1,090-ton, 314-foot-long Wickes-class flush-decker (Canadian sailors called them four-stackers) did see some serious action in the Second World War. In July 1943 the *Tattnall* was transformed into *APD-19* after conversion into a high-speed "Destroyer Personnel Transport." She took part in a number of actions in the Mediterranean, including the disembarking of "Frederick's Freighters," the handpicked Americans and Canadians of the 1st Special Service Force, the "Devil's Brigade," at the heavily fortified Hyeres Islands, east of Toulon, France. Reassigned to the Pacific War in the spring of 1945, she joined the picket line of ships protecting the invasion fleet's anchorage off Okinawa in April 1945. *APD-19, Tattnall*, won three battle stars for her Second World War service.

Off the end of the breakwater, by the disjointed and broken sections of the three CPR vessels, lie the remnants of one, if not two, Consolidated Whaling Company whalers—the 102-ton, 92-foot-long *Blue* and *Black*. It is estimated that some 25,000 whales were taken by vessels like these throughout the 52 years that the shore-based whaling industry operated in British Columbia. From 1911 until their final disposal in 1947, these small ships were often seen during their winter lay-up at the Consolidated Whaling docks beside the Point Ellice Bridge in Victoria. Very little remains to identify them as whalers today—only a jagged hole in a foredeck of one entirely collapsed hull where a harpoon gun was removed many years ago by a local diver.

The largest component of scrapped hulls lying at Royston consists of four Royal Canadian Navy (RCN) ships that all arrived at the site in the post-war years of 1947 and 1948. The history of these ships—the frigates HMCS *Prince Rupert, Eastview* and *Dunver,* and the 1,370-ton, 326-foot-long E-class destroyer HMCS *Gatineau*—is discussed in detail in the previous chapter.

Another scrapped hull at Royston that saw service in the Second World War was the US Navy fleet rescue tug *ATR 13*. This "auxiliary tug rescue" was one of nearly 100 ocean-going fleet rescue tugs built in the United States during the war. These 164-foot salvage vessels were originally designed for firefighting and for towing damaged ships from the scene of battle.

Seventeen-year-old Leo Murphy, looking to his first draft and fresh out of navy diesel school, boarded the brand new *ATR 13* in December 1943 only to discover she had a steam power plant, not a diesel. He caught on quickly, nonetheless, and *ATR 13* crossed the Atlantic the following March to join a fleet of tugs with tandem tows of barges all required for the invasion of Fortress Europe.

Murphy and the rescue tug saw their first action off the D-Day beaches in the summer of 1944. In September that same year, already a seasoned veteran of Sicily, Salerno and Anzio, as well as Normandy, *ATR 13* was sent to the war in the Pacific where she became one of the first Allied ships to enter the Sasebo naval base on the island of Kyushu following the Japanese surrender in August 1945.

Deemed no longer "essential to the defence of US," the tug was sold to the Pacific Salvage Company of Vancouver, BC, in late August 1947. The company quickly renamed their new acquisition *Salvage King* and fitted her out with the latest in electronic equipment and 350 fathoms of two-inch steel cable. Since the deep-sea tug also had a towing radius of 7,000 miles, her new owners proudly claimed she was "the best equipped salvage ship afloat." Unfortunately, her firefighting equipment—consisting of two pumps and five monitors capable of discharging 3,000 gallons of water per minute—proved useless when she herself caught fire in Victoria Harbour in October 1953. Found too damaged to repair, the charred ruin was stripped by Capital Iron and eventually towed to Royston in 1959. The wooden hull of *Salvage King,* ex-*ATR 13,* finally succumbed to the elements some years ago and there's little left to identify her anymore.

In the centre of the breakwater, surrounded by rock ballast, lies a massive wooden hull with large timbered ribs, the last remains of the five-masted barquentine *Forest Friend* (whom we met in Chapter 14), which arrived at Royston sometime in the late 1950s. Built in Aberdeen, Washington, in 1919, the 1,614-gross-ton, 243-foot *Forest Friend* was one of a large fleet of wood schooner-style vessels constructed along the Pacific Northwest during the First World War. For some 75 years, US sawmill owners built up a sizeable fleet of lumber schooners and barquentines for both the coastwise and trans-Pacific trades. As a result, the lumber industry in the US northwest was able to rely on a fleet of some 300 sailing vessels

In 1922, a 17-year-old Bent Sivertz signed up on the five-masted barquentine *Forest Friend* while she was loading lumber at Hastings Mill. He recalled that the *Forest Friend* was "wartime construction—no frills," but nonetheless "she was fortunate in having an excellent naval architect and first class shipwrights." In this photo the towline has just been dropped and all sails are nearly set as she passes out of Juan de Fuca Strait headed across the Pacific with a load of lumber. SAN FRANCISCO MARITIME NHP, J.8,990N

Forest Friend (on the right in this photo) probably arrived at Comox Logging & Railway Company's hulk break-water sometime in the mid-1950s. The last remains of the Cape Horn windjammer *Riversdale* stand beside her, scuttled at the site in November 1961. COURTESY COURTENAY, BC, NATIVE SONS HALL

registered to both lumber mill companies and independent ship owners to freight their product to local and overseas markets.

In late September 1922, a young Bent Sivertz happened to see *Forest Friend* berthed alongside the Hastings Mill dock in Vancouver preparing to load a cargo of lumber for Sydney, Australia. Sivertz was able to secure a berth on the ship as an ordinary sailor after skilful exaggeration of his knowledge on the points of the compass and of knotting and splicing. Once she had set sail, the teenager was soon going through the purgatory of "learning the ropes" that every new sailor faced on a sailing ship.

Forest Friend remained in the offshore lumber trade for four more years and was then laid up idle on the Fraser River for a number of years before being sold to the Island Tug & Barge Company in 1937. The retired lumber freighter was subsequently cut down by the big forest product towing company and converted into a wood chip and hog fuel barge. Once she had reached the end of her working life, sometime in the 1950s, she was picked up by Comox Logging and shoved in next to the A-frame at the new truck log dump that had just been built at Royston.

The most prominent remaining feature of the Royston hulk collection, standing just off the beach, is the proud Victorian bow of the steel, three-masted Cape Horn windjammer *Riversdale*. Launched from Liverpool, England, in 1894, the 2,206-ton, 276-foot *Riversdale* was a prime example of a British-built square-rigger of the late nineteenth century. In the days before steamships came to dominate the sea lanes of the world, thousands of windjammers such as *Riversdale* were running before the trade winds in the deepwater trade.

Riversdale was in and out of ports around the world over the next 20 years, wherever sailing ships were required to transport the bulk cargoes then in high demand, such as coal, coke, lumber and wheat. While carrying coke to the Gulf of Mexico in the summer of 1914, as the German-owned *Harvestehude*, the ship found herself in the smelter port of Santa Rosalia when war broke out in Europe. Along with 11 other German square-riggers, the Cape Horn windjammer remained interned in the hot and desolate harbour, her decks drying in the Mexican sun and barnacles collecting on her anchor chains, for the duration of the war.

In 1924, after the Santa Rosalia collection of German windjammers were awarded to the victors of the Great War, *Riversdale* was bought by American lumberman Robert Dollar, but she was laid up in San Francisco and never sailed again. In 1924, the deteriorating ship was bought by the Coastwise Steamship & Barge Company of Vancouver, who cut her down into a barge and used her for hauling ore from the Anyox mine in northern BC to a Tacoma, Washington, smelter. Then, in 1935, she joined a fleet of 12 other retired sailing ships owned by Island Tug & Barge Company, all purchased as cheap bottoms to haul chips, hog fuel and logs along the coast.

Eric Lawson, who had an extensive career specializing in wood conservation in the field of historic ship preservation, inspects a scupper door along the port side of the barquentine *Forest Friend* at Royston in 1994. RICK JAMES PHOTO

By the late 1950s, *Riversdale* had passed into the hands of the Crown Zellerbach Corporation, who renamed the log barge *Crown Zellerbach #3*. When her hull started to show its age and began to give out after withstanding years of being smashed and beaten by logs dropped into her holds, Crown Zellerbach towed her into Comox Harbour to be scuttled on the outside of Royston's hulk breakwater (the big American forest company Crown Zellerbach now owned the site, having bought Comox Logging & Railway Company in the early 1950s).

Just to the seaward of *Crown Zellerbach #3* (ex-*Riversdale)* lie the remains of another massive log barge, *Crown Zellerbach #2*. This hulk was originally launched as the four-masted barque *Comet* from a shipyard in Port Glasgow, Scotland, in 1901. The massive steel square-rigger was purpose-built to carry "case-oil" kerosene. By the late 1880s the worldwide demand for case-oil was growing at a phenomenal rate and ever-increasing quantities were being shipped from Standard Oil refineries along the US eastern seaboard. Eight large sailing ships specially designed as case-oil carriers were some of the largest square-riggers ever to be launched from British shipyards. The four-masted steel barque *Comet* measured some 318 feet in length and was registered as 3,017 gross tons. Later, while in the hands of a German shipping company as *Orotava*, the big Cape Horn windjammer also found herself interned in the Mexican port of Santa Rosalia for the duration of the Great War.

Lumberman Robert Dollar, who bought all 12 square-riggers interned in Mexico and brought them up to San Francisco, had *Orotava* (ex-*Comet*) make one lumber voyage across the Pacific, but commercial sailing was no longer viable and the barque was sold off to Pacific (Coyle) Navigation Company of Vancouver in 1929. She was promptly cut down into the barge *Pacific Forester* and remained with Pacific (Coyle) until sold to Island Tug & Barge in 1936 to become *Island Forester*.

After the Second World War, Island Tug mounted three large steam cranes on the *Island Forester*'s deck for loading and unloading logs. Like *Riversdale*, *Island Forester* was finally sold to Crown Zellerbach who renamed her *Crown Zellerbach #2*, and in 1962 the old windjammer joined her sister barge at Royston.

The weather and sea have taken a harsh toll on the breakwater's fleet of hulks, and every passing year weakens the structural integrity of yet another hulk to the point at which it collapses into more broken and rusted rubble. Field Sawmill has vacated the mill site on the Courtenay River, so the breakwater no longer fulfils any useful purpose anyway. All the same, the ships served useful roles far beyond their original builders' expectations, and with their varied histories reaching well back into the nineteenth century they have not only provided more than 50 years of service as a hulk breakwater but also constitute an important maritime heritage site.

Chapter 18

The *Brig. Gen. M.G. Zalinski*: 60 Years Lost in Grenville Channel, 1946

Archie McLaren couldn't sleep one particularly stormy night in September 1946—he was quite disturbed about the weather conditions as his ship, *Brig. Gen. M.G. Zalinski*, ran full speed ahead up Grenville Channel in BC's Inside Passage. As the Transportation Agent (purser) aboard the steamer, McLaren was so convinced that they were headed for a disaster that he woke up the ship's clerk to help him prepare to abandon ship if need be. The two wrapped up the ship's records in heavy paper and ensured that all the cash aboard was in the money bag and ready to grab at a moment's notice. McLaren also had the foresight to slip some other valuables into the bag—two bottles of bourbon. His disturbing premonition held true. Disaster struck *Brig. Gen. M.G. Zalinski* within a couple of hours.

Around 3:00 a.m. on September 29, the crew of *Brig. Gen. M.G. Zalinski* were shaken from their sleep when the ship suddenly received a severe jolt that was quickly followed by emergency blasts of the ship's whistle. *Zalinski* was already listing to starboard and taking on water quickly by the time the crew lined up to get in the lifeboats. The US Army Transport ship had struck rocks off Pitt Island, a few miles from Lowe Inlet.

The cargo ship *Brig. Gen. M.G. Zalinski* was originally launched in 1919 as the steel freighter *Lake Frohna*, hull #759 of the American Ship Building Co., Lorain, Ohio, for the United States Shipping Board (USSB). Built as a Laker-class ship, she was a full canal-sized ocean freighter of the common three-island, four-hatch, two-masted type. The canal-sized ships were limited to some 260 feet in length in order to access the Atlantic ocean via the American and Canadian canal and inland waterway systems.

Severe shortages of ocean-going ships brought on by the onset of the First World War had resulted in the creation of the USSB in September 1916. When the US entered the war in April 1917, a subsidiary of the Shipping Board, the Emergency Fleet Corporation, was assigned government authority to acquire, construct and operate merchant vessels. Its job was to build a "bridge of ships" across the Atlantic Ocean to deliver munitions and supplies to the US troops in Europe.

By the time *Lake Frohna* was completed in 1919, however, the Great War was over (the Armistice was signed on November 11, 1918). Apparently the USSB had the Laker on a trans-Atlantic run for a short time but then, in 1924, *Lake Frohna* and three other surplus cargo ships were purchased from the USSB by Alexander McDougall of the Minnesota Atlantic Transit Co. in Duluth, Minnesota. *Lake Frohna* was renamed *Ace* while the other three were renamed *King*, *Queen* and *Jack*, and the four ships became known as the "Poker Fleet." They were operated between the Lakehead at Duluth and Buffalo, Ohio, on Lake Erie

Brig. Gen. M.G. Zalinski is shown here as a US Army Transport Service vessel, probably at Seattle's Port of Embarkation during the war. According to crewman Archie McLaren, the former Great Lakes freighter, formerly *Ace*, was well suited to her role hauling supplies to Alaska, being highly manoeuvrable. PUGET SOUND MARITIME HISTORICAL SOCIETY 1050-1

carrying package freight—any freight that was sacked, bagged, bundled or cased—as well as other general merchandise and assembled goods. However, the Poker Fleet became best known for hauling automobiles by the thousands throughout the 1920s, and the freighters were often seen departing Detroit, Michigan, with deckloads of shiny new Ford Model Ts. The package freight industry itself went into a slow decline and finally disappeared during the Second World War when traffic on the Great Lakes began to carry bulk materials.

With the US about to enter WW II late in 1941, *Ace* was purchased by the US Army in September of that year and, after requisitioning by the Quartermaster Corps, the ship was renamed US Army Transport (USAT) *Brigadier General M.G. Zalinski* and transferred to Seattle. The old Laker was used throughout the war primarily for transporting supplies to Alaska. *Zalinski* remained on this Alaska run right up until the night it was lost.

The Puget Sound Pilots' movement cards revealed that *Brig. Gen. M.G. Zalinski* was assigned late in September 1946 to carry perishables to Alaska because a strike was tying up Puget Sound ports at the time. The ship was destined for Whittier with 1,115 tons of meat, fresh fruit and vegetables in its refrigerated holds and 778 tons of general cargo aboard, including household goods for military personnel.

In the March 1988 issue of *Sea Chest: The Journal of the Puget Sound Maritime Historical Society*, Archie K. McLaren, an officer on *Brig. Gen. M.G. Zalinski*, related his first-hand account of the ship's loss. He began by pointing out that *Zalinski*, as a former Laker, ". . . was considered very adaptable to the Alaskan trade as it was only 260 feet long and easy to maneuver in restricted areas."

McLaren recalled that on previous voyages *Zalinski* had usually called at Seward in order to discharge cargo to railcars destined for Anchorage, but that on the final voyage the ship was bound for Whittier, closer to Anchorage. The ship left Seattle in the early morning of September 26, and McLaren described the rain that night as ". . . so heavy that one could not distinguish rain drops falling. It was more like a wall . . ." To make matters worse, only one of the ship's two pilots had boarded in Seattle, a Captain Thorvick who ". . . was well past 70 years of age . . ." and who, the crew soon realized, was also past his professional prime. As McLaren described it, from the moment of departure from Seattle, the voyage seemed to be jinxed and ". . . there was only one kind of weather . . . BAD!"

Brig. Gen. M.G. Zalinski was not equipped with radar and was attempting to navigate the Inside Passage the old-fashioned way—by bouncing the ship's whistle-blasts off the shore and measuring the elapsed time for the returning echo to determine distance from land. "To this day, I can recall the gaunt

The *Lake Frohna* became the *Ace* as part of the Minnesota-Atlantic Transit Company's "Poker Fleet." The *Ace*, *King*, *Queen* and *Jack*—while primarily occupied transporting packaged freight around the Great Lakes—were best known for hauling automobiles out of Detroit. LAKE SUPERIOR MARITIME COLLECTIONS, UNIVERSITY OF WISCONSIN-SUPERIOR
MCK #15389

face of Captain Thorvick after two days or more standing watch . . . around the clock," McLaren remembered in his account.

The ship dropped anchor for a brief respite but Captain Joseph N. Zardis, impatient to be underway again before daylight, sent for Thorvick after only four or five hours of rest. The elderly pilot protested, noting that they were very close to Grenville Channel where it would be next to impossible to navigate with the heavy rain muffling all sound, but the captain ignored him. As he listened to the rumble of the anchor windlass Archie McLaren was certain that the ship wasn't going to get through the night without eventually hitting one side of the channel or the other.

On Monday, September 30, the *Prince Rupert Daily News* reported that *Brig. Gen. M.G. Zalinski* had ". . . gone aground and sunk by the bow within minutes early Sunday morning. Running (full speed) parallel to the shore, she grounded on rocks, crumpling her steel plates amidships like paper and opening a hole through which the water poured rapidly. The veteran transport sank 25 minutes later . . . without even the final salute of exploding boilers."

All 48 of *Zalinski*'s crew and a red setter, which was being shipped to Lieut. Col. G.E. Dawson of Anchorage, were able to get away in the two port-side lifeboats. Drifting in the channel, they watched their ship slowly settle into the sea. Two or three hours later they were picked up by the fish packer *Sally N* and were taken to the Canadian Fishing Company's cannery at Butedale, and then to Prince Rupert aboard the Union Steamship's *Catala*.

In Prince Rupert, winch operator Bernard Boersema told a reporter, "Driving rain made it so black we couldn't even see the bow when we struck. The force of the collision broke No. 1 and No. 2 holds clear open—a tear about 40 feet long. When the mate asked me to sound the bilge in the two holds there were already seven feet of water in No. 1 and more rushing in like fury." Boersema was told to forget about sounding No. 2 hold and to head for a lifeboat.

With Captain Zardis apparently in a state of shock it fell upon Archie McLaren to contact the Seattle Port of Embarkation by radiophone and make a report. When asked whether it was possible to salvage the ship, McLaren replied, "Sure, if you know of a company that could pull it off in some 400 to 500 feet of water."

Brig. Gen. M.G. Zalinski remained forgotten on the sea bottom off Pitt Island for 60 years. Then, on May 11, 2006, the ship was back in the news once again. The *Vancouver Sun* reported that, "The Canadian government—fearing a 700-tonne oil spill and even a massive underwater explosion—is seeking international help to deal with a bomb-laden, oil-leaking American army transport vessel . . ." Apparently Canadian Coast Guard officials were alerted in 2003 when an extensive oily sheen was spotted on the surface of Grenville Channel near the wreck site. Twice divers were sent down to seal the leaks but no further work was carried out because of concern about the unexploded ordinance believed to include a dozen approximately 500-pound aerial bombs, as well as .30 and .50 calibre ammunition.

While the depth in Grenville Channel is approximately 300 feet, the wreck came to rest on a ledge only about 100 feet below the surface, depending on the tide height. A warning was issued in January 2004 ordering mariners to avoid anchoring or fishing within 650 feet of the wreck. One of the fears was that the ship was well within reach of recreational divers. There was also concern expressed for the numerous cruise ships that pass through Grenville Channel, sometimes only about 300 feet from the hazardous wreck's location.

Chapter 19

A Stranding on Porter Reef: The Loss of the *North Sea,* 1947

As *North Sea*, an American cargo and passenger steamer, made its way south across Milbanke Sound in the early evening of February 13, 1947, it was raining so hard that the lights at both Susan and Vancouver Rocks were obscured. A 30-knot southeaster was blowing on the starboard beam and the seas were choppy. As she turned into Seaforth Channel, the Ivory Island and then Idol Point lights were momentarily visible but then vanished from sight in the rainy haze.

Finally, at 21:43 hours and travelling at full speed under the command of Captain Charles C. Graham, *North Sea* slammed into Porter Reef on the north shore of Seaforth Channel and came to a stop with a

The passenger and freight steamer *North Sea* was on a regular run from Puget Sound to Alaska in the late 1930s, with voyages usually terminating at the historic city of Sitka. To the great interest of the tourists aboard, the *North Sea* also stopped at cannery ports during the summer salmon season. On one trip the ship returned to Seattle with 56,000 cases aboard, along with her full passenger list. VANCOUVER MARITIME MUSEUM PR 3476

crashing jolt. Bilges were sounded immediately and, when it was discovered that #1 starboard was taking on water fast and #2 hold, which contained ice boxes, was flooded up to the 'tween decks with water still pouring in, an SOS was immediately transmitted. As well as 60 crew and 85 passengers, there were some 167 tons of frozen fish, 50 tons of general cargo and 70 tons of baggage aboard.

North Sea had departed Seattle on January 29, 1947, with a full load of cargo and passengers aboard. A northerly gale with blizzard conditions had buffeted the ship as it progressed north up Lynn Canal, and it was necessary to break ice through the narrow channels leading to Sitka. On the return trip south the weather finally warmed up but it began to rain hard once *North Sea* left Ketchikan, and the rain persisted all the way to Milbanke Sound and into Seaforth Channel where *North Sea* ran up onto Porter Reef.

At the time of the stranding the 1,903-ton, 299-foot *North Sea* was nearly 30 years old. She was originally launched in 1918 as the standard three-island type steel freighter *Plainfield* by S. Moore & Sons Shipbuilding Co. in Elizabethport, New Jersey. During the First World War the ship was under the control of the United States Shipping Board, but whether *Plainfield* went into lay-up after the war with hundreds of other American freighters is unknown at the time of writing. It is known that the vessel entered commercial service when the Baltimore and Carolina Steamship Co. purchased two Shipping Board vessels, *Tipton* and *Plainfield*, in 1922, renamed them *Esther Weems* and *Mary Weems* respectively and converted them into passenger vessels for service on a Baltimore–Charleston–Miami run.

Around 1927 both ships were sold to the Pacific Steamship Company of Seattle. *Esther Weems* became *Admiral Benson* and *Mary Weems* was named *Admiral Peoples*. The latter ship was soon recognized as one of the line's finest, with her private bathrooms, shower and toilet facilities. Clinton H. Betz, in his history of the Pacific Steamship Company in the September 1990 issue of *Sea Chest: The Journal of the Puget Sound Maritime Historical Society*, commented, "The ships were far from being graceful or good-looking vessels, possessing no rake or sheer and with straight up-and-down masts and funnels. Clearly noticeable was their origin as freighters. They were rated as 'fair' passenger ships."

By early 1930 *Admiral Peoples* was on a California–Puget Sound route and in 1934 she was sold to the Northland Transportation Company of Seattle and refurbished to carry 500 tons of cold storage cargo. Renamed *North Sea*, the passenger and freight liner was placed on the Puget Sound to Southeast Alaska run. For the duration of the Second World War the Northland Transportation fleet was under the control of the War Services Administration, but with the return of peace in 1945 the ships were released back to Northland. With her machinery overhauled and accommodations refurbished to passenger-liner standards, *North Sea* was returned to the Alaska run.

As it happened, on the night of her mishap BC Packers' herring fleet was tied up at Bella Bella waiting out the foul weather and, upon hearing *North Sea*'s distress signal, some of the larger boats (*North Isle*, *Bernice L*, *Cape Henry*, *Three Aces*, *Nishga* and *Otter Bay*) raced to the scene. Between 0015 and 0100 hours a rescue fleet composed of fish boats, tugboats and a Fisheries patrol boat evacuated all 85 passengers and most of the crew and returned them to Bella Bella. (The corpse that was being shipped south and reposed in the baggage locker wasn't to be "rescued" until two days later.) A day later, the southbound Canadian National steamer *Prince Rupert* stopped at Bella Bella, picked up the passengers and crew and took them to Vancouver. The *Prince Rupert* reported that she had just gone through "the worst storm in her history."

Meanwhile the stricken *North Sea* was starting to pound while water rapidly filled her engine room and holds. As the tug *La Garde* stood by, the tug *La Pointe* held a line secure on *North Sea*'s bow while anchors were put out in case the ship showed signs of shifting on the reef. The pumps on board were activated and additional pumps arrived with the Pacific Salvage Company's *Salvage Chieftain* on February 16. Efforts to

Loaded with tons of fish that soon began to decompose, the stranded *North Sea* became home to hordes of rats that descended into the holds to eat their fill each time the tide receded, as Syd Woodside, the customs superintendent in Prince Rupert, was to discover. VANCOUVER MARITIME MUSEUM

wrest the *North Sea* free on the high tides proved futile. Also, as recorded in Chief Officer Frank Huxtable's report: ". . . Strict Watch was kept to protect ship's property from salvage crew . . ."

He noted further on February 28, ". . . Rechecked all rooms and crew's quarters and found several doors unlocked and rooms broken into . . . 4:00 p.m. found Chief Engineer's room broken into and several items missing. Reported to salvage boss and Canadian Customs."

On March 5, tugs *Salvage Chieftain* and *J.R. Morgan* made fast to *North Sea*'s stern and made several attempts to pull the ship off Porter Reef. On the third try *North Sea* began to pound heavily in the seas, and finally rolled 40 degrees to port, which dislodged the foremast. Then, at 1600 hours, loud cracking noises were heard. At this point all pumping was stopped as it was feared *North Sea* was about to break in two. Two hours later the salvage superintendent reported that the fire-room bulkhead had been carried away and a 40-foot crack had appeared along the port side. At this point, he declared the vessel a total constructive loss. On March 7, the ship's owner ordered the ship abandoned.

The Coast Guard investigation concluded on March 20, and Captain George Hansen, the pilot, was cleared of the charge of "inattention to duty." *North Sea* was insured for $500,000 at the time of loss. Stores and other items aboard the derelict steamship were soon looted, while the hull itself was sold to BC interests who stripped the wreck of its winches, all moveable machinery, lifeboats etc., as well as anything of value from the passenger accommodations. What remained of the steamship was sold to an Oceans Falls agent for a Victoria scrap firm.

Later in the summer of 1947 Syd Woodside, customs superintendent in Prince Rupert, went on board *North Sea* and discovered swarms of rats as the sole occupants. Apparently, they were descending into the holds at low tide to take their fill of the 15 car loads of rotten fish and then making their way topsides again on the incoming tide. "I had thousands of them watching the last time I was on board," Woodside said. "It was an eerie experience."

Campbell River resident Bob Logan, who happened to live at Shearwater from 1947 to 1950, thinks the Ocean Falls agent who acquired the salvage rights to *North Sea* was named Harold Hunter. He was also told that it was Andy Carrie of Oceans Falls who took Hunter out to *North Sea* with his tug *Bonnie Belle* to take a look at the propeller. Carrie thought he could position a barge directly behind *North Sea* and, once they had removed the propeller nut and rudder, blow the propeller directly off onto the barge. Logan figured they were successful since Carrie returned from the adventure with the propeller on board the barge.

Once Hunter had finished salvaging what he wanted, he turned over the rights to Andy Widsten of Widsten and Logan Marine. They went alongside the derelict with a 56-foot landing barge and some salvage gear two or three times over the next couple of years and managed to retrieve lengths of cable and deck-benches, which they used around Shearwater until they finally rotted out. They also recovered the ship's gangplank, which was used for many years as a Shearwater wharf ramp. In his Letter to the Editor in the July 2009 *Western Mariner,* Logan noted that when they were aboard *North Sea* salvaging what they could, they never saw any rats.

North Sea stood out on Porter Reef as a sentinel to passing ships for years afterward. When passing the wreck at night the CPR coast steamers would floodlight the remains of the forlorn steamer for the benefit of their passengers but, by 1963, time, tide and weather had taken their toll and *North Sea* collapsed and disappeared beneath the waves.

UASBC diver Sheldon Boyd explores the wreck of the *North Sea* in the waters close to Porter Reef. JACQUES MARC PHOTO

Chapter 20

Coastal Treasures: Fred Rogers, BC's "Wreck Diver Emeritus," 2008

When Fred Rogers slipped into the turbulent waters of Porlier Pass, the narrow tidal passage between Valdez and Galiano Islands in BC's Georgia Strait, he was in for a shock. "The force of the tide was alarming, holding us out on a horizontal plane like a flag on a pole," he describes in his book *Shipwrecks of British Columbia*. Even worse than that, Fred recalled, ". . . any attempt at turning our head sideways to the current was trouble; it would tear away your face-mask or mouth-piece."

It was Easter 1955 and Rogers was making his very first wreck dive with buddy Pat Moloney. Their target was the steam tug *Point Grey*, which had struck a reef and sunk in Porlier Pass in February 1949. The wreck, shuddering in the tide and appearing as if it might topple off the reef at any time, held Rogers in awe of its violent beauty. Even now, more than 50 years later, he still defines his *Point Grey* experience as, "The one that opened my eyes; we were now addicts for more adventure."

The hunt for shipwrecks became an obsession that was to take Rogers along most of BC's heavily convoluted coastline. When asked how many wrecks he actually dove on over his career, he simply points to the bookshelves loaded with his logbooks and glibly says, "It's all up there if you want to count 'em!" Still, even without an accurate tally of his efforts, Rogers was always aware of the significance of what he was doing and kept meticulous records. When he hung up his tank and flippers for good, he sat down and published all his West Coast diving endeavours in three books.

Fred Rogers' lifelong curiosity about the mysterious world beneath the ocean's surface started at an early age. When he was growing up in the Grandview district of Vancouver in the 1930s he would often take the streetcar down to Stanley Park to fish for bullheads. There Fred observed his first real divers. They were laying a high-pressure water line across First Narrows. As he watched, fascinated with the hard-hat divers, it occurred to young Fred that there was far more on this earth than just the terrestrial world he inhabited.

The 15-year-old caused quite a sensation when he arrived at Stanley Park with his own homemade diving helmet. He had scrutinized photos of the internationally renowned diver William Beebe and realized that his dive helmet looked quite similar to the top of a galvanized hot water tank, so the teenager cut the top off a discarded water tank to fashion his own helmet. To make it more comfortable he wrapped a section of garden hose around the edge as a seal and had his dad cut a square for a viewing glass. Then

Fred Rogers purchased his first dry suit, mask and snorkel in the mid-1950s and saved money by making his own compressed air tank from a fire extinguisher. Diving soon became an important part of his life. FRED ROGERS COLLECTION

Fred proceeded to wade into Burrard Inlet up to his neck. But he slipped on a rock, fell over, and his home-built hard hat instantly flooded with water. Diving was suddenly a less appealing pursuit. Fred decided to postpone his sub-sea experiments until some future time.

It was well into the 1950s when Rogers, again eager to see beneath the sea, purchased his first dry suit, fins, mask and snorkel in Seattle. It was an early Bell Aqua dry suit made of a very thin rubber that was easily punctured by barnacles. To save a few bucks he made his own weight belt and compressed air tank. The belt was straightforward, but the tank? His solution was a $5 fire extinguisher from the local junkyard. Once he had the gear and had taught himself how to dive, Rogers started picking up small jobs, such as clearing cable or rope caught in the props of towboats to supplement the family income. Following a wartime stint in the Royal Canadian Navy, he had found full-time work as a welder and pipefitter, so diving was still primarily a hobby that he had to schedule time for on weekends and holidays.

Then Pat Moloney got Rogers interested in hunting for shipwrecks. Moloney had begun compiling an inventory of wrecks from the Vancouver Pilotage office and Fred was amazed at the staggering number of vessels that had been lost along the BC coastline over the previous century. The wreck diving would obviously require a very systematic approach. The two divers began by exploring the waters around Vancouver. Off Prospect Point in Stanley Park (where the teenaged Rogers had donned his first homemade diving gear) Rogers and three other divers were the first, in September 1960, to see the remains of one of the most famous ships on Canada's West Coast, the Hudson's Bay Company's SS *Beaver*. She had grounded there in 1888 and, four years later, the wake from the side-wheeler *Yosemite* had swept her off the rocks into deep water.

When they finished exploring local Lower Mainland waters and were ready to work further afield, Rogers and his diving partner Ed Seaton built themselves a 35-foot steel boat to take them upcoast in the winter of 1961–62. The following summer, their first major excursion would be to the wreck of *Themis* near Scarlett Point lighthouse off the northern end of Vancouver Island.

Aware that they were probably the first ever to see the wreck, the two divers were dazzled by what they found. "It was a mass of colour with its profusion of sea life," recalled Fred. "Then, as we moved along the side, a towering shadow confronted us through the disintegrated hull plating—the huge triple expansion

When they had finished exploring local Lower Mainland waters and were ready to work further afield, Fred Rogers and his diving partner, Eddie Seaton, built themselves this 35-foot steel boat in the winter of 1961–62 to take them upcoast. Here, Seaton is pictured alongside the wreck of the *Drumrock* in Takush Harbour. FRED ROGERS COLLECTION

steam engine, leaning as if about to fall over." While finding and exploring shipwrecks certainly had its romantic appeal and adventure, Rogers soon learned that it also had extreme hazards.

In the summer of 1964 Rogers, with his son Glenn and Ed Seaton, took their dive boat about 350 miles up the Inside Passage past Bella Bella to where the former freight and passenger steamship *Ohio* had been run ashore in Carter Bay in August 1909 after hitting a rock at Steep Point in Heikish Narrows. For a week the wreck divers gradually worked their way into the dark bowels of the *Ohio*, overwhelmed by all they found. One of the most unusual and puzzling relics was a large white bathtub containing hundreds of bottles with some of the necks protruding out of the black muck that permeated the wreck. Some of the bottles were still sealed with their corks and later Rogers and Seaton sampled a couple. It was hard to determine the type of the 55-year-old liquor but Rogers recalls it was likely cognac or scotch, was definitely overproof and really "hit the spot!"

Exploration deep inside the decaying wreck of *Ohio* required lights, as the slightest touch would dislodge material and stir the water into inky blackness. It was during one of their final dives that Rogers learned the hard way how dangerous wreck diving could be. Forty-five years later he remembers his "mighty close call" vividly. He was three decks down in the total darkness of one of *Ohio*'s holds and, in hindsight,

Built as a trans-Atlantic steamer in 1872, the *Ohio* sailed for Seattle in 1898 to take part in the Klondike gold rush. She remained operating on runs from Seattle north to Alaska right up until her loss in August 1909. She is pictured here at the coal bunkers in Nanaimo before steaming northward. VANCOUVER MARITIME MUSEUM PR 3521

Rogers and Seaton explore the bow of the *Ohio*. It was here that Rogers had a "mighty close call" after being far too eager to get at the treasures in a storeroom three decks down. After losing his lifeline, and in total darkness, he was down to the last breath of air in his tank and barely made it back to the surface. FRED ROGERS COLLECTION

far too eager to get to the treasures in a storeroom—brass navigation lamps, lanterns, chandeliers and "other fancy stuff." It almost cost him his life.

Rogers had taken a night-light diver's lamp with him but, not totally trusting the light, he had also tied a line to the dive boat. Trailing the line out behind so he could follow it back out, he proceeded down into the ship's holds. When he reached the storeroom he temporarily tied the line to a pipe, but the pipe broke away and disappeared—with the line—into the blackness. As he groped around with his light trying to find his lifeline, Fred was keenly aware that his air supply was getting dangerously low and he was fast running out of time. He abandoned the search for the line and concentrated on trying to locate the door through which he'd entered the storeroom. Fighting off panic Rogers felt for the hull structure around him. The layout of deck beams enabled him to partially orient himself and, using his light up close, he was able to make his way along the hull plating toward what he hoped was the entrance. Fortunately he calculated correctly and was able to escape the hold and head for a dim light in the murky distance. By this time his tank was providing its last puff of air and Fred was barely able to make it to the surface.

Regardless of this near-death experience, Rogers and Seaton continued wreck diving until 1972 when they finally decided they'd had enough, sold their boat and parted ways. In just over 15 years, during any spare time they could find together, the two scuba divers had accomplished an incredible feat. They had explored much of Canada's underwater West Coast, from southern Vancouver Island to as far north as the Alaskan border, in their search for shipwrecks. The pair accumulated so much data that, along with his detailed wreck charts, Fred Rogers was able to fill three books. The first, *Shipwrecks of British Columbia* published in 1973, was updated 20 years later with *More Shipwrecks of British Columbia*. In 2004, well into his eighties, Fred published yet another book, *Historic Divers of British Columbia*, the culmination of 50 years of research on the subject.

Even when he was well into his late eighties Fred Rogers still had projects on the go. Here he is in 2008 with one of a number of model steam engines he has built. JACQUES MARC PHOTO

Because of Rogers' meticulous work mapping and documenting BC's countless shipwrecks, the on-going research projects carried out by the Underwater Archaeological Society of BC always commences with a phone call to the society's "diver emeritus" at his Qualicum Beach home. No use going over old ground, as chances are Fred Rogers has already "been there, done that."

Chapter 21

That Old Easthope Down on the Tideflats: Keeping the Easthope Engine History Alive, 2009

Ask any old-timer down on the dock what he considers to be the most famous West Coast marine engine from the first half of the twentieth century and chances are he'll reply, "Easthope." Heavy-duty, slow-turning and easy to repair, Easthopes proved a natural fit for the hundreds of "misery stick"-propelled (powered by oars) fish boats. They also happened to be the first gasoline engine to be manufactured in Vancouver, BC.

While the hundreds of Easthopes may have been the power plants of choice for the small boat fleet 75 years ago, now the only place you might come across one of these engines is in a small handful of classic craft, in a private collection or perhaps in the bilge of a long-abandoned gillnetter beached in a backwater next to an upcoast village. As artifacts from a bygone era, many of these cast-iron engines are long past any hope of restoration, and anyone who stumbles across one is often left guessing about its early history.

Today it's possible, thanks to the efforts of Joe Holmes of Richmond, to determine not only when a particular Easthope was built but also who it was originally manufactured for. It's a simple matter of retrieving the details from the engine's brass serial-number plate. Holmes was fortunate to acquire the old company records that allow him to identify each and every Easthope. Around 25 years ago he was looking for parts to keep some old Easthopes running and got in touch with Bill Easthope. Word had it that Bill had a lot of old inventory stored around his White Rock property. Once the two men realized they shared a common interest, they began buying and trading parts.

Bill Easthope happens to be the great-grandson of Ernest Easthope who, along with his sons Vincent and Ernest Junior, founded Easthope & Sons in Vancouver in the early 1900s. (Government records reveal that the partnership was formally declared on February 13, 1906.) After they sold the company and it subsequently failed, Easthope family history has it that two Easthope brothers, Percy (Peck) and Ernest Jr. (Vincent had died in 1907) bought back the name. They started up the company again in 1909 as Easthope Brothers and began manufacturing four-cycle engines. (Ernest Easthope, Jr. made a Declaration of Partnership for Easthope Brothers on February 23, 1909, as ". . . the only member of the said firm.") Their brother, George Sr., apparently joined them soon afterward.

They operated out of an Easthope Bros. shop on West Georgia Street by Coal Harbour until it closed in 1951. At that time, the whole operation was moved out to the Easthope Sales and Service outlet in Steveston, which Bill's uncle, George Easthope Jr., had opened in about 1930. (Easthope Bros. Ltd. also happened to be incorporated at this time.) Then, in 1978, when both Bill's father Gene (who had been out at Steveston since 1942) and his brother George Jr. decided they wanted to retire, the entire family-owned and operated company was sold to Ron Dodd of Richmond Machine Works on No. 2 Road in Richmond and the company name was changed to Ebros Holdings.

Now living in 100 Mile House, Bill notes that while the last Easthope gasoline engine was manufactured in 1950, the company continued manufacturing commercial fishing equipment, such as the Easthope trolling gurdies and drum-drives, for a few more years out at Steveston. Bill was working there (primarily making and repairing gurdies) when he and Dodd decided to try re-manufacturing two of the small gasoline engines (the 4–6 horsepower single cylinder and the 8–14 horsepower, single-casting twin cylinder) on their own. While they were initially encouraged by the interest in Easthope engines still out there in the fishing and pleasure boating fraternities they had to abandon

This is one of the few operating Easthopes left on the coast—Al Mason's 10–18 Easthope engine in his gill-netter, *Eva*, built by the Suzuki shipyard on Annacis Island in 1937. The present two-cylinder 10–18 engine replaced the original single-cylinder Easthope in the 1950s so that the boat could highball up to Rivers Inlet and elsewhere on the coast. ULRICH GAEDE PHOTO

the venture after a couple of years when the costs of manufacturing were found to exceed the retail prices.

The Steveston Sales and Service outlet ran into financial trouble in the 1980s and it all came to an end on July 31, 1987, when the company closed and the machinery and buildings were sold. As a result, a lot of what was left of the Easthope parts inventory ended up in the dumpster. Bill saved what he could but Joe says most of the "good stuff" is long gone.

Eventually, in the late 1980s, Bill told Joe (who had been buying parts from him for years), "You know, you're my best customer. Why don't you just buy everything that's left. I'm tired of this!" Bill insisted Joe take all the engine patterns too, along with most of the rest of the stuff he'd saved. Joe was reluctant at first to take the historic patterns due to the amount of care and storage he figured they'd require for proper preservation but he finally agreed to it. Bill Easthope did keep some choice parts and engines for himself, though, such as one of the only 12 "new-style" 8–14 hp engines (serial #81:5695, manufactured in 1981 and sold to D. Smith of Vancouver) and a 5–7 hp (#ZA5283, produced July 7,1948, and sold to R.M. Rasmussen of Port Hammond, BC) that he had restored for his father. (The "new style" engines came with enclosed valve rockers and push rods.)

The *Eva's* brass engine plate confirms it as a two cylinder 10–18 Easthope. Bill Easthope says that the best way to imitate an Easthope running is to repeat "two bits, two bits, two bits . . ." To watch and actually listen to the distinctive sounds of the *Eva* and her Easthope, enter "Easthope engine running in *Eva*" into your web browser to see the videos filmed by Finn Slough photographer Ulrich Gaede. ULRICH GAEDE PHOTO

When Bill showed him all the old company ledgers, however, Joe got really excited and he was quick to let Bill know he'd love access to the records so he could enter all the original engine and owner details into a registry on his computer. The surviving company records and patterns went all the way back to 1911 but not to the early years when the Easthope company first started out building two-cycle engines. (Joe says he has only ever seen one of these early Easthopes "in the flesh"—it was rusting away in a field.) In the end, because of the difficulty of deciphering some of the entries in the old handwritten ledgers, it took a year to painstakingly enter all the information into a computer database.

Also in the collection were the original notebooks the engine assemblers and mechanics kept in their pockets for ongoing records of each job. Even if they just tweaked an engine a little, an entry would be made in the greasy, handwritten pages. Holmes observed that the company also maintained books that kept tabs on their clientele. "They had a lot of agents and repeat customers and they would grade these guys—A, B, C, D, you know." It was a great way to keep track of who was reliable and easy to deal with and, more importantly, who was trouble or a deadbeat and rated a "D."

Joe Holmes encourages people to send him the serial numbers of Easthopes they've come across or own as collector's pieces so he can provide them with the engine's background. Every time he learns about another old Easthope still out there he adds it to the registry, but he's adamant about one thing. "I don't need any more engines! I'd just like to know what's still out there—what's alive and what's not."

If you happen to own, or know of, an old Easthope and you'd like to learn its history, contact Joe at 604-649-1270 or email him at joeholmes@shaw.ca. Joe is also an active participant on the online Old Marine Engine Discussion Board at: www.oldmarineengine.com where he answers questions on Easthope engines posted to the site.

This 15–18 Easthope is seen at George Sawchuk's Fanny Bay property on the east coast of Vancouver Island. Sawchuk paid Fanny Bay boatbuilder Martin North $100 for the engine "years ago." From the serial number (VA 4848) on the engine plaque, Joe Holmes used the old Easthope records to identify the engine as a two-cylinder 15-hp (550 rpm) completed by Easthope engine fitter V. Easthope on September 4, 1945, for the Canadian Fishing Company. RICK JAMES PHOTO, 2008

Selected Sources & Reading

Oral History Tapes, Rick James Collection
Joe Quilty: September 1, 1996; Alan Heater: July 27, 1996; Fred Rogers: May 30, 2007.

Personal Communications
Janna Brown, Bob De Armond, Barrie McClung, Mike Burwell, Ronald A. Burke, Michael Mjelde, Barry Gough, Stanley Wardill, Ruth Masters, Ray Stockand, Bob Briggs, Newton Cameron, Fred Corneille, Norman Hacking, Glen Olson, Bill Franklin, Charles Nordin, Bob Logan, Jack Bruno, Frank Clapp, Art and Don Elworthy, Harold D. Huycke, John Henderson, Allan Heater, Joe Quilty, Mrs. R.W. Draney, Ronald A. Greene, Art Twigg, Bent Sivertz, Fred Rogers, Bill Easthope, Joe Holmes.

Unpublished Material
Vancouver and New Westminster Ship Registry volumes, Transport Canada. Burnaby, BC: Pacific Region Federal Records Centre, Library and Archives Canada.

Victoria Ship Registry volumes, Registry of Vessels, Transport Canada, Marine. Victoria: Transport Canada.

Vancouver Shipping Register (1890–1945). British Columbia Archives and Records Service, GR 1333, Canada, Marine Branch, reel B-2530.

Books
American Lloyd's Register of British and Foreign Shipping. American Shipmasters' Association. Available online annually to 1900. www.mysticseaport.org/library/initiative/VMSearch.cfm

Bureau of Navigation, Department of Commerce. *Merchant Vessels of the United States.* Washington, D.C.: Government Printing Office, annually.

Canada Department of Marine and Fisheries. *List of Shipping* ("Blue Book"). Ottawa: King's Printer, annually.

Canada Department of Transport. *List of Shipping* ("Blue Book"). Ottawa: Queen's Printer, annually.

E.W. Wright, ed. *Lewis & Dryden's Marine History of the Pacific Northwest.* Portland, Ore.: Lewis & Dryden Printing Co., 1895.

Gough, Barry. *Gunboat Frontier: British Maritime Authority & Northwest Coast Indians.* Vancouver: UBC Press, 1984, pp. 198–204.

Huycke, Harold D. *To Santa Rosalia Further and Back.* Newport News, Va.: The Mariner's Museum, 1970.

Lloyd's of London. *Lloyd's Register of British and Foreign Shipping.* London: Lloyd's of London, published annually since 1764.

Lubbock, Basil. *Last of the Windjammers: Volume I and II.* Glasgow: Brown, Son & Ferguson, Volume 1, 1927; Volume II, 1935.

Macpherson, Ken and John Burgess. *The Ships of Canada's Fighting Forces 1910–1993.* St. Catherine's, Ont: Vanwell Publishing, 1994.

Mitchell, W.H. and L.A. Sawyer. *British Standard Ships of World War I.* Liverpool: Sea Breezes, 1968, pp. 150–6.

Newell, Gordon, ed. *The H.W. McCurdy Marine History of the Pacific Northwest: 1895–1965.* Seattle: Superior Publishing, 1966.

Rogers, Fred. *Shipwrecks of British Columbia.* Vancouver: Douglas & MacIntyre, 1973.

Rogers, Fred. *More Shipwrecks of British Columbia.* Vancouver/Toronto: Douglas & MacIntyre, 1992.

Taylor, G.W. *Shipyards of British Columbia: The Principal Companies.* Victoria: Morriss Printing, 1986, pp. 84–93.

Twigg, Art. *Union Steamships Remembered 1920–1958.* Campbell River: A.M. Twigg, 1997.

Selected Journal and Newspaper Articles

John MacFarlane. "Capital Iron: Scrap Dealers in Lotus Land." *Resolution: Journal of the Maritime Museum of British Columbia*, 18 February 1990, pp. 4–8.

Clapp, Frank. "British Columbia's Early Log Barges: Beginning with British Pacific Transport Company Ltd in 1924," Part I & II. *The Sea Chest: Journal of the Puget Sound Maritime Historical Society*, vol. 34, no. 3–4, March–June 2001.

James, Rick. "*Geo. S. Wright*: Part I and II." *The Sea Chest: Journal of the Puget Sound Maritime Historical Society*, vol. 44, no. 2–3, March and June 2011.

Wells, R.E. "West Coast Barges," *Victoria Daily Colonist*, 27 February 1972, pp. 12–15.

Newspapers

19th-century US newspapers: www.infotrac.galegroup.com/itw/infomark
Puget Sound Daily Courier. 19, 26, 29 March 1873
Vancouver Daily World (1888–1924)
Vancouver Province (1898–)
Vancouver Sun (1912–)
Victoria Daily British Colonist (June 25 1866 – Dec 31 1886): www.britishcolonist.ca
Victoria Daily Colonist (Jan 1 1886–): www.britishcolonist.ca (1858–1910)
Victoria Daily Times (1884–)

Since this is no more than an abbreviated list, I highly recommend those looking for a more comprehensive bibliography to refer to the Underwater Archaeological Society of BC series of reports. In particular, *The Ghosts of Royston* (2004) and *Historic Shipwrecks of the Central Coast* (2010), where many of the stories in this volume were originally published in a more scholarly style and format. To order copies go to: www.uasbc.com.

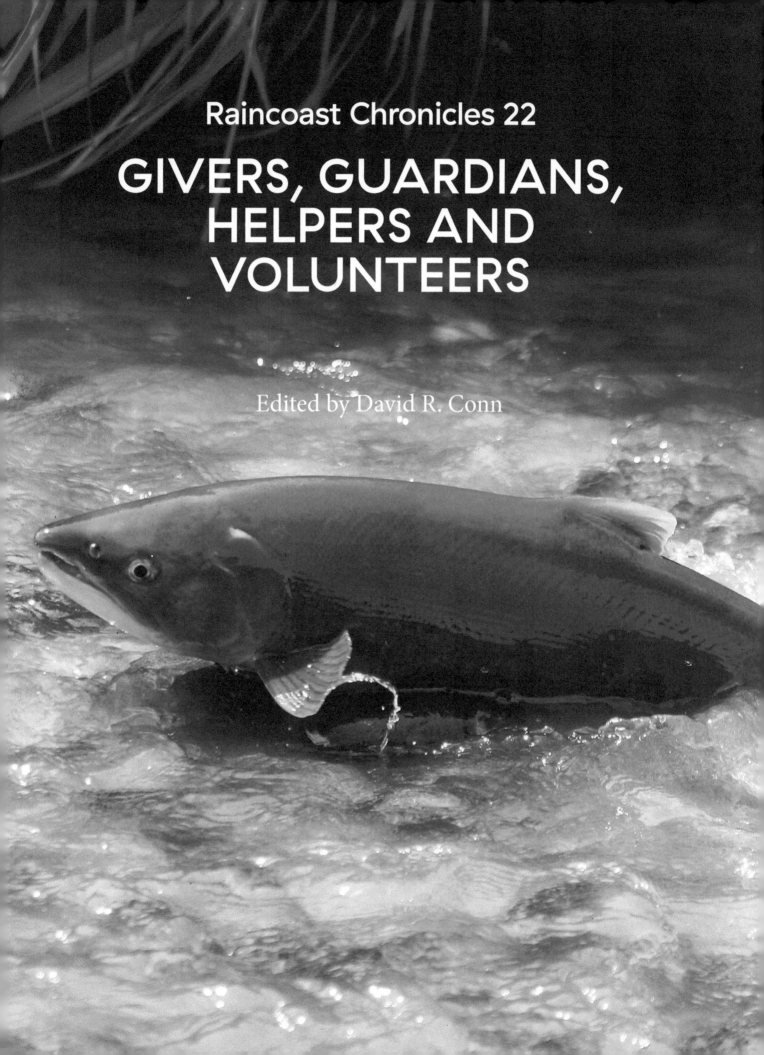

Raincoast Chronicles 22

GIVERS, GUARDIANS, HELPERS AND VOLUNTEERS

Edited by David R. Conn

HARBOUR PUBLISHING
INTRODUCTION

Back in 1977, when I was dedicated to writing poetry about Vancouver shipyards, Howard White of Harbour Publishing invited me to also produce some articles about the waterfront for Harbour's signature anthology, *Raincoast Chronicles*. I began by recording and editing memories of former Vivian Engine Works and Boeing Canada employees. I found that rewarding and have been writing articles ever since.

When I approached Harbour last year about writing more pieces for *Raincoast Chronicles*, I was offered the opportunity to guest edit an issue. We decided to highlight service people. Much of the economic activity in our region has been about the challenges and rewards of harvesting or processing its fabulous natural resources. At the same time, a human infrastructure has developed here, including what we now call armed forces, clergy, health care professionals, hospitality providers and transport workers. The toil of volunteers has also been important in many fields, such as conservation and recreation. This issue of *Raincoast Chronicles* collects nine service experiences that helped shape our coastal culture.

Tips by Harbour staff and my own network produced these diverse perspectives. Thanks to former magazine editors Alan Haig-Brown and Vickie Jensen, as well as writing mentors George McWhirter and Tom Wayman, for their suggestions and encouragement. I'm grateful to the writers, photographers and subjects for these efforts, and for their patience while I learned about producing an anthology of articles.

David R. Conn
Vancouver, BC

1

SINGING "THE SONG OF THE REDEEMED"
Creating Christians at the Chinese Rescue Home

by Stephen Ullstrom

The Chinese Rescue Home in Victoria, BC, later known as the Oriental Home and School, operated from 1886 to 1945, when it closed because of the Japanese evacuation during World War II, shifting priorities and lack of residents. Founded by John Endicott Gardiner, an American missionary and customs officer fluent in Cantonese from having grown up in China, the Home was originally intended to rescue Chinese prostitutes. Typically described as underage, these girls would have been brought to Canada by pimps, often under the guise of being someone's wife or child. Also rescued were women sold to be wives or domestic servants.

The first rescue was described this way: It came to Gardiner's knowledge that "a young girl only nine years of age had had her wrists broken, her back whipped until it ran sores and the sores irritated and burned with lighted tapers by an old hag of a procuress because the girl failed to bring in as much money by soliciting and prostituting herself as her procuress or keeper thought she should." And so, with the help of the chairman of the Police Committee, Gardiner rescued this and another girl.

The news spread among the prostitutes that salvation was at hand and word came that more of them wanted rescuing. Though the police chief refused to assist, Gardiner, with the help of sympathetic Chinese men, managed to spirit additional girls away. Suddenly finding himself, a single man, with an inappropriate number of female charges (not to mention not being a housekeeper), Gardiner rented a house, hired a matron and by the end of the first year had seven girls in residence ranging in age from eight to nineteen. At this point his friend, supporter and co-conspirator, the Reverend J.E. Starr, wrote to the Women's Missionary Society (WMS) of the Methodist Church of Canada asking for help.

Chinatown was a lively, exotic and at times forbidding place for the surrounding white population. Here, Chinese vendors have set up shop on Fisgard Street, a scene straight from China, in about 1898. Yet the West is trying to make itself known, as seen by the Methodist Chinese Mission building behind the vendors on the left.

City of Vancouver Archives, Str P351.1

The Home was often a lively place, with residents of all ages staying for different reasons. This group shot from 1902 shows the community at a point of transition, when rescue work was still important, but accepting women and children as boarders also became common. The matrons pictured are Kate Morgan (back left) and Ida Snyder (back right)— no-nonsense Canadian women who nevertheless dedicated themselves to their cross-cultural work.
United Church of Canada, BC Conference Archives. BCCA 13-24

Gardiner's actions were extremely controversial. Politically, the authorities tended to stay out of Chinese affairs, while also seeking to limit immigration based on fears that white jobs were being lost and western culture supplanted. Socially and religiously the rescues were lauded due to strong moral objections to the Chinese trade, as tersely represented by Mrs. Chapman, an upstanding citizen and secretary of the Home's first advisory committee: "This demoralizing traffic is like a leprosy that will contaminate our own white community if allowed to go unopposed." The reality, however, is that Asian prostitutes were a small minority (though perhaps more visible) compared to their white counterparts. The two ethnicities would often work together, servicing the same clients, and the types of prostitution ranged from the elite call girls to the survival sex workers on the street, as we see today.

The rescues were also controversial in the Chinese community, as these women and girls were significant investments for their owners. The Chinese had a centuries-old tradition of buying and selling women, as well as state-regulated prostitution, so the brazen kidnapping of their women by the nosy white Christian devils was almost beyond belief. Since snatching the girls back was difficult, the Chinese often resorted to the courts, even going as far in one case as the Supreme Court in Ottawa. Interestingly, the Chinese often won, though the WMS persevered. About one girl on whom $120 was spent in legal fees, Kate Morgan, the matron at the time, asked, "Can we estimate the value of one human soul in money? As we hear the house ring with the merry laughter of those rescued ones and see their bright

smiling faces, we feel, indeed, that God has used us in this work, and we believe that some day they will sing with us the song of the redeemed."

Still, the Chinese elite had their own reasons to be worried about prostitution. While it was regulated in China, on the wild West Coast it was controlled by gangs and secret societies. San Francisco had already suffered violent "tong wars" over the control of prostitution, gambling and opium. Hoping to avoid a similar fate, in 1884 a group of merchants formed the Chinese Consolidated Benevolent Association, the constitution of which included the stipulation that, "if a young girl has been kidnapped and brought to Canada, she must be surrendered to the association. The association will pay for her fare back to Tung Wah Hospital in Hong Kong and notify her relatives to take her home. If she does not have relatives, the Tung Wah Hospital will arrange . . . adoption." This did not cover all instances of the buying and selling of women, but it was an attempt to end the worst abuses.

As for servants and wives who had been bought, the WMS admitted that "many of these girls are quite as well cared for, if not better treated, than many domestics in European homes," and so these, except for evangelistic attempts, were left alone. As the missionaries realized, "it is useless to attempt rescue until the girls themselves wish for it."

The back view of Chinese houses along lower Cormorant Street (now Pandora Avenue) that impoverished Chinese labourers, predominantly male, would squeeze into for accommodation. This photograph, taken in 1886 by Édouard Deville, partially explains the negative impressions the white community had of the Chinese, compared to the western ideals of space, privacy and sanitation.
Image B-06853 courtesy Royal BC Museum, BC Archives

The interior of a Chinese joss house, or temple, in Victoria. It was not just prostitution that the Home and the Methodists wanted to uproot, but also the "heathen superstitions" of Confucianism, Buddhism and Taoism, which the missionaries held to be contrary to Christianity and western enlightenment.
Image D-05668 courtesy Royal BC Museum, BC Archives

But who were the members of the Women's Missionary Society, and why did they care? The WMS, founded in 1881, grew out of the Evangelical Protestant movement of that time to save the world by introducing Jesus Christ to all those who had not heard the salvific news. Later, in the beginning of the twentieth century, the focus for the Methodist and then United Church (in 1925 the Methodists merged with three other denominations to form the United Church) shifted toward social justice, with an emphasis on creating God's kingdom on earth.

The WMS's purpose was twofold: to financially support the missionary endeavours of the male-led General Board, and to recruit and support female missionaries and ministries for situations closed to men, such as immigrant women and children in Canada, or for gender-segregated societies such as China and Japan. In BC, the WMS first became involved with Thomas and Emma Crosby's ministry to Natives in Port Simpson, running a girl's home. Other Native work followed, as did missionary work in the mining communities of southeast BC. The WMS's takeover of the Rescue Home took place in 1888, as well as assisting with the adult night school started by Gardiner. A day school for children was added in 1896. The missionaries were also expected to visit the Asian communities up-island and in the Lower Mainland, and a permanent presence was eventually extended to Vancouver with the opening of a school and girl's home.

Yet evangelistic zeal was not the only driving force. The WMS was also a largely middle- and upper-class organization, based in Ontario and the Maritimes where Protestant Anglo-Saxon values were well established. It was believed that in order to maintain the strength of the nation, immigrants, whether from Asia or non-Protestant Europe, needed

Models of Methodist womanhood, and wives of prominent leaders in the community, (left to right) Mrs. W.H. Burkholder, Mrs. W.J. Pendray, Mrs. David Spencer, Mrs. Frank Adams and Mrs. E. Chapman served as the Chinese Rescue Home's first advisory committee.
United Church of Canada, BC Conference Archives. BCCA 13-39

to be assimilated. Thus, even in 1925, one missionary superintendent, N. Lascalles Ward of the Anglican Church, could write, "It is quite possible that in the future through the rising tide of colour, the 700,000,000 Asiatics will flood Western Canada. If they come as pagans, it will be the death to Western civilization, but if we do our part and christianize Asia and the Orientals now, we can trust God to over-rule any race war that may arise."

All of the women recruited by the WMS were single, as married women were expected to support their husbands. Also important was a strong sense of personal salvation, as well as a calling from God to be a missionary. For work in China and Japan, considered to be a more prestigious posting, as well as more physically demanding, the WMS tended to recruit professionals, such as doctors and teachers. Good health was also important, and preference was given to daughters of prominent Methodist leaders. In contrast, though cross-country domestic moves to the less civilized west would have been just as taxing, domestic missionaries were typically less educated and from lower classes.

For the Home, a job posting that included running a boarding home, engaging with different cultures and languages, possible court appearances, teaching academic subjects and homemaking skills, and conducting evangelistic visits in Chinatown, the WMS deemed that a middle-aged matron capable of exerting control was most desirable. None had university training. Instead, housekeeping, teaching or nursing experience was sought. Curiously, knowledge of Cantonese or Japanese seemed not to be a priority, though how many Canadian women would have had the opportunity or inclination to learn? Instead, the missionaries seemed to rely on translators as well as their own ability to teach English, though occasionally a missionary from China or Japan would be temporarily reassigned to help in Victoria.

The first matron was Annie Leake, a forty-eight-year-old Nova Scotian schoolteacher. Describing herself as "tired of the school room having had twenty-seven years of service, my heart turned to Mission Work of some kind." Through a friend she heard about the newly acquired Rescue Home, and, much to her surprise because the WMS typically favoured younger candidates, she was accepted.

Annie Leake ran the Home for five years, much of that time by herself, though she did convince a friend and a relative to join her at different times, and later a missionary from Japan, Martha Cartmell, was also sent to help. Her first decision, in January 1888, was to move the Home to Cormorant Street, on the edge of Chinatown, given that the original house was "in such a condition, and so poorly arraigned for our work," and to spend time and prayer soliciting better clothes and furniture. After all, "to civilize those girls we must live like civilized people, and to do so means some outlay." Leake then set about getting to know her charges despite the language barrier, protecting her charges from attempts to win or kidnap them back, as well as taking part in new rescues. Mr. Gardiner came weekly to preach in Cantonese, and, as part of her attempt to teach the girls to be "industrious and obedient"—prime Methodist values—Leake taught reading and writing, arithmetic, knitting and other household chores and skills.

One year later Leake was able to report that, following visits from a Chinese evangelist in Vancouver, most of the girls had requested baptism, which Leake believed to be genuine due to the "throwing off of old superstitions, doing willingly what before was a task [and] real delight in religious worship," as well as "the girls retiring at different times for private

The original house on Cormorant Street, in 1906, two years before a new facility was built on the same lot. Befitting the Home's desire to serve the Chinese community, the sign over the front door is in Chinese characters. Barbed wire topping the fence on the left can also be seen, the legacy of a decision by the advisory committee in 1898 to protect their charges by preventing escape.
United Church of Canada, BC Conference Archives. BCCA 13-28

prayer." Though eventually forced to resign because of undisclosed conflicts, Leake was able to write in her memoirs that "I consider those five years among the most remarkable & successful of my life's work . . . I had no more doubt of their conversions than I had of my own, and of my own I had full assurance." She also added, contrary to her first impressions, that her experience with the Chinese "led me to have a very deep and abiding interest and respect for the Chinese as a people and a nation. I felt often that we had many things we could learn from them to our profit." Yet, the work was still often fraught with misunderstandings and an inability to fully bridge the cultural divide. Martha Cartmell, for example, once suggested strong coffee for a woman struggling with tobacco, opium, alcohol and gambling addictions. Presumably, the cure failed.

As the Home became established, daily life was very much construed as home life. First on the daily agenda was morning worship. "Cleanliness and good conduct" were valued and taught, as were "all the ordinary [subjects] . . . and if some of the higher studies are ignored the more useful ones are substituted." In 1896 a separate day school was established, though still closely associated with the Home. At the request of parents, Chinese and Japanese languages were taught in addition to English. The older residents also did all of the chores and cooking under the supervision of the matron.

The matrons and other workers emphasized the freedom that the residents had to come and go, yet they were concerned about protecting their charges from former owners or others with dishonourable intentions. Imparting Christian and Anglo-Saxon values was also important. When possible, the Home did gain the legal guardianship of the children, and in 1898 the advisory committee passed a motion to install barbed wire on the fence, as well as more locks on the doors and windows, to prevent escape. The matrons were also not shy about expecting their rules to be followed. These strict measures seem to have been phased out in later years, however, once the need for rescue had passed.

The Home was also caught in the often fiercely contested debate over the desirability of Chinese immigration. Chinatown wasn't completely ghettoized, with Chinese servants and pedlars common throughout Victoria, and Caucasian gentlemen often enjoying a spot of entertainment by playing the lotteries in Chinese shops, yet politically the spectre of the Asian menace was frequently raised. This resulted in the Chinese head tax, followed by the Chinese Exclusion Act of 1923. While church leaders, at least tacitly, supported the government, the missionaries were much more outspoken in their defence of the Chinese people. As expressed by Miss Churchill, a teacher at the school, "time and time again the question has been put to me by visitors, "Do you really think these people can be Christianized?" My answer has been, undoubtedly, yes. More than that . . . the moral effect of Christian teaching is felt by the whole community." By remaining in Chinatown, the missionaries tried to serve as a bridge, a way for the Asian communities to integrate, while also educating and dispelling myths about the Chinese in the wider Canadian society.

In response to the discrimination, the Chinese became nationalistic, started promoting Confucianism over Christianity and founded their own schools and organizations. This did not seem to affect the attendance at the Home's day school—perhaps a reflection of the Home's reputation or of the increasing number of children in the community—though

Mr. and Mrs. Hamaguchi, newly married at the Home. Canada required mail-order brides to be married as soon as possible after arrival, and the Home proved to be a safe place for the brides to stay until the wedding could occur.

United Church of Canada, BC Conference Archives. BCCA 13-1

attendance at the Chinese church did plunge. What did change was the increase in Japanese women that the Home served, soon to form the bulk of the Home's work. In the early years, from roughly 1895 to 1906, it appears that Japanese prostitutes also stayed at the Home while transiting to the US. Some of these seemed willing to go, and the matrons were unable to convince them to stay, while others did seek protection from their "husbands." Later, the Home became a destination for mail-order brides, sent by immigration officials to await a Christian wedding as required by Canadian law. Between 1903 and 1915, for example, 697 weddings were recorded, with each couple being given a Japanese bible.

Rescue work gradually gave way to serving more as a boarding house, school, women's shelter and evangelistic centre, which was reflected in the name change in 1909 to the Oriental Home and School. Some women were brought by their husbands for shelter and safekeeping, as the husbands were in debt or needing to leave town to find work. For these, if the husband was financially able, the matrons would charge a boarding fee. Others were brought by their husbands so that they could learn English and housekeeping skills. Another time, a policeman brought three boys who had been found sleeping outside, while a new widow with two young children sought support until she could move on with her life. The missionaries also shifted from direct evangelism to organizing the existing Christians into various Sunday schools, auxiliaries and prayer meetings with the hope that these would encourage the Chinese and Japanese to engage in missionary work themselves.

The Home also celebrated what successes it could claim. The original goal, when Annie Leake first arrived, was to train the converted women as "bible women" who could be sent back to China as evangelists. It was soon realized, however, that most prostitutes and servants were of low class and would not be listened to. Also, most of the older women rescued proved resistant to or incapable of change, and did not stay long. Still seeking a positive impact, the goal was revised to impart the glories of Anglo-Saxon womanhood and then marry the women to upstanding Chinese Christian men so that the redeemed household

Children from the Oriental Home and School on a field trip to a Japanese warship in Esquimalt, 1915. With the head tax and then Chinese Exclusion Act, the Chinese population in Victoria declined, leading the Home to widen its focus to include the growing, and unimpeded, Japanese population.
United Church of Canada, BC Conference Archives. BCCA 13-14

could be a shining light for the surrounding community. Indeed, the first girl ever rescued apparently became the wife of one of the first Chinese pastors in BC, and "proved an efficient helper in missionary work as long as she lived." Still, training and marrying the girls and women didn't always prove so easy. Of two girls it was said, "we have many suitors . . . but find it very difficult to make a choice; and indeed we wish to keep them with us as long as possible, that they may be more settled in their habits." When marriage did happen there was still some ambivalence about the results, as reported in 1908: "The homes of our married girls present a striking contrast to the homes of the heathen Chinese . . . and although they do not come up to our standard, much to the annoyance and disappointment of our efficient and worthy matron, yet they compare favorably with the homes of the white people of the same class." The situation seemed to have improved four years later: "We consider it an encouraging fact that many of our Chinese families are moving out of Chinatown into nice roomy homes in good parts of the city, where their children have plenty of playground and fresh air. These homes are furnished in Canadian style, and we have been more than pleased to see how beautifully clean and orderly the women keep their houses, and how proud and happy they are to be in 'a real home.' Here they will have true home life, something which I fear is little known in the crowded apartments of Chinatown."

Some residents, though, especially those who came as children, did become missionary doctors, nurses and teachers in China, including Canada's first Chinese-Canadian nurse and female doctor. Victoria Cheung was the daughter of one of the first Chinese converts, and initially came to the Home for a short stay when her baby brother was born. Later she returned for her education, and then got a scholarship to study at the University of Toronto Medical School, where she became a doctor and went on to become the first female intern at Toronto General Hospital. She worked as a doctor in China for almost forty years, surviving the civil war, the Japanese occupation and the Great Leap Forward under the Communists, until her death in 1962. In contrast, Agnes Chan arrived as a slave girl. One of five daughters, she was sold three times, eventually being brought to Victoria where she escaped to the Home. After completing her education, and after borrowing money from the WMS to free her younger sister, who had also been sold, Agnes studied nursing at the Women's College Hospital in Toronto, graduating in 1923, about the same time as Victoria. Not as much is known about her career, but she also served at a Methodist hospital in China, and survived the civil war and Japanese occupation. Of those who did fulfill the original dream, it was written, "It is a wonderful encouragement to the workers here to see the girls, one by one, rising to their duty and responsibility and catching the vision of 'service.' It proves the worth-whileness of the work, for every one that thus 'passes on the Light' multiplies our work and influences and spreads it far beyond the boundaries of this immediate field."

The beginning of the end came as a shock with the evacuation of the Japanese in 1942, though this must have come somewhat as a relief too, as the Chinese and Japanese were increasingly antagonistic toward each other, reflecting the political realities in Asia. Of the Home's twenty-four residents, eighteen were Japanese. Since "eleven of the children were under twelve years of age," and "practically none of the children had mothers, and any fathers living had already been sent to road or labor camps," the WMS decided that Miss

Agnes Chan's 1923 graduation photo as Canada's first Chinese-Canadian nurse. A success story for the Rescue Home, Agnes fulfilled the Home's original vision of creating native Chinese evangelists by returning to China to serve in a Methodist hospital. *United Church of Canada, BC Conference Archives. BCCA 13-23*

ORIENTAL HOME and SCHOOL

Staff, residents, students and supporters gather in about 1938 for a group photo in front of the new building on Cormorant Street. They don't know it yet, but with the start of WWII and the evacuation of the Japanese, prominent in this picture, to the Interior, the Home will soon be closed.
United Church of Canada, BC Conference Archives. BCCA 13-23

Daniels and Miss Herbert, two of the workers at the Home, would evacuate with the girls to a WMS home in Assiniboia, Saskatchewan, which was apparently a dorm for high school girls. So, with "forty-one pieces of baggage . . . two parcels sent express and five boxes of school books freighted," as well as "eighteen pieces of hand baggage, our lunch and a gallon thermos jug of milk, [the Japanese residents] left the Oriental Home in cars for the boat."

Left with an almost empty building, and only a small Chinese community to minister to, the WMS decided to relocate. The building on Cormorant Street was rented to the Knights of Columbus as a "service club" for soldiers, and a new house, at 1120 Pembroke Street, a little ways away from Chinatown, was bought and officially opened on November 17, 1942. Reflecting a shift of priorities given the lack of residents as well as changes in society, the new centre was to serve as the missionary's home, as a meeting place for Chinese church groups, and for young ladies to stay as needed, such as if they were between jobs or attending high school. But after providing shelter and a home for hundreds of women and children for nearly sixty years, the residential focus was clearly over. The last girl moved out in 1945. A few months later, Lottie McRae, a "returned missionary from China," became the new resident missionary. She kept active in the Chinese community and in the Chinese United Church, but the Home quietly disappeared from Victorian life.

2

THEY CAME TO FISH
Snapshots from the First Fifty Years at Painter's Lodge

by Constance Kretz

Young Joe Painter was working as a dock-boy at his parents' resort in July 1947 when he noticed fishing guide Les Macdonald rowing back in from the Tyee Pool with long-time Painter's Lodge guest Ray Slocum in the boat.

"Get anything?" he called out as they approached the dock.

"Yeah, we got a seventeen and a half," he heard Mr. Slocum reply.

Eleven-year-old Joe didn't think too much of that. It was a small fish—nowhere near the 30 pounds necessary to be classified as a tyee.

Never mind, it was early in the season. As the youngest child of Ned and June Painter, he had been working on the dock since he was six or seven and knew the rhythm of the season well. Tyee fishing wouldn't start to get serious until August.

As the rowboat drew alongside he reached out to steady it against the dock and let Mr. Slocum step out. He glanced down at the fish in the bottom of the rowboat and stopped short.

"I couldn't believe my eyes," he said.

Joe had misheard. Mr. Slocum's fish wasn't 17½ pounds, it was 70½ pounds—a record.

"It was like a big pig laying in the [boat]—and it was a beautiful fish," he said in an interview sixty-five years later.

"So I just ran up to the lodge and told everybody."

You never knew what might happen at Painter's Lodge.

The salmon Mr. Slocum caught that day held the record for the biggest registered tyee for the next twenty-one years, until another regular Painter's Lodge guest managed to break it.

But that was in 1947. Before then, before the record fish, before Joe Painter was born and before there was a dock and a lodge, there was a small beginning: a one-room cabin and a

Ray Slocum with his 70½ pound tyee, caught on July 29, 1947. It held the Tyee Club's record from 1947 to 1967.
Image 9993 courtesy the Museum at Campbell River

boatworks built by his parents, June and E.P. (Ned) Painter, on the other side of the Campbell River estuary. From that place, they started the business that would become Painter's Fishing Resort, a landmark fishing lodge built around the tyee salmon that returned to the Campbell River every year.

Beginnings

"Mr. Painter, late of Port Alberni, arrived last week and is now busy installing his boat building and repair plant on the spit at the mouth of the Campbell River. The heavy machinery came by rail via Courtenay and by truck to its destination. Mr. Painter is a first-class builder and there is no doubt will work up an excellent business here."

—May 11, 1922, edition of the *Comox Argus*

Ned and June Painter met in Port Alberni. They married in 1921. She, slim with red hair, had grown up in Kelowna. He was born in Vancouver and apprenticed in boatyards there, becoming a naval architect. He served as a Navy diver in World War I and on his return to Canada went back to building boats, setting up in Port Alberni. Afternoon winds there limited his boat rental business to mornings and evenings though, so he began to look for another place.

He checked Campbell River, hearing it had excellent fishing and lighter winds. It was decided. He negotiated a year-to-year lease on a spit of land at the river's mouth, next to the fishing grounds known as the Tyee Pool, where massive chinook salmon gathered every August. On May 18, 1922, he and June arrived in Campbell River, stepping off the Union Steamship at four in the morning with their three-month-old baby girl, Joan. Soon, June got her first look at their new home. She remembered it as a beautiful morning. "To my great delight the Spit was covered with wild flowers. The Spit was to be our home for the next eighteen years. The first year we were more-or-less camping, as my husband was busy getting his boat shop ready."

June and Ned built both their first home—a one-room "shack" (her word for it)—and the boat shop that year. With no running water, June would row across the river once or twice a day to fetch some from wells at one of the farms opposite. On the Spit, their closest neighbours were families from the Campbell River Band, the Wei Wai Kum First Nation. June remembered a row of cabins that faced one another and a large potlatch house.

With his boat shop up, Ned began building. He designed a 14-foot rowboat for the Tyee Pool with low gunwales that made it easier to haul a 40-, 50- or 60-pound tyee into the boat and a hull that tracked well through choppy tide rips. Visitors could rent the boats by the day ($3 per day in the 1940s plus extra for rods, with fishing guides earning $8 per day around that time). His design stood up well and remains in use in the Tyee Pool to this day.

After World War I, fishing visitors increased. Anglers came from around the world to try for a tyee—from author Zane Grey of California to the Governor of Bermuda, Sir John Asser, and many others. In 1924, three men who wanted to both protect and promote the fishing in Campbell River decided to establish some rules for catching the great tyee. They

Ned Painter's boat shed on the Spit with several tyee rowboats pulled up on the beach.
Courtesy R.D. Berger

formed the Tyee Club of British Columbia, basing their requirements on those of the Tuna Club of Catalina Island, California. The tackle restrictions they set out (on rod length, type of hook and line weight) gave the tyee a sporting chance. The rules also levelled the playing field for an annual tournament to catch the biggest fish. Membership was achieved by catching a fish of 30 pounds or more under the Club's rules and Ned Painter became the first weighmaster.

That same year the Tyee Club began, June gave birth to their second child, John, in the house on the Spit on August 1, 1924. As Ned's boat rentals grew, visiting anglers began asking the Painters to provide a place to stay on the Spit next to the fishing grounds. Given their leased land, Ned and June decided on tent accommodation. Ned built 14- by 16-foot frames to support the canvas tents, which had wooden floors, walls and patios. They started offering the tents to rent in 1926, the same year their third child, Ann, was born. The resort side of their business had begun.

Over the next few years the Painters' business continued to expand and in 1929 Ned and June bought land on the west side of the estuary from farmer Tom Hudson. There, they built their first permanent lodgings: six cabins and a tearoom. Not long after, they added three more cabins and an office. The lodge they became famous for would not be built until almost a decade later, by which time June, Ned and their five children had set a standard for excellent fishing and service to guests from around the world. From Hollywood stars and corporate magnates, to politicians and trophy-hunting anglers, you never knew who you might run into at Painter's Fishing Resort, but one thing was sure: they were there to fish.

The Painter Family—Working Together

"They were a good pair. My Mother was very capable and could work hard and was very good with people. She had had a tough upbringing in Kelowna as her Dad was sick and she had to care for the horses and do the chores. Dad was a skilled builder and very good at maintenance. He left the entertaining to my Mother. He preferred to be at his own projects, which were many."

—Beth Hughes (nee Painter), June and Ned's youngest daughter

Once the cabins were built on the west side of the estuary, Ned and June rowed between there and the Spit camp on the east side of the river mouth to manage both their properties. "Our home was always at the Spit but it was back and forth all summer," Beth said. She and her older sister Ann would row over to the cabin side for meals.

The Spit remained their home until they moved into the lodge in 1939. As the kids got older, they had jobs at the resort. Eldest daughter, Joan, was key. She was "my mother's right hand," Beth recalls. Joan looked after the younger children, would bake or do laundry for the lodge, and fill in for her mother as needed. She had taken a business course in Courtenay and could be found in the office looking after the company books, or helping to organize things like corporate Christmas parties. "I don't know how Mother and Joan did it," Beth said.

Eldest son, John, laughed when asked what work he did at the lodge: "God knows every kind of thing!" He milked the cow (there was a milk shed on the hill behind the teahouse), hunted deer and grouse for the lodge, shovelled coal in the basement when the delivery truck came, and kept the tent camp coolers filled with ice delivered from Courtenay. He built boats with his father, too, and as he got older guided many guests into the Tyee Club.

Middle sister, Ann, was dock "boy." She was good with the guests and strong enough to pull the rowboats up on the dock. Beth worked in the laundry room and when she was sixteen moved over to the dining room to waitress. Joe, the youngest, started out as dock boy and, like his older brother, later hunted and helped his father build boats.

Painter children Ann (standing) and Joan and John (kneeling) among the flowers on the Spit. *Courtesy the Painter family*

The Painter family in the lodge lounge at Christmas time around 1944. June and Ned Painter are seated on each end and the children are, from left to right, Beth, John, Joe, Ann and Joan. Timmy, the cocker spaniel, sits on the floor. The photo was taken by a photographer for Finning Tractor Company. Mr. Finning was a client of the lodge and he told June Painter, "Come on, you have to have a picture of your family," so they gathered all the kids together. It's believed Mr. Finning had brought the photographer up to Campbell River to take pictures of machinery.
Courtesy the Painter family

Ned's brother, Joe, also joined the family, living on the Spit in a cabin. In the 1930s he met his future wife, Madge Petter, who was a cook in the teahouse, the guest dining area before the lodge was built in 1938. Their courtship started in the teahouse's staff dining room, Beth remembered. "She [Madge] kept a bottle of scotch to add to their coffee after hours. One day the rest of the staff put tea in the bottle. All hid waiting for the outburst when he had his coffee. I don't know what happened but they all giggled about it for a long time. I was very young at the time but the memory of their joyful giggling still remains with me. So Madge married Joe and became part of the family."

It was a lot to run. Ned looked after the wharf and boat repairs, and the coal furnace for the lodge. He set up a windmill and water tank to supply the lodge and cabins, and a generator for electricity. In the boatshed, he built about fifty rowboats each year, selling many so that the rental fleet was renewed every season. June meanwhile took care of the guests and all that it entailed.

"Cooks were always a problem," the Painters' youngest son, Joe, said. "One guy was a good cook and a chef, and he came in one morning and . . . he had the whole of that big stove covered with hotcakes. No orders or anything and he was just absolutely dead drunk. So they had to ship him off to bed and she [June] just had to pull all that stuff off the stove and start taking orders."

"And guides were always a problem. They would sleep in or something," he said. "And it was hard to get guides, especially during the war." The Painters provided meals for the guides at that time, as well as lodging for some of them.

Still, June did make time for other things. Family friend Mary Haig-Brown, who was close to their son Joe's age, has warm memories of her. "In the spring she would take us to the rocks above Duncan Bay to see wildflowers and tell us their names. 'How,' I wondered, 'does she know where each one is?' We always found what we looked for—the sea blush, the chocolate lilies, the blue ones. What were the blue ones called? I didn't worry about the names; I was worried about sliding off the rocks and over the cliff. But I never did. Mrs. Painter was there to see that I didn't."

The Lodge

"The lodge was beautiful and exciting and safe. The dining room with fresh flowers on each table, the wide cedar paneling, the plates on the walls, the abalone shells on the window sill, the French doors leading to the lounge with the comfortable chintz couches and chairs and the huge stone fireplace. The curving staircase which we slid down on our tummies, the guest rooms with more flowers and wooden match holders that looked like little witches cauldrons, but especially the family dining room off the busy kitchen, always full of people talking, visiting, and drinking tea; the books, games, goldfish—it was magic. I, younger than most, was never squished or overlooked. I sat on her [Mrs. Painter's] lap and was safe."

—Mary Haig-Brown, family friend, from the eulogy read at June Painter's memorial service in 1997

Construction of the lodge began in 1938. A three-storey wooden building with a basement, it stood on the top of a ridge overlooking a row of cabins, the dock and Discovery Passage. In 1939, the Painter family finally moved from their home on the Spit to live at the lodge.

Beth writes: "There was a *porte cochère* at the front entrance which led into the office and hall with stairs to the bedrooms upstairs." On the main floor, the front desk was on the right as you entered the building and the walls opposite were filled with photos of guests and fish going back decades.

If you walked past the desk you'd enter the lounge with its large stone fireplace, moose trophy mount, chintz chairs and views over the water. Turning right through French doors would take you into the dining room. The main guest rooms were on the second floor. The third floor had four rooms, but these shared one bathroom so were used less. Beth Painter and her sister Ann had a bedroom on the third floor, but during the busy tourist season they would move to a tent behind the laundry room.

The lodge became the centre of the resort and even after the Painter family sold it in 1948 the spirit of their time there remained, in the photos of favourite guests, the wooden beams and the stone fireplace. Just walking in those front doors, guests knew they'd arrived at someplace special.

Above: A sketch of the lodge from a 1950s brochure.
Courtesy Joe Painter

Left: A view of the lodge under construction in 1938.
Image 11878 courtesy the Museum at Campbell River

Below: A view into the lounge. The stones for the fireplace were hauled up from the beach below the lodge.
Image 11883 courtesy the Museum at Campbell River

The Fishing

"You came to Painter's Lodge to fish. Fish hard. And they did."

—Butch Dunstan, Painter's Lodge fishing guide starting from 1967

If you worked at the resort, you'd start to know: Colemans' tents were always the first set on the very end of the Spit; Mr. Smarsh's table in the dining room was the one nearest the kitchen; Mr. Shutts liked porridge every morning. "Can I have my Tiger Oats?" he'd joke with the waitresses. Among staff there was a genuine, respectful warmth for the guests who returned year after year, and whether at the tent camp in the early years or in later times at the lodge, the fishing was always the priority.

On the Spit, the tent camp faced the tyee grounds and going fishing meant rowing out a hundred feet or so from the beach to reach the Tyee Pool. Guests could sit on their tent patio, drink in hand, watching for the tide to be just right to fish. At the lodge, everything was geared to making the fishing easy and pleasurable, from the timing of meals to the pairing of guides with guests.

The list of people who rented the first tents in those early years catalogues some of the top fishermen and women of the time. Bill Coleman of Seattle was one of them. He was Tyee Man in 1927 (the Tyee Club's title for the person who catches the biggest fish of the year) with a 54½-pound fish taken on August 16. He always had the first three tents at the very end of the Spit: one for cooking, the other two for sleeping. He'd move in for the summer, bringing a cook, furniture and numerous friends.

Bill Coleman's patio at the Tyee Spit camp in 1936. From left: Herbert Pidcock (sitting on steps in black bathing suit), Bill Coleman, Heber Smith, Julie Dodge Nelson and Darrell Smith. Herbert, Heber and Darrell were sport fishing guides for Painter's Resort.
Image 18528 courtesy the Museum at Campbell River

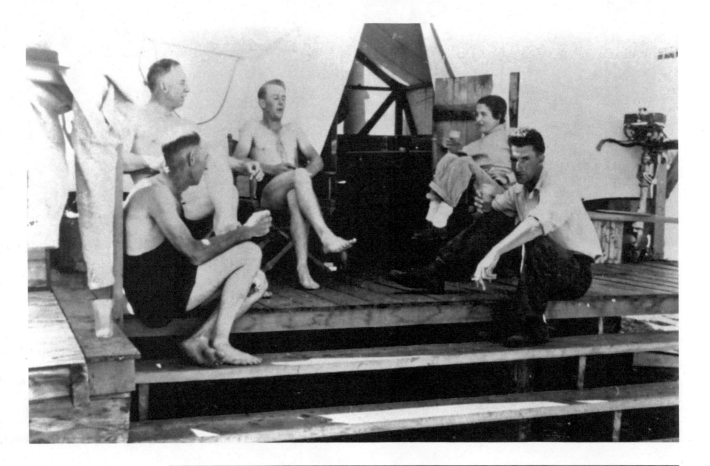

Other regulars in the tent camp were the Schuttses from Seattle and the Wolvertons of Vancouver (A.N. Wolverton: Tyee Man 1938; 58½ pounds). The Ballantines had a set of tents (Mrs. H.R. Ballantine: Tyee Man 1954; 60½ pounds), as did Mrs. W.C. Butler of Everett, Washington (Tyee Man 1934, 60½ pounds), who would arrive in a chauffeured Rolls Royce with an entourage.

They made themselves comfortable but were serious about fishing.

"It was a pretty exclusive group," Joe Painter said. "You know, you'd never get any of them to use bait. I mean all the guides knew how to do that . . . But these people just wouldn't have thought of using—in fact the clubs all used single hooks, so they really gave the fish a chance."

And they came back year after year.

Butch Dunstan's experience at Painter's Lodge began four decades after Ned and June Painter set up their first tents on the Spit. The resort had changed hands twice by then but the pattern of catering mainly to wealthy or famous clients had continued. But no matter the income level, fishing was the shared passion.

Aerial photo of the Spit with the Painter's tent camp visible on the end, at the bottom left of the image.
Image 15468 courtesy the Museum at Campbell River

Above: The cover of a 1950s brochure for the resort.

Courtesy Joe Painter

Right: Butch Dunstan (left) and fellow Painter's staff in front of their guide shack at the resort.

Courtesy Butch and Terry Dunstan

Dunstan started guiding at Painter's in 1967 when the Corbett family owned the resort. The Corbetts had bought the resort in 1963 from the Maclean family, who had been the first owners after the Painters sold it in 1948.

The selection of guides was deliberate. Mr. Dunstan was recruited when he was at the University of Victoria. Corky Corbett, the lodge's owner, would often hire guides from the universities. Mr. Corbett's daughter, Daphne, who lived and worked at the lodge with her family during that time, said her father sought guides who could do more than just fish.

"He was looking for people that could carry on intelligent conversations, that were outgoing so that if there was not good fishing there was somebody in the boat that our guests could talk to . . . and maybe [find] other things for them to do," she said.

Mr. Dunstan moved to Campbell River that summer and lived in a guide shack on the resort grounds. Guide shack accommodations included a bed, a hot plate for cooking, a fridge and some roommates (other guides).

One favourite guest during Mr. Dunstan's time guiding was Edward Smarsh of Garfield, New Jersey, who had been coming to Painter's for at least twenty years. Mr. Smarsh, who called himself a "stationary engineer"—his joke about being a janitor—would stay at Painter's Lodge for two weeks. Mr. Dunstan remembered him warmly and would go to town to pick up his liquor order when he arrived each summer. Mr. Smarsh's largest tyee was a 49½-pound fish on August 3, 1968.

The dining room. The best table was in the corner with the windows. In the 1960s it was dubbed the "Crown table," as this was where guests of the Crown Zellerbach–hosted parties were seated. The company was the resort's top corporate client at the time, renting three to four cabins all season long.
Image 11894 courtesy the Museum at Campbell River

R.D. Berger started working for Painter's Lodge in 1965 when he was still in high school. His job interview with Mr. Corbett took place at the lodge: "What do you want to be here for? Gardening or fishing?" Mr. Corbett asked the teenager pointedly.

"I almost said gardening," Mr. Berger said, laughing, but overcame his youthful nervousness to say these important words: "I want to guide."

There was a hierarchy and as a new guide, Mr. Berger was first assigned to "jump parties"—guests who had come to the lodge without a reservation and usually stayed only a few days. The longer-term regular guests were assigned to the more experienced guides.

"You had to work your way up in terms of guiding and your people powers," he said. He did, staying on through his university years to become one of the top guides.

Inside the lodge, arriving guests would be greeted at the front desk. When they were settled the guide would get a phone call: "Your guests are here." Dunstan remembers receiving those calls in his guide shack. He would get "tiddlied up" and meet the guests at the lodge to discuss the next day's fishing. Usually he would arrange to meet them at the dock at 6:00 a.m.

The dining room opened three times a day for an hour and a half each time. In the 1960s and 1970s breakfast started at 6:00 a.m. and lunch at noon. Dinner was from 5:00 p.m. to

Staff at Painter's Lodge in July 1970. Owners Corky and Joan Corbett are seated in the centre of the front row (Mr. Corbett in dark suit, Mrs. Corbett with dark hair). They are flanked by June Painter (left) and Madge Painter (right), with their daughter Daphne Corbett beside Madge. In the back row are the fishing guides. Second from right is head guide Mike Rippingale, third from right is Butch Dunstan and fifth from right is R.D. Berger.
Courtesy R.D. Berger

6:30 p.m. but guests would often show up before five, "because they'd want to eat right away and get out fishing to catch the last light," Mr. Dunstan said.

The guides would be waiting on the dock for their guests to come out after their meal. "You dare not be late," he said.

The service was formal in the dining room, said Terry Dunstan, who became head waitress in the early 1970s. Tables were covered in white linen, with polished silverware and napkins neatly folded into a sailboat. She wore a pale yellow uniform that was so starched "you couldn't sit down!" After breakfast the wait staff changed into a work uniform to clean the dining room, wiping down the salt and pepper shakers and the chairs.

She remembered this about the dining room guests: "You were there to fish. You weren't there to drink. And you weren't there to have a leisurely meal. It was a whole different mindset than now."

Despite the formality and high standards, it wasn't stressful. It was more like a family, she said, because the guests would stay a week or more and you had a chance to get to know them.

Painter's Lodge guides host a football game on the resort lawn in 1974 against then-rival April Point Lodge.
Courtesy R.D. Berger

Guide R.D. Berger said of working there: "It was a team . . . you were quite proud to be working for Painter's."

Daphne Corbett added, "We were very, very fortunate, I would say, that in the period of time that we had the lodge we retained the same core staff." This included the kitchen staff, wait staff, housekeeping staff and the guides. "So there was a family environment because we all got to know each other so well."

She and her brothers would eat dinner with the staff before the dining room opened in the evening and "it was always lots of fun and we always ate exceptionally well." During off-hours she would sometimes play pick-up football on the back lawn with the fishing guides.

Famous, Wealthy, Powerful

"You never knew what might happen in a place like that."

—Eileen Lornie, maid at Painter's Lodge in the 1950s

From the beginning, Campbell River's tyees drew the wealthy and the famous to Painter's Lodge. Eileen Lornie was a maid at Painter's in the 1950s when the Maclean family owned the lodge. She was cleaning cabins and knocked on one door, supplies in hand. Her jaw dropped when Hollywood star Glen Ford opened the door. He told her, gently, that she could come back the next day. Ms. Lornie left quickly and found a spot to sit down for a few moments to recover.

Mike Rippingale started as a fishing guide at Painter's in 1956, hired by the Maclean family. Over the years, as he became one of the more experienced guides, he was assigned to take many top clients fishing, including Glen Ford, actor Harve Presnell, former prime minister John Diefenbaker, Toronto Maple Leafs coach Punch Imlach and others. He described Mr. Diefenbaker as "a truly amazing man, extremely quick-witted and with a fantastic memory," in a 1969 newspaper interview.

Butch Dunstan remembers Mr. Diefenbaker going to the pool area with books every morning when he stayed at Painter's. "He sat and made notes and read."

Actor Harve Presnell, known for his version of the song "They Call the Wind Maria" from the 1969 movie *Paint Your Wagon* (which also starred Lee Marvin, Jean Seberg and Clint Eastwood), came to the resort a couple of times, Daphne Corbett said. He stayed in one of the cabins and guests walking by couldn't help but stop to listen when he sang in the shower.

While movie stars often came to the resort to find fish, on one occasion it was the other way around. Actor Vincent Price had stayed at the lodge a few times and on September 4, 1966, a call came in from Hollywood. Mr. Price was having a barbecue with friends and wanted to serve salmon. Were there any big fish available? It happened that Daphne Corbett

Guests from Boeing Corp. relax for a barbecue lunch at "Picnic Beach" on the Quadra Island side of Discovery Passage after a morning of fishing in the early 1970s.
Courtesy Butch and Terry Dunstan

Painter's Lodge head guide Mike Rippingale (centre) with Glen Ford (right) and his son Peter Ford (left) after a day on the water. *Image 20282-124 courtesy the Museum at Campbell River*

had caught a large tyee the day before. "My 42½-pound tyee was packed up and flown to Hollywood for Vincent Price," she said.

In 1965, Corky Corbett asked Mike Rippingale to be head guide for Crown Zellerbach guests, beginning a new era of major corporate clients at the resort. The lodge became part of Crown Zellerbach's strategy to win business from US paper buyers for its Campbell River pulp and paper mill. These included buyers for big newspapers like the *Los Angeles Times*

Salmon Marinade

(used at Painter's Lodge beach barbecues in the 1960s and 1970s)

Combine in a shaker:

½ cup oil

⅓ cup rye whiskey

2 tbsp soy sauce

1 tbsp garlic powder

1 tbsp sugar

Salt and pepper

Shake to combine and pour over salmon fillets. Recipe is for one coho, sockeye or small spring. Marinate in the fridge for four to six hours. Grill skin side down on medium high on the barbecue.

Courtesy of Butch and Terry Dunstan

and the *Seattle Post-Intelligencer*. The company rented three or four cabins for the season and brought in potential clients for a week of all-expense–paid fishing, including guides, meals and accommodations in cabins that were stocked with top-quality alcohol.

As head guide, Mr. Rippingale knew that if the guests "had some good fishing and a good time, chances are they would probably buy paper from Crown Zellerbach. Because we used to compete with Powell River and we always figured we had Powell River beat every single time."

A day out fishing for corporate guests like the Crown Zellerbach parties started after breakfast with the guides taking guests south of Quadra Island to fish for coho (Francisco Point, Butler's). Returning to Discovery Passage they'd stop for lunch, pulling their boats up at "Picnic Beach" on the Quadra Island side north of the Wei Wai Kai Village Bay. There, the guides unpacked coolers full of gourmet food prepared by kitchen staff, including steaks, salads and buns, plus beer and wine.

The guides would dig a small pit and light barbecue briquettes, and soon guests would be enjoying grilled steaks, salmon done in a beautiful marinade and sometimes fresh oysters, all served on real plates, with silverware and white linen napkins, Terry Dunstan said.

After the guides had cleaned up, it was time to head out fishing again.

Endings and a New Era

It was Joe Painter's dog that woke him on the night the lodge burned down. Joe's home is next door to the lodge property and on December 24, 1985, at about four in the morning, Rufus was outside and wouldn't stop barking. Joe got up to see what was wrong. As he walked toward his back door he saw bright orange reflected in its glass panes. No! Flames. The lodge was on fire. His wife, Eileen, called the fire department but the wooden lodge his parents had built was going fast. They watched as the building became engulfed.

Initially the fire was ruled accidental but new information led to a 1997 court case, which determined the fire to be arson. In 1999 a former employee confessed.

In the meantime, the resort had come under new ownership and in 1988 the Oak Bay Marine Group opened a new lodge. It was a bigger take on the original, but with deliberate nods to its design, such as the *porte cochère* at the entrance and the stone fireplace in the lounge. Some of the old photos of movies stars were restored and in the main lodge they line the walls going up the stairs to a trophy gallery on the second floor. The Tyee Club's awards and more photos and mementos of celebrities and record fish are here, and it is open to the public. It's worth a look, for a taste of the glamour and traditions the Painter family established, and the continuing passion of those who come to fish for Campbell River's tyee salmon.

HELP FROM ABOVE
The Early Years of BC Helicopter Rescue

by Kenneth I. Swartz

Before the helicopter, many life-saving missions were simply impossible, or required a lot more time to complete. From the first search and rescue (SAR) missions by underpowered helicopters in the late 1940s to the highly coordinated Royal Canadian Air Force (RCAF) operations of today, BC's helicopter rescuers have saved hundreds of lives.

Over six decades, the approaching rotor beat of four generations of RCAF helicopters—the Sikorsky S-51, Piasecki H-21, Boeing Vertol CH-113 Labrador and AgustaWestland CH-149 Cormorant—has often been a signal that another life-saving mission was under way.

These SAR helicopters have become symbolic for their rescues, but it's the pilots, flight engineers, rescue technicians and maintenance mechanics who really make these missions possible.

Mercy Flights

In 1920, Ottawa established an Air Board as a government flying service to operate aircraft on behalf of various federal and provincial agencies. A seaplane base was soon constructed at Jericho Beach in Vancouver to support Air Board flying in BC.

From this scenic location, many of BC's first generation of aerial explorers embarked on bold missions to map the province, detect forest fires, spot illegal fishing boats, track smugglers and provide mercy flights to citizens in need. When the newly formed Royal Canadian Air Force took over the base in 1924, the uniforms of the aircrews changed, but humanitarian flights continued.

Search and Rescue

World War II brought an exponential increase in flying activity across the nation, and a corresponding increase in accidents. In British Columbia, the RCAF made coastal patrols and logistics flights, while providing operational training for bomber, flying boat and transport aircraft crews heading to battle overseas. Thousands of American warplanes overflew the province on their way to Alaska, as did some eight thousand lend-lease warplanes being delivered to the Soviet Air Force via Alaska.

Wartime searches for missing aircraft demanded a lot of resources. The rugged mountains, dense forests and poor weather contributed to many accidents, and concealed some crash sites for decades.

The first helicopter rescue in Canada occurred in May 1945. A US Coast Guard Sikorsky R-4 Hoverfly picked up the crew of an RCAF PBY-5A Canso flying boat that crashed in the wilderness 120 miles from Goose Bay, Labrador.

In late 1945, the RCAF received a mandate to establish a national search and rescue service. Then in 1946, the territory to be covered increased when the International Civil Aviation Organization (ICAO) required countries to provide search and rescue coverage over adjacent oceans. The ICAO also recommended the acquisition of helicopters for rescues in inaccessible areas.

In 1947, Canada was divided into five SAR regions managed by new Rescue Coordination Centres (RCCs) established in Halifax, Ottawa, Winnipeg, Edmonton and Vancouver. Vancouver's RCC was located at No. 12 Group Headquarters on West Fourth Avenue, near Jericho Beach. Each RCC region also received dedicated SAR aircraft and crews that could rapidly respond to air, land and sea emergencies. An international conference was held at Jericho Beach to develop Canada–US search and rescue procedures for aircraft lost in BC or neighbouring American states.

BC's First Helicopter Rescues

Helicopters are so much a part of the modern transportation system in BC that it's hard to imagine a time when they didn't exist. Prior to the arrival of the first RCAF example in 1949, the Rescue Coordination Centre in Vancouver had to request helicopters from US agencies and commercial operators for SAR missions.

The first major postwar aerial search in BC was mounted for a Trans-Canada Airlines (TCA) Lockheed 18 Lodestar, bound from Lethbridge to Vancouver with fifteen passengers and crew. TCA Flight 3 disappeared while on approach to Vancouver Airport on April 30, 1947. More than thirty aircraft, supported by ships and ground parties, combed twelve thousand square miles of southwestern BC.

On the third day of the search, American pilot Angus E. McArthur arrived from Seattle with a new Bell 47B helicopter, to fly local spotter Ted Stull over the dense forests around Buntzen Lake and Mount Coquitlam. The Bell was owned by Central Aircraft of Yakima, Washington, and was outfitted with inflatable floats.

The pioneering nature of these operations led to some tragedies. Soon after returning to Washington, McArthur and a passenger died when they crashed into Lake Union.

In spite of the comprehensive search, TCA Flight 3 was not found. The wreckage of the Lodestar was finally discovered in 1994, on the heavily wooded slope of Mount Elsay in Mount Seymour Provincial Park, North Vancouver.

Bell 47B helicopter, NC106B, on floats at Vancouver's Sea Island Airport and flown by Angus McArthur with local spotter Ted Stull, May 1947.
Gordon Peters photo, courtesy Kenneth Swartz collection

US Air Force air rescue unit Sikorsky H-5 from the McChord Air Force base at Vancouver Airport, August 1947, for the Charles Shiverick recovery mission.
Gordon Peters photo, courtesy Brent Wallace collection

Two more US helicopters visited BC on a humanitarian mission in August 1947. Their crews intended to recover the body of Charles Shiverick II, an American student fatally injured by an avalanche while climbing Mount Serra in the Coast Range with the Harvard University Mountaineering Club.

A Sikorsky H-5 from the US Air Force air rescue unit at McChord Air Force Base near Tacoma arrived in early August, followed by a Bell 47B from Central Aircraft, flown by Carl Brady. Both teams believed arrangements had been made to carry Shiverick's body down to the Tidermann Glacier so it could be flown to the coast. However, the Harvard climbers decided the recovery operation was too risky, and buried Shiverick on the mountain.

First Successful Rescue

The first successful helicopter rescue in BC took place on October 4, 1947.

Skyways Services pilot James Sampson flew a Bell 47B, CF-FZN, to the headwaters of the Capilano River. There he evacuated an injured employee of the Greater Vancouver Water Board. Skyways had shipped the helicopter from Winnipeg to Vancouver in late summer to try to find work.

Gordon Oram had been working at Palisade Lake, high above the Capilano River, when he injured his leg with an axe. Dr. J.S. McCarley hiked five hours up the mountain to provide medical assistance. Oram lay beside the lake for thirty-six hours before he was rescued—torrential rain made it too hazardous to carry him down the trail. The helicopter evacuation

Skyways Services Bell 47B, CF-FZN, made its first rescue flights in the Vancouver area in 1947 and 1948. It was bought by Okanagan Helicopters and in 1949 used to carry construction materials to the Palisade Lake dam, and in the early 1950s to train RCAF pilots to fly in mountains. Vancouver 1949. *Gordon Peters photo, courtesy Brent Wallace collection*

took just fifteen minutes, landing in Boulevard Park, where an ambulance waited to transport Oram to North Vancouver General Hospital.

A few months later Paul Ostrander, using the same Skyways Bell 47B, flew injured skier William Lehrie from Grouse Mountain to the front lawn of Shaughnessy Hospital for treatment of a fractured collarbone. It was the first time a skier had been flown to hospital in BC.

Skyways sold that Bell to Okanagan Air Services in 1948. One of its first tasks was flying construction supplies to a new dam site on Palisade Lake. This operation brought early worldwide attention to the use of helicopters in the mountains of BC.

The RCAF Sikorsky S-51 Era

British Columbia finally gained its own SAR helicopter in May 1949, when two new Sikorsky S-51s arrived in Vancouver by train. They were taken to the RCAF's Sea Island base for reassembly. One remained there, while the other was sent to northern BC to support army surveyors.

No. 123 Search and Rescue (S&R) Flight welcomed the arrival of its new S-51 (No. 9606), which joined an eclectic fleet of wartime aircraft at Sea Island. They included an Avro Lancaster, Beech Expeditor, PBY-5A Canso, Douglas C-47 Dakota, Lockheed Hudson III, Lockheed Ventura, North American Harvard, and a Noorduyn Norseman on floats.

The Sikorsky S-51 had a fuselage of just over 41 feet, a 48-foot diameter three-blade rotor, and was powered by a 450-hp Pratt & Whitney R-985 radial engine, the same model that powers the Beaver bush plane.

A pilot required strong arms to fly an S-51, since the control system was purely mechanical with various linkages, chains and gears. Air loads on the rotor were transmitted to the pilot's control stick. The S-51 had a cruise speed of 85 mph, a range of 260 miles and could carry a maximum load of 1,450 pounds including pilot, up to two passengers and fuel.

The first mission for the new, bright yellow S-51 was in June 1949. F/L Hugh Campbell, DFC, flew to Vancouver Island to undertake the first of several searches for a missing US Navy Lockheed Neptune patrol aircraft and nine crew members. Those searches were unsuccessful. The wreckage of the Neptune was not found until 1960.

On July 1, 1949, Vancouver's Chief of Police Walter Mulligan and Alderman Hal Wilson were delivered to the police games at Brockton Point in Stanley Park in the S-51, piloted by Hugh Campbell.

"This novel means of transportation appealed in no small manner to the large crowd present. A general flying display was the hoisting of one of the crewmen into the helicopter by means of a bosun's chair and cable actuated by an electric winch in the aircraft. During this demonstration the helicopter hovered at a height of approximately 40 feet," wrote No. 123 S&R Flight's daily diarist.

In late August, F/L Hugh Campbell demonstrated lowering a man by winch over the outdoor theatre at the Pacific National Exhibition, and then on December 24 he flew along Vancouver streets as part of Christmas celebrations!

The S-51 flew up and down the south coast and as far inland as Penticton on SAR calls and mercy flights, as well as hoisting para-rescue crews out of the bush. In January 1950, the S-51 flew a doctor to a pneumonia patient at the north end of Vancouver Island, then evacuated the patient to Port Alice Hospital. Later in the month it took a sick man to hospital in Squamish.

On February 13, a giant six-engine USAF B-36 Peacemaker nuclear bomber declared an emergency. En route from Fairbanks, Alaska, to Fort Worth, Texas, icing commenced, and three of the engines caught fire or stopped over the north Pacific. The pilot jettisoned an unarmed nuclear bomb, and later all seventeen crew members bailed out over Princess Royal Island.

The next morning F/L Hugh Campbell took off in the Sikorsky S-51, heading north. Mechanical problems forced him to make emergency landings on a golf course in Parksville and a field in Qualicum Beach. Once the helicopter reached Bella Bella, it embarked on a barge towed by the 95-foot RCAF supply vessel *M-468 Songhee*. This improvised aircraft carrier provided accommodation, fuel and meals for the S-51 crew and for USAF helicopter crews also searching.

Twelve members of the B-36 crew were rescued, but the other five were never found. The wreck of the bomber was not discovered until three years later, near Hazelton.

The concept of a floating SAR helicopter base got a second look in August 1950, when a temporary landing pad was installed on the aft deck of the *Songhee*. F/L Hugh Campbell

F/L Hugh Campbell flies RCAF Sikorsky S-51 No. 9606 with F/O Dan Campbell as passenger during experimental landings and takeoffs from a temporary helicopter deck installed on the RCAF supply vessel M-468 Songhee to expand the helicopter's SAR capability. Burrard Inlet, August 1950.
Courtesy Daniel Campbell collection

made several landings and takeoffs as the *Songhee* steered around Burrard Inlet. The concept was a mini aircraft carrier to provide a helicopter crew with fuel, food and accommodation during prolonged searches, but it was never put to use.

During the early 1950s, several RCAF pilots from the Sea Island base learned to fly helicopters at the Joint Air Training Centre in Rivers, Manitoba. They included Flying Officers S.H. "Shorty" McLeod, Gerry McKenna, Daniel Campbell and K.C. Lynas. The RCAF realized that more training was required to fly in the mountains, and in 1951 began sending pilots to Okanagan Helicopters' advanced mountain flying course. The first mountain courses were taught by Okanagan's legendary Carl Agar, with senior pilots Deke Orr and Fred Snell, on Mount Garibaldi (elevation 8,786 feet) 50 miles north of Vancouver.

"We did our initial mountain flying training in an Okanagan Bell 47D operating from the Diamond Head Lodge," recalls Dan Campbell, who trained with Gerry McKenna in February 1952.

"Our instructor would go over the lesson plan in the lodge, and then we'd fly up and practise mountain landings and takeoffs on Mount Garibaldi—which, unlike the North Shore mountains, didn't have any skiers to get in our way. Whatever we were taught in the

Right: F/O Dan Campbell flying S-51 No. 9606 approaches the improvised landing pad at the 5,100-foot-level site of an RCAF B-25 Mitchell crash near Widgeon Peak, west of Pitt Lake, in mid-September 1953. Operating from a schoolyard in Port Coquitlam, the S-51 flew five bodies out one at a time and supported the accident investigation team. *Courtesy Daniel Campbell collection*

Bell we would then duplicate on the S-51. To prevent the S-51 from sinking in the snow, 'bear paws' [small skis] were attached to the wheels to spread the weight of the helicopter."

It was also very important for aircrews to be proficient in hoist rescues, which required a lot of practice. The S-51 could often be seen winching RCAF personnel off the dykes of Lulu Island and in the Fraser Valley. The unit was renamed No. 121 Communications and Rescue Flight.

On January 29, 1953, a B-25 Mitchell bomber, with a five-member crew from No.1 Advanced Flying School at RCAF Saskatoon, disappeared while on a training flight to Vancouver. When the snow melted in late summer, the wreckage was found near Pitt Lake. Crashes on the West Coast were not usually very forgiving, and it was the sad but necessary duty of the SAR aircrews to remove bodies.

Between September 17 and September 24, F/O Dan Campbell flew the S-51 from a school playground in Port Coquitlam to the crash site, to take the bodies of the Mitchell crew off Widgeon Peak and to re-supply the accident investigation team.

Sikorsky S-51 No. 9606 was destroyed in a hangar fire at RCAF Sea Island on April 29, 1954. Within a few years most RCAF S-51s were relegated to flight training.

Piasecki H-21 "Flying Banana"

By the early 1950s, the RCAF recognized that the S-51 was inadequate for SAR missions, and ordered six new Piasecki H-21As. RCAF Sea Island received its first example, No. 9613, on January 22, 1955. Local aircrews began immediate training on Canada's largest helicopter of the 1950s—later known as the Vertol H-21A.

The twin rotors of the H-21 provided more stability for hover rescues. Two 1,425-hp Wright R-1820-103 radial engines allowed it to fly farther (350 miles), faster (up to 131 mph) and higher (8,450 feet), which provided a tremendous boost in SAR capability.

The H-21A fuselage was 52½ feet long and had two 44-foot diameter rotors. The aft part of the fuselage extended upward so the long blades of the two rotors could overlap. Inside, it had a two-seat cockpit and a large cabin that could accommodate twenty-two passengers, twelve stretchers, or four thousand pounds of cargo. Maximum takeoff weight was three times that of an S-51.

The H-21 was flown in BC with one or two pilots, a flight engineer and a rescue specialist. During start-up, pilots needed to carefully engage a mechanical clutch that transferred engine power to the rotors. If the clutch engaged too abruptly, the jolt could break all the wooden rotor blades.

In April, Sea Island's H-21 was needed at RCAF Cold Lake, Alberta, to provide coverage during spring breakup. It departed on April 20 for Penticton, but tragically crashed the next morning on Santa Rosa Mountain, 20 miles west of Rossland. The crash killed No. 121 C&R Flight pilot F/O Donald West and crewman Cpl. Eric Ericson, as well as civilian Robert Chesney, an H-21 expert from the Piasecki factory in Philadelphia. Co-pilot F/O K.C. Lynas and Cpl. J.S. Stredecki survived.

British Columbia was left without a rescue helicopter until December, when a replacement H-21A, No. 9611, arrived in Vancouver.

Opposite bottom: RCAF Piasecki H-21A "flying banana" helicopters served BC from 1955 to 1965, performing many rescues and evacuation flights. Some of the pilots that flew H-21s in BC between 1955 and 1965 included Daniel Campbell, Max Chapin, Chris Cooling, Pete Fuller, Bob Goldie, Ted Harris, Bob Hughes, K.C. Lynas, Pat Mathews, S.H. "Shorty" McLeod, Craig Miller, Don Park, Ron Peterson, Ed Riley, Ray Rasmussen, Roy Saunders, John Thompson and Donald West and certainly others, supported by a dedicated RCAF team of flight engineers, rescue specialists and helicopter mechanics.
Courtesy Daniel Campbell collection

For the next ten years, the "flying banana" became BC's SAR workhorse. These red-, blue- and white-painted helicopters responded to hundreds of air incidents, maritime incidents and air evacuation requests. Their loud rotor beat signalled their presence even if they could not be seen.

H-21 crews were routinely called out to winch lost or injured hikers off Vancouver's North Shore mountains. In October 1956, F/O Don Park and his crew made Canada's first recorded night rescue. They used belly-mounted searchlights to help keep the helicopter clear of the trees, while hoisting a hiker found after six days on Mount Seymour.

Tragedy again struck BC on December 9, 1956. A Trans-Canada Airlines Canadair North Star, operating as Flight 810 from Vancouver to Calgary, turned back to Vancouver with an engine problem, but disappeared after passing over Hope.

More than fifty military and civilian aircraft searched for the North Star, which had sixty-two people aboard. H-21 crews spent many hours over the mountains east of Vancouver. TCA Flight 810 was not found until six months later, when climbers chanced upon the crash site on Mount Slesse. Then the H-21 supported a base camp nearby, while nimble Bell 47s flew accident investigators up to the site at 5,700 feet elevation.

In the spring of 1957, the RCAF received approval to make point-to-point trips to carry critical patients to hospitals. This was a major breakthrough, shifting many medical flights from ambulances and airplanes to helicopters. The front lawn of Shaughnessy Military Hospital in Vancouver became a frequent landing spot, and community parks were often used in other towns.

In October 1958, the Vancouver search and rescue flight was renamed again, as No. 121 Composite Unit.

British Columbia's SAR helicopter fleet doubled in early 1960 when a second H-21A, No. 9614, arrived in Vancouver. This delivery ensured that one helicopter was available for most emergencies, while the other was receiving maintenance.

The largest helicopter rescue of the H-21 era in BC happened in early 1962. On New Year's Day the Greek freighter *Glafkos*, inbound from Japan to Vancouver, got far off course in a storm and hit a rock near Ucluelet. The engine room flooded, but the anchors were quickly dropped to prevent the ship from being torn apart on Jenny Reef. Salvage tugs *Sudbury* and *Island Challenger* arrived and tried to tow her to safety. On January 3 the situation was still a standoff, with *Sudbury* and *Glafkos* both anchored and connected by a towline.

A helicopter evacuation was undertaken by F/L Dan Campbell and his crew, Major John Thompson, Cpl. Ken Matson and Cpl. Vic Hodge. They made several trips to *Glafkos* to hoist sailors off the heaving deck in batches of five or six. Then they lowered two local volunteers, who set up an extra towline for *Island Challenger*. The disabled *Glafkos* got off the rock, and was towed to Victoria by *Sudbury*.

Two days later, a USAF F-89 Scorpion jet interceptor crashed on a snow-covered mountain northeast of Penticton. The same RCAF crew, assisted by para-rescue personnel, rescued the pilot and recovered the body of the radio operator.

Through the early 1960s, the Sea Island base had five helicopter pilots working rotating shifts. Generally only one helicopter was flown at a time.

Opposite: No. 121 KU sent an H-21 No. 9614 to Inuvik, Northwest Territories, in May 1963 to provide SAR support during flood season on the Mackenzie River. While in the NWT the crew of H-21 salvaged a Cessna 170 from its accident site on May 29 and flew it 100 miles back to its home base in Aklavik. *Lynn Garrison photo, courtesy Daniel Campbell collection*

Following pages: A welcome sight to many folks in trouble: an RCAF Search and Rescue Labrador at close range. This helicopter served with 442 Squadron at Comox during the 1970s. It was retired in 2004. *Photo by Kenneth I. Swartz*

Right: Some wartime BC wrecks became museum displays. H-21 helicopters 9611 and 9614 were both involved in the salvage of a rare US Navy OS2U Kingfisher aircraft from Calvert Island on March 12, 1964. The aircraft went to the Air Museum of Canada in Calgary and later to the US for restoration and display on the battleship USS *North Carolina* in Wilmington, NC.

Courtesy Daniel Campbell collection

Below: No. 121 Composite Flight's new Boeing Vertol CH-113 Labrador No. 10402 at the 13,000-foot level of Mount Kennedy in the St. Elias Mountains, Yukon Territory, March 27, 1965.

Courtesy Daniel Campbell collection

In March 1965, 121 Composite Flight flew and supported a party that included the late US senator Robert Kennedy and members of the National Geographic Society when they climbed Mount Kennedy, named in honour of President John F. Kennedy. Here some climbers and the RCAF crew members pose in front of Labrador 10402 at the Base Camp on March 22, 1965. Left to right: James Whittaker, the first American to summit Mount Everest; Senator Robert Kennedy; Brad Washburn, Director, Museum of Science, Boston, who first climbed the St. Elias Range in 1935; Flight Engineer Dave Mader; F/L Dan Campbell; Co-Pilot F/L Bob Hughes; and Flight Engineer Vic Hodge.
Courtesy Daniel Campbell collection

The Canadian government selected the turbine-powered twin-rotor Boeing Vertol 107 as its new search and rescue helicopter. Six of these CH-113 Labradors were ordered for the busiest rescue units serving BC, Atlantic Canada and Ontario.

The introduction of the Labrador coincided with a major cut in the national defence budget. The Sea Island RCAF base was closed in July 1964, and No. 121 Composite Unit relocated to Comox on Vancouver Island. The Labrador took over from the hard-working H-21A in BC at the end of 1964.

In February 1965 there was an avalanche at the Granduc copper mine site near Stewart. Twenty-six workers were killed, and many survivors were left in urgent need of evacuation. In spite of blizzard conditions, the Labrador was able to get them to safety, including thirty-two passengers in one load. For most of the Labrador's career, it was flown by 442 Squadron, a historic number that was revived and applied to No. 121 Composite Unit in July 1968.

For forty years the Labrador was the symbol of air rescue in the province, until it too was retired in 2004 as the three-engine AgustaWestland CH-149 Cormorant SAR helicopter entered service.

4

YOU DID WHAT YOU COULD
A Practice on the Gulf Islands

by David R. Conn

Dr. John Ankenman and Dr. David Boyes have been close friends since the 1940s, when they studied medicine at Queen's University in Kingston.

Their first general practice was challenging enough: in 1950, they took on BC's southern Gulf Islands. A provincial government subsidy paid some expenses. John and David, and their wives, Jo and Louise, settled on Lower Ganges Road, Salt Spring Island. At the time, the island had a population of two thousand. Patients ranged from wealthy aristocrats on large acreages to welfare recipients renting cabins or squatting.

Medical facilities were basic: the old wooden Lady Minto Hospital in Ganges lacked offices or elevators, and boasted just two bathrooms. Yet formality was still the rule: the young doctors wore ties and jackets. As the designated healers of this isolated region, they were at times called on to provide coroner, dentistry, psychiatry and veterinary services. Both couples started families on Salt Spring Island. Change came slowly, but the Ankenman-Boyes practice saw the wide availability of antibiotics, the beginning of prepaid medicine through the provincial government and policing contracted to the RCMP. Infrastructure improvements at the time included paved roads and a few town street lights.

Dr. John Ankenman: I was an Ontario farm boy, and David was a Vancouverite. David convinced me to come to Vancouver General Hospital to do an internship, and along the way we decided we would go into practice together. After internship, we looked at Anchor-

David Boyes (left) and John Ankenman (right), medical students in 1948, horse around with their landlady.
Courtesy John Ankenman

age, as well as Abbotsford, Comox and Alert Bay. Dr. Jack Pickup at Alert Bay was anxious for help, and he offered us $500 a month to go there. As an intern at VGH, I had a patient from Salt Spring Island who said, "The elderly doctor needs to go, and we're looking for younger doctors." David and I decided to go over.

We went by boat to Ganges, and Ira White was a local retired doctor who entertained us. They put us up at the Harbour House Hotel. We went to see the hospital, and Dr. White introduced us to Barbara Hastings, the head of the hospital board. Gavin Mouat, who owned the Salt Spring Real Estate Company, arranged for us to buy Dr. George Meyers's practice and house for $12,000. Dr. Meyers retired right away—he was anxious to get out of it. Dave and his wife, and my wife and I went to auctions in Vancouver and bought the cheapest furniture we could get.

Dr. David Boyes: I bought beer parlour chairs for our office for two bucks apiece. We flipped a coin to see who'd be in the upstairs and who'd be in the downstairs. The office was in the house. We were anxious to get to work and pay off our debts. John bought a used Dodge convertible, and I bought a car that was a joke.

At the hospital, there was an operating room and fifteen beds. There was no laboratory, and a very modest little X-ray machine . . . it was hardly strong enough to go through a chest. We had to do our own lab work in our office. We had been taught how to do white blood counts and even simple urinalysis. We would go up to the hospital every morning, do our rounds, and then sit and have coffee with the head nurse and usually two others. It was rather social. We used Goodie's [Don Goodman's] place for a morgue. I had to carry some bodies in there. He had the ambulance. Dr. Ira White was able to do anaesthetics for us.

After we finished going over the patients' needs, then we would go back to our office. We had a nurse in the office who served both of us. She came in about eleven o'clock and tidied things up, so we were ready to start seeing patients. We would keep seeing patients until

Lady Minto Hospital
1914-1958

The old wooden Lady Minto
Hospital, Ganges.
Courtesy Salt Spring Island Archives

they were all gone. Then we'd go up to the hospital again. Almost always there were house calls at night. I remember one night getting sixteen calls while I was having dinner. That was a bit unusual, but it was a busy practice.

There was a movie every Saturday night, which finished usually at ten o'clock. For a lot of people, that would be one of the few times they were in Ganges. They expected the doctors' office to be open, and so we kept it open. We saw three or four patients after the movie.

JA: The head nurse at the hospital was Beth Petersen, who was a widow at the time. She was on call 24/7, and she was a wonderful nurse. It didn't matter, day or night—if somebody was in labour, we had to call her. Ellie Kellman was a doctor's widow from Fernie, so she'd been around the block a few times. She was a wonderful help for me—with somebody in labour, she could tell when it was time to call me.

As an intern at VGH I had delivered over a hundred babies under supervision, so I felt quite competent to deliver my first island baby. When someone was admitted to hospital in advanced labour, I was delighted to deliver a healthy boy. However, when I went to retrieve the placenta, I was surprised to find another head. The mother was even more surprised. She hadn't known she was carrying twins!

We had a very ambitious public health nurse from Victoria, and she was anxious to get our view on cleaning up. There was some question about people dumping their sewage into the ocean, and she wanted to make sure everybody had proper septic tanks. I inquired around to our neighbours to see if they had septic tanks, and they said, "Doctor, before you go too far, just check and see what you've got." Our wives were up in the bathroom, David and I were down on the bank in front of a pipe, and it just flushed straight out!

DB: We were given some responsibility from the province. I think we got $1,000 a year for public health. I went to the restaurant across from us, and they were flushing directly into the harbour. I did get the septic tank operating.

My grandparents had a place at Langford Lake, so I was sort of brought up in the woods there. I'd always used guns, so I was comfortable with the idea of shooting deer for meat, which was common on the island at that time. It was very rural. We liked the deer in May and June. That's when the meat was the best. What you did not want to shoot was deer in the late fall, because they were tough then.

There was no liquor store on Salt Spring, which was a serious matter for us, even at that time of our lives. You had to buy from the local taxi driver, and it was expensive.

JA: There was a United Church minister, Reverend Bompas, and he was organizing petitions against getting a liquor store. One Saturday afternoon my wife and I were at a friend's—Hattie Jenkins—and the minister drove up. Hattie went out to meet him and said, "You might as well turn around; I'm enjoying a cocktail with my friends."

David and I tried to make fig wine in our kitchen, and then tried to distill it, which worked out so-so. But finally a dear old lady said to me, "Dr. Ankenman, I have to tell you, your patients say your office smells like a brewery."

David and I were together there from 1950 to 1951, and then in 1952 David went back to do postgraduate work at VGH, and I supported him. In 1953, I went to Victoria for post-graduate training, and he supported me. Then we sold the practice in 1953.

We used to make our house calls to the other islands, if there was an emergency, with a Seabee or a Taylorcraft. We had an arrangement that the person who called paid for the pilot on the other side. Anyway, one day I took off with the pilot in the Seabee; I'd made a house call on Miners Bay on Mayne Island. We got up in the air, and the engine conked out. We weren't going fast enough to glide, and we dove right into the sea and up. We surfaced and nobody saw it happen. We drifted for the longest time, until finally a fishboat saw us and pulled us ashore. I was black and blue from head to toe.

DB: We were invited to this wedding, and I had to do a house call. We took the Seabee. Bill Sylvester, the chief pilot for BC Air, was with me. We were going to drop confetti over the wedding on our way. So we both opened our side windows and we were leaning out. There were dual controls, and each of us thought the other was flying the airplane! We pulled out about 50 feet above all the visitors. They thought it was wonderful, but we scared ourselves.

I was driving back at night from Fulford, having done a house call. There was a guy lying beside the road. He was big, but I was fairly strong at that time, so I put him in the car and got to the hospital, then phoned John to come and help me. The guy had a completely rigid belly. He'd been drinking—I could smell that. So I thought I'd better try and do something, or he'd die. John came and agreed with me, so I opened him up, and John had to hold the belly open because we had no retractors. We scooped gallons of beer and peanuts and stuff

Above: A Republic Seabee, the type used for emergency visits to the other Gulf Islands.
Courtesy Douglas Tait, Canadian Museum of Flight and Transportation

Left: A Taylorcraft, the type used (on pontoons) for emergency visits to the other Gulf Islands.
Courtesy Douglas Tait, Canadian Museum of Flight and Transportation

out of his belly, and sewed up the hole, and he survived. I used fourteen cans of ether. It was the sort of thing you had to do. You did what you could.

One of the Akerman women came to me with a pregnancy, I had her in labour in the hospital and she insisted on sitting up. I had her sitting up until the baby's head was coming then I delivered her. I thought, well, there's something to that. There was an old operating table in the basement of the hospital. I rigged up some stirrups for it, and had Ted Ashbee make some legs out of fibreglass. I started delivering babies in that. I took it to VGH when I went back in my residency. I delivered thirty-five babies in it, and I kept records. It really reduced the analgesic level, because the patients were aiming downhill. But as soon as I left, they abandoned it.

JA: The year that David was away in Vancouver, I developed acute appendicitis. I phoned Ira White. At midnight, he gave me a spinal anaesthetic, rolled me over and took out my appendix. I have two scars: a high one where it didn't take, and a low one where he finally got in. My wife was on the phone to David, and he chartered a plane. He was there at day-break, and he took over the practice for a week.

DB: We were paid to do clinics on Galiano, Mayne, Pender and once in a while on Saturna. We did regular afternoons on each of those islands. We had to do house calls. Vic Jackson had a 30-foot gillnet boat, *Crackerjack*, that he put a little cabin on, and he had a good motor, and if it was something like just going to a clinic, we'd use that. A nice little boat and we used that a lot. If a call was urgent, we'd use an airplane.

JA: When we made our calls to the other islands on *Crackerjack*, we used to fish, coming and going, and we always got lots of cod and some salmon.

DB: I had one near miss on that boat. I was working on Galiano, it was a house call, and I was coming home. It was about two in the morning, and I was sleeping and Vic Jackson was steering. I woke up and went to the stern, and I looked up, and there was a freighter. His bow was only about 20 feet behind our boat. He didn't know we were there, and we didn't know he was there. We were going about seven knots; he was going ten.

Once I was doing the clinic on Galiano, waiting for Vic Jackson to pick me up. This very large logger said, "Dr. Boyes, I hear you pull teeth." I said yes I do, but I charge five bucks. I had a universal forceps with me, and I pulled his tooth, which was really loose and just came out. "God, you did that good, doc. If you're not in any rush, here's another." So I pulled about thirteen teeth. He said, "Don't mind the blood, doc." He paid me right there.

There was no vet, and so we got called to look after animals sometimes. This farmer had a cow that had just delivered, and she was thrashing about. I went over, but I couldn't even examine her because she was jumping all over the place. Then I went to the drugstore. Peggy Wells was a very good druggist, and I asked her if there was anything that might help the cow. She said, "I think that might be milk fever, and if you gave it a lot of glucose it might help." I got a litre of glucose 10 percent, quite strong, and I shoved it into this cow by racing around the barn after her. She just cleared right up.

The druggist's husband, Austin Wells, was a PhD, as well as a real baron. Artificial insemination of cattle had just come to the province. He was given this job. I spoke to a farm couple about having one of their cows inseminated. We arranged for Dr. Wells to take

A Ganges scene, with cenotaph, pharmacy, gas station and store.
Courtesy Salt Spring Island Archives

his equipment to the farm when the cow was ready. As he was inseminating this cow, the little English lady came up to me. She said, "This is the happiest day of my life. I've always wanted to have pasteurized milk!"

JA: A patient had six registered boxer pups. At that time boxer ears were cropped. He contacted me because of the high fee that a Victoria veterinarian was going to charge. I thought it not ethical to compete, and after considerable thought I said I would do it for the pick of the litter. David and I anaesthetized the dogs with intra-venous Nembutal and the deed was done. That is how I got my boxer, Brenda.

Late one Saturday night, a very inebriated husband and wife came in. She'd split her scalp open. I used silk sutures to sew her up, and told her to come back in a week or so and I'd take them out. Well, I forgot about it, and she didn't turn up. Six or eight weeks later she came in all infected, and said, "There's something wrong with my head—I don't know what it is."

The people at some of the Cusheon Lake cottages were pensioners or on welfare. They wouldn't come in to the office, because it cost them money to get in. So we made house calls you'd never make nowadays.

DB: I learned basic economics from the taxi business there. I noticed that I was getting suddenly far more house calls from Fulford Harbour. I talked to the cab driver about it, because patients used to use him. He said, "If you raise the price of your house call by a dollar, they'll take the taxi to your office instead."

The cost per day in our hospital when I went there was $2.75. When prepaid medicine came in, and the province assumed responsibility for the hospital, within six months the cost for a day in the hospital was $18. We would send out bills every month, and we knew the finances of most of our patients, so we'd reduce our rates from the fee schedule. Then we got half of that, when the bills came in. Prepaid medicine came in while we were there, and suddenly we were getting 75 percent, whereas before we were getting less than 50 percent.

JA: But the problem was, not everyone could afford the medical insurance plan premiums. We were often paid in kind. We'd get meat, and I used to get cream from Mrs. Dodds.

DB: I got a suit from the local clothing guy, for doing his son's appendix. I got a rabbit every week for four months, for doing a hysterectomy.

When people went to jail, you had to go in and examine them. A doctor friend from New Westminster got really drunk, and the RCMP officer, Gordon Graham, had to put him in jail. Then a patient came in with appendicitis, and I needed to operate. John wasn't there at that time. So I said, "Gordon, will you let me take that guy out of jail for a couple of hours?" So this doctor helped me do the appendix, and then we put him back in jail.

One day the CPR ferry came in from Vancouver. The first mate came up to see me in the office. "Dr. Boyes, would you please come to the boat with me? I think my skipper's gone crazy." So I went to the boat, and he was right off his head. I had to authorize the first mate to take over the ship. He had the skipper tied down so he wouldn't jump overboard. I gave him something.

The nephew of British Field Marshall Wavell lived on Mayne Island, and I got a call late in the day that he had burned himself very badly. I got to his house in a taxi. He had a police dog, and the dog wouldn't let me in. The taxi driver refused to help. I got a piece of firewood that felt good in my hand, and I hoped the dog would go for my head. I approached him and he went straight for my throat, and I whammed him. I took this guy out by taxi. He had a terrible burn, so I sent him to Victoria. They grafted him and did all sorts of fancy things. He'd dry his wood by putting it on top of the stove. Then he'd forget and it would go on fire. About three months later, I got another call. He'd done it again, but this time he'd killed himself.

JA: I learned that I shouldn't transport patients in my car. I got a call one night to see an old man. When I saw him, he was having chest pain. I thought he was having a coronary, and I said, "Look you've got to come to the hospital with me." I insisted, and we got in my car and we chatted about his life. About halfway to the hospital, I realized he wasn't talking to me anymore. He was gone.

I got an emergency phone call to see a lady who lived on the road to Fulford Harbour. I went down, and she was in advanced labour. I put her in the car and was taking her to the hospital when her membranes ruptured. So I decided after that, I'd call an ambulance.

There were a lot of remittance people on the island. There was only one other doctor there—Arnold Francis. He was semi-retired, and very supportive of our practice. He spent a lot of time fishing on his cruiser. He ran a nursing home and frequently supplied his patients with salmon. His favourite expression was "bugger thee."

Lewis Larsen was an American prospector who hit it rich by discovering gold. His daughter Giovanna, a concert violinist, was married to Laurence Hanke and they managed a six-hundred-acre cattle ranch. Mr. and Mrs. Larsen lived in Seattle, but spent summers at Salt Spring on his yacht. We became good friends with the Hankes.

There was a patient of mine called Tiny Conover. He was an American. As a child he had camped on Wallace Island, and his dream was always to own that island—which he did. He was an army photographer, and he was taking pictures in a munitions factory and spotted a beautiful girl. That's how he discovered Marilyn Monroe. They remained friends, and she came up and visited him on the island.

The Kellogg family had a retreat at Musgrave Landing, and they hosted Adlai Stevenson. Warren Hastings, a British naval architect, and his wife, Barbara, had retired to a twenty-acre estate on Ganges Harbour, where they built a manor house. David and I became good friends of [Warren and Barbara], and frequently enjoyed their hospitality. As chair of the hospital board, Barbara was very supportive in getting hospital equipment that we needed.

The Athol peninsula is 550 acres, with six miles of waterfront. When I lived there, the property was a sheep farm owned by Captain Qvale and his wife. The captain was very ill and I made frequent house calls, always admiring the setting.

Ganges as the young doctors saw it from a seaplane on their emergency house calls. Note active log and booming ground. Harbour House Hotel and Hastings House are on the bay at upper right.
Courtesy Salt Spring Island Archives

Top left: left to right, Dr. John Ankenman, Jo Ankenman, Louise Boyes, and Dr. David Boyes at farewell reception, Harbour House, Ganges, 1953.
Courtesy John Ankenman

Top right: Dr. David Boyes and Dr. John Ankenman visiting Yorke Island, 2004.
Courtesy John Ankenman

From my viewpoint, the practice was one of the highlights of my life. I have never regretted it. Now let me tell you why I left. It was the year that David was away, and I had spent a Sunday making house calls from one end of the island to the other. One of those very busy days, and I came home very tired, and my wife had roasted a chicken and set it up in front of the fire in the living room—it was seven or eight o'clock at night, just a special dinner. Just as we sat down, the doorbell rang. An elderly lady came and said, "I was visiting town, and I need my toenails clipped." I said to my wife, "This is the last year I'm going to spend here."

DB: I left because I was out of it—getting behind. There was no way I could keep up. There were new drugs and new diagnostic things coming on. So I went back into obstetrics and finished my training.

When the doctors sold their home and practice in Ganges, a farewell party was held at Harbour House Hotel. Each was presented with a sterling silver cigarette box from Birks. The engraving read, "In appreciation with good wishes from the residents of the Gulf Islands—June 1953."

John Ankenman became head of urologic sciences at UBC Health Sciences Hospital. He also joined a group of investors who developed the Athol Peninsula as Maracaibo Estates. He and his family kept a boat there, and enjoyed Salt Spring Island for many more summers.

David Boyes became director of the Cancer Control Agency of BC, and a world authority on cervical cancer.

NOTES ON WOODEN FORESTRY BOATS

5

by Rick Crosby and Rob Morris

Coast Ranger
The Last Wooden Forestry Vessel
by Rick Crosby

When the BC Forest Service's (BCFS) 52-foot wooden patrol vessel *Coast Ranger* was launched in 1967, it was a part of the Service's fleet that had numbered, since its formative years in the 1920s, about sixty traditionally constructed, plank-on-frame vessels. The *Coast Ranger* was the last one built, and, from the late 1980s to 2008, the last of that fleet in service on the BC coast.

Based out of Prince Rupert in the North Coast Forest District, for close to twenty years the *Coast Ranger* transported timber cruisers and scalers out into the coastal forests, delivered seedlings to tree-planting crews and carried out fire inspections. There were few roads providing access to the coast and into the logging camps. The vessel was primarily used as accommodation for BCFS personnel, with as many as nine on board, including the skipper and cook/deckhand. When coastal logging activity was at its peak, the *Coast Ranger*, like the vessels stationed in other Forest Districts, also served as a self-contained office for the forest rangers. They had their air photos, charts and files on board and worked right off the boat.

In its last two decades, the *Coast Ranger* continued to serve the North Coast Forest District in a most utilitarian fashion. Positioned in remote inlets so BCFS staff could monitor road-building activity, timber sales contracts and forest stewardship operations, the vessel could relocate readily as logging camps were moved. The *Coast Ranger* covered the entire northern forest district, which stretched from Stewart in the north to Princess Royal Island in the south.

On the isolated north coast, the *Coast Ranger* was also used to patrol for log theft. Forestry crews could see certain features of the coast far more easily from the decks of the vessel. While doing shoreline inventory work they patrolled slowly, and this allowed them to spot the cut stumps of poached trees that wouldn't show from the air.

The *Coast Ranger* gave the BCFS a presence on the coast, but a large portion of the rationale for continuing to operate the vessel came down to dollars and cents. While increased road and aircraft access in the more southern forest districts, as well as maintenance costs, were the main reasons for the retirement of virtually all of the fleet, the *Coast Ranger* remained viable. The *Poplar III*, the second-to-last retired, was auctioned off by the BCFS in 1987.

Given the *Coast Ranger*'s mobility as transport and accommodation on the remote coast, a strong case for its continued operation was in the notorious weather conditions on the North Coast. Weather permitting, a crew can be dropped off just about anywhere by a helicopter or floatplane. But it's costly to have that equipment do standby time and, if the weather turns stormy or low visibility sets in, the crew can be stuck until it eases and the aircraft can safely fly again. The *Ranger* provided a safe, comfortable work platform that could withstand anything the weather threw at it.

The *Coast Ranger*'s daily running cost was the same as that required to charter a helicopter for just one hour (plus its fuel costs). Floatplanes, while their rates are lower than helicopters, are more restricted in their coastal access. In addition, the daily costs for *Coast Ranger*'s skipper and a deckhand, plus meals for them and the BCFS personnel on board, were less than half the going rate to charter one of the private vessels on the coast offering remote accommodation for crews.

Weather conditions, isolation and difficulty of access will always be impediments to the BCFS's North Coast operations. With ingenuity, careful maintenance and upgrading, and an eye to the bottom line—and not a little fondness and dedication to their fine wooden workboat—the North Coast Forest District personnel kept the *Coast Ranger* working for them practically and cost-effectively for twenty years. However, with declines in coastal logging activity on the North Coast, it became harder to justify the *Coast Ranger* being used only a few weeks a year, as well as the vessel's significant costs for annual maintenance. So the last wooden BCFS vessel was finally taken out of service in 2009, and was sold in a Crown assets auction in 2010 to a new owner, Rick Weston of Cobble Hill. He immediately enrolled *Coast Ranger* in the Ex-Forest Service Vessel Squadron alongside other surviving wooden vessels from the proud BCFS fleet.

The *Coast Ranger* in Portland Canal on BC's North Coast, c. 2005. The 52-foot, traditionally constructed vessel was built and launched in 1967 by the BC Forest Service's Marine Depot on the North Arm of the Fraser River. The Port Hardy–based *Forest Patrol*, a fibreglass 52-foot vessel built by Canoe Cove Manufacturing (Sidney, BC) in 1974, now covers the coast for the BC Ministry of Forests and Range.
Courtesy North Coast Forest District

The *B.C. Forester* at Toba Inlet
with the Forest Service's Captain
Avery on board, 1957.
NA-16830 courtesy Royal BC
Museum, BC Archives

The Forest Service's Wooden Fleet
by Rob Morris

The BC Forest Service's (BCFS) first depot was established at Thurston Bay on Sonora Island in 1914. There, the shipwright crew began building wooden boats for the patrol fleet.
Courtesy Tom Edwards collection

The *Sitka Spruce* was the first 32-foot Gardner diesel-powered ranger launch built at the depot in Thurston Bay, along with the *Douglas Fir* and *Red Cedar* in 1918–19, and the 30-foot *Check Scaler* built in 1924.
Courtesy Tom Edwards collection

The 1923-built 65-foot *BC Forester*, now called the *Kwaitek*, was the first headquarters launch and the flagship of the fleet. It is the only Thurston Bay–built vessel still afloat.
Courtesy Tom Edwards collection

Eleven assistant ranger launches, a proven model nicknamed the "blimp," were constructed at the Fraser River facility from 1944 to 1952—*Red Cedar II, Cherry II, Douglas Fir II, Alder II, Arbutus II, Silver Fir, Western Ash, Oak II* (shown here), *White Birch, Cottonwood II, Sitka Spruce II.*
Courtesy Tom Edwards collection

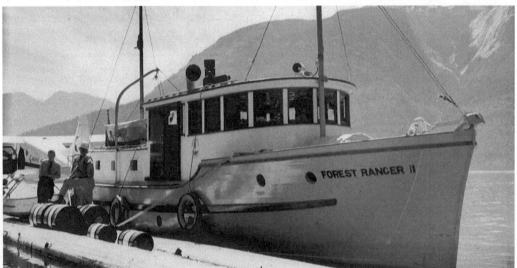

The 46-foot chief ranger launch *Forest Ranger II* was launched in 1953 and the 40-foot twin-diesel vessels *Western Hemlock* and *Forest Dispatcher* entered service in 1958 and 1961, respectively. Commissioned in 1967, the *Coast Ranger* was the last wooden vessel built by the Marine Depot crew.
Courtesy Tom Edwards collection

The BCFS also acquired existing vessels for their fleet over the years. The *Yellow Cedar* was launched in 1914 as the Fisheries patrol vessel *Bonilla Rock* by the W.R. Menchions shipyard in Coal Harbour, Vancouver. Acquired by the BCFS in 1948, it served as the Tofino-based forest ranger launch for many years.
Courtesy Tom Edwards collection

The Ex-Forest Service Vessel Squadron
by Rob Morris

When the Ex-Forest Service Vessel Squadron (EFSVS) held its first rendezvous at the Garden Bay Marina in Pender Harbour in June 1992, the owners of the vessels, all retired from the BC Forest Service's fleet, were there to share common interests in their classic, BC-built, wooden vessels. But more importantly the Squadron recognized collectively that its role as custodian of a BC coastal heritage and way of life grew on the strong backbones of their sturdy vessels, and remains alive with the boats and in the memories of the Forest Service personnel who walked their decks.

For many years a large fleet of "public service vessels"—hospital and public works vessels, Fisheries and police patrol boats, the church mission vessels and the BC Forest Service's fleet—provided much of the connective sinew of the coast's society. Together with the coastal freight and passenger services, they linked the hundreds of small settlements, logging and mining camps and homesteads clinging to the shoreline in bays and inlets up and down the coast. After World War II, however, roads were pushed through to the coast and floatplanes began to provide unlimited access. The public service fleets dwindled in size and importance. The Forest Service fleet was deemed inefficient and gradually auctioned off to private owners.

In most cases the new owners realized what they had acquired—well-constructed, solid vessels in prime condition. It was the Forest Service's unflagging pride in, and respect for, their vessels and the personnel that crewed them, that was translated into the highest

Tom Edwards (top) worked as a shipwright at the BCFS marine station at Thurston Bay, Sonora Island, from 1939 until 1941, became boatbuilding foreman in 1946, then superintendent of the Forest Service Marine Depot on the Fraser River until 1979. The Marine Depot closed in 1988 when it became Celtic Shipyard. Edwards oversaw the building of many of the BCFS vessels and was responsible for the high standard of maintenance of the fleet. He came to see "his boats" at the 2011 rendezvous of the Ex-Forest Service Vessel Squadron at Steveston, BC, and passed away the following year.
Courtesy Doug Mitchell

standards of construction and upkeep in the fleet over the years. One Squadron member summed up a common understanding at the first rendezvous when he said, "If it wasn't for the Forest Service, my vessel would have been on the bottom long ago."

The Squadron vessels proudly retain their classic and original configurations, and some still have their "Forestry grey" hull paint. In 2012 the EFSVS rendezvous coincided with the BC Forest Service Centennial celebration. As a sign of appreciation and respect for the manner in which the Squadron owners have kept up their vessels, the Forest Service's centennial committee had a brass plaque cast for each member vessel. It was most fitting that a plaque was also presented to the family of Tommy Edwards, the man who oversaw the building and maintenance of the fleet for many years.

There are currently approximately forty Ex-Forest Service vessels (wood, fibreglass and aluminum constructed) still afloat, the majority in BC waters, the rest in Washington state. As of March 2013, fourteen wooden vessels (ten in BC, four in Washington state) are members of the EFSVS:

Above and bottom opposite page: The Ex-Forest Service Vessel Squadron's rendezvous in Victoria Harbour in 2012 coincided with the BC Forest Service's Centennial celebration. The Forest Service presented each vessel and former Marine Depot superintendent Tom Edwards (posthumously) with a commemorative brass plaque (inset).
Courtesy Doug Mitchell

Alpine Fir II	*Oak II*
Cherry II	*Silver Fir*
Coast Ranger	*Sitka Spruce II*
Dean Ranger	*Syrene*
Forest Ranger II	*Tamarack*
Kwaitek ex BC Forester	*Western Yew*
Maple II	*White Birch*

The EFSVS is reasonably certain that the following wooden vessels from the former Forest Service fleet are also still afloat:

Cottonwood II	*Poplar III*
Douglas Fir II	*Sea Ox*
Forest Surveyor	*Wells Gray*
Hecate Ranger	*White Spruce*
Nesika	*Yellow Cedar*
Oliver Clark II	

6

THE NON–UNION JOB

by Alan Haig-Brown

After dropping out of high school to go commercial fishing, I eventually finished grade twelve with the help of Vancouver's Shurpass College. In 1963 I moved to Vancouver to start at UBC. As a former commercial fisherman and a country boy, I looked for a place to live on the waterfront. I found it under the Granville Bridge, at 1801 Granville Street, in a shack that had once been a floathouse. Clay's Wharf was squeezed between Girody's Sawmill and a little bite of False Creek, beside the causeway to Granville Island. Today there are condos where the sawmill was, a sea-wall walk where my house was and a bunch of plastic boats where the marina was.

Above: Clay's Wharf as seen from the Granville Bridge in the early 1960s. I spent three winters living there either on a boat or in the house at the end of the dock.
Courtesy Alan Haig-Brown

Left: The chip conveyor for Girody's Sawmill and the Burrard Street Bridge in the distance.
Courtesy Alan Haig-Brown

Above: Me, at twenty-one years old, trying out a beard at Clay's Wharf.

Vicki Robbins photo, courtesy Alan Haig-Brown

Right: The wharf and house stretched along what is today a seawall path. Girody's Sawmill has been replaced by condos and the ragtag collection of wooden pleasure boats and work boats have been replaced by upscale plastic models.

Courtesy Alan Haig-Brown

For many years, Harold Clay ran his little marina on a sliver of leased waterfront. The industrialized creek was filthy, with rats that were big enough to eat cats. But it was a great place to live rent-free in return for caretaking, with no neighbours objecting to parties, and a little kicker boat to explore the local waters. The marina customers kept a ragtag flotilla moored on floats around Harold's five charter boats. The charter boats were all painted a rich turquoise, and ranged from the 52-foot *Arrawac* to the boxy cabin cruiser *Arrawac V*. These were rented out through the summer months, but remained moored through the winter. It wasn't much of a living, but Harold got by with frugality.

Then, in an attempt to move his marine game up a notch, he bought the classic 77-foot *Beatrice*. Built in 1891 as a sealing schooner, she had served time as a tug, and latterly as a coastal freighter. She came with freighting contracts, but Harold incurred some bad luck when he changed the veteran's name to *Arrawac Freighter*. Not only did he lose the contracts, but ran the boat up on the shore whenever he tried to move her.

Finally Harold made a deal with another marginal company called Loggers Freight Services Ltd. I never knew the arrangement, but it was likely as haywire as the deal he offered me. "I need good crew on the *Freighter*," he told me. "I will pay you 6 percent of the gross proceeds for each trip."

Left: Moored on the Granville Island side *c*. 1964.
Courtesy Alan Haig-Brown

Below left: The fleet of charter boats with Harold Clay on left and his dogs to the right.
Courtesy Alan Haig-Brown

Below right: I worked on the *Arrawac Freighter* in 1964.
Courtesy Alan Haig-Brown

In 1964, coastal freighting, like tugboating, was a good job. It paid union wages and you got a day off, with pay, for every day worked. I had spent three years as a commercial fisherman, where we fished whenever the government allowed, and we were paid a share of a union-negotiated price. A deckhand got one-tenth of the catch. I was finishing my first year at UBC in April, and needed work to carry me through to the salmon season at the end of June.

Although I have never heard of such an arrangement since, shares on a freighter sounded like my fishing work. On top of that, Harold offered my wife, Vickie, a half share to do the cooking, with no deck work. I accepted and Clay explained he wouldn't need a cook until the following week, but I could start the next day, as the boat was loading for its weekly trip. "I also want to get someone that I can trust on the boat," he added. "I don't know what they are doing up the coast, but I need a report."

With some trepidation I joined four crew members at the loading dock on Granville Island. It was located beside the Arrow Transfer warehouse that is today Bridges restaurant. A yacht broker now uses our big yellow loading crane as part of his sign. In 1964 this was a dirt parking lot where we sorted the freight from delivery trucks onto pallets. These were then slung over the side and into the freighter's forward hold.

We had been working a few hours when I joined the mate, Gus, and the cook, Riley, in the galley for coffee. Riley was reading a letter and Gus was cussing. I asked what the trouble was, and Gus explained that Riley had been given a one-week notice. Riley had been working hard handling freight, and I suddenly realized Harold had been less than forthright with me. A full-share cook/deckhand was to be replaced by a half-share cook. I told the crew what I knew of the situation, and joined Riley as he went up to the office to phone the boss and, not having a union rep, threaten Labour Relations Board

The main deckhouse of the *Arrawac Freighter* before the walk-in freezer was added. This image was taken by folksinger and photographer Stanley G. Triggs, whose album *Bunkhouse and Forecastle Songs of the Northwest* on Folkways is still available from the Smithsonian Institution in Washington. *Stanley G. Triggs photo, courtesy Alan Haig-Brown*

and other dire mayhem. I took the phone and, as men did in those days, spoke for my wife, saying she would not sail under these conditions.

Sometime after dark, the cargo—a mix of groceries, totes of bottled beer, tools, engine parts, boom chains, propane tanks and other essentials of coastal life—was loaded. As the new man I was assigned to the captain's watch. Gary, the captain, had expressed some reservations about having a "college kid" on the boat. When we rounded Point Grey he gave me a compass course to steer to Porlier Pass. Although a lot of coastal travel on fishboats and freighters alike was point-to-point or light-to-light, according to the indispensable *Captain Lillie's Coast Guide*, I had done my share of wheel time in fog and darkness where compass courses on radar-less fishboats were the norm. During the last few hours of the skipper's six-to-twelve watch, Gary and I established a mutual respect that would grow into genuine friendship.

We took a side trip to the Gulf Islands to visit the dynamite factory on James Island, where we picked up a ton of 70 percent dynamite for a mine on Texada Island. The dynamite was stowed as deck cargo, well forward, and a red "dangerous-cargo" flag was hoisted.

On the stern, just behind the deckhouse, was a large walk-in freezer. The workers from James Island told us to stow a cardboard box of blasting caps in the freezer, and to be very, very careful how we handled those volatile little devices. Recalling a schoolmate who blew off his fingers with a single blasting cap, I let one of the other crew stow the box.

By the time I came back on for the second afternoon's six-to-twelve watch, we were back out in the Gulf of Georgia and headed north. Riley had served up a good lunch, but when I went down to the galley to fetch coffee for the skipper and me, he was well into a twenty-sixer of rye, and he had a .303 Enfield lying on the galley table. In spite of the gun and the booze, Riley seemed to be in good spirits as he followed me up to the wheelhouse. "Captain," he asked, "do you suppose that if I was to fire a round into the caps on the stern they would touch off the dynamite in the bow?"

Gary smiled and allowed that it might well do just that. "Good," replied Riley, "'cause I don't want there to be anything bigger than a matchstick left."

I did my best to appear as nonchalant as my skipper about the threat, but I felt a lot better once we had off-loaded the explosives at Texada. If that was one of the scarier events in my life, Riley was soon to deliver one of the finest. It was probably the next day, as we were travelling through that narrow pass called the Hole In The Wall. It is indeed as its name suggests, bordered by steep walls covered with a thick wash of dark green second-growth fir. It was a beautiful sunny day with our boat making a steady nine or ten knots through the glassy waters. Riley's bluster had turned to melancholy and he was still rye-mellow when I stopped in the galley for coffee. He had his harmonica out and was playing a tune with a

The Hole In The Wall pass on a grey day.
Courtesy Alan Haig-Brown

lilt that fit the surrounding beauty. I had recently discovered the great Carter family tune "Wildwood Flower" and its less well-known version "Reuben James" that told of a wartime sinking. I suppressed the urge to ask if Riley knew the tune, not wanting to ask too much of the moment. The next tune that he played, without my prompting, was "Wildwood Flower." I was beginning to like this freighter life. Kristofferson had yet to write "Me and Bobby McGee," but this day between Maruelle and Sonora islands, Riley was blowin' soft trying to forget his blues.

Some of the crew remained a bit reserved around me, but I chalked this up to suspicion of a "college boy" that would dissipate with time. Highway access to the BC coast ends at Lund, and our regular work started there. In addition to logging camps, we stopped at a number of stores located in little bays and inlets that were too out of the way for the boats of the Union Steamship lines. It was hard work, with multiple stops on each watch. The deckhand was responsible for preparing the correct freight for each stop in advance, and then handling the hooks or pallet bars for the union rig to off-load the freight in all shapes and sizes. For larger stops the off watch would generally come on deck to help.

There were a few unscheduled stops as well. One was the pub at Minstrel Island. We would come up through the Yacultas and then out into Johnstone Straits via Chancellor Channel above West Thurlow Island, before going back into Havannah Channel at Broken Islands. After a stop at a large float camp on Chatham Channel we came into Minstrel Island. With a long government wharf and freight shed, this little settlement was served by

Minstrel Island was a gathering place for area residents. The bar had a sign on the door telling loggers to remove their caulk boots before entering.
Courtesy the Swan family collection

the big *Northland Prince II*, but our captain liked to go up and flirt with the barmaid, and didn't mind the crew coming along.

The sign on the door required loggers to remove their boots before entering, but seaman wore rubber-soled Romeos made by Vancouver's Leckie Boots. They were similar to those fancy boots that today's yuppies get from Australia, but they cost a lot less, and had steel toes for when we dropped a propane tank. Leaving Minstrel Island, Gary liked to take a shortcut through the Blow Hole, a twisted little pass with a lurking boulder nearly blocking the end. This is not navigation that they teach in maritime schools; it is all local knowledge—the stuff of stories of boats that didn't make it. There was beauty in the harmony and dexterity with which a skipper like Gary could handle a heavy old wooden boat like the *Arrawac Freighter* in such tight places.

The *Northern Prince* was one of Northland Navigation's boats that took freight into the "larger" ports like Sointula and Sullivan Bay. *Dave Lewis photo, courtesy Alan Haig-Brown*

Things had warmed up for me with the crew, but there was still a little reserve. The Minstrel Island stopover gave me enough liquid courage to tell Gus, the mate, that I had been hired to spy on the up-coast behaviour of the crew and report back to Harold. Gus's craggy bearded face broke into a smile. "He has tried this before," Gus laughed, "so we were waiting for you to say something."

After passing through the Blow Hole, we wound our way around Turner and Village islands. We made stops day and night in little out-of-the-way bays and coves where a float camp or a rare isolated homestead still clung to a dream. The hippie invasion had not begun yet. Heading up Knight Inlet, we stopped at a deserted cannery with fading blue-trimmed buildings in Glendale Cove to deliver a new propeller shaft for a gillnetter named *Chiba*. Then it was on up to the glorious spectacle of Knight Inlet, past Cascade Point with its waterfall, and to the head of the inlet where, just outside the shallows, a log raft was moored. We off-loaded a bunch of groceries and a set of Cat tracks there, to be picked up later by the loggers from the Klinaklini River that flows through the mountains from the Chilcotin country.

On my return to our little False Creek shack for an abbreviated weekend, I got my phone call from Harold. He asked me what I had learned about the crew. Exaggerating my experience somewhat, I declared, "Harold, I have worked a lot of different boats on this coast, and this is the finest crew I have ever seen." He never called again.

On that first trip and each weekly trip after, I was overwhelmed with the coastal inlets. Fishermen tended to go back to the same places in Johnstone Straits, or north to Namu or Wales Channel where the fish would come. With the Loggers Freight Service we searched out some of the most isolated holes where loggers needed grub and spare parts. After coming back down Knight we turned in to Tribune Channel and Thompson Sound, making our deliveries. On the north side of Gilford Island we had a favourite stop to off-load the weekly shipment of one hundred cases for the beer parlour there. I recall only one time that it was open so we could go up for a drink. Most often we arrived in the morning, but if we avoided breakage we were rewarded with a case of beer for the crew. There was never any breakage.

From the *Arrawac Freighter* we delivered one hundred cases of beer per week. If we didn't break any, we got to keep a case.
Courtesy Alan Haig-Brown

The free beer was nice, but I soon discovered that my skipper seldom went through an evening watch without a beer or two, and he was kind enough to share with a lowly deckhand. I suppose in some part that was my reward for a couple of stops where he would take a bottle of rye and head up to visit a logging camp or an isolated store. The crew speculated on all sorts of nefarious or sexual exploits, but we stayed on the boat.

This area of the coast that towboaters call "the jungles" and modern yachters call Broughton Archipelago is a great place to spend some time. I remember one day in Drury Inlet the skipper came into the wheelhouse and abruptly ordered "Hard to port!" followed by "Cut the throttle and kick her out of gear." As the boat slowed and drifted toward a big kelp patch, he walked out on deck, retrieved a fishing rod from under the tarp of the lifeboat, and cast a jigger toward the edge of the kelp patch. "There's a good kelp reef here," he said. He really did know every rock.

Between visiting, stopping for a drink here and there, a bit of fishing and once, an unsuccessful bear hunt, it was taking six days to cover the thousand-mile route that was supposed to take only five. We often arrived in Vancouver on a Friday night or Saturday morning with our load out and departure scheduled for late Sunday. But it was great fun, the money wasn't much, and there certainly wasn't any day off for every day on. I suppose each of us had a reason for being on that boat. The older guys had often left more legitimate jobs for reasons unspoken. For a young guy like me, being paid to work on a commercial boat was reward enough.

Riley, the cook, took the "You can't fire me 'cause I quit!" approach to Harold's letter. My wife didn't come on, and we had a series of unsatisfactory cooks. But life on the boat was good. One day we left Vancouver with a huge deckload that included an outboard motor-boat. We were heading into a stiff summer westerly that was kicking up a good chop off Howe Sound. When it started breaking over the bow and threatened to wash the small boat overboard, Gary slowed the freighter and sent two of us forward to lash down the motor-boat and other deck cargo. As we finished, he pushed the throttle forward, and a particu-larly big swell curled up over the bow to soak the other deckhand and me.

That afternoon I was on watch when we headed up Lewis Channel, just past our stop at the Teakerne Arm log booming camp. It was a nice sunny day and Gary had just opened us each a beer from his stash. I asked if he had a spare cigar, as it was in the times of rum-dipped and wine-soaked Old Port cigarillos. Gary kindly provided and I lit up, declaring that it was a good ship where the skipper waited hand and foot on the deckhand. The next thing I knew Gary was charging at me with a hypodermic needle raised and ready to strike. I dashed out of the wheelhouse and escaped. I was never sure of the needle's contents, but was pleased to have escaped finding out.

One of our stops shortly after Lewis Channel was the Surge Narrows store on Read Island. We carried in all of their groceries on our weekly visit. Their shipment, like others in rural stores throughout BC in the days before rural liquor outlets, routinely included a case or two of large bottles of vanilla extract. We never helped ourselves to that or any other freight. The groceries that we carried to the camps were a lifeline in which we took pride. We also knew that we would be back the next week, and already our skipper or mate knew the wrath of a logger's wife whose frozen strawberries had been run over by a forklift back on Granville Island. At times we were blamed for wrong orders from the suppliers, but mostly the arrival of the boat was cause for people to stop what they were doing and

At Surge Narrows in 1964 when I was a deckhand.
Courtesy Alan Haig-Brown

come for a visit. In the evening it was not uncommon to see a young logger all washed and dressed in his going-to-town clothes, including shiny black shoes, so that he could pace up and down on the float.

The *Arrawac Freighter* had few of the navigational aids that are routine on newer vessels. We had a compass, a depth sounder and an ancient radar. One night coming down Knight Inlet, Gary decided to show me his thirty-five millimetre slides from the time he spent running a tug in the Arctic. The only AC outlet on the boat was on the radar set. The pictures of icy seas and hard-working tugs were fascinating when projected onto the back of the wheelhouse, but we had only watched a few when the fuse on the radar blew. This ended our slideshow, and led to a near mutiny when the mate's watch came on an hour later, and threatened to drop anchor rather than sail in those narrow channels without radar. None of the fishboats that I worked on had radar, and Gary and I were able to shame them into accepting the old coastal navigation method of steering point-to-point and light-to-light.

Arrawac Freighter didn't have an autopilot either, so even in the beautiful June weather we would have been confined to the wheelhouse. However, Gary lashed a boathook to the top spoke on the wheel. After that we were able to sunbathe on the railing outside the wheelhouse and steer with the boathook. Another time our skipper demonstrated his boat-handling prowess was the morning we arrived, late as usual, back in Vancouver. In those days the Kitsilano Trestle rail bridge, with a swing span, crossed False Creek just inside the Burrard Bridge. The swing span was left open, and Gary knew the heavy four-by-twelve–inch planks that protected the pillars could indicate the depth. The bridge was built on the ledge of a hard bottom. By counting the horizontal planks Gary knew how much water was on the ledge. On this day we had been trying to make the tide to get to our pier on Granville Island, but the tide was ebbing, and it looked like we were half a plank short. Throttling up the big heavy vessel, he pulled the throttle back and kicked the boat out of gear just as our bow passed the bridge abutments. There was a gentle thump as the keel hit the ledge and bounced the boat over the shallow.

I had been on the boat about six weeks when we got a new cook. He was a lonely sort of guy. He wasn't a very good cook, but that wasn't all that raised suspicions. He told me his last job was as a part-time night guard in a jail up in Peace River country. This was not a man to be trusted. That week we made our usual stop at Minstrel Island. We all headed up to the beer parlour but the cook stayed on board, saying he had to prepare dinner. He was such a loser, and the rest of the crew was so sure he was a bad apple, that I took pity. I left the pub ahead of the others and brought him down a beer under my jacket. He took the beer but refused the invitation to talk. I wanted to give him the opportunity to admit his role, but there was only a dour face concentrating on the mashed potatoes to accompany the handsome roast that was browning in the oven.

When the crew came back, the skipper said that he would take the boat through the Blow Hole while the other watch had lunch. As I was on his watch, that meant I would eat later. "And bring me a plate of that food," he commanded the cook as he climbed up to the wheelhouse.

A short time later, just as we were approaching the sharp turn to avoid the boulder in the middle of the Blow Hole, the cook arrived with a plate of roast and mashed potatoes. He set it on the compass table just as the skipper spun the big wooden wheel. I didn't see if it was his hand or one of the wheel spokes that hit the rim of the plate, sending it spinning into the air and spreading meat, potatoes and vegetables all over the small wheelhouse. "Now clean up the fucking mess!" ordered the skipper. He had clearly made up his mind about the cook.

The next week, there was a new cook. Things were peaceful for the next couple of weeks. We continued our rounds of the sixty-five stops in the islands and inlets of the southern

I was a deckhand when I took this photo in May or June of 1964. We were waiting for the tide to come up so that we could get into the dock and off-load groceries for the store. The shipment always included cases of large bottles of vanilla extract for bootlegging.
Courtesy Alan Haig-Brown

Our captain, Gary, had me nail the board over the word "Clay's" on the ship's side, saying that it was illegal to have anything but the vessel name displayed. There was a lot of tension between the office and crew. The dog in the wheelhouse door was freight.
Courtesy Alan Haig-Brown

coast. I think at that time Kingcome Inlet was about as far north as we went. It was at a logging camp there that the skipper had one of his regular whiskey visits. Then, just at the last week of June, when life seemed to have returned to normal, we arrived back to see termination notices with most of the paycheques. I was spared but quit in support of my comrades. It was almost time to go fishing anyway.

I did agree to help with the loading and stowing of the cargo. Harold also asked me to show the new skipper where all our stops were on the chart. I took him up to the wheelhouse on the boat moored at Clay's Wharf, and began to show him the southern part of our route. "You go up through the Yaculta Rapids," I said.

"Oh yes, I've been through there on one of the Union Steamship vessels," he said. Impressed, I asked, "Were you the skipper?"

"No, I was a passenger," he replied.

"You've got to be kidding me," I thought and maybe he was, but I decided I had best take him over to the Loggers Freight Service office to see Gary, our laid-off skipper. Once there, he persuaded Gary to give him sailing directions by invoking their mutual guild membership.

That evening, when I went down to the boat to help with the stowing, it was a madhouse. Our mate, Gus, was up on the dock, slightly inebriated and daring any of the new crew to come up off the boat and fight him. He was loudly expressing some beer parlour logic to explain why he could legally beat the shit out of them on the dock, but not on the boat. The new mate was in the hold, and kept correcting my stowage plans. In disgust, I climbed out of the hatch, only to find our old jail-guard cook hiding by the deckhouse and signalling me to come over. He was terrified of Gus, and told me that he was hired back on as engineer. Then he pleaded, "Can you come below and show me how to start the auxiliary engine?"

That's when I knew my non-union service to the up-coast logging companies on the *Arrawac Freighter* had come to an end. I had a few days before salmon fishing started. I went up on the dock and collected Gus, who had a car, and we picked up my wife and drove to the Williams Lake Stampede. And that was a whole other story.

PLEASE PUSH THE GATE
Driving Vancouver Trolley Buses

by Angus McIntyre

My earliest memories of urban transit vehicles start in Toronto, and then our family moved to Windsor, Ontario. By the age of nine I was allowed to take the bus from our neighbourhood to downtown—this was a Fageol Twin Coach on the Lauzon bus route. Most Windsor routes terminated at the downtown bus terminal, and I spent time there watching the action. I knew then that this was going to be my future career. After five years in Australia, we moved back to Canada, and I finished grade twelve at Point Grey High School in 1966. That summer I had my first real job as a deckhand on the *Sudbury II*, an ocean-going tug that hauled barges of limestone from Texada Island to Astoria, Oregon.

Fageol Twin Coach buses ran on gasoline and had a very bouncy suspension that used "Torsolastic" rubber mountings rather than springs. This 1966 view shows the rear door gate.

Courtesy Angus McIntyre

But I knew my true calling was to drive Brill trolley buses in Vancouver. I continued my post-secondary education at Vancouver City College, and when my family moved to Winnipeg I was able to remain in Vancouver. My father was a business executive, and wanted me to obtain a university degree.

In July of 1969 I applied to be a bus driver with BC Hydro, just after the first man walked on the moon. The interviews followed quickly, and then I received a call to come in to the Oakridge Transit Centre (OTC) for the "trainability test." This was a session where an instructor was assigned to the applicant, and I was taken out to the yard where there was an old Fageol Twin Coach gasoline bus. A series of instructions on how the bus worked was given, and then the instructor drove the bus to Forty-first Avenue just east of Main Street. At this point I sat in the driver's seat, and for the next half-hour drove around the southeast part of Vancouver. The instructor watched closely to see how well I remembered his directions, and even though I had never driven a bus before, I was being assessed to see if I was "trainable." The next step was a medical exam, and my final interviewer told me he was pleased with everything, except that he felt I was shy by nature and might have trouble throwing drunks off the bus! Radios were over twenty years in the future, and it was often hard to find a working pay phone. I learned that it was easier to use a bit of psychology, but when that didn't work, I hauled problem passengers out of the bus. Not only were we expected to maintain order, but each trainee had to climb up the folding side steps onto the roof of a Brill trolley bus. An instructor had taken a trolley pole and let it go straight up in the air. While on the roof we were told to take hold of the trolley pole and contact the 600-volt DC trolley wire with it to show that the vehicle was insulated by the rubber tires! Then we had to walk the pole down and hook it under the pole hooks. We learned how to rewind the trolley rope into the retriever on the back of the Brill. Using caution, we were expected to keep trolley service running. Training was four weeks; present-day training is six weeks, including one week for the air brake ticket. In 1969 we were required to operate an air brake–equipped vehicle for a certain number of hours, and we received a Chauffeur's

A trolley pole has jammed in the trolley overhead, and a transit supervisor is on the roof attempting to free it. Drivers were expected to climb up onto the roof by using fold-out steps on the side of a trolley bus.
Courtesy Coast Mountain Bus Company

Rob James shows the correct method to rewire a trolley pole. This is done facing the traffic and allows the driver to stand closer to the bus. This is a 1983 Flyer trolley coach built in Winnipeg.
Courtesy Coast Mountain Bus Company

When a parade or disruption caused a detour of a trolley bus, "pole pullers" were used to bridge a gap in the overhead wires. The detour could take place at speed and required the right technique to pull the poles down at just the right moment. When the trolley finished the turn, the pole puller "rewired" the poles. Newer trolleys had battery power to make a detour.

Courtesy Angus McIntyre

"A" licence, with a new badge issued each year. This badge had to be visible to the passengers.

Another interesting part of training was the "detonator test," where the trainees were taken out in a Brill trolley bus to Forty-first Avenue west of Kerrisdale. A metal box was attached to the front bumper and wired into the brake light of the bus. I got behind the wheel and drove up to the speed limit, and then the instructor pushed a switch that fired a chalk mark on the pavement. As soon as I heard the shot I floored the brake pedal, which fired another chalk mark, and held the pedal to the floor until the bus stopped. We then got off the bus and used a tape measure to check our stopping distances. Traffic was so light on a weekday morning that we had the street to ourselves.

We also drove the Brill diesels into Richmond, and it was my turn on the way back to drive through the Fraser Street swing span bridge. This was so narrow that two trucks or buses could not pass in opposite directions at the same time. There was more give and take on the roads in those days.

One of the challenges of driving a bus in Vancouver until 1971 was that the buses did not have a mirror on the right-hand side. If we had to change lanes to the right, we were instructed to leave the turn signal on for half a block, and then do a "test manoeuvre," where we would start to make the change but only go partway. If we heard a screech of brakes or a horn, we were to back off and try again. We learned to use the inside mirror to help, or ask a passenger at the front to look out the side window and see if the next lane was clear.

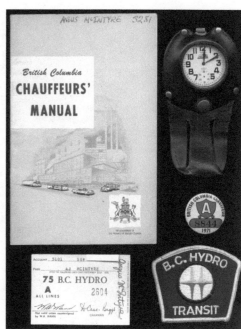

The author demonstrates the method of walking the pole down on the roof of a Brill trolley. If a trolley rope broke, the driver was expected to climb up steps onto the roof, hook the pole down and repair the broken rope. We also learned how to put up each pole in sequence with just one rope.
Courtesy Brian Larrabee

At that time Hydro hired one in ten applicants, a ratio that still holds today. Standards were not as stringent, and one man in my class of six confided to me later that he had not finished elementary school, and was functionally illiterate. I was the youngest at twenty-one, and he was the oldest in his early forties. We were paired for training. He had operated streetcars, trolley buses and subways in Toronto for twelve years, and knew more about the job than any of us. He said he did not answer a single question on the IQ test, but did well on the trainability test.

Our uniforms were made to measure, and our class of six went to Gordon Campbell's at Second Avenue and Quebec Street for fitting. The jackets were military-style Eisenhower "Ike" in navy blue. We wore pale blue shirts that were 100 percent cotton and had to be ironed. We had heavy grey wool slacks that were warm in winter and hell in summer. Uniform shorts did not appear until 1991. Black or brown shoes only, no flashy socks. The blue tie was compulsory until daylight savings time, when it could be removed while wearing a short-sleeved shirt. We were issued a peaked cap with the BC Hydro logo on it. An instructor explained that while it was not compulsory to wear the cap, we could notch up our authority level by wearing it when we went to the rear of the bus to deal with "problem passengers." One winter day I arrived at Broadway and Alma on a 9-Broadway bus, and was met by a transit supervisor. My clip-on tie had fallen off somewhere and was missing. He said, "If you can't get a tie we'll have to take you off the road!" He then asked where I lived, and I told him at Tenth and Spruce. As this was right on the line, he said, "Leave five minutes early and go home and get a tie." I did just that, and later he waved to me at Cambie Street when he saw I was now "properly dressed."

Oakridge Transit Centre was virtually unaltered from when it was built in 1948. The cafeteria in the basement was open for meals until 8:00 p.m. and was a social centre for drivers and other late-night workers. It was not unusual to go there in the early morning

Above: A 1949 vintage Brill T48 trolley bus is shown at Granville and Dunsmuir on the 10-Tenth route. In this 1969 view BC Hydro buses still lack a right side mirror. The man at the rear door is holding the gate for alighting passengers.
Courtesy Angus McIntyre

Right: In between rush hours, trolley buses rest at Oakridge Transit Centre at 41st Avenue and Oak Street. By 5:00 p.m. the yard will be almost empty.
Courtesy Angus McIntyre

A Canadian Car Brill trolley bus is shown at Oakridge Transit Centre ready to leave on an enthusiasts' trip in 1970. From left to right: Seattle Transit driver Keith Daubenspeck, Angus McIntyre and Brian Kelly.
Courtesy Wally Young

hours and find policemen, ambulance drivers, cabbies and other "night owls" sharing a coffee and conversation. Smoking was permitted everywhere, and a large exhaust fan in the drivers' report room, known as the "bullpen," attempted to clear the air. The north wall had movable boards with all the running times posted on blueprints—we had to copy down our own running times from these. In 1971 BC Hydro became the first transit system to print drivers' schedules by computer.

All six trainees were taken in a Brill diesel bus down to the booking office at the police station, where we were fingerprinted by a burly police constable. We were bonded to carry from $120 to $150 of the company's money to sell tokens and make change. At the cashiers' wickets in the bullpen, we were each issued $120 in rolls of tokens and coins in a cloth banker's bag. This would be equivalent to about $800 today. We could also cash in with the cashiers at the downtown bus depot on Dunsmuir Street. Once out of training we earned $3.40 an hour.

The class also visited the main office of the Street Railwaymen's Credit Union (STRY) at Eighth and Quebec, and we were encouraged to join. Facilities included a five-pin bowling alley and a coffee shop. We were told that as employees of BC Hydro, if we wanted to buy a house in the city, STRY could facilitate the purchase. And I did just that in 1977, when a bus driver's salary could buy a house on the west side of Vancouver.

We were advised that a metal tackle box from the Army and Navy fishing department would be suitable for our supplies. These had tilt-up trays for tokens and coins, and a space at the bottom for the changer, maps and other items. Some drivers had homemade boxes, ammunition cans or even briefcases. A friend who started on the job four months before I did had a memorable start to his shift one day. He had a small padlock on his tackle box, and when he arrived at work he realized he had left the key at home. He ran over to the maintenance shop to have the lock cut off, and when that was done he picked up the box and it sprang open, spilling coins and tokens all over the shop floor and into the pits.

Marie, a streetcar conductorette from World War II, drove the Stanley Park–Powell–Nanaimo route during evenings. She wore her changer on her belt and you could hear her coming before you saw her. When I started on the job there were still six women drivers. They started as streetcar conductorettes during the Second World War, but when the city streetcars stopped running in 1955 a number of them became bus drivers. The last of the women drivers of that era retired after the first women of the modern era were hired in 1974.

It was necessary to learn how to load the changer as you drove the bus. This was accomplished by steering the bus with your left hand, and, while watching traffic, you took a roll of tokens or coins and carefully let them slide into the top of the barrel. The Granville Street Bridge, a red light or a train at a railway crossing also provided opportunities to perform this task. After two weeks of learning the basic skills of driving buses and trolley buses, we were assigned shifts with regular drivers to learn the various routes. A "line instructor" would help you learn details about the trolley overhead wires and switches on that route, and give you a chance to deal with the public. Monday mornings were challenging because people would buy a week's supply or more of tokens. In two stops both "B" token barrels could be drained, so as you drove to the next stop you reloaded. Many people bought tokens since it saved a nickel on four fares, half the price of a cup of coffee!

We were all issued a punch with a unique punch mark that allowed it to be traced if there was a transfer dispute. I was the junior driver in my class, and when the punches were handed out everyone was given a brand new, heavy chrome punch except me. A special presentation was made by the instructor to give me my punch. It was smaller, all the chrome was worn off and it had a small piece of chain attached to it. Everyone laughed until the instructor explained that I had been given a historic punch that dated back to streetcar days. We also had to memorize the codes for punching transfers: D for Main–Robson, X for Stanley Park–Powell, and so on.

1969 TRANSIT FARES:

Student "A" tokens: ten for $1
Adult "B" tokens: four for 75¢
Child "C" tokens: four for 30¢
Cash fare: adult, 20¢; students, 15¢; children, 10¢

At this time we had fare boxes known as Grant Money Meters. When a passenger paid a fare, the fare box enunciated the coins and tokens thusly:

1¢: *buzz*
5¢: *bong*
10¢: *bong-bong*
25¢: *bing-bing*
"A" token: *bing*
"B" token: *brrringggg*

"C" token: no sound. These tokens were blue plastic the size of poker chips and had to be emptied manually.

One advantage of this system was that the driver did not need to view the fare paid, but could just listen for the correct sounds. School kids could be a problem sometimes. Word would go out in a school to have a "penny day," and when the kids all got on the bus to go home the old Grant Money Meter would buzz like crazy, until we dumped all the pennies manually.

Drivers could ask a cashier for "three bags of chips" to get "C" tokens. When cashing in, you had to be sure that all the bills faced the same way. On a busy run you could start with four quarters, and count out 250 by the end of the shift. We were encouraged to have all transactions conducted through the change dish. It was felt there was less chance of dropping coins that way.

Needless to say, with handling all this money, Hydro had a group of Company Representatives (we called them "spotters") to oversee our duties with their money. It was hard to pinpoint a spotter, since they travelled incognito. From anywhere in the bus a spotter could determine how much money was deposited by the fare box sounds. I was written up for letting someone on for fifteen cents, who the spotter felt should have paid an adult fare.

Hydro had the right to check your change fund at any time during your shift to be sure the full amount was there. I was once checked by the "Popsicle Stick" supervisor at Broadway and Granville. He had a set of Popsicle sticks with marks on them to show how much was in each barrel of the changer he dipped. He would quickly see how much you had in your changer, count up rolls of tokens and coins, view wads of one- and two-dollar bills, and say, "That's fine. Go ahead." If a driver was short on his change fund, he was disciplined with paycheque deductions.

While most passengers were reasonable, of course there were a few who were not. I recall pulling into the eastbound Hastings and Abbott stop at Woodward's, which was always very busy. The first man through the door asked for change for a five-dollar bill. I said, "Do you have anything smaller?" He reached into his pocket and pulled out a handful of coins. From all the dimes and nickels he could have used to pay the fare he plucked out a quarter and dropped it into the dish for change. We bit our tongues at moments like that.

A malfunctioning changer was serious—it either short-changed the driver or the passenger. I quickly discovered my Johnson changer was giving six "A" tokens at a time instead of five, so I took it into the operations office on the main floor at OTC. This small space hadn't changed since 1948: there was still the clatter of manual typewriters, carbon paper copies and old-fashioned file cabinets. Drivers brought their changers in to Eva, a secretary who was also the changer technician.

A few words about the problem, and she opened her desk drawer and pulled out an array of tools: needle-nose pliers, screwdrivers and rubber mallet, and lined them up on

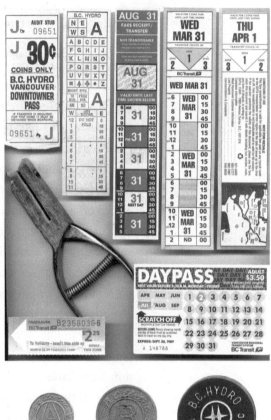

Top: A collection of passes and transfers. Each metal punch had a unique punch mark that allowed it to be traced to a specific driver if there was a transfer dispute.
Courtesy Angus McIntyre

Above: "A" tokens were for students at 10 for $1, the "B" tokens were the adult version at 4 for 75¢, and the "C" tokens were plastic discs the size of poker chips, and were the children's token at 4 for 30¢.
Courtesy Angus McIntyre

her desk. She then tested the changer and attempted to solve the problem by rearranging the interchangeable spacers at the bottom of the "A" barrel. After no success at this, she said, "I'll put on a new barrel." She pried a lock pin over, stood up and proceeded to hammer the offending barrel on the edge of her desk to force it to slide off the changer assembly. The desktop bore evidence of many previous operations like this. Once removed, a new barrel was hammered into place, tested and passed. The changer never malfunctioned again.

Before changers were phased out, some internal thefts took place. If a robbery happened in front of witnesses, you were compensated by the company. In one case a driver's friend pulled off a pre-planned robbery, but the driver was found out and he no longer had a job. One night the run in front of me was robbed at Stanley Park Loop, and on the next trip the run behind was robbed. As the frequency of such events increased, it was inevitable that "Exact Fare" was soon to arrive.

Most trolley routes had a two-minute "headway," the interval between buses, at 5:00 p.m. The rush hour was shorter but more intense then. Imagine an eight-hour shift on a Broadway or Granville–Victoria bus, up to one thousand passengers, manual steering, heavy foot pedals, bench seat, no right-hand mirror, fare box tinkling madly away, and add to this a non-stop demand for tokens, change and information. At age twenty-two I remember staggering off the bus at the end of a shift some days in a state of mild shock. If your thumb or arm was starting to go numb, you were told, "You'll get used to it!" Carpal tunnel syndrome had yet to appear in the dictionary.

By early 1970 many American cities had already converted their transit systems to Exact Fare. Thefts and other issues led BC Hydro to announce it would be Canada's first Exact Fare city, to start April 1, 1970. Hydro started a major media campaign and, at the end of March, I sold my last tokens at Cordova and Carrall, changed my last quarter at Nanaimo and Charles, and returned to the garage. At OTC there was a celebratory mood among the drivers that our job was about to improve greatly. One driver became so emotional that he emptied his cash box, placed it in front of the rear dual tires of an old Brill trolley, drove over it and pinned the flattened remains over the cashiers' wickets in the bullpen with a prominent sign that read: *So long fucking changers!*

With the arrival of Exact Fare the adult fare increased to 25¢, with no tokens available. It would be some years before monthly passes appeared. Hydro also had to decide what to do with the twelve hundred changers they owned, and offered to sell them back to the drivers at $5 or $2, depending on age. A surprising number of us who cursed and swore at the things actually bought them back. Change dishes were removed over the next few weeks, though occasionally a passenger would come up the steps with a dollar bill and my hand would lift up in an automatic reflex to the changer that was no longer there!

A few months after I started on the job, I picked up a passenger at Kootenay Loop. We looked at each other, and he said, "Angus, what are you doing here?" The man was Slim, one of the oilers in the engine room on the *Sudbury II*. I replied that this was my chosen career. He commented that he had expected me to spend the rest of my days "on the water." When I finished training, I telephoned my family to let them know of my new job. My mother was

The author is shown at the wheel of a Brill trolley with changer, change dish and Grant Money Meter fare box. The tally counter was used to keep a daily record of passengers carried.
Courtesy Ken Wuschke

pleased that I had made up my mind on a career. My father was initially upset, but years later he felt I made the right decision.

On rare occasions a passenger, often young, would board without any money. This was a genuine situation, and we accommodated them with a transfer. An adult who boarded with no fare or explanation was considered a serious problem, so much so that trolley poles were pulled, service stopped, supervisors and even police attended to deal with the matter. It was not in people's mindset then that they could ever board a bus and not pay.

When I started there were quite a few men and women who had worked on the streetcars. One thing I enjoyed was listening to their stories of those days, and by the time I retired in 2010 I was telling stories of my early experiences to new drivers. Seniority is very important to a bus driver, and it dictates the shifts, hours and days off that can be worked. I worked evenings for most of forty years, and drove four generations of trolley buses during that time. I had four different employers, three unions and four major labour disputes during my career.

Vancouver in the early 1970s was relatively unchanged from the 1950s. There were more than a few eccentric passengers, such as Robin Rear View, The Duchess, also known as the Contessa or the Rubbernecker, the Hat Lady, Rodney Rosary, Coffee Boss, the Gas Mask Woman, The Dinner Roll Man and others. Since I worked the same line for many years—the Stanley Park–Nanaimo route—people often commented on how it must get boring. But there is always entertainment from the passengers.

The author is shown at Oakridge Transit Centre during a three-month lockout in 1984. The following year BC Transit replaced Metro Transit.

Unknown

I was working a 9-Broadway route one Sunday afternoon in 1970 when two women boarded the bus eastbound at Granville. A lady in her eighties said, "We want to get off at Commercial to catch the Grandview car." The woman with her, in her fifties, said, "Don't be ridiculous, Mother, that hasn't run in years. We want to get the Victoria bus, driver." I did not like the daughter's treatment of her mother, so when we approached Commercial, I called out in a very loud voice, "Commercial Drive, change here for the Grandview car." As the two women alighted, the older one turned to her daughter and said, "There, I told you so!" Some older passengers still referred to the transit system as the BC Electric.

Before beer became available in cans, it could only be bought in "stubby" bottles. These were sold by the dozen in cardboard boxes, and were quite heavy. The box had a pop-up handle, or an opening in the side to carry it. I had three incidents in the early 1970s, all at the Princeton Hotel stop at Powell and Victoria. A man would board with a case of beer to take home, having already visited the beer parlour. While standing at the front, he had not secured his pants properly, and it was a choice of having his pants fall to the floor, or drop the case of beer to prevent that. In each incident the case of beer did not fall but the pants did. On two occasions passengers got full exposure.

From 1972 to 1977 I was a line instructor every Friday night on the Stanley Park–Nanaimo route, which terminated at Slocan and Kingsway. I had to warn each trainee about Peggy, who boarded at the Cordova Street stop of Woodward's Department Store. Peggy was in her mid-seventies, and would always get dressed up in her best clothes and have her hair done to go shopping at Woodward's. After shopping, she would pop in to the Metropole Hotel or the Grand Union Hotel "for a few," and often be escorted by one of her gentleman friends to the bus stop to go home. I would be in the front passenger seat and the trainee would be behind the wheel. Peggy was petite, and had a very loud, gravelly voice from an excess of cigarettes and booze. She lived on Slocan with her daughter and grandson. Peggy

and I would chat, and then usually at about Hastings and Nanaimo, she would turn to the seated load of passengers and yell out, "I'm going to get shit when I get home!" The reason I had to warn trainees about Peggy was that when we pulled up in front of her house, which was not a bus stop, she would tip the driver 25¢ for a coffee, and then lunge for a hug and a big sloppy kiss. Waiting at the front door of the house was her daughter, and I would walk Peggy over to the house and carry her shopping bags.

One evening I was driving and pulled up to the Woodward's stop, where there were police cars parked, and a sports car was up on the sidewalk. A regular passenger got on and reported that the car had been speeding and the driver lost control, and everyone got out of the way except Peggy, who was hit. I asked if she knew how badly Peggy was injured, and she said, "I don't know, but as they were loading her into the ambulance, she was yelling: 'I need a drink!'" A month later Peggy was back in circulation to entertain us.

As drivers, we had to use discretion when it came to dealing with passenger requests. I was driving a Powell bus early one evening, and picked up two young men at Cordova and Abbott. They asked if I stayed very long at the terminus at Eton and Renfrew. I replied about eight minutes, and they then asked if they could bring a large object on the bus. Since it was after the rush hour, I thought this would be okay. When I asked what they had to move, the response was "a coffin." Full size. This was a rental casket from a house on McGill Street, and would save paying to move it in a taxi van. I agreed, and sure enough there they were on the

Winters were colder with more snow forty years ago, and the transit system installed grooved tires on the buses for better traction. People rode the Brills down to Stanley Park for ice-skating on Lost Lagoon.
Courtesy Angus McIntyre

return trip with the coffin. It took two minutes to get it in the front doors of the Flyer trolley bus, and I suggested they place it on the floor behind the rear doors to be out of the way, and it would be easier to remove it through the back doors. All went well until I discovered that they wanted off at Granville and Davie, by which time the bus had a seated load of passengers. As it turned out the coffin would not fit through the back doors, and in order to get it out the front doors we had to get people to leave their seats in that area. One lady with limited English seemed to think there was a body inside and was getting upset. It took two minutes to get the coffin out the front doors, to the surprise of people on the sidewalk. The two men explained they needed the coffin for a Fringe Festival play they were producing, which involved black humour. I decided the experience was worth it, since people do not move caskets on the bus system every day.

There were also more than a few interesting bus drivers to keep the job entertaining. "Big Lou" weighed over three hundred pounds, but was agile on his feet. If he had trouble sitting comfortably in the driver's seat, he would use his weight to bend the seat back. Unruly passengers rarely attempted to tangle with him. He was an avid racetrack fan, and since he worked the extra board, he could often sign a two-hour Race Express bus direct to Exhibition Park, enjoy several hours of betting, and get paid to drive a bus back to the garage. He even ran his own lottery in the bullpen once for drivers to guess his weight. A set of scales was brought in to determine the winner.

Doug was a senior driver when I started, and began his career on the old streetcars. He always worked evenings on the trolley buses, and on the busy lines like Main and Fraser. He was in a world of his own, and we marvelled at the things he could get away with. He had a beanbag ashtray that nestled on the dash, and with careful adjustment of vents and windows, he often smoked as he drove. He punched a dozen books of transfers on his bus ride to pick up his shift on the road, although he might only need three. If you asked him the

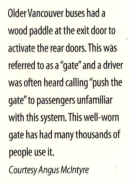

Older Vancouver buses had a wood paddle at the exit door to activate the rear doors. This was referred to as a "gate" and a driver was often heard calling "push the gate" to passengers unfamiliar with this system. This well-worn gate has had many thousands of people use it.
Courtesy Angus McIntyre

Above: After almost forty-one years Angus McIntyre retired as a bus driver. Among other honours he received this bus stop sign that shows the logos of the four companies he worked for. Two vintage Brill trolleys from the Transit Museum Society collection were used on his last day.
Courtesy Susan Roschlau

Above left: Angus poses in front of a Flyer articulated trolley bus in the final months of his career. Compared to the earlier Brills this trolley has a Recaro driver's seat, full power steering and smooth, rapid acceleration.
Courtesy Greg Dixon

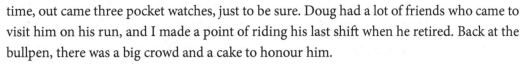

time, out came three pocket watches, just to be sure. Doug had a lot of friends who came to visit him on his run, and I made a point of riding his last shift when he retired. Back at the bullpen, there was a big crowd and a cake to honour him.

Even though I only handled money for seven months, it was an experience I'll never forget. I felt fortunate to be part of the end of an era in Vancouver transit history. I was the senior driver at OTC for five years, and by the time I retired in 2010 there were only four drivers senior to me in the whole system.

I arranged to have two Brill trolley buses that are part of the collection of the Transit Museum Society available for my last run. Co-workers, relatives, friends and neighbours all joined in for two round trips on the 7-Dunbar–Nanaimo that evening. I still maintain my licence, and do volunteer bus trips and community events.

THE MAKING OF TETRAHEDRON PARK

by Heather Conn

Twenty-three years after making what he calls the hardest decision of his life, George Smith leans forward in his living room chair, both to ease his flared-up back and to speak closer to the tape recorder. A gregarious jokester, this Gibsons, BC, resident now looks solemn, his reddish moustache no longer framing a grin. "I went up to the cabins for a week and tried to think of ways that I could avoid my moral responsibility," he says, still with a touch of wryness, recalling his inner conflict in 1989.

The cabins he's referring to are four log structures that stand in the Tetrahedron region or "Tet," overlooking six thousand hectares of mountainous wilderness northeast of Sechelt, BC. (Tetrahedron Peak, named for its shape, is the highest one on the Sunshine Coast at 1,737 metres.) In the summer and fall of 1987, this passionate conservationist and avid backcountry skier, along with friend and neighbour Victor Bonaguro and others, rallied a construction crew and 240 volunteers to build these remote cabins and surrounding trails. The buildings were designed as warming huts and overnight retreats on four separate sites. They were meant for skiers who wanted to access the deep, untouched snow by Mount Steele (elevation 1,650 metres) and elsewhere. They would shelter hikers who came up to enjoy the wilderness forests, fresh blueberries and still beauty in places like Edwards Lake, Bachelor Lake (the spelling's correct; it's a surname) and McNair Lake.

But in 1989, two years after the cabins' construction, Smith saw the logging plans of local Jackson Brothers Logging Company. He realized that this outfit was going to continue logging right down to the edge of some of the area's ten lakes, destroying a substantial part of the Tetrahedron forest. "There was almost no place left [in our forest district] that wasn't

Map excerpt courtesy BC Parks

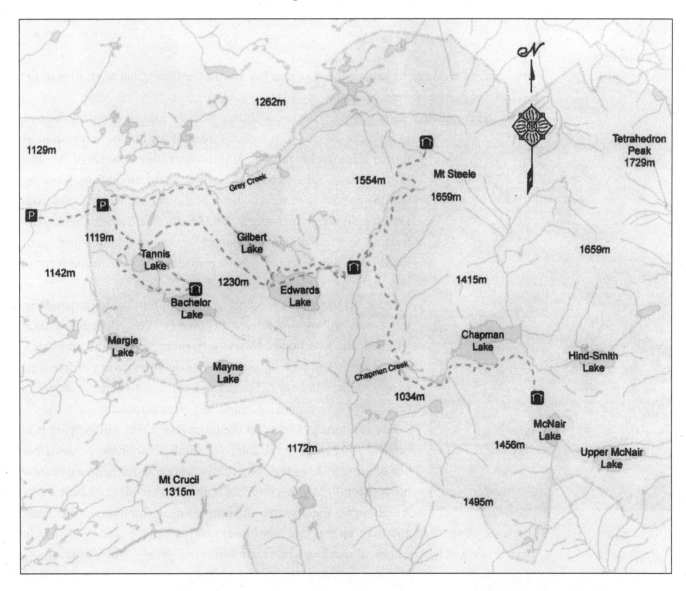

Snow buries most of McNair Lake cabin, May 24, 1999.
Courtesy George Smith

Victor Bonaguro (left) and George Smith, November 2012.
Courtesy Heather Conn

impacted by logging," he says of the area that lies within the traditional territories of the Sechelt and Squamish First Nations.

He didn't want to fight in acrimony but to collaborate with the logging company, he says, to keep the Tetrahedron a cherished spot for outdoor recreation. A former bush worker himself, Smith comes from a family of foresters in the Ottawa Valley. He grew up in a lumbering village, knowing well the kinship of those who work in the woods. Besides, numerous local logging operators—from Ken Sneddon at Sechelt Creek Contracting to the Mainland Logging Division of Canfor—had sponsored the building of the cabins, providing support in the form of logs, industry contacts, labour or advice.

After so much shared effort and community-wide camaraderie, was Smith willing to confront his former allies, challenging their goodwill and livelihoods, by trying to make the Tetrahedron a provincial park? Did he truly want to give up years' worth of free time to take on the Ministry of Forests and a well-entrenched industry to become their version of a *persona non grata* volunteer?

He continues: "I went up the mountain. I was still denying it to myself." After seeking the solace of nature in solitude, he describes one of the wildlife moments in the Tetrahedron that helped galvanize his decision: "I saw this little bear cub and its mom at McNair cabin. It was early in the morning and I was going to climb up Panther Peak. The cub got spooked and went up this tree." Smith says he felt bad for scaring it. "I went back inside and looked out and watched while the mother was going, "Woof, woof, woof," as if saying, 'Get your butt down here.' The little one was squeaking, 'I'm scared.' Finally, the little bear came down. It was in the early morning dew. Both the mother and cub had a beautiful sheen, almost a blue on them. Then they took off, running down toward Chapman Lake."

Fearful of a future that threatened these wild animals and their habitat of mid-elevation mountains, woods, streams and wetlands, Smith says, "I knew I had to do something." That same weekend, while still in the Tetrahedron, the sight of a mother rock ptarmigan and her chicks, at the southern end of their breeding territory, cinched the choice for this expert birdwatcher. "I came down feeling like I had a responsibility to their land," he says now.

Besides providing homes to such creatures, the Tetrahedron region contains the headwaters of the Chapman and Gray Creek watersheds, which provide drinking water to most of the roughly thirty-five thousand residents on the Sunshine Coast. In late 1993, the BC Ministry of Forests' Watershed Cumulative Effects Analysis studied the Chapman watershed and found that about three hundred landslides, mostly caused by logging and the construction of logging roads, had occurred in the Tetrahedron, says Smith. He adds that the Ministry knew in the 1970s that the watershed was already compromised, yet the logging continued. After his solo trip into the Tet, his crisis of conscience was over. He knew that the area needed to be protected. And so began what Smith calls "that scrap": the advocacy campaign to create the largest park on the Sunshine Coast.

But before the community tensions started, before Smith experienced a smear campaign and disturbing middle-of-the-night phone calls from loggers and some disgruntled souls

Young locals, hired under BC Parks' Environmental Youth Team project, peel logs destined to become part of the respective bridges that spanned Steele and Chapman Creeks.
Courtesy Michel Frenette

who had helped build the Tet cabins and now felt betrayed by his push to create a park, hundreds of local volunteers provided an eager workforce in the cabins' construction. In February 1987, volunteers helped a hired crew skin logs of Douglas fir, laid out at the Sechelt airport on a site donated by Sechelt council, for the cabins. In June that year, the shells of the cabins, their flooring, trusses and cedar shakes, plus outhouses, were completed at the airport, using a crew and dozens of volunteers.

That summer, Bonaguro led more volunteers in building the yellow-cedar post foundations for three of the cabins. He oversaw the workers building, sanding, priming and painting doors and windows for the cabins, along with benches, tables and firewood boxes. They also created forty helicopter slings; these triangle-shaped nylon lines, with a hook on the two bottom ends, were used to transport one or two logs at a time by air to the four cabin construction sites in the mountains.

Volunteers helped load logs onto trucks, transport them up the mountain, then unload them at various landings closest to the cabin sites. On cabin assembly weekends, Bonaguro and several other volunteers, including Merrily Corder, would leave Gibsons at four in the morning and be up the mountain at daylight, around five. After creating multi-pages of logistics, Bonaguro, an applied science engineering technologist, ensured that all logs were identified for correct positioning and laid out in parallel rows ready for the airlift. The helicopter would arrive about four hours later. Depending on which of the cabin sites the logs were destined for, there would be only one to five minutes between loads.

Logs unloaded at Edwards Lake, 1987.
Courtesy Merrily Corder

"It was like having a second job for me for a year," says Bonaguro, who worked full-time as owner of Sunshine Kitchens. Today, the sign "Victor's Landing," built and erected in 2012 by the Tetrahedron Outdoor (formerly Ski) Club, stands at this former airlift spot to honour Bonaguro's contribution.

Hard work, not complaining, was *de rigueur* for this volunteer, who laments that people nowadays are soft, exerting themselves less than in decades past. During the project, Bonaguro called himself "The General" while Smith nicknamed him "The Field Marshall" for his officious style in overseeing the airlifts of logs. "Everyone knew what they had to do," Bonaguro says. "That was my job. The helicopter pilot said it was like a military operation."

As project manager, Smith remembers one challenging day while he and his crew were off-loading logs from the helicopter sent by Bonaguro, Corder and other volunteers. "There were personnel problems that day. Things weren't going well. Then we saw one of these logs coming in from the helicopter and dangling down from the thing [sling] was a chocolate bar and a cantaloupe. That made us all laugh."

During the summer and fall of 1987, ski club volunteers, the crew and others from the community—from Girl Guides and Boy Scouts to people with disabilities—built twenty-five kilometres of trails to the cabins. Volunteers cut firewood and built bridges over creeks. Only the people who were bush-wise were allowed to wield a chainsaw. Safety was paramount. "Some didn't know much," says Bonaguro. "You had to kind of help them along."

Guides, Brownies and leaders at Bachelor Lake cabin, October 1987.
Courtesy George Smith

Smith remembers the contributions—in almost Paul Bunyan style—of one young volunteer who worked on the bridge at Mayne Lake. "He was a logger, strong as a horse. He got up there and looked around. He was helping us build bridges. He got in there with his muscles and his saw . . ." Bonaguro continues the story: "I said: 'The snags are over there. Here's the saw. Can you do it?' He said, 'Yes, I can.' He took one huge step. We had to take three steps to catch up with him. He just whipped that [snag] off. That was remarkable."

Volunteers as young as five, along with their families, would come up for a day or a weekend to clear brush for trails. Seniors such as John Hind-Smith, a seasoned outdoorsman and environmentalist, readily lent their expertise or sweat equity. Hind-Smith had been exploring and promoting the Tetrahedron for decades, trying to encourage politicians, academics, the media and Ministry of Forests to recognize its value as a wilderness retreat, worthy of protection. A lake in the park now unofficially bears Hind-Smith's name. In 2006, he was awarded posthumously the Sunshine Coast Conservation Association's Environmental Achievement Award for his exceptional dedication and commitment to the environment and wildlife preservation. Starting that year, the award has been renamed the John Hind-Smith Environmental Achievement Award, in his honour.

Volunteers John Hind-Smith (right) and Jason Winfield clear brush for the Mayne Lake trail.
Courtesy George Smith

"John was delighted to take people into the woods and teach them about the environment, plants and birds, sitting down, surrounded by all these flowers," Smith says. "People were getting into the woods, and it wasn't being spoiled." He adds: "When we were cutting the trails, the volunteers were enthusiastic. It was infectious."

Both Smith and Bonaguro ran a tight but fun operation. Smith let construction crew members go if they weren't willing to work hard. When he was asked to take on a half-dozen "bad boys," who were doing community service for minor crimes, he told them: "I know why you're here. We could use your help. See those guys over there? They know what they're doing. You could learn something and help your community. If you think this is just a game and you're going to slack off and get your hours counted, there's the road. Goodbye. It's up to you. We're not going to babysit anybody. We've got work to do. And you know, they all responded well to the challenge."

Corder, then a child-care worker, remembers these troubled youth blossoming while sharing the work and camaraderie in the mountains. "It was a nice opportunity to compliment them and build their self-esteem," she says. "You could see them growing. They worked really hard and wanted to come back." With extensive backcountry experience, Corder says that she enjoyed mentoring these and other volunteers. She not only shared

Volunteers Merrily Corder (left) and the late Eileen Bonaguro at Gilbert Lake, October 1987.
Courtesy George Smith

wilderness survival skills and tips on safety and proper clothing, but encouraged them to see how rewarding life in the outdoors can be. "I could role-model being present in the moment with the weather, trees, my muscles and breath, and how that ties into being one with the natural world. It's a spiritual thing."

Despite the flies, mosquitoes and sometimes rainy conditions, Corder says that almost every volunteer, including those who had never been in the woods before, thrived while working on the Tet project. "We all learned from each other. There was an all-round good feeling. People from all walks of life were feeling healthy. It's so exhilarating in the fresh, clean air, drinking pure water from the stream. People were experiencing how good they were starting to feel just from being there."

Bonaguro remembers: "Ninety-nine percent of people who came out were really happy. Usually, the weather was really nice, especially in autumn, when all the colours were there. The kids saw the little trees growing. Some of the adults said, 'Oh, look at those pine trees, they're six feet high.' The kids would be running around them and running through the flowers." Back in Gibsons, he'd have volunteers showing up at his home at any time of day to use his private woodworking shop during the cabin construction phase. "They were happy to do it."

In hindsight, this volunteer-driven project offered many of the same elements as an effective corporate team-building exercise: organizational skills, opportunities for personal and group transformation, and confidence-building. A small group of people spends time in the wilderness to develop leadership skills and a shared vision, learn appreciation, commitment and accountability, while gaining empowerment and a deeper sense of connection to nature. But the Tetrahedron project wasn't just a two-day or week-long junket for transplanted urbanites. Some volunteers spent many consecutive weeks and weekends in the Tet as their own wilderness backyard; this land and its waters were part of their natural community. Smith and Bonaguro, who spent ten years with BC Hydro in the north of the province, both came from a resource-extraction background; for them, this work went far beyond mere bush labour. Values of preservation were at stake. Bonaguro says: "I wanted to do something positive—not extraction."

The impetus to open the Tetrahedron's wilderness to public recreation came from volunteers and the allure of Mother Nature herself. It took the remnants of a local ski club and the curiosity of a handful of intrepid telemark skiers, on a quest for high, open tracts of unsullied snow, to launch the plan to construct wilderness cabins in the Tet where none had ever been.

In the mid-1960s, some tradesmen at the mill in Port Mellon on the Sunshine Coast, who wanted to ski free locally with their families, bought a rope tow from Hollyburn Mountain and installed it on Mount Elphinstone near Gibsons. One of these people was Wayne Greggain, a key player in launching the Tet cabins. This group of dedicated skiers and volunteers built a cabin as a warming hut, close to the rope tow. They used a Tucker Sno-Cat and a long rope to haul people on skis up the mountain, plying the steep switchbacks of the local B&K Road in Roberts Creek.

Volunteers George Smith, Richard Chamberlain, Bill Stockwell, Garnet Sully and Aaron Chilton build the Tannis Creek bridge in October 1987.
Courtesy Merrily Corder

Skier Pat Camozzi at Mount Steele peak ridge.
Courtesy Paul Gaulin

But by about the mid-1970s, the BC Ministry of Transport decided that certification was needed to continue this unregulated form of travel. The provincial government increased the club's occupancy permit on Mount Elphinstone from one to five hundred dollars. That's when the Elphinstone operation of the ski club closed, says Bonaguro. However, the club had put a house trailer on Branch Creek, now the Dakota Ridge area near Sechelt, using it as a warming hut for adults and families who skied Dakota Bowl.

By 1984, because of misuse and vandalism, the club removed the trailer. The ski club, which then had fifty to sixty people, dwindled. Still seeking the ultimate powdery terrain, some diehard members decided that they would shut down the Dakota Bowl/Elphinstone ski area and move to the Tetrahedron. By that time, local skiers had made forays into the Tet, but none had skied the summit of Mount Steele. Then in early 1985, resident Ian McConnell made a pioneering trip onto this peak.

That same year, Smith joined him on the June 1 weekend, bushwhacking then skiing up the north side of the same mountain. "When we got up to the top, there was snow to die for there," Smith says. They pitched a tent, skied for three days then came down. He says now, "The light bulb went on in my head. Gee, the snow is wonderful, way better than anything around Vancouver. In the fall, the idea was still percolating in my head: why don't we build some cabins?"

In December 1985, Smith received an informal go-ahead at a basement meeting in the home of Greggain, president of the still-dormant Tetrahedron Ski Club. Nine Sunshine Coast skiers—Greggain, Sneddon, Bonaguro, Randy Dunn, Stan Carsky, Pat Tyson, Bert Sim, Doug Smith and Stuart Nicholls—authorized Smith to try to secure funding to build cabins and a trail system. The group agreed that Greggain would reactivate the ski club to host the project. Smith remembers: "The conversation sort of went like this: 'If we don't do this, somebody else might.' We didn't want somebody to screw it up. We wanted it to be properly done. The basic mood was: You're not going to get the money for this. You're not going to get permission from Ministry of Forests but if you do, well, we'll go for it."

The following year, Smith and Greggain invested hundreds of volunteer hours seeking support and donations for the project. With the help of ski club members like Verna Sim, Marilyn Greggain and Corder, they made presentations to local governments, associations and chambers of commerce. "They had a portable corkboard with pictures of the whole thing [Tet area] with all the mountains: a dog and pony show," Bonaguro remembers. Sned-

Above: Mona d'Amours, project officer for the Government of Canada's Job Development Programme, at the Bachelor Lake cabin outhouse, 1987.
Courtesy George Smith

Right: Crew member Denis Guerin (left) and master cabin builder Paul Anslow at Edwards Lake cabin, 1987.
Courtesy George Smith

don, Fred Gaizley, Doug Smith and others helped successfully solicit support from local forestry companies and small businesses.

"At the time, there was a recession on the coast," Smith says. "Almost nobody believed that we could actually pull this off. But people began talking it up. We began to get more support." Jackson Brothers Logging Company, the Sunshine Coast Regional District, the Ministry of Forests and forty-nine businesses came on board. The project ended up with 240 volunteers.

In late 1986, the project received $152,621 from the federal government's Job Development Programme, thanks to a proposal submitted by Smith. Over the year, he had volunteered his time researching funding opportunities and educational partners to develop a project plan. This money would help pay eighteen construction crew members during the course of the project, enabling them to receive hands-on education in eleven areas from surveying, wilderness survival and first aid to power saw maintenance and safety. Local individuals and institutions had already agreed to provide the project's educational components. "It was starting to look like we might pull this thing off," Smith says.

In January 1987, Smith interviewed eighty-eight applicants for six crew positions and hired local Paul Anslow as the master cabin builder, who developed the initial design for the cabins. As part of the federal funding, Smith was required to hire a First Nations person, a woman, and someone receiving social services or unemployment benefits. "Some of the best employees were women," Smith recalls, adding that one, Janet Robertson, was the best at chainsaw filing of her whole crew. "They were really hard-working. They had to assert themselves. They carved out respect. I was pretty clear: whether you were a woman or First Nations, old or young, or whatever it was, that had to be respected."

Mount Steele cabin under construction, 1987.
Courtesy George Smith

A management committee was formed to oversee the project. Besides Smith, Bonaguro and Greggain, members included chartered accountant Doug Cameron, Pat Tyson, Brad Benson, Bert Smith, Brian Ruben and Jim Wilson. The group received a bank loan from the Royal Bank in Sechelt. Sechelt council donated office space and a phone. But despite these signs of community support, some people were still hemming and hawing, says Smith. Some, scornful of the long hair sported by cabin builder Anslow and others, dismissed their goals as a hippie pipe dream; in their view, these scruffy slackards were exploiting government funds for a dubious project that was guaranteed to fail.

Crew member Larry Smith works on the McNair Lake cabin, 1987.
Courtesy George Smith

The Tetrahedron Ski Club's open house, held at the airport in Sechelt in June 1987, blasted away that attitude. In Smith's words: "When they saw what we had done, they shut up." Besides thanking supporters, the group showed off the top-quality cabin structures that they had built at the Sechelt airport. They held public demonstrations of their construction techniques; Bonaguro, trails foreman Michael Belisle and the whole crew showed people how to cut shakes and how they had carefully created Norwegian half-dovetail notches when building the log cabins. "The councillors, mayors, the press were there, old people, young people," Smith says. "We showed them what we were doing. That was a really big hit."

That summer, the project received $20,000 from the BC lottery fund. Employees from the Canfor (Howe Sound Pulp and Paper) mill in Port Mellon on the Sunshine Coast built and donated stainless-steel chimney pipes, built the foundation for the McNair Lake cabin and brushed out the trail from Chapman Lake to the cabin. Gibsons Building Supplies supplied trucks for free. Industry and community support totalled $117,641. At last, this volunteer-dependent project had gained widespread credibility and momentum.

After the cabins and trails were built, the move to make the Tetrahedron a park began with a pivotal meeting. Smith and local Ric Careless arranged to meet the district manager at the Ministry of Forests office near Sechelt, only to find that thirty-five people were there to greet them. "It was obvious they wanted to squash it [the park plan]," Smith remembers. The Ministry of Forests and logging companies quickly came together, he says, to try and stop the effort to protect the Tetrahedron. Meanwhile, Hind-Smith helped Smith make a detailed map of the proposed park area.

A core group of about a dozen volunteers formed the Tetrahedron Alliance in 1989, which soon had more than one thousand members. In Smith's words: "They decided the Tet wilderness was too important to let it disappear." Essentially, these foundational people launched the conservation movement on the Sunshine Coast, he says. Smith went on to become conservation director of the Canadian Parks and Wilderness Society.

For the next five and a half years, the volunteer organization mobilized a campaign to increase public awareness about the need for habitat protection and forest preservation in the Tet, besides the risk that logging held for the Coast's drinking water. Writers, researchers and others offered their skills to help save the area's old-growth forests of hemlock, fir and yellow cedar. On weekends, local business people and others drove a bus up to the area so that community members could see this wilderness region first-hand. "When more people saw it, they realized it was worth protecting," Smith says. "People were blown away because it's so beautiful."

People soon learned that the Sunshine Coast's forest district had done some of the most extensive logging of any area in the province, relative to the region's size, Smith says. The Ministry of Forests hosted a Local Resource Use Plan process, which included public consultation regarding future use of the Tetrahedron. "Even today, only about 3 percent of our area base is protected. That's one of the lowest [ratios] in British Columbia. Across BC, 14 percent of the land base is parks," says Dylan Eyers, BC Parks' area supervisor for the Sunshine Coast.

During his activism to save the Tetrahedron, Smith says that he endured considerable public criticism—"it got ugly"—yet he and other committed community members persevered. After the cabins and trails were built and the formal job development project ended

A view of Bachelor Lake taken during the Tetrahedron Outdoor Club's twenty-fifth anniversary pancake breakfast, September 2012.
Courtesy Heather Conn

in December 1987, volunteers continued for many years to contribute their skills and time to the Tet. They built trail signs, replaced the cabins' shake roofs with metal roofs, and performed numerous other jobs.

Tetrahedron Outdoor Club members and local hikers on the porch of the Bachelor Lake cabin, part of TOC's twenty-fifth anniversary pancake breakfast, September 2012.
Courtesy Heather Conn

Ultimately, the devoted work of the Tetrahedron Alliance paid off: on June 1, 1995, six thousand hectares of BC wilderness became Tetrahedron Provincial Park. Initially, BC Parks assumed the administration of the trails and cabins. After completion of the park's master plan, the Tetrahedron Ski Club, today's Tetrahedron Outdoor Club, adopted a volunteer stewardship role, under contract with BC Parks, to maintain the cabins and trail system. As BC Parks' 2010–11 annual report points out: "Much of the protected areas system we know today has been built in concert with individuals and groups donating their time and labour."

Today, Eyers praises Smith, Bonaguro and other Tet Outdoor Club members for their leadership and ability to maintain consistency and long-term momentum for maintaining the cabins, fuelled by a spirit of conservation and outdoor recreation. "They've done an outstanding job," he says by phone from his North Vancouver office. "Many groups can't always sustain the same enthusiasm: they get old, they have kids. This is a fun group to be a part of. They've been able to attract people who want to take the leadership role for a few years and maintain the volunteer enthusiasm."

Tetrahedron Outdoor Club volunteers continue to support BC Parks staff by splitting firewood and assisting with helicopter lifts. Each year, they perform a myriad of duties, from cabin renovations and trail-clearing to plowing and maintaining the park's road. In 2012, to help celebrate the twenty-five-year anniversary of construction of the cabins, the club hosted free pancake breakfasts at three of the cabins. It erected a permanent plaque at Edwards Lake cabin that acknowledges Smith and Bonaguro for their decades of work; both men have volunteered to take responsibility for the stewardship of this cabin.

How does Smith feel now, after spending a quarter-century tending a special part of BC's wilderness? "It makes me feel very lucky. It changed my life. I feel blessed by the people I met. The Tetrahedron—that's where my ashes are going to be."

NIGHTTIME SOJOURN WITH SOCKEYE

by Peter A. Robson

A job counting sockeye took this writer into the forest—alone and in the dark.

I sweep the flashlight back and forth across the trail that parallels the wide, shallow stream. The narrow cone of light gives scant relief from the oppressing darkness and the invisible canopy overhead. Suddenly, I'm startled by a loud slap in the water just a few metres to my left. My heart skips a beat and the hairs on the back of my neck prickle. I stop, wide-eyed, and swing the flashlight toward the noise. All I see is a patch of roiled water. Calming slightly, I realize it must be the damn beaver that's scared the heck out of me for a couple of nights now—though I've never actually seen it.

A few metres farther along the trail, I freeze again at the snap of a branch as yet another unknown creature moves through the night. Deer? Cougar? Bear? Even after having walked the hundred-metre trail a dozen times, I am pretty certain I'll never get used to being in the forest at night.

The year was 2002, and I was out of work. Then I was offered a contract to count returns of sockeye salmon to Sakinaw Lake, on BC's Sunshine Coast. I'd done volunteer work to protect salmon runs before—primarily on the small seasonal coho salmon creek behind our acreage on Sakinaw Lake. That consisted mainly of work parties. Under the supervision of our well-liked Fisheries and Oceans community adviser, Grant McBain, we'd made rock and log weirs, added gravel and generally tried to enhance the creek's natural spawning habitat.

Coho salmon returns to Sakinaw Lake were fairly stable. However, returns of sockeye salmon had plummeted and were down to a few fish. Extreme measures were necessary to ensure the survival of the remaining sockeye. That's how my job came about. From the beginning I wasn't convinced I'd enjoy being alone in the forest four hours each night, but I cared about salmon and perhaps I would overcome my fear. It would certainly be a challenge.

Sockeye is one of five species of Pacific salmon, and each has a distinct life cycle. Salmon hatch in fresh water, growing and feeding until their bodies go through a transformation that allows them to survive in salt water. Known as smolts and only a few inches long at that stage, they migrate to sea and range as far as the mid-Pacific Ocean in their quest for food. After spending two to seven years in the Pacific (depending on species) they use a

Sitting alone in the dark forest, one can easily become paranoid, as I came to learn.

combination of magnetism and smell to make their way back to their birth streams. There they mate and deposit their fertilized eggs in stream-bed gravel. Each pair then guards their eggs until they die.

There are thousands of salmon-bearing rivers, streams and creeks along the BC coast, and many have never been documented. Each is host to one or more of the five species. In turn, each of those species is genetically and geographically unique, and programmed to survive the conditions of that particular body of water.

One method of measuring the health of a particular salmon population is to count the number of out-migrating smolts. Another is to physically count or estimate the number of fish returning to that stream. Fisheries and Oceans Canada (DFO) is responsible for saltwater fish in Canada, and this is where DFO field crews, contractors like me, and volunteers come into play.

On some evenings it was still light when I made the hike from the last cottage on the lake, where I parked my car, to the fish ladder, a distance of half a kilometre. However, the return trip was always made in the dark.

There are thousands of salmon-bearing rivers, streams and creeks along the BC coast, and each is host to one or more of the five species. In the past, thousands of sockeye, like those shown here on the Adams River, would return to Sakinaw Lake.

To enter Sakinaw Lake from the ocean, returning salmon have to navigate up the lake's narrow outlet stream. This presents two problems: first, it is a chokepoint where salmon are vulnerable to predators such as seals, otters, mink and bears. Second, the sockeye return each summer when lake water levels are lowest and there isn't much more than a trickle flowing out of the lake. To get around these problems, the sockeye return to Sakinaw Lake under cover of darkness—to help conceal them from predators—and during high tide when there is adequate water to make it up into the lake. This was why the job entailed being down at the creek for the nighttime high tide.

Typical low summer flows out of the lake. This photo shows the narrow path that the sockeye must take to get into the pool below the dam and ladder. The shed was constructed after my summer sojourn, but was built on the place where I spent my nights.
Courtesy Grant McBain

In the early 1950s, during an extended drought, DFO Canada built a small concrete dam and fish ladder just above the high-tide mark, to make it easier for fish to get into the lake. They were maintained by local fisheries officers until 1989, when government cuts eliminated staffing. It wasn't until 1999 that Grant McBain stepped in, due to declining numbers of sockeye. The fish ladder is a series of concrete steps—mini-waterfalls—that allow fish to leap in stages the two metres up to the lake level. The set-up wasn't anything fancy; simply lifting or inserting the dam's wooden planks controlled the outflow from the lake. There wasn't much water behind the dam to begin with in summer, but with carefully timed releases it did provide a little extra flow.

In the light of day, the shallow stream—above and behind the dam—is picturesque as it flows through the understorey of ferns and salal, and under the canopy of cedar, hemlock and fir, before emptying out into a small, unnamed ocean bay. The stream is a popular attraction for cottagers, as they can tie up their boats at the end of the lake and hike to the ocean.

My nightly ritual was always the same. I'd pull one of the dam boards to increase the trickle of water flowing into the shallow pools below the fish ladder. If it was light, I'd wander down the twenty metres to the ocean, carefully looking into the stream to see if there were any sockeye making their way upstream (there usually weren't). Then I'd sit on a drift log on the beach for a few minutes and enjoy the evening—which usually required first applying a dose of DEET to keep the mosquitoes at bay. Often I'd notice a seal swimming just offshore and hope it wasn't making dinner of precious sockeye. I'd then move back up to the fish ladder and prepare for a night's work.

Below left: Looking upstream from the seaward entrance to Sakinaw Lake. The dam and fish ladder are in the background. This photo shows typical spring and fall flows out of the lake, not the summertime flows facing the sockeye.
Courtesy Chris Watson

Below: Fish ladders are designed to make it easier for fish to make their way upstream. All the fish entering Sakinaw Lake must pass through this ladder, which also acts as a funnel where predators often lie in wait.
Courtesy Grant McBain

Dusk at the mouth of the creek. In the background are the Hodgson Islands at the entrance to Agamemnon Channel.
Courtesy Chris Watson

On evenings when tides dictated that I arrive in the dark—which was most of the time—I had a little ritual. I had salvaged some old planks from the bushes and built myself a low seat. There was absolutely no protection from the elements. I'd give the little clearing around the dam a good examination with one of my flashlights, hoping to hear a minimum of scurrying noises, rustling or breaking twigs in the forest around me. On clear nights, a few stars would shine through gaps in the forest canopy; on rainy nights, it was so dark I couldn't see my hand if I waved it in front of my face.

With luck, I'd hear the telltale splash of a sockeye as it entered the ladder. It would often take fifteen to thirty minutes for a fish to make its way through. I wasn't supposed to use the flashlight to observe the fish, but it was hard not to peek instead of simply listening and counting by sound.

Unfortunately, returns were proving very low that year, and the sockeye were few and far between. My best night was nine fish, and most nights there were zero. I considered two or three a good night. This was a far cry from the average of five to ten thousand sockeye that returned in the 1950s and 1960s. At that time, Sakinaw sockeye were so abundant there was a small commercial gillnet fishery in local waters. However, sockeye returns had been declining for many years, and no one was certain exactly why. A DFO report suggested the

primary factors were likely poor ocean survival, overfishing (including incidental bycatch from commercial fisheries targeting other runs) and insufficient water flow or water levels to allow fish to enter the lake.

Sitting alone in the forest in the middle of the night—and having to stay awake—was unnerving. Seldom could I sit still for more than a few minutes before being drawn to the sounds made by scurrying mice and voles or other small creatures. Occasionally something would climb over one of my feet and startle me. By the time I could jump up and aim the flashlight, whatever it was would have vanished into the night. One can easily become paranoid, as I came to learn. On many evenings, the air would be filled with the screeches and hoot-hoots of barred owls. Frequently they were perched on branches nearby, and sat unconcerned as I studied them with the beam of my flashlight. Other times I would hear a *whoosh* as an owl swooped expertly among the trunks and branches. The beavers were never far away, and I think they enjoyed scaring me with the slap of their tails.

Toward the end of the summer, with the lake at its lowest level, I'd return at night to find that in my absence, beavers had left branches, sticks and rocks in their efforts to stop water from flowing out of the dam. I began many evenings by clearing away their handiwork.

The worst threat, however, were the creatures that came to prey on the migrating sockeye. One night early in my sojourn, it was just getting dark as I watched this cute little creature—a little larger than a squirrel—hopping around the edges of the pool below the

Sakinaw sockeye are unusual in that they don't spawn in stream-bed gravel, as shown in the photo. Instead they spawn in sandy areas of the lake where upwelling from underground springs provides cold water and oxygen essential for survival of their eggs.

In the darkness, barred owls would hoot-hoot from their perches in the trees. Occasionally I'd hear and feel the whoosh of flapping wings as predators flew through the forest.

ladder. At the time, a sockeye had just entered the fish ladder. I wasn't the slightest bit concerned until this creature, later identified as a mink, swam up to the sockeye, boldly clamped onto its snout, and then started this kind of death roll that reminded me of TV shows I'd seen about alligators. I jumped up out of my reverie, grabbed a long-handled fish net and jammed it down onto the churning water in the fish ladder. I couldn't see what happened then, but the mink apparently decided to leave the area. I waited forty-five minutes for the salmon to recover and make its way up the rest of the ladder, but in the end, figuring it was totally exhausted and easy prey should the mink return, I scooped it up with a net and carried it above the fish ladder.

The most dramatic events were when a family of river otters would suddenly appear from out of the darkness looking for a meal. The otters had little fear of me, even when I yelled at them and threw rocks and sticks. They had no qualms about diving right into the fish ladder or attacking sockeye in the pool below the ladder, only metres away from my bench. These sleek and crafty seven- to fourteen-kilogram mammals would hiss and chatter threateningly whenever I tried to chase them off. Unfortunately the otters—the same family or others—showed up almost nightly, and I got used to seeing their evil (to me) yellow-green eyes staring at me in the beam of the flashlight.

During several evenings I heard rustling branches and snapping twigs as larger animals moved through the forest. It was the bigger predators such as cougar and black bear that worried me the most. Why shouldn't they like a fresh sockeye as much as the smaller predators? I knew that should a cougar decide to attack, my first clue would be when it sank its claws into me. If it were a bear, I'd probably hear it coming and perhaps I could scare it off

Because it was dark, I never knew what creatures were wandering through the forest, though my biggest fears were bear and cougar.

with bear spray once it was within range, but trying to fight off a bear in the dark wouldn't likely be a winning proposition. My only answer to large predators was to make noise—sing loudly—and keep the flashlight sweeping around like a lighthouse beacon. There was lots of time at night to worry about such things.

As the summer wore on I debated the life and death struggles taking place all around me. I understood that seal, mink, otter and who knows what else out there were simply trying to survive. On the other hand, this particular sockeye run was close to extinction, and every single fish had become vital. I wondered: Should I interfere with nature by chasing off predators, or should I let nature and the idea of survival of the fittest play out, at the risk of the run becoming extinct? Since mankind has skewed what may once have been a natural balance in our environment, and since man was probably the reason for the declining Sakinaw sockeye, it may be too late to let nature take its course. Perhaps protecting the sockeye was a way to help rebalance nature. Yes, there was plenty to ponder on during those long evenings alone in the forest.

All this took place a decade ago, but for some reason the experience seems like it happened yesterday. I could never have guessed that spending a summer alone and awake in the forest at night would have left such strong, lasting memories. I doubt there are many people who willingly spend their evenings as I did, but by taking on a job that required it, I was forced into a whole new world of adventures and discoveries—ones that take place when most of us are tucked into our beds. While I never did get over my discomfort at being in the forest alone and awake at night, the fact that I did the job and faced my fears night after night (and didn't get eaten by a bear) is something I will feel proud of for the rest of my life.

The Aftermath

During the summer of 2002, a total of seventy fish returned to Sakinaw Lake. For the next few years, returns continued to decline and during one year, only a single sockeye was counted. Fortunately Grant McBain, the local DFO enhancement officer, and his assistant Jim Wilson managed to harvest eggs from a few of the last sockeye. Several generations were raised in captivity and their offspring released back into the lake as fry. In 2011 and 2012, an average of five hundred sockeye returned, and indications are that the run may finally be on the road to recovery.

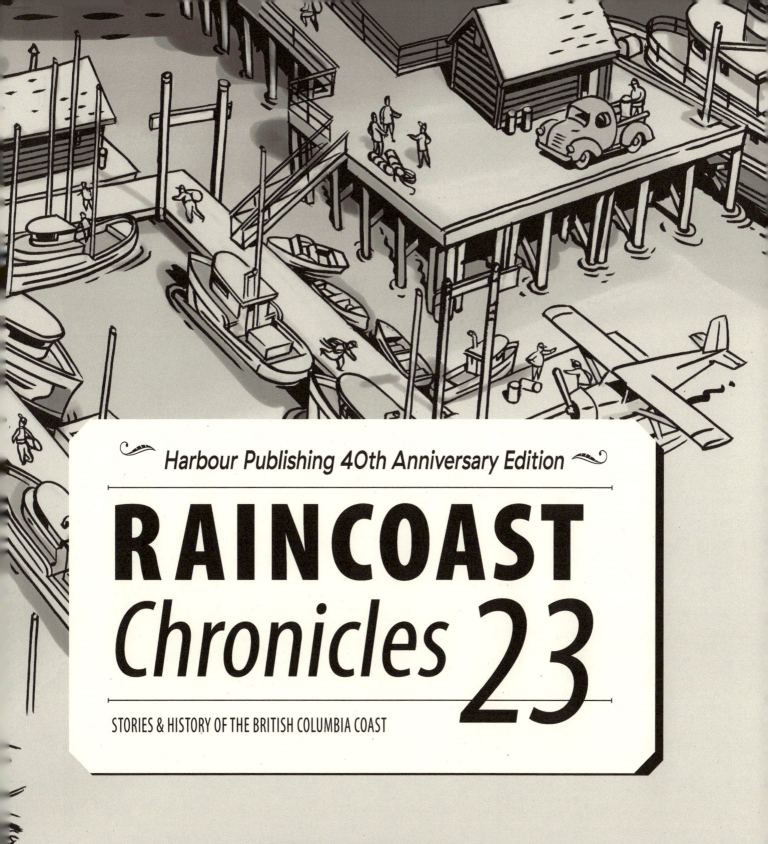

Harbour Publishing 40th Anniversary Edition

RAINCOAST
Chronicles 23

STORIES & HISTORY OF THE BRITISH COLUMBIA COAST

Edited by PETER A. ROBSON

with an introduction by HOWARD WHITE

**HARBOUR
PUBLISHING**

INTRODUCTION

By Howard White

The year 2014 marked the fortieth year that books bearing the Harbour Publishing imprint have been flowing out into the world from our headquarters in Pender Harbour, BC.

My wife, Mary, and I actually bought our first printing press in 1969, started our newspaper in 1970 and published the first issue of *Raincoast Chronicles* in 1972, but it wasn't until 1974 that the first actual book with the first actual Harbour Publishing imprint appeared, so that's what we decided to use as Harbour's official start date. Our very first book (*A Dictionary of Chinook Jargon*, 1972) and the first issues of *Raincoast Chronicles* didn't have any imprint on the spine because we didn't know they needed one. When a concerned reader pointed out the omission, we decided to call ourselves Harbour Publishing because every business in Pender Harbour was Harbour this or Harbour that—Harbour Motors, Harbour Grocery, Harbour Barber. There was also a Harbour Pub and for years the freight truck delivered our books to them, which we might not have minded if they delivered the pub's beer to us, but somehow that never happened.

The Harbour Publishing imprint burst upon the scene with three books in 1974 and nobody can now remember which was first, *Build Your Own Floor Loom* by Steve Lones or *The Dulcimer Tuning Book* by Randy Christopher Rain (a.k.a. Randy Raine-Reusch). These were quickly followed by *Between the Sky and the Splinters*, a book of logging poems by Peter Trower that helped establish a distinguished literary career and became a classic of its kind.

My approach to starting a publishing operation was conditioned by my background in isolated BC coast logging camps where if something wanted making you made it yourself. My first move had been to get a bulldozer and clear a piece of land. Then I tore down an old building supply building in Vancouver and used the lumber to build a print shop on the cleared land. Then I bought a press and learned how to print with it (sort of). Only then did I start looking around for a likely book to publish. And only after the book was printed and bound did I begin to wonder if anybody might want to buy it. I know, I can hear the wiseacres muttering that my approach hasn't changed much. Luckily I am now surrounded by a brilliant and dedicated staff, some of whom have actually studied modern publishing methods in university, and they do their best to compensate for my atavistic habits.

I don't suppose many onlookers, watching Mary and I pulling armfuls of spoiled paper from our antique press late into the nights of those first years, would have given our enterprise much chance of surviving, but four decades and some 600 books later, here we are.

The years went by in a blur. Once we hung out the Harbour Publishing shingle, the stories poured in from all corners of BC, and we were swept away in the tide. We never had time to stop and ask ourselves if this was how we wanted to spend our entire working lives. But any time we have doubt, we find much reassurance in thumbing through the volumes that crowd the bookshelves of our home and next-door office—books like *Now You're Logging* by Bus Griffiths, *Spilsbury's Coast* by Jim Spilsbury, *Fishing with John* by Edith Iglauer, *Grizzlies and White Guys* by Clayton Mack, *Marine Life of the Pacific Northwest* by Andy Lamb and Bernie Hanby and yes, *The Encyclopedia of British Columbia* edited by Dan Francis, to name only a few. Those are the kind of BC-born-and-bred books Harbour has become known for and the kind in which we take the greatest satisfaction because if Harbour hadn't been here to coax them into life, perhaps that whole corpus of regional literature might not exist.

To mark the occasion we have decided to conscript this issue of *Raincoast Chronicles* to reprint some of the more memorable passages from Harbour's forty years of books. It is only a taste, but we think it conveys the unique flavour Harbour has brought to BC's cultural life. We hope you enjoy reading it half as much as we enjoyed creating it.

ON MEETING EMILY CARR

Excerpted from Haunting Vancouver *(2013), by Mike McCardell.*

1

~

This book was written by McCardell using the voice of an imaginary immortal, Jock Linn, a former sapper with the Royal Engineers who came to BC in 1859. Linn needed an eternal job so he decided to become a reporter and interview some of the province's most notable persons. —Ed.

Nutcase. The first time I met her I knew I was not dealing with an ordinary, boring woman. She was a nutcase.

When I walked into her home she was pulling a rope attached to a pulley in the ceiling with the other end of the rope going down to the back of a chair, and the chair was rising.

"I don't like reporters," she said.

I have met many people like that. I don't blame them. After knowing reporters all my life, actually all my lifetimes, do you think I would trust them? You tell them something and you have to put your faith in someone you don't know to tell the story back as you told it.

There was nothing, absolutely nothing, in the life of Emily Carr that might be considered normal, including her pet monkey, Woo.
Image I-61505 courtesy of the Royal BC Museum, BC Archives

Come to think of it, I don't know how I have ever found anyone to talk to me. "May I sit down and talk?" I asked.

"Only if you can fly. Can you fly, Mr. Linn?"

"What do you mean?"

She pointed to the chair now hung near the ceiling. "There is your chair."

Okay, at that moment I was in love. I must clarify that. It was not the kind of love that I had for Pauline Johnson, with whom I wanted to snuggle. Pauline was beautiful, and in the way boys and girls have been behaving since we were creatures in the sea I was attracted to Pauline. Then we could make more little Paulines.

Emily was different. I loved her mind. I hate to say that but it explains it all. I did not want to snuggle with her mind but, for goodness' sake, her furniture was hanging near the ceiling and I loved the mind and the woman who would do that.

I also liked her paintings, though they all looked the same to me. One tree, two trees, one totem pole, two, etc.

"I see you looking at my paintings. You don't like them, right?" she said to me.

I said I liked them.

"You are full of crap," she said. "I can tell a liar when I see one." Then she took a long drag on her cigarette.

"They did not like this when I taught school," she said.

"I heard that was your problem."

"What was my problem?"

"You smoked in school when you were teaching."

"So what? And I cursed the bad attitudes. I cursed them with curse words. You have a problem with that?"

"No, ma'am."

You see, that is why I liked her, in a platonic sort of way. Poor Emily. By the time I met her she was a washed-up artist. Those were her words.

"No one is ever going to buy my work."

"Maybe," I said. "There will come a time when people see the original inhabitants in a different way. They might even like them."

She shook her head, which was covered with a skull cap that she wore all the time.

"Are you crazy? They see them as savages and they will always see them like that."

This was true. The government was snatching the Native children from their parents, which really was kidnapping, and forbidding the potlatch, which was like forbidding Christmas and Easter to a Christian, and not allowing the children to learn their own languages. In a word, the government would erase the savage from the savages, though they did not say it that way.

When I'd thought about that I said, "You're right. So why are you painting totem poles?"

"I like them."

That is the problem with artists. They are out of step with government edicts.

Then she reached out for her monkey, which was her pet, and it climbed on her arm and sat on her shoulder.

You can see why I said she was a nutcase. But she also lowered the chair so I could sit on it.

"You are not so bad," she said. "Not good, mind you, but your face looks like one of those on the totem poles, so you can sit."

Her life in short: She was raised by a Victorian father who transplanted Victorian life to Victoria—high ceilings, pictures of Queen Victoria on numerous walls, slipcovers on the chairs and the couch that covered the legs of the furniture because it would be obscene to see exposed legs, even those of a couch.

Emily did not like that. That upset her father so Emily disliked it even more. Her father went out of his mind. Emily did the only thing she could. She became an artist.

Now being an artist in those days meant that she would paint landscapes, and her father agreed. It was called dabbling in the arts and a daughter should be allowed to do that.

Then her father died. It happens. Her guardian, chosen by her father, said she could go to California to study art, so long as it was landscapes.

She went, but then she got on a freighter going to France. Sometimes kids do the craziest things and you want to kill them. It is a good thing they are faster than you.

She learned amazing ways of painting things, close up and personal and far away and still attached. It had nothing to do with Victorian painting.

Emily came back to British Columbia and painted totem poles far up the coast, in the Queen Charlottes before the name was changed to an aboriginal name. No one wanted her work.

She was broke—that happens to artists—so she quit painting. If she could not make a living of art she would run a boarding house. That was her way of saying "Screw you" to the world and to herself.

But there was income in renting rooms to folks who did not want to be homeless, so she did that for twenty years.

Can you imagine giving up everything you love and want to do for two decades?

This is where the historian and the journalist fail. They say she gave up art for twenty years and ran a boarding house but it was not twenty years, not in the beginning. As with all of us it was one month that became six and became twelve and is it Christmas already? And then two years became six and those became ten.

"I can't believe I have been doing this for ten years. Once upon a time I painted pictures. That's a joke."

We all say that.

And then ten years more and thoughts of a brush and canvas and paint were a distant memory. "I once thought I could paint trees. Now I use the sawdust to keep a fire going so the guests won't complain."

She said that to a mirror.

And then what happens? She becomes famous overnight. The Group of Seven—that was Canada's artists to the world and they all lived in Ontario—got to see Emily's paintings of trees.

"Magnificent. Wonderful. Just what we are trying to do," they said.

Just as an aside, every time a reporter writes "they said" I wonder if they said it

all at once. Imagine the Group of Seven together in a room looking at Emily's trees. "Okay, the official word is, now, all together, 'Magnificent. Wonderful. Just what we are trying to do.'"

"Oh, come on. Someone didn't say it. Let's try again."

Anyway, Emily was made an honorary member of the Group and she was suddenly famous, while she was still running a boarding house.

How the heck did this happen? Out of the blue the famous men with brushes decided that a woman on the West Coast who lives with a monkey was pretty good. Why did it not happen sooner? You only get angry when you think about it, or disappointed, or disillusioned. No, life is not fair.

Anyway, she was closing in on sixty when her fame came. But of course fame at home does not naturally follow. She was closing in on seventy when the Vancouver Art Gallery had a one-woman show of her paintings. The gallery was then a small building on Georgia next to a movie house.

"Totem poles? Trees? Why are we looking at these?" some patrons of the art of Victorian landscapes said.

Three years later she was too sick to paint any longer, and four years after that she died.

The Vancouver Art Gallery now has a permanent display of her trees and totem poles. When it moves to a new and larger building it will have an even larger permanent display. And the Emily Carr University of Art+Design has graduated thousands of students, most of whom look at things in strange and challenging ways.

The only difference is none of them are allowed to smoke in class. Emily would have probably lit up anyway.

THE STORY OF PRINCESS LOUISA INLET

2

Excerpted from The Sunshine Coast: From Gibsons to Powell River
(1996, 2011), by Howard White. Photos by Dean van't Schip

Jervis Inlet, which zigzags deep into the Coast Range like a forty-mile light-ning bolt between the Sechelt Peninsula and the Powell River side, is a clas-sic coastal fjord, shadowed most of its length by mile-high mountain walls. It is very deep and includes a 3,000-foot-deep hole known as the Jervis Deep. How-ever, the feature that sets Jervis Inlet apart from its sis-ter inlets occurs ten miles from the head on the east side. There the mountain walls unexpectedly part and let into a four-mile side inlet—Princess Louisa—sur-rounded by such precipitous bluffs the effect is like looking up at the sky from the bottom of a colossal and extremely gorgeous cavern.

A trip to Princess Louisa is an experience that won't ever be forgotten.

"There is no use describing that inlet," Erle Stanley Gardner once wrote, before proceed-ing to ignore his own advice. "There is a calm tranquility which stretches from the smooth surface of the reflecting waters straight up into infinity. The deep calm of eternal silence is only disturbed by the muffled roar of throbbing waterfalls as they plunge down from sheer cliffs. There is no scenery in the world that can beat it. Not that I've seen the rest of the world. I don't need to. I've seen Princess Louisa Inlet."

I won't fall into the trap of trying to describe Princess Louisa except to say few

Looking out at the entrance to Princess Louisa Inlet. Fortunately, the inlet was mostly ignored by those seeking to extract resources because its only substantial resource was beauty.

Sunshine Coasters would deny it is the Hope Diamond of the area's scenic jewels. It is the place we take those special visitors we want to hook on the coast, the one experience guaranteed to jar the most jaded soul into a full-blown state of awe. I have been visiting Princess Louisa regularly since I was a kid and it never seems enough. Despite going in many different weathers, moods and ages, it has never failed to send me away with a renewed sense of life's promise.

The inlet's rare magnetism draws remarkable people to it and inspires them to extraordinary exertions. Legend has it that it was avoided by the Sechelt people after a small village at the head was buried by one of the inlet's periodic rock slides, but band elder Clarence Joe claimed his people used to visit it for recreational purposes just as the white man would later.

Early on, Princess Louisa was ignored by the more development-minded settlers because its only substantial resource was beauty, which didn't readily lend itself to being canned or milled. This was a challenge inventor Thomas Hamilton would apply himself to later.

Herman Casper just wanted to wake up in the morning and see it. Casper was a deserter from the German army who homesteaded the only decently flat land in the area, the peninsula down at the inlet mouth by Malibu Rapids, in 1900. When he wasn't blacksmithing for local handloggers, Casper whiled away his days spoiling his twenty-six cats and composing songs in praise of the magnificent surroundings, which he was happy to perform with his zither for visiting boaters:

> Beyond Mount Alfred, in ze vest
> Where ze sun goes down to rest
> It draws me dere, I don' know vy
> S'pose it is ze colour in ze sky.
> For zey are purple, mauve and pink
> Howeber it makes me vunder, look and t'ink.

Casper was followed by Charles (Daddy) Johnstone, a towering mountain man from Daniel Boone country who kept edging west ahead of civilization until he and his family of six landed up at Princess Louisa around 1909. There they threw together a one-room split-cedar shack, lived off the land and had three more kids. The Johnstone gang may have succeeded in getting closer to the inlet's soul than anyone since the Sechelt in the days when they had it to themselves. As part of their education, sons Steve and Judd were sent up on the snowy plateau above Princess Louisa without jacket or shoes and with only matches, salt and a jackknife for survival. They would live by their wits for weeks at a time, and explore miles into the interior of the province. After World War One, Daddy began to feel even Jervis was too cramped and carried on to Alaska, where he became famous as a pioneer. But Steve and Judd returned to British Columbia and passed the rest of their days in homage to the fabulous Jervis landscape that had been so deeply imprinted on them in their formative years. Their names became synonymous with the inlet's wild spirit, and Judd in particular became famous for his tall tales of pioneer times.

Judd married Dora Jeffries from Egmont and they stayed up Princess Louisa, sixty miles from the nearest family, through the birth of their first three girls. The sun would disappear behind the inlet crags for two months in the depths of winter, and it would get so cold the salt water would freeze from shore to shore. To get anything that couldn't be obtained from the bush, Judd would have to drag the boat across two

Below left: The beauties of Princess Louisa Inlet defy description, though many have tried.

Below right: The sheer walls of Jervis Inlet can take your breath away.

miles of sea ice and row to Pender Harbour, a hundred-mile round trip. He was always a welcome sight at Portuguese Joe's bar in Irvines Landing and never had to pay for a drink. All you had to do was ask him how things were going.

"Could be worse. Had a hard blow and a cedar tree come down on the shack is all."

"Very big?"

"Naw, only about six foot on the butt."

"Good God, Judd. Didn't it do a lot of damage?"

"Naw. Fell crost the bed right where the old woman was sleepin', but it hung up on the stove before it could git 'er. Tore the roof off is all."

"That's terrible, Judd!"

"Naw. I just took a couple blocks off the end and split up a mess o' shakes. Old woman bin after me fer a new roof anyways."

"What about the rest of the tree. How did you remove it?"

"Didn't bother. It was pointin' in the stove anyways, so I jus' lit the fire and stuck the Gilchrist jack on the other end. Every time the old woman wanted some exter heat, I just hollered at the kid to go out and give a few clicks on the jack. It was auto-feed, like."

"So it wasn't so bad after all."

"Hell no. I got a new roof and a whole winter's heat without once havin' to leave the shack."

James (Mac) MacDonald devoted his entire existence to being the inlet's chief admirer, protector and ambassador to the world. *Courtesy of the Princess Louisa Society, W.A. Stenner photo*

I sometimes wonder if it was due to Judd Johnstone that the entire Jervis Inlet–Nelson Island area seemed to become such a prime bullshit-producing zone. When I was growing up there, it seemed you couldn't get a straight answer out of anybody.

Certainly you couldn't get one out of James (Mac) MacDonald, the globetrotting American playboy who fell under the Princess's spell in 1919. "After travelling around the world and seeing many of its famous beauty spots, I felt I was well able to evaluate the magnificence of Princess Louisa," he wrote in one of his more sober utterances. "This place had to equal or better anything I had seen."

Like many another wealthy American who no sooner spied a thing of beauty in a foreign land than he had to have it, MacDonald promptly applied to the BC government to purchase the inlet head, and the government turned out to be eager to unload it.

The interior of Mac MacDonald's log cabin. *Courtesy of the Princess Louisa Society*

Their appraisal of the 292-acre site, which would come to be called "The Eighth Wonder of the World" and attract 20,000 gawkers a season despite its inaccessibility, was that only 42 acres were flat enough to be of any use, so MacDonald could have the whole thing for $420, if that wasn't asking too much. He took possession in 1927.

Through absolutely no fault of its own, this turned out to be the best thing the government could have done. Within a few years MacDonald would be turning down $400,000 offers from hotel chains and preserving the area for public use with a determination the government would not come to appreciate until 1964, when MacDonald finally had the satisfaction of seeing his beloved charge consecrated as a Class A marine park.

Rich, eloquent and handsome, "Mac" MacDonald could have had his pick of successful careers, but from his fateful encounter with the Princess in the prime of his life until the day he could no longer hobble around on his own, he devoted his entire existence to being her chief admirer, protector and ambassador to the world. He got married in 1939, but the new wife made the mistake of forcing him to choose between the Princess and her, and a Mexican divorce quickly followed.

Mac left the inlet only during the winter months, when the weather becomes much harsher than the coastal norm. At first he rented a *pied à terre* in Pender Harbour from his friend Bertrand Sinclair, and later he established regular winter digs in Acapulco. From May to October he was back at Princess Louisa, continuing his endless study of her moods, cataloguing her wonders and expounding on them to visitors. In time every feature in the inlet, from Chatterbox Falls to Trapper's Rock, came to be known by a name Mac gave it. He became a walking encyclopedia of inlet history and lore, most of it unreliable, but all of it highly entertaining.

MacDonald's presence became an attraction in itself, compelling regulars like John Barrymore to return year after year to pass long evenings sitting on the afterdeck of his splendiferous MV *Infanta*, where Mac would tell stories and point out faces in the rock formations of the bluffs. (Barrymore claimed to have discovered Napoleon, though Mac later speculated you had to be drinking Napoleon brandy to see it.) Hollywood types seemed to take a particular shine to Mac. At various times he entertained the likes of Ronald Colman, William Powell and Mack Sennett, complete with his entour-age of bathing beauties, who filmed part of a movie called *Alaska Love* in the inlet, but MacDonald was equally attentive to locals and kids, reputedly turning down dinner with Arthur Godfrey so he could keep a storytelling date at the youth camp. This is all the more notable considering Mac's legendary appetite for free grub. It is said that from the time the first yacht showed up in the spring to the time the last one left in the fall, he never ate his own cooking.

MacDonald was a great admirer of Judd Johnstone and, after Judd moved south to Hardy Island, of his brother Steve, who stayed up-inlet all his life. He was also a great fan of old Casper. During one of his winters south, MacDonald hired some professional musicians to make a record of Casper's songs, which proved a great hit among inlet fanciers and netted the old smithy a rare spot of cash. MacDonald was outraged in 1940 when Thomas Hamilton talked Casper into parting with his beloved acreage for $500 so the aviation tycoon could build a luxury resort called Malibu Lodge. Mac cheered when Malibu went broke in 1947 and was taken over by Young Life, a non-denominational church group offering low-budget vacations to city kids.

MacDonald was particularly attentive to Muriel Blanchet, the adventuring Victoria widow who cruised the inlet with her five children in the 1930s. With the help of

Hubert Evans she recorded her experiences in the coastal classic *The Curve of Time*, which has a lengthy passage describing Mac as "the Man from California," which of course he wasn't.

Under the inlet's influence MacDonald became one of the most ardent apostles of the creed that humanity was placed on the Sunshine Coast "not to be doing but to be." He even went so far as to dedicate himself formally to "the satisfying state of loaferhood."

"The world needs ten million full time thinking loafers dedicated to the purpose of bringing this cockeyed life back to its normal balance," he declared in his five-point manifesto of loaferdom.

Of course it helped to be the favourite son of a Seattle grocery heiress, a fact MacDonald made no bones about, advising would-be loafers: "Before birth, look the field over and pick out a family in which some member has misspent his life in amassing sufficient do-re-me to permit you to dodge the squirrel cage." In this he differs from the Johnstone boys, who would argue that you could enjoy the best the coast had to offer with no more accumulated assets than a jackknife and a box of matches.

I remember Mac as a pleasant old man with a crown of luminous silver hair who used to keep his houseboat, the *Seaholm*, in Madeira Park while he waited for the inlet to thaw in the spring. I had a paper route, and while it was a bit of nuisance to paddle

Above: A quiet forest trail, part of Princess Louisa Marine Park.

Right: Chatterbox Falls provides a focus for the breathtaking scenery at the head of Princess Louisa Inlet.

over to where he was anchored, it was always worth seeing what nonsense he would come up with. One spring he launched into a big production about a new sport which had taken Acapulco beaches by storm that season, and ceremoniously produced this wonderful innovation he'd smuggled back just for my benefit. I was excited by the buildup but disappointed by the actual item, which looked like the lid of a small garbage can. He said you flicked it so it sort of hovered like a flying saucer. He made me practise it with him until I had the knack, then commanded me to go off and spread the fad among my friends. That was how Madeira Park became the first Canadian beachhead of the Frisbee craze, way back in 1957. To a twelve-year-old, Mac seemed like nothing so much as a great big overaged kid, which I am sure is a judgment he would have been most delighted to accept. The only thing you had to watch was that he didn't lure you inside his cabin and try to make you play chess. As a chess fanatic he was known for his willingness to play with anyone, no matter how incompetent, but I am sad to say even his legendary patience was checkmated in my case.

Mac died in a Seattle rest home in 1978. His ashes are planted inside a boulder at the head of Princess Louisa, beneath an inscription which reads "Laird of the inlet, Gentleman, friend to all who came here."

Kids get a chance to experience the wilderness at Malibu Club. Originally a luxury resort for Hollywood movie stars, the property now serves as an affordable summer youth camp operated by Young Life, a non-denominational Christian organization.

PILING BLOOD
by Al Purdy

It was powdered blood
in heavy brown paper bags
supposed to be strong enough
to prevent the stuff from escaping
but didn't

We piled it ten feet high
right to the shed roof
working at Arrow Transfer
on Granville Island
The bags weighed 75 pounds
and you had to stand on two
of the bags to pile the top rows
I was six feet three inches
and needed all of it

I forgot to say
the blood was cattle blood
horses sheep and cows
to be used for fertilizer
the foreman said

It was a matter of some delicacy
to plop the bags down softly
as if you were piling dynamite
if you weren't gentle
the stuff would belly out
from bags in brown clouds
settle on your sweating face
cover hands and arms
enter ears and nose
seep inside pants and shirt
reverting back to liquid blood
and you looked like
you'd been scalped
by a tribe of
particularly unfriendly
Indians and forgot to die

We piled glass as well
it came in wooden crates
two of us hoicking them
off trucks into warehouses

every crate
weighing 200 pounds
By late afternoon
my muscles would twitch and throb
in a death-like rhythm
from hundreds of bags of blood
and hundreds of crates of glass

Then at Burns' slaughterhouse
on East Hastings Street
I got a job part time
shouldering sides of frozen beef
hoisting it from steel hooks
staggering to and from
the refrigerated trucks
and eerie freezing rooms
with breath a white vapour
among the dangling corpses
and the sound of bawling animals
screeched down from an upper floor
with their throats cut
and blood gurgling into special drains
for later retrieval

And the blood smell clung to me
clung to clothes and body
sickly and sweet
and I heard the screams
of dying cattle
and I wrote no poems
there were no poems
to exclude the screams
which boarded the streetcar
and travelled with me
till I reached home
turned on the record player
and faintly
in the last century
heard Beethoven weeping

From Beyond Remembering: The Collected Poems of Al Purdy (2000),
selected and edited by Al Purdy and Sam Solecki

THE SIMPLE JOY OF RAIN

Excerpted from A Walk with the Rainy Sisters: In Praise of
British Columbia's Places *(2010), by Stephen Hume*

I'm not a guy who faithfully scans newspaper travel sections for winter get-away deals. I don't line up at the airports for a break in Hawaii or Fiji or Palm Springs or some Mexican beach in the Baja and then return with tales of iguanas, golf and too many green swizzles.

Nor am I that guy's gloomy alter ego, hunkered down and complaining about the dark, dank, insufferable months of January and February on the soggy, dreary, dismal West Coast.

What's to complain about?

A little damp is the price I pay for living amid the wonders of North America's temperate raincoast.

All things considered, it's a small price compared to what I fork over to the government to pay for wars in Afghanistan, a retractable roof for Vancouver's football stadium, temporary digs for speed skaters or the latest city hall facelift.

Complaining about winter rains on the West Coast makes as much sense as complaining that the sun rises too early in the morning. Things are what they are. This is a marine climate. It rains.

As for me, I love rain. I love it even when it saturates the slope we're on and we get a surfeit of it seeping into our deepest sub-basement, as it does every so often when downpours escalate to monsoons.

I love the subtle gradations of grey and the filtered light and the ever-changing sky. I love the gossamer drift of fine drizzle and halos around street lights and wraiths of water vapour drifting over depths in which the luminous globes of jellyfish pulse. I love the faint scent of the tropics that sometimes arrives with the Pineapple Express.

I love a shower's dimpling hiss across the still, glassy surface of a woodland bog and the drumming of raindrops on elephant-sized leaves of skunk cabbage. I love the splash and clatter of coho in a seething fall freshet to announce winter's imminent arrival and the massed trilling as the March rains bring out spring peepers to sing winter away.

Suzanne Boyer photo

My own winter mornings are always a surprise. Bands of fog layering the horizon in patterns that are never the same from one dawn to the next, with snow-clad mountains rising out of the sea in their capes of frozen rain: now hidden, now peeping out of the mist, now shining in a ray of sunlight, now draped in streamers of cloud.

What can be more of a feast for the eye than the reflections of clouds racing across the sides of tall buildings after a quick, sharp rain and a sudden blow from the sea, or the gleam of lights reflected from rain-slicked pavement so black it looks like you are about to fall into the abyss?

Who is immune to the sight of a small child in a yellow slicker and red gumboots jumping into the endless, joyous wonder of new puddles or to the hiss of a squall across the surface of Lost Lagoon, rising to rattle against your raincoat, preferably one of those stiff, Irish green poacher coats of waxed cotton?

At night I can think of nothing more satisfying than the staccato spatter of raindrops driven by a brisk southeaster while I lie snug in my bed, listening to my wife's steady breathing, and behind it, to the wind sighing through cedars in ancient voices from our dreamtime that speak to all of us in the same language, a language everyone understands regardless of the self-imposed illusions of racial, ethnic, linguistic, national, religious or any other difference.

The sound of rain is the sound of life. The touch of rain is the quickening of existence. I love it.

TOFINO'S FRED TIBBS: ECCENTRIC PIONEER SETTLER

4

Excerpted from Tofino and Clayoquot Sound: A History *(2014),*
by Margaret Horsfield and Ian Kennedy

The year 1908 marked the arrival on the west coast of a self-effacing young man, Frederick Gerald Tibbs, destined to become one of Tofino's best-known characters. At first glance not a prepossessing character, Tibbs appeared stocky and rather shy, painfully self-conscious about a facial disfigurement dating back to a childhood injury in England and made worse by various surgeries. Benignly good-natured and cheerfully eccentric, Tibbs first settled on land he pre-empted at Long Bay (Long Beach), the area now occupied by Green Point Campground, a considerable distance from Tofino and from other settlers. Strangely keen on physical exercise, Tibbs caused locals to shake their heads when they heard he took a plunge in the breakers at Long Bay every morning, followed by an energetic run round and round a huge tree stump on the beach. Tibbs wrote voluble, friendly letters to Walter Dawley [owner of the store and hotel on nearby Stubbs/Clayoquot Island], including fussy and precise shopping lists. He ordered such items as "limewater glycerine" for his hair, lemons, mousetraps, nails, thimbles, a blue sweater, and on one occasion a can of bright

Right: Frederick Gerald Tibbs, pictured here with his cousin Vera Marshall, stands out as one of Tofino's best-known eccentrics. He settled at Long Bay (Long Beach) in 1908, and later moved to Dream Isle off Tofino, where he clear-cut the island and erected a castle-like home.
Image F-03427 courtesy of the Royal BC Museum, BC Archives

Far right: A sample of wallpaper covered with pink roses, sent by Fred Tibbs to storekeeper Walter Dawley in 1909. Writing from his home at Long Bay, Tibbs requested that Dawley obtain matching pink paint.
Image MS-1076, Walter Dawley fonds, box 9, courtesy of the Royal BC Museum, BC Archives

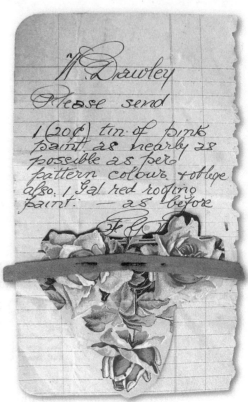

pink paint, enclosing a sample of rose-covered wallpaper providing the hue to be matched. After passing on good wishes to everyone in the "liquid dominion of Clayoquot," as Tibbs called Dawley's establishment, he signed his name in a flourish of calligraphic curlicues. While living at Long Bay, Tibbs gave his return address as "Tidal Wave Ranch." He did no ranching there, but filled his days clearing land and establishing himself in a rough little cabin "built out of driftwood and gas cans and made quite ornamental," according to Mike Hamilton's memoirs, and featuring—if the paint did arrive as ordered—a rosy pink interior.

Early in 1910, Tibbs left Tidal Wave Ranch and took a job on remote Triangle Island off the northern tip of Vancouver Island, which he described as "this mountain top, surrounded by ocean." Tibbs assisted there with the construction of a new lighthouse, sending to Dawley for tennis shoes and a "good deep-toned mouth harp" to be shipped up on the supply vessel *Leebro*. He saved enough money for a trip to England, but by November 1911 he was back at his "ranch," in his spare time busying himself as president of the Clayoquot Conservative Association. The following year Tibbs took a job at the Kennedy Lake salmon hatchery and found himself increasingly drawn to Tofino. A small, 2 ½-acre island in the harbour caught his fancy, so he sold his property at Long Bay and bought the island, which he christened Dream Isle, painting the name in huge white letters on the rocks. Here, Tibbs began to pursue his dreams, with the village of Tofino watching in complete astonishment.

In the first of many unexpected moves, Tibbs set about clear-cutting the entire island, blasting out stumps whenever he could. He had a fondness for using large amounts of dynamite; loud explosions from Dream Isle became commonplace. Ignoring [fellow settler] Jacob Arnet's kindly suggestion that he leave at least some trees

A view of Tofino in 1913, with the recently completed St. Columba Anglican Church on the left and the dock and lifeboat station on the right.

Bert Drader photo: Ken Gibson Collection, Tofino

for wind protection, Tibbs left only one tree in the centre of the island, an enormous spruce that he topped at 100 feet. Over time, he removed every limb, leaving a tall, standing spar. Up this he built a sturdy ladder, almost a small scaffold, mounting all the way, step by step, to the top, where he constructed a narrow platform. According to local legend, he would climb to the platform every morning with his cornet and serenade Tofino with lively tunes, in particular "Come to the Cookhouse Door, Boys." Having first lived in a tent on the island, Tibbs gradually built his dream home, a wooden castle, three storeys high, complete with a crenellated tower and battlements. Painted red, white and blue and held to the rocks with steel guywires, the castle eventually housed a piano and a phonograph, with a garden alongside featuring trellised roses, a loveseat and a sunken well. Inside, the walls were "beautifully ornamented by artistic designs in plaster work," according to George Nicholson, who managed Dawley's hotel at Clayoquot during the 1920s. Tibbs lived on the ground floor; the upper levels remained unfinished and accessible only by ladder. In the years leading up to World War One, Tibbs had just begun all this work; he continued doggedly on, year after year, with each new development establishing him ever more firmly as one of Tofino's leading eccentrics.

Although few could compete with Tibbs's highly visible idiosyncrasies, from the earliest days of settlement the west coast consistently attracted its fair share of oddballs: independent, stubborn individuals determined to go their own way, brooking no interference. Solitary, a little—sometimes very—peculiar, these men (and they were always single men) tended to disappear up the inlets or into the bush, finding remote places to live undisturbed, coming to town only when it suited them.

World War One changed everything. One by one, men enlisted and went off to

Below: In the foreground is Arnet Island, also known as Tibbs, Dream or Castle Island, after Fred Tibbs cut down all the trees but one to build his "castle" and tower.
Image A-05272 courtesy of the Royal BC Museum, BC Archives

Right: Tibbs's dream home was a wooden castle, three storeys high, with a crenellated tower and battlements. Painted red, white and blue, it was held to the rocks with steel guywires.
Image F-03428 courtesy of the Royal BC Museum, BC Archives

Bottom: Vancouver photographer Frank Leonard took this photo of Stubbs/Clayoquot Island in the 1920s. The saltery is at the end of the dock, and Walter Dawley's store, with its square, white front, stands on the far right. The Clayoquot Hotel, rebuilt after the fire of 1921, is the dark building to the left of the store. The beach in the foreground is where the body of Fred Tibbs washed up.
Frank Leonard photo, Vancouver Public Library 16677

fight. Tibbs was among them, joining up with the Canadian Forestry Corps. However, before he headed off to serve, he sounded one final blast on his cornet from his treetop platform, saying goodbye to his island domain. He told no one he was going, simply boarded up the windows of his wooden castle and left. On one window, up in the tower, he painted a picture of a beautiful princess; some say she looked like Olive Garrard. No one knew at the time, but Tibbs harboured secret romantic attachments, not only to Olive but also to Alma Arnet. Some thought he also fancied Winnie Dixson. "Oh, he tried all of us, all the different girls," Winnie later commented. "I didn't have much interest...I had about 300 chickens."

Neither Alma nor Olive had any idea what lay ahead. Tibbs had made his will before setting off to war, leaving the island "and everything thereon, excepting the house and ten feet of land on either side of the house site," to Alma Arnet, "because she is the nicest girl I know." He left the house and contents, except for his gramophone, to Olive Garrard, "because it was built for her." If Olive married, the house should go to Alma "if she is still single." Returning intact from the war in 1919, Tibbs resettled on his island and resumed his land-clearing, his gardening and his risky experiments with explosives. On New Year's Eve in 1919, he tried to explode dynamite from his tree platform, to "blow the old year to the four winds," but the explosion did not go off with the bang he had hoped, the dynamite being frozen.

In his wooden castle, Tibbs entertained visitors who came to listen to his gramophone and drink cocoa, and he often went to Tofino to collect mail and to "have some music, as there are two or three damsels here who play very nicely." He attended community events and dances—though he never danced—and he also took up a new job. Rowing his skiff around the harbour, he tended the navigation lights, coal-oil lanterns mounted on tripods on wooden floats. Every second day when the lanterns required refilling, Tibbs would tie up to the floats and clamber on to fuel the lights.

In early July 1921, Francis Garrard noted that Tibbs had been blasting rock on his island; "he had got badly powdered and had been quite ill from the effects." Immediately after this, on July 4, the Clayoquot Hotel went up in flames. Along with every other available man, Tibbs rushed over to Stubbs Island to assist in fighting the fire. The following day he went out to tend the lights, but after landing on one of the floats, his skiff drifted away. He dived in to swim after the boat. Not realizing what had occurred, a Tla-o-qui-aht man who saw the empty skiff towed the boat to Opitsat. Tibbs turned and made for the nearest land, on Stubbs Island. Perhaps overexertion, combined with the effects of the dynamite powder, had weakened him, for although he was usually a powerful swimmer, the effort proved too much. "He made the spit alright," Bill Sharp recalled. "He crawled up on the sand and lay there." A Japanese fisherman alerted the authorities; the telegram sent from the Clayoquot police to their superiors in Victoria read "Frederick Gerald Tibbs found exhausted on beach at Clayoquot by Jap fisherman early this morning." Tibbs could not be revived. "When the Doctor arrived...," wrote Francis Garrard, "Tibbs was already dead...it was a very sad affair." The gravestone for Frederick Gerald Tibbs stands in the old Tofino cemetery, on Morpheus Island.

Following Tibbs's death, the Garrard and Arnet families reached an agreement

Fred Tibbs limbed his one remaining tall spruce, and then built a ladder up it, which he ascended regularly to a narrow platform where he played his cornet.
Image F-03431 courtesy of the Royal BC Museum, BC Archives

Tibbs Island as it looks today. In 2015 it was listed for sale for $698,000.

Donna Fraser photo

about his unusual will. Olive Garrard relinquished her share of the inheritance, his castle home, to the Arnets, and Dream Isle became Arnet Island. A group of men went over to the island shortly after Tibbs's death to cut down the 100-foot-high "tree rig," deeming it unsafe, and as time passed the clear-cut island slowly greened over. A few others attempted to live on the island, renting out Tibbs's castle, but the place became associated with bad luck and sudden death. According to Anthony Guppy, after several unfortunate fatalities and mishaps there, the "strange little castle remained unoccupied for a long time…People began to believe it was haunted. It became a sort of game for young people to go over there, get inside, and make the most hair-raising ghostly noises." The stories of Tibbs lingered and grew; by the late 1920s, "Fred Tibbs had already acquired the gloss of a legendary figure," according to Guppy. The year after Tibbs died, Alma Arnet married; Olive Garrard also married in 1923. Had Tibbs lived a bit longer, perhaps he would have reconsidered his will. He certainly would have enjoyed the livelier social scene that began to emerge in Tofino in the ensuing years.

WHAT THE SEA PERHAPS HEARD
by Rachel Rose

Killer whales hunt a blue whale calf
and eat his tongue. As he bleeds to death,

blood seeps without a sound into my body.
Gulls come, screaming their belly-greed,

small fish unstitch flesh with needle teeth.
The mother blue has more grief

in her massive body
than anything else I have held.

No one has seen what I see: how great white
sharks copulate, fitting together in secret method.

When the octopus siphons me inside her,
and I unfurl her delicate legs with warm currents,

she blushes for me alone. I hold the tight curl
of the seahorse's tail as he pivots,

protecting his basketful of life.
Observe the spaghettini arms of starfish

reaching for drifting food. Hear their little song:
the stomach, the stomach! Dear urchins, sweet limpets,

all feast in me. In the heat of my armpit
waves curl their black seaweed, stones groan

as they are ground to sand. I rock them.
In my cold brain I am rational,

I do not weep to feel the polar bears
scrape my frozen cheeks.

From Song and Spectacle *(2012), by Rachel Rose*

COUGAR HUNT

Excerpted from Tales from Hidden Basin *(1996), by Dick Hammond*

Cougars have always held a fascination for the people of the Coast—Native or European. Whenever hunters gather, tales of the secretive cats, of their strange mix of daring and cowardice, of rashness and cunning, are sure to be told.

There are no cougars on Nelson Island, but to brothers Cliff and Hal, they were the most interesting of all animals—even more interesting than the great bear, the grizzly. For just about everyone who hunted had seen one of those, but some men had hunted all of their lives and not seen one of the big cats.

Cliff and Hal's greatest ambition was to go on a cougar hunt with the Old Indian, an event he had hinted might be in the future. But when they heard the familiar *Puff—Puff—* of Charlie's old engine one November morning, they weren't thinking of cougars; they were just glad he was there for a visit. Charlie's visits to the farm were welcomed by everyone. His kindness and sense of humour endeared him to their sisters and their mother. His knowledge—which he was always willing to share—was valued by Jack, their father, who liked the old man and was impressed by his practical wisdom. And the boys could never get enough of his stories of hunting and fishing and of the old times. For his part, Charlie relished the good food and appreciative audience.

Alistair Anderson illustration

But certain chores had to be finished, so by the time they got to the float the boat was tied up, and their father and Charlie had been talking for some while.

"Charlie, hey Charlie!" The grin on the face of the old man disappeared. He said severely, "Lazy boys. Boys no good. Not come down to meet Old Indian. Probably sleeping."

"We weren't sleeping. We were working. Ma wouldn't let us go 'til we'd finished."

"Yes. That's right, Charlie. You know we'd have been here if we could!"

'Well-ll, maybe Old Indian believe you. He not very smart. Try to make hunters out of farm boys."

"Farm boys! We're not farm boys. Just because we live on a farm..."

They were almost speechless at the insult. Charlie grunted, "Hmph. Real hunters eat'm fishy duck, like it."

"I like fishy duck, Charlie. It's good," said Cliff.

"Me too," lied his younger brother manfully.

Their father spoke. "Charlie thought you might want to go on a cougar hunt with him." His eyes twinkled. "I said I didn't think you would be interested, but that he could ask you himself."

He watched with amusement their frantic attempts to correct this second monstrous misapprehension.

"Well, perhaps I was mistaken. If you're going to go, you'd better hurry and get your things. The tide's dropping."

There wasn't much to get. Coats, hats, hunting shoes. Gun.

As they turned to go, Charlie said, "No gun. Old Indian have gun. One gun enough."

"Aw-w, Charlie..."

"No gun," firmly. No gun it was.

It all happened so fast. One moment doing chores, the next gliding over the smooth surface of Hidden Basin, with the *Puff—Puff—* of the boat's engine echoing from the rocky shore.

"Where's the cougar, Charlie?" "Where're we going, Charlie?" "How long will we be gone?"

The old man ignored them, his attention on the tricky business of guiding his boat past the rock in the rapids leading out of Hidden Basin. That done, he condescended to notice his passengers. He looked them over, stern-faced.

"Noisy boys. Worse than seagulls. Like crows with owl. Cougar hear, he run away, never come back."

"Aw-w, Charlie. You know we don't make any noise when we're hunting."

He relented somewhat. "Maybe so. Maybe could be worse. We see how quiet boys be when tired, hands cold, shoes full of snow." His voice lost its bantering tone.

"Cougar go after old lady's chickens in Pender Harbour. Old lady's dog bark. Cougar go into hills. Dog follow, not come back. Old lady call police. Cougar hounds all away somewhere. Police remember Old Indian, say, 'Get cougar.' Old Indian say, 'Sure.' New snow, easy track cougar. Come get boys."

Charlie.
Alistair Anderson illustration

There was no wind. The boat slipped easily along, making about four miles an hour—the speed that Charlie found most fuel-efficient. It seemed that he wasn't in any hurry. At the rate they were going, it would take about three hours to get to Pender Harbour. The land slid by, looking like a picture postcard of Christmas with the still, reflecting water and the dusting of snow on the trees, which became thicker as they rounded the point and turned north. Time passed quickly as the old man—stimulated as ever by an appreciative audience—told them stories of hunting and the old times. All too soon they arrived at the dock.

As the old boat had no reverse, docking could be an occasion of some excitement. You had the choice of making a one-eighty turn to kill momentum, which took a good deal of water, or stopping the engine, gliding up to the dock and leaping out to "snub" the line on whatever was convenient. As Charlie's lines were almost as old as his boat, they tended to snap under tension, giving added drama to already tense proceedings. This time, having deck hands, Charlie chose the second method. The ropes held, the boys knowing enough to let them slip a bit to ease the strain.

Safely docked, Charlie donned his wool jacket. Sanctified by many hunts, the wool retained traces of every odour with which it had ever been in contact. Then he took his old gun from its corner. Smelling heavily of the ratfish oil he kept it soaked with, it was loaded, hammer cocked, ready for any emergency—such as a potential dinner presenting itself within range. The boys were horrified. They had been taught, with great firmness, that one never kept a loaded gun around, much less one that was ready to fire!

Cliff said hesitantly, "Ah, Charlie, do you always keep your gun like that?"

"Like what?"

"You know, with a shell in the chamber, and cocked."

"Sure. Why not? Who going to pull trigger? Come around point, see seal, click of hammer maybe make dive. Boys know nothing."

They subsided. This would take some thinking about.

Years later, Father would say, "You know, it's a funny thing, but I found out as I got older that people who really use guns, and have lived with them all their lives, are the most careless with them. You see someone doing all the right things, checking the chamber, safety on, that sort of thing, chances are he's a weekend hunter. I don't say it's right, mind you, but that's the way it is."

As they started off, Hal—always the practical one—asked, "How about food, Charlie?"

The old man grinned. "Oh," he said enigmatically, "I think we find plenty of food for hungry boys."

He hung a rolled-up blanket over his shoulder by a strap, but it was obviously just a blanket.

They walked briskly along the shore on the trail that led to the old lady's house. There was about an inch of snow on the ground, but though there were many footprints, there was no other sign of life. A dog barked somewhere, and there was a faint smell of woodsmoke. They passed several houses, seemingly deserted, and came to a cottage with a red-shingled roof. Smoke drifted from the chimney. The snow in the yard and around was heavily trampled.

"Sh-sh," whispered Charlie. "This house of old lady. No spook-um."

He led the way to the back of the house where the chicken pen was. There were many tracks in the snow: dogs, people, chickens. Charlie pointed to a track like a large dog's.

"No claws. Cougar."

The boys were immensely thrilled. Their first cougar track! Charlie walked toward the chicken pen. The chickens, made nervous by the cat's visit, cackled and clucked at the strangers.

Immediately a door opened. There was the old lady, an impressive-looking gun grasped firmly in her hands, the muzzle pointing more or less in Charlie's direction. She peered at them as they stood frozen.

Lowering the gun, she said, "Well, it's about time! I don't know what you men do; it takes you so long to do anything. It's been a whole day almost that my Hopsy has been lost, but does anyone care? They do not! What are you doing there scaring my chickens? Why aren't you out rescuing my Hopsy?"

With his inscrutable look firmly in place, Charlie weathered the wordstorm. When it finally subsided a bit, he said with great dignity, "Old Indian come many miles to help find little dog. Travel over water, over land. Never stop. Now we are here, not worry. Old Indian find dog." He finished gravely, "We go now."

"Well, I should hope so. My poor Hopsy out in the woods all alone. I don't know why someone couldn't have done something before this..."

Her voice faded as Charlie hastily led the way around the corner and up the trail. The words became indistinct, but her voice could still be heard until they went around a rock outcrop. When it could be heard no more, Charlie sighed. "Cougar fool to come here. Old lady talk 'm to death, sure."

As they went up the trail, he pointed to the marks in the snow.

"Cougar come up here. Dog come after. Dog go '*yap—yap—yap*.' Cougar not like noise. He not afraid of dog, not go very fast. Head for high ground soon."

They went on another 100 yards or so. The boys studied the tracks with great care, scarcely able to believe that they were actually following the trail of a cougar. Charlie walked steadily on, not bothering to look at the trail at all, or so it seemed.

The right-hand side of the trail became steeper until the bank was almost vertical for the first fifteen feet or so. Charlie said, "Boys, watch. Cougar's trail go away soon." Sure enough, in a few more paces there were only dog tracks going back and forth and running around in circles. Then the single track of a running dog led up the trail.

"What happened, Charlie? Where'd he go?"

"I'll bet he jumped away off down there in the brush," guessed Cliff.

The old man shook his head sadly. "Boys use mouth. Not use eyes. Even dog not use mouth until he have something to talk about."

The embarrassed brothers kept silent and began to study the trail. In a moment they found, half obscured by dog tracks, two deep parallel gouges in the ground, with well-defined claw marks facing the steep bank. They looked up. There was a ledge about three times their height, but there were no marks in the light cover of snow on the bank.

"You mean it jumped up there and didn't touch the bank? Ah-h Charlie, you're joking. Nothing could jump that high!"

The old man shrugged. "Boys so smart, maybe teach Old Indian how track cougar? Maybe first go up bank, look for cougar tracks, eh?"

They looked up at the steep slippery bank. Hal said doubtfully, "If we try to go up there, we'll get all wet and muddy and make a lot of noise. Why can't we just follow the dog tracks? The dog knows where the cougar went, I'll bet."

Charlie grinned. "Maybe some hope for boys yet. Okay, we follow after dog."

The dog tracks led only a little farther up the trail, then disappeared into the brush as the bank became lower. Charlie turned to the right, back along the way they had come.

"But Charlie, the tracks go that way!"

"Boys, come, maybe learn something."

So they stumbled along the slippery broken rock with its coating of wet snow. Strangely enough, it didn't seem to be as slippery to the old man, although he wore boots much like theirs. Soon they were at the ledge above the marks on the trail. Charlie pointed, and there, plainly to be seen in the snow, was the mark where the big cat had lain. It had crouched there above the trail, watching the dog.

Charlie said, "What cougar thinking about? Why not jump on dog? Maybe too close to house. Maybe just not hungry enough!"

The boys looked at each other. They'd had visions of finding the lost dog and bringing it back to the old lady. But suddenly the woods didn't seem quite so friendly, nor the prospect of a happy ending so certain.

They were both wishing right then that they had the nice comforting heft of a gun in their hands. Hal was sure Old Charlie knew just what they were thinking. Why else would he have been grinning like that?

Back they went to follow the dog and cougar tracks. It was hard going. The trail headed almost straight up the hill. The ground was rough and covered with thickets of salal and salmonberry brush.

They had turned north around the shoulder of the hill, and the snow was now about four inches deep. They were soon sweating under their wool coats. Snow found its way down their necks, up their sleeves and into their boots. They were forced to make the most heroic efforts to keep from gasping or panting, for Old Charlie was strolling along as if he was on a good level trail, his breath coming and going silently, his footsteps almost as silent. This was a humiliating experience for two boys who prided themselves on their woodcraft! They began to watch how the old man walked. He never seemed to be looking at the ground just ahead of him, but he never slipped. Always his step took advantage of some foothold, a rock or a root, a stem or a branch, or a bit of log. They began to study the ground ahead, to plan their steps.

Several times the tracks showed that the cougar had leaped to a high place and watched as the dog came trotting busily along his trail. Suddenly, Charlie put up his hand in the signal to stop. He spoke very quietly.

"I think we find dog very soon. Maybe cougar too. Boys, stay here, make no noise."

He looked at his gun, slid the lever enough to see the shell in the chamber. Though the barrel showed rust, the action worked smoothly and quietly. He took off his wool mittens and put them in his coat pocket. Then he moved off. They thought he had moved silently before; now he was like drifting smoke. It seemed impossible to the boys that a human could make so little sound, even in snow.

About 100 feet ahead, a good-sized fir tree had blown down many years before. Though almost prone, it still lived. The top was against a rock bluff, the middle some twenty feet from the ground. Charlie went up to the root of it, where he stood still for a long time. The boys were in an agony of excitement. Finally he moved, just a shadow in the falling snow.

He was gone only a few minutes, but the boys had never known minutes to last so long. He reappeared and beckoned for them to come. He stood patiently as they slipped and scrambled up to him, all caution forgotten.

"Did you see the cougar, Charlie? Do you think he's around here? Maybe it's watching us! What did you see? Why'd you make us stay back?"

The old man raised his hands in mock horror.

"Boys not need guns. Old Indian right about that. Bad as old lady, find cougar, talk 'm to death!"

They subsided, waiting for him to tell them in his own time.

"Well," he said matter-of-factly, "anyhow, we find old lady's dog. Old lady's dog find cougar."

He pointed to the tracks. Those of the cougar had disappeared.

Alert this time, they looked at the fallen tree. Not near the root, but well up off the ground. Cliff pointed. The snow was disturbed. Charlie nodded approvingly, led them farther on. He said, "Dog find cougar; cougar find dinner."

There was blood on the trampled snow, and drag marks leading to a dark shape already whitened with new-fallen snow. It was the dog, partly eaten.

"We camp here," said Charlie.

The boys looked around them. In the excitement of the hunt, they hadn't paid much attention to anything else, even discomfort. Now reality came back to them. It was late in the afternoon, perhaps four o'clock. Already the shadows under the trees were growing dark. Everything was covered with wet snow. It hung on the branches and clung to the trunks of the trees. The whole woods were wet. The boys were soaking wet, their wool Mackinaws heavy with water. These famous coats were supposed to protect the wearer in all-day rain. Indeed, they were very good. The raindrops caught in the dense wool and trickled down to drip off the lower edge. The wet wool kept its wearer warm and absorbed sweat. However, the brothers' coats were old, thin hand-me-downs, and their shirts—also wool—were soaked. This didn't matter while movement kept them warm, but as soon as they stopped moving, they felt the damp. There is an old Irish saying about wool that goes, "No matter how cold and wet you get, you're always warm and dry." It has some truth to it, inasmuch as you will probably never, in our coastal conditions, die of exposure while dressed all in wool. But you can get very cold and uncomfortable.

And uncomfortable the boys were. Their wool pants were sodden, their boots full of partly melted snow. They had eaten nothing since breakfast, but if Charlie had any food, it was well hidden. They had no tarp and no blankets. Charlie had the tightly rolled blanket on his shoulder strap but it was small and very wet. Wet snowflakes were coming down quite fast now, and there was no shelter in sight that seemed the least bit adequate. They looked at each other.

"Well," said Cliff, "now we'll see how a real Indian Woodsman builds his camp."

"I hope," said Hal, "that we'll see how a real Indian Woodsman finds dinner!"

Meanwhile, Charlie had been ambling about the line of broken bluff against which the tree had fallen. Now he called to them.

"Boys, come."

They scrambled up to where he was standing in the partial shelter of a slanting rock face. He was scuffing the snow away from an area about two feet square.

"We build fire here. Come," he ordered.

He led the way back to the fallen tree where, taking the little hatchet that he always carried from his belt, he walked along until he found some dry ribs of fir bark to his liking. Splitting off some of the cork-like bark, he handed the pieces to Cliff and indicated the direction of the fire-to-be with his thumb. Finding a pitch-soaked place by a knot, he gouged out a handful, which he gave to Hal. He then walked back to the root where there were some bushes of leafless huckleberry, cut several bunches and gave them to the waiting boy. Again, he indicated the camping place with his thumb.

The boys delivered the loads, and seeing Charlie walking away, rushed to join him. They didn't want to miss a thing.

Hal could stand it no longer. "Charlie, what are we going to eat? Why didn't you tell us to bring some food?" (They thought this hardly fair, for he had told them at the boat not to worry about food.)

"Well, never mind. Old Indian know there be food here."

Charlie led them over to where the dead dog lay, now just another white mound in the snow. He took out his big clasp knife, reached down and, seizing the dog's hind leg, rolled it over. Its entrails flopped about messily. The cougar had eaten the soft underparts.

"Cat lazy, eat soft bits, leave good meat for boys." Expertly, he cut away the hind leg he was holding.

Hal felt his stomach flop over and try to slip up to his throat. He looked at what was left of the dog.

"Charlie," he stammered, "we're not going to eat that dog, are we? Not really? Dogs are pets. We don't eat our pets!"

The old man looked at him, his face showing no expression at all.

"Boys, listen. Dog NOT HERE. Dog go away someplace. Indians tell lot of stories, but they not know where dog go. White men say they know, but they lying. They not know. But Old Indian know one thing. Dog not here. What is here is dog MEAT. That good to eat. Okay?"

Back at the rocks, Charlie put down two pieces of bark with a bit of pitch between them. He fished a tin of matches out of a pocket, extracted one and put the tin back in his pocket. He struck the match on his thumbnail and applied it to the pitch, which blazed up quickly. Then he carefully placed a few more bits of bark on the little fire. In a few minutes, he had a small, hot, almost smokeless fire going.

Cliff asked, "Do you want us to get some armloads of bark, Charlie?"

The old man laughed. "Just like a white man. Build big fire, stand away back, carry wood all night. Indian make small fire, stay close."

With a few quick knife strokes, he skinned the leg, sliced the meat and cut out the bone. Handing them each a slice, he then took the bunches of huckleberry and cut off three of the biggest stems. Taking a third slice, he shoved the end of the stick through it and held it over the fire.

"Boys, eat," he said.

In a moment there were three dog steaks sizzling in front of them. It didn't smell all that bad. In fact, the smell of roasting meat made Hal's mouth water.

At length, Charlie said, "Enough cooking. Too much cooking, all good gone from meat." He sniffed his meat appreciatively. "Dog meat, good. Make boys strong. Not get very often."

He handed them each a bunch of the huckleberry stems, and taking one for himself, put a bunch of tips in his mouth and stripped off the dormant buds with his teeth. "Boys, do same," he commanded. "Buds good for you; all meat, no good. Next year's leaves good for you. Taste good too."

Hal contemplated his piece of charred dog steak. He looked at his brother. Cliff had just taken a large bite and was chewing strongly, swallowing the mouthful as his brother watched. Cliff wasn't fussy about food. He would eat just about anything, usually with great enthusiasm. But Hal had always been very critical about what he ate, and he was very doubtful if dog meat came under the right heading.

He thought, "Well, if Cliff can do it, I suppose I can." So he took a bite of dog.

"I knew I was in trouble as soon as I took the first bite. As soon as it touched my tongue, it reminded me of wet dog. I made myself chew on it, but the more I chewed, the bigger it seemed to get until my mouth was completely full of this lump that tasted like wet dog."

He decided to swallow it whole, but distinctly heard his stomach say, "You send that down here and I'm sending it right back up again."

He slipped it out of his mouth into his hand, and flung it under his arm onto the snow behind him. He looked over at Charlie. He was watching with a wicked little grin on his face. Hal's mouth still tasted like wet dog. He took a handful of the huckleberry tips and suddenly there was a taste that reminded him of spring and fresh berries.

Cliff threw away a bit of gristle.

"Aren't you going to eat your piece, Hal? Can I have it?"

Wordlessly, Hal handed the piece of meat to his brother. His supper consisted of huckleberry tips. Nothing else.

It was now dark. Small as it was, the fire of bark gave out quite a bit of heat, which the sloping rock face reflected back at them. Their wet clothes were steaming a bit, and the boys realized that they weren't nearly as uncomfortable as they had expected to be. Charlie picked up his blanket from beside the fire and unrolled it. It turned out to be three small wool blankets about five feet square. He handed one to each of them and folded the other around his shoulders. Then he began to talk. He told them stories of the days when there were no white men, of tribal wars and sudden raids, of warriors and hunters, gods and demons.

Hal later said, "I sat there on a rock, soaking wet to the skin with an empty stomach and wet feet, and dozed off into a sleep as sound as if I was in my own dry bed at home."

Hal woke up once about midnight. Charlie was carefully putting a small piece of bark on the fire. Cliff was lying on his side, curled up toward the warmth. He was covered with about half an inch of snow. It was warm and comfortable under the blanket. He went back to sleep.

He woke to a gentle pressure on his arm. Embers glowed where the fire had been, and there was just the faintest trace of light in the morning sky. Cliff was rubbing his eyes sleepily.

Charlie spoke, his voice just audible. "Boys, stay. Be quiet. No move, no talk, no breathe." With this somewhat impractical admonition, he stalked off as silently as any ghost, carrying his rifle, ready for action.

The minutes dragged endlessly. They huddled there in damp clothes on rocks that seemed to have grown much harder overnight with wet snow on and about them. They were cold, stiff and hungry but daren't whisper so much as a word to each other about it. Just as they could begin to see around them in the growing light, they heard footsteps in the snow as Charlie crunched up to them, making much more noise than usual. He was talking to himself, using guttural words they'd never heard before. He leaned his gun against a rock and, not saying anything to the boys, picked up the rest of the pitch and put it on the still-warm ashes. When it began to smoke, he blew on it and it burst into flames. The air became filled with the smell of burning pitch. He put dry bark on the pitch, and in a few minutes he had another cheerful, smokeless fire. Reaching into his coat, he pulled out the other leg of the dog and with a few deft moves had it skinned, deboned and sliced.

"Eat," he growled.

Cliff was never one to be slow to speak. Even though Charlie's manner gave him little encouragement, he dared to ask, "What happened, Charlie?"

The old man looked at them from where he squatted by the fire. For a while, they thought he wasn't going to answer. His face appeared as if carved out of a piece of hard, dark wood. Finally, he growled, "Old Indian getting too old. Bad as foolish boys. Forget to throw out shell when last shoot gun. Try to shoot cougar with empty shell!"

With the meat about half cooked, he kicked the fire apart and began to eat, Cliff following his lead. Hal hadn't even pretended to want any. Charlie picked up his gun.

"Okay. Boys ready? Had nice rest, good breakfast. Should be able to walk fast."

He watched sardonically as they scrambled to roll their blankets with muscles half paralyzed by cold and soreness. They were ready quickly, but he started just soon enough to make them scramble to catch up. Running uphill in the snow did have the very salutary effect of getting their muscles warmed up and ready for work.

And work it was to keep up with the old man. He cut diagonally up the hill, apparently with a definite goal in mind. He didn't speak, and the boys couldn't, needing all their breath to keep up. After travelling for almost an hour, Charlie stopped. The boys threw themselves down on the snow, their wet clothes steaming from the exertion. After a few minutes' rest they got up and went to where Charlie was standing, his back toward them.

He was looking down a steep, narrow draw. They could see about 100 yards down it through scattered old-growth fir trees. There were a few small clumps of salal, but the ground was mostly clear.

"Why are we stopping here, Charlie?" asked Cliff.

Charlie looked at them. His face was relaxed, and when he spoke his voice was mild.

"This, our last chance. This draw has deer trail that lead up hills to cedar swamp. Deer winter there. Eat cedar branches to keep belly full. Cedar, no good food. Deer get weak, easy to catch. Cougar know this. Old Indian think he head for there by easiest trail. This trail. He not here yet. We wait."

He hunched by a fallen tree where he could see down the draw with only his head showing, and rested his rifle on the log.

"Boys, find place to sit," he ordered. "Can look down trail but only with one eye," he chuckled. "Now we see what kind of hunters boys make!" His voice became stern. "No move, no make noise. Breathe slowly through mouth. If itch, no scratch. If cramp, no move. If nose run, let drip, no sniff. Blink eyes quietly! If cat come up trail, then turn and run away, Old Indian go home with two skins instead of one!"

He puffed out a cloud of breath, which drifted slowly off to their right and up the trail. He pointed to it. "Wind right. Now we wait."

They waited. Remembering it as a grown man, Hal said, "I never thought just sitting could be such misery. Cliff and I had done this sort of thing before, watching deer, but we didn't have Old Charlie watching us then! I had got myself into what I thought was a comfortable position, but pretty soon my 'comfortable position' seemed like the worst sort of torture. I knew I had to relax, but I itched, especially my back and arms. If you can scratch when you want to, you never even think of it, but when you can't...and we were wearing wet wool! My nose started running, but I daren't move a hair to stop it. I could see Cliff's face out of the corner of my eye. He looked as a man might, sitting on an anthill. That made me feel a little better!"

He was so wrapped up in his misery, he almost missed seeing the cougar. Suddenly it was just there, about twenty feet from where he should have first seen it. It was all he had imagined one to be, and more. It belonged there in the woods more than anything else he had ever seen, and he had a feeling that they didn't. He had never felt that way before. He wondered why Charlie didn't shoot, then he figured he had the gun

Alistair Anderson illustration

pointed at a certain spot and wasn't going to move it. All of a sudden Charlie made a quiet sound, something like a low whistle. The cougar stopped in its tracks, looking up toward them. Charlie fired, and the cougar turned and leaped, all in one movement. It soared through the air, all grace and wildness. It hit the trail about twenty-five feet down, but it was dead when it landed, and it hit all limp and crumpled. Charlie had shot it right through the heart. It was a good shot, about eighty yards, and downhill. The boys hadn't thought that either he or his old gun had it in them!

Before the echo of the shot had come back, Charlie was up and trotting down the hill. Cliff and Hal followed, but Hal's legs were so cramped he thought he was going to go down the hill head first. Cliff was staggering as badly as he was. Charlie was by the cougar before they were more than halfway there, but they soon limbered up and ran down to him. He was kneeling by it, having first made sure it was dead. He stood up. His left hand was cupped, and the boys saw that it was full of blood. He stepped over to them, dipped two fingers of his other hand in the blood and drew them across Cliff's forehead, then down both cheeks in a sort of pattern. Then he did the same thing to Hal. As he did it, he said something in the strange language he had used that morning.

Then Charlie put his hand up to his mouth and licked the blood out of it. All of it. Hal felt a bit squeamish, but somehow he felt it was right.

Charlie said, "Old Indian forget exact words, but good enough. Spirit of cougar satisfied. Boys not be full hunters, but got good beginning. Old Indian think might be hope for them yet!" He pulled out his knife, went over and squatted beside the cougar. He looked back at them.

He said, "Now, boys, build fire. Old Indian skin cat while still warm." He grinned. "Small fire," he said.

They got pitchy bark from a fir tree, split some wood from a cedar windfall with the hatchet. Then they found a flat spot, brushed away the snow and carefully built a fire between three rocks as they had seen Charlie do. A small one.

Hal said, "I don't think we should use cedar. You know how it sparks and crackles."

"I think you're right. Charlie wouldn't like that, would he?"

So they went back and got more fir bark. Charlie called, "Bring hatchet." He took it and cracked the thighbone after slicing the meat around it. They looked with awe at the huge jumping muscle of the hind legs.

Cliff said, "I wish I had muscles like that." Charlie looked at him, his face impassive.

"Boys' legs make pretty good meat just like they are." He cackled at his own joke. Charlie was in a fine mood. He had guessed correctly. He had made a fine shot. The bounty for the cougar plus the hide would bring a fair bit of money. And they had fresh meat!

These were much bigger steaks than the ones from the dog. They toasted them on forked sticks of hemlock, peeled so the bark wouldn't give the meat a bitter taste. Hal had no qualms about this meat. It was dark and wild tasting, but at the first bite his stomach informed him, "Yes, you can send some of that down, and the sooner the better."

While they were eating, Charlie picked up a handful of the split cedar and threw it on the fire. "Cedar make nice crackle," he remarked.

The boys regarded him silently. The only thing you could predict about Old Charlie was that he would be unpredictable!

After they had eaten, he chopped off the other haunch. "Too good to leave."

He sliced a hole between the bones of the lower leg and shoved a stick through for a carrying handle. Then he rolled up the hide, tying it in such a way that the legs formed carrying straps. Tossing it to Cliff, he said, "You carry hide." He tossed the rest of the meat from the haunch they had cut to Hal. Then he put the stick with the untouched one on his shoulder and started off down the draw.

When they had gone a little way, Hal remarked to his brother, "It seems kind of a shame to leave all the rest of that meat to go to waste."

Charlie heard. "Meat not go to waste. Listen."

They listened. A raven croaked not far away. Another answered from the flat below.

"Nothing go to waste in the woods."

They went a bit farther. A raven called almost over their heads.

"Raven say thanks. Maybe even send good luck."

The grey sky began to send down a fine mist of rain, and though it wasn't enough to make them really wet, it made the snow more slippery. But the way back seemed short, as the way back always does. They reached the trail in less time than they would have thought possible, and soon enough, there was the house of the old woman. Charlie went to the door and knocked. Her face peered out of the window suspiciously. Then it disappeared and the door opened. She was talking as it opened.

"Well, you're back. About time, too. Where is my Hopsy? Did you find him? You've been gone long enough!"

Charlie backed off a few steps.

"Ah-h-h—" he said, then stopped and looked desperately around at Cliff and Hal. They looked back at him silently.

Suddenly Hal was inspired. Perhaps it was the adventure stories he had read. He spoke out boldly.

"Ma'am," he began, "we found your Hopsy but we were too late to save him. He died fighting that savage cougar. He put up an awful fight but it was too big for him. Mr. Charlie buried him and put a cross on his grave. He carved 'Good Dog' on it. He thought you would like that."

Cliff and Charlie were looking at him with awe. He almost began to believe it himself, it sounded so good. He continued, warmed by their appreciation, his voice solemn. "Mr. Charlie swore he would get that cougar to revenge poor Hopsy. We tracked it all that night. In the morning it climbed a tree and Mr. Charlie shot it, and there is the skin!" He pointed to Cliff's shoulder. The old woman was actually speechless. There were tears in her eyes. Finally she spoke to Charlie.

"I knew he was dead. I could feel it. But it was so good of you to do what you did, I'm going to give you a special reward."

She turned and went into the house. Charlie's eyes glittered brightly in his impassive face. He hadn't expected this! In a moment she was back, carrying an envelope in her hand.

Cliff whispered, "I wonder how much she's going to give him."

She pulled out a square of cardboard, handed it to Charlie. "This is a picture of my Hopsy. You may have it to keep."

The two boys looked at Charlie's face. Then they looked at each other. It was too much for them. They ran across the yard, down the trail and on around the bend. There they stopped. They had to—they couldn't run for laughing.

Charlie came around the corner, walking with great dignity. He looked with disapproval at the boys. Cliff was lying on the wet ground, out of breath from laughter. Hal was trying unsuccessfully to remove the grin from his own face.

Charlie said sternly, "Foolish boys. Boys know nothing." He shook his head sadly. "Poor boys. No one teach them sense. Only Old Indian, and he think maybe too big a job for him!"

He took the picture out of his pocket, handling it with great care.

"Indian would know that this is great thing. Old Indian hang picture in cabin of boat. Spirit of dog be glad, bring good luck. Even foolish boys know that good luck is best thing you can have!"

He headed down the trail. The cougar hunt was over.

6 WHAT NOT TO WEAR TO A NUDE POTLUCK

Excerpted from Adventures in Solitude: What Not to Wear to a Nude Potluck and Other Stories from Desolation Sound *(2010),* by Grant Lawrence.

Beginning in the 1970s, CBC radio personality Grant Lawrence spent his summers at the family cabin in Desolation Sound (north of Vancouver) after his father purchased a block of land for subdividing. —Ed.

"Pot" would in fact be the keyword to Aldo's potluck invitation. Much to their consternation, my parents were figuring out that besides apples and oysters, there were a few other crops that could be successfully harvested in Desolation Sound. With its rare coastal microclimate of warm, wet air and long, hot summers, Desolation Sound is perfect for growing bountiful bushels of marijuana.

Aldo's potluck was a five-minute boat ride away in the next bay. As our motorboat rounded the rocky finger that separated our bays, we heard the potluck before we saw it. The caterwaul of a party in full swing danced across the open water like radio waves. As we drew closer, my innocent young eyes widened upon seeing a scene of total hedonism.

Intertwined brown bodies lay outstretched all over the sun-drenched shoreline, smoking, drinking, laughing, singing, making out and making love. Seemingly wild, long-haired children ran among the cavorting adults, leaping off the rocks into the green ocean water. The aesthetic that united the party was a revealing one: every single man, woman and child was totally and utterly nude. It was like the moment Charlton Heston discovers the humans at the oasis in *Planet of the Apes*. Just add a cranked-up Deep Purple cassette and matching purple bong smoke that hung low across the bay: "Smoke on the Water," just like the stereo blasted. This outrageous scene was more than enough for Dad to start vigorously turning the boat around, but Mom wouldn't let him, reasoning that:

a) she was bringing banana bread;

b) we were going to have to meet the rest of our neighbours eventually;

c) how would it look if the big, bad developer and his family suddenly swung their boat around in full view of the entire party and left without even saying hello?

We tied our skiff to a makeshift barge of boats, a barely floating, pell-mell parking lot of rafts, canoes, kayaks and rowboats in various states of sunken disrepair. We had to climb through several of them before we could make our way up the gangplank to shore.

Throughout my childhood, whenever I was extremely uncomfortable or frightened, I developed a strange nervous reaction: my teeth would chatter like I was locked in

Keith Milne Illustration

a freezer. Walking up that gangplank on that hot summer night into a foreign, naked scene of hippie strangers, my teeth sounded like a death rattle. My little sister cowered behind me, pulling on the back of my E.T. turtleneck. We were greeted by a beaming Aldo and his festive, long, white beard, flowing down over his bulging brown belly, both of which almost covered his dangling penis. Almost. He gripped a half-full bottle of label-less red wine in one hand and waved in the other a giant doobie, which he transferred to his lips when he extended his leathery, brown hand in welcome. My sister and I stared in shock, eyes like Keane Kids in pale, expressionless faces. My teeth continued to chatter uncontrollably.

Everyone at the party warmly welcomed us with extremely uncomfortable hugs, introducing us all around. Pungent pot clouds filled the air like a skunky London fog. Elaborate bongs gurgled and hissed, threatening to stain Mom's pink pedal-pushers. Mom later said she had never maintained such steadfast eye contact in her life and took extra caution when reaching out to shake hands with the guys. When Aldo sat down on a stump and spread his legs like Santa in a sauna, she strategically placed the pan of banana bread directly on his lap. Painfully, my sister and I were torn away from our parents' side when two gregarious, naked kids bounded up to us and insisted that we try their rope swing. They pranced barefoot down the rocks with the effortless agility of nimble forest creatures while we gingerly followed as if blindfolded. At the edge of a cliff overlooking the water was a lineup of more naked brown children of various ages, all shrieking happily while taking turns on a thick, bristly rope swing that was looped around a branch of a giant fir tree that grew out over the water. They'd place a foot in a loop at the bottom, grab the rope with their hands, swing out over the ocean and let go just at the right moment to plunge into the warm, green water below.

My sister and I were expected to follow suit. My teeth had stopped chattering long enough to politely refuse, but these friendly naked children with names like Sunpatch and Birdsong urged us on, insisting that we remove our clothes and join in the fun. (Similar pressure in far more adult situations was being put on our parents back in the heat of the bash.) For whatever bizarre societal reason, being the only clothed individuals at a nudist party at the edge of the wilderness felt as uncomfortable as if one were to be suddenly dropped naked onto a downtown sidewalk. And there would be no "Grin and bear it"—literally—for the Lawrence family on this night. The closest thing we got to public nudity was in our bathing suits once or twice a summer on a Vancouver beach, and even then I would never dare take my shirt off.

I struck a deal with the Lost Boys. Neither my sister nor I would remove our clothes, but I would try the rope swing. A pair of naked, deeply tanned identical twin boys with matching shocks of shaggy black hair held the rope for me. I pushed my glasses up from the end of my nose and nervously placed my shaking Keds sneaker inside the loop. I took hold of the rope. Its fraying fibres bit into my silky city palms. With a simultaneous shove from the twins I was suddenly airborne, hanging on for my young life, all my tiny muscles contracted, my body wrapped around the rope in a kung fu grip.

As I arced out over the ocean, the setting rays of the sun spilled across the surface, turning it to gold, illuminating the shoreline rocks with an illustrious shimmer. I felt something deep within let go and give in. Panic turned to acceptance, then calmness, then serenity as I hung over the glimmering ocean, frozen in space. Time stood still and all sound ceased. As if in a dream I gazed back toward the cliff edge at my sister and the naked children. They were calling to me . . . waving, yelling something and making hand gestures. The moment of serenity evaporated as quickly as it began. Real life, sound and motion roared like a train from a tunnel. I heard the words "Jump! Now! Jump! Let go of the rope!"

I didn't jump, and I didn't let go. I held on. Momentum swung me back toward the ledge filled with children like a nerd pendulum. I heard the words "No!! No!!" as they began to scatter. I slammed into the crowd, knocking kids off the ledge, sending them plunging into the water like lemmings. My runners' toe grips scraped the rock ledge but couldn't hang on.

The rope took me swinging out over the water again. I shut my eyes and hung on so tight the fibres cut into my palms. This time, when momentum swung me back toward the cliff, since I had cleared it of children, I slammed face first into a wall of granite. My glasses clattered to the ledge. Blind and stunned, I dropped to my hands and knees and searched until my fingers found them, bent but not broken.

My sister was pushed out of harm's way thanks to a very kind, older, fully developed naked girl, who also helped me with my bleeding nose, her perky brown breasts at my direct eye level. While the rest of the kids pulled themselves out of the water below, the kind girl suggested we head back to the main party and find our parents. Both my sister and I readily agreed and followed her round brown bum back to the party.

We spent another ninety excruciating minutes at the party. Since the only pot my parents touched sat on our stove simmering Kraft Dinner on Friday nights, they weren't blending in any better than Heather and I were. After the umpteenth uncircumcised male member bounced past my sister's eye level, she eventually slipped into something akin to a catatonic shock, desperate to escape back into the 1880s' world of heavily clothed bonnet-to-boot characters of *Little House on the Prairie*. I pushed my bent glasses up my nose to get a better look at the bronzed, pregnant hippie ladies, spread out on the rocks like melted candles.

Mom eventually signalled our exit . . . "Aldo! Thank you so much for having us!" in a volume shrill enough to frighten birds into flight. "We'd better get the kids home now, but this has been an absolutely fabulous party!" On our mostly silent boat ride home, Dad muttered that the party had been an unpleasant cross between *Helter Skelter*, *Apocalypse Now* and a *National Geographic* special on orangutans. I have had a deep, personal aversion to potlucks ever since.

Christy Nyiri Illustration

7 JAPANESE FISHERS AND WORLD WAR TWO
Losing Licences, Vessels and Livelihoods

Excerpted from Spirit of the Nikkei Fleet: BC's Japanese Canadian Fishermen *(2009), by* *Masako Fukawa with Stanley Fukawa and the Nikkei Fishermen's History Book Committee*

I was visiting my friend. It was Sunday noontime. They had a radio going and we heard, "Japan attacked Pearl Harbor." We couldn't believe it, you know. "Ah, that's a hoax," we'd say. They kept repeating and repeating all the time...we couldn't believe it. My friend and I were saying, "It can't be." ...Then that night a truckload of soldiers came. —Takeshi Uyeyama

The year 1941 was the beginning of a nightmare for Japanese Canadian fishermen.
Canada. Dept. of National Defence/ Library and Archives Canada/ PA-134097

Nikkei [Japanese Canadian] fishermen's knowledge and familiarity with coastal waters made them the chief target of rumours and suspicion of fifth-column activities, and as a result they were the first to feel the impact of Japan's bombing of Pearl Harbor.

In 1941 all of them were either Canadian-born or naturalized Canadians, but although not a single one was detained by the RCMP or the military, they were accused of having within their number Japanese naval officers in disguise. The first act of the federal government under the *War*

Measures Act was to impound the Nikkei fishing fleet and suspend the licences of the Nikkei fishermen. Ironically, in 1938 when Hitler invaded Europe, the Canadian government had ordered all vessels to be marked with NW numbers on top of the cabin and on each side of the boat. This now made it easy for aircraft to identify the vessels belonging to Nikkei fishermen.

At dawn on December 8, 1941, the Royal Canadian Navy proceeded from port to port disabling beached vessels. The few boats that were still out on the wintry seas were ordered by radio to head immediately for one of the nearest of thirteen official fishing ports on the coast. There the vessels were searched for weapons and maps and immobilized. Some 2,090 licences issued to 1,265 Nikkei fishermen—including those held by thirty-seven World War One veterans—were cancelled, and 1,137 vessels owned and operated by them were impounded.

Meanwhile, Japanese Canadian fishermen up and down the coast offered their assistance and declared their loyalty to Canada. In Steveston, the dantai [the 1897 *Regulations of the Fraser River Fishermen's Association*] volunteered their boats for coastal defence. The Northern British Columbia Resident Fishermen's Association, a Japanese Canadian group in Prince Rupert, followed suit on December 11. They "unanimously affirmed their loyalty as Canadian citizens and offered themselves for any service which Canada may desire of us." On January 10, 1942, *The Province* reported that even during the period when their boats were being stripped, rounded up and impounded, "young men in Steveston voiced their allegiances and services

A soldier raises the Union Jack on a confiscated boat.
Canada. Dept. of National Defence/ Library and Archives Canada PA-170513

to Canada." The *New Canadian* reported on January 12, 1942, that a mass meeting of Canadian-born Japanese residents in Steveston passed a resolution without a dissenting voice and directed Hiroshi Nishi, president of the Japanese Canadian Citizens League, to send a telegram to the Standing Committee on Oriental Affairs in British Columbia stating their confidence in the Canadian government and the RCMP and that "we earnestly desire to contribute our utmost to Canada's war effort and thereby offer our services in any capacity the government may decide." On January 14, 1942, the headline of the *Marpole-Richmond Review* read "200 Steveston Japs Offer Services for War Effort." Just days before the bombing of Pearl Harbor, the Upper Fraser Japanese

Above: Tatsuo Oura and his granddaughter, Christine, in 2004.
Stan Fukawa photo

Top: Koji Takahashi's *Mary H* was confiscated and sold, and Takahashi was relocated to sugar beet farms in Manitoba.
Courtesy of Ken Takahashi

Fishermen's Association had donated 3.8 tons of canned chum salmon for distribution in Britain. Yet within twenty-four hours of the bombing, Japanese Canadians were being rounded up and their boats impounded.

Within a week of the seizure of their boats, all Nikkei fishermen were ordered to take them to New Westminster. Those on the west coast of Vancouver Island in Tofino, Ucluelet and Clayoquot were the first to leave. On December 15 their trollers and packers departed for New Westminster, each with a soldier on board. In that flotilla was Yoshio "Johnny" Madokoro (1913–2000) on his troller, the *Crown*. He had been enjoying the good life in Tofino as one of the executives of the Tofino Trollers' Co-op, whose members had prospered over the previous two decades by delivering their catches to the fresh markets of Vancouver and Seattle. The boats belonging to his brother, Hiroshi "Thomas" Madokoro, and his father, Kamezo Madokoro, were also in the flotilla. The soldier on Johnny's troller was a prairie boy and was seasick throughout the voyage. They found many of the soldiers to be "decent enough" and were bewildered as to how "individual *hakujin* (Caucasian) Canadians could be so decent, and yet" the newspapers and radio repeatedly said that "Japanese Canadians were all traitors." The Madokoros reached New Westminster without incident.

Tatsuo Oura was born in Steveston and trolled for the Ucluelet Japanese Fishermen's Co-op. Years later, he still remembered the knock on his door and the shock of opening it to an RCMP officer. The officer accompanied him to his boat, the *TO*, searched it for firearms and removed everything that might possibly be used as a "weapon." Oura argued with him about the removal of the iron bar he found there because it was needed to crank-start his engine. The officer, new to the sea, had no idea what Oura was talking about. In frustration, Oura hid the iron bar under his shirt because without it his boat would have no power and could not be controlled.

The flotilla consisted of sixty or more boats under guard of the navy vessel HMCS *Givenchy*. The weather was foul, as it often is in December, and they were caught in a storm and had to wait it out in Bamfield without food, warm clothing or any means of keeping warm. Their every step was watched with a rifle pointed at them. Oura says, "Thankfully, Kenneth Miller who had worked as an engineer on a Japanese packer boat in Ucluelet heard of our plight and he and another fisherman, Thompson, brought supplies to Bamfield for us." The flotilla waited there three days before the storm subsided.

The usual day-and-a-half trip from Ucluelet to Steveston took five days. All the boats except one reached Steveston, and on December 23 the *Givenchy* started the search for Tsunetaro Oye and his boat; they located him the following evening on the United States side of the border. The US Coast Guard handed over a mortally injured Oye to Canadian officials, who brought him by car to the Vancouver General Hospital where Kanzo and Larry Maekawa, as former and active officials of the Ucluelet Japanese Fishermen's Co-operative, visited him. He was completely covered with bandages and, though conscious, was unable to speak. He answered queries with gestures, confirming he had been beaten and his throat slashed by his captors in the United States. He subsequently died and was cremated without his bandages being removed.

Harold Kimoto, who left from Clayoquot with a sailor on board his ship, found that except for one sailor who stole a fisherman's wallet, the navy men were nice enough individuals. However, when they reached New Westminster, "a whole gang came on board and they took everything that was left on the boat. They took batteries, everything. I didn't care because we were leaving the boat anyway, but gee whiz." Others reported similar lootings. Tommy Kimoto said, "Those navy guys stole everything. They even stole anchor chains." Another said, "You could go into New Westminster and hear that compasses were selling for two dollars. It used to be a joke. Buy a Japanese compass cheap. Or a spotlight anywhere, cheap. Batteries. Hard to get. You could buy them anywhere. These navy guys were looting our boats of everything they could tear off and selling it for beer. I guess it is natural. I've seen it happen in other places. But the navy was supposed to be the protectors of our property."

On December 14, Masao Nakagawa and Isamu Kayama were cutting wood for the winter at Port Essington when the police arrived and ordered them to take their boats to the Inverness Cannery. Thinking that this was as far as they had to go, Nakagawa on his father's boat, Kayama on his own boat and Jitsuo Uyede on the *J.U.* started out prepared only for a short trip. They were given no time to inform their families or to take on provisions, and having stripped their boats for the winter, they had no food, warm clothes or fuel for their stoves on board. At the Inverness Cannery they were ordered to Tuck Inlet near Prince Rupert, where they waited for two days until sixty gillnetters had been assembled. They were not allowed to go ashore. When they learned they were going to New Westminster and that the navy was confiscating their boats, they were sick to their stomachs.

Just one hour before they left the inlet on the 16th, Minoru "Min" Sakamoto and Juichi Matsushita, who were young boys at the time, were given permission to obtain provisions. They returned with bread, canned goods, sugar and tea from the Yamanaka store in Prince Rupert and three sacks of coal for the fifteen boats with stoves. The food lasted them for two days. They left that morning at 8:30 with two Canadian Navy Fisherman's Reserve vessels, the *Leelo* and the *Kuitan*, towing the gillnetters in two long lines, the boats stretching for about three-quarters of a mile. They were joined by the corvette HMCS *Macdonald* and the tugboat *Stanpoint*. The fishermen had no idea that the journey ahead of them would take fifteen long days and that their lives would be in danger all the way as they fought wind, fog and ice floes.

As soon as they left the harbour, they ran into trouble. A strong westerly wind blew all day and the waves became so high they seemed to come from the sky. At about 2 am they sought shelter and anchored near Lowe Inlet. On December 18 the flotilla ran into heavy seas again at the mouth of Milbanke Sound that made navigating a nightmare, and twice the *Stanpoint*'s tow line broke. The corvette crew spent three hours repairing the damage. Meanwhile, six boats had drifted loose and the sea became so rough that they had to seek shelter in a nearby channel. At this point the *Leelo* proceeded to Bella Bella to obtain gasoline for the twenty boats with engines still in running order.

At midnight the rest of the flotilla reached Bella Bella, managed to purchase groceries and left again in the dead of night. None of the skippers had suitable clothing and, cold and wet, they huddled for warmth in their cabins. As they had slept little since they left home and they had no food left, there were now tired and hungry men at the wheel, bracing against the waves that hit their bows. They ran all night through log-strewn waters, and as only a few boats had lanterns on board, they began colliding in the dark as the rough seas lifted them and brought them down with a terrible thud

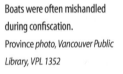

Boats were often mishandled during confiscation.
Province photo, *Vancouver Public Library, VPL 1352*

that shook their bones. Now and then a propeller would spin helplessly in mid-air. Near Namu a fisherman from North Pacific Cannery, having closed his cabin too tight to ward off the cold, was overcome by gas fumes and his boat was observed running in circles. Another boat took her in tow. The sea became rougher. Many of the men became seasick.

Although wind data is not available for 1941, Jim Attridge, a former meteorologist who has researched the weather for this period, says that based on the known temperatures and rainfall at that time, the weather must have been similar to the conditions that existed in December 2004, when virtually all weather stations in coastal BC reported above-average temperatures and copious amounts of rain. The data from Solander Island off the northern tip of Vancouver Island shows that on December 15, 2004, the average daily wind speed was 37 miles per hour (mph) gusting to 66; 37 mph would produce "near gale" conditions with mounting thirteen-foot waves and foam blowing streaks downwind. By the time the wind speed reached 56 mph, there would be waves of nearly thirty feet, a heavy sea roll, a generally white surface, and visibility would be impaired. Wind gusts of 66 mph produce waves as high as thirty-six feet, and this is classified as a "violent storm." It was just such a storm that Masao Nakagawa and Isamu Kayama experienced during their "terror-filled" trip down the coast to Steveston, and Roy Ito recorded and wrote about it for the *New Canadian*. Although all Japanese-language newspapers had been shut down immediately after war was declared, the *New Canadian* was still allowed to publish but it was heavily censored. When the censor killed this story, Ito saved it to recount in *Stories of My People*, published in 1994.

The day that the flotilla stayed in Takush Harbour was spent playing cards while the temperature dropped lower and lower. Some of the fishermen broke up their cabins for fuel while others boiled water in tobacco cans and hugged them for warmth. Christmas was a day they would never forget. Seven fishermen pooled their resources and bought the only meat they could find in Alert Bay—one chicken. Combined with a little cabbage boiled in salt water, it became their Christmas dinner. They left Alert Bay that night, and sometime during the night one of the boats from Prince Rupert submerged until only the cabin appeared above water.

They reached Steveston on December 28, and as some of the fishermen had left home with no money, they had to borrow from friends and relatives in Steveston for the return fare. "We spent New Year's Day in the same clothes we wore when we were cutting wood fifteen days before our long voyage south," Masao Nakagawa said. "We went home to Essington wondering what the future had in store for us. Losing our boats meant our livelihoods were gone. Why was it necessary to impound our boats? Why was it necessary to take them to Steveston? We wondered how this could happen to Canadian citizens." His father, Sasuke, had been born in Shiga-ken and was working on the Skeena when he volunteered to fight for Canada in World War One. He served in France with the 10th Battalion and was wounded. Now he, too, had been declared "an enemy alien."

In Nanaimo, the Mizuyabu family was living a relatively tranquil life when all Japanese fishermen were ordered to stay in port. Yukiharu Mizuyabu remembers that:

soldiers equipped with bayonets on their rifles stood along the waterfront road to ensure that the Japanese Canadians abided by the curfew imposed upon them. A few weeks later my father and the other fishermen were ordered onto their boats and escorted by the Canadian navy to the mouth of the Fraser River where the boats were impounded. They were forced to return to Nanaimo by ferry. Without their boats, all Japanese Canadian fishermen were suddenly deprived of their only source of income, but the callous politicians made no provisions for families affected by these actions.

Many fishermen would relive the traumatic events of the confiscation until they died. Amy Doi says that her father, Ihachi Hamaoka, "tells with shame his story of being forced to lead the fleet of Japanese fishboats [from Powell River] through a dangerous pass that the fisheries people would not dare navigate in order to take them to be impounded." He was incarcerated in Hastings Park until he was sponsored by Mr. Oishi, a farmer, enabling the family to be relocated to Kamloops. "Our family has been here ever since. My mother refused to go back to the coast and fishing after the evacuation order was lifted."

Nikkei fishermen of the inner coast, including the Fraser, were similarly ordered to return to port. Their vessels were searched by naval personnel for firearms, and they were told to remove their valuables and personal effects. Their boats were then immobilized, tied together and towed to the Annieville Slough, where vital engine parts and certain navigating instruments were removed.

Yoshio "Joe" Teranishi, twenty-eight years old, was putting the finishing touches on the roof of the new house belonging to his uncle, Mo-yan (Mosaburo Teraguchi), in Steveston when he heard from his cousin that war had started. They were given instructions to run their boat to Annieville and tie it up. He cannot recall how he got back home

Japanese men reading enemy alien notice.
Province photo, Vancouver Public Library, VPL 1343

without the boat. He observed that there was no watchman at Annieville, and some of the boats were sinking. After witnessing this scene, he sold his own boat for $400, $200 less than its real value, and he never returned to Annieville. "I heard it was awful."

Tatsuro "Buck" Suzuki described the incomprehensible actions of the government and his own feelings to Barry Broadfoot, who published them in *Years of Sorrow, Years of Shame* in 1977. Suzuki had been the secretary of the Upper Fraser Japanese Fishermen's Association when he received a call to report to naval headquarters at nine the next morning. The commander told him quite frankly, "Mr. Suzuki, we were caught with our pants down," and then he ordered all fishing vessels to be turned over to the authorities immediately. Suzuki told Broadfoot, "Don't think that the authorities weren't waiting for us when Pearl Harbor came. Within two hours things began to happen. Two hours. To this day I don't know what they thought about those fishing boats. They were our living. They were small boats, made of wood. We had no radar, no radio, no echo sounder. Why, we could go into Vancouver any time and buy British Admiralty charts of every single mile of the coast." Suzuki tried to convince the authorities that the Japanese fishermen were not spies, that "we were just ordinary fishermen…[but] as far back as the late 1890s they had determined that one day they would kick the damn Japs off the river. There was one common statement you could hear along the river: There's only one damn good Jap and that's a dead Jap."

In *Wild Daisies in the Sand*, Tom Sando (Tamio Kuwabara) wrote:

On the chilly morning of Saturday, December 6, 1941, my father, younger brother Shig and I, Tamio Kuwabara aged nineteen, traveled across the choppy waters of the Georgia Strait on our small fishing boat Hokui No. 1. *We tied our boat down in Steveston Harbour…We had a bright outlook and big plans. We were going to buy a larger boat that would permit us to fish all year round. Of course, we would be spending the salmon season, the months of July and August, in Skeena River, but we would return to fish the BC coast for halibut, cod and shark for the remainder of the year…Our bright future was shattered the following morning when we heard the shocking news on the radio—Japanese planes had bombed Pearl Harbor…Ten days later we received a notice from the RCMP to remove our fishing boat to an impound yard near New Westminster. We tied down our small fishing boat upstream on the Fraser River. It was heartbreaking to see our beloved boat left behind.*

In 1948, Shiromatsu Koyama's *Hawthorne II* sold for $195.50.

Courtesy of Faye Ishii

Harry Yonekura recalls his final farewell to his boat as it was being towed to the Annieville Slough in New Westminster.

Standing beside me to witness this travesty was Unosuke Sakamoto, president of the Fishermen's Association, and Yoshio Kanda, a district representative of the association. The three of us decided to complain to the commandant at the Garry Point Naval Base. Reluctantly, the commandant admitted that he had placed inexperienced men in charge of towing our fishing vessels. He also told us that he had been placed in charge of impounding all 1,137 boats and his deadline for this mission was December 27, 1941. It was now December 14. This meant that he had only thirteen days left to deliver the remaining boats. There were about 450 to 500 fishing boats to impound in Steveston alone! Tentatively, Mr. Sakamoto suggested that the Japanese Canadian fishermen be allowed to sail their own boats to the Annieville Dike. The offer was readily accepted. There was just one hitch in the plan—how would we get back to Steveston? The commandant did not hesitate to offer us passage back to New Westminster on a naval ferry, from where we pooled our resources and paid for transportation back to Steveston.

I guess we all needed one last voyage on our own boats before bidding them farewell, possibly forever. I will never forget the overwhelming sadness and sense of disbelief I felt at the Annieville Dike as I patted my boat and tied it up securely one last time. Then I quietly said goodbye and got up, resolving to put aside my emotions and accept the situation. My country was at war and I had to do whatever was necessary to prove my loyalty.

The scene at the Annieville Slough was chaotic. Ann Sunahara wrote that vessels arrived at the rate of 125 a day to facilities that were totally inadequate to handle the numbers, and they were moored some fourteen abreast without regard to their respective size or relative draft at low tide. Some 980 boats remained idle there for six weeks, some swinging at anchor while others were damaged and lying waterlogged on the banks of the Fraser at

JAPANESE FISHING VESSELS DISPOSAL COMMITTEE

RELEASE AND DISCHARGE

FISHING VESSEL: "Hawthorne II" CLAIM No.: 522-828

REG. or LIC. No.: Victoria 1438 Owner at Time of Impounding: Shiro KOYAMA, #09929, File 1507

NAVAL No.: VE 045-A

CLAIM PAYABLE TO: Shiro KOYAMA, #09929 Present Owner: Abandoned Vessel

This vessel was damaged while in the custody of the Royal Canadian Navy, and was declared a total loss by the surveyors for Naval Service and Japanese Fishing Vessels Disposal Committee.

The owner has agreed to accept $200.00 in full settlement of his claim for the loss of his vessel, which is considered fair value by the surveyors aforementioned. The sum of $195.50, being $200.00, less expense charges of $4.50 is approved by the undersigned and accepted as adequate compensation.

In consideration of the payment of the sum of ONE HUNDRED AND NINETY-FOUR DOLLARS AND FIFTY CENTS ----------------------------- ($ 195.50) (of lawful money of Canada) (the receipt of which is hereby acknowledged), we, the undersigned, being the owners and/or mortgagees, shipyard repairers and all others having any interest, claim or demand against the said motor vessel registered at the Port of Victoria, B. C. Official or License No. 1438 DO HEREBY RELEASE and forever discharge His Majesty the King, as represented by Royal Canadian Naval Service or any patrol or auxiliary service, acting through or under the authority of Royal Canadian Naval Service, and all boards, commissions or departments of His Majesty's Canadian Government of and from claims which we may now have or which hereafter may arise and which now could or at any time hereafter be made in consequence of damage sustained or any alleged damage sustained, to the above-named motor vessel while in custody of His Majesty's Royal Canadian Naval Service or any auxiliary patrols, commissions, boards or departments hereinbefore named.

AND FURTHER, we covenant that we are the owners and/or mortgagees, shipyard repairers and all others having any interest, claim or demand against the said vessel and are the only parties or persons having any interest, claim, lien, demand or charge over the above-named motor vessel, and should any claim hereafter be made by or through any parties whatsoever, we hereby agree to indemnify and save harmless His Majesty the King as represented by any of the naval services, boards, patrols, departments, or commissions hereinbefore referred to.

AND FURTHER, that this discharge and release enures to the benefit of and is binding upon all the parties hereto, their respective heirs, executors, administrators, assigns, successors and representatives.

DATED at Montreal Quebec, British Columbia, this 3rd day of January 1948.

low tide and awash at high tide, their engines sludged with silt. Equipment and gear were stolen despite an armed naval patrol, and by the time the boats were re-moored six to eight weeks later, 162 had sunk. It was heartbreaking for fishermen to witness their beloved boats being so ill-treated and it was beyond their comprehension why they had been confiscated.

These events were all the more devastating to the Nikkei fishermen since, after enduring half a century of racist government policies, their lives had started to improve. The fishing in 1941 had been good on the Fraser, and 1942 promised to be even better because it was the year of the big Adams River sockeye run. At the same time, the war in Europe had increased the demand not just for canned sockeye but also for pink, coho and even chum salmon. The fishermen's new confidence was reflected in the fact that they had been spending heavily in improving their equipment and gear so that they now owned some of the best vessels in the industry.

The Nikkei fishermen had fully co-operated with the navy because to do otherwise would have been considered unpatriotic. But they also thought that the issue of national security would soon be resolved and that their boats would be returned to them in time to have them back in operation for the fishing season. "We still had our nets and gear in our net lofts, so a lot of Japanese fishermen thought it was just a temporary thing and when it was straightened out they'd get their boats back and we'd be fishing by spring. After all, they still had their nets."

The value of the 1,137 impounded boats and their equipment was between $2 million and $3 million. The table below shows the vessels impounded, by gear type.

Gear Type	Number of Boats Confiscated	Number of Japanese Canadian Owners	Number of Boats Released to Non-Japanese Owners*
Gillnet	860	715	145
Troller	120	115	5
Seine	68	67	1
Packer	147	138	9
Cod, other	142	102	40
Total	1,337	1,137	200

*A number of vessels belonging to non-Japanese were rounded up by mistake and impounded. They were subsequently returned to their owners.

With the removal of 1,265 fishermen from active participation in West Coast fisheries, the government of Canada faced a production crisis just when an uninterrupted food supply was necessary for the war effort. The government's response was to issue Order-in-Council PC 251 to return the Japanese vessels to active fishing in the hands of fishermen "other than Japanese origin" by charter, lease or sale. This was followed by PC 288 that ordered the establishment of the Japanese Fishing Vessels Disposal Committee (JFVDC).

To overcome the belief still held by some Nikkei that they would be getting back

NOTICE OF SALE

The Custodian of Enemy Property offers the following boats for sale:

Fishing Boats

"S. I."	No. 6603	Vancouver
"Bumper Catch"	No. 152918	Vancouver
"B. Y."	No. 3363	New Westminster
"Departure Bay III"	No. 154949	Vancouver
"Departure Bay V"	No. 155241	Vancouver
"Gardner M"	No. 154669	Vancouver
"Garry Point No. 4"	No. 154971	New Westminster
"Gigilo"	No. 154554	Vancouver
"Holly L"	No. 152459	New Westminster
"I. M. P."	No. 973	Vancouver
"Izumi No. 3"	No. 153369	Vancouver
"Izumi No. 8"	No. 170430	Vancouver
"Kamtchatka"	No. 153169	Vancouver
"Merle C"	No. 154384	Vancouver
"Otter Bay"	No. 155110	Vancouver
"Yip No. 2"	No. 154972	New Westminster
"K. K."	No. 3368	New Westminster
"Kimio"	No. 6598	Vancouver
"K. N."	No. 3364	New Westminster
"Lion's Gate"	No. 1359	Vancouver
"Mizuho"	No. 134292	New Westminster
"Point Yoho"	No. 154539	Vancouver
"Three Queens"	No. 155094	Vancouver
"Kanamoto"	No. 141788	New Westminster
"Newcastle 4"	No. 138688	Vancouver
"George Bay"	No. 154349	Vancouver
"Rose City"	No. 138305	Vancouver
"Jessie Island No. 9"	No. 155231	Vancouver
"Kitaka"	No. 138608	Vancouver
"Moresby 2"	No. 150875	New Westminster
"R. K."	No. 2776	Vancouver
"Worthman T"	No. 152919	Vancouver
"Y. O. 3"	No. 2779	Vancouver
"Y. O. 5"	No. 2780	Vancouver
"Y. O. 6"	No. 2781	Vancouver
"Fragrance"	No. 6602	Vancouver
Gas Fishing Boat	No. 3362	New Westminster
"Y. O."	No. 2777	Vancouver
"Y. O. X. 2"	No. 2778	Vancouver
"Newcastle 8"	No. 150252	Vancouver

Other Boats

"Blue Fox"	No. 154927	Vancouver
"Louise"	No. 2907	New Westminster

All offers must be in writing, for individual boats, and accompanied by a certified cheque for 10% of the offer.

Offers for fishing boats, if accepted, will be those from bona fide fishermen or Fishing Companies who are entitled to own vessels of Canadian Registry.

The highest or any offer not necessarily accepted.

Arrangements to examine the boats may be made with the undersigned. All offers should be addressed to the undersigned and will be accepted up to 12 o'clock noon the ninth day of March, 1942.

G. W. McPherson,
Authorized Deputy of the Secretary of State and/or Custodian, 1404 Royal Bank Building Vancouver, B.C.

FRANK A. CLAPP COLLECTION

After the vessels were confiscated, they were leased or sold to fishermen "other than Japanese origin."
Courtesy of Frank A. Clapp, The Province, February 21, 1942

into fishing, district representatives were appointed to obtain signatures authorizing the sale of their boats. The Nikkei fishermen had no option but to sign over their boats because their families were being separated and dispersed with no means of support, but it was not until January 25, 1942, that any hope they had of fishing the 1942 season was finally dashed. In *Steveston Recollected*, Unosuke Sakamoto described the procedure adopted by the JFVDC:

Each district chairman was responsible for getting signatures on the proc-uration forms, and since all the Japanese knew they had to leave the Coast, they signed them. The Government then advertised for buyers. They listed all the boats—so much for this, so much for that—and white men and Indians chose the boats they liked. At first it was all right. The Government asked us to set prices so they would know the actual value of the boats. Then they let us know the offered price and we notified the owners in the places they had been sent to. I would write to them telling them the price and asking them what they wanted to do. They all knew they had to sell their boats cheap, so they sold them—with tears. But by the end if someone wanted a boat which we priced at $1,000 and if that person didn't have that much money he would say, 'I have only $500, but I want this boat so sell it to me.' The Government would then make the bill of sale on its own authority. A lot of boats were sold this way. Nothing could be done about it because we were all under the War Measures Act.

The release of over 1,000 boats created a glut in the market in which buyers could more or less dictate their prices. *The Province* reported on March 17, 1942, that "the commission has full power to force Japanese owners to sell. Any white Canadian who cannot reach a settlement with a Japanese owner has merely to write to the commission offering to buy and naming a price. The commission will do the rest. If the offer is judged fair, the Japanese owner will have to sell."

HARRIET'S GRAVLAX WITH MUSTARD SAUCE

8

Excerpted from Seasonings: Flavours of the Southern Gulf Islands *(2012),*
by Andrea and David Spalding

The run of spring salmon is eagerly awaited on the West Coast. Springs—also known as chinook salmon—make their way to our waters as early as March. A favourite West Coast way to serve this salmon is in the form of gravlax, and it is found on many restaurant menus. However, it is rarely prepared at home, except by British Columbians of Scandinavian descent who have grown up familiar with the process.

We hope that this recipe will demystify gravlax so this moist and succulent dish is available to everyone. The recipe is very easy, but it takes time—three days—so plan ahead. Don't panic, though, as for most of the time the salmon sits in the fridge and you ignore it! Gravlax is "cooked" in brine and the juices it generates. Served in very thin slices, gravlax is delicious as a dinner appetizer. It can also be served at breakfast, with a poached egg, buttered toast and a topping of Mustard Sauce.

Our Pender Island friend Harriet Stribley, originally from Sweden, gave Andrea this recipe many years ago. As is the way of recipes, adaptations crept in. Now we don't know what Harriet's original recipe was, but this one is an easy, terrific way to impress guests with a West Coast staple food.

Makes 10 servings

Gravlax

1 spring salmon fillet, approximately 2.2 lb (1 kg)	4 Tbsp (60 mL) sea salt
⅓ cup (80 mL) aquavit*	4 Tbsp (60 mL) sugar
Sprigs fresh dill (lots—Harriet said you cannot have too much!)	2 Tbsp (30 mL) lemon zest
	1 Tbsp (15 mL) freshly ground pepper

*A Scandinavian liquor available in liquor and wine stores.

Three days before you plan to serve the gravlax, rinse salmon fillet in cold water. Pat dry and carefully remove bones. Score skin side in four places, and freeze fillet, laid flat, for at least 24 hours (freezing will reduce the risk of illness caused by parasites).

The next day, defrost fillet. Pour aquavit into a glass or ceramic baking dish large enough to accommodate the fillet. Place some dill sprigs in the dish and lay the fillet, skin-side up, on top. Cover and marinate in the refrigerator for at least 6 hours, basting the top side with the juices every couple of hours.

Turn fillet skin-side down and sprinkle the remaining ingredients evenly on top. Baste with the juices. Cover tightly and marinate another 24 hours in the refrigerator. (This "cold cooks" the fish.)

On the third day, drain the fish and lay it skin-side down on a serving platter. Slice as thinly as possible through the flesh at an angle, down toward the skin. Start slicing from the tail end, letting the knife curve away at the skin so you don't cut through it.

Mustard Sauce

4 Tbsp (60 mL) Dijon mustard	2 Tbsp (30 mL) lemon juice
4 Tbsp (60 mL) sweet mustard	½ cup (125 mL) olive oil
4 Tbsp (60 mL) sugar	2 Tbsp (30 mL) chopped fresh dill
4 Tbsp (60 mL) vinegar	Salt and pepper
2 Tbsp (30 mL) aquavit	

Place all sauce ingredients in a blender and process to combine.

Assembly
Chopped fresh dill
Twists of lemon

Garnish the gravlax slices with chopped fresh dill, drizzle with the sauce and top with twists of lemon.

FRENCHY AND SIMPSON

9

Excerpted from Fishing with John *(1992), by Edith Iglauer*

~⁀

We awoke in the morning to rain brushing against the windows. Right after breakfast, John started the Gardner diesel and we ran back down Cousins Inlet to a marine crossroads; this time, we took the left-hand waterway, the much wider Dean Channel. Our goal, three hours away, was a pocket-sized opening called Eucott Bay. It was 1973 and the United Fishermen and Allied Workers' Union was on strike, but John had obtained written permission from the strike committee before we left Namu to food-fish for ourselves while we were travelling. It was almost noon, and I was preparing a salmon chowder with one of two small cohos John had caught, along with one fair-sized spring salmon, fishing briefly on one line on the way to Ocean Falls. He looked in the red stewpot on the stove. "We'll take some of this to two old fellows who live in a floathouse at Eucott," he said.

Almost immediately afterwards, he slowed down and turned left into a small bay hiding among the trees and stopped a few feet inside. At the far end, I could see what appeared to be marsh grass and a sandy beach. Beyond, through a V in the low hills covered with green firs, I glimpsed snowy mountains blending with a mass of white clouds floating across a bright-blue summer sky. It had stopped raining.

John anchored, and pulled down a chart. We were in fourteen fathoms, but directly in front of us it was only three. He said, "We'll have to wait for high tide to call on Frenchy and Simp*son*, because right now it's low tide and their dock is resting in mud." He pronounced the latter name with emphasis on the *son* to give it a French twist. "They live in a floathouse, an old abandoned fish camp that's been pulled up on the grass. It's just out of our sight now, beyond those three pilings over there." Farther ahead of us, perhaps 200 yards away, where the chart showed a depth of half a fathom, was a small unpainted frame house on floats with a ramp to the beach. "A retired fisherman lives there, when he's around," John said, "but he doesn't like visitors much. Don't mention him to the old men when we visit them. They aren't speaking."

"Who else lives in this bay?" I asked.

"That's all," John said. "All winter long, just the three of them are here, except for an occasional visitor from Ocean Falls or when the United Church boat, the *Thomas Crosby*, stops in to check up on them."

"There are only the three of them in this bay and this man and the two others don't speak?"

"That's right."

"Why?"

John shrugged. "It could be anything, but I think it was a political disagreement. It doesn't matter; they may not even know themselves. These guys living in isolated spots like this tend to get paranoid."

In the afternoon, John put the dinghy over the side and said, "It's high tide, so we can go over to see Frenchy and Simp*son*." He poured some of the salmon chowder into a container and put it in the dinghy along with a bag of apples and oranges, the custard pie, a six-pack of beer and the bottle of Scotch he had bought at Ocean Falls. At the last minute, he went below and got the spring he had caught on the way, and brought that along, too.

I took off my Stanfield's, put on my red turtleneck sweater and got into the dinghy with John, who was resplendent in his Norwegian cardigan. He started rowing us across the bay toward the three pilings. There we entered a channel in the flat, grassy

Taking a break from picket duty during the fishermen's strike, the author and John travel from Bella Bella to food-fish and to visit Frenchy and Simpson.
Harbour Publishing Archives

marsh. At the far end, half hidden among the trees, was a low, flat-roofed, oblong wooden building with a covered porch. It was dark red, with white trim on the eaves, the frames and the mouldings around the six panes of glass in each of its small square windows. The building, a foot or so off the ground, was on a scow that was on skids; and in the grass behind were an indeterminate assortment of half-ruined, unpainted small shacks. We came slowly to the rough plank dock in front of the scow as a slight, somewhat bent little man rounded a corner of the porch, hurrying toward us. He was wearing the usual dark wool fish pants, held up with suspenders; and a yellow, red and black plaid wool shirt wide open at the neck, with a broad expanse of dingy-grey underwear showing underneath a medal on a chain. A wide-brimmed felt hat was pulled down to his large, long ears, and his welcoming smile revealed toothless gums below a hooked nose. He had a small, deeply lined face, with a day's growth of beard. I climbed out of the dinghy to the dock on my knees, and when I stood up I was looking straight into his bright, dark eyes; we were the same height—five-two. He bowed low and removed his hat, revealing a bald head encircled by white hair.

"Hello, John, we see you come in today, and now you bring your lady to see old Frenchy and Simpson, yes?" he said, speaking with a pronounced French accent. He turned to me. "My name is really Leo Jacques, and sometimes they call me Jack, but people know me as Frenchy. My friend's name is Albert Simpson. You want to see Mr. Simpson, John?"

"We came to see you both, Frenchy," John said, as he straightened up from tying the dinghy to a rotting plank. He handed me the custard pie and chowder, and gave the spring salmon to Frenchy, then picked up the bag with the beer and whiskey that he had set out on the dock, tucking it under one arm and holding the bag of fruit with his other hand. He looked fondly at Frenchy. "You look very well—better than the last time I saw you. You were having trouble with your stomach."

The author and John on the stern of the *Morekelp*.
Harbour Publishing Archives

"Boy, I wish I had a stomach like that old man Simp*son*," Frenchy exclaimed. "Oh, well, I am *cer*tainly okay and I do a lot of praying for Simp*son*. He's my friend." He started walking ahead of us, then stopped and said to me, "That old man, he looks like Chur*chill*. I'm eighty-four this month, but that man Simp*son* is eighty-eight." He held up the spring. "I'm sure glad to get fish. We haven't had any for long time."

The dock teetered drunkenly when we walked across it, and the plank connecting to the grassy shore quivered when I stepped on it. We passed rows of neatly piled firewood, uniformly cut alder, on the way up the path, and crossed the rotting porch. Frenchy opened a door, and we went into the house. It was so dark inside that it took my eyes a minute or two to get adjusted. We were in what must once have been a store, with a counter and shelves behind it just past the entrance. There was a calendar on the wall with a picture of a Japanese girl in a white kimono, and above it a green pennant that said, "Alaska, 1969." Farther along the wall was a magazine cover with a picture of de Gaulle, and above that a set of antlers was mounted on a board. An oil lamp hung from the ceiling, and several dark socks were draped along the sill of a dusty window.

"Come on, old man, see what company I brought you!" Frenchy shouted. I looked down the narrow, rectangular room in the direction he was shouting and saw a large, elderly gentleman wearing an old-fashioned brown fedora. He had a round moon of a face and looked absolutely like Winston Churchill. He was sitting up rigidly erect, smoking a cigarette in a holder held upright between two fingers, thin, stuck straight out. He was dressed in a blue-and-white-checked flannel shirt and grey pants, and his feet, which were swollen, were encased in bedroom slippers. A crutch was hooked to one arm of his chair.

Frenchy drew up two chairs, then darted over to Simpson, leaned over him and pulled up the open fly on his pants with the tender gesture one would reserve for a child. We sat down facing the big man, who was staring at me. Frenchy seated himself on a bed against the wall and mopped his brow. "I get so nair-vous and excited," he said apologetically. "Just with people I like. The others I don't give a damn about. I pay no attention." Simpson, meanwhile, had finished his cigarette and was fumbling to pick another out of the package he held, but he dropped the package on the floor. Frenchy jumped to pick it up, took out a cigarette, lit it and handed it to him, saying to me, "This old man fell off a roof t'irty years ago and landed on his hands, so he broke them, and they aren't much use. He can't walk, neither. Since he had his stroke, he's partly—partly—" Frenchy paused, searching for the word.

"Paralyzed?" John suggested.

"Right you are, sir. That's the word for it." Simpson spoke for the first time, slowly, in clipped, precise English. His voice was unexpectedly deep and clear. "I have been living in this bay with Frenchy for fifty years, since we met and teamed up together." He turned his head toward me, paused to move his hand slowly to his mouth and puffed on his cigarette. "I am of Scotch background, from Nova Scotia. We were a family of eight, and most of my family is around Boston now. I have a sister who writes often, and another sister who left a hundred thousand dollars to her church."

"The money we have, we decide to leave it to hospital," Frenchy announced.

"What hospital?" John asked.

"Oh well, whatever hospital we decide to die in," Simpson replied. "We split everything fifty-fifty. Frenchy's a smart man. He's a Frenchman, but he's honest."

"That Simpson, he's not a very good trapper, he's no good at all," Frenchy said. "He has trouble even catching a mouse!"

Simpson removed his cigarette between stiff fingers and gave a deep easy laugh, revealing gums as toothless as Frenchy's. "Yes, I could learn a lot from Frenchy," he said.

"Have you been back to Nova Scotia often?" I asked.

"I never wished to go home again," he replied. "I worked first in Alberta, but I wanted to fish, so I came to BC and went trolling. Frenchy is from Trois-Rivières, in Quebec. We used to troll together, but he's had traplines as well, trapping marten and, later, mink. He made five hundred dollars one month."

Simpson stopped talking, and Frenchy jumped up again. "Do you want a bottle of beer?" he shouted at Simpson, and Simpson nodded. Frenchy opened a bottle from the six-pack that John had put on the counter, and handed it to him. Simpson raised it clumsily between his two hands to his mouth, took a healthy swig and managed to set it down on a table beside him. Frenchy offered us some, but John shook his head, so Frenchy poured us each a mug of coffee from a pot on a kerosene-drum stove under the window.

"I never went back to Quebec, neither," Frenchy volunteered. "My father was a doctor, and my mother died when I'm two year old, and he had a nurse take care of us children. My older brother had a big farm, but I left home very young and crossed the country. I never went to school. I got shot in the First World War." He opened his shirt. "See that hole?" He leaned over so we could get a good view of a small round scar. "The bullet went out back. And I got slit with a bayonet right across here." He ran his finger across his neck, then pulled back his shirt collar to show us that scar, too. "Only four or five come back, but, by jeez, this crazy Frenchman, he come back! I got a bunch of medals, but they sank in my boat."

"Show them the document that was presented to you with your King George medal," Simpson said.

Frenchy went to a drawer and took out a folded sheet of faded paper, which he handed to me. "Old King George and the Queen came to see me when I was pretty near dead in University Hospital, London," he said.

I opened the paper. "Read it out loud," John said.

Below the Royal Crest in red at the top, and the words "Buckingham Palace, 1918," I read, "'The Queen and I wish you Godspeed, a safe return to the happiness and joy of home life, with an early restoration to health. A grateful Mother Country thanks you for faithful services.'" It was signed "George R.I."

Frenchy nodded proudly while I read. He pulled a card out of his shirt pocket and handed it to me. It was a holy card, with a picture of the head of Jesus wearing a crown of thorns, above a prayer in French, printed in green ink. "I had this in my breast pocket when I got shot," Frenchy said. "I kept it from 1918, and I been all over the world with it on them freighters I used to go on—especially on the Great Lakes." He patted it and put it carefully back in his pocket.

"I had half my army pay going to my sister, a very lovely woman, and when I came home I find she give two hundred dollars I send to help her priest to say prayers for me," Frenchy went on. "So I never send her more, and when I leave, I tell her, 'You won't hear from me, because you worry too much.' I never been back to see her—not since 1919—and I never wrote, neither. Not to my own sister."

It started to rain. Two or three raindrops hit my shoulder, so I slid my chair an inch or two back from a leak in the roof. Frenchy leaped up and put a tin can on the floor to catch the drips, and from then on, the patter of rain on the roof was accompanied by a musical *ping*. Frenchy sighed. "Someone brought this old fish camp here on a scow and left it all to rot. When we move in, she look like hell. I pull her up here and push some cedars under her when the tide is in. I patch the roof real good, but I guess I have to do it again. Last winter, John, we live real nice. Someone from Canadian Fish Company tow a fish camp with a store here, and we look after it, so we got to live on it until spring. Especially because it have an oil stove, it is much more comfortable than this old wreck. I have a lot of work carrying five-gallon drums of oil inside for the stove, but it's good all the same to wake up in a nice warm house, and we had very little snow." He laughed. "By golly, I sure never want to go back to Quebec. Too cold!"

A sudden crash. Simpson, lifting his cigarette to his mouth, had knocked over his beer bottle. Frenchy scrambled after it as it rolled away, and he muttered, "We have more trouble from morning to night." Without warning, he burst into song. "Ho! Ho! Ho!" Then he sang it in a faster rhythm—"Ho-ho-ho!"—smiling at Simpson. "We get some good laughs," he said.

John Daly catches up with correspondence at an out-of-the-way bay near Namu.
Harbour Publishing Archives

"Yes, we do," said Simpson, with a deep chuckle. "We'll have the Seventh-Day Adventists in here soon and have a gospel night." We were all laughing now; Simpson's heavy body was shaking with mirth. "The United Church boat, the *Thomas Crosby IV,* stops in here every three weeks to see us," he said finally, taking out a blue bandanna and wiping his forehead. "I know that boat," John said, still smiling. "It's a big steel one, eighty feet long, that goes anywhere in any kind of weather."

Frenchy went on singing little "Ho-hos" to himself as he skipped back to the bed where he had been sitting. He picked up a handsome patchwork quilt and a yellow-and-blue crocheted blanket there and brought them over for me to see. "We asked the *Thomas Crosby* to bring us sleeping bags," he said. "The one they gave us for Simp*son* was too small, so the United Church at Prince Rupert sent us these and I put them on this old man's bed instead."

"We had quilts like that in Nova Scotia," Simpson interjected. "Mother used to make them."

Frenchy ran to an alcove behind me, which was evidently his bunk, and came back with an armful of quilts, announcing, "I got two or t'ree more quilts that the Church brought us, and the five girls who crocheted blanket come to see us. One of them church girls give me a kimono, but I don't say not'ing." The quilts were handmade and beautiful.

Frenchy removed his old fedora, scratched his head and put the hat on again, but Simpson never removed his for any reason. In fact, I never saw Simpson without a hat. (Later, when I asked John if he had ever seen Simpson without a hat, he said, "No, and nobody else I know has, either.")

Frenchy said, "We hire a guy to bring our groceries every four weeks—wintertime, too. He's a paperworker from the Falls, a Prussian with a nice boat that takes an hour and a half to go twenty-eight mile to the Falls. He do everything for us." He chuckled. "When I used to go to Ocean Falls, I used to go to the Happy House, right around the bend at what we call Pecker Point. The alders have *cert*ainly grown over that Happy House fast since it closed."

Simpson was frowning, shaking his head at Frenchy, who suddenly stopped talking.

Looking amused, John picked up the conversation. "That German you hire must have a powerful boat. It took us three hours to get here with my seventy-two-horsepower, five-cylinder Gardner," he said.

Simpson leaned back in his chair, cackling. "Oh, I know that one. It's a good one."

"I used to have nice boat, troller, for seventeen years," Frenchy said. "The *Albatross,* built at Sointula, on Malcolm Island. In 1936, I get twenty-four cents a pound for springs and six cents a pound for coho in Namu—forty cents for a whole coho. A lot of people were living in this bay then, in small shacks in winter, mostly loggers and fishermen, but there was a woman here who sold baths. She had bathtubs in little huts, and you could take a bath for two bits or a dollar—whatever you thought it was worth. She would lend a towel to you for ten cents, or sell it to you for twenty-five; the only thing, she was such a bad cook. I know because I used to chop her wood to have a cup of tea and whatever she gave me to eat."

"What happened to the *Albatross*?" I asked.

"I sink it, I t'ink in '43, maybe '44," Frenchy said. "The manifold and exhaust and fumes, they put me to sleep and *bingo!* she went on the rocks. I get out in a rowboat, and someone from Bella Coola in a gillnetter came along and picked me up. No insurance, so I lost the whole works. I bought another boat the next year, and someone walked on it and stole eight hundred dollars." He shrugged. "Fishing from daybreak to night was too long, anyway. I got dizzy from the exhaust and from looking up at those lines."

He got out four glasses and poured us each a Scotch, handed them to us and said, "There are some nice big ducks around and we don't even shot one. We like to see them around. We used to make homebrew and then t'row away the corn, and when ducks came around they'd get drunk and go round and round like this." He lay down on the floor on his side and flapped his arms, hopped up and sat down again on the bed, still talking. "They was fat and in good shape, and once in a while a hawk or owl came around and got one. We used to have lots of owls at night, but no more now."

"Every night, they used to howl 'Hoo! Hoo!'" Simpson said. "Another thing, we used to have a lot of Japanese here from the Falls. There was this old fellow who was

eighty-four, a gillnetter, who used to hang around here in the winter. He wasn't a bad fellow, either. Better than that fellow that's over there now."

Frenchy leaned over and said to me in a low voice, "I don't mind, but him and Mr. Simp*son* don't get along well."

My eye had been attracted by a white ceramic angel with a gold halo on the shelf behind Simpson's impressive head, and when my glance shifted to binoculars hanging from a hook on the wall next to it, Frenchy said loudly, "From here, Mr. Simp*son* can see a bear way up at the head of the bay without glasses. He's got to do somet'ing, that guy. I shot two black bears last year. There used to be a lot of deer, too. They would come in evening at low water and drink, but I don't see none now. I fish for Simp*son*, but I wait until there is more than one fish in the water and then I don't make too much noise. Seals and otters come right up to your boat if they t'ink you have fish. They walk on the bottom, those otters—I see the tracks—and they say when seals come like that, fish are coming in. Seals walk one-and-a-half mile to this lake above here, and then another mile to another lake. We saw twenty wolves in one bunch, too; they come down for fish. They howled right alongside here, right around our door."

Simpson signalled for more Scotch. Frenchy poured some into his glass. "Thank you, sir," Simpson said. He held the glass up between both hands and drank, put it down and said, "We had the best cat in the country, and the wolves got him. Oh, he was a wonderful fellow."

"When anyone came, he just sat by Simp*son* and growled!" Frenchy said.

"Oh, the wolf caught him right at the door—I know he did," Simpson said mournfully.

"That black-and-white cat, Ta-puss, would sleep up on the pillow against Simp*son*'s head and would snore," Frenchy said. "Simp*son* would wake up and say, 'Quit your snoring,' and push that cat to the wall. One night, he was sleeping right beside Mr. Simp*son*, snoring, and Mr. Simp*son* tried to push him off once too often and Ta-puss bit him in the hand." Frenchy began to laugh, rocking back and forth. He laughed so hard he had to wipe his eyes with his sleeve.

Simpson wiped his eyes, too, and said, "Ta-puss would push on the doorknob and then push the door open."

"Old Ta-puss, I wouldn't take fifty dollars for him," Frenchy said.

"I wouldn't take a *hundred* for him," Simpson said, shaking his large head solemnly from side to side. "Oh, I wish we had him now. He would never catch the mice in here. He would just sit and look at them walking back and forth in front of him."

The light coming in through the windows was fading, and the room had become even more shadowy. John rose to go. "Tomorrow, we're going to Nascall Bay. We'll stop in on our way back from there," he said to Simpson, who was looking downcast.

Frenchy walked back to the dock with us. It was now totally dark, and we rowed home in a driving rainstorm. Without my Stanfield's on, I was thoroughly chilled. It was so cold when we got back to the boat that John turned up the stove while we shivered, taking off our wet clothes. We ate supper surrounded by the smell of soggy clothes drying out on a clothesline that crisscrossed the cabin from wall to wall.

We were in bed long before ten o'clock, when the strike news came on. Nothing had been settled. John said gloomily, "It may be another week before the strike is over, but anyway it gave us a good chance to come here. I always stop and see those wonderful old fellows once a summer, even if it means losing a day's fishing. I sure admire Frenchy. It's not easy for a man his age to do all that cooking, and he washes their clothes, too, by hand. Frenchy tells me he has to lift Simpson sometimes; I don't see how he does it, Simpson is almost twice his size. No, no, Simpson is not an easy man to take care of. He liked you, by the way. If he hadn't, he would have sat there like a sphinx, not saying a word."

John moved the *Morekelp* to a different position during the night, because of the wind, and just before we left the next morning, we looked out the window toward Frenchy and Simpson's place. With the tide out, we could see a neat grey speedboat tied up at the small dock that I hadn't noticed before because of the tall grass around it. John said, "It's Frenchy's and it's sixteen feet, with a little cabin and a gas engine. If their floathouse burned up, he could put Simpson on that boat."

10 CANADA DAY AT YUQUOT

Excerpted from Off the Map: Western Travels on Roads Less Taken *(2001),*
by Stephen Hume

As an antidote to the tired assumptions that always seem to colonize our Canada Day weekends, I decide that for the first one of the new millennium I'll take my ten-year-old daughter, Heledd, to Yuquot to visit the place where modern history first collided with the West Coast's ancient and mysterious past. We first drive 165 miles north from Victoria to Campbell River, then another 55 miles through the rugged mountains west of Campbell River to Gold River, where Margarita James, director of cultural and heritage resources for the Mowachaht/Muchalaht First Nations, dispatches us for another hour by boat, dodging deadheads and crashing through glossy swells.

A centre of commerce during the fur trade, Friendly Cove, or Yuquot, now has only one resident family.
Elsie Hulsizer photo

Yuquot is where the compelling Mowachaht Chief Maquinna confronted the European superpowers of his day just over two hundred years ago. A place of stunning beauty, it straddles a narrow isthmus connecting several rocky outcrops to Nootka Island. Think of two crescent moons lying back to back. That's both the shape and the luminous colour of the two great canoe beaches, one opening to sheltered waters, the other facing the booming green combers of the outer coast. The old village site is one of those places that resonates with energy from the moment you step ashore and notice the strange, perfectly oval pebbles that are polished as smooth as glass beads and left in heaps by the tireless sea.

It's a difficult feeling to describe, an eerie combination of history and some less tangible spiritual presence. But perhaps this feeling is merely the burden carried in by the visitor who has taken time to read about the mysterious, mystical whalers' shrine that was located on an island in a sacred lake. It was here, long before Europeans had even arrived in the New World, that Mowachaht inhabitants of E'as and Tsaxis, two ancient villages farther north on the wild, hurricane-lashed western fringe of Vancouver Island, first began hunting and harpooning gray and humpback whales, later bringing their knowledge to Yuquot. Whatever I might have felt from the weight of this history, my carefree daughter is soon wading through the sun-bronzed grass that nods over the ruins of a settlement from this culture that was already ancient when the Greeks went to sack Troy. The surf booms and seethes up the shingle, the breeze makes cat's-paws on the rippling meadow, nectar-laden bees fumble at the Indian paintbrush and blue camas and the air is rich with the sweet scent of clover. Some things never change.

We stop to chat with Ray Williams and his wife Teresa, the last continuous occupants of the site, largely abandoned in 1967 when the federal government moved the inhabitants to Gold River. "The chiefs asked us to move, too, but we said no," Ray tells us. "We stayed. We're the caretakers of Maquinna's lands. That move, that was a

Yuquot, or Friendly Cove, on Nootka Island, as painted by Thomas Bamford in 1897.
Image PDP00705 courtesy of the Royal BC Museum, BC Archives

mistake—a really big mistake. The government moved our people right next to that pulp mill in Gold River. It was an awful place, babies were getting sick." Ray gestures to where his talented son Sanford is at work carving a new totem pole and directs us to where we might look at some ancient poles, now down, moss-covered and already rotting back into the earth as they were meant to do. "This place is our people's spiritual centre," Ray says.

I follow my daughter along the beach and into the trees. Below us glimmers Jewitt Lake, named for John Jewitt, captive of Maquinna for two years after the rest of the crew of the ship *Boston* had been killed by Mowachaht warriors in 1803. It surrounds the island where the whaling chiefs had the shrine that is also known as their Washing House, certainly the most important monument in the West Coast aboriginal whaling culture. The shrine, a spectral structure of carved wooden figures and human skulls, was the focal point of the long and arduous rituals of purification and preparation that had to be undertaken by the chiefly lineages, which, like the kings of Europe with their royal deer and Indian rajas with their tigers, reserved to themselves alone the right to hunt whales. Although the Whalers' Shrine is considered one of the most significant artifacts from that interface between the physical and supernatural worlds inhabited by both mythic and shamanic figures on the pre-contact West Coast of Canada, its power is defined as much by the absence of reference points as by anything else.

Collected by George Hunt at the instigation of anthropologist Franz Boas in 1905, the shrine was dismantled and removed to the American Museum of Natural History, where it resides to this day. Yet even stories about it obtained from First Nations informants are scattered and scarce, as though even those who knew what it signified were reluctant to talk about its origins and the way the rites practised here shaped the society around them. One thing is clear: Like a dark body that's discerned by astronomers through its influence on the space surrounding it, the gravity exerted by the Whalers' Shrine upon the spiritual cosmos of the Nuu-chah-nulth who lived at Yuquot made it a pretty skookum place.

Yet there's another residual power here that affects newcomers, too. This is where, in 1778, Captain James Cook became the first European to set foot on the Northwest Coast. These days it's popular among the politically correct to sniff at the accomplishments of men like Cook, but his voyages of exploration in small wooden ships on an uncharted sea so vast it could drown all the Earth's continents is more akin to journeying to the moon than our technological hubris likes to acknowledge. Cook, in fact, was greeted with enthusiasm by Maquinna, who quickly seized the political opportunity to make himself a crucial power-broker and established Yuquot as a key base in the commercial fur trade that followed. During a visit eight years later, one Mr. Strange, a passenger aboard a visiting sailing ship, gave Yuquot its English name: Friendly Cove. It proved a good name.

Britain and Spain were at the brink of war over rival claims to the Northwest Coast when the Spanish established a fort here in 1791. Maquinna invited Captain George Vancouver and Captain Juan Francisco de la Bodega y Quadra to a formal dinner, helping defuse the tension while a solution was worked out between the two great European powers. In 1795, when Spain peacefully withdrew, the British commissioner presented Maquinna with the Union Jack that had been raised when London's claims prevailed.

Today, Friendly Cove is a national historic site and these great events are commemorated with a cairn and various plaques—not one of which, my daughter observes, makes any mention of either Maquinna or the Mowachaht people who had been there for 4,300 years. But that soon changes. Up at the white glare of the abandoned church with its stained

glass windows depicting the historic events that entangled these three nations forever, we find the pews pushed aside, the smell of fresh paint and a bustle of activity amid the rainbow splinters of light that spill across the age-darkened floorboards. Robin Inglis, director of the North Vancouver Museum, and Bob Eberle, a theatre professor at the University of British Columbia, are frantically preparing for a remarkable event—the arrival of three crates aboard the coastal freighter *Uchuck III.* They contain a gift to the Mowachaht and Muchalaht from the Spanish government. It's a collection of high-quality artistic reproduc-

Stained glass windows donated to the church at Yuquot in 1954 portray the meeting of Captains George Vancouver and Bodega y Quadra in 1792.

Elsie Hulsizer photos

tions of the charts and drawings of Yuquot and its original inhabitants made by Tomás de Suría and José Cardero, members of Quadra's crew more than two hundred years ago. "These are the images you see in all the textbooks," Robin says. "What an interesting thing for the Mowachaht to have this collection of images from the moment of first contact." Robin and Bob are helping to set up a summer-long exhibition at the site in preparation for a celebration when the Mowachaht of Gold River will hold a reunion at Yuquot. Visitors were invited to join them for a salmon feast, traditional songs and dances while the Spanish were to formally present their gift.

In the meantime, an extra set of muscles is welcome and I am pressed into service helping load the heavy crates aboard an all-terrain vehicle and then keeping them in place behind the driver as we bounce our way back up the overgrown plank road from the wharf to the church through the salmonberry canes, blackberry brambles and salal. At the church, a young woman comes down to help unload. Marsha Maquinna, daughter of the present chief, reaches in and lifts out a picture. It is Suría's imposing portrait of her own ancestor, the great chief Maquinna himself. And as my daughter observes, on this coast, you can't stuff much more Canada into a Canada Day than that.

11 THE SCHOONER *BEATRICE* AND THE GREAT PELAGIC SEAL HUNT

Excerpted from Westcoasters: Boats that Built BC *(2001), by Tom Henry*

And since our women must walk Gay
And Money buys their gear,
The Sealing boats must go that way
And filch at hazard year by year.
—Rudyard Kipling

If, as is often alleged, life was slower in the old days, then how did so much get done? In the time it takes a modern urban planner to conceptualize a shopping mall, pioneers built, lived in and abandoned whole towns. Plodding horses, hand-wrung laundry and the slow slap of sail on a windless day may be the ascendant images of the late nineteenth century, but when they saw opportunity, the province's colonists moved at rip speed.

This ability to turn chance to account was especially well developed in the marine industry of the late nineteenth century. Shipbuilders had two great advantages over their modern counterparts (three, if you count gumption). One was easy money. A man wanting to build

After a day's hunt, sealers skinned their catch.
Image B-00619 courtesy of the Royal BC Museum, BC Archives

a ship simply marched into the smoky, red-velvet lounge of Vancouver's Alexandra Hotel, where the wealthy seamen marshalled, and made a pitch. If his idea was sound, he walked away with the cash in his pocket. The other great benefit was lack of regulation. Shipyards were more a matter of attitude than zoning, and certainly unfettered by environmental rules. A shipwright staked out an area above the high-tide line, purchased or pinched a few logs and set to work.

It was this ability to wed capital and enterprise that helped BC seafarers cash in on the great pelagic seal hunt. Sealing was to the 1890s what the gold rush was to the 1860s—a free-for-all pitting men against the elements in pursuit of fortune. The hunt set country against country, made and ruined many men and established Victoria as a major Pacific port. Like the gold rush, it was a pivot in history, anchoring BC in the Dominion of Canada at a time when America was contemplating annexing the West Coast from Washington to Alaska.

The *Beatrice* in its early days as a sealing schooner. Workers appear to be scraping the hull.
D. Hartley collection

Between 1885, when the Canadian sealing industry was launched, and 1911, when Canada withdrew from the seal hunt, no fewer than 125 sealing vessels were built in BC, many in makeshift and obscure yards. These ships were alike: strong, sturdy, simple. Sail-powered, they were between sixty and eighty feet long. They were also beamy, which made them good craft in the rough waters of the Bering Sea where the bulk of the seals were taken. Sailors on the best of these craft, it was said, could wear carpet slippers on deck and never get them wet.

One of these ships was the *Beatrice*. By any measure a remarkable vessel, the *Beatrice* laboured at so many tasks that its registry reads like a mongrel's genealogy: sealer, towboat, fish packer, marine research platform. It was also lucky, outlasting several generations of the seamen who trod its plank decks. Like a centenarian peasant who attributes her longevity to a daily stint cutting cordwood, the *Beatrice* survived on work, work, work.

The Canadian sealing industry was a decade old when the *Beatrice* was launched, from James Doherty's False Creek Shipyard in April 1891. The harvest centred around the migratory habits of *Callorhinus ursinus,* or the northern fur seal, whose undercoat of short soft fur was prized by furriers and costumers. Roaming over the North Pacific in search of food, the animals gathered by the hundreds of thousands each summer at the breeding grounds around the Pribilof Islands in the Bering Sea.

Until the breeding grounds were pinpointed, sealing was a chancy harvest, limited by the sealers' ability to find and keep up with the swift-moving herds. Then in 1885,

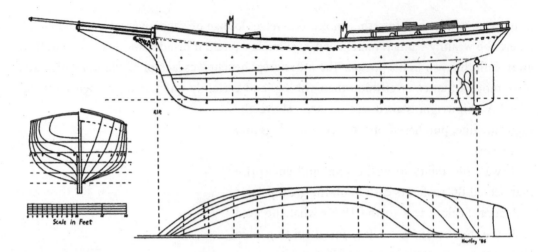

two vessels, the *Favorite*, from Sooke, and the *Mary Ellen*, from Victoria, returned from the Bering Sea with 4,382 skins, worth an astounding $35,000. The industry exploded; by 1892, 122 schooners with three thousand men were taking part in the pelagic seal hunt. The ships ranged throughout the North Pacific, scouring the waters off the Aleutians and down the Siberian coast to Japan.

The *Beatrice* made a number of runs to the sealing grounds—all were more remarkable for accident or intrigue than for harvest. The first trip was under the registry of Charles G. Doering, a Vancouver brewer and rose gardener par excellence, and his bearded, barrel-chested father-in-law, Hans Helgesen, whose long and varied career matched that of the *Beatrice*. Doering bought the ship to make money; Helgesen was in it, as a son later said, to "have one last fling at the sea."

Helgesen was born in a small town west of Christiania, now Oslo, Norway. His father was a farmer and shipbuilder. He had first gone to sea in 1847, at age eighteen. He joined a sailing ship and worked his way via Cape Horn to the American west coast. In San Francisco he caught word of the California gold rush and jumped ship, walking ashore on a pier made out of cookstoves. He panned for gold in California, then came north on the *Brother Jonathan.* In Victoria he built a scow and made his way to Hope. For several summers he panned gold on the Fraser River, camping and keeping company with a polyglot collection of adventurers. On one of the expeditions a companion of Helgesen's shot a caribou—which is, according to one story, how the Cariboo region got its name.

Gold gave way to farming and an unsuccessful attempt at a sedentary life. In 1862 Helgesen bought a fertile section of ground on a south-facing hill in Metchosin, on southern Vancouver Island. Several years later he left to go prospecting in Nevada, followed by a stint cod fishing in the Queen Charlotte Islands. Cod fishing gave way to provincial politics, which gave way to mining in British Guiana. Between stops at Metchosin to father seven children, he had a mini-career as a fisheries overseer on the Skeena River and revisited a lost gold lode in the Cariboo.

Helgesen was sixty-two when he and Doering purchased the *Beatrice.* He knew local waters and had hoped to captain the vessel. But he lacked proper papers. Reluctantly, he hired a Captain Bjaerre, a Danish deep-sea sailor with papers but no local knowledge. Under Bjaerre's command (and Helgesen's watchful eye), the *Beatrice* departed Victoria and headed south until it intercepted the seal herd off California. Then it turned and followed the herd north.

Seamen have long known that a ship owner and a captain make a volatile combination. Authority is vested in one by proprietorship, in the other by tradition. The two mix like guns and religion. Aboard the *Beatrice,* Helgesen had a number of complaints about the way Bjaerre was handling his ship. He thought it was carrying too much sail, and was sometimes near capsizing. He said as much to Bjaerre, but Bjaerre insisted he knew what he was doing. He didn't.

Two hundred nautical miles off the Queen Charlotte Islands the *Beatrice* hit a severe storm. While the little schooner plowed into the heavy seas, Bjaerre ordered the fore and aft staysails set. The wheel was lashed to keep the seas just off the bow. Then he and the crew went below to ride out the storm huddled around the tiny woodstove. Helgesen, too, was below deck. His philosopher's brow furrowed in thought, he watched the flickering oil lamp and listened to the ship's groaning timbers. As usual, he did not like the situation. Only this time he was convinced Bjaerre's boldness—Helgesen would have called it foolishness—was going to end in calamity. The captain had too much sail forward. The risk was that the schooner would pay off—turn broadside to the weather. Once broadside, all it needed was a large wave to send it somersaulting.

The farther the *Beatrice* rode into the storm, the more Helgesen fretted. Finally he donned his heavy oilskins and clambered onto the deck. The only other person there, according to Helgesen's account, was the cabin boy, Joe Devine, who was clearing food scraps. The two were clinging to the rails, watching the sails, when Helgesen spotted a wall of water looming on the windward side. It was what seamen call a rogue wave—a freak of wind and current. Helgesen only had time to bellow and take cover.

Top left: Sealers aboard a vessel in the Smoky Sea. The hard masculine life appealed to author Jack London, but even he found the slaughter excessive.
Image B-000617 courtesy of the Royal BC Museum, BC Archives

Top right: In the rush of the hunt, slaughtered seals were often heaped on the deck of a sealing ship until there was time to skin and salt the pelts.
Image F-05169 courtesy of the Royal BC Museum, BC Archives

A gust turned the schooner broadside, the wave hit and everything was sent spiralling. Devine was launched into the sea. Helgesen, clutching a belaying pin, was dragged underwater as the ship capsized. Below decks, the crew were sent tumbling down onto the galley ceiling. (The ceiling sported their marks for years.)

How long the *Beatrice* stayed under no one knows—for later all felt it was days. But slowly, freighted by wet sail in water, it righted. As the rigging emerged it scooped the flailing Devine and hoisted him aloft. Stunned, the lad was left straddling a backstay. Like the rest of the crew, he was thankful to be alive. From that point on, Bjaerre and Helgesen appear to have had a more harmonious relationship.

Out on the sealing grounds, the *Beatrice* operated much like any other sealing vessel. At the cry "Boats Out!" the sealers clambered over the side of the ship and into specially designed craft they called shells. It took three men to handle a shell: a steersman or gaffer, a rower and the hunter. Some Native hunters used shells, but most preferred canoes. Canoes carried two, the hunter and a paddler. The paddler was often the wife of the hunter. Once overboard, the canoes and shells fanned from the mother ship. The search for seals often took sealers fifteen nautical miles away, until the *Beatrice*'s masts were sticks on the horizon. Each boat was provisioned with a keg of water, hardtack, bully beef and, if the ship's cook was up early enough, prune pie, which was a staple of the sealing fleet. Only the captain and the cabin boy remained on the schooner.

Sealers divided their quarry into three categories: travellers, seals that raced through the water, jumping from wave to wave; moochers, lollygagging seals that raised their heads now and then to look around; and sleepers, seals that lay on their backs snoozing. Sleepers made up the bulk of seals taken. Hunters had to approach silently, so as not to waken the animal. When the craft was close enough, the hunter raised the spear, took aim and sank the metal tip deep into the seal's blubbery side. It was then the gaffer's job to gaff the seal and haul it to the boat. If the gaffer missed, the seal sank. Some hunters shot bullets into the water to force seals under. After several panicked dives, the mammals were too exhausted to evade the spear. When guns were prohibited in the harvest, hunters attached a rope to the weapon's stock. If a patrol boat approached, the gun was lowered over the side.

The first seals caught each day were left whole, for ballast. Any other seals were skinned on sight, the hunter taking care to leave plenty of blubber to insulate the hide from the burning effect of salt, which separated layers of pelts in the hold of the sealing ship. For the first fifty sealskins taken, the hunter received two dollars per head; for the next fifty, three dollars; after a hundred skins the hunter received four dollars apiece.

The money had to be good because the job was hazardous. The North Pacific is not a good place to be in a small boat. Among the many dangers hunters faced, the greatest was fog. Great banks of impregnable white mist rolled over the Bering Sea with such frequency the area was known as the Smoky Sea. Within moments a crew with a clear view of the mother ship would be lost. The greatest aid in overcoming the difficulties of navigating in fog was the intuitive sense of the hunters, some of whom accurately guided their tiny boats through thick fog for several hours to arrive at the side of their ship. The mother ships, too, attempted to help crews home. After the small boats pulled away in the morning, the captain would take the ship downwind, so the shells and canoes were likely to blow to it rather than away from it. If visibility was poor at the end of the day, the schooner fired guns, and the cabin boy was sent aloft to light an oily rag at the masthead.

Back on the ship, unskinned seals were stripped and their hides salted and stowed. It was a grim sight, even by the standards of the day. Author Jack London, who in 1893 travelled for seven months on the sealing schooner *Sophia Sutherland*, described the scene in his book *Sea Wolf*: "It was wanton slaughter…No man ate of the seal meat or the oil. After a good day's killing I have seen our decks covered with hides and bodies, slippery with fat and blood, the scuppers running red; masts, ropes and rails splattered with the sanguinary colour; and the men, like butchers plying their trade, naked and red of arm and hand, hard at work with ripping and flensing knives, removing the skins from the pretty sea creatures they had killed." For London, the horrors of the skinning were compounded by the fact that the entire enterprise was done in the name of fashion, so that the skins "might later adorn the fair shoulders of the women in cities."

On August 20, 1895, the *Beatrice*, under Captain Louis Olsen (and new owners), was working near the Pribilof Islands when it was boarded by American revenue officers from the cutter *Rush*. The *Rush* was one of several American and British gunships in the area, enforcing the terms of an 1893 accord brokered by an arbitration tribunal in Paris that attempted to regulate the harvest. The sealing nations had agreed that all vessels must keep official logs of the harvest and must present the logs for inspection.

In truth, however, the boarding was part of a systematic harassment of sealing ships by American officials. In 1886 the US, afraid of losing a virtual monopoly on sealing, attempted to ban all foreign harvesting, claiming, ludicrously, that since the seals were born on American lands, they were domestic animals. The Russians, who formerly owned Alaska and had tried the same manoeuvre, reminded the Americans of the illegality of their position, and the Americans grudgingly changed their policy—but only technically. In the hold of the *Beatrice,* American officers discovered a number of sealskins not entered in the official log. The ship was seized and, following the protocol set up by the arbitration tribunal in Paris, handed over to a British patrol vessel. It was sailed to Victoria where the skins were sold. The Crown then brought charges against the ship's owners. As punishment for not maintaining an accurate log, the Crown asked the courts to order the ship sold. The owners and the captain were outraged. In court, lawyers for the defence testified that the captain had kept perfect records. The mix-up occurred, they said, because it was a temporary log; when the captain had a moment he would have transferred this information into the official log. He had recorded all the information required, but not in the right place.

The judge hearing the case was unimpressed with the Crown's arguments. He declared the arrest of the *Beatrice* to be unlawful. Furthermore, the judge said that the *Beatrice* was in pursuit of profit and might reasonably have expected further profit. The Crown was ordered to pay $3,163.50 in damages.

Predictably, the judgment made the *Beatrice* a marked ship on the sealing grounds. The following season, on August 5, 1896, an American patrol boat seized it again, this time for killing seals in a prohibited area. Once more the vessel was transferred to Her Majesty's Service and sailed to Victoria. In court, the captain's defence was that overcast skies made it impossible to properly determine his position. He said that a strong current must have nudged the *Beatrice* into the no-hunting zone. The judge pointed out that it was seized six nautical miles within the prohibited area, the logbook contained scratches and crossed-out areas that suggested hasty alteration, and the master's testimony in court was at odds with his own records. The defence collapsed and the owners were required to pay a fine of several hundred dollars.

By 1911 it was clear that the seal population was seriously depleted. Where it had numbered in the millions in the 1870s, it was now estimated to be only 150,000. Japan, Canada (represented by Britain), Russia and the United States signed the International Pelagic Sealing Treaty. This treaty ruled that the Bering Sea was to be closed to all pelagic (open ocean) hunting of seals for the next fifteen years. The aboriginal inhabitants of the area were permitted to hunt using traditional methods, i.e., with spear and canoe. Americans could take a limited number of seals on the Pribilof Islands, and the Russians on Robbens Island. In return for keeping its ships from the sealing grounds, Canada was to be given 15 per cent of the catch.

Thus, with the signing of the treaty in July 1911, thousands of men lost their livelihood. Valuable schooners became floating liabilities. Some, like the *Borealis,* were converted into halibut schooners. Others became rumrunners. Many rotted. However, even before the treaty was signed, the *Beatrice* had retired from the sealing industry. It was rescued from the boneyard when the Butchart family set it to work as a lighter in Saanich Inlet. In 1908 it was bought by Captain Albert Berquist of Sidney, on Vancouver Island. Berquist rebuilt boats for a hobby and a living. He was helped by his sister, a fantastically strong woman who could push a shipwright's plane as well as any man. The two cut down the *Beatrice*'s masts, built a deckhouse and installed a 200-horsepower oil-burning steam engine. Thus began the *Beatrice*'s career as a tug. In 1962, Harold Clay bought the *Beatrice*. The ship had been gutted by fire while laid up at the North Vancouver ferry dock in 1958. At the time the fire appeared disastrous, destroying the wheelhouse and much of the deck. In the long term, though, the blaze may have done for the old ship what fires do to grassland—reinvigorated it. Clay rebuilt the wheelhouse and refitted the ship with a diesel engine. He changed the name to the *Arrawac Freighter* and used it to carry everything from frozen strawberries to diesel engines upcoast.

Keen to use the *Arrawac Freighter*'s ample hold, Joe Moyles bought the ship in 1972 and set it to packing sea urchins and clams on Vancouver Island's west coast.

In 1981, the *Arrawac Freighter* was bought by Doug Hartley, who renamed it *Beatrice* and used it for gentler purposes, including training oceanographers from Royal Roads Military College.

The *Beatrice*'s semi-retirement ended in the early 1990s, when it was sold to David Francis, a former sea urchin diver who returned it to service packing sea urchins. Francis skippered the *Beatrice* on every trip, except the last. In April 1993, the *Bea-*

The *Beatrice*, renamed the *Arrawac Freighter*, moored at Victoria in 1969.
Vancouver Maritime Museum

trice snapped its reverse gearshift and put into Prince Rupert for repairs. Francis, whose wife was ill, flew home. When the shipyard called early to say the ship was ready, Francis told his engineer to take it across to the Queen Charlottes to fetch a load of sea urchins. On the way back the ship was caught in a gale. When the engine made an unusual sound the engineer went to investigate. The engine room was thigh deep in water. A hull plank had opened, and water was coming in so fast two pumps could not keep up. Attempts were made to take the *Beatrice* under tow to Masset, but by the time the ship reached the dock the stern was awash. The vessel was secured with heavy lines and the crew left. But it was too heavy. The hawsers snapped and the *Beatrice* rolled into the current, where it was swept away. Later, using a sounder, Francis scanned Masset Inlet for the hull but came up empty. Because there wasn't a ticketed master on board when the *Beatrice* ran into trouble, there was no insurance. Thus ended the legacy of one of the oldest vessels on the coast.

OOLICHAN GREASE

by Howard White

Oolichan grease gold, you hear about it
how the Tsimshian empire held
the whole coast to ransom for it
brought the poor stick Indians begging
from the interior, beating paths
between the mountains you could
follow in the dark, by nose
the "grease trails" that let the
white man in, later on—
a beautiful woman professor told me about it
paler than butter she said,
but like butter without salt
and not at all repugnant to
the European palate
used as a condiment
but I ask you, are empires
sustained by condiments?
It was their oil, for the flame
in the flesh and more
                    I found it finally
in Bella Bella 1976 price $48/gal.
and it smelled like the cracks
between the deck planks of an old fish barge
if you can imagine spreading that
on your bread—quite enough to hurl
the European palate toward the nearest
toilet bowl which is how far
Indian is from White how far
learning is from knowing how
far we are from this ragged place
we've taken from them, for that,
the smell of fish left in the sun
and let go bad, that is the old
smell of the coast, known, as scent
is the final intimacy known of lifelong mates

take that barge plank, let it toss
ten years on the tide, knock on every rock
from Flattery to Yakutat, bake another
ten in the sun, take it rounded like
an Inuit ivory and grey as bone
crack it open and sniff the darker core
and you will know
what Vancouver knew ducking through
his first Nootka door pole, the essence
the odour of their living here
and however far you are from loving that
is how far you are
                    from arriving

Processing oolichan on the Nass River, ca. 1884.
Image C-07433 courtesy of the Royal BC Museum,
BC Archives

From Writing in the Rain *(1990), by Howard White*

NAMING ROCKS THE HARD WAY

12

Excerpted from The Encyclopedia of Raincoast Place Names:
A Complete Reference to Coastal British Columbia *(2009), by Andrew Scott*

Having a coastal feature named for you is normally a great honour. Having a rock or reef named for you, however, can be somewhat of a disgrace. According to nautical tradition, if you manage to wreck your boat on an uncharted rock, that rock is named for you—or, more commonly, for your vessel. But this really only happens if your boat is quite large or if you are important enough for notoriety to ensue. Usually the rock or reef in question has already been named for some unfortunate earlier wreckee.

The BC coast is littered with rocks that commemorate marine mishaps and enshrine the shame of certain skippers. At the entrance to Mantrap Inlet in Fitz Hugh Sound is Barracuda Rock, where the survey launch *Barracuda* came to grief. The British merchant steamer *Benmohr* "grazed" Ben Mohr Rock in Trincomali Channel west of Galiano Island, and the *Wellington* did the same to Wellington Rock in Seaforth Channel. The venerable Union steamship *Cutch*, originally built as a pleasure craft for an Indian maharaja, had the dubious honour in 1899 of christening Cutch Rock in Metlakatla Bay near Prince Rupert. The steamship *Danube* crashed into Danube Rock in Skidegate Inlet, and later, renamed the *Salvor*, became a specialist in salvaging wrecks on reefs. The list goes on and on.

Danube Rock in Skidegate Inlet is named for the steamship *Danube*, shown here at Port Essington, ca. 1898.

Image D-01382 courtesy of the Royal BC Museum, BC Archives

Most ships with rocks named for them survive their fraught encounters. They are refloated by rising tides or pulled off by tugs and taken to dry dock for repair. Many go on to give long and eventful service. The 130-foot patrol boat *Armentières*, for instance, spent much of its life on the BC coast. In 1925 it struck unreported Armentières Rock in Pipestem Inlet and sank, but was raised, towed to Victoria and refitted. Forty years later it was still at work, though under a different name.

Other reef-bound vessels are less fortunate and suffer tremendous damage. Consider the USS *Suwanee*, an iron sidewheeler that had been built during the US Civil War for river use, with a shallow draft and front-and-rear rudders. On its way to Alaska in 1868, the warship became firmly grounded on an unmarked rock (known today, of course, as Suwanee Rock) in Shadwell Passage off the north end of Vancouver Island. As the tide dropped, the ship broke in half and was utterly destroyed. The crew survived, and salvage operations retrieved the guns, ammunition and machinery. The wreck has been a popular dive site for years, and artifacts from the *Suwanee* adorn the homes and gardens of several recreational divers.

If you're a ship captain, a far easier method of attaching your name to a dangerous rock or reef is to discover the threat without getting wrecked and then report it to the Coast Guard. Thus we have Marchant Rock in Hecate Strait, spotted in 1869 by master George Marchant while he was ashore enjoying breakfast on dry land. Hewitt Rock in Finlayson Channel and McCulloch Rock in Dixon Entrance received their names after captains James Hewitt and William McCulloch, respectively, located these menaces and described them to naval officials.

It is possible, should you end up on some reef, to avoid having your name, or your

A painting by Edward Bedwell, second master of HMS *Plumper*, shows the ship aground at Discovery Island.
Image A-00238 courtesy of the Royal BC Museum, BC Archives

vessel's name, printed on the charts for fellow mariners to chuckle over until the end of time. Just blame the person who sent you on your journey! The success of this strategy can be seen in the name of a rock in Trincomali Channel. HMS *Plumper* was anchored at Nanaimo in 1859 when its master, Captain George Richards, received an urgent order from Governor James Douglas to return to Victoria. En route, at full speed, the *Plumper* hit a rock where there weren't supposed to be any. Damage was negligible, fortunately. Richards and his officers felt that it was Douglas who had ordered the voyage, and Douglas, not them, who should forever be associated with the site of the accident. They named the hazard Governor Rock.

13

DRAMA AT
MISSION POINT

Excerpted from That Went By Fast: My First 100 Years *(2014), by Frank White*

Back in Abbotsford it didn't take long to run through the small savings we had left and I was back feeling the pinch to get some money coming in. I decided to go drop in on Charlie Philp. I'd worked for him before and knew he was always mixed up in some side action in the woods. When I walked into his office, he was on the phone listening to quite a tale of woe by the sound of it. "That bad, eh? That's tough. Well, I wish there was something I could do..." Then he looks up at me and it's like a light bulb went on. "Well, just a minute, somebody just walked into my office—let me call you back."

Me, back in the day.
Harbour Publishing Archives

So he sits me down and pours me a drink and treats me like a long-lost friend and eventually he gets around to talking about this pretty decent little camp on Nelson Island sitting on some damn fine timber but the guys just aren't cutting the mustard—they're a couple of moonlighting teachers and they're screwing everything up. Charlie's got some money tied up in the operation and he needs somebody up there who knows how to get logs in the water. This time Charlie is talking about a partnership deal with me right from the start. So we agree I will go up and size things up, get the camp on its feet and decide whether I want to get in any deeper. I found the idea attractive.

The truck-logging boom that had started back on Vedder Mountain in 1939 was still flooding the BC woods with small operators, and a lot of guys I'd worked with were running their own shows and making good dough. Well actually, it turns out most of them were not making good dough, or any dough, but that was not the story they told when you met them in the beverage room of the Rainier Hotel. It looked good to me and I wanted to get in on it.

I'd proved to Charlie I could run a camp, and logging was the one place I could see where a man could still make it if he played his cards right and worked hard. I had all the tools, I knew that—I knew every part of logging, except the business part of selling the logs, but Charlie could help me learn the ropes there. I was wary of Charlie; if there was a dollar to be had, his idea was not to split it with you but to take all of it, but I should be getting to where I could deal with that by now. If this was any kind of a camp, and Charlie assured me it was a great location with plenty of untouched timber, this might just be the opening I'd been looking for.

I had never heard of Nelson Island before and had to get a map to look it up, figuring it would be one of these little islands you could spit across, of which the BC coast has too many to remember. I was quite surprised to find Nelson Island was actually one of the larger islands in the Gulf of Georgia, bigger than Gabriola, Denman or Lasqueti and only a little smaller than Saltspring. It had hardly any people living on it and no villages, only a few gyppo logging camps and a couple small resorts. It was on the mainland side of the gulf, about sixty miles north of Vancouver, kind of blocking the mouth of Jervis Inlet. It had a lot of bays, lagoons, basins and lakes, and Charlie's camp was tucked into a little nook on the south side called Green Bay. The timber was pretty much untouched except for a little handlogging in the early days, but it was nothing like the first growth I'd seen on Vedder Mountain. It was very stunted and scrubby around the edges where it was exposed to the ocean winds, but the interior had some heavy stands that would make for nice logging once you worked your way into it.

The nearest settlement to Green Bay was the fishing village of Pender Harbour, seven miles down Agamemnon Channel, which had several stores, a post office, schools and a hospital. It was too far from Pender Harbour to get the kids to the schools, which would be a problem since my daughter Marilyn was going into Grade 3 and my son Howie would be starting Grade 1 in a year. My wife, Kay, was game as usual—she was always ready to move on to the next thing, especially if it looked like it might finally work into a decent opportunity. She was in top form and ready to do her part, whatever that might be.

There was a steamer service to Pender Harbour, not Union Steamships, the famous pioneer steamboat company that settled the BC coast, which was already cutting back on its routes by this time, but a newer outfit called the Gulf Lines that had three war surplus ships all called the Gulf something—Mariner, Wing and one they'd already lost when it slammed into Dinner Rock off Powell River a few years before, the *Gulf Stream*. The *Gulf Mariner* and the *Gulf Stream* were minesweepers and the *Gulf Wing*, which we would get to know all too well, was a Fairmile, a smaller, wooden class of sub-chaser around 100 feet long and narrow, maybe twenty feet wide. For a while, the war surplus Fairmiles were all over the place but you seldom see one now.

For this first trip Charlie said I wouldn't have to worry about the Gulf Lines because they had a new camp boat I could run from Vancouver up to the camp. As a Fraser

Valley boy, boats were not my thing and I had never run a boat that far before, so this was a bit of a challenge. Still, I'd run boats for short distances here and there and was at home with motors so I thought that was fine. I packed my bag, picked up the usual collection of machinery parts and logging supplies around town, and drove down to Granville Island where Charlie's truck yard was and where this boat was tied up at a place called Clay's Wharf, a grimy False Creek institution that persisted into recent times.

It wasn't hard to spot my command, even among the peeling derelicts that populated Clay's Wharf. It looked like a typical gyppo logging camp boat, a sad-looking thirty-two-foot hulk on its last stop before the boneyard. It was a long, narrow-gutted, low-slung thing with a drooping bow, long passenger cabin with big square windows—several of which had lost their glass—and a V-to-flat bottom with the chines built out to form little spon-son-wings toward the stern. This was an unusual feature I later found made handy shock absorbers for knocking against logs, although I'm sure the designer had some higher purpose in mind. There was no name or numbers painted on it, though I learned it had been one of a pair of quite famous sister ships, one called the *White Hawk* and the other the *Black Hawk*. I never did know which one this was, because for reasons I could never imagine somebody had renamed it the *Suez*. I should have expected trouble from a boat named after an Egyptian ditch.

What the *Hawk* boats had been famous for was speed. The *Suez* had originally been powered by an Allison V12 airplane engine that was said to push forty knots, making it the fastest boat in Vancouver Harbour. It was supposedly built to serve as a water taxi for running log scalers back and forth between Vancouver and the big log-sort grounds in Howe Sound, although I met people who insisted that had only been a cover story for its real purpose, which was running booze into Puget Sound during Prohibition. Certainly it had the classic design of a lot of rumrunners—their idea back then was to get speed by making the hull long and narrow so it would cut through the water; they hadn't come up with the idea of the planing hull yet.

The big Allison had long since been replaced by the standard cheap boat power of the day, a six-cylinder Chrysler Crown salvaged from a wrecked car, which drove it at a plodding seven knots. The engine conversion was typically haywire with straight sea-water cooling and a dry manifold that used to get so hot it glowed red, which proved handy for brewing coffee. We even used to fry eggs and make toast on it. There was no motor cover—it ran too hot to be shut up and I wondered how they kept spray from coming in through the missing windows and killing the engine.

I didn't know much about boats at that point but I knew enough to see this was a boat best used in calm water, and I had a little twinge of concern thinking about the kind of long crossing through open water I was about to attempt in it. The marina owner's son, a smart-ass kid who manned the gas pump, didn't do anything to ease my nerves.

"You're not taking this thing out today, are you?" he chirped. "Where you taking it? Nelson Island? You're nuts. I wouldn't go across the harbour in this floating coffin today. Have you even checked the weather?"

He jabbered away like a squeaky young crow without waiting for answers. As a matter of fact, I hadn't thought to check the weather beyond the farmer's forecast, which

Once the pride of Vancouver's water taxi fleet, the MV *Suez* was a typical sad-sack camp boat by the time I took charge of her.
Harbour Publishing Archives

consisted of a quick glance at the sky, but I wasn't about to give this sawed-off little shit the satisfaction and made like I knew what I was doing. He just shook his head and said, "So long, buddy. It's been nice knowing ya. Any last words for your wife and kids? I'll keep this space open in case you come to your senses and turn around."

This was Harold Clay Jr., a.k.a. Squeak, who in later years would move to Pender Harbour and carry on where he'd left off getting under my skin. He was honestly one of the most annoying individuals I ever had the misfortune to know, and the most annoying thing about him was that he was just about as smart as he thought he was, at least around anything to do with boats.

I wasn't out under the Lions Gate Bridge before I realized there was no way I should be out there in that punky old wreck. There was a pretty good southeaster blowing up and the clouds were black and menacing. I only had a sketch map that Charlie'd pencilled on the back of a letter because the route was supposed to be so simple, but the vista of low grey humps I saw before me now bore no resemblance to the map. There was an unreliable-looking little car compass mounted on the dash that seemed to be working, and checking it against the map I picked out what I thought must be the left side of Bowen Island and the mountains of the Sunshine Coast beyond.

It looked like a thousand miles of ugly cross-seas I had to survive before I got to the next shelter, and I think I would have turned around and gone back if it hadn't meant having to face the taunts of that smartass kid. The old *Suez* was no good in a beam sea—it was no good in a following sea or a head sea either—and all the cargo

I'd packed was soon flying around and falling into the bilge, and spray was pouring into the cockpit, which was open and had no self-bailers. I couldn't let go of the wheel to run back and save anything or check the bilge, which I could tell was getting full by the sloshing sounds. I had to keep plowing grimly ahead until I was past Bowen and coming up on those little islands off Gibsons where I could get some shelter and stow things a little better and bail the bilge.

I'd been pinning my hopes on reaching Gibsons where I could wait out the blow, but it was still early in the day by the time I got there and I hated to quit. I got things nice and shipshape and figured what the hell, I might as well keep going and at least get a little closer to my destination. The trouble with this plan was that I was about to enter what towboaters call "The Stretch," which is the thirty miles of exposed shoreline between Gibsons and Secret Cove where there is no sheltered moorage. I had a vague idea about this from what some towboaters had told me in the pub but I figured I had a good six hours of daylight, which would be plenty of time to get me to Secret Cove or Pender Harbour where there would be good shelter for the night.

I might even make it all the way to Green Bay if things went well. What did vaguely bother me was this was all lee shore, meaning if the motor conked out the wind would blow you up on the beach, but so far the old Chrysler Crown was purring along like a champ so I figured I might as well keep pushing. I've never been good at resisting the temptation to squeeze in an extra mile before dark.

The weather had all been coming at me from the port side, which was the boat's good side—there were no missing windows. What I discovered as I turned up past Gower Point and started along toward Roberts Creek was that the seas were now behind me. The *Suez* had a full stern and a narrow bow which made it hell to handle in a following sea, and not only that, the cabin was completely open at the back and now the spray was funnelling into the boat and hissing where it hit the hot motor. Again I was in the position where I couldn't take my hands off the wheel, the way the boat was wallowing around. That bleak, menacing shore seemed to go on forever. The boat seemed to be dead in the water, even though the motor was grinding away as normal.

I was discovering what a lot of unhappy mariners discovered about The Stretch—it's only thirty miles but in a southeaster with an ebbing tide it can seem like three hundred. The current runs two knots against you on an ebb tide, reducing the old *Suez*'s net speed over bottom to five knots, and less than that once you subtracted all the zigzags it was making in the following sea. I cut in close to the steamer dock at Roberts Creek but there was no safe tie-up there that I could see. There was a bit of a haywire breakwater around the Jackson Brothers booming ground at Wilson Creek but the tide was out and it looked too shallow so I kept chugging. I don't know what gets into a guy that makes you want to keep pushing, keep heading into a worsening situation rather than pulling back when you have the chance. There's something so tempting about sticking to your plan even after it's gone all to hell, the momentum of the trip that is so hard to resist.

The three hours had stretched into four and the afternoon light was draining away. As I came up to a couple of wave-washed rocks called White Islets feeling very lonely and exposed with nothing but open sea before me as far as the eye could see and foaming shore on my starboard side, the motor developed a miss. I dashed back to give it a ten-second check, saw nothing, then dashed back to grab the wheel as the boat began to yaw. The miss got worse. The motor was now running only on four cylinders.

I crawled along the coast in the fading light, desperately checking the map and the shore for a place to get a little shelter where I could throw out an anchor—I did have a rusty little thing with hardly any chain and rotten-looking rope—and like so many a sailor before me, I pinned my hopes on reaching the Trail Islands off Sechelt, where it looked like a guy might get a little shelter. If I'd been doing it now, I would have swung way out and got as far from shore as possible, but the greenhorn's first impulse when he's in trouble is to hug in close to shore, not realizing that is your worst enemy if you lose power. Too late I saw breakers ahead and realized I was running into some kind of shallows way out in the strait where there should have been deep water. I swung to port and took seas hard on the beam, holding my breath with every sputter and miss of the motor.

I wasn't a praying man, even in a spot like that, so I had to make do with yelling, "Come on you son of a bitch, hang in there, don't quit now…" But quit is exactly what it did. I hit the starter and got it going and it went a few hundred feet then quit again. I birled the starter till it started to run out of battery then went out into the stern. I had almost got clear of the spit, which I learned later was Mission Point, the gravel bar formed by the region's largest watershed, but the tide was pulling me right back into it. I searched around madly in the wallowing boat and found a broken pike pole about six feet long. I was able to hold the boat off for a while but it was a losing battle.

Finally, just as the boat was about to start crunching on the gravel bar, I jumped overboard and stood on the spit trying to hold it off. That worked better than the pole but it took a brutal effort with the boat surging and twisting, as if madly wanting to wreck itself. It was now completely dark. I hadn't passed another boat in hours, though there were house lights twinkling along the shore. I don't know how many hours I stood there in that freezing water. I don't know what I thought I was trying to accomplish. I was just trying to save the punky old wreck of a boat, which Charlie had probably traded for a couple truck tires.

I don't know why a man does things like this. If I'd been thinking straight I would have realized I was risking my health if not my life, risking leaving my wife and kids without a

The author jumped overboard and tried to push the boat off the spit.
Kim La Fave illustration

breadwinner—and for what? Just to complete a mission, just to not have to phone Charlie—a man who'd cut your throat in a minute if you stood between him and a buck—and tell him I'd lost his junk heap of a boat. But you don't think in a spot like that, at least I didn't. I was always ready to sacrifice myself for the worst broken-down hunk of equipment in the most hopeless goddamn situation.

I don't think I actually hatched a plan so much as my feet found it. Luckily Mission Point is a gravel bar with few large boulders, or the boat would have been kindling. But as I kept pushing the boat out, the waves kept shoving it upcoast, the tide was coming in now, and the water started to get deeper. I somehow managed to drag my half-dead carcass back in and went back to the pike pole. I was now around the point and going down the windward side of the spit, which wasn't so rough. I'd been noticing some kind of structure farther up the shore, and as I got closer I could make out another big steamer dock like the one at Roberts Creek, jutting out into the water. After another hour or so I had worked the boat around to the dock, where I got it tied off to a piling.

I was just about done for. I didn't know what hypothermia was then but I'm sure I had it to the nth degree. I couldn't feel myself. My feet were like pieces of wood. My skin was dead, like canvas. My brain felt like I'd been on a week-long drunk. I was shaking so bad I couldn't close my hands on a knife to cut bread, so I just grabbed handfuls. I felt different than I had ever felt before. I felt like I'd broken something inside myself. I was used to asking a lot of my body and it had always delivered, but it felt like this time I had just asked too much. I was scared. I wondered if I would be found in the morning dead from exposure.

Then I got my eyes focused on shore and realized there was something there called Davis Bay Inn, or something along those lines. A warm bed. Hot food. I had no idea what time it was but I figured I better make an effort to get ashore because I might not make it through the night otherwise. There was nothing to do but swim for it, which wasn't as bad as it seemed because it's shallow there and my feet hit bottom before I got halfway in. The door to the inn was locked, so I pounded and shouted till I got somebody up. A guy stuck his head out of a window.

"We're closed," he says.

"Look, I'm in bad shape," I stammered, my tongue so thick I could hardly talk. "I just about lost my boat and I need to get warm…"

"We're closed," he says again. "If you want a room, go up to the lodge. They'll take you."

"Where's…the lodge?" I said.

"Top of the hill. Can't miss it." *Slam.*

So I drag my shivering ass up Davis Bay hill, which seemed like Mount Everest, and I get into this little flophouse where they're not too overly thrilled to see me either, but they give me a bed and I eventually stop shaking enough to sleep.

The next day it's sunny and calm. The boat is sitting innocently alongside the wharf, still as a picture. I find a skiff on the beach and paddle out with a piece of driftwood for an oar. It's easy to see why the motor stopped. It's white with dried salt from the blown spray. Every spark plug is shorted out. It's a wonder it ran as long as it did. I clean up the plugs and wiring real well, knowing I don't have much battery, but it starts right off and purrs like a kitten.

For some time, the asshole from the inn has been standing on the shore shouting about his skiff so I grab the stubby pike pole and paddle it in.

"What the hell do you think you're doing?" the guy says. "That dinghy is for inn guests only."

I get up good and close to him and say, "How would you like a punch in the goddamned nose?" I really wanted to give it to him too, and I guess he could tell because he was suddenly a whole bunch more understanding and agreed to row me back out.

It was a beautiful day without a ripple in sight. It was hard to believe this was the same ocean as the day before, and it also made me realize what a damn fool I was to be out on it. All I had to do was listen to Squeak and wait twenty-four hours. I felt good about having survived the ordeal but I had that strange feeling that I had strained something inside that was never going to be 100 per cent right again. It was an odd feeling, one I'd never had before.

Looking back, I can admit something that I wouldn't have admitted then, and that is that I was past my peak. I was thirty-five and at a point where a man's physical abilities start to go into decline. I'd always been sound as a dollar physically but now I started to have a lot of back trouble. Already I'd lost the ability to sleep, and I was tired a lot. I had stiff joints in the morning. And somewhere around then I started to experience the first twinges of phantom pain in my face, a tic that would become more familiar over the years. I still had forty years of working life in me as it turned out, but it worries a young guy when he encounters his first whiff of mortality. It wasn't an auspicious start to this new phase in our lives.

The *Suez* tied up at the Green Bay logging camp.
Harbour Publishing Archives

14

MAXINE MATILPI: CAPSIZED IN SEYMOUR NARROWS

Excerpted from Working the Tides: A Portrait of Canada's West Coast Fishery *(1996), by Vickie Jensen*

I've been fishing for most of my life. My grandfather Henry Speck was a fisherman. My father, Charlie Matilpi Sr., was a fisherman. All my brothers fished. My first husband was a fisherman. He operated the seine boat *The Star of Wonder*.

The accident happened when we were out on James Walkus's boat *Miss Joye*. It was my first season for herring, and it was probably the third week we were out, near the end of November. There were seven adults on the boat: Kenny Lambert and his father, Forest; Bruce Rafuse; Gary McGill; Fred Anderson (my ex); myself and Kenny's wife, Betty, with her six-month-old baby, Jason.

It was rough that morning, and we had travelled all night from Ganges because James wanted us to go to Deepwater Bay. He'd said that the first boat to catch thirty-five tons would get to go home after delivering to Vancouver and would get the weekend off. *Miss Joye* was the first one to catch the tons, but instead of us going home, James pumped the herring from our boat to his boat and travelled south to deliver while we travelled in the opposite direction.

We were supposed to stop in at Campbell River for at least a couple hours for all the crew

The *Miss Joye* was headed north to Deepwater Bay to seine for herring when disaster struck.
Rick Tanaka photo

members to get proper rest, to get groceries and fuel up. Betty and I and the baby were in the galley, and we thought for sure we were going to pull in to Campbell River. But as we got closer we looked out the window and Betty said, "Holy shit! We're going through instead of stopping." The tide was running at its full ebb through Seymour Narrows, but we kept on going.

It seemed like not even five, ten minutes into the Narrows when we hit the first whirlpool. It was ever so slow. We didn't know what we had hit then, but when we came creeping back to position and travelled farther along, we could see it. We had rolled way over, so that if the window had been open, we could have touched water. We just braced ourselves. Betty said, "Oh my God, I hope nothing happens to me." I said, "Betty, don't talk like that." For some reason she felt fear that day, and she was not a person who was easily scared.

Kenny was the captain. As we were going through, he was on the radio trying to talk to James to tell him that we were going through rather than stopping to wait for the tide to slacken off. We were trying to hug the shore. Bruce was on the wheel. It seemed like it took all his effort to control the boat. I remember looking into the pilot house, and Kenny had his legs braced far apart. Normally, a lot of boats will pull back the throttle, shut the engine off and just glide through. But for some reason that morning while Bruce was on the wheel, the throttle wasn't pulled back until we almost were into the second whirlpool. Fred, my ex, had just gone to bed along with the other crew member, Gary. Forest was awake; he was the engineer. We'd had engine problems that night, so he kept getting up to check on it.

That boat was so cranky, so top heavy, that anything could've happened even before we got to Seymour Narrows. Plus we didn't put the net in the hatch to stabilize the boat. Then we hit the second whirlpool. The first one that got thrown was the baby, who was sitting in between us on a table in a cuddle seat. He went flying and hit his forehead on a counter by the sink. Betty and I got thrown, too. She was the one that was closest to the stove. I remember there was a huge pot of boiling water on, plus there was a big kettle that was almost to the boiling point because we were planning to make stew for dinner that day. We were sprawled out on the galley floor, which was at an angle. She kept on saying, "Keep his head out of the water. Push him up." But by the time we got hold of Jason, he was already limp. I knew right then and there he was dead.

You could feel the boat tipping over more and more, then the water started gushing through. It seemed like it came from the pilot house first. I just remember feeling the cold, cold water. Betty was by the stove, and the big pot dumped all over the right side of her body. All she kept on saying was, "Oh my God, oh my God. Keep his head out of the water."

I could hear Kenny trying to talk to James, but the phone was breaking up terribly. By then the throttle got pulled back. When the engine shuts off, a bell rings in the engine room. My ex heard it and came running up in his underwear, saying, "What the hell is going on here?" We were ankle deep in water. Betty picked up the baby, and Kenny came right behind Fred and said, "Every man for himself. Get out of the boat. Get out of the boat. We're going to sink."

Kenny and Betty and the baby went toward the pilot house to get out that way. Fred and I were in the galley, trying to open the galley door, but there was too much water pressure. So we grabbed a frying pan and kept banging the window by the sink, but it just kept bouncing off. By then we were almost standing on the stove. The water was coming up fast, really fast. We were three-quarters upside down by then. By the time it got to our chests, we were completely capsized. I don't know how many times we tried to get out of that window, and we just couldn't. Finally, we just hung on to the lazy Susan with our noses pressed right up against the floor to get any air.

I don't think it took that boat fifteen minutes to completely capsize. Meanwhile, Bruce, Gary and Forest got out of the boat. The net had already started to unwind from the drum. Bruce had a pocketknife on him so he was able to cut himself out of the net. That saved his life.

Forest got free of the boat but was too exhausted to swim back to it. He hung on to this wooden refrigerator box, but the current was too strong. The last they saw him, he was hanging on to this box. When they turned around, he was gone. He never surfaced again.

In the galley, I could feel somebody tugging at my legs. I thought this person who was tugging on me wanted to breathe, so I kinda kicked my feet to let them know there was air up here. But I was too afraid to go under the water. That happened twice, and then the person just quit. I thought it was Betty, maybe, but it was actually my ex. He had dove under and finally kicked the window out after we ran out of air. The window was quarter-inch-thick Plexiglas; he didn't realize that he had cut his foot badly, all the way around. He cut a main artery. When he got up to the surface, the crew members helped him to get to the keel; that's when he realized that he was bleeding. The cold water saved him from bleeding to death.

All three guys were on top of the bottom of the boat by then. Underwater, I found my way to the pilot house. The interesting part was when I decided to leave the galley, it seemed like I felt my grandfather's presence, Henry Speck. For some reason I just had to follow this

This photo taken from a Coast Guard rescue helicopter shows the upturned hull of the *Miss Joye*, in which Maxine Matilpi was trapped for two and a half hours.

Courtesy of Maxine Matilpi

feeling that told me to get to some light. So I dove down and saw this light like a lantern, and I followed it. I came up to the surface, ready to burst, and sure enough, I had at least five feet of air in the pilot house. I stood on the wheel, but water started coming up really fast. That's when I started to panic and screamed, "Please God. Please God. Don't let me die." I thought of my uncle who had drowned years ago and what he must have gone through.

When water got past my nose, I thought, "Now I'm going to die. This boat's going to sink, and they're never going to find me." So I dove down again. Again I followed this feeling that my grandfather was there guiding me. This time I swam toward the engine room. It was pitch black down there. There's a kind of wraparound stairway, and as soon as I got to it I knew exactly where I was. I just collapsed. I had no energy. I couldn't even lift my legs up.

There was some breathing air. I felt around in the pitch black and knew I was in the engine room. I told myself, "You've got to get out of the water or you're going to have hypothermia and go into shock." I felt around some more and realized I could get myself out of the water completely, so I did.

I started to get super cold. A mattress, clothing, blankets and a sleeping bag floated by. I got back into the water and with all my effort lugged the sleeping bag out of the water, wrung it out and put it around me. The funny part was that I had to pee so bad. I don't know why I didn't just pee my pants, but I struggled to get my pants down before I realized how silly that was. I ended up peeing myself and that's what really warmed me. In the meantime, diesel was coming into my nose, my ears. Every time I touched them, they were just slimy. I could taste it in my mouth. It got into my eyes a bit, and every time I blinked they started to sting. All the fumes were making me really sleepy.

Just then, I found this wooden object and started banging away on the hull. I kept banging away, shouting, "I'm alive. I'm alive. I'm down here." Bruce and Kenny heard me and answered, "We're going to come and get you. You just hang in there." But when they didn't show up, I fell asleep. They thought I'd died.

I must have slept twenty minutes at the most. When I woke up again, that's when reality hit. This wasn't a bad dream. I told myself, "You have to get yourself out of here." So I tried. I got to the washroom and made three attempts to get out of the porthole there. Then I went back to where I was before.

When I got back to the engine room, they yelled to me that four divers were coming through and to stay put but try to be kind of visible, to make a ripple to let them know exactly where I was. So I had to leave the engine room and go back into the water by the stairway. A diver found me and told me that the boat was slowly sinking and we would have to get out within a few minutes. He asked me if I'd ever scuba dived. When I said, "No," he explained how we would buddy breathe. I was wrapped around him as we were going up. I didn't realize how deep we were. I think we were about twenty, twenty-one feet under the surface.

The boat was upside down and the hull was still visible. The diver who saved my life gave me a picture of it later. They got me on *Tamanawas*, a boat standing by, and there was a doctor aboard. I was so cold and all I wanted to do was sleep, but he wouldn't let me. Somebody wanted to give me rum or rye and another suggested a hot shower, but the doctor told them either one would give me cardiac arrest. They took off the wet clothing that I had on, put on these huge pants and a shirt, and got ready to hoist me up to a helicopter.

Today, Maxine Matilpi and her partner, John Livingston, create Northwest Coast Native art and regalia.
Courtesy of Maxine Matilpi

I insisted that the diver who found me come up with me. I hung on for dear life. I remember him telling me not to look down, but I did.

I could hardly believe it, seeing the situation from the air. I had been in the capsized boat for two and a half hours. I had travelled almost the whole of Seymour Narrows going round and round and round. Forest and Betty and the baby were dead.

After the inquest into the accident, I talked to the diver who rescued me. He came up to me and said, "You probably don't recognize me. I'm the one that got you out of the boat." I just gave him a big hug. I got choked up because I wanted to say so many things at once. I thanked him for my life, and he said, "Well, that's my job." I heard that five or six years later he died.

Shortly after the accident, I got pregnant with my son Aubrey and went right back out fishing. But it was with great difficulty, and it was with great pain and fear. Surviving the capsizing has made me appreciate life. I don't take anything for granted. I was lucky to have the two children I've always wanted, and that's what made life go on for me.

Corporal J.C. Lemay was one of three divers awarded a medal for bravery for this rescue effort. Sadly, Corporal Lemay was awarded his posthumously, as he went missing during a training dive and is presumed dead.

SPLIT AND DELIVERED, OR DELIVER AND SPLIT

15

Excerpted from Dogless in Metchosin *(1995), by Tom Henry*

For the woodcutter, there can be no better month than November. The days are cool and, on the end of Vancouver Island, relatively dry. Mornings in the woodlot are marked by the sound of ravens, seagulls, red-tailed hawks. Always there is the gentle patter of leaves falling. If the sun is out, you might even work bareback, as much for the thrill of cheating the season as for any need.

Yesterday, after an afternoon of just such weather, I finished cutting cords number forty-nine and fifty. Then I helped Wayne deliver them to a customer in Colwood. We'd just begun heaving the wood off when the customer—a slight guy in his forties—mentioned it didn't look too dry. "I, um, I ordered dry wood," he said.

He was right, the stuff we were throwing off was a bit mushy. What he didn't understand was that in the topsy-turvy world of firewood, the customer is always wrong.

Wayne paused, mid-toss. "Look, if you don't want the wood, that's fine," he said. "I've got plenty of people who do." He wasn't kidding either. One ad in the paper and we'd got enough orders to keep going for a month. The customer jammed his hands in his pockets. "That's funny," he said. "That's exactly what a woodcutter said last year."

The biggest problem for woodcutters selling unseasoned cords or short cords is to get the wood off the truck and the money in the pocket before the buyer wises up. And the oldest trick to distracting buyers—men anyway—is to ask them about their woodstove.

John Steinbeck once observed that a whole generation of American men grew up

THE BEAUTY OF DAMPISH WOOD IS IT BURNS SLOWER, THEREFORE LASTS YOU LONGER!

Dave Alavoine Illustration

knowing more about the ignition system of a Model T than they did about the clitoris. Same holds true of men today, but substitute airtight woodstove for Model T. The passion longtime wood burners feel for their airtight stoves is surpassed only by their love of bragging about them. How much their Franklin holds, how long it'll burn without restoking, all recounted with a troubadour's affection.

Wood sellers understand this, and if they see a customer eyeing a chintzy load suspiciously, they will make a casual reference about woodstoves. That is usually enough to launch the buyer on a long-winded tangent. Meanwhile, off goes the wood, into the pocket goes the cash.

There's another way woodcutters gouge customers. A real cord should be stacked very tightly, with few air spaces. Just what this means, however, is a matter of interpretation. A woodcutter in Cowichan I worked for used to tell customers that the spaces between the pieces of wood could be large enough for a squirrel to fit through, but not large enough for a cat. That was for good loads. On poorly stacked loads, he'd change the standard to cats and raccoons. Another trick woodcutters use is a variation of the good cop, bad cop routine. Only with wood sellers, it's bad dog, badder dog.

The loaded wood truck backs into a nice surburban driveway. Two toothy dogs bail out. While one heads up the street after the neighbour's corgi, the other starts excavations in the rhododendron patch.

There's your dilemma: see three years of hard gardening ruined, or face five years' frosty relations with the lady up the street who owns the corgi. Either way, the distraction is enough to allow the wood to be heaved off and the woodcutter to collect the money.

Perhaps the best wood-selling scam isn't really a scam at all—unless you consider advertisements that associate drinking beer with fun-loving chicks and muscular dudes a scam.

The idea of sales, as I understand it, is to sell an idea, a concept. Motor homes, missiles, mushy wood, who cares. It's the notion, not the commodity, that needs to be marketed. And this is why so many woodcutters drive boneyard trucks and are missing front teeth. A cord of wood from Walmart? Bah. There's no chance, no adventure in that.

But a cord of wood from a guy named Randy, who returns your call from a pay phone? It's ripe.

The very best wood seller (notice I didn't say woodcutter) I've run into understood the importance of selling the image, not the product. Johnny sold wood in Victoria in the mid-1980s. His motto was: deliver and split, rather than split and delivered. Johnny drove the requisite crappy truck, with requisite dogs, and had the requisite smell. But Johnny went a step farther on the image thing and spray-painted a quote from Virgil on the side of his truck. And he kept a copy of Henry David Thoreau's *Walden* on the dash, cover up.

I sold wood with Johnny now and then, and it was as if people had been hoping all their wood-burning lives to meet such a person.

"You read *Walden*?"

"On your lunchtime? In the rain? On a log? Awwww."

As if *Walden* and dirty Stanfield's made for the ideal woodcutter.

Of course, those customers never wanted to discuss the finer points of *Walden,* which was a good thing, because Johnny knew as much about Thoreau as he did about ignition systems on Model Ts. But that didn't matter: The customer had bought a lousy cord from a real woodcutter. As Johnny himself once said, better that than a real cord from a lousy woodcutter.

But something makes me think customers may never catch on to woodcutters' tricks. Something makes me think that they don't want to. I've been cutting and selling firewood for sixteen years, and more than a few gyppo loads of wet wood have gone to the same customer year after year. "That wood you sold me last year was none too good," they'll say. "Couldn't burn it until February. Hope this is better." "You bet," I say. "Full cord, maybe a little more." This happens year after year. They must figure it's worth the price of a cord to see a woodcutter doing what he does best.

16 BACK TO THE LAND: WHEN HIPPIES CAME TO SOINTULA

Excerpted from Sointula: An Island Utopia *(1995), by Paula Wild*

Meeting the boat from outside was always an important part of Sointula life. In 1958 the Union Steamships were replaced by the *Island Princess*, a vehicle ferry that travelled between Sointula and Kelsey Bay once a day, hoisting cars on and off its deck with a large crane. When the *Island Princess* began unloading strange-looking people in the late 1960s, "meeting the ferry" took on a whole new meaning.

Jenny and Jim Green were operating an art gallery in San Francisco's Haight-Ashbury during the era of "free love" and "flower power" when Jim was drafted. The Greens piled their possessions into a Volkswagen van and made their way north seeking refuge and a safe place to raise their infant daughter. "We got off the ferry in Sointula in the middle of the night and there were lights and people everywhere," Jenny recalled. "It was 1968 and it seemed like half the town had stayed up all night waiting for the boat to come in."

"After we had been in Sointula for a few weeks we went to our first function at the Finnish Organization Hall," Jenny continued. "We opened the door and all this wonderful music came pouring out. At the top of the staircase were a couple of drunks brawling; they fell down the stairs and landed at our feet. It felt like we had stepped back in time into the Wild West."

Sointula residents gawked at the newcomers' funny cars, baggy clothes and beads, and frowned at the long, dirty hair that was prevalent on the men as well as the women. While non-Finns had moved to the island before, they had never arrived in such large numbers and they had never looked so unusual. The Greens and others like them were full-blown hippies, and most of the people in Sointula had never even seen bell-bottoms before. As well as looking odd, the new people acted differently too. They perplexed Co-op clerks by asking for "health food," and it didn't take the Greens long to determine that they were the only vegetarians in the entire fishing village.

The majority of the new people congregated in the outlying areas of Mitchell Bay and Kaleva Road. Some bought old farms; eighty acres with a few buildings, a tractor, a flock of chickens and maybe a cow could be purchased for $7,000. Others camped in plastic lean-tos, teepees or abandoned saunas.

The newcomers stuck to themselves, coming into town every couple of weeks to pick up their mail and shop at the Co-op store where most had their only contact with what they referred to as "real Sointula people." While the early Finns had advertised their utopia in the *Aika*, rumours of a hippie commune rippled down the coast by word of mouth. There was a lot of coming and going, creating the impression that there was a larger countercultural population on the island than there actually was.

As well as offering sanctuary from the United States draft and the lure of cheap land, Canada was also attractive for its socialized medical care. A trip to Sointula to visit some

An old homestead with sauna and boat shed, 1974. Many saunas were located on the beach so only a few steps were required for that refreshing dip in the ocean.
Rick James photo

Above: A traditional Finnish home on Kaleva Road, 1978.
Rick James photo

Above right: Old Tom, the communist logger, lectures a hippie on "the dignity of the working man," 1974. The light bulb over the door indicated whether the variety store was open or closed.
Rick James photo

friends convinced Kit and Stephanie Eakle to have their baby in British Columbia. They moved to Malcolm Island from California in May 1970, and at the end of the summer they were asked to caretake Jane and John McClendon's place. In 1969 the McClendons had bought an old homestead, which they used first as a summer home and later as a permanent residence. Their Kaleva farm was a destination point for a lot of the hippies, many believing that it was the site of an active commune. While that was not true, Jane did let people sleep on the farmhouse floor or in one of the outbuildings.

"People called Jane 'Mom' because she was a little bit older than the rest of us and she fed everyone," Stephanie said. "When Kit and I were caretaking their place, we felt obliged to continue that tradition. People would show up with two pounds of brown rice and ask to stay indefinitely. We were all city people and didn't really know much about living off the land."

The Eakles decided to have their baby at "home," an old sauna at the McClendons' that had been converted into a cabin, rather than at the hospital in Alert Bay. Other pregnant women were invited, Stephanie's parents came from California, and a sister arrived from New York. An ex-Vietnam medic promised to oversee the delivery but showed up two months late. "It was really exciting until complications set in and my parents had to charter a float plane to take me to Alert Bay," Stephanie recalled. "There was no ambulance on the island in those days, and we weren't connected enough with the locals to know anyone with a fishing boat."

In fact, the hippies' connections with the locals were varied. Many of the older generation of Finns were open and friendly. They looked beyond the long hair and strange clothes and saw people who wanted a simple lifestyle, whose dreams echoed their parents' ideals. They observed the newcomers buying the farms that their children had abandoned and watched while they cleared fields of timothy and wild grasses, repaired broken fences and windows and removed the rubble left from rambunctious teenagers dynamiting chimneys.

Willie Olney noted: "The hippie movement gave Sointula a complete freedom of fashion. They wore weird get-ups but they looked so comfortable. Pretty soon it seemed like everyone could wear whatever they wanted. Before the hippies came, women wore nylons all the time. People die in the winter and most of our funerals are outside. Women used to freeze in the wind and rain, but after the hippies were here for a while it was acceptable to wear pants."

While most of the older residents were accepting, their children were suspicious and sometimes hostile. They had worked hard to improve their lives and found it difficult to understand these strangers who turned their backs on the modern conveniences of life. To compound the matter, none of the new people seemed to have jobs, a fact that irritated and puzzled the hard-working Finns. Also, although only a small percentage of the hippies were draft dodgers, the locals believed otherwise. Many of the middle-aged men, more patriotic than pro-Vietnam, viewed the newcomers as cowards who wouldn't fight for their country. And then there were the rumours about drugs and free love.

"We felt frightened when the hippies came," Bonnie Nelson admitted. "We had to start locking our doors; we had heard stories about people going crazy on drugs. It seemed like there were a lot of them and everyone felt that life would change because of them."

"Life did change when the hippies came," Aileen Wooldridge stated. "Up until that time everybody knew each other and most people were related in some way. We were a tight-knit little community and all of a sudden there were all these other people. It couldn't stay the same. There was a lot of resentment because things were changing."

The youth of the island, in the rebellious years of their teens and early twenties, were openly curious about and even attracted to the hippies. Their interest further increased the tension between their parents and the "long hairs," who were held responsible for the drugs that were beginning to appear on the island.

"After we had been in Sointula for a while I screwed up enough courage to go to Granny's Cafe," Jenny reminisced. "I sat there for twenty minutes and was ignored—they wouldn't serve me. For the first time in my life I knew what it was like to be a minority. A few days later, though, I was walking down the street and there was this older Finn man walking toward me. I smiled at him, and his face just opened up in the most beautiful smile. I realized then that some of the problem was my own shyness and insecurity."

Other reactions to the hippies were more aggressive. There was talk of running them out of town. Local logging truck drivers played chicken with hippie vehicles travelling to Mitchell Bay, and a truck that broke down on the logging road was torched.

In the summer of 1971 an old cellar on Kaleva Road, home to an ever-changing group of hippies, was the site of a pre-dawn drug raid. Rumour had it that the RCMP found LSD hidden in the woodpile but chose to let the prime suspect escape. A few weeks later the cellar burned to the ground. No one was living there at the time and, although no charges were ever laid, most hippies believed that the fire was deliberately set by locals.

While members of the counterculture felt that some Malcolm Islanders were not friendly, they did not necessarily expect them to be and were satisfied as long as the hostilities didn't get out of control. Stephanie reflected: "We felt that the town was not friendly but we weren't either. We were raised in the city and didn't expect people to care about who we were. But

Right: Jimmy "Slim" Erickson (left), of Finnish descent, has coffee at Granny's Cafe with Walter Miller, an expatriate of Windsor, Ontario, and Miller's son Devin, January 1976.
Rick James photo

Below: The Geisreiters liked the look of what was going to be their barn so much that they made it their house instead. Wood for the house was obtained from their property and the beach as well as from the mill at Telegraph Cove. No nails were used in the construction of the house; all the wood was notched and pinioned instead.
Courtesy of the Geisreiter collection

the Finns were curious about us and some did want to be friends. I'm sure we alienated some of them with our attitudes."

Not all the newcomers to the island were hippies. There were others, a little older and with children of their own, who longed to return to the basic values of an earlier time. Dick and Bette Geisreiter, residents of Mendocino, California, bought the eighty-five-acre Halminen farm in 1968 and moved to the island two years later. "It was the era when people were going back to the land," Bette said. "We were burned out from working so hard and were looking for a slower lifestyle. All of our relatives thought we had lost our marbles, but really we had found them. The wonderful thing about Sointula was the simplicity; it was another age. When we got off the ferry a lot of people were there, including a woman wearing a big Mexican hat. Years later I found out that Doris Slider had heard that there were people from California on the boat and had worn that hat to make us feel at home."

Dick and Bette Geisreiter and their sons, Billie and John, beginning a new life on Malcolm Island, 1970.
Courtesy of the Geisreiter collection

Like the Tynjalas who moved from North Dakota in 1902, the Geisreiters brought all their worldly possessions with them. Their caravan included five cars, a Volkswagen van converted into a chuckwagon, an old telephone van and a one-ton truck filled with tools and windows for the house they were building. Accompanying the couple were their three sons, friends to drive all the vehicles, Zeke the dog, plus thirteen goats with six kids. Bette said, "We picked the best stock to take with us. To get the goats into Canada, Dick had to dip them in a sulphur solution. I guess that sterilized their skin; it sure turned them a nice lime green."

Everyone who moved to the island attempted to live a self-sufficient lifestyle. Most chopped their own firewood, planted large gardens and canned their surplus produce. "At that time getting back to the land was the Mecca we all said we wanted," one person noted. "Living in Mitchell Bay, we didn't have much choice; that's pretty well all there was."

The Geisreiters, however, were serious about their lifestyle change. "One of our goals was to do as little shopping as possible," Bette remembered. "We grew most of our own food and were self-sustaining to 80 per cent. We sold vegetables and cheese to the Co-op. We also had a milk route and sold milk, butter and eggs. We shopped at the Co-op once a week and every couple of months Dick would go to Vancouver and fill the back of the truck with a couple hundred pounds of flour, sugar and other staples."

The Geisreiters and others like them found that hard work and perseverance paid off in more than just personal satisfaction; it earned them the respect and friendship of the islanders. For many, music was the key that opened doors. "We'd go to Lempi and John Blid's for a sauna and then the gang would come over and we'd play music until 2 or 3 in the morning," Dick said. "There was a mandolin, a banjo, an accordion and sometimes a piano. We played at weddings, funerals and anniversaries. It was a fun way to mix with the community."

Will and Heidi Soltau in front of their army-tent home at Pulteney Point, 1972. Their airtight stove was multi-purpose: it provided heat, sterilized baby bottles and served as the kitchen stove.
Courtesy of the Soltau collection

Although many of the people coming to Malcolm Island were talented, it was soon apparent that backgrounds in Chinese studies, economics and floral design were not particularly useful in their new home. Just as the early tailors and poets struggled to fell trees and operate a sawmill, so the newcomers had to adapt their urban skills to a rural environment. They met the challenge with a combination of hope and confidence, and even those without any practical experience never doubted that they could build a house and live off the land.

The Soltaus moved to Sointula in 1971 after an abortive attempt to go back to the land in Kansas. They were looking for "a hippie haven, an untapped wilderness, where the government was giving away free (Crown) land." With the Eakles they bought fifty-four acres near the lighthouse at Pulteney Point, and in 1972 moved there with their two-year-old daughter and one-month-old son. Home was an army tent with an airtight heater.

"It seemed like an adventure at the time," Heidi said. "I had blind faith in Will's ability to build a house—he had studied architecture and built some chairs."

"I wasn't really prepared to go back to the land," Will admitted. "I'd always lived in the suburbs. I had some drafting experience, a couple of books and a little generator to run a few power tools. A lot of the house was built with a chainsaw."

The two families attempted to limit their purchases to staples like oil and salt. They caught fish, baked bread, raised chickens and goats and always ate their evening meal together. Even after they had built separate homes, dinners remained a communal effort. Roughing it in the 1970s wasn't much easier than it had been at the turn of the century. Heidi's Pulteney Point memories revolve around wet firewood and crying while she milked the goats because her hands had cramped with the cold. She cooked meals and sterilized baby bottles on the airtight stove and remembers the day the goats broke into the tent and took one bite out of each potato.

Members of the Treesing tree-planting co-operative at work in the snow at Frederick Arm, November 1975. Standing left to right: Simon Dick, Janey Lord, Stewart Marshall, Kathy Gibler, Edda Field, Barb Imlach, Ralph Harris, Mike Field, Anthea Cameron. Sitting: Sid Williams and Robbie Boyes. Treesing was formed in 1974 to provide jobs for newcomers to Malcolm Island, particularly women.
Rick James photo

Granny Jarvis, the wife of gillnet drum inventor Laurie Jarvis, was born in the Klondike during the height of the gold rush. Here she is taking a closer look at Rob Wynne (left) and Doug, two recent arrivals to the island, 1974. *Rick James photo*

Sooner or later the newcomers' dream of living off the land gave way to the reality of having to earn a living. Some found employment on government-funded Local Initiatives Programs making street signs, cleaning seniors' yards and landscaping the hall hill (where they were frequently accused of smoking marijuana behind the hall), but the real money was to be made in the logging and fishing industries. Scrambling through the bush and over windfalls, the philosophy graduate learned to set chokers while the weaver mastered the intricacies of mending a seine net. A side benefit to the on-the-job training were the horror stories about accidents and death, widow-makers and snapped beach lines. Jobs for men were plentiful but there wasn't much in the way of work for women.

Jane McClendon moved to the island permanently in 1972. "Unless you were part of a family with a fishboat, women usually didn't get fishing jobs. So around 1974 I started a tree-planting co-op." An island dump fire that got out of control was Jane's first planting contract. She could only find five experienced planters so she and a few others trained forty more. A core group of twenty newcomers bought shares of $50 and formed the tree-planting co-op Treesing. Half of the membership had to be women and all members had to be Malcolm Island residents. Contracts were run on a co-operative basis; on many jobs the crew lived and ate together, often camping in tents and lean-tos.

At first positions on the board of directors were filled by women, but one by one they found other jobs and the nature of the co-op began to change. As more co-op members moved on to other things it became necessary to hire people from off-island. Originally a true co-op with no paid management, a new, all-male board of directors decided that they should be compensated for their responsibilities. On the verge of becoming a business rather than a co-op, Treesing dissolved in 1988.

Before they became involved with Treesing, Kathy Gibler and Anthea Cameron established their own work-protection plan. One summer they decided to apply for fishing jobs but on their way to the dock realized that they would be lucky if there was a job for one woman, let alone two. They agreed that whoever got the job would split her income with the other.

"Anthea got the job," Kathy said. "Later that week I got a job fertilizing trees for a forestry crew. We ran around with big flour sifters on our backs, which spit out stuff that looked like coarse salt. Anthea and I both worked for three days. At the end of that time she gave me $300 and I gave her $75. We kept that up for over a year. We weren't living in the same house but it seemed like a good plan."

In another communal effort, newcomers to the island joined a Vancouver-based food co-op called Movable Feast. An order book was passed around and volunteers compiled a master list pooling everyone's bulk orders. "Someone would take a truck down to Vancouver, work in the co-op warehouse for a few days, then bring the order up-island," Ralph Harris remembered. "A lot of our basics were provided for that way. The Sointula Co-op didn't carry things that we wanted, like wheat germ, nutritional yeast and soya sauce."

Davie and Les Lanqvist keep an eye on the fish tally as the seine boat *The Millionaires* is unloaded at Sointula's Norpac barge, July 1977. Many newcomers to the island broke into the fishing industry on *The Millionaires*. *Rick James photo*

As well as working and purchasing items co-operatively, most of the newcomers became close friends. Sharlene and Roger Sommer and their three children moved to Sointula from Sacramento, California, in June 1970. "Roger was an accountant and I was a housewife who stayed home and looked after the kids," Sharlene explained. "When I first saw the hippies in Sointula I was scared of them, but eventually I became friends with them because most of them were American. Our first Thanksgiving in Sointula I was in tears because I had never been away from my family. All the Americans felt that way to some extent, so we all baked bread and killed our own turkeys or chickens and got together for a big meal. I realized then that family isn't necessarily blood."

But even those who weren't classed as hippies ran into problems with the locals. The first incident occurred in 1968 when a Finn demanded more money from a Californian who had bought his farm. The two men were arguing in the kitchen when one of them grabbed a rifle. There was a struggle, the gun went off and the Finn was shot. Not having a telephone or a car, the American ran to a neighbour's for help and ended up driving the injured man into town on his tractor. In the interim the Finn bled to death. This incident upset the newcomers more than the longtime residents. As an American living on the island at the time, Jenny Green felt that "people looked at us a bit after that, but we didn't really feel like they held it against us as a group until a different American closed the logging road. That really created a lot of hard feelings, more so than the shooting.

"When Roger and Sharlene bought their farm it included an access road linking Sointula to the small community and log dump at Mitchell Bay. Everyone used this road, including the local logging company, which paid a nominal fee to do so. When the lease expired, Roger increased the fee, hoping that the loggers would find another route. The logging company balked, negotiations broke down and Roger barricaded the road. A lot of yelling took

Danni Tribe using a modern, aluminum gillnet drum on the north shore of Malcolm Island, 1987.
Paula Wild photo

place, there were threats of physical violence and rocks were thrown at the Sommers' house. Once when Roger went to Mitchell Bay to visit friends the road was blocked so he couldn't get home. When, in spite of the harassment, Roger refused to change his mind, the 'dump' road was extended to become the new link between Mitchell Bay and Sointula."

By the mid-1970s the Finns' hard edges of suspicion and protectiveness had been worn thin by familiarity. Arriving in Sointula via Port McNeill, Vancouver and Detroit, Mary Murphy said: "The people in Sointula were more friendly than any place else I had ever lived. In the city everyone distrusts everyone else, but here people offer you rides and are curious about what you are doing. I was pregnant, and everyone seemed interested in my health and the baby. I got the feeling that the locals approved of us because we had a garden and were starting a family.

"There was a difference after I worked in the Co-op store," Mary continued. "Here you need to show that you are a hard worker to be accepted. Work is more than just a job, it's almost a community activity."

Over the years most of the hippies traded their long hair for more conventional styles and became involved in the routines that owning a home and raising a family bring. An interest and concern about what was happening found them attending community meetings and volunteering for committees. Although there are still some vestiges of "them" and "us," for the most part the newcomers have been accepted. As one Finn said, "They've become such a part of the island that I can't imagine it without them. Besides, they're not really hippies anymore."

17   EIGHT-DAY WILSON

Excerpted from Whistle Punks & Widow-Makers: Tales of the BC Woods *(2000),*
by Robert Swanson

Since time immemorial loggers have been famous short stakers. At the building of King Solomon's temple the loggers in the forest of Lebanon are said to have quit at the slightest provocation, jumped on their asses and journeyed into the nearest town to go on a wingdinger. This trait in loggers has been evident right down to recent times. During the Roaring Twenties, "Seattle Red" was reputed to have worked for seventy-nine logging companies in the state of Washington in one year.

In the BC woods the character who seems to have been the Short Staker Cup Holder was a logger known as "Eight-Day Wilson." His Christian name at the present writing seems to be unknown. Even Bill Black told me that "Old Eight-Day" just happened, and even though Black hired him out for twenty years, his card read "Wilson, Eight-Day: Country of birth—unknown."

Eight-Day Wilson roamed the big clearing back in the days when they cut the stumps above the swell—ten or twelve feet high—and left the big blue butts to rot in the woods. Those were the days when a logger carried his own roll of blankets and hit town wearing caulked boots, stagged-off pants and a Mackinaw shirt.

He got the name of Eight-Day for obvious reasons—he was a fair-weather, eight-day staker. After eight days on the job in any camp he would usually bunch her and head back to town. He was known to hire to a camp and after sampling the grub and washing his socks, beat it back to the bright lights and go on a tear.

A favourite stunt of Eight-Day's was to hire to a camp as hooktender and lie in camp the first day to sober up. After getting a mug-up from the cook in the middle of the morning he would saunter up the skid road and poke around a little. Being a boomer he was sure to know most of the boys in camp from the PF man down to the whistle punk, from whom he would get the lowdown on what the new outfit had to offer in the way of a logging show. If the ground was rough or he didn't like the donkey puncher he would wander back to camp, roll his blankets and head back to town.

One time at Loughborough Inlet, where Jack Phelps was pushing camp, Eight-Day pulled the pin because a green whistle punk sat in his place at the table—that was excuse enough for even a homeguard to tell the ink slinger to write-her-out, but it didn't take much of an excuse for Old Eight-Day. Once when a flunky handed him old hotcakes he bunched her right then and there.

Eight-Day Wilson worked the camps in the days when the stumps were cut above the swell—ten or twelve feet high. This crew, in the Queen Charlotte Islands (now Haida Gwaii), was felling spruce for airplane construction in World War One.

University of British Columbia, Rare Books and Special Collections, British Columbia Historical Postcard and Photograph Albums Collection, BC 1456/62-32

The kitchen of the 120-man Powell River Company camp at Kingcome Inlet, 1915. At one camp, cold hotcakes were reason enough for Eight-Day to quit. *University of British Columbia, Rare Books and Special Collections, MacMillan Bloedel Limited fonds, BC 1930/276-1*

Bunkhouses like this one did not encourage loggers to stay put for long periods of time. *Museum at Campbell River 13312*

At Cowichan Lake his favourite stunt boomeranged on him. Eight-Day Wilson had hired out for Matt Hemmingsen and had completed the customary eight days. He needed an excuse to quit, so he resorted to the infallible test: throw a caulked boot up in the air. If it stayed up, he stayed in camp for another eight days. The trick had never been known to fail. He even had his duffel bag packed in readiness when he threw up the caulked boot and it went through the stove-pipe hole in the bunkhouse and stayed up. To save face Wilson had to stay another eight days, but he went on a record bender when he hit the bright lights with a sixteen-day stake.

Eight-Day Wilson was the last of the great short stakers. His kind are dying out and loggers are gradually losing the wanderlust from their nature and beginning to settle down. Eight-Day Wilson, ace short staker, embarked on his farewell journey to the camps of the Holy Ghost some years ago. He said goodbye to the bright lights and then walked off the end of the Ballantyne Pier in Vancouver, BC.

THE RECLAIMED

by Peter Trower

Overwhelmed homesteads
lie crushed to the dirt
by adamant snows
their waterlogged boards
mummybrown huddles
engendering moss,
arrogant blackberries
scratch through their ribs.

Tottering fenceposts
like battledrunk troops
groggy with rot
advance into nowhere
stagnating sockets
of bucketless wells
breed in their dimness
an airforce of gnats.

Sometimes a chimney
revealed like a trick
rears redbricked
from a scrimshaw of creepers
winds of conjecture
retrace a room
on the unhindered air
the echoes of fire.

Stricken to phantoms
the feeders of dreams
lost among stars
the sparks of their laughter
all the high hopes
the gadfly illusions
whimper from bedsprings
and rustgutted stoves.

Wordless the epitaph
decades have wrought
vanishing paths
weedthrottled forgotten;
impotent schemes
abandoned endeavours
quick in her seasons
the earth will reclaim them.

Bus Griffiths illustration

From Bush Poems *(1978), by Peter Trower and Bus Griffiths*

18 MORTS

Excerpted from Writing in the Rain *(1990), by Howard White*

Up in our neck of the woods these days, fish farming is the thing. It's the big action and the big argument. Basically the people who're making a buck from it like it, and everybody else thinks it stinks. Well, everybody agrees it stinks, but the argument sticks on the point of whether or not a little stink and mess might be put up with in the name of a few paying jobs. The jobs are kind of crummy and the pay is poor, but this strip of rock and Christmas trees has been kissing goodbye to jobs for so long there is a whole generation that's never known steady work. Big healthy guys in their mid-twenties still living at home, still driving 1973 Trans Ams. Anything that promises to get their wasting carcasses off the living room sofa and out of the house for a few hours a day has to look pretty good to their families.

But that doesn't apply to me. My sons are still playing peanut hockey. I sit a lot myself, but in front of a computer, not on the sofa. I do better tickling the keyboard of an IBM than I ever did pulling levers on a D8, much as my old construction buddies find it hard to believe anybody actually gets paid for this kind of thing. And not having to work outside anymore frees me to think kind thoughts about it. I have actually convinced myself that I liked physical work and miss it, and from time to time this leads me to dabble in it. I keep a hand in a small sand-and-gravel outfit with two other guys and put in the odd shift over the weekend trying to prove I'm as good a man as I ever was.

You might think I run a certain risk by doing this, and you're right.

It was September 1988. Around here it had been a wonderful month—very sunny and dry. The boys over at the Water Board were issuing handbills banning all sprinkling—even days or odd, before 7 pm or after. They were going up every day to the reservoir with their yardstick and measuring the fall and calculating how many more days of dry spell we could stand before water stopped coming out of all the taps in Pender Harbour. The kids were still swimming in the salt chuck.

This had an implication for the fish farmers. With all the pollen and leaves and dust and other end-of-summer goodies blowing around and stewing up in the warm water, the plankton thought the good times were here again and launched on a record-smashing population bloom. Any time one of these clouds of happy plankton drifted down on a fish farm, the fish choked in the pens. A hundred thousand six-pound salmon died at once, costing someone a million dollars. At first the farmers surreptitiously chucked their "morts" (mortalities) over the side, but when the volume got into the hundreds of pounds, then into the tons, this illegal activity became too obvious. They began burying the morts in limed pits ashore like they were supposed to, but in no time at all every scrap of dirt on the rocky shore became stuffed with dead salmon. Fish tails were sticking out from under every rock and leaf. So the farmers began loading the mushy carcasses into one-ton totes and hauling the totes to the garbage dump, two to a pickup truck. But the morts kept coming, and soon the farmers were out of totes and out of pickups.

This was when I got the call. They didn't call me to compute. They called to hire our truck, a twelve-yard Dodge in fair shape for its age.

I don't get many calls about the truck. I am on the phone all day about books, but I don't place much store in that. Getting a call as a truck operator was something special. The regular hauling jobs that came up—clearing lots for new retirement mansions, cleaning ditches for the Department of Highways—were passed around among the serious sand-and-gravel operators with never a nod of recognition in our direction. My sand-and-gravel partners, when they were around, kept the truck going on projects they always seemed to stir up on their own, but when they were away and I was holding the fort as I was now, the truck sat embarrassingly idle. I felt I was letting our side down, but the construction bunch just didn't want to talk to me. I suppose when any outsider stopping by Blueband Diesel mentioned the possibility of getting our truck on a job, some greasy fellow might say, "I think he's too busy writin' books, ain't he?" There would be sarcastic laughs, and that would be as far as it went.

You better believe I was tickled to be called about the truck. "Say, you got some kind of a truck, dontcha?" the gruff voice demanded.

"Yessir, that we do."

"Well, how would you like to have it up here in the morning?"

I was in the last stages of getting away a contract publishing job worth fifty thousand dollars, and even if they took the truck for a whole day, it couldn't be worth more than two hundred dollars. I was also sick. My padded leather chair was shiny with sweat and my heart was pounding and my mind kept evaporating and blowing out the window. It had gone on too long to be anything usual, and later in the month I would finally drag myself off to the doctor's and discover my metabolic system was going mad under the influence of an overactive thyroid, but at this point I was assuming it was all just something that came with turning forty-two. I could barely hold my pen. At the slightest exertion I would collapse in my chair, panting and shaking.

"Wh—what is it you want hauled?"

"Ha-ha. Whaddya think? Fish!"

"Er, how much?"

"Oh, I dunno, seven-eight totes. There's more comin' in all the time."

I knew it was insanity to consider doing this. Nobody who liked me expected it of me, and this guy seemed to be laughing at me even as he asked me to do it. I had made quite a public thing of doubting fish farms and their works, and had every reason to abandon them to their smelly fates, as all the other truckers apparently had. I also didn't have a valid licence. I had a Class 5 licence for driving cars, pickups and mopeds like most people, but for a truck of the Dodge's size you needed a Class 3. I used to have a truck driving licence, back when it was called a "C" licence—I was very proud of the fact I took my original driver's test in my dad's ten-yard Dodge tandem when I was a sixteen-year-old kid, but when they went from letters to numbers I somehow got downshifted. I had pointed this out to the Superintendent of Motor Vehicles in numerous letters, claiming protection under the grandfather clause, but so far I was losing the argument. My partners kept telling me to smarten up and go get a new one, but it was a matter of principle for me. I had been stopped by cops once or twice and they hadn't noticed this technicality, but they could. The fine was $2,500, but the real penalty was getting written up in "This Week In Court." It was just another thing that might have tipped the scales toward saying no to the fish plant.

This was just the sort of deal I could never refuse.

"Yeah, I'll be there," I said.

And of course immediately panicked. What am I, nuts? I asked myself. You can't fill a gravel truck with rotten fish. The slime would leak out the crack around the tailgate. But my mind was running ahead of me, patching the holes. I could buy a roll of 6-mil poly and line the box with that, maybe a double layer of it. It still might squeeze out at the back where the crack was an inch wide. I could jam a two-by-four in there, under the poly. What if the tail-gate unlatched under the weight and let ten tons of rotten fish out on the road? What would I say to my friends in the Save Our Scenery Society then? But if I pulled the chains tight, it would hold the gate shut even if the latch broke.

Conspiring with the enemy gave me a rare kind of thrill. I was a professional, and when a professional receives an honest request for his services, he answers the call. His personal politics stay out of it. There are limits of course—Eichmann went too far—but this little job wasn't going to affect the fish farm issue one way or another. I would come out of it a man with inside knowledge, a guy of substance—unlike the pencil-necks at soss. I would have the wisdom of Tiresias, the old seer with the dugs of a woman and the dork of a man, who lived both sides.

The truck started for me, and I made it up the twisty road to the fish plant only half an hour late.

"Hey—you came!" the foreman laughed. He was burly and bearded like an old antarctic whaler and obviously only half-expected me to show. "I'll back you in under the crane as soon as Fred gets unloaded." He met my eyes for the first time and his voice relaxed into a friendlier, fellow worker tone. "I...I guess loose fish will be okay in that truck, eh...?" It warmed my heart. I didn't expect to see him let his doubts show, not at this stage anyway, but seeing me standing there in front of him, nervous and weak from sweating, I guess it was too much for him. But I was on my way now, I didn't want sympathy.

"Oh yeah, I think so. I got a roll of poly and some boards to seal it up. Long as you don't fill me too full, most of it should stick." I don't think my breezy manner convinced him, but it gave him all the excuse he needed to go ahead. He broke into his tough grin again, and clapped me on the shoulder.

"That's the stuff! I knew you could handle it. Back that big bastard in there!"

I wasn't all that smooth with the truck because I had only driven it around The Bluff to blow the airhorn at the schoolkids. I'd never driven it loaded, and I'd never driven any diesel truck with a thirteen-speed transmission before. But I slid it back under the crane without grinding any gears or knocking over any sheds, and got out while they went about filling the Dodge's twelve-cubic-yard gravel box with rotten fish. I sweatily went over the checklist in my mind. I'd laid the board way across the back. I'd cut it two inches too short, but I'd jammed a square rock in the gap. I'd cinched up the chains as tight as I could. Must remember to unhook them before I dump. The poly was laid out and hanging over the sides, with dirt scattered around to hold it in place while they loaded me. I went upstairs for a coffee and leaned over the rail looking down on the operation, trying to look nonchalant. I was smart enough to know that if I hung around where the fish was, I'd end up with my hands in it. My goal was to get home without a single fish scale on me, or on the truck.

They had a bunch of broad-shouldered kids sluffing around, and the whaler fingered one up into the gravel box to handle the tote-dumping while he worked the crane. The totes were wooden boxes about a cubic yard big; and they lifted them with a sling around each side. They lowered them into the gravel box; then the kid would take the one sling off and they'd lift one side, spilling the tote over. At the first spill the kid doubled over and lost his breakfast. He crawled over the side, white in the face and refusing further service. The whaler looked around and picked another, bigger kid, a good-natured hulk I knew slightly who was on his first day. He slowly made his way up and got the spilled tote away, moving to a far corner of the box and fanning his nose between lifts. Then I saw why he'd been so slow to get in: he hadn't had time to buy gumboots and he was trying to get by the first day with flimsy plastic overshoes. It wasn't long before a look of horror came on his face and I looked down to see foamy pink fish juice pouring over the top of one overshoe.

He returned a sickly smile, then stepped right out of the shoe, plunging his white sock right into a pool of orange fish muck. He made a pathetic noise, and I put my fist to my forehead for him. I couldn't stand any more, so I went downstairs into the actual fish plant. It was just a big shed on the water's edge with totes piled up against one wall, a walk-in freezer, and across one whole end a long wetbench surrounded by about twenty-five slickered locals all hacking up fish with funny-looking blunt knives. I was surprised to see a lot of people who I knew to be strong critics of fish farms working there, including Cam Fisher, one of the table officers of soss.

"I didn't know you worked here," I said, amazed.

"I didn't know you did either," she replied, haughty.

"I guess there's nothing wrong with taking money off them," I said.

"I don't eat their fish, if that's what you mean. You wouldn't catch me dead eating this garbage," she said loudly, her voice ringing around the tin building as she splatted down a ratty-looking jack spring and zipped it open without looking. "None of us do."

Alexandra Burda illustration

There were murmurs of shy agreement along the line. Being mostly oldtimers, they felt salmon should be left the way God made them, and not squeezed into pens and force-fed like pâté de foie gras. When I saw Cam roaring at a forklift putting some boxes down in the wrong place, I realized she was actually inside foreman of the joint.

The truck was loaded with eight totes. I climbed up on top of the cab and looked at the damage. The whole gravel box was about half filled with dead fish, all lying this way and that. They didn't look that bad. It stank a bit, but it was the old smell of the coast. The load looked pretty stable. I folded the edges of the poly over the mess like a Christmas present and chucked some broken pallets on top to hold it down. There was a stream of pinkish juice the diameter of a pencil-lead draining out one corner of the box, but it looked like it was diminishing. There was nothing to do but put the truck in low gear and crawl up the steep driveway. I roared out of the yard and out of their lives into my own, carefully avoiding any jolts that might send dead fish sloshing over the tailgate. I took comfort in the fact this grade was probably the steepest I would have to handle on the trip, and the load made it up with no trouble. I pulled over every ten miles or so to see if anything was amiss, but nothing was. It might have been a load of clean drainrock I had in there. Even the little pencil-leak had disappeared.

It was going so well I decided to take it to the big dump in Sechelt, where it would be less noticeable than at the little Pender Harbour dump and also give me more truck time. It was a bit nervy driving that mess down the busy streets of Sechelt, right under the noses of fish farming's most dedicated opponents, but I slid through without a turned head, and up the hill to the dump. They had a special sump pit set aside for such unpleasantries, and I had gone to the trouble of clearing the load with the authorities, something nobody else bothered to do. I did this the night before, just in case I needed it. That's how good I was.

I even remembered to undo the chains holding the tailgate shut before I hoisted the dump up. I even fished the broken pallets out of the stew so they wouldn't go into the sump. Not that there would be any harm if they did, I just wanted to avoid even the chance of trouble. I wanted to be better than good. The exertion of lifting the pallets had me seeing red in a minute—reminding me for the first time I wasn't quite well—and I did get more than a few fish scales on me at last. But nothing serious. There was a man in a trench coat across the pit surreptitiously taking pictures of me, probably for the soss. I waved at him.

I made it home before 2 pm, hosed down the truck and went back to my thinking, feeling like a powerful instrument. Some sticky negotiations that had been holding up the fifty grand suddenly opened up for me, and I got on the phone to Ontario to close the deal before the people went out for the weekend, then phoned up the printer, got the price I was looking for from him, and set the deal in motion. I had been putting these closing moves off for weeks, but I'd come home from truck driving feeling the power.

The next day they called again. I was no less busy and felt no less ill, but agreed to go without hesitation. I made it on time this time. And went straight into the coffee room to wait for them to load. When I came out and looked down, I noticed two things. The truck was a lot fuller than the day before. And the stuff was a lot juicier. I only had about six inches of freeboard between the muck and the top edge of the gravel box. They had not only thrown in eight totes of very dead salmon from the farms; they had added six totes of offal—fish guts—from the processing plant. Old fish guts, which had been sitting around a week or more in warm weather. I didn't like it. They hadn't asked me. But what could I do now? Tell them to spoon it out? I should have stayed outside to watch, and stopped them half-full like the first time. I wrapped the plastic around, weighed it down like before, got in low gear and ground my way up the hill. I stopped at the top to look it over. Nothing had sloshed over the tailgate, although there were twin streams of pink fish juice the thickness of a cigarette squirting out each corner of the tailgate. I couldn't tell if they were diminishing or not, but I could tell they were really rank. This batch was much riper than the first one.

The old coast had never smelled liked this.

I worked my way over the twisty Egmont Road out to the highway and stopped for a look. The streams of fish juice were still squirting onto the road. The load itself seemed to have levelled off and kind of jelled. But it was all still there. I got underway, keeping a sharp eye behind me in the big side mirrors. A few miles down the highway, I began to notice little splashes of liquid flying out whenever I went around a corner. Then I began to notice it all the time, streamers of spray peeling off behind me as I motored along. A few cars passed the opposite way and I wondered what they saw. If someone came up behind me, they would probably get quite a surprise. I pulled over at the next wide spot.

The upper edges of the gravel box were glistening. The load looked wetter than it had when I started. The jostling of the road seemed to be breaking the stuff down. And somehow the poly had got pulled down into the soup so it was no longer sealing the big crack between the upper edge of the metal and the plank which made up the top eight inches of the gravel box, and every time the stuff surged a little going around a corner, it would splash out through the crack. Very gingerly I pulled myself up alongside the load and began trying to pull the poly back up where it belonged without getting any fish on me. I saw both of my knees turn dark as they touched the wetness. I inserted a couple fingers very delicately into the reeking muck, searching for the edge of the poly, but when I found it I couldn't get a grip. It was very slippery. I had to thrust both hands in to the wrist and rip hand-holds in the plastic. By the time I had it pulled up on both sides, my shirt front and my thighs were saturated with the oil and the stench of rotten fish. I spent a good many minutes scuffling in the dry grass on the side of the road trying to clean my shoes, but to little effect. When I climbed back into the cab, the smell was so strong I had to roll both windows down. It was so strong I soon lost the ability to smell anything, only a rawness in my nostrils and a fever on my brain.

Not ten miles farther on, I looked in the mirrors and saw ribbons of spillage once again trailing off behind me on both sides. My heart sank. I had to go back and put my hands in that rotten muck again. I looked for another wide shoulder and pulled over. The whole outside of the truck was now glistening with fish oil. The streams at the corners of the box had increased to the thickness of a cigar and had created sizable pools on the ground just in the first few minutes the truck was stopped.

I was starting to feel I would be lucky to get out of it this time around. I wished for the first time, but not the last, that I had turned off at the road to the Pender Harbour dump several miles back instead of making for Sechelt as before. I jumped up and plunged my arms into the gooey mess, no longer having anything to keep clean, and pulled the plastic cover up. When my eyes came to rest on the load of fish, I couldn't believe my eyes. When I had first started out, the load had looked mostly like fish. But as I drove and the rotting carcasses fell apart under the jostling of the road and mixed with the gooey offal, it came to look more like fish purée.

Now it looked like nothing I'd ever seen. I had to shake my head and blink my eyes. It was like a field of dandelions gone to seed. The entire fuming mass was bristling with little translucent globes. Hundreds of little pointy sacs waving in the breeze. It took me a minute to figure it out. These things were swim bladders. Each fish has this little bag it can fill with water to regulate its depth, and they're made out of some tough cellophany stuff that doesn't rot. As the rest of the fish parts broke down and went to mush, these little guys had become inflated with gas and floated to the top. It was a most hallucinatory sight, as if the load had suddenly burst into bloom. It disconcerted me. It heightened a sense of unreality that had already gone far enough.

I decided to get back on the road before the puddle of liquid fish under the truck got any bigger. As I drove I began to consider the implications of going through Sechelt with this steaming, dripping mess. Just waiting at the stoplight on Dolphin Street would result in a couple of gallons of rotten fish purée in the middle of the town's busiest intersection. The people in Pronto's restaurant would suddenly lose their appetite. The people in the office of the *Happy Shopper*, the pro–fish farm newspaper, would suddenly get a new perspective on the artificial fish issue. People would swarm round. It would be the event of the week.

The streamers of slime were out again. It was happening faster each time as the load became less and less stable. Going around one corner I glanced in the mirror and saw a little slosh of pink go over. If it kept getting looser, I might not be able to drive it at all pretty soon. I slowed down to 20 mph, 10 on corners. I might just make it to Sechelt in time to have it all go over the side—or suppose a pedestrian stepped in front of me and I had to make a hard stop. Tons of reeking pink glop would surge forward and go cascading up over the front of the truck, flattening the jaywalker and plugging every storm sewer for three blocks. The central core would be evacuated for days while cleanup crews worked overtime, all at my expense. Next week, banner headlines: Glop Truck Driver Had Wrong Licence. Court trials. Crippling expense. Disgrace. No one would ever talk to us again.

A car pulled up close behind me, then punched on its brakes and dropped back fifty yards or so.

I decided to turn around and take the load back to the Pender Harbour dump while I still could. It was no closer by this time, but it would save my having to go through any towns. The problem was to find a place on the narrow, twisting coast highway where I could swing this big bowl of jelly. It had to be level and wide, so I didn't spill the load…

Just then I came to the Election Section. The Election Section is a half-mile stretch of bad curves near Secret Cove, which the government has been promising to straighten for over ten years. Every election they give the local highways office a few thousand dollars to round up all the local contractors and make a show of doing something. Then on the day after the election they're all sent home, leaving the stakes to be torn out and the blasting holes to be silted up for another three years. At this point the Vander Zalm government was suffering at the polls so the Election Section was in business again. New clearings had been made on either side of the road, and a portable office trailer had been dragged in along with a water truck and a few government engineers in orange-and-white pickup trucks. To me it looked like a good place to turn around.

I geared the truck down and slowly reduced my speed to about 5 mph, then slowly eased the nose of the truck off the pavement into the clearing beside the office trailer. It bumped a little bit harder than I planned, but not very bad. I looked in the mirror and saw a flash of pink.

Lost a little juice, I thought. I'll get a hemlock branch and go brush off the pavement. I rolled gently to a stop, popped the maxi brake on and opened the door. There were a few fishtails and bits of flesh stuck to the side of the box, which I thought odd.

I walked around the rear end and looked behind.

My heart stopped.

For 100 feet the highway was covered with fish, fish heads, fish tails and bright orange mush. Both lanes were fully involved.

Some of the fish were whoppers.

And the little swim bladders were bobbing everywhere. Thousands of them, dancing, mocking me, in the hot sun. The car that had been following me at a safe distance was now stopped at the edge of the spill, and there was another behind it. I could see the driver shaking his head.

My heart was pounding like a runaway steam locomotive. I didn't know it, but the condition I had was giving me high blood pressure to start with. When I later had it diagnosed, I was solemnly warned to avoid excitement or sudden exertion lest I pop a blood vessel. This kind of stress was no doubt sending my reading off the scale. My ears were ringing. I was seeing red when I turned my head. But somehow I managed to stay upright. I waved the cars through, guiding them along the left-hand shoulder, clear of the mess. Then I got the shovel off the truck and started spooning the slop toward the ditch. I worked too fast and exhausted myself in seconds, making no discernible difference to the bubbling mass. Cars kept coming and interrupting me.

Then one of the government engineers showed up. He was a youngish chap wearing an orange plastic hard hat and carrying a clipboard. He had been over on the jobsite somewhere, doing his best to put in hours without any crew or equipment to boss. He kept looking at the road, then at me, then at his clipboard, as if he hoped to get some guidance from it. He didn't know what to say. Nothing like this had ever come up in engineering school. But I could see that he was determined to be uncooperative.

"What are you stopping here for?" he said. "You can't leave that stuff here."

"I just pulled in to turn around and spilled a little. I'm on the way to the dump," I said.

"Well I'm going to have to get some information," he said, rolling up a new page on his

Alexandra Burda illustration.

clipboard. Just then cars came shooting around the corner from both directions, braking hard as the vista of salmon chowder opened before them. I ran out to flag them through, one at a time. When I finished and picked up my shovel again, the engineer caught up to me with his clipboard.

"I'm going to need some particulars," he said.

"Look," I said, "we're going to have an accident here if we don't get the road clear. Why don't you let me take care of that, then I'll give you all the particulars you want." Another three cars came squealing to a halt and I had to rush over to signal them through. The drivers all looked sour and shook their heads with disapproval at me. I was the focus of all their anti–fish farm feelings. What am I doing here, I wonder, I kept musing. I should be at home quietly clicking my word processor, whispering pleasant assurances to elderly lady poets over the telephone. Will I ever get back there? Will I escape from this mess alive? My blood pressure was setting a new Olympic record.

The engineer had now come up with a new idea, which was to surround the spill with about three dozen fluorescent orange traffic cones. He encircled the spill completely, blocking both lanes off, so that traffic actually had nowhere to go. This created a very dangerous situation, since he made no attempt to guide the traffic, and within minutes I had to run through the muck waving my shovel to prevent a head-on collision between a rusted-out Volkswagen Beetle and a 36-foot Winnebago-with-everything, both trying to slip by on the far shoulder.

I looked at the engineer. "This is a bit dangerous, don't you think?" I asked.

"I don't want people running through your garbage," he retorted hotly. "I *live* here."

I couldn't quite follow his logic. I guess he was making some oblique reference to the fact fish farmers were outsiders, a lot of them, missing the point I'd lived in the area for thirty-eight years myself. I reckoned if it came to a head-on collision, most people would probably prefer to swerve through the spill and get a little rotten fish on their tires, but I didn't have the breath to argue. I began looking for something better than the shovel because I wasn't getting anywhere with the cleanup. A snow shovel would have been better, or just a plank I could lay down and push like a bulldozer. Beside the engineer's office trailer I spotted a heavy wooden rectangle used as a base for portable road signs. I walked over and grabbed it.

"Hey!" the engineer hollered. "We use that. I don't want you getting your, your...stuff all over it."

It was like the word "fish" had suddenly become unmentionable to him.

"I'll clean it up after," I said, walking past him and banging it down on the road. It made a pretty good bulldozer. A little rusty car stopped on the shoulder and a burly kid got out. He walked over to me with a grin on his face.

"You need a hand?" he said.

I couldn't believe my ears.

"Do I ever," I said, "but it ain't very pretty."

"Ha-ha, little bit of rotten fish never killed anybody," he chortled and grabbed the shovel. Between us we soon had most of the big lumps pushed over into the ditch, leaving only a smeared layer of virulent orange mud over a lane and a half of the road.

"What are we going to do with that?" he asked.

"Dunno," I said. "Maybe we could slosh it off with water, if we had water." I remembered the tank-truck parked beside the office trailer and hollered at the engineer.

"What's the chance of getting some water out of that truck?"

"What for?" he said.

"To clean up your road here before this shit gets baked in and you end up breathing it for the rest of the year," I said. That got his attention. He shuffled over to the truck and opened up a hatch alongside the tank.

"What have you got to put it in?" he said dubiously, still clutching his clipboard.

I couldn't believe my eyes. Under the hatch was a high-volume fire pump hooked to a coil of hose.

"Does that pump *run?*" I shouted.

"Of course it runs," he said.

"Well for Chrissakes, start it up and hose this road off before somebody gets killed! We could have had this road open half an hour ago with that thing!"

Sulkily, he gave the starter a pull and a two-inch jet of high-pressure water burst from the hose. He kept it himself, not wanting to trust unlettered persons with the operation of a government water hose, and within a few minutes had the road gleaming as blackly as if it was freshly paved. While he was carefully spraying off the sign stand, I jumped back in the truck and was out on the road before he noticed. I could see him waving his clipboard in the rearview mirror as I geared into high range. I figured there had just been time for the first cars that had passed through to reach the police station in Sechelt. Now, if I made straight for the Bluff dump as fast as I could go without spilling any more, I might just make it in half an hour. That would give the cops just time to make it back to the spill—depending how long they spent taking a statement.

I should just be able to make it.

The Indy 500 never seemed so long as that fifteen miles. I had to gear the truck up furiously on every bit of straightaway, trying to make time, but brake with enormous care coming into any corners, tender as a waiter with a three-tiered tray full of beer. Another spill of any size would be game over. It didn't help that my hands were shaking with fever and my oily shoes kept wanting to slip off the clutch and brake pedals. I spent as much time looking behind me in the rearview mirrors as I did ahead at the snaking road.

After an eternity I crawled into the dump, drove straight toward the hole up at the far end I'd already picked out in my mind, and put the hoist in gear. The sopping mess slid out the rear into the ground. No constipated sperm whale ever felt greater relief. The evidence was off the truck!

I turned and began rolling down the grade toward the exit.

At that moment a police cruiser came flying into the dump at the head of a huge plume of dust, raring over the potholes like a bucking bronco. It shot past me without making any sort of signal, so I kept on rolling toward the highway and home. The cruiser bounded up to where I'd let off the load, spun around in the gravel, peeled back toward me and put on the siren. I pulled over, popped the maxi and climbed down onto the road.

I was strongly moved to fall down on the ground and pour my sick heart out in the dust, but a tiny voice in the back of my head, barely audible over the pounding of my temples, was whispering, "Don't give it away, don't volunteer anything, act cool, you never know…" The cop walked up looking mean, until he got a whiff of the truck box, which twisted his face up like a prune.

"Wow!" he yelped.

"Bears love it," I laughed. This was a lie, in fact. It was a peculiarity we'd all observed over the past months that the one kind of garbage the dump's considerable scab-ridden army of bears wouldn't go near was fish farm garbage. It was their only taboo.

"Did you just unload a truckload of fish waste in this landfill?" the cop intoned in his cop-like way.

"Can't deny it," I grinned, reeking. "Yes, I did."

"And are you authorized to do that?"

"Yeah, I am," I said. His eyes were watering, and I moved closer to him where the wavy lines coming up off my fish oil–soaked pants would go right up his nose.

"Oh. We were told you weren't…" he said, backing away.

"Well, you just phone the works superintendent at the Regional District and he'll fill you in," I said. I was like ice inside, dreading the next request. If he uttered the words "driver's licence," I would collapse in a heap, my life over. But the wavy lines did their work.

"Okay, well, sorry to bother you," the cop said and hustled back to the car. I let him go on ahead.

It didn't matter.

It was still the worst day of my life.

OLD WOMAN

by Anne Cameron

Old Woman
is working
gathering
the frayed ends of dreams
the ravelled edges of hopes
re-weaving
your soul
Her face
this pale moonlit night
is sharp and spare
her eyes
deep shadowed hollows
her mouth
pursed and wrinkled
and as she weaves
she hums a salt sea melody
that tells of cedar and rock
and the twisted
granite-wood arbutus
clinging tenaciously to cliff face
perched above the crashing waves
gnarled and bent by hail
She does not
waste her time
in recriminations
She does not
waste your time
with sympathy
She hums her song
her gnarled-root fingers
weaving your mind
making whole again
your fabric of being

From The Annie Poems *(1987), by Anne Cameron*

WHISTLING SHITHOUSES
Queen Charlotte Airlines' Stranraer Fleet

Excerpted from The Accidental Airline: Spilsbury's QCA *(1994),*
by Howard White and Jim Spilsbury

Of all the queer collection of aircraft we assembled in the course of our bargain-hunting for aircraft we could afford, it is clear to me the one we'll be most remembered for is the gangling Stranraer, the "whistling shithouses" we set beating their ungainly way up and down the fog-shrouded cliffs of the BC coast, loaded to the gunwales with Chinese second cooks and Finnish chokermen chewing snoose. This is the image that comes to my mind most strongly when I recall the company's salad days, and I am happy to have it as our epitaph.

In a way this is very ironic, because as time went on we were all rather embarrassed about the Strannies and were never so proud of ourselves as the day we finally graduated to DC-3s and left the old flying boats behind us. We thought wow, we're a real airline now. The whole office came out and rolled up their sleeves to help wash and wax the first DC-3; even the cipher girls from accounting got in on the act. But the DC-3s don't remember very well—they just made us like every other airline. The Strannies made us unique. Of all the planes we flew, they had the most personality by far.

We have all read about old-time sailors and their many beliefs and superstitions, and how almost human personalities were associated with the ships they sailed in. Some ships were "lucky" ships and came through the worst storms and the worst battles unscathed.

Docking a Stranraer was always a
panicky manoeuvre.
*University of British Columbia, Rare
Books and Special Collections, Jim
Spilsbury fonds, box 24, plate 4-1*

Other ships were not so lucky and were forever becoming involved in one or another type of marine disaster, not necessarily related to the competence of the crews involved. There were some ships cursed with such bad reputations that owners had difficulty in getting crews to man them.

This sort of thing is not normally associated with aircraft, probably because of the very nature of their operation, and the frequency with which the flight crews are changed. A modern aircraft flies almost continuously, but changes crews every few hours. It may fly halfway around the world and back, and take aboard six or eight different crews in the process. Things just don't have a chance to get that personal anymore.

But in the early days of Queen Charlotte Airlines it was different. Any given aircraft would be doing well to average four to five flying hours a day. The rest of the time it would be in the shop being serviced, so it was not unusual for an aircraft to have only one pilot for long periods of time. Pilots would come to have their favourite aircraft, to which they preferred to be assigned. This probably was particularly the case with the Stranraers, since they flew only in daylight, and their entire flight crew of captain, first officer and flight engineer would stay with the machine for weeks at a time. So individual Stranraers soon took on personalities that stayed with them. Most were good—some not so good. CF-BYJ was a case in point.

I seem to recall that CF-BYJ was the third of all the Stranraers we bought. We originally had two—CF-BYI and CF-BYL—which we were using on the run to the Queen Charlotte Islands and Prince Rupert.

When BYL was lost on a mercy flight from Stewart it left us short, so we got BYJ and immediately flew her back to Montreal for conversion to a passenger plane. It was on this, her first flight, that she got into her first real trouble. On arriving in Montreal and attempting to land in the St. Lawrence River at the Vickers aircraft plant, just above the Lachine Rapids, the pilot, in trying to avoid the broken ice packs in the river, which was very low, taxied her right onto a submerged rocky reef, taking part of the bottom of the hull out and sinking her in shallow water. What was to be a fairly simple conversion now developed into a two-month repair job. To start with, getting her through the ice pack and up on the shore

was no simple task. A channel had to be cut through foot-thick ice with handsaws and, after getting her out, a large canvas and corrugated iron shelter had to be built over her so she could be thawed out and the hull rebuilt. Fortunately we were able to get our old friend Albert Racicot to do the job, and he had access to materials and spare parts. We also sent one of our crew chiefs, Curly Nairn, and another mechanic from Vancouver to oversee and assist.

Finally she was ready to go, and just like new. The ice had almost gone from the river and one of the local types undertook to pilot her out into the main channel. *Carunch!* and she had a new hole in her bottom. The French pilot waved his arms around and claimed that the river bottom was all changed since the thaw! Who

The *Skeena Queen* (CF-BYL), last seen circling Prince Rupert on August 31, 1946.

Harbour Publishing Archives

knows, maybe he was right, but it took another three weeks to get her ready the second time, and she finally arrived in Vancouver after taking the Deep South route via Mississippi, Texas and California. Once out on the coast she was put right to work, and we bought two more Stranraers, BYM and BXO, just to make sure.

Incidentally BXO was the last of the Strannies left whole out of the lot. She was the only Strannie left whole in the whole world apparently, because in the 1970s when the Royal Air Force was looking for an intact copy to complete its collection of historical military aircraft at the Hendon air museum outside London, they came to BC and glommed BXO from a group of antique plane buffs and took her back to the old country in pieces. I visited her there in 1984, all painted in RAF colours as if she had never been built for the RCAF in Montreal or had a glorious career flying for QCA at all. I tried to bring this to the attention of the museum officials but they obviously didn't believe a word I said.

I felt badly about this, but I didn't say anything because who would understand? Here in the west we have a very tenuous sense of history, and even when we do end up staring it in the face we think it's just our own personal history, of no significance to the world. But it was surprising how many people came up to me and expressed indignation that the Brits had scooped the last living Stranraer on us and stuck it in their museum when it should have been in ours. Still, how could we really complain? A few of these flying history buffs, including the filmmaker and sometime TV weatherman Bob Fortune, had tried to raise enough money to keep BXO here and hadn't been able to. As recently as the 1970s the awareness that this old plane might represent something worth saving still hadn't really developed in BC. For a number of years it just seemed we had been too slow off the mark and lost our chance to preserve what the Strannie represented, until BYJ changed that. But I'm getting ahead of my story.

After her second sinking in Montreal, BYJ got back home and flew the line relatively routinely for a few months. I say relatively because this plane couldn't seem to go two weeks together without throwing something at us. One hot summer day in 1947 the boys were welding up a crack in her exhaust ring just outside our rented TCA hangar on Sea Island when a spark went the wrong way and something started burning. In the time it took to grab the nearest fire extinguisher and hose down the flames, three wing panels had been destroyed, at a replacement cost of $12,500. The incident also convinced TCA we weren't the type of neighbour they wished to have sharing their classy digs and they threw us out, leaving us without adequate covered work space for several months. It was perhaps around this time BYJ got her nickname. We had been in the habit of naming all our aircraft "Something-or-other Queen." The *Skeena Queen*, the *Nimpkish Queen*, the *Haida Queen*, and so on. BYJ spent so much time in maintenance she was dubbed the *Hangar Queen*.

Then she encountered her third sinking, and this was a dilly.

It started as a regular scheduled flight from Vancouver to Zeballos, via Gold River, Tahsis and Ceepeecee. Andy Anderson was the pilot with Bill Oliver, co-pilot, and "Boost" Coulombe, flight engineer, and there was one passenger aboard when she came in for a landing at Ceepeecee on a grey February morning, with reduced visibility in sleet and rain.

Strannies CF-BYI and BXO docked at Sullivan Bay.
University of British Columbia, Rare Books and Special Collections, Jim Spilsbury fonds, box 20, QaCA-1

The approach was normal, but right after touchdown she struck a partly submerged hemlock deadhead, with the top barely breaking water, ripping a five-foot gash in the bottom of the hull. The flight engineer saw what had happened and yelled at Andy to pour on the coal and keep her steaming for the closest beach. Andy opened the taps and bumped her as far as she would go up on the clam beach in front of the cannery, where she settled immediately in about five feet of water.

Andy said that locals appeared from behind every stump. Just before going up on the mud, they had passed a small boat with two people in it and had practically swamped it with the waves they made. It turned out that the boat contained our one outbound passenger, who had engaged an Indian dugout to take him out to the aircraft. When the plane roared right on by, the anxious passenger thought he was going to miss the flight and urged the oarsman to "Follow that plane." When the plane stopped, the passenger jumped right in through the open door with his suitcase and landed up to his waist in water inside the hull.

"It's okay, Mac," Andy said, "we're not going anywhere right now!"

Our inbound passenger didn't fare much better. He had been standing up in the aisle when the plane touched down, and when she hit the deadhead, a great stream of water and wood chips hit him square in the chest, filling his eyes and mouth and soaking him to the skin, but he took it all as part of his day's work. He was an official log scaler, employed by the BC Forest Service, on his way to the camp at Tahsis to scale some timber. According to the story our crew told, he just mopped his face off and spat out the water and wood chips, but he stopped to chew on a particularly large sliver of hemlock. Then he spat it out and shook his head, commenting to himself, "Just Number Two Common. Must be out of the cull boom."

The first word of the mishap reached us in Vancouver by radio, but the message was, of necessity, very meagre and completely lacking in detail. It just said BYJ suffered slight damage at Ceepeecee and suggested that our superintendent of maintenance, Charlie Banting, come over and take charge. We should have been better informed, but it was by now company policy to say as little as possible on the radio, since too many people were listening and if Carter Guest got hold of it there would be no end of complications. As it was, the mere suggestion of needing Charlie Banting confirmed our suspicion that all was not well.

It was quickly decided that John Hatch would fly over with a Norseman, taking Charlie Banting, another mechanic and lots of tools; Johnny thought I should go too—just in case there were any higher politics involved. We arrived the same afternoon. It was a dismal sight. The tide had come in to cover the entire hull and cockpit. Only the wings and tail structure were above water. There was still intermittent rain and snow.

Our first problem was to provide enough flotation to get the aircraft up on the beach as far as we could, so we could work on the hull when the tide dropped. There was a lot of talk about air bladders, which we didn't have, and oil drums, which are hard to harness. My contribution at this point was to visit the local logging camp and arrange to borrow two large spruce logs, which we got a fisherman to tow into the bay for us. Then we borrowed a lot of heavy rope from the fishing company. When the tide went down we floated these logs under the lower wings, one on each side, and then passed the rope over the logs and under the hull many times to make a sort of rope cradle. When the tide came in she gently raised off the

After the crash at Ceepeecee, CF-BYJ was refloated with the aid of two logs. The photo at left shows the aircraft with the first log in place. The photo at right shows the aircraft with the second log in place. Ropes joining the two were used as a cradle to help float the hull.

University of British Columbia, Rare Books and Special Collections, Jim Spilsbury fonds, box 24, plate 7-2 (left) and 7-3 (right)

bottom, and we were able to move her ashore so that on the next low tide she was high and dry on the beach. We of course released the rope slings and floated the logs out as the tide fell. Low tide was around midnight, and it gave us a total of about three hours to repair the hole in the hull. It was about five feet long and a foot wide.

At this critical moment in history we were joined by a very useful chap who was travelling for the Standard Oil Company, doing repair and maintenance work on their marine refuelling stations. He was a marine engineer by trade and had a wealth of experience in ship salvage work. He offered his help and we decided to go along with his suggestions. It was very simple: plug the hole with concrete. We didn't think it would set in time, but he had an answer for that. You mix caustic soda with Portland cement and use boiling water, and this would set up in half an hour, he said. The canners had both the caustic soda and the Portland cement, so we were in business. All we had to do was dig our way under the bottom of the hull and screw on a large sheet of galvanized iron to act as a retaining form while the concrete set. It all worked just like the man said, and the morning's high tide floated her off high and handsome. It never leaked a drop.

Telling about it now makes it sound so easy, but the undertaking had its moments. Bear in mind that the actual patching job was carried out at night with the aid of a borrowed Coleman gas lantern, and with a chilling mixture of rain and sleet coming down. Charlie Banting came from Manitoba, and he didn't mind cold weather or snow, but he hated rain. He was still wearing his prairie-style overcoat. It was very thick and heavy, came down to his ankles, and the collar turned up around his ears. But it was not rainproof, and during that night it must have taken on about twenty pounds of water. It sagged right to the ground like a tent, and Charlie could hardly move in it. The hem bulged out with water. Charlie was standing holding the lantern while Boost was lying on his back under the hull in a trench we had dug in the clam bed, working with a hand drill, fastening this large piece of galvanized iron to the hull with PK screws.

The trench was only about a foot deep and had filled with water, and Boost hardly had room to turn under there. Then I noticed something peculiar. Every now and again the

With her new concrete bottom, CF-BYJ is ready to fly once again. *University of British Columbia, Rare Books and Special Collections, Jim Spilsbury fonds, box 24, plate 7-1*

steady stream of water running into the trench would suddenly swell to a subdued gush, and I noticed bits of paper mixed in with the dirty water. I began tracing this stream uphill with my eye, and a few feet up the beach I spotted the partly covered outlet of the cannery building sewer. Every time someone flushed a toilet, poor Boost got a soaking. It was running in the neck of his Mackinaw shirt and out his pant legs.

I pointed this out to Charlie and commented that we couldn't have picked out a worse spot on the whole beach. He looked things over slowly, with the rain running off the end of his nose, and then looked at me over the top of his glasses.

"Wahl," he drawled. "You cain't have everything *absolutely* perfect."

In the morning she was floating like a cork—no water coming in. All seats, floorboards and lining had been stripped out of her. All the wiring in the hull and all the instruments in the cockpit had been under water and ruined, but fortunately the engines in a Stranraer are mounted in the upper wing and this had been ten feet above water, so they were undamaged. The only question was how to start them. The wiring that ran the electric starters was out of commission and there was no way to crank the engines. This was no problem for our Charlie. He moored the Strannie alongside a log float. Then he got a fisherman's gumboot and made a fifty-foot length of rope fast to it. He had someone climb up and slip the boot over the upper propeller blade of the far-side engine. Then he commandeered four enthusiastic locals and got them on the other end of the rope. He signalled to Andy for prime, and "Switch-On," yelled "PULL YOU BASTARDS!" and they did. The old engine fired first pull, the process was repeated with the near-side engine and Andy was on his way back to the hangar and a third new bottom for BYJ.

Up to this point no one had been hurt in any of BYJ's tantrums, but a very definite pattern was emerging. In all three incidents sinking was involved, and in all cases snowy, icy weather was a factor. The fourth and final episode was true to form as far as sinking and snowy weather were concerned, but this time there was no happy ending. In retrospect, it was just as though old BYJ was trying to tell us something and we wouldn't listen, so finally she threw the book at us.

It was Christmas Eve 1949; the weather—reduced visibility in wet snow. Pilot Bill Peters

Jim Spilsbury aboard his yacht, *Blithe Spirit*, in his later years. *Harbour Publishing Archives*

was heading north from Sullivan Bay with four passengers. While landing in the little bay in Belize Inlet–Alison Sound where Oscar Johnson's floating logging camp was then located, something went wrong: just after touchdown, as Bill started his "round out" at about seventy-five miles per hour, the nose dug in, sheered sharply to the right and the big machine executed a complete cartwheel. The whole nose section of the hull broke off. Bill got thrown through a hatch but was fouled in the wreckage and dragged partway to the bottom before struggling free. Co-pilot Jack Steele and flight engineer Sig Hubenig were momentarily stunned but managed to recover in time to swim out through the break in the hull. Two passengers, Gordon Campbell and Gordon Squarebriggs, were able to save themselves but the other two, Ralph McBride and John Buckley, were pulled down and drowned. The ship sank in three minutes with only the very tip of the upper wing showing. Oscar and his crew were able to get a line round it, and dragged it to the surface with a boom-winch to remove the bodies of Buckley and McBride, who were still strapped into their seats. We theorized that they might have got out if their safety belts had not been fastened, and for this reason we generally advised seaplane and flying-boat passengers to leave their belts unfastened during takeoff and landing, but to secure them in flight in case of turbulent air. After this, Oscar lifted the wreck out with a logging donkey and A-frame, and piled it on the beach.

I am not a superstitious person, but by the time I was finished with BYJ I had almost become one. Her ghost lay quiet for thirty-five years.

In September 1981 I was taking an extended cruise up the BC coast with three friends, all of whom were already previously well acquainted with the coast but, like me, always willing to see more, so this was one of our "Voyages of Adventure and Discovery" in the good ship *Blithe Spirit*, which I had purchased after I left aviation. None of the other three had ever heard of BYJ, and I had no idea that there was anything left to see or on what part of the sixteen hundred miles of shoreline in the Seymour Inlet complex it might be.

We had been looking for a suitable spot to set our prawn traps, but after about twenty miles it was still too deep so we decided to find a spot to anchor for the night. The Seymour Inlet group had not yet been charted, so we were quite on our own. It was about 10 pm, and after crawling along with both echo sounders running we found our way into a narrow entrance. We felt our way through several right-angle turns, located a secluded bit of channel in which we were able to get our anchor down in a convenient twelve fathoms of water, and secured for the night. In the process of positioning the ship I had been sweeping the shoreline with the searchlight, and in doing so had picked up an unidentified object on the beach that might well have been the wreckage of an old building or something. In the

morning I put the binoculars on this object and my spine just turned to ice. I launched the dinghy and rowed ashore before the others were up, and there it was: the remains of CF-BYJ, covered with moss and seaweed, but with part of the QCA speed-line and name still readable in black and yellow on the side of the hull. The spectre of Christmas Eve 1949 back to haunt me! Scavengers had been at it but, Belize Inlet being uncharted, it is not frequented by either pleasure boats or commercial fishermen, and the wreckage was still recognizable as a Stranraer. Some of the parts were remarkably well preserved.

In 1983 a tug, scow and crane owned by Bill Thompson of Pender Harbour picked up all that was left of BYJ with the intention of rebuilding it at the Canadian Museum of Flight in Langley, where Thompson was a founder.

Subsequent to the publication of this story, and due to a lack of storage space and funds at the museum, restoration efforts were stalled and the remains of BYJ languished at Bill Thompson's property for several decades. However, recently BYJ was moved to the Shearwater Aviation Museum in Nova Scotia, where volunteers are hoping to restore this historic aircraft. —Ed.

Former Queen Charlotte Airlines ship CF-BXO on display at Hendon's Royal Air Force Museum in London, England. She is painted in Royal Air Force colours despite having been built for the Royal Canadian Air Force in Montreal and having enjoyed a glorious career flying for QCA.
Harbour Publishing Archives

20

CLOSE CALL WITH A GRIZZLY

Excerpted from Grizzlies & White Guys: The Stories of Clayton Mack *(1996),*
compiled and edited by Harvey Thommasen

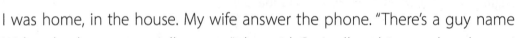

I was home, in the house. My wife answer the phone. "There's a guy name Walmark who want to talk to you," she said. So I talk to him on the phone. I know the guy, I seen him before. He came here once before that. He said he had two guys who want to hunt grizzly bear in Kimsquit. "It's okay," I said. "Sure, come in."

They came in, fly in an airplane to Bella Coola. They get in my pickup. They get out a gun case. Nice gun case. They open it, there was a nice little gun in there. They said they didn't know how accurate it was or if it was any good for grizzly bear. I asked him, "What calibre is it?" .350 Remington Magnum. Short rifle. That gun kick like hell. Uses shells that aren't very long, but they big around—thick. Them guys want me to use it, they want me to tell them how good it is for grizzly bear, and write down where I hit them grizzly bear. Then they want me to send them a report, tell them how good the gun is.

"Okay," I said. I asked him how much that gun was. "About seven hundred dollars in the store," he said. But it was special made for me. Short barrel, my name on shoulder mount: "First class guide—Clayton Mack."

I took them to Kimsquit. George Anderson, my son-in-law, came with me as my assistant guide. We took two hunters out the first day, got two grizzly bears. George got one, I got one. And then I took this guy, he was the youngest of the bunch. I took him quite a ways up the river. Lot of grizzly bear up there. Lot of fish spawning up there. And he shot at one grizzly bear. Gut-shot it, I guess, shot it through the stomach. We try and look for him, we see the blood all right, but we couldn't find him. George, he doesn't like guys like that, who gut-shoot the bears. He don't like to take them out. I try to tell George, "You take him out."

"No, you take him out," he said. "That bear was very close and he gut-shot him. Make the bear mad."

So we decided I would take that young guy out the next day. We finish skinnin' them two grizzly bears we got and then took the skins down to the boat. Spread them and salt them down.

We still got to get one more bear for this young guy. I took him up by myself the next day. I went up the Kimsquit River about a mile. There is a side stream, breaks in from the main river. Right close to the mountain. Trees are all small here, biggest about a foot through. I walked through some trees and came to a riverbed. A little water in there. A few fish in there, few dog salmons. I saw a bear go into the timber, I saw him walking. This young hunter was pretty clumsy. Noisy, clumsy, fall down and get his gun barrel stuck in the mud. You have to take that mud out of the barrel or else it blow open. He don't seem to care. I tell him to be care-

Clayton Mack at Kwatna in 1940.
Courtesy of Cliff Kopas

ful, he's going to ruin his gun. They told me later, "He has too much money, he doesn't give a damn what he does to his gun. Got so much money, he don't care." He was so clumsy I was worried he might get hurt.

There was a logjam. I put him in there. "You stay right here, I'll go back down and chase the bear up toward you. When he comes out of the woods there, shoot him," I said. I went down, walk down the river. I thought I was quite a bit below the bear now. That grizzly, he's behind me now I thought. So I went in the timber and started yelling like you chase cattle, *Ai, ai, ai!* I walk up, I don't see any sign of fresh bear track. Lot of old tracks. I was about

Alistair Anderson illustration

a hundred yards to the guys when I heard something behind me. *Woof, woof, woof.* Every jump she make, she made that noise.

I look back and saw a pretty good-sized grizzly bear coming toward me. I had this brand new gun. I stop and stand still. She keep coming, I didn't shoot right away. She stop about twenty, twenty-five feet away, and she stand up on her hind feet. About eight feet tall. Then she walk toward me on her hind feet. Look like she was gonna try and grab me up. I lift the gun up, try and shoot her in the chest. That gun slip. Barrel slide up her chest, and go off. Shot her under her chin, above her neck. She fell down, touched me a little bit on my leg. Dead. Big gun. I look at it. It was a sow, a female.

I stand there, and I hear sticks breaking, noises where this bear came from. Sound like a person blowin' their nose. He snorting. I look back, by God, I see another grizzly bear coming. Running toward me. This time I run. I run as fast as I can. There was a riverbed—ditch, like—about six feet deep. I jump down into it, I slide down on the bank, like, and hit the bottom. No water, dry riverbed.

I look up. It was a young grizzly bear, about four year old, I guess. Stand right there, right on top of his mother. He put his foot on her and he look at me. Pret' near as big as the other. Pretty big, too. I look beside me, there was a hole under the ground. It was a bank, overhanging bank. Flood, I guess, washed out quite a bit under the bank.

I look up and see that bear start circling around toward me. Joe Edgar told me that's a bad sign. Means he's a real bad bear. I shot the mother, you see, so he was mad at me. He wants to come after me. I thought, "He's gonna jump down." Gun loaded. I go under the bank. I hear the bear on the overhang, over my head. That bugger come right on top. That overhang roof about ten inch thick. I was afraid the overhang bank would break and bury me alive. The bear could smell me underneath here. I stayed in there looking up. Like a roof over me. I waited. If he comes down, I shoot. But he didn't, he was still on top of me, on the overhang.

He smell me, try and put his head down little bit once. Then he reach, try and put his hand down to feel for me. Then he came down with both front legs, try and feel for me underneath there. I see yellow jackets then, comin' out of his hair. They buzz all over me. The air was yellow with yellow jacket bees. I was scared to move too much. If I run that grizzly bear will get me; if I stay, I get stung. Then he came down, slide down, in an awkward way, like. He came down with his head down and then I see his jaw. I see his whole head is over toward me now. I shot him right between his jaw. I just about touch him, then I pull the trigger of that short .350 magnum rifle. *Bang!* He keep still there, I think I got him.

Clayton Mack with a grizzly bear, 1965.
Courtesy of Cliff Kopas

Talk about yellow jackets! Buzzing and flying all over. I came out of there, walked a little bit and climbed up the bank. I got on top of the bank and walked back toward the bear. I put my foot on the bear, spread the hair apart. He was just yellow inside the hairs. I guess he been raiding a yellow jacket nest. They like that, to eat the nest of yellow jackets. Lot of honey in that, and young yellow jackets.

I was standing there looking at all those yellow jackets in that bear when I heard something again, coming. I think, "Another bear coming. Must of had two young ones—two full-grown young bears." I started to yell at him, "Go on, beat it, I don't want to kill you." I went down little bit back to that clumsy guy. He asked, "What did you shoot?"

"Two grizzly bears," I said. "They try and get me. Come on, let's go look at 'em." He came over with me. That other third bear was still there. Sitting beside the mother. I heard my walkie-talkie, somebody talking on the walkie-talkie. They heard me shooting from the boat. They asking who shooting. I said, "A bear try and go after me." My son-in-law told me, "Better get out of there." We went down for the night.

We eat, had breakfast. Then went back up with the jet boat to skin them bears. We skin the mother, no yellow jackets on it. Just the young one. We try and skin the young one but you can't touch it. Not for the yellow jackets under the hair. They come fly in your face. So we drag that grizzly bear to the boat, sink him in the water to drown the yellow jackets, then we can skin him. I never seen anything like it. Just yellow inside the skin.

21 TRIANGLE ISLAND

Excerpted from Keepers of the Light *(1985, 1990), by Donald Graham*

While they watch winter winds scale shingles off their roofs, lighthouse keepers from Race Rocks to Green Island on Alaska's doorstep can always console themselves with the maxim: "It could always be worse, we could be at Triangle Island." Triangle Island light was the worst ever. In the annals of West Coast navigation the very name conjures up savage weather, disaster and death—complete and utter triumph of the elements over mankind. Established with a gush of enthusiasm under an ill omen in 1910, crowned with the worst calamity in the Department of Marine and Fisheries' history, Triangle would be abandoned as its costliest blunder ten years later.

Maritime events were always hot news in Victoria. When readers opened the *Colonist* or the *Times*, they first turned to the "Marine Notes" or "Shipping News" columns, which heralded arrivals and departures and served up lurid accounts of wrecks. Reporters were permanent fixtures in the outer offices of the marine agency down on Wharf Street, constantly hectoring the agent and his underlings for scraps to carry back to their editors. They could also be found at any time of day down on the docks, rubbing shoulders with burly stevedores, notebooks at the ready as they waited for ships' officers and crew to disembark.

Late in the afternoon of June 23, 1909, their patience paid off when the lighthouse tender *Quadra* lumbered up to the government pier, home at last from laying plans for the "ultimate lighthouse." H.C. Killeen, the man of the moment, came down her gangplank and regaled them with an account of how he had staked out a site on Triangle Island—forty-two miles northwest of Cape Scott, 650 feet above the sea—for a powerful first-order light which he was sure would "ultimately develop into one of the most important lighthouses on this coast." Rightfully predicting the "great development" of steamship traffic, the engineer declared that Triangle Island would serve as "a leading light which will be first picked up by the steamship captains and will give them their bearings whether they are bound for Puget Sound or Prince Rupert."

Triangle, as a special *Colonist* Sunday supplement exalted, stood out as "the furthermost western point of the Empire." It was the opposite bookend of British imperialism to Bombay's great gateway to India: a malevolent cone-shaped crag which had escaped the Ice Age, lurching out of the waves in flagrant, baiting challenge to the Marine Department's chief engineer, W.P. Anderson. After Anderson's heady architectural triumph at Estevan Point, there was nowhere to go but up. And what kudos might come from humbling that awesome outpost, five times higher, destined one day to become "the key to wireless communication on the Pacific"! Crowning it with one of his distinctive concrete phalli would surely propel him into the ranks of his heroes—Great Britain's Stevenson, Douglas and Halpin, the greatest lighthouse builders of all time, men who counted Eddystone and Skerryvore among their brainchildren. In a heated meeting on March 5, 1909, other members of the Lighthouse Board tried in vain to dissuade him, suggesting he build on Cape Scott, a more accessible site at the northern tip of Vancouver Island, instead. Their chairman was having none of that.

It was one thing to draw the plans but quite another to translate them into steel and concrete on the cutting edge of a ceaseless hurricane. Gales howling down the Hecate Strait and Queen Charlotte Sound linked arms with storms swirling in like dervishes from the open Pacific to collide with Triangle Island. Jet-force winds crashing up its steep flanks enveloped the summit in updrafts from every point on the compass at once. Straining at her anchor chains in the heaving grey sea, ss *Leebro* disgorged supplies and gangs of navvies in workboats that summer.

They laid a ton and a half of steel rails that climbed 1,820 feet up the rock face to a winch and donkey engine above.

During their off-hours the workers explored the island. Crawling into a cave near the

The light station at the forbidding summit of Triangle Island.
Courtesy of the Canadian Coast Guard

shore one evening, they held up their lanterns and recoiled in horror from a skeleton sprawled against the dripping rock wall, leering back at them, clad in a battered lifebelt and gumboots. No one ever uncovered the identity of the hapless "sentinel of Triangle Island," only that he was a white man who had somehow made his way ashore years before. After an eerie lamplit ceremony, Captain Freeman of the halibut vessel *Flamingo* interred his bones in the cavern, but not before a radio operator with a grotesque sense of humour tucked the skull under his arm as a souvenir.

Up on top of Triangle, the crouching workers dug, drilled and blasted water cisterns, and framed a duplex dwelling and wireless shack. Fierce winds pried shingles and siding off almost as fast as the men nailed them down. Carpenters harnessed in safety belts hammered up forms for the tower, then mixed, poured and tamped the concrete. Once stripped, the tower stood forty-six feet tall. For three months they battled the shrieking gales to haul up and wrestle fifty-two half-inch-thick curved panes into place around the huge beacon room. Some days the battering wind vibrated putty out of the frames faster than it could set. The iron lantern chamber was braced inside with stout beams, and anchored by cables and turnbuckles to the rock.

The first decade of this century seemed to promise that all Nature would be subjugated, bent to man's will through an enlightened partnership of labour, capital and technology. Encyclopedias of the day portrayed a universe understood in all its complexity. This was the age of the *Titanic*, after all, the crowning era of steam and steel. In November 1910, the *Colonist* proclaimed in shouting capitals "TRIANGLE LIGHT IS SHOWN NOW," echoing Killeen's confidence in "the largest and most powerful of North Pacific Coast lights." And so it was. Its gargantuan lens, an identical twin to Estevan's, with outer prisms nine feet in circumference, rumbled around on a tub filled with nine hundred pounds of shimmering mercury, and focused a million-candlepower light from the kerosene wick through its bull's eye in a slender cone that stretched fifty miles out toward Japan.

Back on Triangle, however, huddling out of the barbarous winds' reach, lightkeepers and radio operators looked down in disbelief upon the furrowed banks of cloud and fog, while mariners underneath searched in vain for the mighty flash in the night. The light was too high. As ugly rumours piled up, Colonel Anderson came west to inspect Pachena, Estevan and Triangle, all built since his last tour of inspection. If he had any reservations about Triangle, he kept them carefully to himself.

Life soon became unbearable for the tiny colony, which inherited the dubious concrete achievement of Anderson's obsession. James Davies took over the station in July 1910 with his wife and three daughters. His assistant, A. Holmes, and the two wireless operators, Jack Bowerman and Alex Sutherland, doubled as schoolteachers.

Every hour after dark, Holmes or one of the Davies family had to climb the tower and wind up the counterweights, which spun the monster lens until they hit the floor. Sleep was often impossible thanks to the shrieking gales and the constant "evil lament of the huge sealions." Seven-foot deposits of guano rendered Triangle's soil so caustic that it burned like lye and rotted leather boots. Occasional halibut, dropped off by sympathetic fishermen, were the only relief from their monotonous fare of canned food, but approaching and landing at Triangle was always a perilous venture. Davies once tried to enhance his family's

The tramway at Triangle looked like the world's worst roller coaster.
Courtesy of the Canadian Coast Guard

diet by ordering a large consignment of apples, oranges, bananas and vegetables. When the *Leebro* unloaded, the precious cargo oozed out from under thirty tons of coal. Two apples and half a banana survived. They tried keeping chickens and a cow, but the animals were driven over the cliff by the wind.

Since isolation magnifies trivia to gigantic proportions, it was hardly surprising that men confined under such abysmal conditions would turn upon each other, snarling like rats in an overcrowded laboratory. A dispute over a ton of coal soon escalated, on that wind-scoured outpost, to fisticuffs. When word of the rumpus reached Victoria, an exasperated Captain Robertson, the new marine agent, issued standing orders to Davies: "You and your family...have no communication whatever with the wireless Station on Triangle Island, except when business necessitates it." The navy's Radio Telegram Branch reinforced the shaky truce with similar instructions to their men, so the people manning the very nerve centre of Pacific communications lived next door to one another, incommunicado.

In February, James Davies called next door "on business" and sullenly handed the operators a message for Victoria: "MRS. DAVIES DANGEROUSLY ILL SOME TIME PAST, BAD HAEMORRHAGE CANNOT STOP, ESTEEM IT A FAVOUR IF VESSEL SENT DIRECT AS MATTER IS SERIOUS." Captain Robertson wired his superintendent of lights aboard the tender *Newington*. Gordon Halkett in turn ordered Captain Barnes "to proceed with all despatch to the station."

As she plied her way full speed toward Triangle, a freak wave overtook the *Newington*, poured over her fantail, filled her decks to the rails, twisted and wrenched out steam pipes, and swept away all the deck cargo. Cringing in terror, the crew clutched railing and

The supply ship *Newington* almost sank as the result of a freak wave during an emergency evacuation at Triangle.
City of Vancouver Archives, BO P397

bulkheads, and held its collective breath as water rose chest-high. The ship shuddered, then rose groaning from her grave under tons of the North Pacific.

Once at Triangle, Halkett leaped from the workboat, scaled the tramway and found Violet Davies up at the house, "very weak from loss of blood." The deckhands lashed her to a mattress and lowered her down to the beach. They had a tough time hoisting her up the side and over the rails "owing to the *Newington* rolling badly." Halkett brought a doctor aboard at Alert Bay and he urged the superintendent to waste no time getting her to hospital. Fifty-six hours later, an operator came across to Davies' house to tell him his wife had arrived safely in Victoria.

After signing on for two-month stints at Triangle, radio operators were often marooned, still living out of their suitcases a year later, bitterly complaining they had been "shanghaied." Even when, at long last, a ship came smoking over the horizon, weeks would slip by while the crew gambled their wages away, waiting for safe landing conditions. While their mother ship cut lazy circles offshore, workboats often stood little chance of abetting the islanders' escape, swamping in the surf and beating their way back to the tender.

The buildings atop Triangle looked like shrivelled bugs, snared and sucked dry in a spider's web of cables and turnbuckles fastened into deadeyes grouted into the rocks. All the buildings were linked by cables—lifelines with burrs that sliced cruelly into fingers and palms. Even so, the dwellings teetered and swayed on their foundations so violently that their occupants became seasick. Windows bulged inward like lenses before they shattered. As a matter of routine, no one ever opened a door alone. Men grovelled along on hands and knees between the buildings. To vacuum her house, Violet Davies needed only to open

Left: The huge first-order light shone in vain
above Triangle's fog.
Courtesy of the Canadian Coast Guard

Above: The telegraph operator's dwelling with makeshift
bracing against Triangle's hurricane-force winds.
Courtesy of the Canadian Coast Guard

a window. The wind barged down chimneys and through walls to snuff out fires and spew billowing clouds of soot through the houses. Everything on the station stood poised to rush over the cliffs to the raging sea 608 feet below.

On October 22, 1912, the anemometer registered 120 miles per hour before the wind, furious at having its temper recorded, ripped it from its mounts, then assaulted the buildings, cleaving off six brick and iron chimneys at the roofline. A shed leapt off its foundation next to the tower and fled, somersaulting end-over-end over the side into the sea. The wireless mast snapped like a straw, cutting off all communications. Down on the beach the raging surf reduced two storehouses to kindling. The two-ton donkey engine for the tramway crawled several feet away from its base.

Praying and shouting encouragement to one another, the two radio operators crouched in their dwelling like lunatics sharing a padded cell, becoming hysterical when the gale bashed in their windows and yanked the flapping doors off their hinges. The house shuddered and split in two. The attic water tank ruptured, flooding all the rooms. Preferring James Davies' company to the prospect of staying to be crushed, they inched along the walkway to the keeper's house, chins scraping the ground. And his dwelling "absolutely rocked in gale," he wrote, "not safe to be inside."

While the gales caught their breath out at sea between storms, Triangle's stark terrain held other dangers. Frank Dawson, another radio operator, went for a hike and tumbled two hundred feet over a cliff to a rock ledge. He had nearly screamed himself hoarse before a search party discovered his perch and hauled him up by rope.

By December 1912 Davies had clearly had enough. He begged Robertson for a transfer from this pest-hole of fear to "more congenial surroundings" as a reward for nineteen years' service. "Triangle is very hard on our nerves and a great strain on our constitutions," the former keeper of Egg Island confessed. Only two years old, his dwelling was already "unfit for habitation." Rain driven horizontally by the incessant gales "swamps us out," he complained, "as the building leaks, and it is an utter impossibility to keep a fire, as the place gets smoked out and we have sometimes to go a week at a stretch without a warm meal." Three winters at Triangle were too many; Davies wanted off before a fourth. "The way the wind circles around the buildings in whirlwinds makes keeping a fire out of the question," he told Robertson, "and you can imagine what a trial it is to myself and mine."

Davies escaped with his family in March. In late January 1914 his successor, Thomas Watkins, sent a message off to Victoria, reporting that a gale had flattened the storage shed on the beach again, strewing 450 oil cans and five kegs of nails along the shore. "The roof is blown about 300 feet along the beach," he reported, "Sides & Floor about 150 feet from original position." Both dwellings "got a severe shaking"—the door of the spare house blew off its hinges and the chimneys were scattered all over the ground again. By March there were only "two habitable rooms, a bedroom and a kitchen," in Watkins' house. That October the keeper was eager to transfer to a new station planned for Bonilla Island up north in Hecate Strait—a "much more suitable place for a man with a wife and young children than Triangle is."

Watkins was succeeded in his turn by Michael O'Brien, who had spent five years down in the hold of the Sand Heads lightship, where he had contracted rheumatism "owing to the confinement and dampness." He was "very desirous of being exchanged to Triangle Island" where he could live with his wife and family.

Triangle Island light may have been a nightmare for its keepers, but when the verdict came in on Anderson's accomplishment, his peers were unanimous. In 1913 F.A. Talbot published his definitive *Lightships and Lighthouses*, an ambitious study of the world's leading lighthouses, the latest and best survey of the state of the art. "Probably the most important light and certainly the loftiest on the Pacific seacoast north of the equator is that on the summit of Triangle Island, British Columbia," Talbot reckoned. He also lavished praise on the "Engineer-in-Chief of the Lighthouse Authority of the Canadian Government" for Estevan Point, placed in "a most romantic setting," and told how Anderson had laid a tramway through a "grand primeval forest" to haul concrete to the site.

The two lights confirmed Anderson's revolutionary reinforced-concrete designs, with their ornate and functional buttresses, as "the last word in lighthouse building." Naturally neither could compare with Eddystone or Skerryvore as engineering feats, yet there was no denying that Anderson's "most powerful beacons" were of "commanding character, representing as they do the latest and best in coast lighting." Never one to rest on his laurels, Anderson altered Triangle's plan, stretching the tower out to twice its height and tapering the central column, for a master plan to build new towers at Point Atkinson and Sheringham Point, each offering easy access for an appreciative public.

The nine years after Triangle Island first captured the public's imagination were nine years of war for its keepers and nine years of exquisite agony for its creator. For all his official preening, Anderson must have seen that Triangle's light was too high when he inspected his masterpiece the very first time, when he watched the shed on the beach slowly shrink to the size of one of his prized stamps as he rode up on the tramway. The chief engineer may even have ascended through the grey stratus that clung like cotton candy to the top two hundred feet of the eyrie most of the year. Surely he knew his mistake. The cardinal rule of lighthouse construction—never build higher than 150 feet—could be read on blackboards and in notebooks in every first-year engineering course in Canada. In his own annual report for 1906, only three years before he unrolled the plans for Triangle Island light, Anderson had reiterated, "*They should not be placed at an elevation exceeding 150 feet above the level of the sea on account of the prevalence of fog.*" So what must he have felt when all the praise pouring in was poisoned by rumblings and (even worse) derision in wheelhouses and shipping offices from Shanghai to San Francisco?

No one will ever know. Any complaints had to be put on paper and mailed off to the chairman of the Lighthouse Board of Canada. There was, of course, an endless barrage on every conceivable subject during Anderson's tenure. Petitions "praying" for new lights, complaints about existing ones, requests for foghorns, beacons, buoys, lifeboats, semaphore stations, and suggestions for changing characteristics of lights—handwritten pleas from lowly fishermen's co-operatives, or demands typed under the imposing letterheads of the world's most prestigious shipping lines—all piled into that in-tray in Ottawa, each one numbered and placed by harried secretaries on the Lighthouse Board's agenda. But there was not one letter about Triangle Island.

The patrol vessel *Galiano*, just prior to its sinking in 1918.
National Defence/Canadian Navy Heritage E-46568

Whatever the explanation for the absence of any reference to the blind cyclops in the Board's minutes, Triangle Island was about to loom up and confront them all as the naval patrol vessel *Galiano* dropped anchor off the station shortly after noon on October 29, 1918, and sent off her workboat with supplies. It should have been a long-awaited day of deliverance for the radio operators. Sid Elliot was ecstatic—he was scheduled to "come off." Jack Neary would see his brother Michael, serving as a radio operator on the *Galiano*. For the lightkeepers there would be a sack of mail. But no one was permitted to go aboard or stay ashore since eight crew members had been left behind at Esquimalt, laid low by the dreaded Spanish flu running rampant in Victoria. Crestfallen, Sid learned that his stint would be continued; he plodded back up the thousand steps "home" while Jack caught up on news of friends and family.

By 1:30 that afternoon, southwest winds began to muster their forces for another assault. The shore party hurriedly transferred cargo while clouds piled up on an ominous, dirty black anvil on the horizon. As the storm struck, Jack and Mike Neary quickly embraced and shook hands goodbye. Seamen dumped the remaining cargo onto the beach, snatched up Miss Brunton, a housekeeper who had been teaching the O'Brien children, thrust her into the workboat and bucked the roller-coaster swells back to their ship. *Galiano* wasted no time hoisting her anchors. As she steamed away, the keepers piled freight on the tram, then climbed home to open their mail.

No one will ever know why the *Galiano* headed for the open sea rather than seeking shelter in Shushartie Bay. She was a "cranky bitch" at best in foul weather, with decks and alleyways always awash when the wind was on her quarter. Her crew had long complained about their captain's inscrutable preference for riding out storms at sea, tempting fate.

Two hours later Art Green, the radio operator on watch, jerked upright in his chair, clamped his headset tightly to his ear and grabbed for a pencil to scribble her last feeble message: HOLD FULL OF WATER. SEND HELP. He called Sid Elliot over and both took turns signalling till sunrise. There was no reply. Art looked over at Jack Neary snoring on his cot. "Shall I wake up Jack?" he asked. "No, let him sleep," Sid advised. Why wake him up to a nightmare? No one ever learned the *Galiano*'s fate. Fishermen on the halibut steamer *George Foster* gaffed Wilfred Ebbs's body out of the water with a pike pole two days later; two other bodies were later found drifting two hundred miles away, east of Cape St. James.

Michael O'Brien left that winter to keep his own appointment with tragedy at Entrance Island light, and Alex Dingwell came down from Green Island to preside at the dismantling of Anderson's monumental mistake. In 1920 the Department of Marine grudgingly conceded defeat to Nature's fury and human error, a decade after the *Colonist*'s editor had gloated, "Triangle Island is at last to be put to the uses for which Nature apparently designed it from the beginning of things." Many of the same men who had bolted the beacon room together scaled it again to wrench off the rusted nuts. Piece by piece the curved glass panels, the nine-foot lens crystals, iron frame, copper sheeting, clockworks and pails of mercury went down the tramway and out to a ship's hold. Some deckhand-photographer with a keen sense of history documented the surrender, capturing the last boat on its way out from Triangle Island.

The hulking lantern from the West Coast's "leading light" has been resurrected upon the tarmac at the new Canada Coast Guard base in Victoria, where it dwarfs tourists on Coast Guard Day. And way up in that punishing corner of nowhere, Colonel Anderson's squat monument still stands above the clouds, futile and permanent, a twentieth-century Tower of Babel waiting to intrigue archeologists a thousand years hence. Who would have built it there, and why?

REMEMBERING GWYN GRAY HILL
Legendary Coastal Sailor

Excerpted from The Inlet: Memoirs of a Modern Pioneer *(2001),*
by Helen Piddington

There are all manner of ways of travelling this coast by sea. Fishermen head north in flotillas nose to tail, often without charts, following the leader. We hear them talking, sometimes, to keep themselves awake, almost incoherent with weariness. Tugs too keep in touch with their buddies travelling at snail's pace, usually alone but sometimes in procession, sharing good tides through rapids. Locals dart across these southeast-northwest paths in and out the inlets to Vancouver Island. Most have small, fast boats and no time for chat. The coast guard and police have large sleek vessels and travel alone, silently, at speed. They zoom up inlets, then down again in minutes, mission accomplished. It makes you wonder what could have been so serious or so easily solved?

Tourists often travel in clumps, chatting non-stop about engine speed, the weather, their next meal at the next resort. We hear them on the radio, days before they get to us, if indeed they sidetrack off the main route north. Most go straight between marinas and resorts, concerned only with creature comforts: food, drink, water, garbage disposal, showers and laundry. If they notice the country they are passing through it is rarely, if ever, mentioned. Many come fully provisioned from home base. Why bother with perishable local produce like prawns or crab that requires cleaning or cooking? Or, horror of horrors, organic lettuce that might contain slugs!

The largest boats, with anxious skippers or well-paid crew, go solo. So large, some of them, that when they make fast to our wharf, the boat shed and auxiliary wharves strain so much their moorings are almost torn free.

Those who sail the coast usually avoid resorts and anchor out, preferring to be alone. This group does its own fishing, buys less than powerboats but is more apt to ask us aboard for a drink or a meal.

Over the years, people from all these groups have become dear friends. We look forward to their annual appearance north and south. Some make us their destination, "the highlight of their summer." We hear their triumphs and disasters, their illnesses and hopes. How sad when boats are sold and friends stop travelling.

There is another group again, and these I call "explorers." They come off-season, as early as April, as late as October. More welcome then because we are less busy. They may stay a day or two, taking part in what's going on ashore—glad to stretch limbs and be of use. Some we've known since our sailing days, encountered first in some remote northern anchorage. Their visits weave warm patterns through our lives. They seem like family and as important in our children's lives. This group is self-sufficient, ignores resorts, always anchors out unless visiting. Travelling perhaps half the year they keep in touch with world affairs. They have opinions. They read. They know and love this coast, can handle her many moods—her hazards—enjoy the scenery, the wildlife and the birds. And they venture inland, always on the lookout for clues to local history. This is the group we left when we became landlubbers and so are the ones we understand most easily.

And of this group there was one very special person: a Welshman by the name of Gwyn Gray Hill. Our paths had crossed often while cruising, and once we settled here he came faithfully twice a year on his trips north and south. He would arrive, a cloud of black smoke on his yawl *Cherie,* painted with aluminum undercoat so she would blend in. Though nearly blind he missed nothing. Would call out as he approached: "I can't see—I can't see!" then comment on some obscure, minute detail. Apparently the thick lenses looped to his ears with strips of black inner tube showed him what others missed. Or he'd begin questioning: "What about Colonel So-and-So who vanished at the head of Loughborough in '28? Have you heard any more about him? And what about Bill Baker? Did he actually drown? Was his body ever found?" All this was ancient history—well before our time and sometimes his. But to Gray Hill the past was as precious as the present, to be pondered over, sorted through, treasured. And if there was no mystery then one must be found.

Gwyn Gray Hill's yawl, *Cherie,* at Boussole Bay, Alaska, in 1976. His yawl was painted with aluminum undercoat and, if annoyed, he'd crank up his oil stove to produce clouds of black smoke. Some called him "General Smuts."
Courtesy of Helen Piddington

Gray Hill gave different versions of his past. Some say he grew up in a castle in Wales, was taught at home by private tutors. Others claim he was actually English and went to boarding school in Switzerland or Germany. Some are convinced he was a remittance man, an only son paid to stay away from home, or the illegitimate son of his "sister." Who knows? But one thing was sure—he led a charmed life. As a lad he survived that famous Scottish botulism case of 1922. His father had taken him fishing at Loch Maree and requested something other than pressed duck for their lunches. Eight people who ate the duck became ill and died.

Whatever the other details, it is known that Gray Hill arrived in Victoria in 1931, a young man with means. He tried commercial fishing with a family connection out of Comox but did not enjoy it. Then lads like the Rodd brothers, interested in boats and the sea, became his friends and he spent the next few years with them in wild adolescent fun.

Gradually these lads grew up, became concerned with work, careers, their wives and children. But Gray Hill, with no responsibilities and no need to earn a living, did not develop. Wanting always to carouse, he became an aggravating nuisance—then a recluse.

His first boat was *Charmer,* a lifeboat from a vessel of that name. On *Cape St. Elias,* his second boat, he began what became annual cruises up this coast. As his sight was poor and getting worse, he memorized the outline of the entire landmass between Maple Bay and Alaska.

Benita Sanders and I heard about Gwyn Gray Hill on our first trip to the Charlottes in 1968. One day, struggling along the shore to Kaisun, we caught sight of *Cape St. Elias* underway in the distance and never for one minute imagined that either of us would meet him—much less be friends.

Above: Gray Hill's *Cherie,* as illustrated in *Character Boats of the BC Coast: Series 1,* by Stephen Jackson (Harbour, 1973).

Above left: Some say Gray Hill grew up in a castle in Wales; others claim he was actually English and went to boarding school in Switzerland or Germany. Some are convinced he was a remittance man or an only son paid to stay away from home. Who knows?
Courtesy of Helen Piddington

After some fifty years of sailing, when he could no longer distinguish between land and sky, he gave up travel and lived aboard *Cherie* at Maple Bay. Eventually he moved to a rest home in Duncan and was put next to the Rodd brother who disliked him most. But at this point both were too old to realize or to care.

During all those years he visited countless people whose meals, I'm sure, kept him alive. For between stops he survived on a liquid diet, or so he claimed. And while his questions were repetitive and sometimes annoying, we were always pleased to see him. Nothing fazed him, everything intrigued him—the weirder the better. And when he came, wolves sang from the hills across the inlet.

Gray Hill liked the shape and size of our son Adam as an infant. Felt him a perfect candidate for the Northumbrian pipes. He had given his pipes to Peter Rodd, another baby he'd admired, but now it was imperative that our child fall asleep to pipe music, to get it into his system early. Thus one evening after Adam was tucked in, Dane turned on the generator so the vacuum cleaner could provide air for Gray Hill's chanter. The noise was extraordinary. Adam slept on. He has yet to try the pipes.

I've claimed elsewhere that we got scant help from anyone. Gray Hill was the exception. During our first summer Dane realized the kitchen ceiling was sagging dangerously. So he cut a beam 4 inches by 14 inches by 15 feet. One end fitted easily into a slot in a central wall but the other was the problem: How could he raise and position it alone? It was enormously heavy. A young, strong inlet dweller who came by that morning was asked to help but refused. His back, he said, might get hurt; he could not take that risk. Then up came Gray Hill from the wharf. A tiny man, who appeared to have little or no strength, he saw the solution immediately. Taking a stout timber some five feet long, he raised the beam with Dane then held it upright—fingers interlaced, back and arms straight, knees bent—supporting the entire weight of that beam while Dane edged it in place. I have photos of him holding it and others of him resting afterwards, unscathed.

Gray Hill was as grubby as his boat—greasy, sooty and reeking of fuel. When he came up for meals I longed to pop him in a hot bath. He would arrive at table empty-handed, unthinkable on this coast, but with his own sharp penknife, like a European peasant. And always he teased me about our spoons and forks—knowing full well their history and provenance. It was just one of his rituals. Then he would keep us up, entranced, till all hours. When he left I would give him jam—"Oh, yes please. Rhubarb—I love it!"—bread, cakes, fruit and vegetables until we discovered he gave it all away at his next port of call.

Gray Hill gave everyone on this coast a nickname. After we got the wild boar we became the Piggwigglingtons or variations on that theme. And between visits, while he could still see, he would write long letters to each of us in his beautiful copperplate script, changing his own name from Gray Hill to J.W. Roast to Rost and back again at whim. He never married but fell in love with other men's wives—the tall slender ones, especially, and all along the coast he promised his mother's rings. The one to get them deserved both rings and boat, for when his cruising days were over she fed him, washed him, drove him where he needed to go and kept him comfortable.

The last time we saw him was very sad. He was seated on a clean boat, in clean clothes, his skin pink and fresh, almost unrecognizable. But his mind was vague and blurry.

Sure he was aggravating, time-consuming and sometimes downright rude—as when pristine yachts pulled up behind him he'd sully them with puffs of soot—but he was also endearing and endlessly entertaining and we miss him very much. Gwyn Gray Hill will always be part of our lives, part of this coast, part of Loughborough and her mysteries.

HERON

by Russell Thornton

In the deep-cut, swerving ravine
the hour before dawn. Creek more spirit than water
pouring white down the bouldery creek path
at arm's length toward me and past.
                              Out of the grey dark
a heron rises, a grey lopsided bundle,
a tent suddenly assembling itself and, in a split-instant,
collapsing and assembling itself again in mid-air.
There it is, opening its near-creek-spanning wings,
trailing its long thin legs, carrying its neck
in an S-shape, head held back: silent heron
flying away farther up the ravine.
                              Is it the same heron
I saw once before—the slender, sensitive-still,
blue-grey mystery alone in front of me in bright daylight?
I watched it until the houses, people, streets and cars
faded into the fringes of the light,
faded, and reappeared along with this same creek
spilling out of a pipe and flowing for a block
through old backyards and into another pipe—
and then saw the still one gone. The entire creek unbroken
could be the heron's home, these waters
of the snowmelt and rain that gather and surge
and twist their way down to the sea.
                              The heron
alights somewhere, disappears, and lifts again
as I come around a turn—and I see it again. And now
I see it at the shallow creek-edge, in an eddy
where the current swings out around a boulder and is lost—
all calm attention standing there, searching
through the creek waters' sunless rays.
                              It finds a fish—
the fish swims quick into the poised long bill.
The heron lifts, the dark tasting itself, the ravine
flying through the ravine—living sign,
secret heron of the beginning, morning bird.

From House Built of Rain *(2003), by Russell Thornton*

THE SAD SAGA OF
COCKATRICE BAY

23

Excerpted from Full Moon, Flood Tide: Bill Proctor's Raincoast *(2003),*
by Bill Proctor and Yvonne Maximchuk

Cockatrice Bay is located on south Broughton Island on Queen Charlotte Strait, north of the entrance to Fife Sound. The bay was well known for its run of big coho salmon, some weighing as much as twenty pounds.

In 1951 a logger named Art McIntyre came to Cockatrice looking for timber, and he found what he was looking for around May Lake. Art, being a man who liked to dam creeks and use water to move logs, liked what he saw. He had already dammed Scott Cove Creek and Marion Creek in Tsibass Lagoon. To Art, this was just another creek.

Cockatrice Creek is 1,980 feet long and it drains Phyllis Lake. There is a swamp between Phyllis Lake and May Lake, 2,310 feet in length. The idea was to build a dam at the tail-out of Phyllis Lake to raise the level of the swamp so logs could be towed from May Lake to Phyllis Lake. Once the dam was built, the level of Phyllis Lake rose fourteen feet. When the dam was completed, Art built an incline railway to the beach.

The remains of the log cradle and railway at Cockatrice Bay. It is believed that the upside-down boat, fitted with an Easthope 10/14, was used to tow logs across Phyllis Lake when Art McIntyre was logging there. When they were finished, it was put on the railway and abandoned at Cockatrice Bay. *Bill Proctor photo*

An incline railway has only one car, which is pulled by a winch, in this case a steam winch. The car would go right into the lake, the boom man would shove the load of logs onto the car, and the winch would pull the load up out of the lake to the top of the hill and from there downhill to the beach. The car, loaded with logs, would go right out into the sea and the logs would float off. Then the winch would pull the car back up the hill and down to the lake for another load of logs.

Art logged this way for five years. Needless to say, that was the end of the big coho of Cockatrice Bay. When Art moved away in 1956 he left the dam in place, and also the railway and the steam winch. The railroad was 1,980 feet long and built on cedar logs, so there were a lot of logs, plus there were a few loads of big logs that had spilled on the way to the sea and been left to rot.

In 1964 a man named Ed Brandon, a shake cutter, came to Cockatrice Bay with his old boat, *Fearless*, and saw all the big logs. Ed was an old loner for the most part but he could see that this was too big a job for one man, so he went to Vancouver to find someone to help him, and he came back with a man named Bob Savage, an Englishman who had never been out in the woods. Bob was forty years old and had a good job in town, but he quit his job and bought a gas-powered winch for $2,000, and some power saws, and came to Cockatrice to make his fortune.

The two men got the winch ashore and tried to drag the logs down to the beach, but the logs were too big. They cut them into short lengths, but this made the work too slow because the short logs were always hanging up on something.

At about this time Ed hired another man, a shake cutter named Joe Walters. Joe was

These are the remains of the dam on the creek at Cockatrice Bay. The dam killed large runs of coho, and though the creek has been cleaned and restocked, the salmon runs have never returned to their historical levels.
Bill Proctor photo

seventy years old and all he knew was how to split shakes by hand. When Joe arrived he built a nice little cabin on the shore by the mouth of the creek, and while Bob and Ed were still trying to get logs to the beach, Old Joe was splitting up a storm. Bob could say to Joe that splitting by hand was too slow, but all Bob and Ed had to show for two months of work was a lot of broken cable and a few blocks. Old Joe had built a cabin and split ten cords of beautiful shakes.

Now Ed took off and went to Vancouver to buy a barge to haul the shakes and blocks and also the rails from the old railroad. Ed was gone for three weeks and all Bob and Joe had was a rowboat, which neither of them could row very well. Both of them chewed snuff, and while Ed was gone they ran out of snuff. It was right at this time that I went to Cockatrice to fish. I got there in the evening, dropped the anchor and was cooking supper when this man came rowing out and circled my boat. I went out on deck and invited him to come on board.

He looked like a wild man and seemed scared but he came and sat in the cabin and I gave him a cup of tea. He said his name was Bob Savage. Then he told me all the things that had gone wrong, all about Old Joe and the snuff, and apparently three nights before I came along, Joe had said to Bob, "We only have a half box of snuff left so there is none for you tomorrow." They got in a fight and Joe had arms like an ape and Bob ended up out in the bush, and that's where he had slept for three nights.

Bob asked me if I would take him to Alert Bay because he was leaving for good. As it happened, I planned to go to Alert Bay to see my wife, Yvonne, who was there waiting for our second baby to be born. So the next day Bob loaded all his stuff aboard and I took him to Alert Bay, and that was the last I ever saw of him. He gave me a seven-foot plywood rowboat for taking him in and left Joe the big rowboat.

About the time Bob left, Ed came back with an old sailing schooner, the *Joan G*, originally the *Maid of Orleans*. (The 129-foot-long ship had a long and interesting history. Built in 1882 in San Francisco, she served as a slave ship and went seal hunting in the Arctic, where she spent two winters locked in the ice. She was used in the fur trade by the Hudson's Bay Company, served as a rumrunner, towed logs here on the coast and worked as a herring packer.)

No sooner had Ed come back than he fell and broke his leg and had to go back to Vancouver, leaving Old Joe there all alone.

The remains of the historic *Joan G* (originally the *Maid of Orleans*) can still be seen at Cockatrice Bay.
Harbour Publishing Archives

I thought about Old Joe a lot, and then one day I got a letter from Bob asking me to go and take Joe to Alert Bay. He sent me fifty dollars with the letter. When I got there, Joe seemed to know I was coming. He had everything packed and ready to go and he had even had a shave that morning. Joe was a nice man and a hard worker, but he left Cockatrice Bay with nothing to show for ten months' work. He had no way to get all his shakes out and he did not even own them, for everything was in Bob's name.

Now there was no one at Cockatrice Bay, but there were tools, chainsaws and lots of other good stuff: blocks, drums of gas, the winch and the old *Joan G*. I brought home what I could pack and wrote to Bob, telling him I had a lot of his stuff in my shop and that when he came back I would bring it out to him. At the very same time, he wrote to me and told me to take possession of everything: all he wanted was his chainsaw and a few odds and ends. I took the letter to the police and they told me to go ahead and take everything and store it, but if Bob came back I would have to return it to him. I thought maybe I could buy it all from him, so I made him an offer of $500 for everything and he accepted it.

I went out and beachcombed some logs and lashed them into a float, then moved the winch and all the other gear aboard. I thought that was the end of it, but I had no sooner got home than I got another letter from Bob wanting me to buy the *Joan G*. It was Bob who had paid for it and it was anchored up at the head of Cockatrice Bay. It seemed that Ed thought he owned it, but Bob had paid $3,000 for it and he sent me a copy of the bill of sale. Bob wanted me to buy it for $1,000 and take it home and look after it.

So I went back again and took a look at it, but wondered what the hell I would do with it. It did not leak and it was a bit of coastal history, so I left it where it was.

Sometime shortly after that, DFO [Department of Fisheries and Oceans] hired a man with a skidder to go in and pull the dam out of the creek. To do this he had to build a road in to the lake. He got within about 300 feet of the lake when the funds ran out. Ten thousand dollars already spent just on the road, but the dam was still in place. Then DFO went in with a powder man and they blew one big log out of the centre of the dam. This brought down the level of the lake some, but there was still no way a fish could get up. There were no fish anyway, so it didn't really matter.

Then Ed came back and found the DFO road there, so now he could get the logs out. He went back to Vancouver and bought a small tractor and found another partner, Ken Olsen, who had an old tug named *Pacific Foam*. The two men got the tractor ashore and loaded the old *Fearless* with shake blocks. Then they began loading the rails on *Joan G*. They piled all of them—about a hundred—on the deck, which made the *Joan G* top heavy. They were going to load the hatch with shake blocks but the tractor broke down, so Ed loaded it aboard *Fearless* and went to Vancouver, leaving Ken in Cockatrice.

Ed never came back for two years. Ken finally left, and the *Joan G* washed ashore during the winter of 1967. All the rails slid to one side and she rolled right upside down and sank.

In the spring of 1968 two men came from San Francisco to see me, to find out whether the *Joan G* could be refloated and repaired and towed to San Francisco, but by then she was too far gone to do anything with. The men had wanted her for the San Francisco museum and they offered me $5,000 if I could save her. I sure wished then that I had bought her from Bob for $1,000.

For two years nothing further happened in Cockatrice Bay, but then some shake cutters came and started to split shakes up the creek. They took a load out and left a hell of a mess right in the creek. Then Ed came back once again and poked around looking for some junk. Sometimes he would find a bit, before it was lost forever.

On the stern of the *Joan G* there were two big bronze rudder plates that weighed about a ton each. At low tide Ed put a cable around them and a stick of dynamite inside and blew the stern off. The old boat can still be seen lying there, but time and tide are taking their toll on what the people have left.

In 1973 two men with a tug and a skidder came to Cockatrice. They put the skidder ashore, planning to pull out all the remaining logs. The fact was that they had no salvage sale, so the Forest Service ran them out.

Then all that was left at Cockatrice Bay was a few logs, a hell of a mess and a little cabin by the creek. Someone shot the windows out and then someone burned the whole thing down. The mess and the remains of the dam were still there.

In 1987 DFO and all the patrolmen in the area and myself went and worked in the creek to clear a bit of a channel. In the spring of 1988 the Mainland Enhancement of Salmonid Species Society hatchery planted 25,000 coho fry into May Lake. We did the same thing every year for four years until there were coho coming back every year.

There were still two problems: a big log in the creek, and the tail-out of Phyllis Lake. In the summer of 1996 a group of sportsmen from Sullivan Bay hired Don Wilson to clean out the mess once and for all.

Now Cockatrice Creek is cleaned and restocked, and all that remains to be seen is whether the salmon run will rebuild to historical levels.

24 OYSTERS AND ST. VALENTINE

Excerpted from Notes from the Netshed *(1997), by Mrs. Amor de Cosmos*

They say it was a brave man who ate the first oyster. But I know that once he ate it, he ate many more. Say what you will, they are delicious molluscs. I have eaten them smoked, fried, raw, stewed and even baked in a loaf of French bread.

I thought about all this as I went on the ferry from Horseshoe Bay to the Sechelt Peninsula, or as the locals like to call it, the Sunshine Coast. The sun wasn't shining but that didn't bother me. I knew I was in for a good time visiting my cousin Leroy on his oyster farm.

Okay, his name isn't really Leroy and he's not exactly my cousin. The name Leroy was of his own choosing. As a kid he found it meant "the king" in French, so he chose to switch over, finding Leroy much more regal than the name "George" that his mother had given him. He always felt himself to be a self-made individual, so why not a self-made name? As for Leroy being my cousin—well, he is actually more like a shirt-tail relative by marriage, but it's kind of a long story so I just call him my cousin.

Tidal flats at Oyster Bay at the head of Pender Harbour on the Sunshine Coast. It was here where early oyster cultivating experiments proved a runaway success.
Harbour Publishing Archives

Leroy is always interesting to be around. He has a personality beyond the ordinary, and somewhere he has picked up an education to match. But more than that, he has one of the sharpest wits I've ever met. Unfortunately, he started his career as a fisherman, and as a fisherman he was a bust. On a troller he tended to get seasick. On a gillnetter he exerted a peculiar magnetism that could attract the only drift log for miles around, and sea lions were his constant companions. As soon as he stepped aboard a seiner, either all the fish in the neighbourhood disappeared or the engine broke down, or both. Once, in the middle of a particularly bad season, he told me that he was going to take an oar out of his skiff and start walking, and as soon as he got far enough inland that people would start asking him what that thing was he was packing, he would stop and settle down. Evidently that's how he got to the Sunshine Coast. It's not exactly inland, but at least oysters don't swim. Leroy felt he could cope with species that stayed in one place.

After some years labouring in the oyster business, Leroy had bought his own oyster farm. I was going to set up his books for him, and he would explain the world of oysters to me.

I took the ferry over to see him on St. Valentine's Day—the day set aside for lovers. Oysters, of course, have a connection with that amorous saint, as they are considered an aphrodisiac. Everyone seems to know this, although none, including companions I have shared oysters with, has ever offered me any actual proof.

Leroy met me at the ferry and we drove to his "farm." An oyster farm is really only a lease from the province to grow oysters on a piece of shoreline. As such it is mostly out of sight, at least at high tide. On the shore there will be a small shack to store tools and trays and stuff, and somewhere there is a skiff to go out to the floats from which are hung strings. In Leroy's case, he also had an old herring punt with an outboard.

At Leroy's place we set up his books. The finances of an oyster farm are not too complex. The capital equipment is the skiff and the outboard and the floats. The oyster spat (the "seed") is quite cheap. You can get into the oyster business with only a few bucks, but the trick is to make money at it. From what I could see, what with harvesting and so on, the business is highly labour intensive. For this reason oyster farms are usually family owned. Nobody gets rich, but then nobody starves either. Leroy's analysis was short and sweet: Buy a farm and you buy a job for life.

Leroy brought me up to date on the salmon farmers, who are now mostly gone. In the 1980s a bunch of salmon farms started up, but for once the Sunshine Coast lived up to its name. Each summer, the sunshine brought with it a plankton bloom in the water that wiped out many of the salmon farmers. This did not affect the oysters, although the oyster farmers have had their share of problems with the red tide. Most of them survived because their operations were small and they had already found ways to diversify their income, so they could stand a season with little or no cash. If the red tide came, Leroy would find something else to do until it passed. Small can be beautiful, if you find beauty in positive cash flow.

When we were done with the books we went to the local pub and I met some of Leroy's fellow oyster men. On the whole they were not like Leroy. They were older and somewhat slower. If you asked them how they were, they thought the question all the way through before replying. I guess the occupation attracts a certain type.

But the oyster farmers were not dull, and because it was St. Valentine's Day the jokes about love and oysters were flying fast and furious. I got them going a bit by noting that the oysters they grew were not the true BC oyster, but imports from Japan. One guy countered with the comment that, like most people, I knew next to nothing about oysters. He was right, but whenever anyone says this about any subject I simply dare them to enlighten me.

Did you know that an oyster will not die of a broken heart? The reason being that they can and do change their sex. They start as females, become males and then go back to being females again. This would be a boon to some people I know. If you're unsuccessful in one area, no problem—just go over to the other side. Apparently European oysters can change their sex indefinitely, but the big BC ones, the Japanese imports, get only two chances. That's still one more than you and me. I think if I were an oyster, St. Valentine would be my patron saint.

BEACH OYSTERS AND FANCY OYSTER STEW

25

Excerpted from One-Pot Wonders: James Barber's Recipes for Land and Sea
(2006), by James Barber

On a low tide and a rocky beach almost anywhere north of Lasqueti Island, you should find beach oysters. They're not the little ones you slurp raw in fancy restaurants; they're big and they need to be cooked.

The simplest way is put them on the barbecue, flat side of the shell up, and cook until the shell opens. Sprinkle with Tabasco sauce or lemon juice or mayonnaise or sesame oil or Scotch, and eat either with a knife and fork or stuffed between two slices of bread. Messy but nice.

Or you can fry them. Opening beach oysters onboard can be very bad for decks, so be careful. I suggest you put them on the barbecue until the shells open just a little bit, when you can pop in a kitchen knife and sever the muscle.

Kim La Fave illustration

Fry them in butter over medium heat, sprinkle with pepper and lemon juice or soy sauce or teriyaki sauce or Tabasco sauce or Worcestershire sauce, and eat.

Fancy Oyster Stew
Serves 4

An oyster stew made of beach oysters is a wondrous thing on a cold winter's day. It sounds a bit complicated, but it's dead easy. You've read the tide tables, you know where you're going to find the oysters (this is a winter trip, an occasion well worth advance planning) and you have bought a couple of extra ingredients, like a small carton of cream, some fresh dill and a decent loaf of bread. I've also taken (at various times) gin, champagne, Jack Daniel's and Captain Morgan rum, and one Christmas in Heriot Bay, when the guests missed their plane and didn't arrive with the cooked turkey they'd promised, we ate this stew, with a bottle of Scotch, for Christmas dinner.

> 4 or 5 big beach oysters (or a 1 lb/500 mL tub if you don't want to take the boat out)
> 2 Tbsp (30 mL) butter
> 1 large onion, chopped
> 1 stalk celery, chopped fine
> 1 clove garlic, chopped fine
> 1 large potato, diced ½ inch (1 cm)
> 1 sweet red pepper, diced
> ½ tsp (2 mL) salt
> ½ tsp (2 mL) pepper
> 1 tsp (5 mL) paprika
> ½ cup (125 mL) white wine *or* water *or* canned clam juice
> 1 cup (250 mL) milk
> 1 tsp (5 mL) Worcestershire sauce *or* Asian fish sauce
> ½ cup (125 mL) half-and-half cream (or, if you're desperate, evaporated milk)
> juice of 1 lemon

Open the oysters while you heat the butter in a pot over medium heat. Fry the onion, celery and garlic 5 minutes. Add the potato, red pepper, salt, pepper, paprika and wine. Cover and cook 10 minutes. Cut the oysters into 3 or 4 pieces and add them to the pan with their juices. Cook 4 minutes. Add milk and Worcestershire sauce, heat through almost to the boil, lower heat and stir in cream for no more than 30 seconds (boiling will make it curdle), and remove from heat immediately. Sprinkle with lemon juice and eat.

Once you've made a good oyster stew, you'll want to do it again.

PADDLEWHEELS ON THE PACIFIC

26

Excerpted from Fishing for a Living *(1993), by Alan Haig-Brown*

In 1977 the international community of nations recognized a new convention granting coastal states exclusive fishing and other rights to the 200 miles of water directly off their shores. While this rule reserved the 200 miles off the west coasts of Haida Gwaii (formerly the Queen Charlotte Islands) and Vancouver Island for Canadian fishermen, it limited their access in the Gulf of Alaska and Bering Sea where many, like Edgar Arnet, had built their careers and their boats on the rich halibut grounds.

"Going out west" had a long tradition among Canadian fisher-men. When the boats loaded ice and left Prince Rupert for the halibut grounds, they steered a course westward from Dixon Entrance across the huge, open expanse of the Gulf of Alaska. Alone on these very cold, rolling seas without radar or satellite positioning, the crews survived monster waves, frozen rigging and breakdowns. With little chance of outside help, they relied on their creativity, courage and calm. Perhaps the most famous tale is the account of Edgar Arnet's paddlewheels—a story still told around galley tables and anywhere fishermen gather.

The *Cape Beale* leaving for a trip to the halibut grounds, January 1957.
Courtesy of Edna (Arnet) Simpson

By 1924 Edgar Arnet had decided to build his own boat. With a partner, John Berg, he had a Norwegian immigrant draw up a set of plans and make a model for a halibut boat. Because the boats must often work in heavy seas to haul the longlines to which the short gangen (lines) with their hooks are attached, the sea-keeping qualities of the boat are all important. After some debate with the builder over the best design for the stern, they went ahead with the construction of a classic halibut boat. A small cabin was set well back from the bow, but in a departure from tradition the cabin was ahead of the hatch. The long propeller shaft was in two parts; the main shaft, which ran through a series of bearings under the floor of the fish hold, was coupled to the tail shaft, which extended out through a stuffing box and the heavy timbers that formed the keel and stern post. A steel shoe ran out from the end of the wooden keel to hold the bottom of the rudder in place.

The *Cape Beale*, as it looked in its early years.

Courtesy of Edna (Arnet) Simpson

The boat was built in a rented Vancouver shipyard near what is now the north end of the Burrard Street Bridge. By the end of February 1925, they had the hull planked, caulked and painted. The deck beams were in place, although the deck hadn't yet been laid. After launching, they towed her around to Coal Harbour and rented space at Andy Linton's boatyard, where they completed the decking, built the house and rigged the boat in time to leave for the Alaskan halibut grounds on June 3. They picked up crew, ice and bait in Prince Rupert and headed out to fish around Kodiak Island, Portlock Bank and Yakutat. John Berg, who had made a couple of trips to these waters on a small Seattle boat, served as skipper.

The following summer, in what was to become a familiar pattern, they got work for the boat packing salmon before going out to fish halibut again. Halibut could be fished virtually year-round with a ten-day layover between trips. John Berg died in 1927, so it was Edgar running the boat on that fateful trip in 1928.

They had been fishing out around Kodiak Island. Fishing had been good and when time came to deliver the trip, Edgar set a course directly across the Gulf of Alaska for Dixon Entrance at the top of the Queen Charlotte Islands. "We were just about in the middle of the Gulf of Alaska, over 250 miles from the nearest land. The darn thing broke right in the shaft log where you couldn't get hold of it. The propeller slid back from the speed that we were making and jammed up against the rudder. The rudder was useless. So then I thought of this side-wheeler. I talked it over with the crew and they thought I had something wrong upstairs.

"We were seven men, some of the crew were in favour of trying to work out something. So we started to make this side-wheeler. Three of the crew wanted to take off in the dory and row for land. We objected to that, so they couldn't. We worked on this jury-rig. It took us about two-and-a-half days until we finally got it going.

"By golly, we were making about two miles an hour. This winch we had, you could turn it so that the heads were fore and aft or athwartships. This made it a lot easier. We used a rope messenger from the winch head to a drum in the middle of the boom, which we had laid across the gunwale to use for the shaft with paddlewheels on each end. We took a couple of turns of rope around the drum and the winch with an endless rope. Well, the darn ropes couldn't last forever. A couple of hours and they were all chaffed up. It was our tie-up lines that we were using.

"When they were all gone we took the cable off the anchor winch. It was quite flexible, not too stiff, so we rigged that up with a couple of turns around the drum and the same on the winch with a tightener up the mast for the slack. This was just a snatch block on the end of a line for the cable to run through. The line ran through another block at the top of the mast and could be tightened from the deck.

"It worked fine, but then it started to chew up the wood on the boom that we were using for the paddle shaft. We saw that wouldn't last very long so we thought

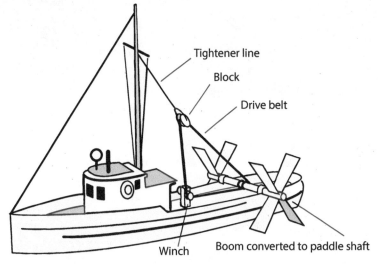

of the funnel that the exhaust pipe went through. It was about two feet in diameter. It wasn't welded, it was riveted, so it wasn't hard to knock the rivets out and wrap the sheet metal on the drum. That went fine, but the steel cable would wear the eighth-inch metal, so we would move it over. In a couple of days there was no more funnel left, it was all chewed up.

"We had a bunch of fishing anchors with one-inch stocks. We took these and lashed them about four or five inches apart, like a Jacob's ladder. We wrapped that around the drum and it worked fine. You could go a couple of days before moving the anchor stops.

"We had tried to make course for Dixon Entrance but the darn wind was against us and was pushing us up into the Gulf, so we decided to make for Sitka. We still had a southeaster, and one day it was blowing about thirty or thirty-five miles an hour. It got quite rough and, with the boat rolling, the paddles would dig way down in the water. On one roll that she took, the boom that we had made for the paddles broke off on some cross grain. So we had to put our dory overboard and fetch it back. We managed to bolt it and tie it together. The paddles were too big so we cut them down to half the size.

"The winds were still taking us up the Gulf and we couldn't make Sitka. On the seventh or eighth day we saw the top of some mountains so then we knew we were getting close to the east side of the Gulf. In the evening we saw a boat in the distance. The tide and wind were taking us right for him. We got there before dark, launched our dory and rowed over to him. It was an American boat from Petersburg called the *Baltic*. They'd had a good day's

Above: Edgar giving instructions aboard a halibut boat, likely the *Cape Beale*, with skates of halibut gear behind him.
Courtesy of Edna (Arnet) Simpson

Top right: Edgar (second from left) and one of his early halibut crews.
Courtesy of Edna (Arnet) Simpson

Right: The *Cape Beale* with her steadying sail raised.
Courtesy of Edna (Arnet) Simpson

fishing and had gone to bed. The skipper got up and I told him what went wrong. 'Well,' he said, 'there's a passenger boat coming down the coast tomorrow.'

"But I didn't figure he'd stop for us so I asked the skipper of the *Baltic* if he would tow us to the first cannery down the coast. This was the Libby, McNeill and Libby cannery, about a hundred miles south and just in from Cape Spencer. He agreed so we dismantled the paddlewheels and he put a line on us. I thought we would get one of the cannery tenders to tow us up to Juneau, which is only about seventy miles. But the cannery manager said no way he was going to let any of his tenders go as he was too busy getting his traps set. So I talked the skipper of the *Baltic* into towing us up. He was reluctant because he was on good fishing. But I told him the insurance would pay.

"In Juneau we sold what fish we had—we had a fair trip—and contacted the insurance.

Edgar at the outside steering station of an early pilchard or salmon seiner.
Courtesy of Edna (Arnet) Simpson

Edgar built the steel-hulled *Attu* in 1959, well before the 200-mile limit, and named her for the island in the Aleutians.
Alan Haig-Brown photo

They allowed us to have a new shaft installed and aid for the tow. They didn't pay for a new boom or funnel. The newspaper people in Juneau got wind of our trip and wanted us to rig the paddlewheels up again so they could take pictures of it. But we had taken it all apart. After a week in the shipyard we were ready to head back out to the Kodiak grounds.

"On the trip when we broke the shaft, we were fishing alongside an American boat called the *Grant.* The skipper of that boat always sold his trip in Rupert. When we left the fishing grounds and set course for Prince Rupert we figured he'd be leaving the same day, but we never saw him after we broke the shaft. He could have passed just a few miles away and we wouldn't have seen him.

"Twenty-five years later, about 1952 or 1953, the same skipper on the same boat was fishing off Kodiak Island. He was setting a course for Dixon Entrance. When he was halfway

Three generations of Arnets. Left to right: Edgar's grandson Russ, Edgar Arnet and Edgar's son, George.
Courtesy of Edna (Arnet) Simpson

across, just about where we snapped our tail shaft, he came on the air with a Mayday call. His crankshaft had broken. The US Coast Guard came on the air right away. The skipper of the *Grant* gave his loran position and within twenty-four hours the Coast Guard had come, put a line on him and towed him into Sitka or Ketch-ikan. We didn't even have phones in the 1920s. It's a lot different today."

Edgar went on to a long and successful career in the fishing industry. He built the combination seine boat–longliner Attu *with a steel hull and aluminum cabin in 1959. One of the first steel seiners built with an aluminum house, she was fished for many years by Edgar's son, George Arnet, and is now being managed by Edgar's grandson Russ Arnet. But when halibut stories are told in the galley, one of the favourites will always be the tale of Edgar's paddlewheels.*

THE SECRET VICE OF FERRY-WATCHING

27

Excerpted from *When Nature Calls: Life at a Gulf Island Cottage* (1999), by Eric Nicol

This story shows that there have always been plenty of things about ferry travel for people to poke fun at, whether the rising fares, fuel surcharges, cuts in service, delayed sailings, CEOs with fat salaries, poor management, and so on that currently frustrate travellers on BC Ferries or the issues that affected Eric Nicol and others when he penned this piece. —Ed.

It is Polynesia North, but first you have to get to it, which isn't easy. The southern Gulf Islands are a jigsaw puzzle kicked over by a falling angel. Because they are off the reasonably straight line that would be the shortest distance between the two points—Vancouver and Victoria—reaching them can require the taking of several ferries of diminishing size and schizoid schedule.

A couple of the Gulf Islands have been threatened with the building of a bridge to help connect the Mainland with the Big Island. None of the plans has got past the planning stage, because the planners have had crosses burned on their lawns by delegates from whichever island doesn't welcome becoming a viaduct for motor traffic. It is part of the mystique of every island that the island is the sublime destination, not part of a highway system.

Peter Lynde illustration

You come, you stay until fulfilled, you leave. No one-night stand in a motel. You *marry* the island, sir, if you know what's good for you.

This commitment is particularly firm for Saturnans. The permanent residents of Saturna Island almost relish the plight of us Mainlanders who try to have an affair with the island that lasts less than a lifetime. The need to transfer from a large ferry to a smaller ferry, to sit for hours in various transfer compounds, baking in sun or peering through rain for the vessel delayed by any one of the many afflictions to which the BC Ferry Corporation is prone—these circumstances do much to keep Saturna free of the uncommitted.

There have been case-hardened men who have chosen the French Foreign Legion over signing on for Saturna.

So we summer cottagers are obliged to see the Ferry Experience as a major part of the pleasure—a bizarre type of masochism—or a character builder, in the same class as World War Two.

It begins with my having to make a reservation for my car. To do this with any hope at all of retaining a shred of sanity, I must have the current ferry schedule. In my judgment, a large part of the Ferry Corporation's thousands of employees is devoted entirely to changing the ferry schedule. The changes are made after consultation with the Oracle of Victoria, which predicts the seasonal ebb and flow of traffic, with consideration of the influence of the Japanese Current and hunches drawn from a hat.

The obvious place for a person to obtain a copy of the ferry schedule is aboard a ferry. Having to board a ferry in order to obtain the ferry schedule needed to make a reservation to access the ferry: this is how the Ferry Corporation discourages triflers and people who are already hysterical.

In addition—and this may be only a personal observation flawed by paranoia—the schedule pamphlets are placed in parts of the ship not normally seen by the passenger searching for one: in the engine room, under lifeboats, et cetera.

For further backup against its leaking information, as soon as the Ferry Corporation senses that too many would-be passengers are getting hold of the current schedule, it issues a new schedule, with previously unknown constellations of asterisks to ensure that no two days of the week have exactly the same timetable. This schedule is then hidden in new places on the vessels.

The only constant in the car-ferry scheduling is the requirement that your vehicle arrive at the check-in booth at least forty minutes before departure time, which is the stuff of whimsy. Tardiness may be punished by relegation to "standby status," a vehicular kind of Purgatory from which few attain salvation. Whereas the ferry rarely apologizes for leaving late unless summer has turned to fall, the loading crew have little patience with drivers who plead being delayed by gridlock, or a medical emergency such as donating a kidney. In this they have the full support of those of us who have arrived well ahead of the deadline and sit in our cars until turned to stone.

Because of these vagaries of the long wait, it is easy for me, the driver, to doze off, with my hand poised over the ignition key. Not until I jerk awake to see that the cars ahead of me in the line have been waved onto the ferry, hear a public-address voice blaring "Will the small red Honda please proceed?" and note an attendant gesture me forward with an expression of total exasperation, do I panic. I reverse instead of go forward, release wind rather than the brake, try to lower the radio antenna by opening the hood and, at last, lurch forward through a gauntlet of faces clearly not glad to be helping the mentally handicapped.

Barrelling, I catch up with the cars entering the maw of the ferry, just as we hit the speed bumps. These steel ridges rise and fall with the tide, phases of the moon that can neuter a car's suspension system. Watching vehicles try to take the bump too fast—sparks spraying as metal grinds on metal—is one of the more dependable sources of entertainment for the car-deck ferry crew. I've drawn applause more than once.

Now, however, I've learned to traverse the deadly rise as if anticipating the sudden uplift of a tsunami. Disappointment is obvious on the countenances of the crew, but I'm accustomed to being no fun at a party.

Then it's into darkness. I know how Jonah felt, being swallowed into the belly of the whale. Such is your entry into the ferry's car deck. You follow the jittery brake lights of the car ahead, round and round, chancy as the ball in the roulette wheel.

I suspect the Ferry Corporation has me secretly listed as dangerous cargo. Why else would the crew always park me beside a colossal tanker filled with enough propane gas to blow the ship, and possibly me with it, to smithereens?

That highly flammable presence inches from my door persuades me not to remain in my car in company with the dogs and cats and livestock not allowed up on the passenger decks.

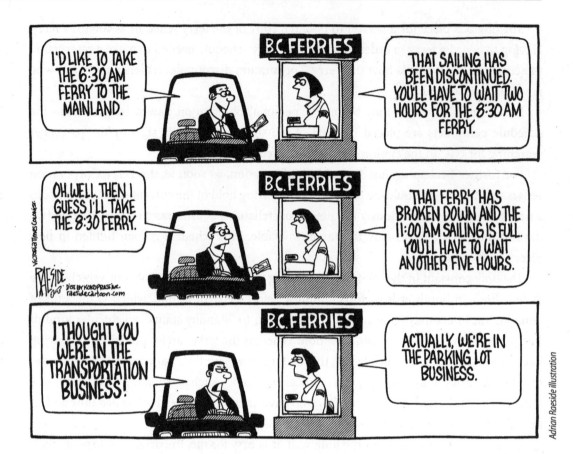

Adrian Raeside illustration

But the decision to abandon the den isn't made lightly. Reason: It is incredibly easy to be unable to find the car again when it comes time to disembark and partake of an even more frantic panic than that inspired by boarding.

They—the ferry people—hide certain cars, you know. While certain drivers are upstairs, trustingly looking for a schedule pamphlet, they somehow move a car that was parked on Deck 3B up to Deck 2B. That's why I find myself trying to run crazed up a down escalator crowded with other passengers—an aerobic exercise with few redeeming features.

So I write the number of my car deck on the palm of my hand to improve my chances of ever seeing my car again. This means not washing my hands during the voyage. Going to the washroom must be carefully thought out, therefore, if not avoided altogether. It may seem overcautious, wearing Pampers in order to find an automobile, but the sea can be a stern mistress.

This fact is briefly forgotten in the excitement of seeing that the ferry is at last moving out of the jetty. She hoots, sharing my surprise at actual movement. Gazing out the lounge window, on the side that will sun-dry me when the ship, giggling, turns around, I'm moved to capture the moment in verse:

Time cannot pale,
nor custom dull,
the oft-told tale
of buoy meets gull.

Thus are some of us stirred by the drama of the ship's leave-taking. More, however, head for the cafeteria. It isn't good form for passengers to bring their own grub onboard to save money. That shows no spirit of adventure. It's like packing a chastity belt for a cruise on the Love Boat.

The ferry cafeteria provides a unique experience akin to losing your virginity. You enter this labyrinth whose minotaur is the cashier and file past a spare buffet of sandwiches, muffins and other delicacies, all wrapped for freshness and, indeed, forever. Trying to extract one of these goodies from its plastic carapace helps to pass the time for most of the crossing of the strait.

It also gives you something to do with your hands while you observe other passengers—a fascinating cross-section of escapees from urbanization. Most of us read, or pretend to. This way we avoid making eye contact with someone who turns out to be someone we know. Or should know. Like a former lover. Or our proctologist. Someone we ought to care about enough to be able to recognize the moustache.

Passengers who have forgotten to bring the survival kit of books or crossword puzzles may be forced to stand on an outside deck, pretending to be fascinated by a passing deadhead.

I have resorted to this escape manoeuvre myself, inhaling both funnel smoke and that from nicotine addicts obliged to puff outside and fume in more ways than one. To be free of all annoyance, you may be required to stand at the bow of the ship, leaning into the wind until your eyebrows blow off.

For me, having my vision impaired by salt spray makes it harder to interpret the symbols on the doors of the ferry's restrooms. These have been designed to minimize any appearance of gender discrimination. The female symbol (skirted) and the male symbol (panted) are barely distinguishable, especially if the ship is rolling. Yet I dare not loiter at the door, peering at a hieroglyphic. Guys have been arrested for harassing the Ladies, which is why I pause only briefly and may run several laps around the deck for confirmative glimpses before actually entering the washroom.

Once in, I hate to leave it. But how many times can a guy comb his hair?

Then, hey, we're there! Arriving at the island! Moment of climax! We sit in our cars, waiting for the ecstasy to begin. For, truly, 'tis better to have felt your ferry dock than never to have loved at all…the penetration of bow 'twixt pilings…the erection of the landing platform…the repeated impact that gives release to our hand brake…then, ejaculation! One last bump and grind up the ramp and we are off to the womb of our island home.

Ferry delayed? Think of it as coitus interruptus. Euphoria is only a ship's whistle away.

28 CLAM CHOWDER THE TRADITIONAL WAY

Excerpted from The Raincoast Kitchen: Coastal Cuisine with a Dash of History *(1997),*
from the Campbell River Museum Society

"This traditional preparation was taught to me by my father, one of the pioneering
Pidcocks at Quathiaski Cove."—Ruth Barnett

Don gumboots and warm clothing. Armed with shovel and pail, make for a
clam bed at low tide. Butter clams thrive in sand-gravel beaches mainly in
the lower third of the tidal range, where they may be found at least 12 inches
(30.5 cm) deep. Unlike oysters, clams are at their best when preparing to
spawn in summer, and at their least tasty immediately after spawning. Dig
up a bucketful, wash them and drop into your pail of sea water. If the clam is
fat, its shells may not be tightly closed. Take home and set pail in a cool place,
after sprinkling oatmeal into it to deal with any sand.

Ready to make clam chowder?

In a large pot, sauté ½ cup (125 mL) chopped bacon until fat is clear. Add 1 cup (250 mL)
diced onion, 2 cups (500 mL) diced potato and sufficient water to boil the mixture.

Above a large bowl, open clams with a dull knife, cutting through the muscles on either
side of the clam's hinge. Open each clam using the knife to loosen the clam from its shells.
Drop into the bowl in order to keep all the clam liquor. Pull away the clam's spout (or

Working at a clam cannery in
Winter Harbour, ca. 1907.
Museum at Campbell River 19410

siphon) and the attached membrane and discard. If desired, chop up clam into smaller pieces and return to bowl.

When potatoes are done, add clams and set pot on a low boil for no more than 10 to 15 minutes. Then add a large tin of evaporated milk, reheat and serve. Of course amounts may be varied to taste. I often add celery and thyme.

A satisfying meal for a cold stormy day.

"Things were tough going in Depression days. We just survived. I ate so many clams I'd swear my stomach started to go in and out with the tide."
—Willie Granlund, Campbell River Museum oral history project

29

A READ ISLAND MURDER MYSTERY

Excerpted and revised from Tidal Passages: A History of the Discovery Islands
(2008), by Jeanette Taylor

When breakfast was cleared away and the children had gone to school, Laura Smith packed her husband's lunch, rifle and bedding. John was heading off in his dugout canoe to hunt for a few days—and they needed the food. It had been another tough summer for the Smiths. John had lost his log boom to the tides, leaving the family destitute. Fortunately Hattie and Edgar Wylie helped out with gifts of salted salmon and venison. The Wylies, their closest neighbours on this remote stretch of the BC coast, could afford to be generous. They had a busy store, a small hotel/boarding house and a bar frequented by the many loggers of the region.

Laura probably watched with some concern as her husband set off on that early fall morning in 1894. She didn't love John anymore and their marriage was just a token. Out on the water, the waves were bunching up into whitecaps and driving against the island's rocky shores. A storm was brewing.

When Laura returned to the house she probably set a coal-oil lamp in the window as a signal to her lover Chris Benson, to let him know her husband was away. Chris Benson was Laura's current favourite, bringing groceries in exchange for her favours. His visits were no secret to anyone in the family, but Chris had become reckless of late, stopping by two or three times a week. Tongues were wagging, which bruised John's pride. One night in bed, John had told Laura she must stop seeing Chris. If she didn't, the children had overheard him say, he'd "deal with him." Laura probably didn't respond. What was the point? They

Edgar Wilmot Wylie was a charismatic fellow who attracted a small community to his remote home on Read Island. Many of them—including Chris Benson and John Smith—were friends from North Dakota, where Edgar had been chief of police before he fled under suspicious circumstances. Edgar died in 1908, leaving his beggared estate to his housekeeper.

Museum at Campbell River 10332

needed the food Chris brought them and, after all, John was no angel himself. Sometime before this he had pulled their neighbour Hattie Wylie into their bed, where Laura lay sick, to have "immoral relations."

Laura's circumstances were complex and abusive. Her first lover, Henry Lang, was, like Chris Benson, a boarder at the Wylies', but he quit visiting Laura after she gave birth to his child, Daisy. That's when Chris Benson, a business partner of the Wylies, started coming around.

Laura's husband had immigrated to Canada with Edgar Wylie, a rotund man with liquid blue eyes. Edgar had risen to the rank of chief of police back home in North Dakota in 1888, when he ran afoul of the law in some grain deal gone wrong. He and John lit out for Canada, where Edgar lived under an alias for a time on remote Read Island. It proved the perfect spot, so both men sent for their families and settled on adjacent homesteads. Edgar may have had some investments to draw on, or perhaps it was his adept hand at cards that bankrolled his businesses. He was soon financing loggers, including John Smith, through credit at his store. In less than a decade, he was ready to build a new hotel on a bluff with a fine prospect, on a corner of John Smith's land.

While the Wylies' fortunes had flourished, the Smiths were barely able to feed their family of four by that fall day in 1894 when John set off hunting with his dogs. Laura stood on the shore to see him off, with the baby on her hip, and then walked up the boulder beach to their cabin. About an hour later she heard the clatter of boots on the front verandah—or so I picture this scene, based on the account she and her daughters gave in a trial a year later. She must have swung around with an expectant smile, but it wasn't Chris at the door. John was back. His dogs had run off, he said, so he'd had to cancel his hunting trip.

The three older children came home for lunch that day, fighting the wind along the rock bluff that separated their cabin from the Wylies' place, where school was held in the hotel parlour. Later John followed the children back to school, to see Edgar Wylie, and he was still away when Laura spotted Chris Benson's double-ended rowboat headed across the channel. Chris veered off to the south, going to a little cove out of sight of the hotel, and Laura was waiting for him when he bounded up the front steps of the cabin. Chris was a big man, who would have had to duck his head, removing his straw hat, to step inside.

"'We're all alone now, ain't we,'" Laura later quoted him as saying.

"'Yes, but the old man did not go off this a.m.,'" she said.

Hattie Wylie was the daughter of a well-known doctor associated with the Mayo Clinic. She helped her father and later served as a midwife and nurse for Discovery Islanders. Hattie left her husband following John Smith's sensational murder trial because, as she said, life on Read Island had become too wild.
Courtesy of Jeanette Taylor

According to Laura's testimony, Chris agreed not to stay long, but somehow one thing had led to another. The baby was probably down for her afternoon nap and the house was quiet, so they had slipped into Laura's bedroom. They were up again and standing in each other's arms in the open bedroom door, with Chris's suspenders hanging loose from his shoulders, when John crept inside with a wooden shake mallet. Laura stepped aside just as John levelled a powerful blow that struck Chris on the left side of his head.

"'Oh, Smith, you've hurt me,'" Chris groaned before he slumped to the floor at the foot of the bed.

"'Damn you,'" John said. "'I'll fix you. You won't come see a woman of mine again.'"

Laura had backed into the kitchen, where she heard John deliver a few more blows. When he joined her, he told Laura not to say a word about what had happened or he'd shoot her. He locked both the outside doors, and in the hour that ticked by until the children drifted home from school, Laura heard the occasional moan from her bedroom.

Ten-year-old Myrtle got home at about 4 pm. She was puzzled by the locked doors but she went to play by the little creek near the house until Laura called her to help gather wood shavings and firewood. They were lighting the cookstove when Myrtle heard a low moan from behind her parents' bedroom door. She drew closer to listen but her father told her to

Edgar and Hattie Wylie built a second hotel/boarding house on a bluff on John and Laura Smith's land, which adjoined their property in Burdwood Bay, on the east coast of Read Island. There is a hint in John Smith's murder trial that Edgar Wylie paid for John Smith's legal costs. This was denied, but following the trial Edgar got title to the Smiths' land.

Photo from Lukin Johnston's Beyond the Rockies

go back outside. When the child was gone, Laura slipped into the bedroom to feel Chris's hands. On a last check, just before the other two children came home at about 5 pm, his hands had begun to go cold.

Laura served the family supper as usual that night, just as dusk began to settle. And though it was getting dark, she urged the children to take the baby and go play among the trees on the hillside behind the house.

"'Let's take this body out to the boat,'" John said when the children were gone.

Laura was shocked by this, but the situation was a "drowned hog," as she later put it. John hefted Chris's lifeless shoulders, and Laura took his feet. They dragged him down to his little skiff in its hidden bay and lay him inside on his back. Then, in the growing darkness, John towed the boat south, letting it blow with the southeast wind into a bay. He hoped that when the boat was found it would appear Chris had fallen in the storm and hit his head. The problem was that John was not a man for details. He left the body in an unlikely position in the boat, where there was no blood to suggest a site of impact. And then there were Chris's clothes. What fool would be out in such foul weather dressed only in his shirt and unfastened trousers?

The next morning Hattie Wylie came to the Smiths', as she often did, and John took her into his confidence. She helped in a futile attempt to scrub Chris's blood from the bedroom floor and she took away a pile of Laura's blood-splattered clothes from beneath the bed. Before she left, Hattie admonished Laura not to talk about what had happened, later adding that if John was sentenced to hang, Laura would have to watch.

It was nearly three weeks before a high tide lifted Chris Benson's boat off a beach and set it adrift in the channel, where loggers found it and towed it to Wylie's Hotel. They sent for Justice of the Peace Mike Manson, who examined the body and made enquiries. Its circumstances and rumours afloat about love triangles made him suspicious, so he shipped the body to Vancouver and sent for the police. When the coroner's report arrived, it confirmed that Chris Benson had died as a result of a massive blow from a blunt instrument. Laura heard the details and later told John the coroner thought Chris may have lived for up to twelve hours after he was struck.

"'He didn't either,'" the children heard their father say, "'because he got a devil of a pounding.'"

John Smith seems to have been the police's prime suspect from the outset but it was hard to get concrete evidence so they arranged for one of the Wylies' boarders to become Laura Smith's next lover. The man was paid what was then a handsome sum, at $125, to extract a confession. He must have feared for his own safety in this tender trap, but Laura's husband turned a blind eye to his visits. The food he brought was much needed.

At first Laura said she knew nothing, but as the weeks passed, with her lover pretending to be very sweet on her, the story emerged. Two months later, Laura gave a full written confession that led to John Smith's arrest. Thereafter, Mike Manson took Laura and the children into his family's care on Cortes Island, and fourteen-year-old Cora and her younger sister Myrtle agreed to testify against their father. They'd heard and seen enough to convince them he had murdered Chris Benson.

The case came to trial in Vancouver about a year later, and though John Smith was impoverished, he was represented by the best lawyer in the province. With the death penalty looming, John stared off into vacant space through the four long days of his trial. Laura described the details of their lives with candour, corroborated by her daughters' evidence. John's chief witnesses were Edgar Wylie and a boarder, who said John spent that day with them, butchering a deer. Later he took a haunch home, which—they proposed—explained the bloodstains on the bedroom floorboards.

The Crown Council prodded Edgar Wylie, wondering if he'd paid John's legal fees, based upon a letter given as evidence. Council also noted that most of John's witnesses were in Edgar's debt. He was fishing, it appears, for a hint that Edgar was an accessory to this crime, but Edgar's steady denials ended this line of inquiry. It was not, after all, Edgar Wylie who was on trial.

When the last of the witnesses had testified, John's lawyer summed up his client's situation in a long, impassioned defence that earned him a round of applause from the packed courtroom. His colleagues later said this was one of the most eloquent appeals ever addressed to a Vancouver jury.

The Crown Council gave a concise but clear summation of the case, followed by a forceful address from the judge. He reminded the jury of their duty and the legal distinctions between murder, homicide and manslaughter. He then gave them his view of the case. He was convinced, he said, that Laura Smith and her children had told the truth. He found it odd that neither Hattie Wylie nor John Smith had testified. The latter, his lawyer had claimed, was in too nervous a state to speak. The judge also questioned the reliability of Edgar Wylie as a defence witness, with his checkered past and a recent conviction for bootlegging to aboriginal people. The other key witness, the judge reminded the jury, had initially said he

Above: Laura Smith's youngest child, Daisy, is seen here with her natural father, Henry Lang. After the murder trial, Laura took Daisy north to Port Neville, where they lived for a time with Henry. Daisy was sent to a Vancouver orphanage when she was about eight, and though she likely never saw her mother again, she remained in contact with her father.

Courtesy of Jeanette Taylor

didn't remember where John Smith was on that day—but on the stand he claimed John was with him and Edgar. These same friends, said the judge, had tried to discredit Laura because she engaged in lewd conversation, but as he pointed out, Laura had made no attempt to hide any of the seamy details of her life. The jury's chief difficulty, as the judge saw it, would be whether to convict John Smith of manslaughter or murder.

The jury filed out of the courtroom and returned one and a half hours later. The courthouse hallways were packed, and when the folding doors were opened a throng of spectators had to be restrained by the police as they made a mad dash for seats. "The prisoner was conducted to the dock and sat with a frightened, hunted look in his eyes," said a newspaper.

"'Do you find the prisoner guilty or not guilty?'" asked the judge.

"As the words 'not guilty' dropped from the foreman's lips," said the newspaper, "a swelling torrent of applause had to be checked by the judge." With the court once again in order, the judge thanked the jury. He did not agree with their verdict, he told them, but he must accept it.

"'You are acquitted, owing to considerable extent, no doubt, because you had a bad woman for a wife,'" said the judge. He warned John not to hurt Laura because he would not get off a second time. "'You can go,'" he said, and a jubilant John Smith stepped out the courthouse doors and into the fresh, cold air of a winter night on the Vancouver streets.

John Smith got off on this murder charge because of gender bias and Victorian mores. The all-male jury, swayed by an eloquent lawyer, were in sympathy with a man who had been cuckolded by his wife.

The lives of all these people twisted into a vortex after this trial, which continued to spin into the next generation. Hattie left Edgar Wylie shortly thereafter because the lifestyle on Read Island was too wild, as she later told her children. A year later, Edgar Wylie was the one on trial, after an aboriginal woman died as a result of his bootleg whiskey. And though Edgar got title to John Smith's land—and his hotel site—perhaps for debts owed, he lost it in a card game.

Laura and John also separated, and the three older children remained with John. Within the year, fifteen-year-old Cora married a Cortes Islander, taking her little brother. Myrtle, whose testimony corroborated her mother's claims, disappeared completely from public records thereafter. As for Laura, she and Daisy lived with the child's natural father for a time, in a logging community to the north. But when Daisy was about eight, she was placed in an orphanage in Vancouver, where her father sometimes visited. Laura moved to the remote mid-coast, where she remarried and lived out her long life in this final relationship. She and Daisy may not have ever met again. As an adult, this separation suited Daisy, who obscured her past by saying that her mother's name was "Hattie" Smith and that she had died in childbirth.

Over a century later, when Daisy's granddaughters began genealogy research, they had few details to work with, save a prideful boast that Daisy was the first white child born on Read Island. That clue led them to my book Tidal Passages, and eventually to stories of their Irish immigrant ancestors who came to the United States three centuries ago.

"I have wondered many times how our grandmother would feel," wrote Daisy's granddaughter Lois Wade, "if she knew we have discovered many of her secrets. I feel a little like we have disturbed the dead. But I am also very happy to give her a story, a childhood and a family. I find myself thinking about [Laura] much more than I would have imagined," says Lois. "Was she good to Grandma? Did she sing to her? Is this where Grandma learned her Irish ditties?"

DANCE OF THE WHALES

30

Excerpted from Whalers No More *(1986), by W.A. Hagelund*

~⌇

The author was born in BC in 1924 and went to sea at the age of sixteen, whaling and working on coastal tugs. He collected stories of whales and whaling lore and added to this his very personal history of whaling on the West Coast. —Ed.

Speaking of whales, there was one favourite story my boys often asked me to tell as they settled in to go to sleep. With a certain literary licence on my part, our boys knew it as "The Dance of the Whales." Few people have seen this phenomenon, and never have I seen accounts of it written, but it was perhaps the most thrilling sight I have ever seen. If I were a painter, I could paint its details in stark shades of colour, for the picture of it is still etched in my mind.

It was during the latter part of the afternoon watch, on a day that had been wet and squally, and I was cold and miserable as I stood my trick on the wheel. Finn John, smoking his old stubby pipe and wearing his brown Indian sweater and his battered old brown fedora, scanned the ocean as we rolled along on an outward sweep, skirting a northerly storm front that had kept us in its frigid grip all day. My eyes automatically came up from checking the compass to search the horizon opposite the direction the mate had swung his head. I snapped alert as my weary eyes spotted a strangeness there that warranted greater concentration.

To the southwest, the storm clouds were lifting and breaking apart as the wind backed around to that quarter. Fingers of sunlight poked down through these rents in the clouds to illuminate the grey, heaving sea, turning the cresting waves a translucent green, and their foaming tops a milky white. Between these shafts of warm yellow were the dark curtains of rain squalls sloping down to the sea. What had caught my eye were small dark shapes that appeared and disappeared in those dark areas of the rain squalls. Undoubtedly fish-shaped, they were so far away that only once in a while could I actually see their tails. This placed them well over five miles away, and the only fish I knew that could be seen five miles off were whales. But I'd never seen whales behaving like this before. Almost a hundred feet in length and as many tons, they were propelling themselves up, completely out of the water.

I cannot recall what sort of hail I made to get Finn John's attention, but when he turned to look, they were gone. He looked back at me, a little bemused, after scanning the area for a good five minutes through his binoculars without sighting a thing; even the sunbeams had disappeared. But he showed respect for my judgment and keen eyesight by hauling the ship around to a heading I indicated and, still at cruising speed, we moved toward that distant spot where the two winds came together.

Alexandra Burda Illustration

Twenty minutes later we were among the rain squalls, and the wind tore the clouds apart with a fury that rent the silence with several long rolls of thunder. It was like the beat of drums, signalling that the curtains were rolling back and the play beginning. Sunbeams poked down onto the sea ahead of us with a brilliance that caused my eyes to water, the dark vertical lines of the rain squalls retreated northward, and the heaving, cresting sea came alive with colour. Then, before us, not more than ten or fifteen cables off, the surface of the sea erupted as sleek black whales nearly as big as our ship hurled themselves up out of the water, some standing as high as our mast, their tails beating the surface into a frothy foam to maintain their momentary posture.

Never had I seen anything like it. Finn John got so excited he literally jumped up and down. Pulling his pipe out of his mouth, and tearing off his hat, he beat it against the weather dodger of the bridge as he roared at me, "Jesus Christ, God almighty! Will you look at those goddamn sulphur bottoms yump and dance!"

He rang down for slow speed, but there was no need to call anyone up; the noise made by the whales had brought them all out from the supper table. There must have been a dozen or more whales in sight at any one moment, and as they dropped back into the sea, others took their places. God only knows how many whales were there, perhaps a hundred. Some of the smaller ones leaped so far out of the water I could see the horizon under their tails, and they terminated their leap in a curve that brought them back to the surface in a thunderous fountain of spray as they landed full length. Sometimes they would rise together in pairs, facing one another, and pause like two huge dancers before our startled eyes, their tails beating the sea into a froth that rumbled louder than any propeller rising to the surface.

Bounding up to the bridge, Louis scowled over at the whales like a tiger held at bay, his jowls quivering, his mouth opening and closing, and his hands clenching and unclenching on the handle of the telegraph. His gunner's instinct to let fly with a couple of harpoons warred with his master mariner's regard for our old ship's aging gear.

Caution won out and, ordering John to skirt the pod of blue whales, he began looking for more suitable whales for our taking. The display lasted less than fifteen minutes; then the sea became strangely silent. Before anyone could retire, however, we sighted several humpbacks breaching to starboard, and pounced on them so swiftly they were lashed alongside before we went to our supper. On our way into the station, we heard that the crew of the *Black* had not resisted the temptation when the pod of blues had surfaced near her, and they were now returning to repair her windlass and replace the whole length of her mainline. There was no doubt they rued their impulsiveness.

During supper, Finn John attempted to explain the phenomenon we had seen by stating the whales were merely throwing themselves out of the water to create an impact of sufficient force to dislodge the encrustations and parasites they hosted on their skin. He said these parasites became more active and worrisome to the whale the farther inshore, to the warmer and less salty waters, they came.

But Jacques-Yves Cousteau, in *The Whale: Mighty Monarch of the Sea*, states that both finback and blue whales couple by facing together like humans, and, to achieve this, they swim up from the depths together, trying to achieve penetration and climax before reaching the surface. I believe that what we had seen was the grand finale, after climax had been achieved, and the inertia of their swift passage upward rocketed them above the surface, where the tail wagging was a burst of ecstasy, signalling fulfillment of this great desire.

Perhaps someday the dance of the whales will be performed within range of a camera, and this amazing spectacle will be recorded for all to behold. Nothing less would convey the true magnificence of these great creatures.

JUDITH WILLIAMS · RAINCOAST CHRONICLES 24

Cougar Companions

BUTE INLET COUNTRY AND THE LEGENDARY SCHNARRS

HARBOUR PUBLISHING

Acknowledgements

Cougar Companions was developed with the generous help of Glen Macklin; Pearl Schnarr Macklin; Glen, Helen, Norman and Albert Fair; and Homalco Chief Darren Blaney. Marion Schnarr Parker compiled Pearl Schnarr's *Cougar Companions* album, which Christa Ma loaned me. Sylvia Rasmussen Ives, Rita Rasmussen, Vern Logan, Rolf and Heather Kellerhals, Randy Bouchard, Dorothy Kennedy and Mike Moore contributed important information and photos. Thanks to Bonnie MacDonald and the Cortes Island Museum and Archives Board and volunteers, and Sandra Parish, director of the Campbell River Museum and Archives, for the opportunity to mount *Naming and Claiming: The Creation of Bute Inlet*, where Schnarr photographic material was first exhibited.

My husband, Robert (Bobo) Fraser, was my companion on all Bute Inlet expeditions. In 1991 the late Sam Smythe drove us deep up into the Homathko Valley. Chuck and Sheron Burchill made our later Homathko Camp and Bute visits rewarding in every way. John and Cathy Campbell helped us collect waterway samples and navigate the Southgate River.

I greatly appreciate Audrey McClellan's thoughtful editing of a third manuscript of mine.

Bute Inlet from the alpine to Fawn Bluff, 1925.
August Schnarr photo. Image MCR 14399 courtesy of the Museum at Campbell River

Bute Inlet Map

Klinaklini Glacier

West Klinaklini River

Franklin River

Mt. Roovers ▲

Mt. Geddes ▲

Mt. Hickson ▲

Projectile Mtn ▲

Scimitar Creek

Mosley Creek

Nude Creek

Tatlayoko Lake

Strikelan Pass

The Three Sisters

Dumbell Lake

Tellot Creek

▲ Mt. Lowwa

Homathko Peak ▲

Nostetuko River

▲ Mt. Moore

Mt. Waddington
(Xwe7xw / Mystery Mtn)

Mt. Tiedemann ▲   ▲ Claw Peaks

Tiedemann Glacier

▲ Rainbow Mtn

Mt. Munday ▲

Waddington Glacier

Coola Creek

▲ Mt. Queen Bess

Nine Mile Creek

Franklin Glacier

Scar Creek

Mt. Klattasine ▲

Majestic Peak ▲

Deschamps Creek

▲ Howard Peak

Homathko Icefield

Allaire Creek

Whitemantle Creek

Stanton Creek

Hidden Mtn

Brew Creek

Jewakwa River

▲ Cambridge Peak

Smythe Creek

Mt. Stanton ▲

Heakamie River

Teaquahan Mtn ▲

▲ Plateau Peak

Southgate Slo

Wahkash Point

Wahkash Creek

Homathko River

Cumsack Mtn ▲

▲ Gunsight Peak

Bishop River

Knight Inlet

Stafford River

Bear River

Snowcap Creek ●

Mt. Bute ▲

Waddington Harbour

● Ward Point

Southgate River

▲ Mt. Raleigh

Apple River

● Purcell Point

Icewall Creek

Knight Inlet

Bute Inlet

▲ Needles Peaks

Orford River

Filer Cr

Mt. Van der Est ▲

Paradise River

Tahumming River

Toba River

Phillips Arm

Moh Creek

Nodales Channel

Blind Channel

Shoal Bay ●

Bute Inlet

Brem River

Loughborough Inlet

East Thurlow Island

▲ Mt. Eliza

Toba Inlet

West Thurlow Island

Arran Rapids

● Thurston Bay

Stuart Island

● Rock Bay

Sonora Island

● Church House

Homfray Channel

Okisollo Channel

● Owen Bay

Raza Island

Discovery Passage

Maurelle Island

Calm Channel

VANCOUVER ISLAND

Kanish Bay

Surge Narrows

West Redonda Island

East Redonda Island

Quadra Island

Read Island

Lewis Channel

Waddington Channel

Refuge Cove ●

Sutil Channel

Cortes Island

Desolation Sound

Heriot Bay ●

Marina Island

Squirrel Cove

Powell Lake

Campbell River ●

● Quathiaski Cove

Goat Lake

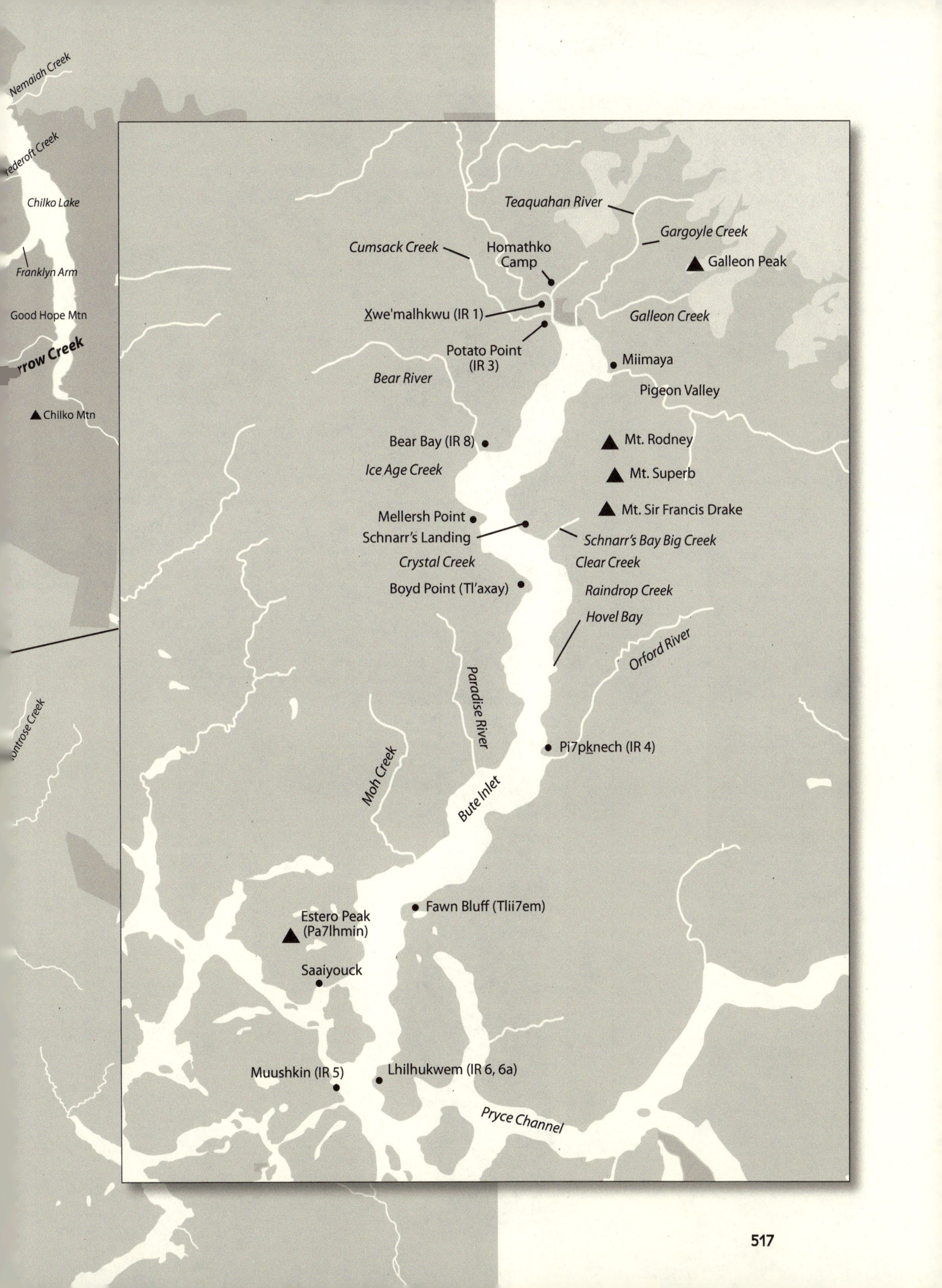

Nemaiah Creek

ederoft Creek

Chilko Lake

Franklyn Arm

Good Hope Mtn

rrow Creek

▲ Chilko Mtn

ontrose Creek

Teaquahan River

Cumsack Creek — Homathko Camp

Gargoyle Creek

▲ Galleon Peak

X̱we'malhkwu (IR 1)

Galleon Creek

Potato Point (IR 3)

• Miimaya

Bear River

Pigeon Valley

Bear Bay (IR 8) •

▲ Mt. Rodney

Ice Age Creek

▲ Mt. Superb

▲ Mt. Sir Francis Drake

Mellersh Point

Schnarr's Landing

Schnarr's Bay Big Creek

Clear Creek

Crystal Creek

Boyd Point (Tl'axay)

Raindrop Creek

Hovel Bay

Orford River

Paradise River

Pi7pḵnech (IR 4)

Moh Creek

Bute Inlet

Fawn Bluff (Tlii7em)

Estero Peak (Pa7lhmin) ▲

Saaiyouck

Muushkin (IR 5)

Lhilhukwem (IR 6, 6a)

Pryce Channel

517

INTRODUCTION
SCHNARR'S LANDING

Of the settlers, prospectors, trappers, mountaineers and loggers who came to British Columbia's remote Bute Inlet between the 1890s and the 1940s, few remained long. August Schnarr trapped far up the Homathko and Southgate Rivers and logged the inlet shores from 1910 until the 1960s. His knowledge of the waterways, their navigation and the routes up their valleys to the Interior earned him a reputation as a legendary woodsman. An adventurous photographer, August carried his Kodak camera up the 80-kilometre (50-mile) inlet with the surrounding mountains rising to 2,750 metres (9,000 feet) around him. He strapped the camera to his suspenders during upriver treks into the alpine areas few dared traverse and documented his homesteading and logging achievements. Schnarr's photo collection is a diary of fifty years of an upcoast working life.

Opposite: August Schnarr in front of the "Grizzly" ice formation, at the foot of Klinaklini Glacier, with his Kodak camera case hooked on his suspenders, c. 1913. *"Water Power Investigations: Report on Taseko–Chilko–Homatho project," page 1243, photo 74[1]*

August, born in 1886, was the eldest son of a German-American family of three boys and a girl, Minnie, who settled in Centralia, Washington state. They built a log house in big fir country, cleared land by burning the trees down, and farmed and hunted for a living.

"You worked from the time you was able," August told Campbell River Museum interviewers Joan Skogan and Jan Havelaar in 1977. "Well, of course, living in a place like that you had nothing but woodlot around you [and] I got interested in animals, trapping. And about the only things I had around there was coon . . . You had to do something you know, and so I got this and that. Then I got to hearing about British Columbia. I was in Gastown in 1907 and the whole of Vancouver was Water Street, Pender and Hastings Street. That's all that was there. They were logging . . . Well, in 1909 I came back again and I been here ever since."[2]

Steam donkey in Hovel Bay, Bute Inlet, 2017.
Glen Macklin photo

August rowed up from the United States in a 16-foot double-ended open boat, logged at Port Harvey on Cracroft Island in 1910, then explored Knight Inlet and fished along the coast into Bute Inlet with his brothers Gustave (Gus) and Johnny when logging shut down for the season. In order to continue exploring the wilderness that had captured his spirit, August became a handlogger, hunter, trapper and boat builder in the Shoal Bay area. By the mid-1920s he and his wife, Zaida, had moved their floathouse into Bute and were raising their daughters, Pansy, Pearl and Marion, at what came to be called Schnarr's Landing, two-thirds of the way up the inlet.

Bute is the second longest of the series of fiords that poke crooked fingers into the northwest coast of North America. It averages 3.7 kilometres (2 miles) in width and descends to a depth of 650 metres (2,132 feet). Captain George Vancouver named the inlet after John Stuart, the third Lord Bute, whose grandson Charles Stuart was aboard Vancouver's ship *Discovery* during his 1792 exploration of the BC coast.

From 1926, pioneering Coast Range mountaineers Don and Phyllis Munday, inspired by Bute's vast unexplored mountains, used August's local knowledge and the trapping cabins he had built up the Homathko Valley for the first assault on 4,019-metre (13,186-foot) Mt. Waddington, the highest mountain completely within British Columbia. Hydraulic engineer F.W. Knewstubb, apprised of August's woodcraft, employed him to guide a BC government survey party examining the hydroelectric potential of Bute's rivers in 1928–30.

Once such doughty coastal adventurers are gone and the wilderness fills in their tracks, what is left? Perhaps a moss-laden roof composting down in an alder grove surrounding a rusted-out "steam donkey"—used to haul logs from the woods. And if a writer is lucky, an articulate descendant will pull from a drawer a family album containing a photo of that steam donkey in action.

Since their invention, photographs have been mined long after they were snapped for social data, point of view and an atmosphere intended or felt by a viewer from a different time and place. Whether candid or staged, they become half of what we can know and use to picture and colour past lives. The cornucopia of photos, negatives, interviews and household ephemera donated by

Steam donkey, 1920s. The tiny man to the left of the donkey, beside August's overturned dugout canoe, provides scale.
August Schnarr photo. Image MCR 20447-17 courtesy of the Museum at Campbell River

the Schnarr family to the Campbell River Museum and Archives has provided remarkably informative and reverie-inducing material for an exploration of the Schnarrs' lives and has led me up the Bute river valleys that have fascinated and occasionally consumed other travellers.

Why did August, a self-educated, hard-labouring and prickly character, purchase a camera and source film and its processing from his remote location? Why make such an effort to picture his world? Talking to his family, friends and adversaries, one gets a sense that August *owned* "Bute," which stood for this wide-ranging world in which he was more at home and with which he was more enduringly engaged than most other residents and explorers. His careful imaging of the very activities needed to earn a living within that landscape—moving a float camp or cutting down a huge tree by himself—seemed to satisfy an aesthetic, ego-gratifying or even spiritual need I am sure he would not have described as such.

For a viewer schooled to value and to parse a photo for motivation, composition, social import and documentary value, a significant selection of the Schnarr photo collection allows for extended "readings." Social documents in the broadest sense of the word, when combined with the Schnarr ephemera in the Campbell River Museum Archives they allow exploration of the skills demanded for this bone-crushingly hard life and the complexity of a pioneering coastal character that could sustain it. Gratifyingly, the Schnarr images often reveal that daily life with an unstudied beauty of composition and mood. The mountaineering Mundays and the hydro survey crew produced stunning images of the mountain splendour they all moved through, but they tell us nothing of residing *in* grandeur, raising pet cougars and earning a living in the Coast Range while continuing to be awed by the surroundings, as August most determinedly does. *Look*, he says, turning from the icy "Grizzly" to us. *Look at THAT!* August's photos are love letters to the northwest Pacific Coast.

PROLOGUE

COUGAR COMPANIONS

THE GOOD PHOTOGRAPH IS NOT THE OBJECT,
THE CONSEQUENCES OF THE PHOTOGRAPH
ARE THE OBJECTS.

—DOROTHEA LANGE

Fall 2010

He was angry. On the phone, in silences between half sentences, I heard his laboured breathing.

I got his name wrong at first: "Ben?"

"I'm Glen," he said. "Glen Macklin, Pearl Schnarr's son."

Several years earlier I'd met August Schnarr's grandson Glen Fair on a fishboat in Doctor Bay. "Ever read a book called *High Slack* about Bute Inlet?" that Glen had asked.

Girlie, Marion,
Pansy, Pearl
and Leo.

Marion, Pansy and Pearl with cougars Leo and Girlie. From Pearl Schnarr's *Cougar Companions* album. *Image MCR 2006-8 courtesy of the Museum at Campbell River*

There was an awkward pause. "I wrote it," I said.

"Well," he continued, not missing a beat, "I'm the son of Pansy Schnarr, one of the sisters who had the cougars as pets up there."

Had August's oldest daughter, Pansy, and second daughter, Pearl, both named their sons Glen? The one now on the phone, the angry one, had to be Glen #2. I listened, said nothing, until I finally realized he was angry about the *Cougar Companions* photo album a friend had loaned me for my research on a Bute Inlet project for the Cortes Island Museum. She had said it belonged to Glen.

"I called Glen Fair," I said. "He gave me permission."

"It's not his, he's not part of the family," the phone voice said.

I was puzzled. Then I remembered Glen Fair had said his mother, Pansy, was not August Schnarr's daughter. "No, she was not," he'd repeated as if it was a new idea.

"He's not a member of this family," said Glen #2. "He gave the album to the museum. I had to fight to get it back. They kept the old photos—well, they're better there, but . . ."

Now I wasn't sure who to give the album back to. What had happened?

"I wanted to copy some of the photos," I said.

"No."

"I haven't copied anything yet."

"Good. You see, there's three albums made by Aunt Marion," Glen #2 said, "each different. This one you have is Pearl's, my mom's."

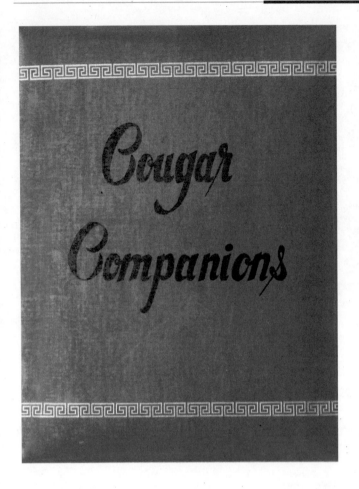

Pansy, August, Marion and Pearl on top of their gasboat, Loggerette.

Bernice (Biddie) Belton getting her picture taken with the cougars.

Above left: *Cougar Companions* album cover.
Image MCR 2006-8 courtesy of the Museum at Campbell River

Above right: *Cougar Companions* album page.
Image MCR 2006-8 courtesy of the Museum at Campbell River

As he explained more, and my long fascination with the inlet reached him, his tone changed. He was still angry, but his voice softened, became interested.

"I want to meet you," he said.

Marion Schnarr Parker made three *Cougar Companions* albums, for her sisters, Pansy and Pearl, and her father, August Schnarr. As I turned the pages of Pearl's album in 2010, August's magnificent landscape photos made it easy to slide up the liquid spine of Bute Inlet into a coastal history that paralleled my mother's 1917–1930s Texada Island childhood and my early experiences there in the 1940s. Men held fish up to be photographed. People posed on wooden gasboats nudging log booms. Houses were towed across water, and a woman holding a child leaned against a rock by the sea and laughed. But the album's startling 1930s pictures of the Schnarr girls with their pet cougars opened a very singular track to the past.

After Glen Macklin demanded I return Pearl's album, he took me to hand it back to her. She wanted to tell her story, and together they helped me follow the family tracks through the inlet I had previously explored for its violent 1860s history.

I was first captivated by Bute Inlet in the 1990s, when I travelled up the inlet to collect material for *High Slack*, a visual art installation at the UBC Museum of Anthropology that evolved into a book. Both centred on events in the inlet during the 1860s, when entrepreneur Alfred Waddington, abed with gout, a ruler and a rough map, conceived a plan to build a toll road up the Homathko Valley at the end of Bute Inlet to Interior goldfields in Tŝilhqot'in territory. Giving little thought to climate and topography, and none to the inlet's Indigenous inhabitants, he sent Royal Engineer Robert Homfray to do a survey for the road in the winter of 1861. Suppressing Homfray's reports of Bute's mercurial wind and temperature fluctuations, an attack by hostile Tŝilhqot'in, the loss of his canoe in the rampaging Homathko River, and his stranded crew's rescue and return to Victoria engineered by a Klahoose chief, Waddington started road construction the following year.

When August Schnarr explored and trapped up through the same territory, he searched for and photographed evidence of that road and the killing of the road crew by Tŝilhqot'in warriors who, responding to a threat to infect them with smallpox, declared war on the intruders. The People of the River, now known as the Tŝilhqot'in National Government, still maintain that the abuse of women also contributed to their decision to attack the interlopers, and they demand a pardon for the men the BC government hunted, duplicitously captured and hanged.[3]

August's daughters, the strong-faced young women in *Cougar Companions*, hugged their cougars, built boats, towed logs, photographed their party dresses and created a life in the wilderness in which they found themselves. Fascinated by these images, I wanted to learn every detail of the Schnarr sisters' domestic, private and working lives, and their unique experience raising the big cats. How had the 1930s media attention and representation of handsome cougars attended by attractive girls affected their view of themselves? And once the album photos made me aware of the extent to which August had documented his life from 1913, I parsed the photographs for clues to his life-defining bond with the inlet geography and history that I share. The album was the key to a clock, allowing me to rewind time.

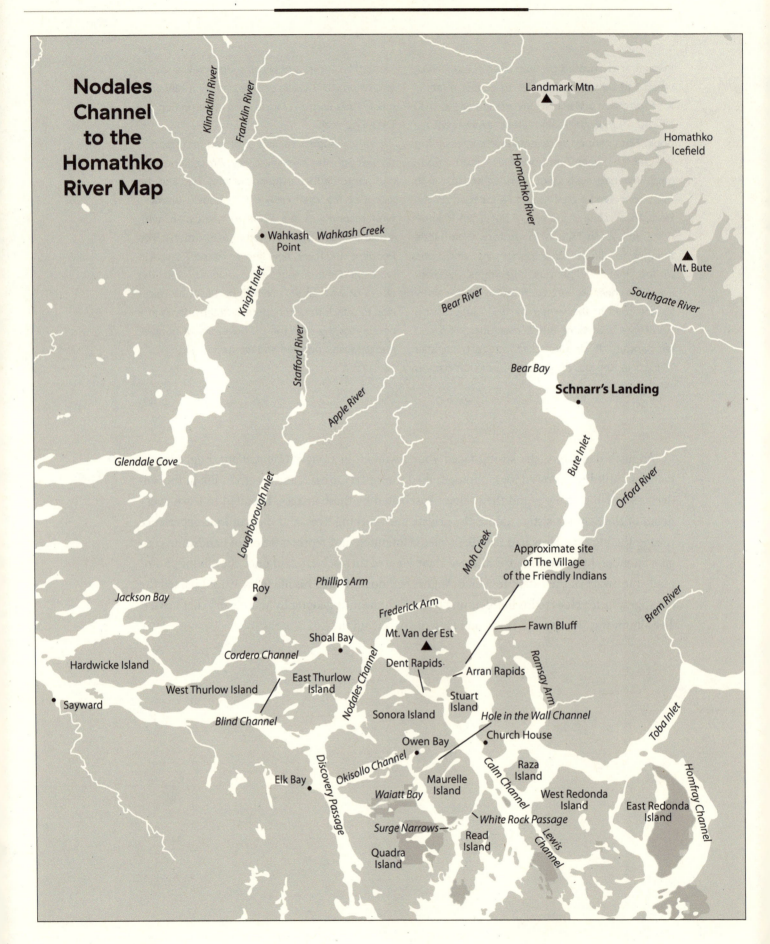

Nodales Channel to the Homathko River Map

Klinaklini River
Franklin River
Wahkash Point
Wahkash Creek
Knight Inlet
Stafford River
Apple River
Glendale Cove
Loughborough Inlet
Jackson Bay
Roy
Phillips Arm
Frederick Arm
Shoal Bay
Mt. Van der Est
Dent Rapids
Cordero Channel
Hardwicke Island
West Thurlow Island
East Thurlow Island
Nodales Channel
Sonora Island
Sayward
Blind Channel
Discovery Passage
Owen Bay
Okisollo Channel
Elk Bay
Maurelle Island
Waiatt Bay
Surge Narrows
Quadra Island
Read Island
White Rock Passage
Stuart Island
Arran Rapids
Hole in the Wall Channel
Church House
Ramsay Arm
Calm Channel
Raza Island
West Redonda Island
East Redonda Island
Lewis Channel
Toba Inlet
Homfray Channel
Moh Creek
Approximate site of The Village of the Friendly Indians
Fawn Bluff
Bear River
Bear Bay
Schnarr's Landing
Bute Inlet
Orford River
Brem River
Southgate River
Mt. Bute
Homathko River
Homathko Icefield
Landmark Mtn

1

MEMORY AS THEATRE

MEMORY IS NOT AN INSTRUMENT FOR SURVEYING
THE PAST BUT ITS THEATRE.
—WALTER BENJAMIN, *BERLIN CHILDHOOD*

Glen Macklin was late.

"Boat ran out of gas out in the saltchuck last night," he said as he opened the pickup door. "Slept in."

We drove up from Heriot Bay, where August Schnarr had moved his floathouse when he left Bute in the '60s, and turned onto Macklin Road. Glen parked next to a swath of grass decorated with a wooden propeller that he said August had carved to drive his canoe up the Homathko River.

Upstairs in the bungalow, his mother, Pearl Myrtle Schnarr Macklin, crept from the living room to sit at a chrome kitchen table by a window overlooking the lawn. Her sweet face was framed by long grey hair tied back in a girlish way, her spine twisted by osteoarthritis.

Pearl was eighty-three and she was tired. She rested one hand on a pile of old photo albums she had assembled for me, slid over a smaller one given to August by the mountaineering Mundays he had guided, and opened the *Cougar Companions* I handed back to her.

"My album, with pictures from our childhood," she said. "I still have the camera he took everywhere. Here's my mother, Zaida."

Merry-faced Zaida stands behind Pansy in a cedar-stake-fenced yard. August holds baby Pearl, born in 1923. On January 5, 1922, August had married Zaida May Lansall from Thurston Bay on Sonora Island, where settlers from Ontario had been given land. Pansy was born in its inner bay, Cameleon Harbour, in 1921.

August acquired a floathouse from a site on the mainland between Phillips and Frederick Arms and moved it across to East Thurlow Island, somewhere around Shoal Bay and Nodales Channel. The complex of sheds was winched up to a roughly logged area just above the high-tide line, and the young family lived there for about two years. August or Zaida took a photo from the house of tugs yarding a boom across the entrance to Phillips Arm.

Pearl identified another photo that showed the buildings making up the house, along with two more structures and an outhouse, all on floats and tied to a pier that, given its length, must be the one at Shoal Bay. That community, laid out on East Thurlow Island in 1895 after a gold find, once boasted three hotels and bars. August's old negative has printed up such deep space I

August Schnarr's wooden propeller and metal stand.
Judith Williams photo

Right: Pearl and Leo, c. 1937.
August Schnarr photo. Image MCR 2006-8 courtesy of the Museum at Campbell River

Far right: Zaida, August, Pearl and Pansy Schnarr.
Schnarr family photo. courtesy of the Museum at Campbell River

The Schnarr floathouse near Nodales Channel.
August Schnarr photo. Image MCR 11640 courtesy of the Museum at Campbell River

Left: Lansall pole cabin, Cameleon Harbour, Thurston Bay, Sonora Island.
Schnarr family photo. Image MCR 14392 courtesy of the Museum at Campbell River

Below: Log tow, entrance to Phillips Arm.
August Schnarr photo. Image MCR 20447-5 courtesy of the Museum at Campbell River

The Schnarr float camp at Shoal Bay.
August Schnarr photo. Image MCR 20447-20 courtesy of the Museum at Campbell River

can count the pieces of laundry on the line and pick my way back, as I did when I visited the bay in 1990, to abandoned boxes of mining cores at the mouth of the road into that draw. Pearl said August laughed about what fools he thought men were, staking their lives on finding gold there.

The hand-hewn 30-foot-long, 5-foot-wide dugout sitting on the fore-edge of the float would become August's propeller-driven airboat.

"That white cruiser's our first boat, called *Hope*," Pearl said. "Don't know why, maybe because of the children. Sometimes we called it *Hopeless*, and later we called our boat *Loggerette*. Well, if there were loggers, we were loggerettes."

Even though the outfit looks ready to move, smoke rises from the floathouse chimneys and the sea looks a bit choppy. Maybe it was not a day to tow anything anywhere, or they may have been waiting, as they must if moving south to Bute, for a slack tide needed to traverse the rapids. Sometime around 1924/25 August did hitch the floats to a tug that towed them down Cordero Channel, through the Dent and Yuculta Rapids at Stuart Island and into the opaque, jade waters of Bute.

"That house was moving all the time," Pearl said. "For a while we were north of Fawn Bluff in lower Bute. Oh!" She and Glen laugh. "There were stories about a cave there. The Leask brothers put all their stuff inside. A rock slide closed it up."

Was this a backcountry treasure myth? The three Leask brothers were real enough to be photo-

The Schnarr floathouses, the gasboat *Hope* and the longboat at Fawn Bluff, Bute Inlet.
August Schnarr photo. Image MCR 20447-9 courtesy of the Museum at Campbell River

Below left: Leask Homestead, Fawn Bluff, painted by Charles Leask.
Easthope Brothers collection

Below: The Leask brothers, c.1920s.
Photographer unknown

graphed in the 1920s, and brother Charles painted their large homestead and waterpower shed in the bay at the mouth of Leask Lake, immediately south of Fawn Bluff at the entrance to Bute Inlet, opposite the mouth of Arran Rapids. When the Schnarrs anchored on the north side of Fawn Bluff, they would have met the three elderly Scots out and about in their 45-foot launch.

The country from Church House to Stuart Island, past Fawn Bluff and up Bute Inlet and river valley complex to an interface with the Tŝilhqot'in territory in the Chilcotin Plateau constituted the Homalco People's ancestral land. With the Klahoose and Sliammon Peoples, the Homalco

The Leask brothers, Henry Graham (born in 1851), Charles Hardy (1862) and Alfred (1863), were born in the Orkney Islands. Henry had been a sea captain, Alfred a banker and Charles an accountant. Intrigued by the Pacific Coast, the brothers moved to the mouth of Bute Inlet from New Zealand around 1913, during August Schnarr's first series of inlet explorations with his own brothers. Over sixteen years the well-educated Leasks, with more funds than most locals, built stone walls, walkways and a net shed with a set of boat ways, and laid water pipes from the lake to run a Pelton wheel, a small sawmill and a kiln so they could melt and pour a glass lens they were grinding for a telescope. Vegetarians, they tended a large garden and orchard. The Leasks' modest home was lined with bookshelves containing complete sets of Ruskin and Shakespeare. They became friends of the Easthope family, famous for their engines, and Easthope Brothers purchased Charles's painted panorama of the CPR steamships entering Burrard Inlet, and two more paintings looking into Bute Inlet and across the Strait of Georgia. Charles died at Fawn Bluff in early 1930. In the winter of 1933/34 both Alfred and Henry broke their legs. The brothers were taken home to Scotland.

are the most northerly grouping of Salish-language speakers. Current Homalco Chief Darren Blaney's recognition of the collapsed cave story and its relation to his family's claim to ownership in that area raises a question: Why were road builders, loggers and homesteaders like the Leasks and Schnarrs encouraged by the government to move right into Homalco village sites at the Orford, Homathko and Southgate Rivers and onto other locations they'd occupied for millennia? Bulletin #7, a 1924 Province of British Columbia Department of Lands publication, advertises land available for settlement from Toba Inlet, the home of the Klahoose People, to Queen Charlotte Sound. It promises arable land, mineral deposits and post offices at Bruce's Landing on Stuart Island at the mouth of Bute and farther up-inlet in Orford Bay. Another post office, a store and a steamer service are said to be available at the modern Homalco settlement of Church House, south of Fawn Bluff. Otherwise, the Indigenous people living throughout the entire area are not mentioned.

Pearl said the Schnarrs' Fawn Bay float camp was moved up the inlet after it was blown out by a big wind, and they squatted in upper Bute from 1925 until August obtained a twenty-year lease on April 11, 1928. Situated at A17, Range 1, Coast District, it contained 17 acres: "Commencing at the most southerly Southwest corner of Lot 556, Range 1, Coast District, being a point on high water mark of Bute Inlet: thence east 20 chains more or less along the south boundary of said Lot 556 to the south corner thereof; thence south 10 chains; thence 15 chains more or less to high water mark; thence north-westerly along said high water mark to the point of commencement." That site, south of Purcell Point on the east shore of Bute Inlet, came to be known locally as Schnarr's Bay or Landing. The floating complex seen in photos taken at Shoal Bay and Fawn Bluff was hauled ashore there, with the outhouse out over water as was common. August's plan was to handlog in summer and trap in fall while clearing land and building a garden and orchard. Once the family was established in Bute, Pearl said, he spent weeks alone exploring and trapping the Homathko Valley or up at Chilko Lake in cabins and lean-tos he'd built.

Top: The Schnarr house complex at Schnarr's Landing, c. 1927/28.

August Schnarr photo. Image MCR 20447-21 courtesy of the Museum at Campbell River

Left: A page from the Schnarr family record books, 1928.

Image MCR 79-1 courtesy of the Museum at Campbell River

Above: One of three Schnarr trapping cabins in the Homathko Valley.

August Schnarr photo. Image MCR 20447-22 courtesy of the Museum at Campbell River

Alfred Waddington's Gold Road, Homathko Camp to Mosley Creek

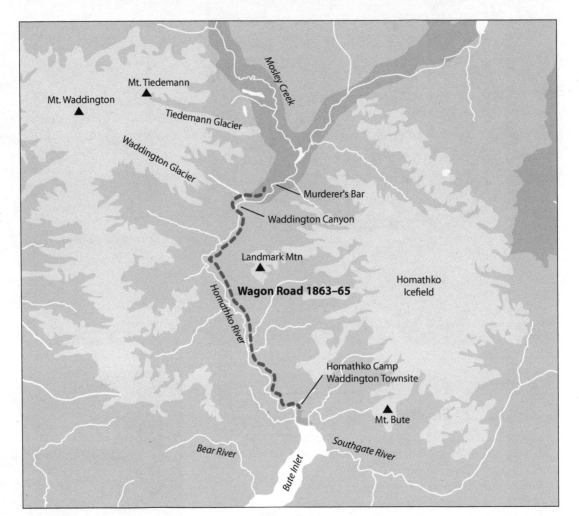

A neat hand recorded the family income and expenses for 1928 in one of a clutch of school notebooks the Schnarrs retained from their early years.[4] A number of furs were sold to the Hudson's Bay Company, a surprising $160 received as cougar bounty, $314 from a survey party August guided and $15 paid for boarding Pansy on Thurlow Island for school. The $2 paid for an official timber mark—"Stamp Hammer 34A"—indicates August had a handlogging sale, and he paid wages to A. Holm and H. Tallgard.

Both Glen and Pearl say that while trapping up the Homathko Valley, August searched for remains of the road Alfred Waddington tried to build in the early 1860s, and one of the cabins he built was near what came to be called "Murderer's Bar" in recognition of the road crew killings.

In the interviews about his life taped in 1977, August, precise about movement through the territory, said Waddington built a road from the Waddington townsite, at the head of Bute Inlet, along the Homathko River, "32 miles up, and bridges across all the creeks. And there's one or two bad creeks on the way up there, ones that clear the streams . . . [Waddington's road crew] had what they call a ferry crossing, almost at the [Homathko] canyon . . . Then above that there's a high bank of gravel, the river hitting against that. And you get up on this bank, there's a big bear trail of course, there's always a big bear trail along the river.

"Where the [Waddington] road leads up again towards the canyon . . . [It's] within a quarter of a mile of there, and there's a little creek comes in from the wood, from the river. Whenever I build a cabin I want water, and wood of course too. So I went right back in there against those mountains . . . about 400 feet . . . and built a cabin."[5]

When interviewed by Maud Emery for Victoria's *Colonist* newspaper in 1960, August laughed at those who told him he should never travel alone in such a landscape. "In that country, where mountains, canyons, valleys, lakes, rivers and river-jams hold traps for the unwary and inexperienced, if you make a mistake, it's your last. I never leave anything to chance. 'We might make it' is not good enough for me. A man is just as safe alone, perhaps safer. Suppose I broke my leg up there in that frozen mountainous region and I have a partner with me. Can he help me? No. He can't pack me out over that kind of terrain, and if he leaves me to go for help, I'd be frozen to death before he got back."[6]

However, August's trips were not always solitary. Pearl's album contained a photograph of Wardy MacDonald, storekeeper at Shoal Bay, and Teddy Hill, a forest ranger from Thurston Bay, sitting in the bow of August's longboat. The 30-foot dugout is bunted up to a gravel bar, likely in a Homathko back eddy. Looking at the next photo, Pearl said, "That's Dad's canoe with August and Teddy Hill making fun of people photographing their large fish." The camera case for August's Kodak 3, a portable of its day, sits on the boat bow. There are paddles and poles, and although that trip may be a story, his longboats, appearing over and over in August's photos, were a bigger story, an ongoing experiment allowing him to move himself and materials far upriver.

Wardy MacDonald, left, and Teddy Hill in the bow of August's longboat. *August Schnarr photo. Image MCR 14414 courtesy of the Museum at Campbell River*

This was not August's first dugout. In his photo notes he explained he'd seen Indigenous people carve long, flat canoes for travelling up the Klinaklini River in Knight Inlet. A cedar log dugout, the centre charred and hacked out, then steamed to flexibility and widened, as cedar can be with water heated by hot rocks, was ideal for navigating inlet rivers. The current in the Homathko is extremely swift, and poling or paddling any distance upstream was arduous for one man. An outboard engine required a propeller and rudder that took space below the waterline and caused strandings on the seasonally shifting sandbars. Sometime after these late 1920s photos, August carved an airplane-type propeller out of wood to be used with an inboard engine, transforming the dugout into an airboat. August's first propellers were too heavy, but the final set, now on Pearl's lawn, carved from the light, clear-grained cedar planks he used to make stretcher boards for curing animal skins, has the elegance of necessary form. Did he learn something of aerodynamics from his brother Johnny, who installed airplane engines in the high-speed boats he used to run booze into the United States during Prohibition?[7] Pearl said

Teddy Hill and August Schnarr, with August's dugout canoe, poling pole and camera case, upriver.
August Schnarr photo. Image MCR 14389 courtesy of the Museum at Campbell River

Zaida with Pansy, Pearl and baby Marion, Arran Rapids, c. 1926. *August Schnarr photo. courtesy of the Museum at Campbell River*

her father took a correspondence course in engineering around 1927; despite having had almost no schooling, August got 100 per cent on the course. "He would work and work on a problem, like building an electromagnet to pick up the heavy boom chains needed in his logging show."

The final airboat propeller was attached to an elaborately pieced wooden hub connected to steel bearings. Everything was bolted to a welded iron tripod that sat at the back of the boat. In early models, four narrow belts connected the propeller wheel to a Briggs and Stratton gas engine placed inside the boat below the pedestal. A lever at the stern of the boat raised and lowered the rudder in shallow water. When a metal cage surrounded the prop, the ensemble resembled a skookum North Woods cousin to a Florida Swamp airboat. August carried loads of lumber and tools up the Homathko to build trapping cabins, and with the airboat he could transport material up the inlet at 10 miles per hour.[8]

Pearl turned to a new album page. "That's Zaida," she said, "sitting on a rock with Pansy, me, and Marion, born in 1926, in her arms." In the photo, the Arran Rapids, west of the mouth of Bute, can be seen ebbing north between the mainland and Stuart Island.

Eighty years later, Pearl bent down into the next image's sepia-toned room. It's the only photo, museum archivists say, of an old floathouse interior, and a nice one at that. A crib, high chair, table and two kitchen chairs hover in light drifting through sunshine-filled curtains. The head of a two-point buck is mounted on a water-stained wall. Below, to the right of the crib is, . . . "a box," Pearl said, "used for Marion to sleep in when she came along. I slept in the crib. The box slid under in the day."

Did life with laughing Zaida prompt August's domestic photos, or is this sole interior image Zaida's eye and her photographic voice? The album contains images of the girls in a tub on the

Top left: Interior of Schnarr floathouse.
August or Zaida Schnarr photo. Image MCR 11639 courtesy of the Museum at Campbell River

Top right: Pearl, Pansy and Marion in a tub on the floathouse deck, Bute Inlet, August 19, 1925.
August or Zaida Schnarr photo. Image MCR 14411 courtesy of the Museum at Campbell River

house float, with rabbit and marten cages, or standing next to a dead cougar. Pearl said Zaida made the children rabbit-skin clothes and canned the rabbit meat no one would buy. "We ate it for years!"

"Did you like it?" I asked.

"We didn't know any different."

"We don't really know very much about our mother," Pearl said. "We were sent off to school and she and Dad stayed in Bute. We never saw them. When my mother died of cancer in 1932 and Dad was left with three girls, he decided to move to Owen Bay. He brought the house down inlet, towing it with a little old Easthope engine he had. Coming down, about at Stuart Island, a wind came up. He couldn't do anything about it. It just broke up the float and the house went down to the bottom. Lost everything. At Owen Bay he found some sheds, took them apart and made a house. We'd been alone a lot in Bute, and now we had the Schiblers next door, but we girls still spent summers alone in Bute while Dad went fishing. As he got older, Dad's desire to be in Bute became absolute, and when I was thirteen he moved us all back up Bute permanently."

"Why did he do that?"

"To avoid pregnancies."

That was one of Pearl's conversation stoppers.

"The Landing had a nice gravel beach, rare in Bute," she continued. "It faced directly south and the big joke was that across channel was the Paradise Valley. Dad said it was one of the worst places he'd been. Buggy! There were Indians living further up-inlet at Cumsack Creek then, in those sorts of houses they built, not much. They never seemed to build a real house. At Orford Bay I saw those hieroglyphics they made up on the bluff next to the river mouth. Way up on the cliff.

"We always had nice trim houses, always a full woodshed, that was the kind of man he was. Big garden. Grew raspberries and loganberries. Canned everything. We also had a root shed, double-layered walls filled with sawdust to keep stuff all winter. Made jam and the Indians traded fish and baskets for jam."

She pulled clippings out of a folder to add to those pasted in the album. The girls became known in a larger world after Quadra Island writer Francis Dickie published the article "Cougar Pets" in 1936.

"Oh, we were in different papers, *Maclean's*, all kinds of write-ups. It didn't mean much to us kids. They were just cats. Now we wish we'd taken more pictures."

Marion titled a *Cougar Companions* album photo of Pearl holding the cougar Girlie "Happiness is . . ." I was so startled by the image I wasn't sure I could read their emotions properly. Is the cougar purring, as she said they did, that they loved being petted and stroked? Is the mutual affection big news? Pearl, looking closely at the photo with me, was eye to eye with herself eye to eye with the cat, her arm lightly around it, holding Girlie up to her, left hand soft on soft fur. Pearl's face pressed to the cat's could be her son Glen's, could be Zaida's, so alike do they look.

Above: *Cougar Companions* **album page.**
Image MCR 2006-8 courtesy of the Museum at Campbell River

Left: Pearl Schnarr and Girlie.
Pearl Schnarr album. Unknown commercial photographer. Image MCR 15626 courtesy of the Museum at Campbell River

Pearl may have been showing off a bit for the photographer, and why not? She looks confident and the cat is sure about Pearl. August said the girls could do anything with them; they'd just snarl at him. In another photo you see the two cougars, each attached to enormous stumps. The chains were needed at Owen Bay to protect the neighbour's livestock and to keep the cats from following the girls to school. They were careful not to let them kill anything, not to give them raw meat. They fed them fish and oatmeal.

Two alder leaves at the left foreground of the photo establish distance between cougar and photographer. That's where I am, a careful distance away on the surface of the print, but I'm dying to be there, holding that cat at Owen Bay. Or are they up Bute? They took the cougars everywhere with them on boats, let them roam free while underway. Girlie once fell overboard and had to swim until they came back to get her. Where the photo was taken depends on how old Pearl is.

"I stayed at home in Bute until I couldn't stand it," she said. "Not one more fight with him. I said, 'I'm a chip off the old block.' Mad. Left at fifteen, went to Vancouver, married a military

Jack McPhee and Ed Adkin with a dead wolf.
August Schnarr photo. Image MCR 6697 courtesy of the Museum at Campbell River

man, moved to Winnipeg. Pansy married Lloyd Fair to get away. Married at Redonda Bay on the *Columbia*. Aunt Flossie came."

Remembering, she was angry again.

I turn back to an earlier album photo, a black shape dangling by a cruelly broken leg from a tripod, a haunting foil to Pearl and Girlie's affectionate embrace.

"August said he could call a wolf," said Pearl, suddenly proud of his skills. "It would come, could be shot. Fur was money, $2.50 for any pelt. You could buy a sack of flour with that. For wolves you got $150.00!"

Wolves eat deer, people eat bread and deer. No one eats wolf. Wolves you wear. Low sun casts an arced shadow of that wolf, the tripod and two men who aren't alike. On the left, an upcoast dude— "Jack," Pearl said, "that rascal Jack McPhee"—hat in hand, sticks a knife in a tripod leg. August said, "McPhee pretended to be almost anything and wasn't anything, claimed to be a trapper but he was just a nuisance."

"Lots of people don't know some wolves were black like that," Pearl said. "The other man is Ed Adkin who ran a logging camp at Eva Creek, as the Teaquahan was then called."

Small and compact, laced into white rubber boots, a roll-yer-own hanging from his lower lip, Ed stands straight, gun upright, facing forward as if on parade, hamming it up. The abrupt rise behind them makes me think the men are up the Homathko River, perhaps in 1928, when Ed was witness for the Schnarr lease.

Looking at a photo of Ed with a cougar, his son and a girl, Pearl said, "That child is me," rather firmly, as if there were some dispute. In a second related photo including August, Pansy appears about five, so it could be 1926.

When Pearl tired, Glen took me out to the big shed to show me August's extra propellers, herring rake and pelt-stretching boards that all retain a fine, dark brown surface attributable to a coating of the Bute wax that is unique to the inlet. This naturally produced substance, appearing on the surface of the inlet water only in conditions of extreme wind and cold, was used as an all-round grease and preservative. "Dad would completely fill that canoe with those Bute wax balls appearing in Bear Bay in bad weather," Pearl had said. Glen dug a soft, buttery sample from a barrel August had moved to Heriot Bay and slid it into a jar.

Late in life, on Quadra, August used Bute wax to grease the rails for hauling his last long-

Ed Adkin's son, whom Pearl called "Brother," with August, a dead cougar and Pansy, Bute Inlet, c. 1926.

August Schnarr negatives. Image MCR 14424 courtesy of the Museum at Campbell River

Glen Macklin with Bute wax.

Judith Williams photo

boat, which he often drove without the propeller's protective cage. He once came into the dock at Hill Island full speed, removed the brightwork off the side of a yacht with this rotor and walked away without a word. He hewed a dugout bathtub at Heriot Bay to keep his carving hand in. "I burned it," Pansy's son Norm Fair told me, "cleaning up after he died. Then I thought, I should have kept that wooden tub!"

The longboat became smothered in blackberry bushes after his death, but the propeller sitting on the Macklins' lawn still turned smoothly in its pieced wooden shaft.

It was late when I got back to Cortes Island after visiting the Macklins that day, and Glen's buttery Bute wax sample had melted into amber oil. Pearl died three months later.

Pearl remembered the longboat as a container for the mysterious Bute wax balls. Her rich explication of the album images led me to assemble a different kind of container: a Bute dossier based on prints from the Campbell River Museum's Schnarr negative files and copies of household ephemera donated by the family. I found more of August's photos in "The 1928–1930 Water Power Investigation of the Taseko–Chilcotin–Homathko," a report prepared for BC's Water Rights Branch. F.W. Knewstubb, the province's chief hydraulic engineer, set out the findings of the survey group August Schnarr guided up the river valleys.

I began to position images in time and place, interleaving Marion's *Cougar Companions* album stories about life with the cougars, her dates and locations, with the water report and Pansy's 1938/39 diary from the Schnarr fonds.[9] Then, using prints of August's photos as playing cards, I laid out images in suits in a skewed variant of the game Patience. I wanted to formulate a Schnarr photo taxonomy based on date, sequence, subject, archival documentation and August's tools and inventions. As I boated through the area again, I was able to anchor the Schnarrs' peripatetic floathouse camp at Shoal Bay, Fawn Bluff or deep in Bute Inlet and connect images to material related to the trapping, logging and gardening that sustained the Schnarrs through the Depression and into the 1960s.

The photograph collection begged to be examined as a social record of the remote location and the role of the three girls in their economic system, but I also developed an appreciation of the photos as conceptually and aesthetically intriguing images. I wondered to what degree August had consciously staged his photos, and from what point of view? The striking photographs of cougars hugged, treed by dogs or skinned could not help but lead me to an uneasy consideration of our complex relationship to animals we kill, wear and/or eat and those we do not. August's agenda was different.

Pearl had stressed that the media images of the girls and cougars presented the girls' life differently from how they experienced it. Journalists unnecessarily romanticized and softened a story that, given the grinding, hard-logging way August and the girls lived, planting potatoes, canning fish, making jam, building boats, booming logs, hauling 100-pound boom chains and raising cougars, all in water-access-only isolation, was already remarkable. "They even got the cats' names wrong," Pearl said, "and called me Daisy," imprecisions irritating to August's competent and necessarily pragmatic daughters.

In the process of laying out image suits, I found that the subject of one photograph might extend sideways, connect to another image and open a new track; memory might stage a small drama, usher in a new character or send me on a historical or theoretical sidetrack. Some stories are just too good not to follow. The dossier shook free of the *Cougar Companions* albums, and with the voices of remaining family members and their inlet neighbours adding commentary, I assembled a broader version of the Schnarrs' lives in Bute's exhilarating, taxing and isolated environment. It takes note of how the girls and our views of them were and are affected by their unique circumstances, by their own staging and making of images, and by being photographed by Zaida, August and outsiders. In the memory theatre, photographs can replace actual events for the Schnarrs, their descendants or me.

INTERLUDE I

THE KODAK WITNESS

AT FIRST PHOTOGRAPHIC IMPLEMENTS WERE RELATED TO TECHNIQUES OF CABINETMAKING AND THE MACHINERY OF PRECISION: CAMERAS, IN SHORT, WERE CLOCKS FOR SEEING.

—ROLAND BARTHES,

CAMERA LUCIDA: REFLECTIONS ON PHOTOGRAPHY

August Schnarr's Kodak #3 camera and case.
Judith Williams photo

June 10, 2011

The pickup skidded to a halt in the yard and Glen Macklin held two objects out the window. "Want these? In a hurry, but I dropped by Dad's and picked them up."

One was the camera Pearl had saved. "Oh yes!"

He got out, handed me a small wooden stand holding a horseshoe, propped a brown leather case on his knee and slid out the camera.

"It's August's. There's a picture of it in the canoe up the river. He took it with him. It says 1910 somewhere, I think. This is how you open it."

He clicked slick little levers and slid the bellows out. The interior was immaculate. I wanted to take a picture of Glen opening the camera with the camera August had carried up in the wilderness to picture his world and add that to Pearl's *Cougar Companions*.

544

"I've seen a great photo taken upriver at the Homathko Canyon by August," I said. "Because it shows the problem Waddington faced trying to put the road through to the Interior, it's reproduced everywhere. This must be the camera that took that and most of the album photos. Where would he have gotten film developed?"

"Don't know. Brought you this mule shoe. It's from the 1860s. Carl Larson found it way up on Waddington's road works and made the stand with wood from one of August's trapping cabins he found. Larson walked into the Interior following Waddington's proposed road and the old grease trail, walked in on the Mosley Creek route, the right way to go, he says. Found the mule shoe and gave it to me. I tried to fit the propeller at Dad's into the truck today but I couldn't get it in."

After Glen left, I worried about that propeller. He had loaned me August's pelt-stretching boards and pole and steel spikes from the Southgate rail line

Above: Mule shoe and stand.
Judith Williams photo

Left: The formidable currents in the Homathko River canyon forced Waddington's 1860s road crew to climb up and over the cliffs and construct a cantilevered road south along a sheer wall from the north end.
August Schnarr photo. Image MCR 14405 courtesy of the Museum at Campbell River

for my Bute Inlet museum installation. He knew the wooden propeller should be saved, but the steel stand was a wide-stanced, awkward thing.

I turned over the abutted pieces of wood. The dainty shoe was hung on a brass tack set on the upright piece above an engraved plaque: "Waddington's Wagon Road, 1862–1864. Found Sept. 7, 1992."

History in the hand.

People say August was the only person to master Bute Inlet's fierce winds and boat far up the seasonally shifting rivers. He was hired to rescue others who tried. The hand-hewn, propeller-driven airboat illustrates his compulsion to work and work at something until he'd solved the problem. The camera, a circa 1910 Kodak #3, using a twelve-image roll of film, is another tool, a clock to tell us his time. Where and when he bought it is unknown. Photographer Henry Twiddle operated a store, post office and hotel from 1911 until the early 1950s at Granite Bay on the west side of Quadra Island. It was accessible south from Nodales Channel and west from the Schnarrs' 1930s home in Owen Bay, on Sonora Island, via Okisollo and Discovery Channels. Pioneer coastal photographer Francis Barrow bought a Thornton-Pickard cine camera from Twiddle in 1936 to shoot movies during his yearly upcoast cruises. Did Twiddle stock film?

August Schnarr's Kodak #3 camera.
Judith Williams photo

A "David Spencer" negatives envelope in the Schnarr fonds provides one clue to the source of August's camera. Spencer opened his Hastings Street store in Vancouver in 1907, the year August first arrived in British Columbia. Its photography department sold cameras and film, and offered developing. It became Eaton's in 1948. A "Woodward's" photo envelope indicates some developed film came from Woodward's Store, also on Hastings, which did a lively mail-order business of foodstuffs and general merchandise that arrived upcoast on the Union Steamship from Vancouver. When the ship docked at Surge Narrows, Stuart Island or Church House, locals like the Schnarrs boated in from all over the area for mail, groceries, gas and social interaction. The family fonds contain a number of Woodward's order books and waybills.

2

READING IMAGES

What do I mean when I say I am "reading" the Schnarr images? If I lay the photographs down in suits, adding August's late–life commentary, Pearl's explications and Pansy's and Marion's notes, I create a shaky timeline. What can I learn? Person, place, perhaps a date? If I really look, I might discern a tonal or psychological ambiance, a reason for the photo, perhaps a larger meaning. Here is young Marion around 1928–30, with a caged mink, a note says. Or is that a marten? How about those striking diagonals and dreamy layers of sun–filtering mesh? How does Marion, or how do I, feel about caged animals raised for fur? An image like this, suggesting a more complex depth to an early Bute family photo sequence, can send me off on a new image run. Conflicting stories can send me running in circles. Memory is not a science. A "reading" is not necessarily conventional history.

Marion with mink or marten at Schnarr's Landing animal sheds.
August Schnarr photo. Image MCR 11641 courtesy of the Museum at Campbell River

The oldest dated image in Pearl's *Cougar Companions* is said to show August at the "Grizzly" on the Klinaklini Glacier (see photo on page x). In the interview he gave the Campbell River Museum in 1977, August said he'd trekked there in 1913, which was when the photo was taken with his camera. It was *not* taken when he was guiding surveyors for the BC government's Water Rights Branch up the Homathko and Southgate Rivers. However, the same photo is in the BC government's "Water Power Investigation" report labelled "Foot of Tiedemann Glacier, Homathko River." On the same page of the report is a Schnarr photo that *could be* the Tiede-mann Glacier, and these two images illustrate the caution needed when dating August's work based on his, Marion's or Pearl's later memories and the notes of others. The negative of August looking back at us looking at him and the glacier formation is in the museum's Schnarr col-lection, donated by his family, and as important to me as the location is seeing the case for the camera he used from 1910 into the '60s strapped to his suspenders. A companion shot *is* firmly labelled "Schnarr standing on the Kleena Kleen Glacier."[10]

August told his interviewers he was last in Knight Inlet in 1915/16, and while there he learned to carve and pole the long, shallow dugouts the Tenaktak People used on the Franklin and Klinaklini Rivers. In their earliest coastal days, when logging ended in the fall, August and his brothers, who had joined him in British Columbia, took themselves as far into the wilder-ness as they could to hunt and trap. I had asked Pearl where August learned his woodcraft.

"They lived down in Centralia, Washington," she said. "German Americans. August was eldest. When Dad and Johnny and Gus got older, they chased their father away with his own gun. Drank. They farmed and hunted for a living. Marion wrote *Rumrunner* about Johnny's

Ray Walker with grizzlies shot by August, Knight Inlet, c. 1915/16.
August Schnarr photo. Image MCR 20447-42 courtesy of the Museum at Campbell River

activities out of Victoria during the US alcohol Prohibition from 1920 to 1933. He visited Bute sometimes. Smart aleck! They didn't get along."

Like any person wishing to survive in the backcountry, August was precise about location and distance. While in Knight Inlet he told interviewers Skogan and Havelaar that he "caught the Klinaklini River there clean through the canyon to the Interior. At the head of Knights there used to be an Indian reserve, great big totem poles. I used to take the canoes upriver, and that's where I learnt how to . . . make canoes and handle them. I used to take them up the canyon to that big glacier. I had a shack there right at the canyon mouth. There's a creek comes in from the Klinaklini Glacier, over all the way down to the gravel bar. Then it comes onto the river and just there, there's a canyon. Well, just above that, in there, I had a shack."

August and his interviewers were usually looking at his photos to spark such memories, as Pearl and I did going through *Cougar Companions*.

"There's Ray Walker [with] three grizzlies I shot up in Knight," August said. "Shot at the old one but she ran off."

Pearl said August partnered with Ray Walker, and the men trapped together in Knight during 1915/16. The photo of Ray with three grizzlies may be August's first image promoting his hunting skills. He was convinced he could earn a living in one of the inlets.

When August returned from trapping in Knight in 1916, he logged around Port Hardy on Vancouver Island, and in Shoal and Rock Bays. He was handlogging in Blind Channel, between West and East Thurlow Islands, when the larger world intruded and he and Johnny, who had moved back south, were drafted into different outfits to fight in the Great War.

"Year of '16? '17?" August said. "I went overseas in the First World War. I was in the American Army . . . I wasn't a [Canadian] citizen yet. They drafted me from this side. I coulda been back in the woods here and I wouldn't have known . . . but I went over and . . . it was quite an experience all right. I shoulda died there. Like they said, 'It's hell on you boys'! Most of them died with

Homesteaders on the Southgate.

Image B-05985 courtesy of the Royal BC Museum and Archives

In the 1960s, Ray Walker's younger brother, Dennis, related how their family and other settlers took up land at the Southgate River Township in Bute in the 1890s.[11] Homesteaders claimed sites at the Homalco village Miimaya (*MEE–a–Mian*), an important Homalco fishing area, where two types of tidal traps were used. Previously, when intertribal warfare ended, Interior Tŝilhqot'in People camped there in fall with the Homalco to smoke–dry fish for winter storage.[12]

Dennis's father, W.G. Walker, was living in England in 1892 when he heard of a proposed Grand Trunk Pacific (now the CNR) railway route from Chilcotin territory to the head of Bute Inlet. He brought his wife and eight children to Vancouver. Then, Dennis said, "Father left for the upcoast to 'land hunt' in a sailboat with two men who were going prospecting. They put him off at the head of Bute Inlet where three trappers, Ben Franklin, Tony Bernhardt and Mart Blanch–field, lived."

Franklin, a pioneer trailblazer and old–time trapper, owned a ranch at Tatla Lake in Chilcotin country. It is said he and his wife came from the Chilcotin over a well–used but dangerous Indigenous trail to take up Bute land.

Dennis's father liked the Southgate and moved his family there in March 1893. They stayed with the three trappers, who built them a log house where a shallow flat of land swings west of the river mouth. Mr. Walker bought 40 acres upriver from Ben Franklin.

"As soon as we were settled in," Dennis said, "we had to start clearing land. How we managed is beyond me, for we knew nothing about back–woods life, but we got by."

On June 25, 1895, the *Vancouver News–Advertiser* claimed settlers were coming "in fairly large numbers." The reporter noted that the local merchant had paid out $5,000 for the best bear skins he had ever seen, and "now that bear season was over, he had several of the Indians logging for him. They appear respectable, well dressed, have plenty of money and are erecting some good houses. Their gardens are also look–ing well."

With the help of Homalco People they employed, the Southgate settlers raised pota-toes, but the spuds shipped to Vancouver barely paid for their freight. A newborn Walker baby died, and then two of their daughters; the rail-way took another route; and the family, like the rest of the settlers, moved on.

pneumonia and dysentery. There's nothing to eat, laying on the cold ground . . . you see, when you read about things like that, you never get the truth. You always hear about battles they're fighting and how they get their wounded out. The wounded are left lying there! I got pneumonia, just got sicker and sicker . . . they picked me up . . . took me back behind the hill . . . behind the shelling, but the shells came right over the top . . . killed thirteen. Well, the next morning I was half covered with dirt."

Invalided out to a hospital, August eventually made it back to the Shoal Bay area.

"When I was drafted I had a 30-foot canoe and trapping stuff I left with George Bruce to sell for me while I was away. When I got back he had nothing. I said, 'When I get you one day we'll settle this.' If I want to fight, I must be in the right. Then I am determined to carry it through. [Holds up fist.] It never failed me. I wouldn't back down for anyone.

"I saw him one day in Shoal Bay. I was working in a mill. He came out of a store wearing a big overcoat, had his hands in his pockets. [I said,] 'Now I've got you. Now—Mr. Bruce, here it is.' He tried to push by me. 'Get on your guard,' I said, and he pushed by and I landed one right on him. Down he went! Three times I knocked him down. A bunch came over. He said, 'This man hit me without a warning.' They all got in a boat. I got in the boat. I said, 'Every time I see you I'm gonna hit you.'

Hastings logging crew, Rock Bay. August is at front right.
Image MCR 6696 courtesy of the Museum at Campbell River

"Well, there was one thing and another. I got married. [When] I saw him again he was working in a hardware store as a bookkeeper. Mr. Bruce . . . [when he] saw me, he was gone."

August must have carved another dugout, the one Pearl identified in the 1920s Shoal Bay photo as his "30-foot canoe." Now, with a wife and two children, August struggled to make his float camp and boats help him work for himself. "I trapped in the winter and handlogged in the summer." To facilitate his economic plan, August wanted trapping cabins or shelters every 10 miles up the Homathko Valley, where the winter furs were best, and a homestead nearby.

In a photo Pearl let me copy, two handmade paddles lean against a raft pulled up on a snowy bank out of an opaque stretch of water. An axe is stuck in the raft, and a gun leans against a rucksack at an angle I can't recommend. Behind the canvas rucksack is a beautiful young man. Fingering the torn edge of the photo, Pearl said, "That's Rankin Robertson from Cortes."

"Rankin Robertson? A kind of lady-killer," Marion said on the phone in 2010—remembered that, even though she insisted she remembered nothing.

I want to climb right into that sepia scene and join Rankin as he bends a little forward, ready to go. According to Robertson family lore, when he was sixteen, in the fall of 1920, Rankin went up Bute from Cortes Island to stay with August and help look for trapping cabin locations. When he didn't return, his family feared he'd died, but his mother noted in her diary that he strolled in for his June birthday.[13]

Rankin Robertson, Homathko Valley, 1920.

August Schnarr photo. Image MCR 20,447-31 courtesy of the Museum at Campbell River

The big rucksack on the raft in the photo would be heavy even empty. August was fussy about his gear; everything he floated and hiked up the valleys had to work. "Good enough is not good enough," he said. There was no room for mistakes. Grandson Norm Fair described how August sometimes used round barrels, covered in waterproof canvas, to which were attached two bucksaw blades that curved forward over the shoulders, to carry gear up the valleys. He wanted dry food and supplies. Firewood was essential.

Where *is* Rankin? He and August are going to, or have come from, somewhere that necessitated a raft. Contemporary Homathko Valley explorer Carl Larson said August crossed smaller high tarns like Law wa Lake between the West and East Forks of the Homathko by falling 10-inch trees and rafting them together with cross-braces. To cross rivers he entered the river so it swept the raft downstream but to the opposite side.

Elmer Ellingson, son of the inventor of the Ellingson jack that August used when handlogging, said Rankin told him, "August Schnarr and I were travelling on foot up the Homathko River where August had a trapline, and we travelled relatively easily on one side of the river, until we reached the steep walls of a canyon. At this point August said the trail was much easier on the far side of the river, and he proposed we cross the canyon. He took his axe out of his pack and chopped down a tall Douglas fir to fall across the canyon to form a temporary bridge high above the wild water below. August then donned his pack, climbed up on the trunk of the fir with his axe in one hand and walked steadily across the bridge, knocking a few limbs off the tree trunk as he went."

Elmer said, "Rankin, watching this display of confidence and balance as Schnarr crossed the canyon, felt less confident and put his pack on the 'bridge' ahead of himself and 'cooned' it across the log on all fours."

Elmer's son Andy added, "This description by Rankin Robertson was very impressive as we knew him to be a very capable woodsman himself, not easily backing down from a challenge. He was clearly impressed with Schnarr's ability and self-confidence."[14]

Pearl identified men in another album photo, suggesting an adventure in a warmer season: "That's Rankin, Dad and Charlie on the right." Surrounded by frypan, billy-can of milk, plates and utensils, they sit on a gravel bar on some thread of the mercurial Homathko River, which will likely blast that bar and its tangle of stumps into another position in next July's melt. We get a good look at four boot soles. Pearl's "Charlie" is identified by Rita Rasmussen as *her* father, Charlie. He has one foot in the air and rolls toward his right arm, which is obscured by a serpentine branch. August crouches, one

Rankin Robertson, August Schnarr and Charlie Rasmussen, upriver.
Pearl Schnarr album

knee on the ground, his right hand casting strong finger shadows behind the head of Rankin, who lounges like a sharply foreshortened odalisque, lush lipped, looking straight at the camera, handsome as a star.

If this was another 1920 trip scouting for trapping cabin sites, August was thirty-four and his hair had begun to recede. Who took the photo? The Kodak may have had a timer, but it doesn't look as if August had a long flex, as Francis Barrow did during the same period, allowing him to take photos that included himself. With money and leisure to travel all summer, then boat back to the comfort of a Sidney winter house, Barrow was touring: drawing and photographing pictographs, chatting up the locals and documenting logging shows. *His* trip up Bute was a day

August, standing in the longboat, shows off a good catch so a companion can take the shot.
Pansy Eddington collection

553

**Two cougar hounds
on the floathouse
before move to
Bute, early 1920s.**
*August Schnarr photo.
Image MCR 20447-93
courtesy of the Museum
at Campbell River*

cruise aboard the steamer *Cassiar* only as far as the Orford River.[15] August, in his dugout and on foot, was imaging a deeper upcoast world he'd learned to move through out of stark necessity, but which, approached with extensive wilderness skills, could produce an abundance he liked to display. He was ready for a permanent family move up into Bute.

Once August located his trapping cabin sites, he and Zaida began the floathouse move from the Nodales Channel/Shoal Bay area into the inlet. Another set of images indicates how their first house was set up so it could be dismantled, moved onto floats and towed to a bay where a handlogging licence had been obtained.

One of the photos features two recumbent cougar hounds. The dog on the left lounges on a wide plank set on the lower skid logs. The photo shows how the smaller building, upper left, is skidded on top of the cross logs below the shack to the right, thereby creating their often-photographed internal porch.

In another shot the smaller building has been slid left and turned so it could be winched on or off the logs beached in front. Since August is walking behind the big logs needed for a float, Zaida is likely the photographer. Washing is hung behind the outhouse on the right, and rising smoke indicates nothing is going anywhere right then, May 28, 1924.

*Below: A note on
the negative says,
"Moving buildings,
Nodales Channel."*
*Zaida Schnarr photo.
Image MCR 20447-24
courtesy of the Museum
at Campbell River*

Another photo in Pearl's *Cougar Companions* has the floathouse complex at Fawn Bluff, and a later photo places the four buildings onshore at Schnarr's Landing below the garden. "Big garden," Pearl said. "Grew raspberries and loganberries. Canned everything."

Proud of their family, Zaida and August posed with Pearl and new baby Marion against neatly stacked firewood. Then the three girls, a little older, hug Jack McPhee's puppies and a cat on the Landing beach below the distinctive small building.

A photo taken after Einer Johnson logged August's land east of the buildings shows the top

Logging done by Einer Johnson and his steam donkey at the Landing. Animal shed with waterline in the foreground.
August Schnarr photo. Image MCR 6700 courtesy of the Museum at Campbell River

Schnarr trapping cabin, Homathko Valley.
August Schnarr photo. Image MCR 6703 courtesy of the Museum at Campbell River

corner of the garden, perhaps potato hills, and the waterline to the rabbit, mink and marten shed. It must date from the 1928–1932 period when the lease was certified, the garden established and August could log his land.

While Einer logged, his wife, Beryl, sat with Zaida behind a very dead bear draped over a log. I shift the photo to begin a suit of dead-creature images I line up under August's photograph of one of the Homathko Valley trapping cabins he used each winter. The camera's lack of focal depth makes the women seem mobile and cheerfully chatting behind the inert, sharp-focused bear.

My friend Esther, looking over my shoulder, labelled this photograph "The Quick and the Dead." She pushed a different print below it. "This is it," she said. "This is the cover of your book about Schnarr."

A cougar pelt, the head propped on a shake wedged into a chair back, is hung over a pole suspended so the legs almost walk along the deck of the porch. "Dead and alive," my conceptually minded pal titled it. Schooled in theories of photography that posit a photo as a vanished moment endlessly recurring, she saw this photo, staged to animate the expired, as illustrating that duality. More schooled in Schnarr family history, I questioned what kind of cougar August had in mind, the hunted or the hugged?

"Consider the image from a position within the backwoods economy," I proposed. "In those

Beryl Johnson and
Zaida Schnarr,
c. 1928–1931.
August Schnarr photo.
Image MCR 14421
courtesy of the Museum
at Campbell River

557

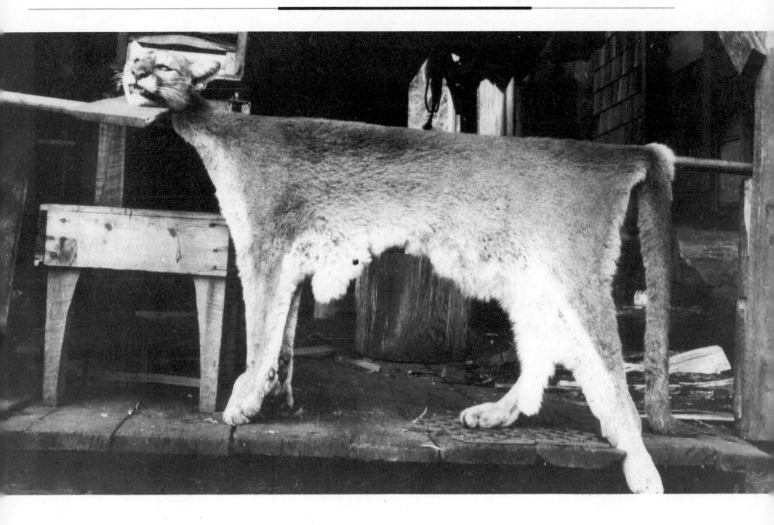

Cougar pelt.

August Schnarr photo. Image MCR 20447-41 courtesy of the Museum at Campbell River

days you had to turn in the cougar nose or ear to receive the bounty, but could sell the pelt. Although August said cougar pelts were not much valued then, according to his 1927 accounts he received forty dollars for one from Mr. Tipton at Surge Narrows Store. A trophy hunter he guided might pay more for a complete head to mount with the pelt. Perhaps that was what August had prepared, what he wanted to show."

"What's a bounty?" Esther asked.

"Vancouver Island once supported the largest and most aggressive cougar population in North America. Until 1958," I say, "cougars were labelled vermin, and the government bounty once rose to forty dollars for each nose turned in—a lot of cash during the Depression. The phenomenal number of animals eradicated through the bounty program reduced predation on domestic animals and deer, animals we wanted for food. Aligning this image with the one of Pearl and Girlie demonstrates our complicated attitude toward animals we hug and feed, those we kill and eat, and some we kill, don't eat, stuff, mount, admire and sometimes wear. We *can* become prey.

"During one solitary hunt, August climbed up cliffs high above the entrance to the Homathko River to hunt goats. A black bear charged him and August almost fell off the cliff. He reached for the Luger he kept in the top of his backpack and shot the bear. But he was puzzled by the charge as bears usually avoided him. Then he saw there was more than one bear and they were trying to run goats off the cliff. Stripped down to his white long johns due to the heat of the day, he'd been mistaken for a goat."

August's staged game photos suggest he is advertising available Bute furs to buyers like Pappas Furriers on Granville Street in Vancouver, whose letters to him regarding prices are in the Schnarr fonds. "If your skins are Mink—we can use them from $6.00–$7.00 per skin, but it relies a lot on the colours," T. Pappas wrote in February 1940. "I would suggest you ship your skins here and I want to assure you that you will have nothing to worry about, we will allow you every dime that is in them." Pappas was also interested in "extra large" and "large" marten skins ($18.00–$22.00), "smalls" ($12.00–$13.00) and beaver, for which they'd pay "up to $30.00 for fine, large, good skins."

"I never went up the Homathko trapping with August," Pearl had said, "but I did go up the Southgate on a way into the Interior in the '30s. There was a cabin. Dad's trapline was seven hours in and out. It was Marion who went up the river valleys with him the most, went up in the series of longboats, Dad's canoes. Marion was a good shot, always carried a gun."

August also guided a government survey party up the Homathko in 1928–1930, and in 1929 he and Charlie Rasmussen would spend three months trapping for marten up that river.

INTERLUDE II

THE WIND HAS ALWAYS BLOWN

Charlie Rasmussen's Bute wax.
Judith Williams photo

When my *High Slack: Waddington's Gold Road and the Bute Inlet Massacre of 1864* was published in 1995, I received a call from Charlie Rasmussen's daughter Sylvia Ives, inquiring about my reference to Bute wax based on a paper by M.Y. Williams in the *Transactions of the Royal Society of Canada*.[16] Williams wrote that the balls of Bute wax, which Pearl said August had loaded into his canoe, rolled in "scow-loads" along the shores of Bute Inlet and collected around log booms during frigid weather in the 1950s. When the inlet temperature ameliorated, the substance melted and could not be found. Williams claimed Bute wax was a plant-based derivative. Sylvia wanted to show me her father's treasured sample of this inlet substance, as well as a diary he kept of his 1929 winter trapping trip up the Homathko Valley with August Schnarr.

With the map from Charlie's tiny, handwritten record opened on the table of the café where we met, Sylvia and I followed him and August up the Homathko toward the BC Interior. The diary entries vividly described the difficulties of boating and trekking up the wild river, and of snow camping to trap marten in the alpine.

Then Sylvia reached into her bag and pulled out a small bottle of a viscous golden substance that flowed imperceptibly down, coating the glass. Bute wax was gorgeous! I wanted to eat it or rub it all over my body. Although I had noted its existence, this was my first sighting of something I came to feel stood for the inlet. No one had seen it for years.

"Dad had three samples of the Bute wax material you wrote about," Sylvia said. "I have one more sample like this, but another more transparent one has disappeared. I'd say 98 per cent of the wax we had came from the water. It collected around the log booms of Len Parker, August Schnarr's cross-inlet neighbour in Bear Bay, where it was easiest to get. Everyone thought it was

a local form of petroleum. Dad was involved with trying to get samples analyzed, and he and Len were dissatisfied with a Dr. Jain they'd transported up-inlet sometime between 1965 and '70. My brother has a map of the location of a smouldering stump impregnated with the material. The locals felt it indicated some kind of onshore source that Munday McCrae, Parker, Ed Adkin, the Moulds, Schnarr and that handsome devil Jack McPhee, all living up Bute during that period, searched for. He wouldn't let me bring it."

Sylvia's aureate jar fired my senses. It was easy to imagine Len Parker and Laurette, the third Mrs. Parker, who Sylvia vividly described as the "Dolly Parton of Bute Inlet," wallowing in it under the stuffed sea lion said to thrust out into the living room of their Bear Bay cabin. Paired with Charlie's diary map of the Homathko Valley expedition, it gave me the same physical rush I got in Bute Inlet's vast spaces, where I was awed by the sudden "Bute" wind, the bottomless anchorage problem, Bear Bay's luminous jade waves and the astounding

FROM JOHNSTONE'S ROUGH CHART
231, Part 4, on Ac1

x ----------- = latitude at head
50° 43' 12"

James Johnstone's survey chart, 1792.
Map by James Johnstone

Homathko waterway to peak mountain extremes. The wax and diary were time bombs, opening tracks in dozens of directions. Sylvia quickly saw I was hooked on the inlet mystique and left Charlie's wax sample with me to get its contents analyzed.

Over the following years, as I learned more and more about August Schnarr, the girls and the cougars, I realized Bute wax, the mystery of its substance, origin, storage and performance, created the very kind of puzzle August thrived on. According to Charlie's diary, August used his trapping trips to tease out coastal systems and follow their threads. Was that stone platform he found part of Waddington's road? Where *was* that on-land, grease-soaked, burning stump the old-timers thought *had* to be connected to some petroleum source?

Everybody speculated about why this useful substance was found in Bute Inlet and nowhere else on the coast, but Bute is exceptional in many ways. Second longest of the West Coast fiords, Bute is surrounded by mountains that rise precipitously from the water and plunge steeply 300 to 650 metres (1,000 to 2,100 feet) below the surface. The 80-kilometre (50-mile) channel regularly becomes a 4-kilometre-wide (2.5 miles) wind tunnel. Blowing down the Homathko Valley off Mt. Waddington, the highest peak completely within British Columbia, the wind is so famously ferocious its blow is known as a "Bute" in English and Xwe7xw to the Homalco, who say, "We have always lived here and the wind has always blown."[17] A Homalco story of the

The 120-metre spire alongside the main summit of Mt. Waddington, photographed by legendary British mountaineer Doug Scott when he and Rob Wood climbed Waddington in 1978.

wind's source blames Raven for everything. Tired of the strong wind that makes it difficult for them to travel, Raven, Heron, Seagull, Crow and Grebe journey to the northern country, where Wind-maker lives with his wife and son. Heron kills Wind-maker and his wife, but Raven takes the young boy home as a slave. According to Homalco elder Noel George Harry, "Today there are many winds because Raven took Wind-maker's boy home with him."[18]

Xwe7xw is also the Homalco People's name for Mt. Waddington. Located 60 kilometres (37 miles) up the Homathko River Valley, at 4,019 metres (13,186 feet high) it is the tallest mountain entirely in British Columbia. The Homalco believe Xwe7xw is the keeper of the infamous north Bute wind. Don't make fun of him or throw things in his direction or the "Bute" will blow. Xwe7xw was an important Homalco hunting ground for mountain goat, bear and deer. The magnificent 120-metre (400-foot) rock spire flanking the peak may have inspired their belief that the mountain was once a man who frequently wandered around. His wife, daughter and dogs are the individual peaks on the southwest side of Southgate Peak on the east side of the inlet. A dog-shaped stone, now under the road, reportedly graced the Southgate's bank.

The abrupt Bute temperature drops that allowed Bute wax to surface and harden are attested to in the story of a tug that arrived in Waddington Harbour to pick up a boom during the 1950s. It was so suddenly struck by a glacial wind that an ice carapace formed all over one side. In order not to capsize the tug, the captain had to release the boom and periodically turn the boat end to end, running south in reverse half the time so the ice buildup evened out.

Nothing small ever happens in Bute. The wind blows the hardest, the temperature drops the quickest and furthest. The whole place is Guinness World Record material.

James Johnstone's 1792 survey for Captain Vancouver correctly indicates Bute Inlet takes a jog west after Schnarr's Landing. At Purcell Point it rounds out to its widest point at Bear Bay, where the wax seemed to collect. Where the inlet narrows to the Waddington Harbour shallows, copious runoff from three glacier-fed rivers deposits silt and creates a layer of fresh water 9 metres (30 feet) deep, extending 50 kilometres (30 miles) south. This may have caused the wax's accumulation at Bear Bay.

Upper Bute Inlet and Homathko Valley

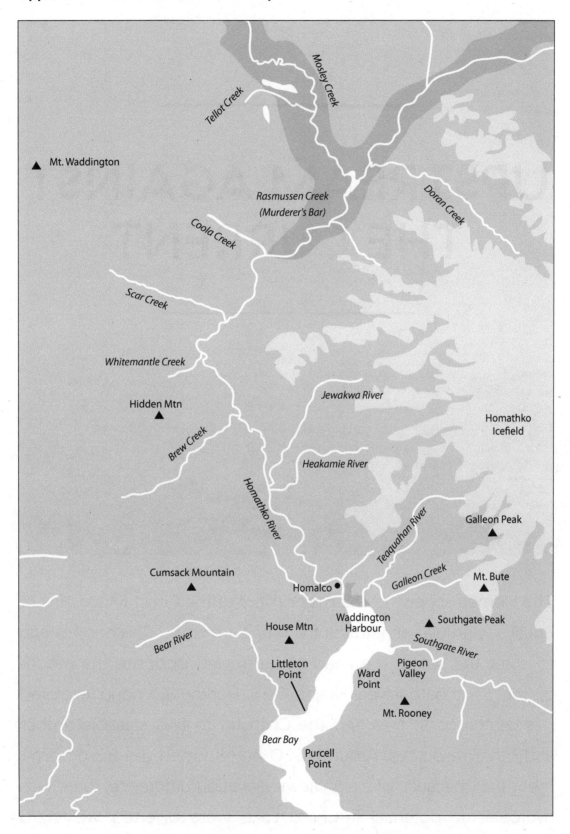

3

UPSTREAM AGAINST THE CURRENT

The Homathko, one of the major rivers of the Coast Mountains of British Columbia, penetrates the range from the Chilcotin Plateau to enter the sea at the head of Bute Inlet, opposite the mouth of the Southgate River. Major Cecil Harlow Edmond explored this central coast area and the Chilcotin to find saleable timber and other resources. Around 1920 he informed the BC government that, because of a significant elevation difference, there was hydroelectric potential if Chilko Lake were diverted westward from Franklyn Arm via Tatlayoko Lake into the Homathko River.[20]

Edmond Creek, flowing northwest into the south end of Chilko Lake, is named after Major Edmond, whose family has owned Lot 108 at the head of Bute Inlet since this time.

Since Edmond's report, the 5,335-square-kilometre (2,059-square-mile) drainage area of the two rivers has tantalized hydro engineers. When a government hydro survey was sent up the Homathko in the summer of 1928, chief hydraulic engineer F.W. Knewstubb noted that "Mr. August Schnarr [who] had trapped and hunted the lower part of the [Homathko] West Fork . . . gave the party the benefit of his experience." August ferried the group up the Homathko and outlined the route a survey party could take to the Interior.

Knewstubb edited the survey report, "1928–1930 Water Power Investigation of the Taseko–Chilcotin–Homathko," which contains location photos, panoramic vistas and elegant hand-drawn maps. A handful of photos from August's negatives, alongside some spectacular photos from the surveyors, create a subset of the Schnarr family taxonomy. One survey photo shows a narrow chasm up the Homathko canyon, a necessary crossing on Waddington's route to the gold fields, and one a hydro survey would have to consider. August had found that crossing the river on a tree felled for the purpose made the up-valley route considerably shorter. In the related West Fork (Mosley Creek) image, men move packs along a log over a river while holding on to a rope guide-rail, something August ordinarily disdained.

On the survey party's return from the Chilcotin, the group ran low on supplies. Knewstubb must have come down to the inlet with, or to get, August, as he wrote in his report:

> An arrangement was made whereby Schnarr, with an assistant [Charlie Rasmussen] for his long riverboat, and Knewstubb, Chief Field Engineer, forming . . . a "rescue party," met the survey

Left: Canyon, West Fork of the Homathko River. *"Water Power Investigations: Report on Taseko–Chilko–Homatho project," page 1226, photo 72*[21]

Right: West Fork, Homathko River. *"Water Power Investigations: Report on Taseko–Chilko–Homatho project," page 1226, photo 65*[22]

August's expert handling of backcountry hazards contributed to the wilderness reputation that led pioneering coastal mountaineers Don and Phyllis Munday to seek his advice. For their May 1926 first assault on Xwe7xw, then known as Mystery Mountain (now Mt. Waddington), August laid out the climbers' route to his trapping cabin and the glacier up which they must travel. Don Munday reported their upriver difficulties with 40-acre logjams, river quicksand and the waterway crossings August habitually made that defeated most folk.[23]

"Oh! Those glacier creeks are wild," Phyllis wrote late in life. "Carrying a sixty-pound pack on your back on a log over a wild glacier creek and the end of the log was just on the other shore and the water was so swift it was shaking the log! Oh, and to stay on the log with your pack on your back and get across . . . well, there wouldn't have been a hope in the world of course, if anybody had ever got into it."[24]

Chief hydraulic engineer F.W. Knewstubb setting out on the 1928 survey.
Frank Swannell photo[25]

party working down from the Lake—near the Forks. Provisions, tobacco, boots and clothes (stated in order of necessity) were about all done for. Schnarr helped out considerably by baking bread in his famous outdoor bakery which, with fish caught in the river, was about all the party had to live on for the last few days. The party travelled downstream, walking or relaying ahead with the longboat, to Gilkey's and Adkin's logging camps near the mouth of the river, where they were all well fed and well treated generally.

According to Charlie Rasmussen: "Schnarr and I met Knewstubb, Chief Engineer of a survey party, in 1927–28, at the point where the main 1860s massacre occurred [and] escorted them out. We brought in about 800 pounds of supplies by canoe to the survey gang."[26] Charlie noted that "Murderer's Bar," the location of the killings, would be shown as Rasmussen Creek on maps.

August's input allowed the surveyors to record evidence of Waddington's 1860s gold road. The road crew had built a log bridge across the Homathko Canyon, and the surveyors photographed what they thought were its remains, as well as relics from the cabin belonging to the ferryman killed at "Murderer's Bar" in 1864, near where August built his trapping cabin.

The intensity of the Homathko River current, caused by the canyon constriction, has always made boat passage all but impossible. When trying to push the road through in the 1860s, Waddington's crew found building anything from the lower end unfeasible and constructed a pack road that switchbacked up from just south of the canyon, over the 2,000-foot rise and down.

A photo taken in 1875 by Charles Horetzky, after the road was abandoned, shows where Waddington's crew drilled holes along the canyon side, cemented in steel pins and cantilevered a track out for the mules. Mules? You remember that shoe Carl Larson found, which Glen Macklin

Knewstubb included a photo of "Schnarr's B.C. Bakery" in the survey report. Pearl proudly told me August was unique in making sourdough bread in camp by building an oven that sat over the fire. BC Archives identifies the location of this photo as Orford Bay, dates and locations being notoriously unstable in the memory theatre.
August Schnarr negatives

Remains of Waddington's road bridge near bottom of canyon, Homathko River, 1928.
Image A-01578 courtesy of the Royal BC Museum and Archives

The Great Canyon of the Homathko, proposed Damsite #G.2.
"Water Power Investigations: Report on Taseko–Chilko–Homatho project," page 1033, photo 94[28]

Remains of Waddington's road after a flood, looking downstream from the north, 1875.
Charles Horetzky photo, Vancouver Public Library 8545

brought me? Carl says elements of the pack road on dry land up over the canyon can still be traced, even after 130 years, because the trees grow so slowly. He based his search for remaining evidence of the road and the massacre in the canyon on a statement from the Homalco man Qwittie, cook for the foreman of the road crew, who testified at the trial of the arrested Tŝilhqot'in concerning the killing of the crew.[27] Carl didn't get a reading with his metal detector until he came to a very old cedar near the trail. He dug up a broken iron pot and found an axe head that an expert later authenticated as having been made in 1850 by Collins and Co. Climbing up a rock slide at the top of the canyon above Waddington's ferry, Carl pulled rock away so it wouldn't fall on a man behind him and found two new mule shoes wired together. He speculated that after killing the ferryman, the Tŝilhqot'in warriors smashed the pot and took the shoes, which they later threw away.

Knewstubb's survey party climbed up over that canyon and took a remarkable photo down into the Homathko gorge, where they proposed situating Damsite #G.2.

The canyon remains a challenge when moving upriver to the northwest and is difficult to traverse downstream. In the 1970s a group intending to kayak down to the inlet was dropped above the canyon, but members found they had to rock-climb through it sideways, trailing their crafts on leads. The canyon stymied the progress of Waddington's road, as bridges and tracks were blown out over the winters. The 1930s hydro project was shelved due to what Knewstubb admitted would be unjustifiable construction expense for the financial return.

Even today the area's extreme weather and the seasonal variation of Homathko River flow may impede proposed run-of-river hydro projects. Although the Homathko's volume peaks in July due to snowpack melt, disgorging the third-largest flow of water of any river in the province, a flowmeter above Homathko Camp indicates it can be reduced to 10 per cent of that in

winter. An unusually hot day or a massive rainfall, winter or summer, can send the river many feet higher in hours. When we foolishly anchored our 60-foot seiner *Adriatic Sea* off the river mouth near Scar Creek Logging's booms in late summer, a heavy overnight rainfall raised the river so much that, combined with a high tide, it lifted our anchor. By morning *Addy*, with more luck than we deserved, had drifted safely into the open arms of boom logs. A couple of years later a sudden melt caused a glacier lake to collapse; a 20-foot wall of water reportedly swept down the Homathko. Don Munday wrote that "the valley is an ongoing cycle of destruction and reclamation."[29]

To get into this volatile wilderness to trap, August had learned to leave his canoe below the canyon, follow bear trails up above the river, and climb up into the alpine and onto glaciers in winter—sometimes alone, at least once with Rankin, occasionally with Charlie Rasmussen, later with Marion. One Cortes Island visitor, Doug Dewar, said he and August were on a steep bear trail, one behind the other, in the 1950s when a bear came roaring toward them. When August shot it, they had to step sharply aside as it rolled wildly downhill, threatening to bowl them over.

Pearl had told me that the winter after the survey, Charlie Rasmussen and August, desperate for cash, teamed up to trap marten.[30] Frigid winter conditions developed the thick marten pelts furriers marketed as Canadian sable. I found a photo of a string of pine marten in Pearl's *Cougar Companions* album and in Charlie Rasmussen's 1929 trapping diary file that Sylvia loaned me.[31] The two men trekked up the Homathko River and into uninhabited territory behind Mystery Mountain from October 1 to mid-December.

In a letter to Dorothy McAuley, Charlie wrote: "We ran trap line from foot of Tiedemann Glacier in many branch lines around mountains and valleys, 60 miles total and got 85 fur marten and weasels in 4 weeks. Additional 2 months was used in relaying supplies in and returning December 20, 1929. The Waddington Trail which had been linked through from head of Bute Inlet to Tatla Lake was still visible in parts, but not of any assistance to us as the 2 canyon cliff roads were destroyed over many years by weather conditions."

Charlie's diary map (see page 53) traces the trappers' route from Bute Inlet (top), along the Homathko Valley to two lean-tos on the north side of the Homathko and a cabin above Coula

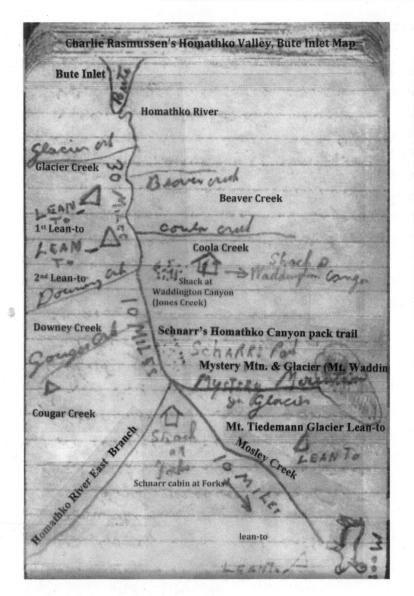

Charlie Rasmussen's Homathko Valley, Bute Inlet Map

Bute Inlet

Homathko River

Glacier Creek

Beaver Creek

1st Lean-to

Coola Creek

2nd Lean-to

Shack at
Waddington Canyon
(Jones Creek)

Downey Creek

Schnarr's Homathko Canyon pack trail

Mystery Mtn. & Glacier (Mt. Waddin

Cougar Creek

Mt. Tiedemann Glacier Lean-to

Mosley Creek

Homathko River East Branch

Schnarr cabin at Forks

lean-to

Above: Pine marten.
© jimcumming88 / Adobe Stock

Left: Charlie Rasmussen's diary, 1929.
Charlie Rasmussen collection

Creek. They left the canoe, blocked up out of the flow, at Jones Creek. The map indicates a trapping cabin above the Homathko Forks and a 10-mile trip up the West Fork (Mosley Creek) of the Homathko to a lean-to at Mt. Tiedemann Glacier, then another 10 miles toward Tŝilhqot'in territory to another lean-to and a moose sighting. Trekking up the East Branch to Tatlayoko Lake, an obvious route on a map, is described as a tougher journey by those who've tried it.

The energetic Charlie, twenty-three, raised at the Rasmussen Bay family homestead north of Lund, writes of the cold and hardships during the trip with remarkable good humour. A Schnarr photo in Charlie's Bute file shows a pile of gear and a clinker-built rowboat, perhaps his up-inlet transport, on the south-facing beach at Schnarr's Landing. His diary begins:

> October 1, Tuesday. Left Schnarr's 1:00, arrived mouth of river 3:30. Camped at Gilkie's Camp 5:30. Started next morn 8:00. Arrived Beaver Creek 5:30. Red sky in the morning so will use lean–to tent tonight.
>
> Oct 3rd, Thursday. Started to rain last night and has poured down since. Divided load in two. Took first load as far as Schnarrs lean–to, which is in an ideal spot under huge cedars.

571

Brought up second load after dinner. Schnarr's watch 3 hrs., faster than mine. Do not know which is right.

By October 4 they'd canoed 500 pounds of supplies 10 miles up to the next lean-to below Downy Creek. The river was so wild they had a few close shaves, and Charlie writes of many aches and sprains, but he also saw four bears and two wolves on the river bar, and a few seagulls 25 miles upriver from the head of the inlet.

On the 7th, Charlie took "a wild and wooly" canoe ride back downriver to the first lean-to. Poling the canoe alone against the current, it took him seven hours to bring supplies back up. His diary lists the many provisions they brought and broke up into separate numbered packs for different locations and time periods, but in spite of the hundreds of pounds of supplies they carried, they still had to hunt and fish to supply enough protein for such packing and poling. On the 8th, Charlie caught seven Dolly Varden trout in an hour. He cut wood and baked bread to go with the trout and boiled potatoes. After tea, pilot bread and jam, he went to swamp out an easier trail over Homathko Canyon (which was then known as Waddington Canyon). After that they'd be on foot.

From Charlie's diary:

The Homathko Valley from Great Divide.
August Schnarr photo. Image MCR 20447-74 courtesy of the Museum at Campbell River

October 9, Wed. Took pack over to great divide. Cached it by old surveyor's camp. Found Bear had opened can and spoiled coffee. All set for tomorrow's hike. Each pack 60–70 lbs.

On the 10th the travellers cut trail from their cache along what August called the "Caribou Road to the top of Great Divide," Waddington's intended route. Charlie fell over a sleeping bear on the way back to camp, but even without a gun they scared off its grumpy attack. August washed clothes.

October 11th, Left cabin at 7 am. Arrived cache 2 pm. Stopped for lunch at Giant Rock, Saw three goats across canyon. Highest point of trail over divide 1500–2000 feet above sea level. Schnarr still trying to pick up loose ends of Caribou Trail. Woke up one night and found mice busy chewing my hair.

Giant Rock was a huge granite slab located right on the trail that must be followed over the canyon to get farther upriver. They deposited packs there and headed back downriver to relay more supplies. On the 12th, Charlie noted:

Back at [lower] cabin at 3:30. Had shot of coffee and fixed canoe and had supper. Chased three raccoons up cedar tree 50 feet from cabin. Two rotten trout there that they were eating. Puff puff! Just sneaked up on one raccoon . . . made a dash at it and chased it for a hundred feet or so into [a patch of] Devils Club.

Back at Giant Rock with supplies, the trappers cut wood and dried their clothes. Heavy rain had raised the river's level three feet in two days and turned it into a muddy torrent. To continue travelling close to the river they had to cut a new, higher trail above the Homathko that took them by what they called "Castle Rock." The noise of the river tearing loose huge log-jams, and the ceaseless reports of boulders striking against each other in the torrent, reminded August of gunfire in the fields of France. Dinner was rice and raisins, pilot bread, jam and tea; supper and breakfast, beans and more beans!

Oct. 17, Thursday. No rain today, saw sun for a min. Good signs this eve for good weather. Schnarr stayed in camp and baked bread, while I took three packs up to Castle Rock. Great excitement 1 p.m. Hear airplane and rushed madly for a clear lookout but could not see it. Schnarr saw it upriver eight miles circling East and West Forks. Great curiosity about what it's up there for. River dropped one foot today. Schnarr found horseshoe, souvenir of 1863 Caribou pack train.

On the 18th the men moved camp from Giant Rock to Murderer's Bar, half a mile above Castle Rock, and made a shaky bridge around Castle Rock. It was rainy, and the two were gloomy until they got a tent up and the big fire going. August vowed to get moose, mowich (deer) or goat the next day.

On the 19th, while August went hunting, Charlie took three packs over the pole bridge and cut a trail to Crevice Bluff. He planned to do what he called "a Blondin," carrying packs across the 300-foot Homathko chasm at Crevice Bluff.[32] A Homalco story identifies one such upriver chasm crossing as a test of courage involving a long run, a giant leap and an essential fall as far forward as possible. Failing the latter necessity, one leaper slid down to the bottom of the canyon

Man holding a rifle against a granite slab near Waddington trail.
August Schnarr photo. Image MCR 20447-47 courtesy of the Museum at Campbell River

with not much left of his hands.[33] August's solution was to fall a giant fir across the chasm. On the 20th, Charlie carried eight packs to Crevice Bluff and sensibly built a ladder beside the log to improve the crossing. On the 21st, he moved ten packs over the bluff, noting: "Blondin stunt a nerve-wracking experience. No place for anybody with a weak heart."

The trappers then organized two packs for the heaviest day of packing yet, to "The Forks," where the Homathko branches right toward Tatlayoko Lake and left to become Mosley Creek. Crazy for meat, they hunted ptarmigan and goat, and on the 24th built a bridge across the Tiedemann Glacier runoff while up to their waists in ice-cold water. Charlie shot two small rainbow trout at Lorin Creek and saw coyote tracks on the river bar. On the 28th everything in camp froze. They brought more packs up from Crevice Bluff, and on the 30th Charlie smoked marten traps to remove human scent, while August hunted for more palatable meat.

> Oct. 31st, Thursday. Threatened snow but cleared off in afternoon. Took last pack and lunch kit up today. Two packs over Grizzly Creek to cabin. Nothing left but shoelaces dragging.
>
> Nov. 2, Saturday. Fine clear weather. Worked around cabin all day making bunk table, smoking bacon, baking bread. Mice celebrated our arrival by galloping all over my head during the night and eating rolled oats. Set patent mousetraps tonight.
>
> Sunday. Went up to Lorna Lake. Schnarr shot goat. Lots of trout jumping in lake. Used old raft on lake that is approximately 1/2 mile long.

The trappers undertook a formidable four-day hike up the West Fork of the Homathko. They spotted moose tracks and a big beaver dam and house. Camping out on November 7, they "set fire to a huge cedar that was hollow to the top and had been used by bears for winter quarters. Fire so huge and hot we had to take to woods til it fell completely burnt up. Spent another nightmare night by open fire."

Crossing a glacier on November 8, Charlie was awed by spectacular ice caverns, sunken crevice lakes and rocks piled hundreds of feet in the air. On the 9th he climbed back up to Lorna Lake, below the Homathko's East Branch, to check traps, but the raft had drifted away and he

August Schnarr's main cabin at the Forks between the East and West Branches of the Homathko River. Remains of the supine roof, found by Carl Larson in 1990s, indicate August roofed the cabin with split cedar inside up with spaces capped by inside-down cedar.
August Schnarr photo. Image MCR 14430 courtesy of the Museum at Campbell River

had to climb up over a mountain and back down to the lake to retrieve it. He packed 100 pounds of goat meat to camp while August built cages for live marten he planned to take home to breed.

On November 10 they improved the cabin, putting in windows and adding more chinking. August set to work baking bread.

On November 11 the trappers headed down to the Cougar Creek lean-to in snow and hiked the 7.5 miles back to camp with part of a goat to make a mulligan stew they followed with tea, cocoa, bread, jam and prunes. They were always hungry!

By Saturday, November 16, they were back at the Forks, hoping for clear, cold weather. Checking traps up the last branch of Mosley Creek, they crossed the river twice on a pole bridge, but waded four other streams, with icy water up to their waists.

> Nov. 19, Tuesday. Still clear and freezing. Mystery Mountain looking like ghost in the moonlight. Took sashay up left side [Tiedemann] glacier and got a big, four point buck. 300 lbs. or more. Hot Dog! Some pack.

Charlie and August took turns going up the East and West Branches of the Homathko and onto the glaciers checking traps. Charlie was stiff and sore after another bitterly cold night sleeping out by the fire.

> Nov. 25th, Monday. Heavy Fog. Went up glacier part way. Schnarr working around line to meet me at lean-to.

The next day Charlie went back up the glacier in fog to meet August at the sunken lake. The cracked ice was pushed 10 feet up onto the shore so they were forced to detour around it.

On the back of this photo, Charlie wrote, "Schnarr getting ready for a feast. Homathko River, Bute Inlet, Nov 18, 1929. The main method of fishing was shooting the trout with rifles esp. in winter." August's canoe stretches along the riverbank behind him.
Charlie Rasmussen photo, August Schnarr negatives. Image MCR 11642 courtesy of the Museum at Campbell River

Wednesday. Foggier than ever. Schnarr and I lost for a couple of hours yesterday afternoon but made lean-to all right.

The next day August went to the canyon lean-to and Charlie hiked to the Forks shack via the West Branch. He mixed up a batch of sour-hots (pancakes) and started bread, but the oven collapsed and one loaf fell in the fire.

Dec. 1st, Sunday. Still mild and clear. Schnarr and I sashayed up West Branch. Left him at 12:30 and went to Tiedemann Glacier lean-to. Picked up one trout on way, two more over river.

Wednesday. Heavy fog. Left Giant Rock 8:05. Arrived cabin [below Homathko Canyon] three hours forty minutes. (Eight miles as the crow flies.) Picked up live female marten today. Didn't have cage so used lunch can. We had a hectic time! Arrived cabin 12:30, tussled with marten and cut her teeth. Roasted front quarter of nanny goat and had great feed. Dried goat carcass and made cages.

On December 8, Charlie and August went downriver below the Homathko Canyon, where they found the flooding river had moved the blockings under the canoe at Jones Creek, though the craft was still there. The wind was howling and everything froze up.

Dec. 9, Monday. Left Waddington cabin [at Jones Creek] 8:30 am. Arrived Forks 1:50. Two hours sleep last night. Caught on fire. Burned to skin on my back and very near took to creek. Just managed to pull off shirt before getting burnt. Also burnt up bag, toque and one mitten in scramble. Oh, what a night!

Tuesday. Slept like log last night. Warm with five blankets, two goatskins and three shirts on. Water freezing three feet from fire. River and creek frozen solid.

The dauntless Charlie trekked farther up the valley to meet August on the 11th.

Arrived river crossing where Schnarr had fire going 11:30 am. Still colder up there and Schnarr looking like old man Bute tonight: overalls sagged at his knees and two inches of ash on his face! Had dinner with him and left for Glacier lean-to while he went back to Chilcotin.

Arrived at Glacier lean-to at 2:10. Cut three logs then axe-handle broke. Heavens! Brr! And, of course, I had forgotten lunch so had beans straight, no soda to take snap away either. Lit fire to big, hollow cedar 20 feet from lean-to. Burned for five hours before it fell and me

Charlie Rasmussen
with the same
string of fish seen
with August on
page 575.
*August Schnarr photo.
Image MCR 20447-35
courtesy of the Museum
at Campbell River*

watching it like a hawk for fear it would break over camp. Was wishing I had not set fire to it as my wood lasted to 7:30 am, but it was pretty to watch. After it blew a couple of holes through it sounded like giant blower and lit up the woods for 100 yards.

Dec. 12th, Thursday. Ouch! Still colder and what a night! Thank the lord it is one of the last ones out by fire. Left lean–to 8:00 am. Arrived at cabin 1:30. Tired and ravenously hungry. No lunch and lean breakfast. Picked up line, got two Marten, four Weasels.

Over the next few days Charlie pulled the rest of the traps. On Friday the Homathko River and Tiedemann Creek froze over; Saturday it snowed six inches and August arrived "looking like an iceberg."

Dec. 15, Sunday. Taking stock and storing away grub. Leaving in morning for Waddington [Homathko] Canyon.

Careful Charlie listed all his trapping hours in the notebook. The marten had proved plentiful, but by the time he returned to the small community of Lund for Christmas, the stockmarket crash had caused the bottom to drop out of the fur market.

Like the Butites' dreams that the Bute wax suddenly appearing under extreme cold and wind conditions was a petroleum product and would make them rich, the fur market failed them. In Charlie's file is a 1929 photo of him with Fred Filander's wife flanking a magnificent cougar. Its bounty nose was worth more than its pelt.

For three decades August continued to climb up into the challenging winter conditions Charlie described to earn what he could. "My father," Marion said, "was an exceptional man. Sometimes he didn't know others weren't." Young Charlie was his match.

In 1937 Charlie Rasmussen was hired by Mr. Richard M. Andrews to supervise construction of a log house on Twin (Ulloa) Islands in Desolation Sound.[34] The Andrews family turned their New York/Tokyo import/export business over to their employees because of the impending war. Having built a log house in Japan, they arrived at the island purchased for them by a Vancouver lawyer and confidently laid out a rambling house form with string.

Charlie hired three expert log-house builders from Quebec and fifteen local woodsmen to construct the house, its furniture and a five-room caretaker's cottage out of island wood. With a horse he got from Fred Thulin, owner of the Lund Hotel on the mainland, they hauled logs to the water and floated them to the big island site. Powell River pioneer John D'Angio told of peeling these logs with a spud, steam-cleaning them, then smoothing them with steel wool and oiling them.[35] Len Parker was hired from Bear Bay to work with D'Angio, improving the view from the house by using a bucksaw and spring rig to lower the hundreds of big stumps left from earlier logging. Charlie took workers up Toba Inlet in his boat *Lauritz* to cut cedar shake bolts from the Big Toba River for the roof. During the eighteen months of construction, Charlie used carrier pigeons to communicate with his mother at Rasmussen Bay.

The Andrewses' daughter, Marion, told me her mother outfitted the enormous log house with furnishings from the Vancouver Hudson's Bay store to complement her father's extensive collection of African animal heads and pelts, and the pole furniture built by Alec North. A great deal of the decor, including a decidedly Canadian moose head, remained where her mother had placed it up to and through the island's ownership by Maximilian, Margrave von Baden. Charlie visited the von Badens, bringing stories of the house construction and the murder of an earlier island owner, a minister mysteriously shot in the jaw through his boat's porthole. The mothers of the margrave and Prince Philip were sisters, and Queen Elizabeth stayed in the house Charlie built.

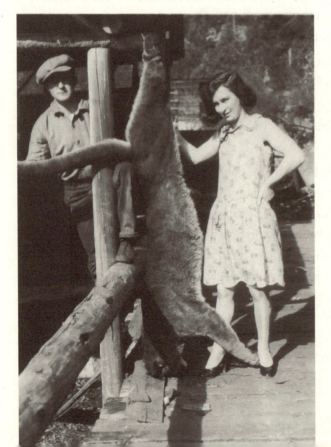

Charlie Rasmussen and Fred Filander's wife, 1929.
Charlie Rasmussen collection

The drainage entering the Homathko near August's cabin at Murderer's Bar was later named Rasmussen Creek. In 1976 a summer expedition coming down from the Interior, trying to trace Waddington's road, almost came to grief crossing the creek from Tiedemann Glacier, which everyone reports is the hardest part of any trek. Out of supplies, like the 1928 survey crew, they desperately needed to make a Murderer's Bar rendezvous with their downstream food suppliers.

"That creek is deep and fast," one of them reported, "and there are punch-bowl-sized chunks of ice floating down at you. It took twenty

Murderer's Bar, 1875.

Charles Horetzky photo, Vancouver Public Library 8547

minutes to get each person across. Later we were following Rasmussen Creek and doing fairly well. But then it dropped into a sheer rock waterfall about 1,000 feet down this narrow canyon. It was dark and we were working out way down and we just came to a dead end. We put carbineers in and roped ourselves to the rock face for the night."[36]

Although logging roads were pushed up both sides of the Homathko, alder is now reclaiming the land I drove on in 1991, and the territory Charlie and August beavered though in 1929 remains a challenge. In July 2018 the Canadian Exploratory Heritage Society attempted to re-enact the Mundays' first Mt. Waddington assault using handmade period gear. After three weeks of slogging through the wildly tangled Homathko Valley, they discovered they couldn't make it far enough inland to cross the river to reach the glaciers. Like all Bute trekkers, they ran low on food.

Mountaineer Rob Wood, who accomplished the precipitous descent of Rasmussen Creek and was photographed triumphant down on Murderer's Bar, said, "Everything in Bute is extreme!"

INTERLUDE III
HOMATHKO BLUES

It's time for Charlie's lifelong pal Len Parker to come to the front of the stage. A new parallel photo run begins with an image titled "Len's Steam Donkey" from Charlie's trapping diary file. This monster land-boat was able to drag logs and itself through the forest, carrying its own water in the tub that Charlie is inspecting on the right.

Len, an enthusiastic Bute wax collector, was August's nearest and longest-enduring neighbour. He acquired property on the south side of the Bear River in Bute looking across the channel to the grand peaks of Mts. Rodney, Superb and Sir Francis Drake, a spot August had coveted

Len Parker's steam donkey.
Charlie Rasmussen collection

for his homestead. Len established himself as a trapper, prospector, logger and poet during the period when the Schnarrs lived at and around Schnarr's Landing. Len and his wife, Mary, who he called Pearlie, had two sons. After Mary died, his second wife, Anne, a Texas schoolteacher, helped publish his poetry. After they divorced, Len married Laurette in 1959.[37]

Charlie's diary file contains a photo of Len and Betty Vaughn, cook at Ed Adkin's Eva Creek logging camp, riding Len's steel-wheeled logging truck along log rails. Charlie and August had taken Knewstubb's survey crew to be fed at the Eva Creek camp on their return from the 1928 survey.

Top left: Len Parker and Betty Vaughn, Eva Creek, 1928.
Charlie Rasmussen collection

Top right: Len Parker aboard his boat at Twin Islands, c. 1937.
John Harrison collection

Below: Butites of the late 1930s lounge on an old gasboat at a log boom when Charlie and Len were working on the Andrews family house at Twin Islands. Charlie Rasmussen standing; Jack McPhee at the left, an unknown man, Len Parker and another unknown person, c. 1937/38.
Charlie Rasmussen collection

In *Mountain and Forest Philosophy*, published at Stuart Island in 1947, Len evokes the isolated inlet life in the logger-poet rhymes of "Homathko Blues":

Moonlight glistens on the river
Stars look down from Mountains high
Wild geese honk, the while I shiver
Lonely bedtime lullaby.
North wind sweeps down the Homathko
Cold as the summit of Waddington Peak,
Lone wolf howls from a windswept plateau
Life of the wild, forlorn and bleak.
Boom chains snap on log boom swifters,
Snow drifts in through the roof at night,
Glowing red, the oil–drum heater
Cannot subdue the North wind's might.
Northlights dance o'er Mystery Mountain
Eerie the gloom of canyons deep,
The camp grows still as a statue fountain
Lonely and dreaming, at last I sleep.

Len gave the Andrews family a wood-bound, wood-paged copy of his poem "Fir Tree Philosophy" from this book. The text is burned into the pages.

In *Shadows Lay North*, dedicated to Anne, Len introduced one poem with the inscription, "August Schnarr, a friend for many years, has been the author's companion on numerous trips far into unmapped mountain country."

The cover of *Shadows Lay North*, by Len Parker, 1954.
Courtesy of Rita Rasmussen

August, a mountaineer, rested his pack.
Until his gaze, so intent and afar,
Seemed to be peering beyond things that are.

This sage of mountains, weathered and wise,
What did he see with those age–dimming eyes?

What brought him there above thicket and creek,
Timberline, boulder slide? What does he seek?

Despite Parker's poetic empathy for his neighbour's wilderness fascination, you don't want to imagine that these two lived as sensitive helpmates in the wilderness. Such independent characters always find ways to irritate one another. For some years Len had a tame bear he fed with biscuits to entertain visitors. One day August tied his canoe at Len's dock and strolled to the house. Len, wife and bear came to greet him. The bear, used to being fed, ambled up to August, stood up on its hind feet and put its front paws on his shoulders. August stepped abruptly back, causing the bear's claws to rake his hand. He slugged the bear in the jaw and knocked it out. Nursing his bleeding and bruised hand,

August turned on Len: "The next time he does that I'll shoot it!" He climbed back aboard his canoe and whirled home.

Although Len moved around for his logging, fishing and trapping work, he was still at Bear Bay when Marion and August were engaged in logging, trapping and animal husbandry in the late 1930s and '40s and when Dennis Walker's grandson, tugboat captain Vern Logan, visited Len in 1970.

After inheriting the Twin Islands house whose construction Charlie and Len had worked on, Max, Margrave von Baden, with his wife, Valerie, youngest granddaughter of the last Hapsburg emperor, and their four children, would boat or fly up Bute Inlet to visit Len and Laurette Parker. Creating an image I treasure, Valerie recalled waiting on Mrs. Parker, a late riser, until she was sufficiently accoutred and made up, apparently a lengthy process.

Parker Camp, Bear Bay, 1970.
Vern Logan photo

4

COUGAR TRACKS: THE HUNTED AND THE HUGGED

Pearl and Marion in longboat, Southgate Slough, Bute Inlet, c. 1924/25.
August Schnarr photo. Charlie Rasmussen collection

In early *Cougar Companions* photos, Zaida Schnarr is usually laughing and touching or hugging her girls. She was in the hospital for six months in 1931 after an operation, and following her death from cancer in 1933 at age thirty-one, images of the girls are scarce until the cougars become news. Pansy was coming up to twelve, Pearl ten and Marion about seven when Zaida died.

584

Pansy described the family's spartan Bute life to Maud Emery, a writer for the Victoria *Colonist*, in 1960, and later in tapes she made for the Campbell River Museum.[38] Like Pearl, she emphasized that she did not know much about their mother as she was boarded out for school at age six, and it was often far too dangerous to travel up the inlet by boat in winter. "I used to go to dances when I was six years old with the lady I lived with in Shoal Bay," she told the Campbell River Museum interviewer. "And she'd put me to bed, when it was time to sleep, behind the piano. That was Mrs. Bryants."

She remembered seeing the Indigenous people living up in Bute in the summer. The family traded them jam for fish. An old couple, Tom and Jenny, who went everywhere in their canoe, "made these baskets for us. This one she made for my Mother . . . made each of us little girls a basket, made of bark.

"In Bute we never knew what it was to go hungry. We canned fruit without sugar—too expensive. Made [our] own smoked fish by [the] root house. We canned tomatoes, carrots, beets, turnips and cabbage. We canned our own meat, made stews. We ate a lot of stew, my dad liked it and it was the easiest for us kids to cook. We were always quite healthy really."

After Zaida died, August, forty-seven, lost everything. Towing his floathouse down inlet, he was hit by a sudden wind at Stuart Island and it sank. The Schnarrs moved to Owen Bay, where there were five or six families and a school.

"Dad tore apart old camp buildings, we straightened nails and August built a house, three rooms and a cellar below. He logged and trapped. Never knew if we'd have gas for the next trip. [We] were struggling and worked hard and steady. It was slim pickings. My dad would never go on relief, no way. He'd fend for himself.

"He taught us to handlog, we bored boomsticks with the old crank auger, we were just as strong as men. We helped him bark logs. We'd run the boat all the time, go and pick a log up, handlogged into the water, we'd run down, start the gasboat up, go on, dog it, tow it in and tie it up on the shore."

Pansy told Emery that after Zaida died and their Aunt Flossie, who had looked after them, left to get married, Flossie's mother-in-law, Mrs. Godkin, became the Owen Bay housekeeper.

August liked to train his cougar dogs around Owen Bay in winter. In the introduction to her *Cougar Companions* albums, Marion describes August setting out from Owen Bay with cougar dogs Rover and Spot on a winter morning in 1934. After boating west out of Okisollo Channel to Barnes Bay, he walked a logging skid road toward Cameleon Harbour on Sonora Island. Fresh snow made tracking easy and he quickly found cougar tracks crossing the road.

"The dogs followed the tracks quietly into the forest, while August continued on his way, listening for the baying of his hounds. After walking through the snow for some distance he came to another set of tracks crossing in the opposite direction. While he was pondering which set of tracks were freshest, he heard the dogs start baying fairly close to the left of the skid road. They didn't run far until it sounded as though they had something at bay. When August made his way to where they were, he saw a large cougar crouched on the limb of a tree. Later, while skinning the beast, he discovered that it had recently been nursing young. So he backtracked to where his hounds had jumped her from under a fallen log and found four hissing kittens."

August took the four handfuls of spotted fur home to his daughters, and Mrs. Godkin cleaned them with damp paper or rag, just as the mother would lick them. Although the local

Top left: Mrs. Godkin feeding one of the cougar kittens at six weeks, c. 1934.
Cougar Companions album. Schnarr family photo. Image MCR 2006-8 courtesy of the Museum at Campbell River

Top right: Pansy and Mrs. Godkin with three cougar kittens, c. 1934/35.
Cougar Companions album. Schnarr family photo. Image MCR 2006-8 courtesy of the Museum at Campbell River

Right: Pansy, Pearl and Marion with Pat Walsh. Cleo and Leo are six months old.
Cougar Companions album. Schnarr family photo. Image MCR 2006-8 courtesy of the Museum at Campbell River

community was captivated by the newborn cougars and supported August's plan to raise them as pets, which had never been done, a few critics thought he was unnecessarily exposing his children to savage animals.

"For the first few days the baby cougars were given milk from a spoon, a method they did not like. Then some kind neighbour brought a nipple and the feedings went much better. On the fourteenth day their eyes started to open. At the age of three weeks one of the two females died. The other three were named Gilmore, Leo and Cleo. Gilmore lived three and a half months."[39]

Cortes pioneer Dunc Robertson was eighteen when he went up Bute to visit the Schnarrs (c. 1934/35). August was away, and Dunc met the housekeeper, who was embarrassed because she was wearing slacks. She said the cougar kittens were ripping her legs. If the cougars were kittens, Dunc must have met Mrs. Godkin.

In a picture of Gilmore, Leo and Cleo at three months, a worried girl holds a big, spotted kitten, while a smiling woman with shiny, waved hair barely contains two spotted furry creatures. This is Pansy with the nurturing Mrs. Godkin. Pansy doesn't even know why she's worried yet, but Mrs. Godkin was becoming fed up with three girls who were not so careful of their hair, and here were kittens to raise as well as girls. It was not long after that "we became bratty, she quit and then I was the mother," Pansy said.

"We made collars for [the cats] out of heavy leather like they use for saddles," Pansy later remembered. "They would break their chains, then hide in the bush and jump out at us when we walked home from school. It would startle us for a minute. Then we'd just take them by the chain and hook up again. When that was enough of that, my dad put heavy anchor chains on them.

"We cooked mash with fish in it for the cougars. They had to eat something, they weren't really well fed but they got nice and fat. We never gave them anything alive, never allowed them to kill anything. They were nice pets, we could pet them and they'd purr just like a cat, and they kept pawing you, don't quit, don't quit. Girlie had a different face to Leo. There's a difference. She's got nice eyes, a kinder look, it's like a tom and a female cat. They didn't like anybody but us three; they didn't like my dad at all. They were just like cats to us, we didn't think of them as anything special, nothing but a bunch of work. We had ten pigs and six dogs and two cougar. The dogs grew up with the cougars. Didn't bother them."[40]

In *Cougar Companions* Marion wrote: "They were kept in the house during the winter and ran about the rooms playing hide and seek. In the spring a wire enclosure was built close to the house and the young cougars spent part of the time there. They were fed in it all the time by then . . . Each would grab their portion and run about snarling savagely, finally settling down to eat. They still slept in the house at night.

"In the summer Leo and Cleo (called Girlie) were put on light chains and had a house of their own for shelter. This was done to safeguard the community livestock. They were close enough together to be able to play and keep each other company . . . they never tangled their chains on anything.

"They made a small, sharp sound for a greeting and purred loudly when they were petted. The cougars were always friendly with the girls, but did not want to be touched by strangers and made their wishes known by hissing. They loved to be played with like a cat and learned easily."

A contemporary view of the Schnarrs comes from an interview with Betty Yerex on another Campbell River Museum tape. When Betty was a very small girl, her father was killed in an accident and her mother, Dorothy, got a job cooking for a logging camp at the head of Bute in "Comack Slough." They'd come up on a steamer to Church House and then up-inlet to a big camp with "lots of food: bear, deer, a hospital and library." Seven miles of rail brought logs down the valley. "August Schnarr was trapping up there," Betty said, "and he came over to camp to visit with his three daughters. His wife was dead then. He used a dugout canoe with a motor to visit."

The cougar cubs were chained to a water tank while Dorothy cooked and sent them away with homemade food. When that camp closed down, Betty said, "a new group came in and Dorothy married the new Camp Super."

It's tempting to speculate that August's visits to the vibrant, independent Dorothy (who I knew as Dorothy Thomas in the 1970s at Refuge Cove) involved courting a new wife. Maybe he was just finding a friend for his girls, but without a new mate, Pansy said, "Our dad raised us like boys. We only had a man's life, we worked like men, he had us handlogging, trapping—we had a pretty rough life."[41]

With Mrs. Godkin gone, the girls shared housekeeping chores. "Pearl was the breakfast cook," Pansy said. "I did lunch and supper and we all did dishes. I was boss more or less. After the move from Bute we spent the winters on Read and every summer we'd go up to Bute again. Every summer holidays we'd spend up there picking berries. We stayed in an open shed, slept on straw. I learned to bake bread over an open fire; we had a gas stove to cook, can fruit with.

"He just had a boatshed left up there and that was where we lived. It was made of poles for

Marion, Girlie and Pearl, c. 1937/38.
August Schnarr photo. Image MCR 15266 courtesy of the Museum at Campbell River

rafters because he made everything sturdy—we'd climb along those things, no fear in us, chasing wood rats. You know, all we had to do is just roll off that log—we had no way of getting out of there. If we'd broke a leg, an arm, or our neck—nobody'd ever know because we never heard from anybody. We slept outside for six weeks, picking and canning fruit, while he was away fishing up River's Inlet. We had to have it all done when he got back or there's heck to pay. We did get nervous seeing a bear sometime. If you think of kids today living like that when they're 12, 14, 15 years old, it would just shock them to death, but we didn't know any better, we were just used to that way of life."[42]

Behind Pansy and Mrs. G. in the 1935 photo is a logged-off hillside. The Schnarrs killed trees and animals for a living. August killed the kittens' mother for the bounty. He was a logger, and the girls were, as Pearl said, "Loggerettes." In her taped reminiscences, Pansy speaks of the harshness of a trapping life and her ambivalence about killing animals. "When we were a bit older he made us go up his traplines. A two-hour job. He walked for an hour uphill, he'd set ten traps, an hour back. We had to do this by ourselves. I was such a sissy, I was scared the whole time I was gone. Sometimes I'd take my little kitten just to talk to, but I'd be looking behind bushes and scaring myself.

"My Dad liked animals. He liked wildlife, but he had to make his living on it. Killing marten, this is what I hated, when we'd come up to a trap having to kill that little marten that's looking at you. He had his foot in there, he's hurting, and you have to hit him on the head and knock

The Landing.
August Schnarr photo.
Image MCR 2006-8
courtesy of the Museum
at Campbell River

him out and then hang on to his heart 'til it stopped. There's no bruise that way on the flesh. But you know it seems terrible when I think of it now, but it was the way of life then. Shooting deer for meat, we thought that was great sport, and now I think it's the most horrid thing to hear of people out shooting deer.

"Everyone hated the way we were treated, you know, treated like men. I'm glad we weren't men because we would probably have taken a poke at him, but being girls you don't do that. When he took his boat engine apart, we had to be right there so we would know how to fix that Easthope of his. We could run machinery as good as anyone else. We were strong, we used to pull up a hundred feet of that anchor chain, besides a hundred-or-more-pound anchor and a boom chain on it, and we'd pull that up as though we were pulling string."

Pansy said that when they were going to school in Owen Bay, "I would come home during the 10:30 recess, light the fire, stack up the wood, put the kettle on, run back to school, run home at lunchtime and make lunch for my dad and ourselves. The kids would go back. I would do the dishes and run back to school. After school we had chores—dogs to feed, pigs to slop, cougars to look after, pens to clean. There was an acre of garden we had to look after too, then we'd can hundreds of quarts every year."[43]

An undated photo shows the two smaller floathouse buildings, one offset behind the other, in front of the garden. Given the Landing's location in a wide bay on the east shore below a draw running up between Mt. Sir Francis Drake and the "Needles," two-thirds of the way up the inlet, the photo must have been taken from a boat or a float. The water in front of the sheds is calm, which was not often the case, Bute being famously and dangerously windy with regular incoming afternoon swells. The garden stretching uphill has begun to fill out, and the dreamy image suggests a late midsummer afternoon when nothing could go wrong. *Which* summer is the question. Perhaps this image dates from the time after the houses were lost in the tow and the girls spent the summers in Bute alone.

"When we got home to Bute for the summer we'd run all over the boom, and jump in off there and swim around. 'Oh, the water's fine,' we'd say to our dad, 'why don't you come in?' And he'd get in to his knees and couldn't stand it. You get accustomed to it, you're sitting out in the sun all day, getting eaten by horseflies; they're awful up there."

Photographs show how the girls' individual characters became more defined as they matured, but the attitude they display in family photos is slightly different from that in a series taken in 1937–38 for the article by Francis Dickie, a writer living on Quadra Island. A commercial photographer posed the girls on a snowy stage. Pansy and Pearl, overly aware of being represented, confront the camera. Marion holds and perhaps encourages Leo, but the cougars, focused solely on the girls and each other, create a closed pack of five: us here together and you out there. The girls loved those cougars, and the cats were bonded with the girls. It is claimed that cougars are impossible to tame, but Leo and Girlie, imprinted on the girls when they first opened their eyes, knew their names, came when called and could be petted when eating, and the girls could take food away from them.

This image of teenage girls and the cougars—the male cat, Leo, still alive—tells time. The cougars arrived in the winter of 1934; Leo lived for three and a half years, and Girlie for six. The snowy series of photos was used all over the world. An article published in New Zealand produced a pen pal for Pansy and a tempting offer of marriage. "I wouldn't have minded, anything to get away!"

The author of a 1938 article in the *Nashua Telegraph* "Parade of Youth" said the cougars were taught to "jump through the girls' arms, play tug of war, catch food thrown to them." He quoted Pansy saying, "We just let them know who's boss. Anytime we want them to stop doing something we slap them. They quit."

The girls needed to be boss as August was often away. "Dad would be up Chilko Lake trapping for six months in the winter, alone in the snow," Pansy told the Campbell River Museum interviewer. "He made himself cabins all the way through [every 20 miles]. Trap marten inland and mink on the waterfront, otter sometimes. You just took everything you could get . . . Everybody says how grumpy he was and this and that, but you know he had a hard row to hoe. He lost his wife, he lost his house, left with three little girls, no money. Must have been very, very nervewracking for him sometimes, you know. But you don't think of this when you're growing up. But I often think of it now. Of course he was very much 'Do as I say and do it now, not a minute from now but NOW!' And you jumped when he spoke and did it. You didn't talk back. You'd get a backhander if you did. He had to be that way to survive. He was a gruff person."

Emery, writing that the cougars were the greatest pets to the girls—the affectionate animals a consolation in their rough, motherless life—concluded: "It is believed to be the first and only time in B.C. and possibly anywhere else, that cougars have been household pets. The girls' father, who has hunted among cougars for 50 years, says the cougar is not a vicious animal. In fact, he claims, all animals are far more inclined toward friendliness than they have been given credit for. Any savagery they might possess is aroused only from fear of being hurt by man or other creatures. Asked if a cougar really screams like a woman as so many stories would have us believe, August Schnarr says: 'No, but they screech and the screech does not resemble a scream. The only other noise a cougar makes is a squeak when it pounces on a deer . . . The cougar is by nature a friendly animal, but also a timid one, and while it may make menacing threats, he seldom carries them out.'

"To Pansy the cougars were the most lovable, cuddlesome and adorable pets she ever had. 'I'd give anything to have another.'"[44]

5

PAPER TRACKS

**Schnarr fonds
at the Campbell
River Museum
and Archives.**
Judith Williams photo

All the archived materials are links, discoveries, chance encounters, the visual and acoustic shocks of rooting around amid physical archives. These are the telepathies the bibliomaniacal poet relishes. Rummaging in the archives she finds "a deposit of a future yet to come, gathered and guarded"—you permit yourself liberties—in the first place—happiness.[45]

The Schnarr fonds in the Campbell River Museum contain a treasure trove of papers brought along when August towed his house from Schnarr's Landing to Heriot Bay in the 1950s. Out spill intimate details of the family's life, their employees and contacts, dances and dinners attended, food processed and money paid and received.

I can track where they travelled by boat, how they amused themselves, and that a woman deep in that wilderness wanted a girdle for a twenty-nine-inch waist. Written in pencil at the top of the first page of a black school scribbler is "1927." Under the heading "Woodward's Stores" is "$50 sent with order," a fair sum to be earned trapping or handlogging then. A list of supplies, including "20 lbs salt pork, 2 oz. black pepper" and "1 satin night gown, bust 36 in.," gives a glimpse of Zaida's writing, menus and bedtime apparel. Three gas bills indicate trips south down Lewis Channel between Cortes and West Redonda Islands to the Refuge Cove Store, owned by Jack Tindall and later by the Hope Brothers, who sorted mail, operated as fish buyers and sold fresh meat and produce, boots and clothes. These names, locations and occupations "tell" me the landscape and how people lived in and moved through it.

A later school scribbler contains a diary kept by Pansy Schnarr from 1938 into 1939. It begins as August, sixteen-year-old Pansy, fourteen-year-old Pearl and twelve-year-old Marion start building a new gasboat at Owen Bay on Sonora Island and organize moving their houses and sheds onto floats for a permanent move back up Bute.

Why keep a daily record for that period alone? Pansy only mentions attending school twice, and the diary might have been a school assignment to allow her to finish her year. "Dad didn't think girls needed much education," Pansy remembered.[46]

Her diary entries relate date, weather, place, activity and how long it took to travel from A to B. They hint at attendant young men, record a visit of the Fair family—into which Pansy later married—and document the girls' contribution to the family economy. I know more about their daily activities than I do of the lives of my grandparents!

Pansy, summer 1937, "up Bute."
Pansy Eddington collection

In 1937 August had received a Bear Bay log sale licence. Renewed in August 1940 as Timber Sale Contract X2734 in the Vancouver Forest District, it encompassed 716 acres south along the shore from Bear River to northwest of Melleresh Point in Bute. August could cut 75,000 feet of fir, for $2.50 per 1,000 feet of stumpage; 40,000 feet of cedar; and any hemlock, balsam or other species. He paid $18.25 for timber cruising, $2.00 for the log-marking hammer and $16.25 as 10 per cent of expected stumpage. Zaida's brother Chas. A. Lansell witnessed the contract.

Several gaps with "Can't remember" scrawled across the page allow my imagination to enter Pansy's narrative. I see August in the Owen Bay shed, setting the teeth of his saw after he informed the girls they were moving back up Bute to log. I imagine a feisty Pearl drying supper dishes: Mad!

Marion enters the house with an armload of wood, followed by a cougar. She kneels down to feed the fire, leaves the stove door open a crack so she can see the flames, a forbidden waste of fuel according to August. Sitting, she shifts one leg out toward the heat, raises the other knee and leans back against the settee as the cougar rolls alongside her thigh to encourage a rub. A hand settles into fur.

Pansy is bent over a table, opening a new school scribbler like the one in which her mother, and now she, records the Woodward's orders, payment to men who log for August, log booms shipped south and boom chains returned. In the top corner of the first page she writes:

Bear Bay timber sale

TIMBER SALE X 27,341.
BEAR BAY, BUTE INLET.
RANGE 1, COAST DISTRICT.
SCALE 80 CHAINS = 1 INCH.

BEAR BAY

INSET
Scale 20 ch = 1 inch

X 27,341.
716 Ac.

BUTE

Bear
Bay

Purcell Pt.

Mellersh Pt.

S.T.L.
36984
12728?

S.T.L.
31127
Mellersh Creek
12762?

INLET

1938, Jan. 22. Killed pig.[47]

23rd: Went up to Van der Est's to set four cougar traps after dinner. After we came home, we pulled logs under boathouse.

Jan. 24. We cut pig up this morning. Uncle Charlie came in to ask August for use of a jack. After dinner he worked around in boat shed. Got another log under. It sprinkled pretty near all day. It was very cold. August caulked two bulkheads and stern of his boat. Pulled two more logs under shed. Lent Case two mattocks. Put young pigs in smoke house. Weather mild. Looked at traps but never got anything.

The Schnarrs had begun beefing up their boat shed with new log floatation in preparation for towing their camp up Bute.

On January 26, August went to Blind Channel in a light north wind and bought a keel for the new boat, bilge strakes, a keelson, gas and candy, for a total of $8.07. A far jaunt in an old gasboat of the day, his route was north out of Owen Bay through Gypsy Shoals, west down Okisollo Channel and rapids, north through Discovery Channel past the Walkem Islands and into Mayne Passage to the sizeable cannery and sawmill at Blind Channel. Rumour has it there was a still.

Jan. 28. Mail day today and Mrs. Van der Est was in, so was Mike. Of course August got nothing done. Mike for dinner, Logan for supper. North wind blowing today. Rather cold. Got settlement for logs.

29th. Went up to look at traps but had no luck. August never got much work done on boat. North wind blowing.

30th. August brought some lumber over from the mill and put it upstairs to dry. Worked in boatshed. It snowed last night and today. Made settlement with Logan on Southgate supplies: $100. To be received later.

31st. August worked on his rowboat. Snowed a little today . . . Still North wind blowing.

The Okisollo and Hole-in-the-Wall rapids make Owen Bay on Sonora Island one of the most difficult communities to access in Discovery Passage. Loggers settled there in the 1900s and established a school in a settler's house in 1927. Needing more students to keep it open, they advertised for a teacher with children. Alma Van der Est, her husband, Bill, and their six children arrived. Alma and her children rowed across the bay to the school, where wind blew through cracks in the walls, and water flooded the floor during high spring tides. Mt. Van der Est lies between the heads of Phillips and Frederick Arms.

On February 1, Pansy complained, as she did all winter, that August spent the day talking to their neighbour, Schibler, and not working on the new boat. After school the girls had a snowball fight in five inches of snow.

Two days later August and neighbour Mike went cougar hunting at Barnes Bay, where August had killed Leo and Girlie's mother, and then on by boat to Tipton's Store at Surge Narrows. It snowed 12 inches more during that day.

Feb. 4. Got ten little pigs today. Made house for Boliver (the boar). Stopped snowing. Milder.

Feb. 5. August made stove for steam box. Brought his winch and [drag] saw float from the pass as it got loose. It's been raining all day. Tonight it hailed. Blowing South Easter

August and Mike installed the stove and steam box in the boatshed. A boat builder, Mr. Whitfield, arrived on the 11th, and that night they all went to a lively whist dinner. Pansy sent Eaton's store $9.95 for a banjo.

Below left: Marion, Pearl and Pansy with cougar. When you look away, what do you see: the pyramidal grouping, teeth, the chain or snow? Unknown commercial photographer. Image MCR 15625 courtesy of the Museum at Campbell River

Below right: Treed cougar. August Schnarr photo. Image MCR 14437 courtesy of the Museum at Campbell River

Above: Jean Schibler and Leo.
August Schnarr photo. Cougar Companions album. Image MCR 2006-8 courtesy of the Museum at Campbell River

Feb. 12. August and Mr. Whitfield worked in the boatshed. They cut out the keel and frame. Made another coil [for steam box] and made it backwards. Snowed pretty near all day.

13th. Yesterday we all went up to Van der Est's for dinner. So, of course, there was nothing done. Snowed all day. Put down 6 inches. North wind.

The essential steam box didn't work. August spent several days trying to fix it. When he finally got it working, they built a rock fireplace and boiled a drum full of water to make steam to bend the planks for the new boat.

On the 19th, Mr. Van der Est came to help Mr. Whitfield put the boat keel on, and August went to Stuart Island on the 26th to ask Uncle Charlie to put some cedar logs in the water so he could build a big float to transport their houses up-inlet. By the 28th the girls had brought a maple bow-stem from the Van der Ests and started planking the boat. On March 1, Pansy wrote that "A. J. Spilsbury came in and August bought a radio from him." This $59.95 radio would facilitate the remote logging show, but Pansy fussed that they were still planking the boat necessary for the up-inlet move to begin logging.

March 5th. Worked around boat. Put another plank on and puttied nail holes. Dance tonight.

6th, Did we have fun!

March 8. Putting the last few planks on. We took pictures of the boat yesterday. Took pictures of us three girls in our dance dresses. We spoiled a whole roll of film. The sun was lovely and warm. Battery on radio is dead.

Raised on Savary Island, north of Powell River, Jim Spilsbury built his first crystal radio set at seventeen. By 1938 he was boating the coast in the *Five B.R.*, selling, installing and maintaining radios for private clients and logging companies. That same year Spilsbury was amazed to be able to install a radio connection from Twin Islands to Kyoto, Japan, via Vancouver. This was in the Twin Islands house Charlie Rasmussen built for Richard Andrews. When the war began, the RCMP instantly ripped out this connection. After World War II, Spilsbury, as well as Jack Tindall, who had owned the Refuge Cove Store, created Queen Charlotte Airlines to move loggers in and out of remote areas, transforming the industry.

Above: Francis Barrow photo of Jim Spilsbury's *Five B.R.* in Bute Inlet below the "Needles."
Image MCR 20110-19 courtesy of the Museum at Campbell River

Left: *Cougar Companions* album page with Francis Dickie article.
Image MCR 2006-8 courtesy of the Museum at Campbell River

Warmer weather allowed them to putty nail holes for painting. Three days later August took to bed with a hot water bottle on his hip as it was bothering him.

14th. Turned boat over.

On the 15th Pansy noted that the previous night's terrible southeaster had wrecked many things and was still blowing. She did not know that *Maclean's* magazine published "Cougar Pets" by Francis Dickie that day. The article was illustrated with two photos of the girls and cougars in snow, taken by a professional photographer.

Loggerette in process, Owen Bay.
Schnarr family photo. Image MCR 14390 courtesy of the Museum at Campbell River

The wind picked up at Owen Bay on the 17th, so August cancelled a trip to Stuart Island and went deer hunting. When the wind fell on the 18th he did go to Stuart Island, and Pansy, annoyed he didn't come home until nine on the morning of the 19th, grumbled at another delay.

Margaret (centre) and Jack Parrish (far right) with their children—baby Ron and Roy—and Amy and Francis Barrow, Stuart Island, c. 1936.
Francis Barrow photo. Image MCR 10345 courtesy of the Museum at Campbell River

Mar. 20. Pearl and Marion went out after dinner to paint the boat. We went up to Van der Est's for supper. Snowed about one inch while we were up there.

22nd. August had Mr. Case over helping him make the shoe for his boat. Mr. Van der Est and Mr. Whitfield building deck.

24th. August took part of his engine over to Parrish's Machine Shop. Us three girls went out and puttied. Mr. Whitfield is still making deck and Mr. Van der Est mixed paint and painted bottom.

Jack Parrish's Stuart Island machine shop was a regular upcoast boat repair stop. The engine Pansy refers to must have been for the new boat. Parrish or blacksmith Case, also on Stuart Island, could have welded the metal tripod that supported the propeller in the airboat, although the first stand was wood. August had money in hand to pay men to build the new boat and repair engines so he could prepare for a more remote life.

Pansy's gnomic March 24 diary entry, "Allan (Game Warden) punched our cougar. Skin (Leo)," is difficult to deconstruct. Leo seems to have died sometime during 1937 or early 1938. Did Game Warden Allan Grenhome "pinch" them for not turning in the nose for bounty? That was illegal. Did he "pinch" the pelt to show off the remains of a hand-raised cougar, a feat never previously accomplished? That the family would keep their pet's pelt may seem gruesome, but not to a trapping family that killed, skinned and butchered animals regularly. Pearl said August conducted an inconclusive post-mortem on Leo to ascertain why he died. Pansy wrote no more about Leo but says that, as the weather improved and the boat neared completion, they framed up a cabin at Owen Bay to stay in once the houses were moved to Bute. August retrieved his engine from Stuart Island and moved what Pansy calls "his boat," the canoe, out of the boatshed so they could lower the new boat into the water. They planed boards for the new cabin and built doorways.

> Mar. 30th. Getting tar ready for decks and front of boat. Cabin nearly finished. Doors and windows to put in yet. Wind is coming from the west still. Weather very warm.
>
> Apr.1, April Fool's Day. Finish tacking canvas on [boat deck]. Mr. Whitfield made hatchway.

After Whitfield finished the hatches, August paid him $265.00 and took him to Stuart Island to catch the steamer. The Schnarrs went to a party and August slept all the next day. On the 5th they put guardrails on the boat and August went to Stuart Island to bring home his new engine.

> April 7th. Us girls went out to boathouse after dinner and puttied and painted part of cabin. The weather was just fair today.
>
> 8th. Mail day. August got the stuff for his boat that Mr. Whitfield sent up. One piece of glass missing.
>
> April 9th. Sent report of cougar down to Allan [Game Warden] to get bounty. The two girls went out to finish what they didn't do on Thursday. After dinner Pearl and I planted Early Rose Potatoes. August still putting engine in boat.
>
> 10th. We went "hooter" hunting today over to Barnes bay. We caught four grouse. Marion shot two of them. Got boom-chains today.
>
> 12th. Worked on boat and engine. After supper we killed the bore [boar] Boliver.

The next day they cut up and salted the pig. On the 14th Pansy put the pig head and other bones and meat on to boil all day while they planted nearly a sack of potatoes in rain. August helped them tie up loganberry plants.

On the 22nd Marion cleaned the shavings and chips out of the inside of the boat and they dug more garden. Next day their teenage friend Frankie Colbard came from Read Island, had supper and stayed the night.

Below left: Pansy, Pearl, Marion and Frank Colbard display a giant Pacific octopus in front of potato hills, Owen Bay, 1938. *Pansy Eddington collection*

Below right: Pansy, August, Marion and Pearl on top of their new gasboat, Loggerette. Cougar Companions album. Image MCR 2006-8 courtesy of the Museum at Campbell River

After Frank left on April 24, the weather was good enough for the girls to spend the next three days puttying and painting the boat grey with green trim. Then there's a big gap in diary entries. On May 19 Pansy wrote that August had put the house sheds on the float a week earlier, and he and Frank were going down to Surge Narrows to phone for a tug. Uncle Charlie was paid $10.00 for helping move the house.

Although handloggers' floathouses were regularly shifted on and off land up and down the coast to follow new log sales, a successful move required a nice sense of timing in relation to the tides. An extra-high daylight tide, available in May and June, was necessary to winch buildings onto a float, tow them to the new site and haul them back onto land. They could then be jacked up on pilings above the highest tide and levelled. Massive pulleys and winches, a nicely developed expertise and a degree of luck were needed to ease the wooden buildings along and not pull them apart.

August's 1934 loss of his floathouse due to a wind at the mouth of Bute must have been uppermost in his mind. The tow route out of Owen Bay is unnervingly documented in the *Coast Pilot*, which states the course is subject to stiff currents and overfalls along the Upper Rapids that flow into the bay and east through the narrow entrance to Hole-in-the-Wall rapids. I have seen the narrows sport a spectacular five-foot-deep hole in the ocean. Organized movement at slack water was called for. Pansy remained as patiently impatient as possible about the move.

> May 20. Tug came to take the houses up Bute. August isn't home so we wait. August and Frank came home at a quarter to one and we were leaving at one. August, Frank, Pearl and Marion went back to get the cougar in the cage. Got up Bute at 11 PM.

A bill from M.R. Cliff and B.C. Mills Towing Company is dated May 21, 1938, "for a tow of camp from Owen Bay to Bear River, Bute Inlet for the period May 20 at 4 to May 21st at 3,—$50.00."

> May 21. We're up Bute, tied where the boom was last year. After dinner August and Frank towed the buildings down to the slides in the corner. The sun still shines as hot as ever.

The handlogging August practised at Bear Bay was part of a dynamic, almost freebooting, period of BC forestry history. Due to the necessity of steep slopes and sheltered waters for booming and towing, it was mainly a Canadian enterprise. When August first came to the coast, the logger could cruise the shore in a rowboat and just set up shop, but the government soon taxed handlogging licences. Given the terrain, Section 22 of the Forest Act, pertaining to handlogging, reads like a dare: "The holder of a license granted under this section shall not use any machinery propelled other than or operated otherwise than by muscular power to carry out lumbering operations under this license."

The many operations tucked into small bays up the coast could use only an axe, saw, jack, wedge, gravity, ingenuity and a considerable degree of enterprise to send a felled tree shooting downslope into the water to be boomed and towed to mills. If there was a second logger, the two could use a crosscut saw to fell the trees. No logger would fall a bad tree because the picky market wanted clear timber. The aim was to fall a clear tree as close to the beach as possible on a slope providing enough momentum to send it all the way down to the water. Higher up, trees were felled across smaller trees and limbed and barked on the underside to make them run. The down-end butt could be bevelled around so it would not catch. A log dump or chute would be

set up to guide logs into a boom bag made of other logs chained together. If a tree did not run, but hit a stump or rock, steel-tipped peaveys and a jack were brought to bear, and the logger had to be nippy to get out of the way when the log took off again. Opportunities for accidents were endless. The last handlogging licence was given to James Stapleton of Toba Inlet in 1965.

On May 24, with the house still on its raft, August and Frank began logging while the girls cleared brush for the house site. On the 31st they moved the house over below the site, and on June 1, with the tide high and the persistent inlet swells at ease, they winched the house off the raft. The next day the bunkhouse was moved up on land and levelled. The Swanbergs, whose camp was across the channel, dropped in with mail.

On June 3, August and Frank worked thirteen hours boring holes into boomsticks to hold the chains that would create the boom bag to contain logs. Pansy put Girlie, who'd been wandering free, on a chain.

The Schnarrs now regularly travelled out of Bute on the *Loggerette* for mail and supplies. Pansy is particular about travel times because it was close to 35 miles from the Landing down to the mouth of Bute and along the east side of Stuart Island to Harbott Point, with its government wharf, post office and steamer stop. If the tide was truly slack they could cut through the narrow Arran Rapids between Stuart and the mainland and down to the Big Bay community. However, the Arran Rapids' nine-foot overfall at extreme tide changes was a serious navigational hazard.

On a June 4 trip they headed for Owen Bay about 9:15, stayed in the new Owen Bay cabin, left at 8:30 the next day, hit slack tide at "the Hole" and arrived at Stuart Island about 3:30. On the return, they waited in "the Hole" for the tide and got back to Owen Bay about 8:45. Leaving there at noon the next day in calm, warm weather, they reached Bear Bay at 7:30.

> June 6. August and Frank put the [water] pipeline in and were brushing out for walk. We killed a pig this evening. Weather very warm.

The next day August and Frank put up the walk and porch. Pansy drew her single diary illustration of the outhouse propped up over the water on tree rounds.

Above left: Bunkhouse move, Bear Bay, 1938.
Pansy Eddington collection

Above right: Levelled floathouses, Schnarr Camp, 1938.
Pansy Eddington collection

Schnarr's hand auger.
Judith Williams photo

June 8. The wind and swells were pretty rough today. Before dinner the men fixed the anchor and after dinner took a couple of jacks up the hill. They were jacking a log when a sharp boulder squashed August's big toe. So he came home and lay around.

10th. August hasn't gone to work because of his toe. Frank pretty nearly got one [log] to the water. The pig got too close to the cougar pen and the cougar took a chunk out of his ear. Frank came home with his nose bleeding because the jack handle flew up and hit him in the nose.

On June 11, August and two of the girls fixed the boom. Frank went to work, and later August, Marion and Pearl went up the hill to fall some trees that were sent into the chute. On the 15th Pansy towed three trees into the boom.

June 16th. Men went to work. Got one tree in the water in the forenoon. Girls tied it to boom. Afternoon got two logs in. The weather is cloudy today.

17th. This morning August stayed home because of his eye. After dinner he fell a tree. Changed anchorage of gas boat. The sun was fairly warm. Swanbergs came over and borrowed 10 cans of milk.

On the 25th they travelled to Stuart Island for gas and went to Owen Bay, where they had supper and breakfast at the "Vans." Their mail did not turn up on the steamer, but they bought fish and headed home in rough weather. On the 29th, August and Frank got two logs to the water's edge and Pearl painted the table. They picked blackberries but a bear ate August's. Pansy tried to tow trees into the boom but the inlet swell was too great.

July 1. Frank cut his finger. Ten trees altogether today. August and the two girls went down to take trees out of the chute. Frank had to stay home on account of his finger. They got four trees in and fixed boom as one of the lines broke. The weather was nice and warm.

July 4th. Fairs were here for breakfast and took us over to camp to get our order. After dinner Frank came home as his finger bothered him. The sun shone brightly today too. After dinner us three girls went blackberry picking and just before we got to the patch we scared out a bear. Killed pig last night. Charged battery.

Schnarr boom
with "riders."
Looking south
down channel
with longboat at
bottom right.
*August Schnarr photo.
Image MCR 20447-12
courtesy of the Museum
at Campbell River*

5th. Cut pig up this morning. Frank came in at 4 PM this evening with a cut in his head. A rock dropped on it. Just cut the skin. August felled three trees and undercut three more. One came out but split in half. The other one smashed at the bottom. One stuck up above.

July 13. Pulled riders on boom today. Frank lost the stamping hammer over-board. We had a little over half of them stamped.

14th. After dishes and pigs were done, Aug and us three girls went timber cruising. I got stung with a Hornet. August never found any good timber . . . Fired Frank today.

Accident-prone Frank got his boat ready and left. The loss of the stamping hammer was more serious than might be evident. Its mark consisted of a number and one of three letters, x y or z, and with the hammer the handlogger branded the butt-end of his logs. The incised code told who cut the log, where the log came from, what kind of land it came off and what royalty was due to the Crown. Each log in a boom had to be stamped if the logger were to be paid and fulfill his licence obligations. The Schnarrs had to obtain a new hammer, by mail, before the boom could be sent south and sold.

August now had to fall trees alone. In her album, Pearl identified a "silent partner" set-up he used when cutting down a large tree by himself. In the photo (see page 88) his springboard is cantilevered out from the tree (lower right) so he can stand on it above the root flare. He's made the undercut (at right above the springboard) in the direction the tree is to fall, and strung his limber line, usually a sapling, with a string to the right end of the saw (from the top right and down). The bark is cut away so he can see where he is sawing from another springboard (hidden at left).

"The preferred wood for springboards was strong, light, yellow cedar," August said when he described this falling technique to the crew taping him at the Campbell River Museum. "They would split out the board and taper it down and curve it in here to lighten. A metal shoe went on the end with a lip that stuck in and levered into the tree. The whole thing had a spring to it that helped.

Top: "Silent partner" logging rig set-up.
August Schnarr photo. Image MCR 14432 courtesy of the Museum at Campbell River

Below left: Drawing #1 "Silent partner" logging rig.
Judith Williams illustration

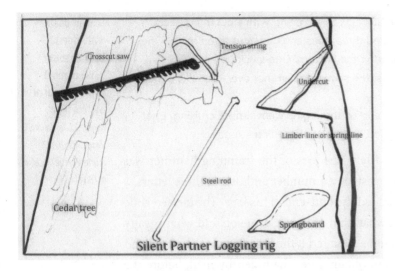

Crosscut saw

Tension string

Undercut

Limber line or spring line

Steel rod

Cedar tree

Springboard

Silent Partner Logging rig

Above right: August with a felled tree, thought to be that shown at the top of this page.
Glen Macklin collection

"I felled all kinds of trees with a spring pole . . . Well, let's say this is the tree here and you're gonna fall it just downhill. You walk straight in [from the water] and then . . . put an undercut in and fall that way [toward the water] . . . Then you put a spring pole, a limber pole, out there in front. And from that pole, you put a string, down to your saw . . . with tension on it to pull [the saw back and] . . . up at the same time, not straight over, 'cause then your saw would go straight down [and] make a cut this way, you see. And then, oh boy, that's hard. You want to keep your cuts straight, like this table. Then it's easy! . . . You'd just keep cutting around, make sure you put your cuts straight. And then this [spring] pole . . . pulls up on your saw . . . And then you keep moving your [spring] pole over as you go in. I'd rather do that myself than have most [any] other person on the other side. All this is my ideas when I was working for myself trying to get stuff accomplished."

About the considerable dangers of handlogging, he said, "Do something reckless, that's what you shouldn't do. I wouldn't be here today I guess if it wasn't for that, and even then I got hurt sometimes. We used jacks in handlogging. I got the Ellingsons; they're a better jack, you see. They got gears in them, you know. You can double your power."

By midsummer 1938 it was hot. On July 21 August worked only half a day. He put the clutch band on the engine and the Schnarrs boated to the head of the inlet.

> 22nd. August fell two trees before dinner. Laid around till 3:30 [then] went back to work. I canned 15 quarts meat.
>
> 24th. After supper we went over to the old place to get some logs and apples. We picked 3 boxes off one tree. Sun very warm.

Above: Swanberg logging camp, 1938.
Pansy Eddington collection

Left: Pansy in Bute Inlet. *Loggerette* **at anchor on the left, circa 1938.**
Courtesy of Albert Fair

Pansy's "old place" is the Schnarr's Landing homestead with its extensive orchards on the mainland south across from Bear Bay. They slept over in the boatshed, had breakfast on the beach and cleaned a fish they took out of a net they'd set. The girls picked three more boxes of apples while August rolled logs off the beach. Back at Bear Bay he went to work, and the three girls went over to Swanbergs' float camp to get mail.

One evening Pansy notes that Gunner, Alex, Red and the boatman came over from Swanbergs' to look at the cougar. On August 6th the Schnarrs went to Owen Bay and had supper at Mrs. Van der Est's. Next day, after digging some of the potatoes they'd planted at Schiblers', they took the *Loggerette* to Stuart to await the steamer, got their order and left for Bute in the rain. At home they began to make up the boom, with August and the girls boring boomsticks, cutting down another tree, and bucking up and stowing logs.

Aug. 12, Aug and girls pulled rider on and tightened up boom. After dinner we went over to our old place to pick berries and apples and get six swifter chains. Got a pail of berries and a couple of boxes of apples.

On the 19th the tug came for this boom and the Fairs arrived for a visit. Next day the Fairs took them, in their *Sally-Bruce*, to the head of the inlet and came back for supper in a typical inlet afternoon wind.

Aug. 21. Canned 26 quarts meat this morn. After dinner we went up to the head in our own boat. Blackford's came up afterwards. Spent night there. Sun shone.

22th. Pretty hard night as we slept on the floor. At noon we came home. Blackford's came out to see cougar. Then they left and I made some supper. Gunner brought mail over and box of chocolates. Weather was warm.

After dinner on August 27 the Schnarrs went to Stuart Island, carrying on the next morning to Owen Bay, where they stayed for a picnic. They got their order at Stuart Island and spent the night afloat at Fawn Bluff. Despite thick smoky air from a forest fire, they made it home on the 29th. August went right out, cut down a tree and sent it down to the water to start another boom of logs.

Aug. 31. Aug fell two trees but only one came in. Three boys came over from camp. Joe Bassett rowed over too. I washed floor and clothes. Weather hazy.

Sept. 1. Aug fell five trees and three came in. Girls towed them down to boom. I washed four blankets. Sprinkled a bit.

2nd. August fell three trees and one came in. I made apple jelly and washed kitchen windows. Thundered and rained today.

On September 3, Marion's birthday, August got the biggest tree on the claim in the water.

Girlie at Bear Bay.
August Schnarr negatives. Image MCR 2006-8 courtesy of the Museum at Campbell River

The girls took the mail over to the Swanbergs and picked up ten boxes of plums and six of good apples. August filed a saw while the girls canned 66 quarts of plums.

> September 5th. Aug got 3 logs in boom today. We canned 65 qtrs. of plums. Jim Smith brought our mail over. Aug received scaling slip for cedar boom. Also selling prices. It rained. 1938.

Pansy's diary skips a year and starts again on what I believe to be Marion's fifteenth birthday, September 3, 1939. They went to Stuart Island in fog for mail and then to Tipton's, where they got three drums of gas.

On September 4 and 5 Pansy made many more quarts of apple jelly while August fixed a steam donkey she had not mentioned before, a considerable mechanical upgrade from the year before. Marion and August oiled some machinery before dinner, and later Pearl and Marion oiled the pipeline. They split new shakes for house repairs. Her note that "After supper dogs were chasing cougar but never got it" suggests Girlie ran free most of the time.

> Sept. 6. Logan was in for breakfast. We bought 13 fish from him. We got 12 quarts canned, and saved one to eat. Logan was in for dinner. Slept rest of afternoon. 5 PM, Ranger Grenhome came in and brought mail. Washed flour sacks. Cloudy. August's log split.

On September 7, 1939, Logan returned for breakfast with a gift of eleven fish, and the diary ends.

The diary and the time and financial record books tally skills the girls added to the overwhelming range of logging tasks, but I feel Pansy writes everything down and leaves everything out! She never mentions Leo had died. "Girlie pined away after and in two years was gone," Pearl said, and then she herself fled, at fifteen, to Vancouver and then to Winnipeg where, she said, "I married a military man."

There is a stiff 1941 letter in the fonds from Mr. Van der Est to August concerning an ongoing payment dispute regarding his son John, his own 1938 work on the *Loggerette*, and eight days Alma cared for the cougars. This undermines the sense of Owen Bay neighbourliness the diary records. August was a very difficult man.

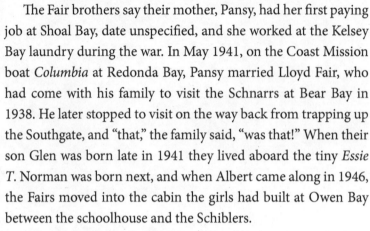

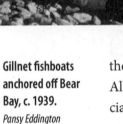

Gillnet fishboats anchored off Bear Bay, c. 1939.
Pansy Eddington collection

The Fair brothers say their mother, Pansy, had her first paying job at Shoal Bay, date unspecified, and she worked at the Kelsey Bay laundry during the war. In May 1941, on the Coast Mission boat *Columbia* at Redonda Bay, Pansy married Lloyd Fair, who had come with his family to visit the Schnarrs at Bear Bay in 1938. He later stopped to visit on the way back from trapping up the Southgate, and "that," the family said, "was that!" When their son Glen was born late in 1941 they lived aboard the tiny *Essie T.* Norman was born next, and when Albert came along in 1946, the Fairs moved into the cabin the girls had built at Owen Bay between the schoolhouse and the Schiblers.

Albert says that just after he was born, Pansy was sunbathing down on the dock at Owen Bay with the newborn nearby. There was a small noise and, opening her eyes, she was horrified to see the tentacles of a giant Pacific octopus come up over the float toward the babe. She grabbed Albert and ran. He survived to start logging at twelve in Okisollo Channel with his dad, in specially made small boots.

Pansy enjoyed the Owen Bay social life the move provided. "We loved dances," she said, "local music. Somebody would play the violin, somebody the guitar once a month, and you got

Marion and Girlie, Bear Bay.
August Schnarr negatives. Image MCR 2006-8 courtesy of the Museum at Campbell River

to know everybody. The loggers, we were loggers. Lloyd, he worked in the bush. Some fishermen would come. It was really nice. I lived right next to the school and I could leave my kids, just run back and see if they were asleep. When we went to Stuart Island we took the kids."

The period of the late 1930s and early 1940s when the girls matured was before the Canadian government passed the Medical Care Act in 1966, and the Schnarrs' medical receipts tell tales. One fonds envelope contains many slips from a Vancouver chiropractor for August, and evidence of an X-ray by the Columbia Coast Mission. August talked tough, but a handlogger gambled his body on his fate and skill.

According to many family members, when Marion was "fourteen," she helped care for the first Mrs. Len Parker while Len trapped. Norman Fair said, "They got to fooling around." Marion became pregnant. In his "resume"[48] Len says his wife "Pearlie died in 1948." Truthfully, official dates and Pansy's diary do not satisfactorily support Marion's rumoured age and condition. A medical bill indicates that on April 3, 1940, "Miss Schnarr had measles" at St. Michael's Hospital, Rock Bay, and returned there April 21. However, birth records indicate Marion had a daughter, named Lennie, on May 29, 1942. She was adopted out. In 1943 Marion was again in the Rock Bay hospital. A bill for $51, dated December 3, 1945, indicates Marion was in St. Vincent's Hospital in Vancouver for fifteen days. There was an additional surgeon's bill for $175.

Cashbooks and tax returns indicate that she continued to log and go up rivers and traplines with August during the '40s. Marion's draft for a letter dated March 12, 1945, indicates they attempted to grow fur by bringing home a group of code-numbered mink from a Vancouver breeder.

> Dear Mr. Hoppe.
>
> Received your letter of the 27th last boat & the bill of sale. We made it out of town O.K. & home in 3 days. All the mink seemed O.K. but two, which were a little slow about eating their food. That was one female and male A.7.1 The trip & handling didn't seem to bother them tho.
>
> Around the first of the month we tried A.7.1. with 3 of the females & he seemed awfully slow. The same day we tried the other male on the other 5 females & he seemed awfully anxious but they did not.
>
> After we put the males back we noticed that one of the females was over on her side kicking. We thought maybe the male had bit her. But she came to again & in a little while appeared allrite. (After being sick to the stomach for a while) . . .
>
> On the seventh we tried them again. Using A.7.1. first. This time he appeared very disinterested. So tried the other male & at the very first cage we put him into he keeled over on his side & took a fit. (Now this male had appeared in very good condition.) So, of course, we took the female out til he came around. Then he was sick for a while & seemed O.K. While we were watching him, the female passed out in the runway and acted much the same, being sick after.
>
> This discouraged us very much & we began to watch them closely. A.7.1. appeared sicker every day until we put him in a small cage and brought him in the house. The first day in the house he looked pretty bad. The second day he looked better & today he really looked well until about 10.00 A.M. Then he took a fit & and one rite after the other for an hour at the end of which he died. We cut him open & and examined him and could find nothing wrong inside at all.
>
> We sure would like some advice on this. They have been fed nothing but codfish & and mostly red cod or snapper. We tried it ground and whole. We have not tried to mate them at all since the 7th.
>
> If there is anything we can do, send a telegram or write & take the letter rite down & put

it on the Union boat. (If it goes in the mail it may not catch the boat.) Hoping you have some solution. Will close, Yours Truly

August was often asked to help search for people lost up the inlet valleys. Another of Marion's draft letters, dated August 3, 1945, firmly states a claim they made after helping the provincial police search for the body of Trygve Iverson, who had left for Twin Lake on July 15, 1945, with two timber cruisers to ascertain the Homathko's utility for floating down pulpwood. The police report states: "It is a treacherous river and he was drowned on July 29th by the upsetting of a raft on which he and his companions Einer Bergan and Erlund Green were floating downriver." Green and Bergan reported the death and returned upriver with the police in the longboat "of August and Marion Schnarr."

"We made four trips up the Homathko R," Marion wrote. "First to meet party coming down. The second after T. Iverson was drowned Aug. 3, Mrs. Iverson paid. Two other trips were made later. Because the river was too high at the time to make a thorough search we waited til later as requested and searched after the river dropped. These trips were exceedingly dangerous and required a special boat and knowledge of the river. I might mention that on the last trip we nearly got caught ourselves.

"We are only working people and had to drop our own work to do the service. As Mrs. Iver-

Log boom at mouth of Homathko River.
Charlie Rasmussen collection

son has paid for two of these trips, we think it is only proper that the Provincial Police should stand for the other two."

Mrs. Iverson paid the Schnarrs $200 for two trips, but the police only ponied up $50 for both of the subsequent two. The body was never found. The active river logging Iverson had been exploring continued until the 1960s, when the first roads were pushed up the valleys.

A notice in the *Owen Bay News* states Marion and Len Parker's son Bert were engaged on November 14, 1946. Both are identified as from Bute Inlet. They married January 31, 1947.

The challenging complexity of Marion's life from 1938 to 1946, combined with Pearl's remark to Glen about being taken advantage of by "those old guys up there," fills me with a fierce, protective rage. I cannot be sure of anything except official records, but I am proud of how these young women worked, coped and grew! Dad was a demanding curmudgeon or worse, and Len Parker is described by more than one observer as a charming, conniving old goat, but the girls were tough. They escaped and became competent, admired adults despite a minimal education and a rough raising.

You sense the determined firming up of Marion's character as you learn of her 1940s life in Bute. Her nephews recall Aunt Marion as a straight speaker, not shying away from correcting them, but also warm and caring. Marion was thoughtful enough to compile the family members' *Cougar Companions* albums, portraying the sisters' unique life with the cougars, and to co-author a book about her controversial uncle, Canadian rumrunner Johnny Schnarr. She and Bert Parker made a life with their three other daughters. Lennie, the daughter born in 1942, tracked her down, claimed Len Parker's First Nations heritage and brought her children to see their grandmother.

I am awed by the girls' extraordinary years with Girlie and Leo, and the hard, physical workdays described in Pansy's diary. Her children treasure the *Cougar Companions* albums and the diary that records an upcoast world they experienced differently, and they are proud of their mother's competence within what they acknowledge was a very demanding life.

INTERLUDE IV

GOLD

Pearl's *Cougar Companions* album contained a print of August's 1926 photograph of Butite Charlie Mould in his cocked fedora and fringed logging boots, propping up a dead grizzly on a float. That's a pretty big bear, and Charlie Mould—well, some folks say he was a pretty big liar.

When I asked Pearl if she remembered the Moulds, she turned and looked out the window. "Ooo-whooowff!—Jackie," she sighed. The girls, of course, knew Charlie and his son, Jack, all their lives. A second photo of Charlie and the grizzly includes a small Pansy at extreme left.

Charlie Mould told evolving tales concerning an Indigenous man he'd once seen kill another to gain a giant gold nugget. He said that man later tracked him for *his* gold, and Charlie may or

Charlie Mould, 21, trapping on the Southgate River, 1926.
August Schnarr photo. Image MCR 20447-43 courtesy of the Museum at Campbell River

may not have killed his tracker to get the giant nugget. The thing about oral history, a wise First Nations chief once told me, is that you can remember differently.

Charlie believed the nugget's source was in Bute, and when son Jack was sixteen, Charlie took him up the inlet to see a wood-framed "Spanish cave" hewn into a mountainside to enlarge its natural size, a wooden door said to be carved with "Spanish helmets," and a hide-lined bucket of a kind used for smelting. There were strange markings on a tree. The Moulds insisted the Spanish had mined and smelted gold in Bute in 1792, and the commanders, somehow informed of the imminent arrival of British ships, scuttled a gold-loaded galleon in Waddington Harbour silt for safekeeping. Maps showing a "Galleon Creek" joining the Teaquahan River north of Southgate Peak may have influenced the Moulds' theories: two of Jack's mining claims lie directly south of that creek.

The "Spanish" material, Jack said, was proof of their mining activity and gave credence to a Bute location for a lost gold mine. Well, maybe. But coastal First Nations encased cadavers in cedar boxes, sometimes grooved or engraved, that were hidden in trees, caves or crevices. Carved planks were erected to mark territory and gravesites, and arbourglyphs, faces and signs were carved into live trees. Any worked wooden surface could be of Indigenous origin but, as is usual in treasure stories, all this provocative evidence was buried, according to Jack, in the construction of a Southgate logging road. That Jack couldn't locate Charlie's "evidence" proved a stumbling block when soliciting mine investment.

The foundation of this whole edifice rested on folk tales concerning the Katzie/Nanaimo man Slumach, who appeared in New Westminster during the 1890s with a plentiful supply of gold. He lived it up in bars and cathouses until his funds were gone, then headed out to the bush with a young Indigenous girl and reappeared with more gold the next year. Although rumour placed his gold vein in the Pitt River area, the Moulds were convinced it was in Bute and that Slumach had found the Spanish gold.

Now, Slumach was no sweetheart. The girls he took away never returned, and records show that at 8 a.m. on January 16, 1891, Slumach was hanged at the Royal City Jail for the murder of the "half-breed Louis Bee." His body was claimed by his nephew, the respected Katzie shaman Simon Pierre, and buried within the old jail. On the scaffold, before he died, eighty-year-old Slumach is said to have called out "Nika memloose, mine memloose" (If I am dead, the mine is dead), cursing anyone who dared search for his gold.

Slumach's curse is said to have claimed its first victim after San Francisco miner John Jackson reportedly found the gold. Jackson returned to civilization, and on May 28, 1924, wrote to a

The tent-shaped rock.[49]

Southgate River cabin painting.
Mike Moore photo

Detail of cabin wall painting, Southgate River, 2011.
Mike Moore photo

friend that his gold cache was buried under a tent-shaped rock facing a creek that came straight out of a mountain, bubbled in places over bedrock bright yellow with gold, and disappeared. This site could be found by lining up three specific peaks. Jackson died two years later without having retrieved his cache.

In 1931, Volcanic Brown, a sprightly eighty-year-old prospector from the Kootenays, acquired a copy of Jackson's letter. Brown never returned from his last trip to the Pitt River area. His body wasn't found, but a jar containing 11 ounces of pure gold was discovered in his last camp.

Jack claimed that during a helicopter reconnaissance he'd found the tent-shaped rock, the bubbling creek and the three peaks near BC archaeology sites EeSf3 and EeSf4, which contained rock shelters with "Spanish remains." The archaeology site reports note male and female human remains, fragments of boxes and scraps of matting consistent with Indigenous burials. Jack's mining claims map, now attached to these particular government archaeology files, situates two "Jackson's Mines" north and south of Southgate Peak near the burials, and four "Slumach's Mines" around Southgate Peak. Jack conflated useful elements of the archaeological information to raise more funds, and he said that in the process of installing a landing stage for renewed surveying, he and his nephew had found the scuttled Spanish galleon. Jack tantalized his lawyer by describing a video he said he had of the ship, sunk in the silt of the Southgate delta. The lawyer complained, "Jack says the underwater video is on its way, but it never arrives."

Raising money to continue exploration was a constant problem, but minute amounts of gold flake, the promised but never delivered underwater video, tales of the misplaced Spanish cave and photographs of the tent-shaped rock were strewn in front of enough prospective investors who could not resist a gamble, and Jack forged on. The green-gold grow-op back in the bush helped.

Twirling a bookstand in the Lund Store one day, I found *Jack Mould and the Curse of Gold* by Elizabeth Hawkins. The book explicated Charlie Mould's conviction that the mine that supplied Slumach with the gold he spent in New Westminster in the 1890s was located in Bute Inlet and had been mined by Spaniards. Over the years the cockeyed logic of Charlie and Jack's gold stories, and local raconteurs' tall tales regarding the misadventures and misdemeanours of the Moulds, *père et fils*, built up a legend about Jack, exploratory dynamiting and gold. Recently, a painting was discovered in the Moulds' old cabin up the Southgate. If you allowed yourself to give the tiniest amount of credence to the Slumach's mine story, the artwork's dated tombstones (for Slumach, second from left; Jackson, third from left; and Brown, fourth) and the scene of men madly digging in a graveyard by lantern light under a spiral-tracked mountain surmounted by a tropic island lunette and ascending bird would have sucked you further along the trail. It was a hoot.

The cabin painting may date from the 1990s, when Jack Mould had attained, both in his own mind and in the minds of some observers, legendary status. Pearl was right to sigh! In and out of jail for things that were always someone else's fault, he surfaced in a variety of local tales. Jack, it is said, was once sitting in a Vancouver bar with a pal, drinking beer, when a third man entered and shot the pal. "Jack," he gasped, "I think I'm dying!" Jack looked him over, remarked, "I believe you are," downed the rest of his beer and left. He was, after all, a busy mining entrepreneur devoting every hour to planting rumours, digging up funding and salting gold claims.

Jack Mould and the Curse of Gold is the lasting result of all these efforts. It contains photos purporting to be this and perhaps that. However, Jack's mention of his heavy use of dynamite in and around his claims attracted my attention when I was compiling *Dynamite Stories*, a book about the enthusiastic use of nitroglycerine in the development of the coastal BC economy.[50] Character-revealing Mould stories popped up unexpectedly. When Bobo and I boated up Bute Inlet in the late 1990s, we'd pass a lopsided grey barge hauled onto the Southgate mud flats. It seemed deserted, but Chuck Burchill, who'd taken over running the Homathko River logging camp up the other river, assured us it was occupied by Jack Mould. Relations between the two men were tense, as Chuck had heard Jack dynamiting the Homalco Band's burial area at Potato Point, at the mouth of the Homathko east of X̱we'malhkwu Reserve, and called the RCMP. Jack claimed Chuck was poisoning him.

Detail of cabin wall painting, Southgate River, 2011.
Mike Moore photo

Chuck once drove us beyond the Teaquahan River to see the marbled murrelet nests in old-growth hemlock. On the way back he picked up two hikers who'd set off six days earlier on a walk into the Interior along the rumoured Homalco grease trail. When supplies and enthusiasm ran short they turned back, taking a shortcut across the tidal flats below Mould's barge. Jack emerged, shotgun cocked, and demanded they get off his property or he'd set an unseen dog on them. "Normal behaviour," Chuck laughed, "should anyone seek to disturb Jack's ruminations."

After I included a censorious note about Jack's generous deployment of explosives at Potato Point in *Dynamite Stories* in 2003, his dossier dropped into deep storage, but a writer's discourtesies have a way of coming back to haunt her. Near the end of August 2007, I was standing on the Refuge Cove Store porch on West Redonda Island, idly watching a floatplane dock. Out hopped the pilot, two shirtless young toughs sucking on their beers, and a burly, bearded older man in scruffy shorts leading a small canine, perhaps a Peekapoo, on a pink leash. They strolled up the dock into the store and the bearded man disappeared into the back. I joined Lucy Robertson, who was behind the till, as he reappeared brandishing a copy of *Jack Mould and the Curse of Gold*.

"They've got my book," he crowed. "The one I wrote!" He waved the paperback energetically in front of the pilot. "It's my book, the one I told you about. Got to buy a copy."

"Surely you get them from the publisher," the pilot said.

Jack turned on him. "*That* bastard! No, gotta get this for a friend."

I sidled up to Lucy and whispered, "Don't say my name!"

Of course I wanted to talk to the legendary Jack Mould, but I most emphatically did not want to be known as the person who'd written about him in a critical way. He was a man widely rumoured to sue or shoot those who crossed him, although I did not think the attendant dog was going to be the kind of threat he'd indicated to the hikers it could be.

"So where you off to?" I tendered as an opener.

"Ah! Nowhere. Just taking the boys out," said Jack, who, at the end of the pink leash, looked rather like an untidy teddy bear. "They've been working hard surveying for me up Bute. Thought I'd come for the ride."

With my tongue firmly in my cheek, I asked, "So, what's your book about?"

"Yeah! I wrote that, all about my search for gold. Don't know—I just have to find it. I wanted the gold all my life and I want the glory."

After years of hearing stories about Jack, now, looking at his aging face, the slumped belly, the Peekapoo—for heaven's sake! I realized all I really knew about Jack Mould came from the accounts of others. The Peekapoo was disorienting.

Three weeks later, Lucy called my attention to an item in the September 12 *Campbell River Mirror*. A week after Jack had been at Refuge, a member of a hiking party had been severely injured during a rock slide, and a rescue party arrived in Bute. A Jack Mould was helpful. The hiker's body was retrieved and removed. A week later a timber survey crew flew in and found Jack's truck by the river. Its doors were open and a large number of water containers lay around. A pair of shoes were found downriver, one in the water and the other high and dry on the bank. The Peekapoo, curled up inside the cab, was pretty happy to see anyone. Jack was nowhere to be found.

Two weeks on, the same paper reported that J&S Kulta Mining of Nanaimo had applied for a permit to explore for gold. President Sulo Poystila said, "Senior members of the company have been prospecting in the area for 50 years." He requested permission to put exploration teams in Bute at an existing base camp at the head of the inlet across Waddington Harbour from Hamilton Point: the location of Jack's barge.

What was going on? Hikers came in. One was hurt and everyone, including Jack, swung into action to rescue him. Jack disappeared. The police arrived to question Chuck closely and demanded a list of loggers and visitors at Homathko Camp during the relevant time frame. The Homalco complained they had not been consulted and the fishing lodges decried the effect of mining operations on salmon spawning, but finding seventy-one-year-old Jack did not seem to be anybody's top priority. In the old days it would have been August, the territory expert, hired to search, but bodies ending up in upcoast waters are seldom found.

6

?ANAQOX TSEN GWAIADTEN: TRAIL TOWARD BUTE INLET

What routes did August and the girls follow up the Homathko and Southgate Rivers to the Interior? Pansy's confirmation of her dad's winter trips up to Chilko Lake, Charlie Rasmussen's diary of the 1929 trip and the Moulds' belief in Slumach's route down from the Interior all suggest it's useful to shuffle August's inland photo images with those in Knewstubb's hydro survey report to see where they correspond and indicate plausible routes up both valleys to the Chilcotin.

Head of Franklyn Arm, south end of Chilko Lake, c. 1929.
"Water Power Investigations: Report on Taseko–Chilko–Homatho project," page 1637, photo 41[51]

Due to the topographically controlling terrain, every usable route inevitably intersects with and overlaps sites and trails used for millennia by the Homalco and Tŝilhqot'in Peoples. It seems obvious August's route to Chilko Lake would make use of established Indigenous trails when useful. It is revealing to position First Nation place names, images and activities within economically purposeful non-Indigenous usages to indicate how concepts of territory, ownership and exploitation shifted as the incoming Walkers, Moulds, Schnarrs and hydro surveyors or logging companies competed for inlet resources.

Before contact, the Homalco (X̱we'malhkwu), a member of the Coast Salish group that included the Klahoose and Sliammon tribes, spoke Éy7á7juuthem, a dialect of the Mainland

Village of the Friendly Indians, Bute Inlet engraving based on an original ink-and-wash drawing made by Thomas Heddington, July 1792.
Judith Williams photo

Chilko Lake, Chilcotin drainage and Indigenous trails to tidewater

Source: BC Parks, Ts'il?os Provincial Park Master Plan

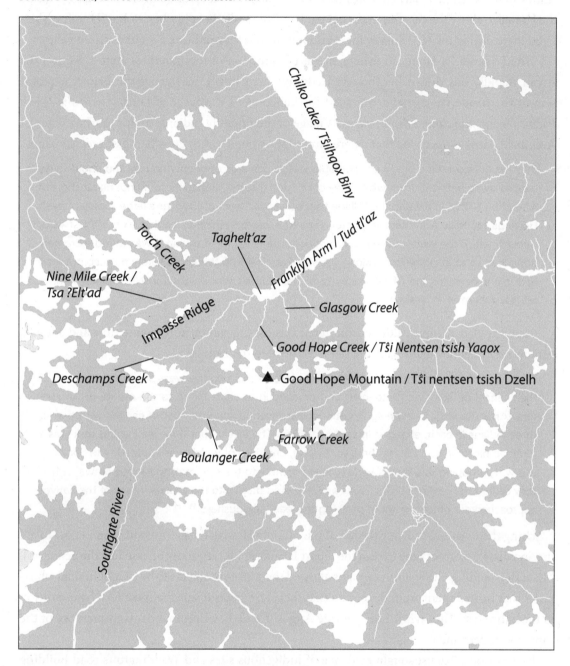

Chilko Lake / Tŝilhqox Biny

Torch Creek

Taghelt'az

Franklyn Arm / Tud tl'az

Nine Mile Creek / Tsa ?Elt'ad

Impasse Ridge

Glasgow Creek

Good Hope Creek / Tŝi Nentsen tsish Yaqox

Deschamps Creek

▲ Good Hope Mountain / Tŝi nentsen tsish Dzelh

Farrow Creek

Boulanger Creek

Southgate River

Comox language. The Homalco wintered in their Bute Inlet territory, where all species of salmon ran up the rivers to spawn in feeder creeks. Subgroups went to sites at the Miimaya River and Pi7pknech at Orford Bay, and seasonally to Saayuick Village on the mainland west of the Arran Rapids. Some Homalco owned Tatapoose village and fort in White Rock Pass, between Read and Maurelle Islands, where the east pass entrance is marked by a First Nations pictograph panel. From Tatapoose, people could move north through Surge Narrows Rapids to Waiatt Bay on Quadra, still ringed by Aboriginal-built clam gardens that have been cultivated for millennia to increase production of butter clams.[52] There are few clam beds in any of the inlets due to the lack of beaches, and the people necessarily travelled out of the inlet seasonally for shellfish. Anthropologist Homer Barnett states that the Homathko Valley underground houses, built by the Homalco above the canyon, were occupied by Tŝilhqot'in People when Robert Homfray sheltered there during his 1861 survey for Waddington, and they indicate a regularly used valley.

"The Lookout," a Homalco fishing site at the junction of the mouth of Bute Inlet and the Arran Rapids, was drawn by Thomas Heddington in July 1792 during the British exploration of the Inside Passage and engraved for Vancouver's *A Voyage of Discovery to the North Pacific Ocean, and Round the World* as "Village of the Friendly Indians." In his journal, botanist Archibald Menzies recorded that where James Johnstone's survey crew had first seen smoke,

> they now discovered a pretty considerable village upwards of twenty houses and about thirty canoes laying before it: from which they concluded that its Inhabitants could not be far short of a hundred & fifty. In passing this Village they purchased from the natives a large supply of fresh Herrings for Nails & immediately after entered a narrow Channel leading to the Westward, through which the water rushed in Whirlpools with such rapidity that it was found extremely difficult even to track the Boats along the shore against it, & this could hardly be accomplished had it not been for the friendly activity of the Natives who in the most voluntary manner afforded them every assistance.

Captains Galiano and Valdes encountered this fishing station at the same time and added a parallel set of Spanish names for the same territory to their maps.

> They saw a large settlement situated in the pleasant plain on the west point of the mouth of the channel of Quintano [Bute Inlet] and proceeded to coast along to the mouth of Angostura [Arran Rapids]. In the neighbourhood there were a large number of canoes with two or three Indians in each, engaged in sardine fishing. The instrument they used in this task was a rounded piece of wood some three yards long, one third of which was studded with hooks. In this way, dropping this kind of wide toothed comb into the sea, making various draws with it, they caught the sardines on its hooks and gathered them into the canoes. Many of the natives approached our officers without showing the least nervousness.[53]

The fishing described by the Spanish was done with the kind of 10-foot rake August made for himself, substituting wire for the bone spikes. *Judith Williams photo*

Using their arms to indicate the arc of the sun, the Homalco fishermen made an effort to tell the Spanish the correct time to pass the Stuart Island rapids (regularly finessed by the Schnarrs). Misunderstanding, the Spanish captains allowed their 46-foot goletas to be caught in tidal whirlpools that turned them around so often that their text states it was the most terrifying portion of the entire trip. They named the passage Angostura de Los Commandants in memory of the captains' understandable agitation.

Ever curious, August sought evidence of Indigenous sites and Waddington's road-building activities as he moved from his Bear Bay and Schnarr's Landing homes upriver to trap. Initial information about the violent conflict that followed the road-building intrusion into this territory was written up by English artist/alpinist Frederick Whymper and published with his engraved paintings in the 1875 *Illustrated London News*. Whymper arrived by boat at Waddington's Homathko Camp on March 22, 1864, a month before the Tŝilhqot'in attack on the road crew, to make "views" of the grand landscape. One of his watercolours places two First Nations people in a canoe on the Homathko River opposite a traditional Indigenous house and two post-contact-style buildings at Indian Reserve (IR) #2A, below the start of the road and the present Homathko Camp.

Homathko River Facing Upstream, **watercolour by Frederick Whymper, 1864.** *Image PDP00109 courtesy of the Royal BC Museum and Archives*

Whymper hired Tŝilhqot'in Chief Tellot to guide him up the zigzag pass above the canyon to sketch glaciated areas where Charlie and August later trapped. "On reaching the glacier," Whymper wrote,

> its presence was rendered very obvious, by the cracking of the ice and the careening of the stones from its surface. This was incessant; now a shower of pebbles, now a few hundred weight of boulders, and now a thimbleful of sand, but always something coming over. The ice—very evidently such at the cracks where you saw its true colour and its dripping lower edges of stalactite form—yet appeared for the most part like wet smooth rock, from the quantity of dirt on its surface. At its termination the glacier must have been three-quarters of a mile in width; it was considerably wider higher up. Whilst sketching, all around was so supremely tranquil that its action was very noticeable. Rocks and boulders fell from it sufficient to crush any too eager observer. A great quantity of snow was on its surface, but fast melting, and forming streamlets that glistened in the sun, whilst from innermost icy caverns, torrents of discolored water poured. The crevasses were large and yawning. Square hummocks of ice, forced up by the closing, existed in many places on its surface, whilst at the western or upper end pinnacles, peaks and pyramids of ice were seen in the distance.[54]

Descending the valley, Whymper stopped briefly at the road builder's ferry station with "S," the man in charge, then continued down the trail with the pack train to the road crew station at the mouth of the river. The next morning, friendly First Nations packers broke into his room and excitedly reported that "S" had been murdered by the Tŝilhqot'in for refusing to give away his provisions and property.

Dismissing the story, Whymper set off with other men down-inlet in a canoe owned by a

Whymper's engraving of the Homathko River cable-ferry crossing, based on a drawing made in March 1864, before the killing of the ferryman. The Tŝilhqot'in warriors cut the ferry loose to hinder pursuit, and it was swept downstream.

During an 1870s Bute survey Charles Horetzky took a photo of two Homalco men with a canoe 12 miles from the mouth of the Homathko River, as well as an evocative image of the tight Homathko Canyon over which Whymper and later August travelled.

Charles Horetzky photos, Vancouver Public Library 8542 and 8543

"Clayoosh Indian," a hard taskmaster who had them paddle to Victoria in five days. On May 12, 1864, the artist was horrified to hear the ferryman had indeed been killed the morning the packers had tried to warn him, and fourteen road workers were killed the following day.

Members of the Tŝilhqot'in tribe that had been terribly afflicted by the 1860s smallpox epidemic had come to pack for Waddington's road. They were threatened with more smallpox by a road boss who came from Victoria, and were then implicated in the deaths of the road crew.

Over the years, Whymper's story was combined with the Victoria *Colonist*'s reports of the duplicitous capture of the Tŝilhqot'in warriors who claimed to have declared war, accounts of a trial in which the men were found guilty of murder and condemned to be hanged, and an eyewitness tale from Qwittie, the Homalco man who survived the killings, to produce oral versions of these unique BC events. These stories fired the interest of August and many others to search, as I did in the 1990s, for any evidence that brought that history and landscape alive.[55] On Monday, March 26, 2018, Canadian prime minister Justin Trudeau exonerated the six Tŝilhqot'in chiefs who were hanged for murder after being invited to parlay with the British colonial authorities who had invaded their territory.

The Tŝilhqot'in Band, the southernmost of the Athapaskan ethnic groups, occupied the Chilcotin drainage, above Homalco territory, with two major concentrations near Chilko Lake. (Chilko Lake's Tŝilhqot'in name, Tŝilhqox Biny, means "Tŝilhqot'in People's lake," suggesting they specifically claim it as their own and not Homalco territory.) These interfacing tribes are known to have had intertribal conflicts, and in 1990 Klahoose elders and sisters Elizabeth Harry and Susan Pielle said the Tŝilhqot'in had occasionally captured and married Homalco and Klahoose women.

The BC government's enthusiastic encouragement of explorers, settlers, entrepreneurs and developers to do as they wished with the inlet areas caused the abandonment of many Homalco and Tŝilhqot'in sites. When the McKenna–McBride Commission was establishing "Indian

Church House.
Image MCR 19779 courtesy of the Museum at Campbell River

reserves" in the Bute area in 1914, they identified Muushkin, a Homalco village on Sonora Island, as IR #5a, even though the people had already moved across to Church House (U7p), IR #6, at the inlet's mouth on the mainland, after a severe "Bute" flattened Muushkin in 1896. Although the Homalco seldom spent extended periods of time at the old inlet sites, they still lived and fished at the head of the inlet in the 1890s and worked for settlers. Pansy and Pearl spoke of trading with them into the 1940s. The Homalco Band now runs its "Bears of Bute" camp at Pi'7knech at the Orford River.

The Homathko townsite laid out by the Royal Engineers on the north side of the river mouth was abandoned after Waddington died in 1872. Waddington had been in Ottawa, promoting his plans for a transcontinental railway with a terminus at the head of Bute Inlet, when he died of

Waddington's Homathko Canyon Road, drawing by Frederick Whymper, 1864. *Image PDP00105 courtesy of the Royal BC Museum and Archives*

Blasting and metal pins for Waddington's cantilevered Homathko Canyon road.
August Schnarr photo. Image MCR 6698 courtesy of the Museum at Campbell River

smallpox. Remaining settlers on both sides of the inlet head were so desperate the government had to finance their removal, and their buildings stood for many years as a reminder of the collapse of the high hopes Waddington had twice inspired. By the 1920s the Southgate Logging Company was established at the mouth of the Southgate where early Bute settlers lived, and an era of raw resource extraction began.

The 1928–30 survey of hydro power potential within these traditional territories the Schnarrs moved through indicated the largely glacier-fed Homathko River, with its wide seasonal variations in runoff, would not in itself be a reliable source of power. However, Chief Engineer Knewstubb thought a diversion, via tunnels, of a balanced flow from Taseko and Chilko Lakes, which drain into the Fraser River, to storage in Tatlayoko Lake, at the headwaters of the Homathko, would overcome this problem. His report included maps of the proposed dam, spillway, storage and tunnel routes, and plotted a water intake, dam and tunnel from Franklyn Arm at the west side of Chilko.

Knewstubb stated that salmon ran into Chilko Lake, but since none spawned above Homathko Canyon, where they planned a dam for water tunnelled from Chilko, he implied there would be no impact on spawning. However, salmon spawned in all the rivers and creeks feeding into the Homathko below the canyon. Then and now, any road building or logging in the inlet creates landslides and silting detrimental to spawners, and silt moving downstream affects young fish as they exit. After years of logging, Bute runs are now much reduced.

The hydro report included photographs of the remains of Waddington's wagon road within the survey area, including a Schnarr photo depicting the blasted-out rock bench, denuded of any structure. A Whymper watercolour depicts the same section of Homathko Canyon prior to the killing of the road crew.

Regarding a possible road from Chilko Lake via Franklyn Pass to the Southgate River for his proposed tunnel, Knewstubb wrote, "There is a fair trail from the head of Franklin Arm to

The hydro report includes a photo of what Knewstubb refers to, in the racist vernacular of the time, as a "Siwash" crossing of the Southgate River. A companion picture has a man straddling that kind of log bridge over the river. Examination with a magnifying glass suggests the figure is August in his usual long underwear, suspenders and hat, hanging over the chasm on the crossing log. He is seated at the centre of a wonderful three-dimensional star created by the log, an oblique rock fissure and the log-cast shadow emerging from a cavern that, on closer examination, is more a product of a slant of light or trick of the mind than a cavity.

the Southgate Crossing, 4–5 miles below Boulanger Cabin which can be used by horses, and a rough trail continues to the (Southgate) Forks. It is recorded somewhere that cattle or horses have been driven over this . . . old Indian route [to Bute. And] in the lake region . . . it is quite feasible to drive a team and wagon . . . to Nemaiah Valley."

He said a powerhouse might be built either at a First Nations crossing on the upper Southgate or up the Bishop River, which an old map marks as "Klattsassine's hunting grounds."[56] Knewstubb wrote that it was desirable to have a road connecting the several working points and portals of a tunnel. However, the principal difficulty in the case of a Chilko Pass tunnel would be crossing the Chilko Glacier. He said it was quite easy to traverse on foot for about two months of the year on a gentle grade.[57] He cited two crossings to or from Chilko Lake that August would have known and described to him. The first was "by way of Bishop River to the [Southgate] Forks, then over Franklin Pass to Franklin Arm to a second [route], via the low-pass . . . much used by the Indians in the good old oolachan grease days." The second was "by way of Bishop, Southgate Rivers and [the] Boulanger—'Y' Creek valleys." He said the latter would involve shorter water transport and possibly a lower elevation of pass but with a glaciered summit. He noted a lower pass across the range on the south side of Mt. Chilko.

Regarding the Franklyn Pass route, Knewstubb wrote: "From the head of Franklin Arm [extending west about three-quarters of the distance down Chilko Lake] via Deschamps Creek there is a trail route over the Coast Range and down the Southgate River to Bute Inlet. The summit of this trail is 5700 feet high and is clear of glaciers though snow often lies at the summit till well into summer. From Franklin Arm head a flat swampy valley extends several miles westward, in fact to very near the summit [of the pass]."

Knewstubb noted that this route connected to a grade point west of Boulanger Creek, and to the bank of the upper Southgate, one mile above "Burnt Cabin." Below this cabin the Southgate flows through a box canyon and down to a point just above the "Siwash" crossing at the Forks with the Bishop River.

Over the years August would have made use of all the routes and cabins mentioned in the report, and Knewstubb's "much used . . . in the good old oolachan grease days" track would be of considerable interest, as it was said Indigenous people could come down this trail from Chilko Lake in eight days. August laid out traplines around the south end of the lake after packing supplies up in stages to cabins, one known as Twenty-One Mile, and another 25 miles from

Crossing the Chilko Glacier. Looking down the head of Chilko Creek Valley.
"Water Power Investigations: Report on Taseko–Chilko–Homatho project," page 1581, photo 27 [58]

"Siwash" crossing, Southgate River Forks.
"Water Power Investigations: Report on Taseko–Chilko–Homatho project," page 1024 [59]

tidewater. The second cabin is the one Johnny Schnarr says they built for the winter during the brothers' 1911–12 explorations when it was cold enough for "mush-ice" to flow in the river.[60]

In 1960, Mount Knewstubb, northwest of Deschamps Creek, was officially named after the chief hydraulic engineer, but the Tŝilhqot'in name, Yanats'idush, meaning "people freeze while on trail over mountain," suggests that peak should be avoided. August and Charlie Rasmussen set marten traps on Tiedemann Glacier in the winter of 1929, so August may have used glaciers for trapping that the Tŝilhqot'in and surveyors viewed as impediments.

In her research of the 1912 circumnavigation of Chilko Lake by the Indigenous guide Kese and the Seattle dentist and alpinist Malcolm Goddard, writer Heather Kellerhals-Stewart found a reference to a white man taking a number of horses over an unspecified route to Bute. She and her husband, engineer Rolf Kellerhals, investigated possible grease trails south from their cabin near Franklyn Arm on Chilko. Heather discovered a Tŝilhqot'in name, ʔAnaqox tsen Gwaiadten or "trail toward Bute Inlet," in "Translations for Tŝilhqot'in Features," a section of the *Ts'il?os Provincial Park Master Plan*, compiled when the present park around the lake was established. That trail is located near the headwaters of Deschamps Creek where it flows into Franklyn Arm, the only ice-free route connecting Chilko to Bute.[61]

A lower route beginning at the head of Farrow Creek necessitated crossing a glacier between Boulanger and Farrrow Creeks, whose Tŝilhqot'in name, Tsi nentsen tsish Dzelh, refers to "bad mountain you cannot walk on."[62]

Vern Logan, a descendant of the pioneering Walker family, told me of a grease trail via Wolf Creek near his family's land on the north side of the Southgate, some 24 miles from the river mouth. Dennis and Ray Walker's fourteen-year-old sister Daisy insisted on being a member of the party that trekked up that trail to Chilko to bring down horses, making her the first non-Indigenous woman to go up and down the trail. The horses were driven to swim the river at certain points, and all but one perished. That poor animal, in a dispute about its ownership, was shot.

Pearl said Marion and her dad tended August's daunting Southgate trapline to Chilko Lake together into the 1930s and 1940s. When I asked Marion, she said, "Oh! She [Pearl] did too. She doesn't remember." Whew—what tough young women!

Charlie Mould, hunting for gold and trapping marten when August photographed him at the Southgate in 1926, may not have shared all he knew of these inland routes, but August knew Charlie was searching out a trail Slumach would have had to follow from New Westminster to the Interior and to the gold mine Mould convinced himself was in Bute. If, and it's a big *if*, Slumach came into the Southgate area in the 1890s, he would have walked the ancient web of Indigenous trails that August used and Knewstubb considered.

Although Charlie, Len Parker and Jack Mould staked mining claims all over the inlet from the 1920s into 2000, August was considered the territory expert, guiding, exploring and trapping until the 1970s. Studying a photo from that time, August said it was taken when another surveying party came in to make a map of Mt. Superb. He took the group 1,700 feet up to camp and next day took them up on the glacier. He said that, while waiting for the surveyors, "We two built a cairn, there were a lot of big rocks—built [it] nine feet high and my name is in, put a bottle in [the rocks]."

Glen Macklin climbed up to the cairn and found a jar indicating it was built during that

1970s survey. Did Jack Mould conveniently mistake August's cairn for the "tented rock," one of Jackson's three signs for lining up the fabled gold mine?

Carl Larson says the Southgate route inland is a bigger trek than the Homathko trail that August considered the easier way into the Interior. During his hands-on research of the old routes, Carl was told that August not only had a route up to Chilko, but that men came down that way from the Interior to work at a logging camp 26 miles up, where the Bishop River forks off. Schnarr's Owen Bay neighbour Jack Schibler had a trapper's cabin there into the 1950s. On one of Carl's expeditions, he and Andy Alsager were helicoptered up above the forks, convinced they could raft down. "The water was rough," Carl said, "and I tipped the raft, putting us in the water. But then we drifted down for four wonderful days, down from Bishop junction."

7

GREASE, WAX AND WATER

SOMETIMES, TO CONNECT, YOU HAVE TO STRAIN
TO GET THINGS LINKED IN WAYS BEYOND THE
NORM AND HOW EACH DOES THAT EXHIBITS WHO
WE ARE.

—ANNE CARSON

Grease

What were the "good old oolachan grease days" Knewstubb cites in relation to the Southgate/Chilcotin routes he investigated with August? Oolachan, or eulachon (*Thaleichthys pacifics*), are a small fish, a kind of smelt, that provided an oil much favoured by First Nations for binding dried fish or berry cakes and as a condiment into which a variety of foods were dipped. The fish appeared in early spring when other food sources were depleted.

Known as T'leena in the Kwakwalla language, eulachon grease was employed as a salve for burns, insect bites, abrasions and chronic skin conditions. It was said to soften leather, was an excellent waterproofing agent and was traditionally used with moss to help seal cracks in canoes and leaky roofs. Along with salmon, sardine, shad and anchovy, eulachon are recognized as a major source of necessary omega-3 oils.[63] Eulachon must be considered a cultural keystone species for Northwest Coast Indigenous people and is valued for its multiple uses and for the cultural bonding activities of grease manufacture, consumption and trade.[64]

August first observed the eulachon fishery, and the processing technique used wherever they ran up coastal rivers, at Tsawadi Village in Knight Inlet sometime between 1910 and 1916. Eulachon were caught in nets as they swam upstream to spawn. Piled in wooden boxes to ripen for ten to fourteen days, the fish were then transferred to watertight boxes filled with water brought to a near boil by the addition of fire-heated rocks.

When a precise temperature was reached and the fish broken up, the oil rose to the surface, was skimmed off, filtered and, pre-contact, stored in bull-kelp bulbs in bentwood boxes. A highly valued commodity throughout the entire territory, it was carried to trade with Interior tribes along paths called "grease trails." The late-run salmon dried and smoked for the winter were low fat, and without the grease's nutrients it would have been more difficult for coastal people to survive the winter on dried salmon, berries and very small amounts of plants. Although the fish once constituted 12 per cent of British Columbia's annual fish economy, their insignificant economic value in the present cash system provided little incentive to preserve them, and many runs of this wonder food are now depleted. They are still harvested by Indigenous people at

Left: Collaged Bute elements: Pearl and Girlie, Bute wax and water samples, photo of Len Parker, grizzly bear and salmon.
Judith Williams photo

Top right: Eulachon. "This is the most important one—Salmon there are many kind. This one is only one kind." —Chief William Glendale, 1999.
Judith Williams photo

Lower right: Making eulachon oil at Tsawadi in Knight Inlet, 1970s.
Peter McNair photo

Homalco snowshoe.
Judith Williams photo

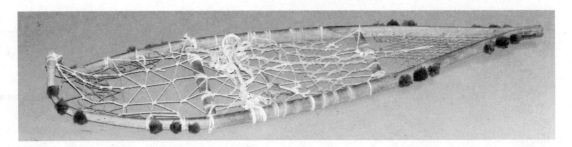

Kingcome and Knight Inlets and up the Nass River, where T'leena is used as a food and condiment, and the fish are smoked. A "grease feast," such as that held by Chief William Glendale of Knight Inlet in 2005, where 200 gallons of oil were given away to mark the rebuilding of his grandfather's Big House at Tsatsisnukwomi, remains a high-status event within the contemporary potlatch system.

In the 1930s, Klahoose Chief Julian told anthropologist Homer Barnett that "the Homalco people used to catch eulachons in Bute Inlet, rendering them for the highly prized eulachon grease," but eight years before Barnett's study of the region, a certain man defied the prescriptions applicable to a widower by catching and cooking these fish the day after his wife died. The eulachon promptly disappeared, with a few returning in 1935.[65]

In Kingcome Inlet a designated regulator of the harvest placed a stick in the river, allowing spawning fish to pass. Only when the stick was removed were people allowed to net and prepare the fish for the famously smelly process of making T'leena. In 2015 Dzawada'enuxw elder Geo Dawson was thrilled to report that eulachon surprised Gwai Yi villagers by running so consistently up the Kingcome River for two spring weeks that the river was black with fish. "Never that many before in my life," he said. "We made grease again!"

There are scattered hints of the Homalco trading grease and smoked salmon to the Interior and returning with baskets, berries, animal furs and snowshoes from the Lillooet People. The Tŝilhqot'in came down to fish the Southgate and, as attested by Robert Homfray's 1861 survey story, occasionally moved into Homalco underground houses to smoke-dry fish for winter. Rare materials, like obsidian for micro-blades, could be carried along the ancient web of trade trails south from as far away as the Bella Coola Valley to be exchanged for grease from coastal people.

In the 1990s the Holmalco Band planned to work with an archaeologist to map their grease trail up the Southgate, and the present chief wants to open the trail for trekking. In recent negotiations with the Tŝilhqot'in, who wished to have access to the lower Homathko due to the events of the 1860s, the Homalco learned some of their people had moved up the grease trail, of interest to August and Knewstubb, to live at Chilko Lake for a number of years.

Long-time Homalco researchers Randy Bouchard and Dorothy Kennedy state they never found information about the quality of eulachon oil formerly obtained/processed at the head of Bute Inlet and had not seen ethnographic or ethno-historic records of the Homalco People trading eulachon oil. But in the late 1970s/early 1980s they recorded Homalco elders Ambrose Wilson and Tommy Paul saying that each year in March the Homalco went to Galleon Creek, which empties into the lower portion of the Teaquahan River, to catch spawning eulachon they both smoke-dried and rendered into oil. According to Bouchard's informants, the Homalco name for Galleon Creek does not refer to the presence of eulachon but to the occurrence of the

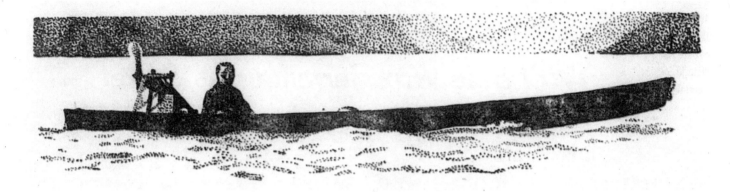

August in his longboat. Drawing from photo for Maud Emery article. Daily Colonist, *October 2, 1960*

red ochre pigment *thuulhminm*. Wilson and Paul said the Bute eulachon run "failed" around 1900 but also said that eulachons were running there again around 1980. Some Homalco reported the fish around the Southgate River mouth and north of Fawn Bluff in 1995.[66]

Young eulachon depend chiefly on copepods (tiny crustaceans found in salt and fresh water) for food. Since eulachon are said to be fatter in glacier-fed rivers like the Nass, it may be that eulachon in some rivers are less worth processing due to scanty output. Most Bute streams *are* glacier-fed, so why only Galleon Creek below Bute Glacier is used by eulachon is a mystery.[67]

Wax

Many creatures, including fin whales, sardines, and young smelt, as well as eulachon, eat copepods. This has led me to speculate that eulachon oil and the Bute wax unique to Bute Inlet might share properties derived from these tiny marine creatures, whose bodies are 70 per cent lipid, a fatty, waxy or oily compound that doesn't dissolve in water.

My consideration that the two substances might be chemically related is a by-product of research on the 1860s events on Waddington's road, when references to Bute wax just kept turning up. My citation of M.Y. Williams's paper "Bute Inlet Wax" in *High Slack* brought Sylvia Rasmussen Ives to me with Charlie Rasumussen's wax sample and diary. Williams's paper emphasized that no one had reported the wax's occurrence elsewhere on the coast except at the mouth of Toba Inlet (Yekwamen). He wrote that an astounding mass of the material was said to have appeared in the winter of 1949/50 when freezing conditions held for *five weeks*. Two men living in Bute said that as the cold and wind increased, the water became full of small flakes of the substance. When thrown together and rolled in the waves, it formed into chunks and balls, which grew larger as the weather became colder. The wax-like material was cast against the shore, forming piles as high as six to eight feet. It came *from* the inlet, not into it. Yet when the Homathko and Southgate Rivers were checked, no sign of the substance could be found. No wax was seen until Purcell Point, 19 kilometres (12 miles) south from the head of the inlet, directly across from Bear Bay and northwest of Schnarr's Landing.

The Butites Williams cited, hopeful of finding the wax source, had explored the valley and

Bute wax, Schnarr collection. *Judith Williams photo*

Article on Dr. Tikam
Jain's analysis
of Bute wax,
Victoria *Colonist*,
December 21, 1968.

SCIENTIST FINDS ELEMENTS 'ABSOLUTELY FASCINATING'

Will Bute Wax Surrender Its Secret?

Times Dec.21,1968 p.12

By ALAN WHITE

One of the mysteries in Dr. Tikam Jain's laboratory at the University of Victoria is a waxlike substance found floating in the waters of Bute Inlet.

He is asking: what is it, where does it come from, has it a use?

Down along the line of scientific investigation, medicine comes upon the scene. But first the wax.

Bute wax — as Dr. Jain has dubbed it — is not in evidence during most of the year. But when waters in the inlet, about 120 miles northwest of Vancouver, fall below 50 degrees, the wax congeals and appears on the surface in tons.

It has not been reported from any other area along the west coast.

LONG STREAKS

Stories told by homesteaders and carried to Dr. Jain tell of the greyish coating being driven in long streaks down the 40-mile inlet ahead of winter winds.

Prospector Frank Lehman, of 1317 Cook St., heard some of these stories and observed the substance "15 or 20 years ago."

It was Mr. Lehman who brought the wax to Dr. Jain's attention.

Engaged in a life-long search for strange chemicals of nature, Mr. Lehman has summarized all the folk-tales about Bute wax.

He has heard a dozen descriptions and explanations in his travels around the inlet.

"There was a lot of talk about it being fish oil — whale oil — or pine oil," he said.

JAR IN HANDS of Dr. Tikam Jain, University of Victoria chemist, holds substance which may be animal, vegetable or mineral in origin, or all three. No one knows what wax or jelly-like compound found in waters of Bute Inlet is yet, but extended chemical analysis at Uvic labs may determine the answers to questions being asked.

"It is generally a grey color, but there are stories of it being in blues and greens."

"After listening to all the stories, I suggested it might be petroleum in the making —

a residual from old, prehistoric oil structures," Mr. Lehman said.

The petroleum theory was only one of several attempts at an explanation.

He also considers it might come from "some bacteria or some sea plant native to that area."

"We know that some bacteria produce wax.

"People up there (Bute Inlet) usually call it Bute Oil. One old-timer had 15 drums of 45-gallon size of it saved up.

FROM WHALES

"One theory they had was that it came from whales who went into the inlet to die.

"Another was that it was some plant peculiar to the area, or pine — but there are none that aren't found in other areas too.

"I have heard a story that the wax is found in one of the fiords of Sweden," Mr. Lehman said. "It may be found in other inlets but not in the same quantity, so it isn't noticed."

'BEFORE MY TIME'

The wax may be a useful substance — and it may not. But discovering its origin and value is part of the fascination of science.

Mr. Lehman said it is one of the things nagging him for an explanation that must come "before my time is up."

Re-enter Dr. Jain ... the chemist—who studied at Agra, India and specializes in plants and waxes derived from them. He wants to break the mysterious substance apart to find out what it is too.

While explaining his work he darts back and forth between his desk and a chalkboard, naming and spelling out chemical elements.

"The origin of its elements are not known," he said recently. "But our chemical investigation will eventually give an answer."

ONE OF 45

He and assistants Robert Striha and Gregory Owen have separated and identified one which makes up about 1 per cent of the wax—called in scientific terms "norditerpene hydrocarbon."

This is the element, only one of 45 in the wax, which may prove the key.

The hydrocarbon has been found in shark livers and in raw petroleum. And Dr. Jain has manufactured it from chlorophyll, found in plants.

"It's a very complex problem," he said. "The 45 constituents in it are absolutely fascinating."

The fascination involves another aspect and brings into consideration medicine—which may or may not be another calculated wild guess about Bute wax.

USED AS SALVE

"I have been told by people in Bute Inlet areas it is used as folk medicine," Dr. Jain said. "Apparently they use it as a salve.

"We don't know what for, or if it works, but we want to find out."

The medical angle explains much of the research under way with Dr. Jain's direction.

---

the shores of the entire inlet. They staked a number of mineral claims, inadvertently discovered Aboriginal archaeology sites, and hired dowser Munday McCrae to survey and make a map of possible wax source sites. They sent samples to various government departments, who said it might be "whale oil" from dead whales, but the locals maintained that whales seldom came up Bute, and the inlet current quickly carried any floating object down-inlet, not up. In the end the analysts acknowledged it was not whale oil but an unknown form of wax ester.

I was struck by a solitary newspaper clipping in the BC Archives files showing Dr. Tikam Jain holding a jar of opaque liquid under the heading "Will Bute Wax Surrender Its Secret?" Jain's wax sample—from "an old timer up Bute who had fifteen 45 gallon drums of the stuff"— was brought to him by prospector Frank Lehman of Victoria. Lehman reported a thick greyish, or occasionally blue or green, coating was sometimes driven down Bute Inlet ahead of winter winds. It might, Lehman thought, be petroleum in the making, residue from old prehistoric oil structures, or produced from some bacteria or sea plant native to that area. Jain, a University of Victoria chemist specializing in plants and the waxes derived from them, said the substance resembled nothing in the known world. He separated and identified one element, 1 per cent of the wax, called *norditerpene hydrocarbon*, which is found in shark livers and in raw petroleum. Jain had manufactured this compound in the lab from chlorophyll found in plants. However, there were forty-four other constituents to the wax.[68]

What was this stuff?

The wax Jain held, like Sylvia Ives's sample, came from August's Bear Bay neighbour Len Parker. Len had recorded the wax's appearance in the winter of 1922, December 1935, January 1936, February 1950, March 1951, November 1955, and during the period of February 14, 1956 to March 1956. He said that in some years he could collect 15 gallons of the substance from 100 yards of beach. Late in May 1951, large, smelly slicks of lodgepole pine pollen were observed in the inlet, and this, along with the golden colour of some wax samples, led to the proposal the substance was pollen based.

In February 1959 the wind again blew with great violence for ten days down the Homathko Valley, from the great icefields surrounding Mt. Waddington in the northeast into Bute Inlet. The temperature dropped nearly to zero, and when the wind suddenly turned to the south, long slicks of Bute wax floated down the inlet and washed up against Len Parker's log boom at Bear River. The wax, collecting around floating debris in the upper three feet of the surface water, created the sixteen-inch balls that rolled against the steep shores at Purcell Point opposite. When the temperature moderated, the balls melted and the material disappeared.[69]

Scientists visited Bute during the summer of 1961 aboard the naval research vessels *Cedarwood* and *Elko* and discovered the inlet bottom was almost entirely of glacial origin and contained only minute amounts of organic material like pollen. No submerged Bute wax was recorded. When samples of Bute wax, all from Len Parker, were analyzed, the scientists concluded the material consisted of esters of fatty acids and fatty alcohols. The material solidified at about 11 degrees Celsius. At the time of testing it was said to be a liquid wax of vegetable origin and from zero to three hundred years old. It is important to note that no scientist was ever in Bute when the wax appeared.

Refusing to be discouraged by the scientists' refusal to declare the wax a petroleum product, Len and August continued experimenting. They washed their hands in it and found it to be powerful cleansing agent. As a paint remover it was unequalled. Despite this, it had a soothing effect on the skin. Used as a waterproofing agent, it rather overdid the soak-in effect and penetrated right into their socks. As a fire starter it blazed up like kerosene. Logging jacks were lubricated, and greased poles seemed Teflon coated. You could burn it as a light, and although its only failure was said to be as oil for engines due to the wax component gumming up the works, Glen Fair mentioned August using it half cut with gas.

Charlie Rasmussen pestered the Department of Mines and Petroleum Resources about the wax well into the 1970s, and stories about its spectacular periodic appearances and useful properties lingered among old-timers. Doris and Norman Hope ran the store at Refuge Cove on West Redonda Island during the '40s and '60s, and the surrounding folk came there by boat for gas and mail arriving on the Union Steamship. Doris recalled August Schnarr boating in one day with a gift of newspaper-wrapped Bute wax that he said was an excellent linoleum floor cleaner. Forgotten temporarily in the warmth of the living room, the substance melted into the rug, and the very fine oil was absorbed by the socks of visiting loggers who were only allowed inside once they removed their caulk boots.

When, sometime later, Doris denied ever having told me the story about Schnarr, I began to think of Bute wax as elusive as memory, unbiddable but emerging under particular conditions. The inlets, not strictly coast and not totally Interior, are a liminal threshold where I felt anything

Think Gum.
Judith Williams photo

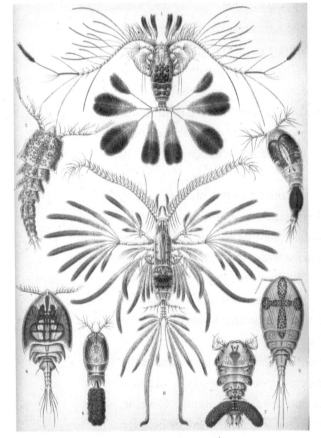

Copepoda, drawing by Ernst Haeckel.
Judith Williams photo

could happen. I saw Bute Inlet holding, like a glacier formed long ago, mysteries that a seismic shift, temperature inversion or the right question could release. Getting a look at the wax in situ, however, entailed being in Bute just when I did not want to be there. From late fall until March the wind was predictably unpredictable. Even the first summer we boated south through Bear Bay, the locus of the wax ball episodes, the sea threw up internally lit, jade standing waves, making a passage south like boating over translucent boulders. We had to turn back up-inlet.

Writing in *The Unknown Mountain* about their 1926 attempts to climb Mt. Waddington, Don Munday said, "Adventure can be very much an attitude of mind." I have had exhilarating boat journeys up the grand Knight and Bute Inlets, but tracking down someone to analyze Sylvia's wax sample became an equally stimulating voyage as I was passed along through a sequence of chatty university and government offices across the continent.

I first called Dr. Michael Healey of the Institute for Resources and Environment at the University of British Columbia. He thought he'd heard of Bute wax but sent me to Steve Calvert, a geochemist in oceanography. Calvert passed me on to Ronald Anderson, a chemist/oceanographer who had been to Bute on a scientific expedition in 1970 and had collected the substance from Len Parker. Although he claimed to have had a wonderful time and been as fascinated as everyone was, Anderson denied expertise and told me to call Andrew Benson at the Scripps Institute of Oceanography in La Jolla, California, who would reveal all.

Dr. Benson speedily returned my call. "Oh no! I am not the real expert," he said but confirmed that the scientific party had concluded Len Parker's substance was derived from copepods. It was a natural wax and oil based on the substance copepods accumulate in a sac in their bodies and use as a metabolic substance in the winter after their food source dwindles. He said at some date, perhaps as long as a hundred years ago, there may have been both a huge bloom of copepods and a sudden die-off. The copepod corpses would accumulate at the bottom of the inlet, where bacteria and time caused the wax sacs to become a more saturated lipid (that is, more oily). Benson told me the brain was mostly composed of lipid. He had produced a few of these lipids in the lab and was amused that one he'd made was being used in a new chewing gum, "Think Gum," that was promoted as a "brain-booster." He was skeptical. Hearing that I was a painter, Benson suggested that since the wax was so stable it would be a perfect artist's medium.

Benson suggested I phone Judd Nevenzel in Los Angeles, who had also been on the Bute trip.

"Nevenzel is an exceptional lipid specialist, although the greatest expert was Bob Bachman in Halifax. We're all friends," he said.

Nevenzel was cranky at first because I pronounced his name incorrectly, but he warmed to the subject and asked if I'd read the article in the San Diego paper. "It's an interview with Andy [Benson] after they had heard about our trip," Judd said. "Andy gave much false information as he'd not actually been on the trip. He insulted this woman. Thing was, he said a woman in Bute used Bute wax as a beauty aid, and even though she was fifty, she looked thirty. Trouble was, she was thirty."

Judd had been doing work in Canada for some time, and in the early 1970s had a chance to visit Bute for research. He and Richard Lee did the collecting and analysis and wrote up their findings for the *Journal of the Fisheries Research Board of Canada*.[70]

"The bodies of copepods are 70 percent lipid," Judd said, "and they bloom in all the inlets, but Bute blooms are thought to be extreme. After a massive die-off, the copepods fall to the bottom of the inlet, and I think the wax that makes up so much of their bodies goes through a natural process of refinement."

Judd thought Richard Lee had taken specimens of live copepods in the spring and fall of 1970–71, but the scientists, who were never in Bute in the winter, received their samples of the wax from Len Parker. They never saw the tree stump that Len and Charlie Rasmussen said acted as a wick to the material's onshore source near Bear Bay, and never saw the wax balls.

Judd said his sample was a naturally refined version of lipid from copepods, specifically *Calanus plumcharus*. Just how the lipid became the waxy substance he could not say, and where the wax was stored when not appearing in the inlet he did not know. Richard Lee proposed that a freshwater deluge from the Bear River, after a sudden thaw melts snow in the mountains, might kill copepods on the water's surface, and their transformation into lipid might be swift. Vast slicks of lipid containing copepod skeletal material have been found in the North Pacific, although no such debris was found in Bute. The mystery of the storage of Bute wax during warm weather, when it is never seen, is perhaps as great as that of its origin. Due to its extreme weather, snowmelts can occur at any time in Bute.

Nevenzel was currently engaged on behalf of Andrew Benson in the analysis of two distinct specimens of eulachon. One was from a river where Indigenous people make T'leena and another from a river where they do not make grease. He was very interested in this analysis because the substance he had found in the fish is a hydrocarbon that survives both the fermentation process and heat and distillation, which he implied were special attributes.

Eulachon oil, like Bute wax, was claimed to have special properties, and certainly the grease's extensive Indigenous use indicates more than mere gustatory necessity and pleasure. To give away hundreds of gallons of grease at a potlatch established the giver as a very high-ranking person indeed. To pour it on the fire so the Big House roof burst into flames was to announce that you and your extended family were the richest and most powerful of all.

I see Bute wax located at a point where environmental reality and narrative overlap to become myth. In many First Nations origin stories, what may seem to be a fanciful narrative turns around to face the observer, "telling" or performing the landscape as the social group's founding site. The "law" of the landscape structure and usage creates the group's social structure. Bute wax is the kind of matter, solid and liquid, hidden and visible, I began looking for in the 1990s to explain to myself the coastal landscape and its processes. Its very un-knowability expresses, perhaps claims, the landscape. It manifests the inexplicable duality of nature in the same way that August's photos of glaciers and waterways, of animals dead and alive, do.

And the wax, with its unknown source, storage and sudden appearance, can act as a key to the memory theatre.

One time, Glen Fair suddenly held his hands out 16 inches apart, saying, "You could grab the wax balls when they were cold, lift them into the boat. August had 45-gallon barrels of it. When Helen and I lived south of Church House we would see chunks of it attached to bits of wood floating out. It would hit on the end of Stuart Island where it was easy to gather. Bute wax fragments were also seen in Basset Bay in Hole-in-Wall, the passage to Owen Bay.

"They always wondered where it came from. There were occasions when the entire inlet would be covered with pollen, so that seemed a possibility. Scientists dragged the bottom but never found a thing. The weather is never now so cold. There was a time August had to carry an axe to chop ice that formed on the canoe from spray, just crossing over to Parker's."

"I saw blobs of the wax once at Surge [Narrows]," Norm Fair said. "It was bitterly cold. I was just a boy."

Water

Eulachon grease was vital to the Indigenous diet. August and Len found Bute wax invaluable. But the nutrient-laden fresh water that rivers, creeks and magnificent thousand-foot waterfalls deliver from the Coast Range glaciers to the inlet are essential, the mother of the fish, grease, wax and much more.

"The 1928–1930 Water Power Investigation of the Taseko–Chilcotin–Homathko" report from the hydro survey August guided was shelved. Another in the 1950s went nowhere, but in

Water sample collection by Judith Williams, Southgate River mouth, August 2010.
Courtesy of Susan Schelle/Mark Gomes

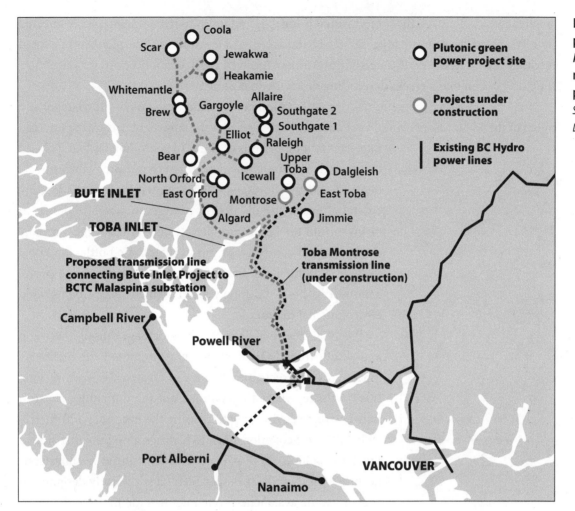

Location of proposed Plutonic/ Alterra Bute Inlet run-of-river hydro project sites.
Source: Vancouver Sun, December 6, 2008

2008 the Plutonic Power Corporation (which became Alterra and was acquired by Innergex of Quebec in 2018) made eighteen applications to the BC government for run-of-river (ROR) hydro projects in Bute Inlet in another bid to create power from inlet waterways. So-called green power from ROR projects is produced by removing water from large creeks and running it through power stations to create energy. It is then cooled and returned to the watercourse. Plutonic/Alterra was already at work in Toba Inlet and wanted to connect power from the two inlets to run south.

Although small, local, well-sited ROR projects, like that supplying power to Homathko Camp, can be built with minimal impact on the landscape, the process of setting up bigger projects creates extensive environmental degradation. The Bute proposal would have three clusters of ROR projects with an overwhelming seventeen river diversions sending over 90 kilometres (55 miles) of streams and rivers into tunnels and pipelines, and require 443 kilometres (275 miles) of new transmission line, 267 kilometres (165 miles) of permanent roads, and 142 bridges. As Knewstubb noted in the 1930s, there is no natural place to store water, and without storage the flow—and the energy production—would be seasonal.

The potential destruction of fish and animal habitat by construction of multiple dams and power lines alarmed many who treasured the inlet's dramatic wilderness and solitude. But the small Homalco Band felt the project would bring jobs and funds to restore salmon runs affected by 120 years of clearing and logging.[71] The band accepted a fee to allow Plutonic/Alterra's initial territory access. At the same time, the government received a rash of applications for water-bottling licences on many creeks descending down the inlet shores.

If all these projects come to pass, what is unique to the inlet waterways will change, and much of the water resources and land access will come under the control of private commercial interests for long periods of time. The commons is being closed off precisely when it is obvious water is a resource in worldwide demand and the storage glaciers are melting in a moderating coastal climate. The disruption of a grand water resource, to be given into the hands of a private and, at that time, partially foreign-owned company, or put in the plastic bottles we know to be environmentally destructive, solely for corporate profit, appeared to be a stunningly short-sighted use of our shared environmental capital.

Potential creek bed disruption and damage caused by erosion and silting from ROR dam building prompted the territory's inhabitants and recreational users to create a "Friends of Bute Inlet" website, where they pointed out the difficulties faced in Bute's extreme environment. Clearing the necessary 120-metre-wide (400 feet) corridor down to bedrock along the east side of Bute's precipitous shore so Alterra could run power lines connecting with their Toba output seemed specifically designed to encourage the avalanche-prone inlet to slide more of the landscape into the water.

Arne Liseth, who'd lived at Skookum Point Logging Camp, three-quarters of the way up Bute's east shore, added an instructive story to the website concerning a 1981 Halloween party. The camp's "backyard" was 7,785-foot Mt. Rodney, sheer from peak to saltchuck. Alterra's power line was projected to run along the side of this mountain.

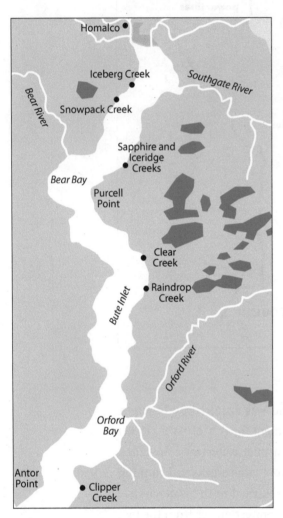

Applications for water extraction allocation in Bute Inlet under the Land and Water Act. *Source:* Campbell River Courier, *December 8, 2010*

October that year had unseasonably heavy snow, but by October 28, a thermal inversion caused air at the top of Mt. Rodney to be warmer than that below. On Halloween Eve, people from many miles around were arriving, and the pre-party started with dinner and drinks and more drinks. Suddenly loud slides were heard a mile or so away from the logging camp, and the tide was observed to go out lower than ever before in a remarkably short time. The smell of sulphur filled the air. Arne and his brother moved their tug to deeper water on the north side of the inlet, but returned it to their dock when the tide appeared to have stabilized. Despite continued rumblings, everyone retired for the night.

About 7:30 the next morning, people at the camp could see vast slides descending in waves from 1,370 metres (4,500 feet) up. The slides turned west at about 610 metres (2,000 feet), headed straight for the inlet instead of proceeding northwest in an old slide chute, and swept

Mt. Rodney, Mt. Superb and Mt. Sir Francis Drake from Len Parker's Bear Bay site on the east side of Bute Inlet, 2011.

Judith Williams photo

old-growth trees into the sea. Chunks of huge fir logs surfaced "loudly and violently from the depths like a broaching pod of whales."

Arne's crew fired up the tug and towed a string of smaller boats to the mouth of the Southgate Slough. Behind them, the waves produced by the slide debris rose to over 50 feet, washing away the camp's saw shop, both porches of the main house and "the fuel dump, containing 500 gallons of gas, thousand-gallon diesel tanks and large eighty-gallon propane tanks." The house itself was untouched.

The Bear River, by Len Parker's old place across the channel, crested at levels not seen for fifty years and rearranged its banks. Late party arrivals found Bute Inlet's entrance plugged with logs and other debris. "A cat could've walked the four miles across the inlet without getting its feet wet!"[72]

Given the inlet's extreme nature, consultation all around is the only strategy that can facilitate entrepreneurial, government, First Nations and environmental actions in Bute, and even then a mountain flank may just decide to roll down on the invaders or shift a river channel. Increasing glacial melt will add new wrinkles to any plan.

Given the inevitability of alteration of the inlet environment by hydro construction, I wondered how an artist might address these issues by making art—but not propaganda. Paintings or photographs of the inlet waterways would always impress, but like glamorous images of brilliantly coloured spawning salmon, they did not seem to inspire serious, ongoing, protective

Run-of-river powerhouse construction, East Toba River, Toba Inlet.

Phillip Wood photo

645

government action. In fact, images of the splendid swimmers seemed to lull the concerned into a sensuous coma. Water in which the salmon spawned and grew would seem to be the primary threatened target of any inlet construction and water export.

I have painted with watercolour paints all my life. What if I collected water from all those systems affected by the hydro and water-bottling licence applications and painted with that alone, not picturing or representing anything, not adding pigment, but allowing the liquids to leave what tone, texture or configuration they could? If I collected again during and after the hydro project, would there be a difference? Could I make an oil painting with just the Bute wax a scientist had suggested was an ideal medium? How big a stretch was it to ask the land itself to reveal a solution to the problem of development?

Bute Inlet water samples, 2010.
Judith Williams photo

On the surface the project seemed more thought experiment than en-actable. I had Bute wax, but getting water samples from such a vast area was a challenge. With the aid of a number of helpers, the water was not only collected, but its collection became a performance of concern, care and focus on a specific terrain. The water paintings I then made created a residue not just of the water (which it did) but, like certain pictographs and petroglyphs, of gentle human intersection with the landscape.

Bute, like the other inlets that thrust their fingers into the mainland and release their essence, is one of the main engines of the coast, sending mineral- and nutrient-laden material down to the hub of islands at the top of the Salish Sea. Since no comprehensive inlet studies have been done, we do not know the full effect that material has on the fertility of this area. Any roads, tunnels, dams or rerouting, and any alteration of water temperature, cannot avoid affecting plant, animal and fish habitat and the water itself. Installing eighteen ROR projects will have considerable impact no matter how well intentioned a construction team may be. The inlet the Homalco, Schnarrs and mountaineers knew will be transformed by hydro towers and lines. Tankers will take water to fill plastic bottles for Detroit or Dubai. Returning tankers will de-ballast stabilizing water somewhere, and what that water contains only heaven knows—and we, as always, will learn too late.

However, it is important to state that should deals between Plutonic/Alterra/Innergex and the Homalco People be stopped by those who wish to preserve the area, some alternate and equal opportunity must, in conscience, be worked out with the Homalco Band. This contemporary phase of First Nations partnering with commercial interests is to a large degree a result of the provincial government dragging its feet settling territorial claims that have resulted from a failure to finalize treaties in the days of Waddington's road building. In 1863, John Robson, editor of the *British Columbian* and later premier of BC, wrote: "Depend on it, for every acre of land we obtain by improper means, we will have to pay for dearly in the end."

8

LOT A17, RANGE 1, COAST DISTRICT

IT BLEW LIKE HECK UP THERE ALL THE TIME, SUMMER AND WINTER. I DON'T KNOW WHAT HE LIKED THAT AWFUL PLACE FOR, BUT THAT'S WHAT HE CHOSE. THE OLDER HE GOT, THE MORE BUTE BELONGED TO HIM.

—PANSY SCHNARR

Precisely when August added a propeller to his dugout to create the airboat is not clear, but his 1930–1960s periods in Bute were facilitated by the speedy trips up inlet waterways it could provide. Only one very old photo shows the prop installed on a stand in the dugout. It was redrawn to illustrate Maud Emery's 1960 Schnarr article in the Victoria *Colonist*.

August in dugout airboat.
Maud Emery collection

Longboat propeller and stand.
Judith Williams photo

After Pearl died in 2011, Glen Macklin and his father, John, gave me permission to move August's last propeller and its heavy steel stand into our Cortes Island shed to dry slowly and let the wood-bugs inhabiting the ingeniously pieced hardwood hub decamp for the bush; the prop had been rescued in the nick of time.

In the installation *Naming and Claiming: The Creation of Bute Inlet* at the Campbell River Museum in September 2011, the propeller loomed like a long-legged insect confronting August's four-inch steel auger, a facsimile of Charlie's diary, and a pelt of the wolverine August occasionally shot. From the museum collection we added Pansy's Native baskets, a surprising pair of Homalco Band's snowshoes and a plaster Station of the Cross from Church House, loaned to the museum by the band. August's grandsons Norman, Albert and Glen Fair contributed a photo of August taken during their 1970s Bute trip and diagrammed the propeller's position in the last fabricated longboat. They noted previous longboats were hollowed logs.

August and the girls used the propeller-powered canoe to trap up the rivers during the winters they logged at Bear Bay. A 1940 scribbler notes that on March 20 they received $564 from Pappas Furs, and another $517 on April 18. They record a total income of $1,433.42 for two log booms towed south to W.C. and V.E. Kiltz on August 26 and October 25. A tax form lists that year's logging and trapping income as $3,399.88.

Pansy's diary and interviews and Marion's letters indicate how the Schnarrs continued to use

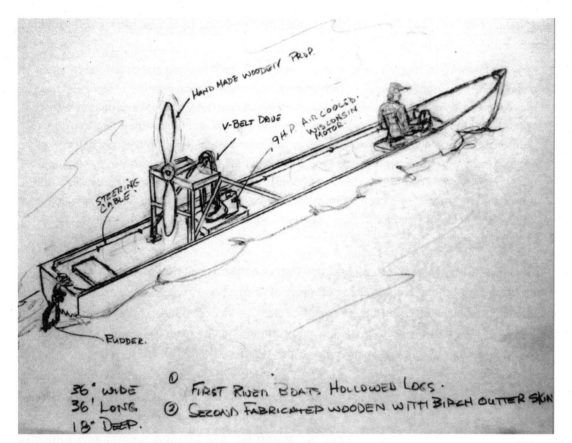

Propeller installation diagram.
Norman, Albert and Glen Fair illustration

Above: Remembering the longboat moored out in Heriot Bay, David Rousseau sketched the prop's cage and baffles.
Judith Williams illustration from David Rousseau sketch

Left: August and Albert Fair camped in Bute Inlet, c. 1970. Last propeller-driven longboat at right with supplemental "kicker."
Courtesy of Albert Fair

the Landing animal sheds, gardens, fruit trees and berry bushes for themselves and for trade. In 1945 August got a further lease on area EFGH, the Landing's original cultivated area, on which he paid tax and rent. In May 1946 he brought a floathouse up from Fawn Bluff to near the Landing. He'd used it to log another sale after Bear Bay was finished.

In 1947 August heard a lumber outfit was to log in behind the Landing, and in June 1947, when he went there to pick raspberries, he accidently met Mr. Vaux, a log surveyor for the

Glaspie Lumber Company. Papers in the Schnarr fonds relating to an ensuing lawsuit provide a *rough* outline of what happened next.

> I had trouble with [a] logging camp that took my place. I got the best bay in Bute Inlet. I sold one right–a–way [right–of–way]. I'd moved my house 2 miles down inlet out of sight and they moved their buildings in. I saw what they were doing. A year later—there were fruit trees—and I told them not to damage them . . . I saw they had a barge and they were going to move it right thru that area. I went home and got my gun, came back, left it on the beach, went up and got in front of the scow and said "you leave it there!" I went down and got the gun, put it down; they quit. The next day the RCMP came and I explained I never pointed a gun, but the Super, who hadn't even been there, said I had. I explained I had not and made him admit [it], I wasn't going to stand for it! Next year they had to buy [the right–of–way] for $10,000. I never did get it all.[73]

Glen and Albert Fair say August and Len Parker had searched the inlet for minerals as well as for a source of Bute wax and staked a number of claims close to the water. Any operator with a log sale licence located behind their claims had to pay an access fee to cross their land to the timber, as Glaspie was forced to do. August used the money he made this way to buy property in the Rendezvous Islands previously owned by Francis Millard, who ran the Redonda Bay Cannery. When Millard died, his widow wanted to sell, and Len thought he had a deal to receive 10 per cent if he found a buyer. That August would not pay Len this fee was one source of enmity between them.

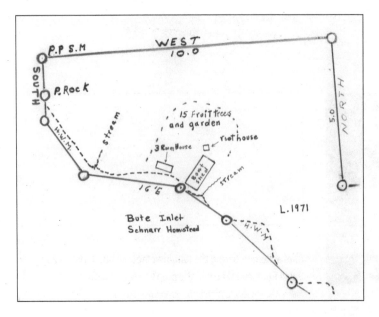

Schnarr's Landing property showing location of house, big boatshed and west orchard.
Judith Williams illustration

The lengthy lawsuit about the 1947 Landing usage by the Glaspie Lumber Company indicates the single incursion August first allowed the company had excluded the house site, orchard and any cultivated area. The loggers ignored his specifications, tore down his old boatshed, drove through the site with heavy equipment, wrecked the garden and destroyed the orchard. They erected nine buildings above the house site, made the point next to the house into a log dump, and compromised his moorage by starting to drive in the pilings to create a booming ground for logs. August hired a Vancouver lawyer and, in a series of affidavits, claimed they had destroyed forty-two to fifty fruit trees, most of the red and black currant, gooseberry, loganberry, raspberry and blackberry bushes, a 100-square-foot garden and his dead wife's flower garden. The soil built up over twenty years had been moved, and the remainder contaminated by oil.

The case went to the BC Supreme Court in 1948. Len Parker gave evidence that the small bay west of the Landing, where the logging company wanted August to have his house and booms, had bad moorage due to the wind direction. He swore he knew the Landing itself had excellent moorage because he was a long-time resident of the inlet. Letters to August make it clear his lawyer felt he had a strong case, but the legal wrangle continued to be thwarted by Glaspie denials. August claimed $5,000 in damages to his trees, but an "expert" hired by Glaspie said they were worth $500. August had, of course, compromised the case by confronting the loggers and implying he was willing to use his rifle to evict them, and he was served notice not to trespass on his land.

August was certainly hotheaded and known for sticking up logging companies so they would pay for access to their sale, but the logging company significantly overstepped the bounds of the initial agreement and destroyed property he'd hand-built over the years. None of the legal documents evince any understanding of the upcoast economy and how food, tools and services could be valued, loaned and traded. Much commerce was "in kind" one way or another.

There was an implication August lost his rights by not always living in situ. In the days of slow boats, handlogging required the logger to live in proximity to his sale. As Pearl said, the Schnarr buildings were moved all over, and other upcoasters shifted periodically, even seasonally, from one fishing, logging and trapping location to another. August moved houses temporarily from Owen Bay to Bear Bay in 1938 but kept up the Owen Bay potato garden and cabin. He also tended the Landing garden and pruned the trees. The Fawn Bluff floathouse was likely the house moved to the Landing's small outer bay in 1947. That poor moorage was life threatening once the big boat shed, used for hauling and securing the boat in winter, was destroyed by the loggers.

Glaspie Logging prevailed, and its site was later taken over by Taylor Brothers and then Don Hayes Logging. Pansy came with her husband, Lloyd Fair, and son Glen in 1951 to pull out some usable cable from the small northwest bay. In the early 1960s, Lloyd Fair moved into Schnarr's Bay, at Big Creek, east of the Landing, to log. Glen Fair and his wife, Helen, bought a house from the Parrish family for $1,200 and moved it next to Big Creek, and Glen logged there with his dad from 1962 to 1965. After one heavy snow a temperature inversion caused heavy rain, and great boulders crashed down the creek bed by the house. "We stayed awake," Glen said, "ready to leave at any moment." Helen's washhouse on a wooden bridge over the creek was swept away. Dennis Walker's grandson, Vern Logan, towed Lloyd Fair's float camp out of Von Donop Inlet in the late 1960s to a tie-up around Beazley Passage at Surge Narrows. It later caught fire, and Lloyd lost his camp. He was killed in a falling accident, and Pansy married family friend Keith Eddington in 1967.

Pearl said she left home at fifteen, soon after they returned to Bute, and went to Vancouver, then Winnipeg. The Fair brothers say she married "Uncle" Albert Linkletter, part Prairie First Nations, who they thought very well of. "I did good, didn't I?" Pearl used to say. Her copy of Len Parker's *Shadows Lay North*, inscribed "to Pearl and Albert," was a wedding present. After the war the couple had an A-frame logging show north of the Paradise River in Bute. While moving logs one day, Linkletter's boat engine kicked back and flipped him overboard. Unable to swim, he drowned in front of their son, Ronny. Following the accident, an unmoored Pearl seems to have lost contact with August. In the fonds is a letter on two sheets of powder-blue stationery, dated October 12, 1952, from Pasadena, California, where she had cousins. Pearl rather formally addressed her father care of Len Parker:

> Mr. Schnarr: You will no doubt be surprised that I'm writing you thru Mr. Parker. Says you don't like to write, but you can write me can't you please? Have been writing Len but the rascal up and married, guess Mrs. can't let him now. I miss hearing from him but hope he is happy. I am very lonely & unhappy about men, married one, and he proved impossible, wanted me to

support him . . . I have my son to take care of, he gets a little money off his Dady who died, but not enough. I am working & am not too good to work.

Well so much for now, hope I hear from you very soon.

Respect, Pearl. — send me photo here.

August must have written back. Within the next year thirty-year-old Pearl sent a Christmas card to "dear Daddy" from the Lower Mainland.

Dear August. How is everything going with you? I sure hope you are catching a lot of marten. How is Moses? Still alive I hope. I am just fine but I get kinda lonesome for the old place at times. Have been out to Fair's three or four times, he is building two houses to sell. Houses sure are expensive down here. I sure hope to see you down soon. Well so long. Lots of love Pearl.

The same year August received a series of affectionate letters and cards from a Therese Hochmuth. She had stayed with him up Bute, wonders about her potted plants and sends greetings to Mr. and Mrs. Parker. Therese said she left only because of "sprains" to her feet, now cured. They are strange letters full of longing for her "dear friend," love of the wilderness, regret and considerable apprehension.

Albert Fair says August married for a second time, and the new wife demanded he move out of Bute. During the shift some of her dishes were broken, they had a yelling match, August hit her and she sued for divorce.

After Albert Linkletter's death and the 1952 letter, August moved the house Albert and Pearl had been building down from Bute to Heriot Bay for Pearl. Young Albert Fair, Pansy's son, often stayed there with his Aunt Pearl. August moved his own house there too, and jacked it up above high tide west of the Heriot Bay Hotel. Pearl, married to John Macklin, moved a house from Sawmill Bay on Read Island to its present location on Macklin Road.

In the 1970s tapes August said, "I had three daughters, all married now. I'm proud of my family, not one went wrong, that's pretty good for these days. One lived up the hill, another in Campbell River. The one in Victoria married Bert Parker. He's the District Superintendent for BC Hydro. Norman Fair was maintenance man at the pulp mill."

August may have been proud, but some say the girls were a little afraid of him, and Albert Fair characterizes him as so suspicious of people wanting something from him that he never had a close friend. After August died, when Albert and his wife were about to have a child, he told his mother, Pansy, "I don't mind what it is as long as it's not like POP."

"You don't have to worry about that, honey," she said.

It was only then that the boys learned August was not Pansy's father.

Pearl and Marion remained close, but the Fair brothers feel Pansy was sometimes excluded from that relationship. She had, as she said, "become Mother" at twelve.

"This house?" August replied to a question about his Heriot Bay cabin. "I've been here in and out. I was up there, moved down here for school. We were at Owen Bay and moved down here and ended here. There was half a shed, Grace Haines owned it. I bought it for $500, built this up Bute and moved it down. Been here since 60s, sixteen years, but in Bute til 60s. Oh yes!"

When he lived on Quadra, August would bring the longboat in from its mooring at Heriot Bay, load it with supplies and travel up the inlet to continue to trap and explore.

Pansy's sons have owned the Landing since 1971.

9

THE WILD IN US

The Schnarr dossier I had built, Charlie Rasmussen's file and the hydro survey, when combined with my photo layouts, created a flowchart of a small group of people moving through place through time. Bute became a storied landscape, each inlet reach revealing the Butites intersecting with waterway geography, its Indigenous peoples, their neighbours and the animal, plant and sea life.

Mouth of the Southgate River, 2014.
Judith Williams photo

A 1941 school scribbler recorded the Schnarrs' "Miscellaneous expenses" after they'd returned to the inlet. On August 2, 90 gallons of oil, and on the 24th, 123 gallons of gas were purchased at the relatively nearby store in the Homalco village of Church House for a total of $53.00. Now that Pansy's diary had clarified for me how that money was earned, I wanted to take a fresh look at where August and the girls lived and what they encountered moving through the inlet and riverine territory to work. Like Charlie and Pansy, I kept a diary and I photographed what I saw.

August 12, 2014, 9:30. My husband, Bobo Fraser, and I headed our aluminum speedboat, *Tetacus*, north from Cortes Island up Lewis Channel to stay again at Homathko Camp on the river August's skills made his own. At the top of Cortes, Toba Inlet's five rivers send water through Pryce Channel into the Calm/Sutil Channel hub at the Rendezvous Islands to meet the northern flood tide, and a boater enters a grander, more demanding water world of rapids, currents and winds. An unusual number of whales were seen south from here to the gulf that year, transient Biggs orcas chasing seals, and humpbacks sieving up enough sea creatures to keep them around.

Our first stop was Church House, the mainland Homalco village site Lhilhukwem, ("basin shaped"), which became Aupe (U7p) IR #6 and 6A when reserves were fixed. During the Schnarrs' Bute years, a steamer landed passengers and store goods here as well as stopping at the public wharf at the south end of Stuart Island, the older Homalco site Chichxwiyakalh ("clear passage between"). Church House was the main Homalco site by 1900, the last village occupied in their territory until their hatchery and bear-watching lodge were built in Orford Bay.

On the north flank of the bay, a sleek black bear swung its nose, sniffing our scent. At the south end a small path of water filtered through the old village and burial ground to trickle across a beach dotted with cold cream jars, pottery shards, bullet casings and a remarkable number of shoe soles, lined up seaward by the tide like footprints of a fleeing horde.

Church House.
Vancouver Province,
January 1966

One day in the mid-1970s my scheduled floatplane flight from Campbell River to Refuge Cove had stopped here. Four women deplaned with their shopping bags onto a dock and climbed up a ramp to a long pier leading to houses, children and mates in a village where Jesus extended his arms from the church belfry. There had been power lines and roads.

The 1896 church had now collapsed, its moss-covered roof blending into the forest floor. There was nothing to indicate the pier had ever existed. A washing machine eyed us from the porch of a lone standing house, and the small 1960s-era white clinic I'd photographed fronting the church when Tom Soames had run a salmon farm there in the early 1990s was now backed by a dark hole in the bush.

The church marks the Homalco move from Muushkin on Maurelle Island after a "Bute" blew the village down. Non-Indigenous schoolteacher William Thompson and his wife, Emma, built a store and a post office here, and in 1911 tried to pre-empt a fair chunk of Aupe that included the graveyard and several Homalco homes. In 1915 Chief George Harry asked the Royal Commission examining reserve lands to stop this pre-emption, enlarge the Aupe reserve and add offshore Bartlett Island for clams and a sheep range. He requested 10 acres at Bear Bay, a traditional herring fishing station, which was not allowed. The band was allotted 29.7 acres at Aupe, later reduced to 20.08, and the schoolteacher was allowed a small portion. Chief Harry told the commission his people spent the winter at Aupe to meet the priest, but went to X̱we'malhkwu (between Cumsack Creek and the mouth of the Homalco) in the summer and to Pi7pḵnech (Orford Bay) for chum salmon in August and September.[74]

The Thompson family continued to run the store and sell the gas the Schnarrs bought. Many Church House residents went to work in the logging industry and at Redonda Bay Cannery, which closed in the late 1940s. The current Homalco chief, Darren Blaney, says Church House suffered a final financial blow in the late 1960s when the federal government imple-

Church House church, c. 1992.
Judith Williams photo

Above left: Homalco men Albert Georgeson and Johnny Blaney carving a racing canoe at Church House.
Courtesy of Homalco First Nation

Above right: Church House 2006.
Cathy Campbell photo

Right: The hand of Jesus in the grass at Church House, 1990s.
Judith Williams photo

mented the Davis Plan, an attempt to downsize the fishing industry through licence restrictions, which penalized small, family-operated boats with general fishing licences. Unable to meet the requirements, twenty-four of twenty-six Homalco boats lost their licences, and families lost their livelihood. Although some residents stayed into the 1970s, and there were attempts to preserve the church in the '90s, the Homalco Band now occupies a site at 1218 Bute Crescent, south of Campbell River. Each time we came to Church House there were fewer people and fewer buildings. Jesus fell from his belfry, and his broken hands lay in tall grass. Like the village, the inlet emptied out as small-scale economic activities practised by the truly independent disappeared.

North, at Fawn Bluff, where the inlet narrows, a kind of magic begins. The silt-charged water becomes a luminous jade path, and seven-, eight-, nine-thousand-foot mountains unfold great scoured-out creek beds and lift glaciers into the sky. A marine sample taken where August anchored in the '20s and logged in the '40s was a vibrant cocktail of fresh water from the Coast Range glaciers mixed with seawater flooding from the north through the Arran Rapids across channel.

656

Water collection, Rainbow Creek Falls, 2011.
Cathy Campbell photo

Fresh water makes up 2.5 to 2.75 per cent of all the water in the world, and 1.75 to 2 per cent of it is stored for our convenience in glaciers, ice and permanent snowfields. There was almost no snowpack in 2014 compared with what Bobo and I had seen in our 2010 and 2011 Bute expeditions, and now exposed ridges of glacial ice gleamed pale ultramarine in midday light. On August 23, 2011, one of our companions, Cathy Campbell, got soaked at Raindrop Creek Falls when we tried to get close enough to collect water. Wind generated by the long, powerful falls blew the boat away. Now the thinnest veil of water trickled onto the surface.

North of Boyd Point an incoming helicopter swung a dangling lanyard over our heads. Moored at shore was the float-camp barge I'd watched being rebuilt at the Whaletown dock the previous winter. Logging had begun again next to Schnarr's Landing, and a new bridge had been constructed over Big Creek where water ran down off the south flank of 2,673-metre (8,770-foot) Mt. Sir Francis Drake.

August had climbed up Big Creek Valley to make a rough, swivelling panoramic photo series above the inlet. Looking at these glacier photos in 1977, he said, "I'm up on Needles Peaks, looking down, 7,000 feet above where I lived. Hot day!"

West of Big Creek, on the long, south-facing gravel beach Pearl said was unique to the inlet, flattish pink and grey stones mounded up to silvered beach logs. This was Schnarr's Landing homestead. It's said salmon roll against these smooth rocks to remove lice before going to spawn in Big Creek, and trout follow along to snitch their eggs. But because the surrounding land

Collaged photos from Needles Peaks.
August Schnarr photos. Images MCR 20447-68, 20447-70, 20447-71 courtesy of the Museum at Campbell River

rise is so abrupt, eggs in low spawning beds are vulnerable to smothering by silt runoff from avalanche-prone slopes being logged again.

The sea was calm and the beach approach easy enough, but thickly suspended silt roiled and clouded the water as if the world was still forming, melting or mixing into something new, which, of course, it was; Bute always exhibiting the world in process. Above the gravel shore, behind a dark hole in the beach brush, rough boulder stairs led up to an alder-shadowed A-frame that Pansy's sons maintain. The building sat on a flat silty bench below a sunny cleared area. Plastic over screen windows hung in tatters, but the floor seemed sound, and I thought the building would not collapse if the tarp under the mossy shakes stayed intact.

In August's old photos of the first house, which sank, two sheds sit right at the beach with two houses hauled up behind. A garden appears to run up to an orchard at the height of the present A-frame. A new survey map (Lot 1971) records a three-room house and a huge boatshed for

Schnarr's Landing animal shed with young Pearl and Marion. The log boom points south, down inlet, c. 1930.
August Schnarr photo. Image MCR 6699 courtesy of the Museum at Campbell River

hauling out the gasboat during winter in front of a root house, garden and fifteen-tree orchard. Glaspie did such extensive bulldozing that the landscape was transformed. No fruit trees were now visible. The Fairs demolished Glaspie's remaining building to build the A-frame. A wavy-grilled '50s truck missing its engine and a blue door refusing to fall into its collapsed building are secondary stage remains giving little sense of Pansy's "old place" gardens where she picked apples for jelly in 1938 and '39.

The Schnarrs' first house was east of a small point where Glaspie established his log dump. The only remaining sign of occupation on the beach was a rotting piling at the east end of the property, a tied-in log below the dump and a solitary, sea-worn shard of green glass. Even the new logging show was temporary. I'll find that floating bunkhouse, helicopter and landing barge again someday at a new log sale when I investigate an out-of-the-way arm or inlet.

We continued up the inlet, motoring past Purcell Point and west into Bear Bay. The light mist had burned off and the mountain peaks sharpened against the sky. A floathouse was jacked up on pilings below Mt. Smith. Could this be where the Schnarrs moved ashore in 1938?

During our 2011 expedition we had tied up to a buoy at Bute Inlet Lodge, south of Bear River. Owners Brian and Mark Gage ran Len Parker's place as a wilderness exploration business. Here Len Parker logged or wrote in the front cabin while Laurette painted in the back shack during the 1970s. There is now a small Homalco reserve on the river's north side.

Below left: Vintage truck grille.
Judith Williams photo

Below right: The Landing A-frame.
Judith Williams photo

In the winter of 2015, a few months after our journey, Bute continued its rearrangement of the landscape. A hydraulic eruption caused by new logging blew out the soil below the A-frame, opening a trench under the floor studs on the left side of the building. The soil shelf Glaspie bulldozed out from the Schnarr orchard and garden collapsed and water and soil, running out from under the front porch, flushed the path I'd climbed up down to the beach. A small area of First Nations shell midden was exposed where Glen Macklin had earlier found what he termed "big stone daggers."

View under the washed-out A-frame, 2015.
Jeanette Taylor photo

Len Parker's two houses, Bear Bay, 2011.
Judith Williams photo

Arcing *Tac* north from Bear Bay toward the Homathko River made the Bute Mountain massif seem to slide left and half block the two-winged Bute Glacier. The visible left wing, hanging above the river mouth like a shaggy pelt, no longer completely blanketed the bald rock as it had done in mountaineer Tom Fyles's 1930 *Alpine Journal* photo. Earlier, in the 1920s, August took a photo from the river that showed the glacier with snowpack. He was afloat close to the present location of Homathko Camp dock, on an initial section of Waddington's road. Each time I came up the river the glacier had retreated more.

Above: Stuffed sea lion head on the wall in Len Parker's cabin, 2011.
Judith Williams photo

Left: View of Bute Glacier from the Homathko River, c. 1920s.
August Schnarr photo. Image MCR 14395 courtesy of the Museum at Campbell River

Above: Bobo Fraser piloting *Tac* at the Homathko entrance; Bute Glacier ahead, 2014.
Judith Williams photo

Left: Bute Mountain from Mt. Rodney, 1930.
Photo by Tom Fyles

Above: Dean Potter jumped off Bute Mountain in a wingsuit for a 2011 *National Geographic* documentary to publicize the grandeur of the area for its protection.[75] Photo looks toward the Whitemantle Range.
Mikey Shaefer photo

Right: Homathko Valley.
Judith Williams illustration

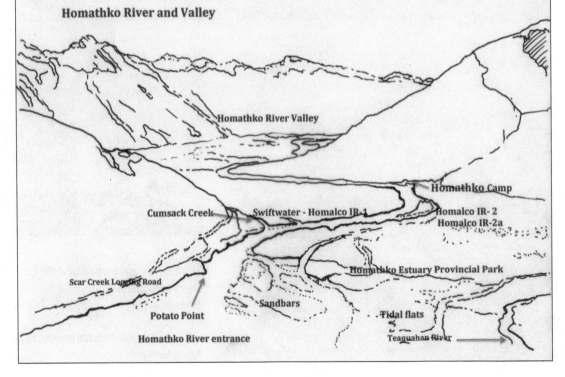

Homathko River and Valley

Homathko River Valley

Homathko Camp

Cumsack Creek   Swiftwater - Homalco IR-1   Homalco IR- 2
Homalco IR-2a

Scar Creek Logging Road   Homathko Estuary Provincial Park

Sandbars   Tidal flats

Potato Point

Homathko River entrance   Teaquahan River

At the south side of the Homathko River mouth, a line of pilings for tying in log booms marks Scar Creek Logging's sort and dump. Now truck logging is closed on this side of the Homathko, the booms have been pulled away and our usual route along that shore into the river proved hazardous. A rock fall below the logging road had cut into the flow and built up a higher river bar. For the first time we ran aground. An oar stuck into creamy, opaque water indicated the depth was a meagre foot. The river swirled a whole leafy cottonwood out into the inlet through what had to be a deeper channel on the north side. I pried us off in that direction, and we drifted back out into Waddington Harbour past a long, new sandbar.

The rising tide allowed us to motor into the river past a 20-foot log stuck into the mucky north shore like a javelin. At the entrance to Cumsack Creek another bar had built up out into the river from the old village site of Swift Water, and at the first valley switchback the water ran fiercely at Homathko Camp dock. The river toggles down Homathko Valley through seasonally shifting sandbars studded with interlocked debris. Passage with an outboard is chancy even in our shallow-draft aluminum boat.

Tac was forced against this flow and in behind the small dock Chuck Burchill had secured in a back eddy. I grabbed the rope hanging from a dock ring, wrapped and tied, snugged in the stern and climbed onto the quivering finger float with the bowline. The river leapt enthusiastically up through a steel mesh surface welded over the four 16-inch steel pipes that constitute the main dock it was attached to, and I gained the ramp with relief. The dock is clever enough and well secured onshore, but the river flows so ceaselessly, implacably and with such indifferent force that I view it with total and humble respect. I am not going to do well if I fall in.

4:30: Safe in camp. Chuck trucked us up to the trailer we had in 2010. Five beds, bathroom, shower and a kitchen we never use. Sheron Burchill's son Wayne cooked pork chops and prepared a big salad from the garden lush with corn, beets, tomatoes, cukes and blackberries. We ate on the lawn in front of the cookhouse. Only a glassed porch has been added since our 1991 visit.

I showed them the one picture I'd found of August in the airboat. Chuck explained how the Homathko monitoring systems indicate it has the third-largest volume of flow of BC rivers, and we considered how laborious and dangerous it would have been to pole upriver alone before August invented the propeller mechanism.

Chuck recognized the location of August's photograph of Charlie Rasmussen at Giant Rock from his hikes. Unless they fly, people intending to go up the left side of the valley past Homathko Canyon must still hike past the massive slab.

We slept in the back bedroom of the trailer, within earshot of the huge sound of Camp Creek, harnessed by Chuck to supply any amount of hydropower to the camp.

August 13. Mist on the river brought me out to the dock at six, where drifting fog slunk down the sides of the Homathko. Its force, still in freshet, underlines August's singular river skills in all seasons. The melt from the Coast Range and the 30-mile-diameter Homathko Icefield begins

Homathko Camp dock, 2014.

Judith Williams photo

in July, but Chuck showed us a photo of Wayne standing on four feet of ice in the much lower winter river, right in front of the dock.

In 1929, August and Charlie came upriver in October and left the boat blocked up out of the water at the south end of the canyon. When Charlie returned on December 8, he found the chocks holding the longboat had shifted in the river rise caused by rain. Descending the Homathko ten days later in the boat, after the higher freeze-up, he notes that he encountered ice jams. Robert Homfray wrote of finding salmon encased in ice balls along the riverbanks around November 15 in 1861. Even today it can be so bitterly cold up the valley that the combination of days of hoarfrost and 160-kilometre-an-hour (100-mile-an-hour) winds dehydrates trees to the point that the slightest spark can create a fire in the dead of winter. Perhaps the trees Charlie described setting on fire were dry as tinder.

Negotiating the river at any time was a challenge, but silt now rebuilding the mouth would not have been such an issue prior to logging and the increasing glacial melt. When August came to trap in low-water season, usable channels may have been more obvious. Still, his and Marion's ability to safely navigate that canoe was and is still impressive.

The previous day's intense flow had made me apprehensive, but the sunlit mist now moving upriver, lifting and blurring the far edge of trees, was enchanting. It would be a fine day. Chuck quickly laid out a logging camp breakfast: grapefruit, eggs, bacon, sausage, toast and their homemade raspberry jam. He was eager to get underway so I could photograph an unrecorded pictograph.

My coastal journeys have led to a fascination with First Nations painted pictographs and carved petroglyphs, signs still in situ of the mind at work in wilderness, the antithesis of decontextualized museum artifacts. Any culture's engagement with landscape becomes layered with various cognitive maps relating to space, time and event. Indigenous people marked their territory with carved or painted images meaningful to them and their neighbours. In 1792 Thomas Heddington drew *The Village of the Friendly Indians*, which William Alexander rendered into watercolour and then engraved to be printed in Vancouver's journals (see image on page 104). August recorded what he cared about in his territory in a medium of his time. Visiting rock art in situ, or a reproduction's or a photo's location, tells how people relate to that world using their iconography and the materials at hand. Interestingly, rock art does not allow one to stay fixed on image alone, since the rock surface also holds our interest, and we flip back and forth between image and ground, more aware of context than we usually are viewing a photograph or engraving. For most Indigenous groups the rock itself was alive and informed any painted or carved image, which was as much a residue of a dream, performance or event as it was a picture in the sense that we might think of them.

Alder is quickly filling in the Homathko Valley roads, but we could drive to the landing strip Chuck kept groomed just above camp. They'd had fifteen planes of a flying club here overnight on August 8. At the south end of the strip a startling stone outcrop rippled a series of galleries up out from a forest mass. The elegantly rounded granitic overhangs, 36 to 46 metres (120 to 150 feet) above the valley floor, are a glacial and epiglacial landform shaped by the passage of glaciers and partially polished by meltwater.

In 1991, when Sam Smythe drove us up the valley on extensive logging roads then in full use, I had seen red marks at one gallery level and taken two fast photos. Chuck once climbed up beside this outcrop with his daughter and rappelled down to the paintings, but the footing was too steep for photography. I could now see two panels with red marks, but a small pine in front of the bottom of the larger panel obscured the main red form. No recognizable image was decipherable, even with a telephoto lens. Alder had grown tall along the road where I took the 1991 shots, and I could now see the rock formation only from the landing strip or faintly as we came upriver to the camp dock. Chuck said it could be seen from other places in the valley. The determined painter(s) must have hung from above with carefully prepared ochre and brush in hand.[76]

Stonefall, pictograph site, Homathko Valley, 2014.
Judith Williams photo

665

Painted stone pictograph galleries, Homathko Valley, 2014.
Chuck Burchill photo

"I can put you on Potato Point," Chuck had said the previous night. We'd been talking about Jack Mould's dynamiting of the protected burial site at IR #3V and his disappearance in 2007. Jack, inclined to dynamite at the whiff of a gold tell, had set off a massive blast that reverberated up the valley to camp, and Chuck boated down to discover the sound's source. Seeing the desecration, he called the RCMP. Jack said he'd been looking for "artifacts" for two "Doctors" who were nowhere to be found. When he disappeared, the RCMP arrived at camp to assure themselves nobody from there was responsible.

After the picto shoot we motored downstream in the camp's aluminum herring skiff. Chuck cruised past Potato Point to indicate the sighting from the Southgate to the point that could guide a boat through the correct river channel. Landmarks are essential; the totally opaque water makes it impossible to see sandbars or deadheads. Then he turned upstream and bunted the skiff against Potato Point's slimy rocks. Wayne pulled me up off the boat bow onto this mound August had passed each time he went upriver. Between tree stands was a razed area where Jack had landed a skidder from a barge and cleared a way uphill. Regrown, the chest-high salmonberry and coastal black gooseberry were so dense we climbed up the side between trees and fallen logs.

At the top of the rise I stopped, smelled . . . *dead*! Whose bones had we trodden on? There were large old trees on the mound that could have held burial boxes—now fallen—if that was what the Homalco used. Where the mound levelled back toward a cliff that might have provided niches for bones, Mould had blasted a rectangular hole, now half filled with water. The back and one side of the cavity suggested a different matrix had been inset within a darker stone, and Jack, suspecting the presence of gold, had blown it out. It was nasty and illegal, but the Homalco chief at the time did nothing. Mind you, some of Jack's gold patrons were reported to be a very rough crew. Anything Jack may have found remains as mysterious as his disappearance up the Southgate.

The vista from the mound across the estuary to the stark, sheer face of Mount Bute was dramatic, and a burial position away from flood-prone village houses built on pilings must have been comforting. There was a swath of what looked to be a slender version of edible arrowgrass growing below in a back eddy.

In the late 1970s, Homalco elders Ambrose Wilson and Tommy Paul told researchers Randy Bouchard and Dorothy Kennedy that Potato Point was known as mimekw'maakw'a, literally meaning "a bunch of little corpses" (because it was the burial ground for the Xwe'malhkwu village), or ch'ilhep, meaning "tangled brush or wood" (because the area had grown over with tangled brush difficult to get through). Paul, born around 1900, said that "in his grandfather's time the Homalco caught seals off Potato Point using special large-mesh cedar-bark nets similar to modern gill-nets."[77] The contemporary name is a bit of a conundrum. Although river meets inlet here, Waddington Harbour has a deep layer of fresh water, and native wapato, a broader-leafed arrowgrass that produces a tuber known as Indian potato, might have grown here, providing the name. But Southgate settlers introduced potatoes to the valley by at least the 1890s, and Indigenous people had learned even earlier to grow them to sell to ships.

Chuck boomed the skiff upstream to the end of Cumsack Creek. A pale blue heron extended up from a stand of silt-coated skunk cabbage and floated across the stream in a stunningly fluid motion no still camera could capture. Later, at the stone table Chuck installed next to the camp greenhouse, I tried to find some painted equivalent for that elemental vision as the opaque river flowed and flowed, unstoppable and irretrievable as the heron's flight.

At dinner Chuck asked if the Homalco made and traded eulachon oil. A visiting Fisheries officer had stated that this habitat was inappropriate, and although there were some eulachon, they did not contain much oil. Interestingly, a 1994–99 Fisheries and Oceans stock assessment study cited Bute Inlet as one of sixteen main eulachon-spawning areas of the coast.[78] If there were eulachon but little grease, what was traded to the Interior along the trails Knewstubb noted?

We discussed other Bute mysteries, like a fish wheel installed on the Homathko that indicated sockeye, contrary to other data, spawned at the head of the inlet due to its deep layer of fresh water. Saltwater steelhead, Chuck said, do not spawn in the Teaquahan as is generally thought, but go there to hunt—perhaps the exiting baby eulachon, whose parents only spawn in its Galleon Creek tributary. Chuck added that fishing guide Randy Killoran shows him trout he catches in high lakes where Charlie and August caught them in 1929. Chuck longed to get up past the canyon to see the newly reported remnants of the underground houses where Homfray and his crew were sheltered by the Tŝilhqot'in in 1861.

I stayed late alone at the table in front of the cookhouse. Cloud moved like a hunting creature in and around and over ridges, pushing apart mountain ranges that read as a mass during the day. Years earlier I'd sat here in hot sun as the glacier across the river dripped down to become a waterfall. There was no snow at this camp in the past winter and blue ice glowed at the glacier's fore-edge. I tried to draw but could not capture the popping dimensionality. The group of minimalist paintings I did with the inlet's water came closer to some essential experience for me; not picturing, but laying another process beside nature's grand gestures. However, drawing

Jack Mould's barge, Southgate River.
Courtesy of Judith Williams/Cathy Campbell

helps learn form that can release meaning the landscape encodes. When it was too dark to see I went to bed, waking again when a moon re-illuminated the glacier.

August 14. Shafts of morning light separated peak, ridge and glacier mass. A strand of cloud dropped slowly down a dark mound, met another and together they slipped out of a hung valley, 1.5 kilometres (5,000 feet) above me, and moved upriver.

After breakfast, Bobo and I slid downstream and across the silken harbour to the mouth of the Southgate River. A new road had been blasted down to the edge of the cliff, marking its south entrance. Raw fractured rock spiralled up to become a rough track east that dropped down to a small camp set where we entered the river proper. The cliff is the log dump for Interfor's long road to Icefall Creek Valley, where huge trees, too big for helicopter retrieval, still stand. A forestry engineer had told us privately that the road and camp were built when salmon were spawning. The blatant prominence of the devastation was staggering. But the road building was closed until fall, and we were the only people moving within the upper inlet's splendour.

The flooding tide made the river choppy where it met the sea, but upstream it swirled glassily through a lazy bend where a cabin hid in thick alder. Farther up, at shallow rapids where the

old northside logging road came down to the bank, Jack left his dog and truck and was never seen again. The tracks of a large creature lined along the opposite sandbar.

Bobo drove northward out of the river across what can be a drying flat of mired logs to a massive rock pier running from Jack's old barge. We tied to the remains of a metal dock strung out to a piling. A bag lay open on the dock spilling out the mud being hand-dug from the river for shipment, a pilot had told Chuck, to a cosmetic company. The long pier road was dotted with bear and wolf scat, and huge tracks from newly introduced elk were churned into mud hedged by encroaching alder. A wispy, bug-spun cage contained crisp orange leaves and grubs wiggling with ugly potential. A sign added to Jack's barge promised twenty-four-hour video surveillance, but the back door flapped invitingly open and shut in the breeze. I waved at the unseen camera and faced out to the slough behind the stone pier—the location, Jack claimed, of the sunken Spanish galleon. Dynamically angled ropes and nets framed the focus across glaucous-green water to House Mountain at the Homathko's mouth, air slipping through swooping swallow feathers the only sound.

Above: Animal tracks on the bank of the Southgate River. *Judith Williams photo*

Below left: Plastic skull and bones. *Judith Williams photo*

Below right: Wooden cross. *Judith Williams photo*

Dock and boats, Southgate River mouth.

Judith Williams photo

I wandered out to Jack's arrangement of dog graves, plastic bones and skulls. The silt bank was collapsing there, and I had the sense it would eventually drop the bones into a fibreglass boat, already capsized below, and eventually entomb them deeper within the silt, as Jack said the galleon was preserved, a plastic offering for the ages.

Bobo was sitting on a stack of wooden pallets. "The collection of batteries is still here," he called.

As I turned, around me rose a period installation, a backwoods cousin to a reconstructed room at the Metropolitan Museum in New York: the dining room designed by Robert Adam in 1761 for John Stuart, 3rd Earl of Bute, when he was prime minister of England.[79] The carefully stacked batteries, five eras of trucks stuffed with vintage chair and machine parts, generations of outboard engines, a blue plastic tarp door and the barge tool-wall were all as much elements of the Mould Room as an Adam chair, nude statues and Boussan rug were of the other. I snapped photos of nets, a boat with its motor in a barrel, a tractor, elk prints, wolf scat and another spun bouquet of wiggling grubs stuck like a wrapped flower arrangement in a tree, objects and processes of our time displayed against a background of implacable stony grandeur. I was as alive with inspiration as August designing his propeller, and as mad as Jack dreaming of gold.

East, up the old logging road, the cabin seen from the river was composing down, burdened with moss and alder leaves. Written on the entrance wall was "Slumach/Jackson Mines Ltd.," the name of Mould's company. Underneath were listed the gold-survey periods from 1952 to 1993. The floor of the inner room, containing the painting of dated gravestones below a spiral mountain, with men wildly digging in a graveyard by lamplight—a projection and perhaps map of Jack's gold dream—was collapsing.

Period room image, 2014.

Judith Williams photo

Left: Detail of cabin wall painting, Southgate River, 2011.

Mike Moore photo

Right: Jack Mould's gold survey timeline, 2014.

Judith Williams photo

Across the inlet, in an open cove of Bear Bay, I saw a tidal shuffling of black/brown branches and twigs loosely distributed across a lemon-lime aquatic plain. Bewitched, I slalomed north through the random debris at full speed, making sharp turns like an exuberant skier to avoid the dark wood. As the prop cut through the sea, some refraction of light caused my wild wake to crest as translucent lemon sorbet. It was my fancy that Bute wax, which once in extreme weather rolled around here as 16-inch wax balls, had returned as dessert.

Once before, heading south in a similar afternoon light, something, perhaps those waxy marine lipids, suspended as they must be somewhere, caught that brightness and reflected it back as a curiously citrus surface. Captivated by the tone, I'd scented the Bute wax trail for a moment. Here it was again.

Len Parker's poem asked what August sought within the mountains. I think August found and engaged with wonders like my lemon-lime plain, places of mind where his wildness, like mine, could live.

The tide had fallen. Back at the Homathko's mouth, getting Chuck's Southgate alignment wrong, I grounded us in eight inches of water. Bobo stepped off the stern and with hefty lifts and pushes shifted the boat into deeper water. As he got back in the boat, one of his Crocs stuck in the muck. It popped up and bobbed along after us as the river flushed us back out to the harbour. Giggling a bit hysterically, I boated it with the fishnet. Bobo correctly lined up Potato Point and we motored upriver, alarmingly close to the north shore's beached trees. He docked well despite the day's sensory overload. I went to the trailer and fell into a lemon-lime reverie.

The Cumsack Range, Homathko Valley.
Judith Williams photo

At dinner a lone cowbird followed Bobo up the stairs into the cookhouse and then ate cake sitting on Wayne's plate. It pecked my arm in a confident way and sat on the back of my chair like a long-time pal. Have they learned to hang out with the Southgate elk in lieu of cattle?

Too exhilarated to sleep, I lay in bed letting the creek's rush sort through swallows' nests, motors, netting, Spanish galleons and August's photos of the Moulds with dead things for the period room in my head. If I added August's 1926 photo of Charlie in front of this cabin to the survey dates I found there, I had the Mould room's timeline.

Charlie Mould, 21, with string of marten, 1926.[80]
August Schnarr photo

August 15. Thick fog on the morning river.

The moment Chuck undid our boat lines, the current hurried us down a blurred waterway and out toward great sunlit cloud strands over the Southgate. The silence was enormous. At Bear Bay we slipped deeper into nothing. Bobo kept his eye on the compass, and I eventually sighted the ghost of a shore, certain we should be at Purcell Point, but an impossible left opening appeared.

"South?" I asked.

"Yes," he said, "yes!"

We'd curved left, then right, and had to be at the west shore, outside Mellerish Point.

Pictograph panel, Orford Bay, 2011.
Judith Williams photo

Down inlet, at Orford Bay, the fog evaporated. I remembered Pearl saying she'd seen "hieroglyphics" way up on the bluff next to the river mouth. Stopping to look for what she'd seen, what the Homalco inhabitants of Pi7pknech had seen and painted, we entered a deeper inlet past. Orford Bay is the only Bute Inlet site manifesting a combined ancient and contemporary Homalco presence. On the south side, a dock and road led to their Bears of Bute Lodge. At the river mouth on the north side was a tall cliff. Parallel red ochre lines 7.6 metres (25 feet) above high-tide mark formed themselves into a serpentine something that I very much wanted to call a creature. Behind a limbed fir tree to its left was painted an extended lipstick-red zigzag.

Projecting image recognition from our contemporary world onto traditional Indigenous images can lead one so far astray that the original intent is lost. I knew I needed to curb what I thought I saw in order to experience what the painter intended. However, if these red marks depicted something serpentine, could it be a Homalco variation of Sisiutl, the two-headed serpent found in Kwakwaka'wakw iconography, or a completely different concept? I knew a wooden Coast Salish memorial box from the Musqueam People of the Fraser River is supported by a spiritually powerful, two-headed serpent they call Sillhqey (S?i:lqey).

The gaze of the Kwakwaka'wakw Sisiutl (one of their highest-ranking crests) was said to petrify the observer. Conversely, a piece of its skin could confer riches and power, or its blood could strengthen warriors. Were these red marks that contradictory something with a long-tongued mouth at the right end and a horned head—or was that a flippered tail or legs or flukes?—at the other? Which was the head?

In the 120-year-old dance hall at Gwai Yi in Kingcome Inlet, a Sisiutl is carved as the main beam. It has a face in the middle and long-tongued mouths at each end. The house itself illustrates the story of a Sisiutl in the river instructing a man how to build the first Gukwdzi or Big House. Villagers told me that snaky creature then climbed out and draped itself between the uprights to become the still-existing beam—thereby creating the time- and mind-bending Möbius strip of narrative I have come to accept in First Nations stories.[81]

But what was I actually looking at here? There are four separate images at Orford. On the left is the horizontal red zigzag with one horned head on the right and a flipped tail. The three-

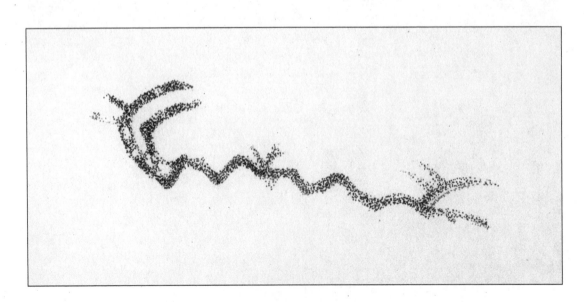

Zigzag "serpent,"
Orford Bay, 2014.
Judith Williams
illustration

foot-by-six-foot double-outlined serpent to its right could have just one head at the left and a tail where I saw a head and tongue. Was that a "blow hole" in the middle of each serpent's back, suggesting whale-like creatures? The middle of the central Orford image was obscured by a branch, but assuming it was a whole creature, was it something seen, imagined, hallucinated or culturally cultivated? Despite seeming a serpentine representation, was it so symbolic I might never guess its meaning?

Could these images be cousins to a Klahoose pictograph of a serpent ridden by a man, his arms outstretched, gleeful at his daring prowess, in Homfray Channel? During my 1986 visit to the channel that winds around the back of East Redonda to Toba Inlet, Sliammon Chief Roy Francis stood on the ledge with one arm identically outstretched as Klahoose Chief Danny Louie said, "My dad used to tell a story of the sea serpent of Homfray Channel." That painted serpent, floating above a wild-haired figure and men spearing a seal from a canoe, makes use of a stone bulge for a big head with a natural indentation painted red for an eye. This splendid gallery poses more than just the questions about content, date and technique. Why do we make

Homfray Channel pictograph gallery, East Redonda Island, 1986. Helen Hanson (most likely), left; Roy Francis, centre; Danny Louie, right. *Judith Williams photo*

images and what are we doing in that act and to what degree does exposure to drawn, painted or filmed representations affect how we perceive the world? For Danny, the picto verified his father's ancient story that stood as proof of his belonging to this territory.

At Orford, below and to the right of the upper images, almost lost behind a small maple, a humanoid holds what might be a small snaky thing. Could this be the serpent-visioning protagonist, the commissioner of the images or the painter? Was the pictograph made to mark the holder of spiritual power derived from something serpentine? Does being present with the images in itself mean contact with the power of the depicted? I tried to enter the mindset of this image-maker, as I want to enter the mindset of August Schnarr when he reduced Charlie to the most transitory significance against Giant Rock, or whoever captured the shared potent glances of the teenage Marion with the cougar Leo.

Below the Orford zigzag is a shallow cave with a small hearth containing calcinated and

Above: Orford River pictograph of humanoid, adapted from photo and Archaeology Site Report #EdSf-1 1967. *Judith Williams illustration*

Right: Cave at Orford River pictograph site. *Cathy Campbell photo*

burnt mammal bones, burnt wood, mussel shells, basketry fragments and a small concentration of red ochre, the pigment used to paint most pictographs worldwide, and locally procurable up Galleon Creek. An inscrutable petroglyph is pecked into a boulder directly outside the shelter.

Naturally occurring red ochre (anhydrous iron oxide) was sometimes burned in the form of limonite to intensify its colour. Some say it was mixed with fat or blood or a salmon egg binder. Recently it has been claimed women chewed the eggs to emulsify them before they were mixed with pigment. It's possible to make excellent egg tempera this way. A palette ledge near the Homfray pictograph complex was used for grinding and mixing paint onsite, and although I sent a sample from it to Conservation Canada, no binding agent could be found. Since it is already oxidized, iron oxide does not fade if it is fixed by the natural mineral runoff that inhibits dark lichen growth and keeps the stone surface whitish. However, it can be buried by the mineral runoff, rock shards can spall off or, if unfixed, exposed pigment can run to blushing mush. Access to the Orford ledges is difficult except from above, but there is the slenderest toehold, and the rocks provide sufficient overhang to allow for the mineral runoff to fix pigment. The central pictograph may have been painted by someone supported from above. Experts have been at work.[82]

When August took the girls to view this rich site, calling them hieroglyphics emphasized the exotic un-readability of the iconography of people whose territory the incomers claimed, but it also suggests there was something that could be read by the target audience that reflected their ideas about their environment and existence within it. Klahoose elder Ken Hanuse told me, "Our name for a single-headed serpent is 'yexa gija.' It had the head of a horse and a basket-like tail. Elder Lill Hill saw one that moved faster than a boat. I heard a 10-foot serpent was seen up in Bute by a Homalco man." The related Tla'amin People refer to Savary Island as a double-headed serpent called Ayhus.

Asked about the Orford picto complex, Homalco Chief Darren Blaney said, "The first Xwe'malhkwu man's name was Gee–thlmatun ('runs to him'). Because he couldn't say no to people who came to him, he was a respected leader.

"During his vision quests he went up to the high lakes in our territory. Like other seekers he would bathe, cut his legs and sweep his body with hemlock or cedar boughs as much as three times a day for up to seven years to get a spirit guide. Marianne Harry's grandfather went way up the Homathko to Tatlayoko Lake on such a vision quest. Some men training to hunt alpine goats learned from bears to eat hellebore to empty themselves and gain strength.

"During a vision quest a series of different guides would come. First might be a grouse, then a bear, or a salmon, which would bring fishing power, but they could go on up to the two-headed serpent, a teaching about leadership ability and making the right choice. The highest vision was the North Star. That was the medicine man.

"In his vision season, Gee–thlmatun, the eldest of the Dog Children, saw a two-headed serpent that showed him its powers. In a dancing power its two heads could be cut off, but it kept dancing until they touched and the body was healed. Way beyond the metaphysical, this power could bring physical results."

Darren feels the Orford pictos have something to do with a serpent vision, but such information was kept secret after contact, especially from the Catholic Church and Indian agents.[83]

People often ask if these pictographs are old. Without datable organic material the answer is that for the most part we do not know. A more trackable question might be, where do iconic Northwest Coast serpent forms come from? The Courtenay Museum on Vancouver Island holds the 6-metre (20-foot) fossil skeleton of an Elasmosaur, a local aquatic creature from the Late Cretaceous period. Indigenous people seeing such fossils might wonder if a sea serpent still haunted nearby waters when a similarly configured log streamed by on an outflow. The local wolf eel does resemble the bulging-headed Homfray pictograph. An impressive 2 to 2.5 metres (7 to 8 feet) long, and oddly curious, eels can be fed by divers, although they are capable of inflicting serious bites. Some Southern Salish Makah People caught wolf eels they called "Dr. Fish" at low tide in the summer months. The sweet/savoury flesh was eaten only by medicine men wishing to enhance their abilities.

In the Pacific Northwest the washed-up, stripped carcasses of the once-common basking shark, all head and 9-metre (30-foot) spine, have occasionally been reported as sea serpent remains. Ancient carvings of sea wolves on Quadra Island, at Petroglyph Park on Vancouver

Orford River humanoid pictograph.
Judith Williams photo

Island below Nanaimo, and far away in Prince Rupert notate the persistence of sea oddity images coastwide. Is the Sisiutl, Sillhqey or sea wolf, like ongoing imaging of dragons, based on the real crossed with the desired or feared or the extinct? What does it mean to reproduce such images through time? To what degree do we see what we are culturally taught to see, and how does that picturing affect how one is in the world?

The wonderful Orford rock art complex pictures a local Indigenous concept, event or belief. August and the girls depicted what was important in their life in film and words. It's popularly said that the first drawing was made by a girl tracing the shadow of her suitor on a wall to capture some essence of the departing lover. Photographing the beloved Leo as a semi-animate pelt after his death attempts to collapse time, but also endlessly repeats loss. To photograph Pearl hugging Girlie captures the cougar's unique relationship with the girls, and being photographed in such an unbelievable affectionate embrace with a wild creature defines the girls' uniqueness for us. Only later did Marion construct *Cougar Companions* to fix positive memories of that period for them. Like the pictographs, the Schnarr images become a theatre of their period in which a person or creature acts out the scene of the image in the memory of those depicted or depicting, and for us.

The existent or nonexistent source of creatures portrayed in rock art opens the door on a curious absence. Considering the extensive representation of most coastal creatures in First Nations rock art, masks, poles and story, and the painted serpentine creatures in Toba and Bute, the dearth of clearly identifiable cougar imagery in Northwest Coast Indigenous art is fascinating. The largest and most aggressive population of cougars in the world was said to live on Vancouver Island until the government bounty program from the 1920s to the '50s, and they are still wonderfully on the prowl throughout the BC coast and into the Interior. Certainly August had little trouble finding them. Johnny Schnarr claimed that in their forays between Knight and Bute in 1910–12 they shot forty.

Gitxsan cougar image, Kitwanga, 1905.
"The Totem Poles and Monuments of Gitwangak Village," George F. MacDonald

Most animals found in coastal BC territory are included in the Dance of the Animals given by certain Kwakwaka'wakw and Oweekino families to indicate the source and validation of family crests. Almost every creature except a cougar is called out by a Wolf or Grouse speaker to dance. Stories or recognizable representations of cougars from those or any other coastal group are almost nonexistent, and they are not normally considered a crest animal.

There are two Gitxsan exceptions. A 1910 photograph taken at Kitwanga in the BC Interior shows a wooden box surmounted by a cougar that wandered north and killed people in Skeena. The cougar was killed and taken by a Kitwanga clan as a crest. A Gitxsan pole shows a cougar at its top, surmounting a wolf.

Negotiating fog, rain and an invisible shoreline while boating southward from Orford Bay had a dampening effect on my fanciful speculation about the meanings of images. We needed to find real landmarks. I drove a compass course north–south to Lewis Channel along what had to be the west side of Raza Island, although it seemed to go on and on.

Suddenly Bobo said, "That's Redonda," and insisted I turn to port.

But wasn't that a house I knew to be *in* Redonda *Bay*? I turned away, west along the shore, found the small island at Redonda Bay's west mouth and rounded the north tip of West Redonda Island to the Redonda light at the top of Lewis Channel. When a faint shadow of Bullock Bluff, across the channel at the north end of Cortes Island, appeared, I scooted over from West Redonda to the Cortes shore and followed it along south, home to Squirrel Cove dock.

August 18. On the water again, at Channel Island off the mouth of Toba Inlet, we saw an enormous floating whale. What looked to be a small flesh-coloured log lay alongside it. Periodically the whale blew and rolled its massive, slightly ridged back forward in the sea to reveal a small sickle-shaped fin but never its tail. Suddenly, out from within the creature whooshed a red material containing bobbing, square, doughnut-shaped white forms.

Still and monstrous in size, the creature, when I reported it to the Wild Ocean Whale Society, answered to all the characteristics of a fin whale, the second-largest creature in the world. Fin and humpback whales, which once inhabited the Salish Sea, were wiped out in a handful of years by whalers from Blubber Bay on Texada Island and Whaletown on Cortes. Fin whales are reported to feed on the oily copepods scientists say bloom so abundantly in Bute, and a vet suggested the "doughnuts" might be undigested fat. The Orford "serpents" may derive from something passing that was as real and as surprising as Pearl hugging Girlie.

WHAT CAN YOU SEE IN A PHOTOGRAPH?

A handsome Mrs. Williams holds the head of a cougar propped up on the lopped-off end of a boomstick. August holds its tail.

The tide is out and the cougar is very dead. You can't see that Mrs. Williams was a follower of numerology and changed her name frequently. I mourn the cougar as Mrs. Williams and August do not. The photo dates from somewhere between the late 1930s and early 1940s. Where are they?

In 1973, Loughborough upcoasters Dane Campbell and Helen Piddington met August in his dusky Heriot Bay floathouse, like that propped up on pilings behind him in the photo. In his shed he showed them a rotary engine from a brand-new Mazda he was installing in his longboat. He calculated its unique configuration would provide superior power to drive the airboat propeller. August was friendly, Dane said, but cantankerous about game laws and the government. "He never mentioned his family, told stories about his days trapping up at the end of Bute and tried to sell me his old boom chains for an exorbitant $40 each." The Mazda sat unused for years.

"I went to that Heriot Bay shed once," August's great-granddaughter Kenna Fair told me. "Oh! It was full of tools and a boat he was building and never finished. There were cougar, wolf and bearskins all over, a great mass of things lost in what to me was a huge space. I don't remember the propellers. It was dark in there and I was very young. I wanted to make a film about them all, but by the time I talked to my grandmother Pansy she had Alzheimer's, and Great-Aunt Marion would not let me visit."[84]

My lined-out "Patience" suits of photographs and papers—the girls and their friends, a pleading letter, a live or a dead cougar—have come to resemble the elements of a Schnarr floathouse that disassemble and shift, become a film flickering through an ancient projector in a dim old community hall. The beam of light expanding from aperture to screen, filled with the grains of dust you seldom see, and the crackle of brittle sprocket holes breaking in old machinery fracture simple chronology or narrative, promote invention. As girls cajole cougars

Opposite: Mrs. Williams, August Schnarr and cougar.
August Schnarr negatives. Image MCR 8493 courtesy of the Museum at Campbell River

Marion and Leo, c. 1937.
Schnarr family photo, Cougar Companions album. Image MCR 2006-8 courtesy of the Museum at Campbell River

across snow to face the professional cameraman, Biddie Belton cringes, afraid, and I invent her visit. I find a picture of Daisy Walker and her child, years after she lived in Bute, and concoct for her a diary of the 1895 Chilko Lake trip, when the excruciatingly doomed horses were brought down the grease trail.

Time's current clusters and re-sorts meaning for me as my wonky taxonomy clanks through the light. Photographs can be analyzed by structuralist, social or psychological theories that can illuminate or obscure the people and eras depicted, but the edges of any such analysis I might have entertained have become ragged as they intersect with the memories of still-living subjects telling their versions of events and my own reading of and projection into the images.

I study the potent image of Marion, who will not now speak, and Leo, who could not. It actualizes what can never again be. Did two creatures from different species ever share such a direct and accessing glance at the same camera, at us? Close your eyes. Do you remember the chain or a glance? Do you think about a cocked elbow? What scenario do you create?

A girl raises one arm over her head and lies back against the settee: Marion in socks and slippers. Pansy stands bent over a table. She stops writing the diary four days after Marion's birthday, September 3, 1939. Leo had died. Tomorrow and tomorrow and tomorrow logs need to be boomed, traps checked, dinner cooked; the pig slaughtered, butchered, salted, canned; potatoes planted, hilled, dug, stored and fed to new pigs to slaughter. The work was endless. Marion only lounges in my head. How desperate were the girls?

Len comes to call. His ailing wife needs help. He can pay. Marion agrees. "We are just ordinary working people," she later wrote. At Bear Bay, under the stuffed sea lion head, the stove glows cherry red. Marion drops down in a chair. Mrs. Parker is dying. Did Len stand in the doorway and read from his poem "Marion Mountain Murmurs"? "I have mothered, fed and sheltered/ All of life that came to me."

I look at this photo of Marion and Leo in the late 1930s, at a faded Xerox of Len's face. How lonely did it get? Something happened. How old was he, how innocent she? Pansy said that when August was away, boys came to visit. I think about Gunner's box of chocolates. "Those old guys up there," Pearl said, "they took advantage of us."

When handsome young Lloyd Fair stopped in at the Schnarr floathouse from trapping up the Southgate in the late 1930s, he and Pansy looked at each other hopefully. At the end of her life she said, "I didn't know what it was to be a wife."

Sometimes I think that . . . I see Pearl taking money from a can up on a shelf, getting on the steamer alone. "Married a military man," she said. Then her Albert drowned. She married John Macklin, lived uphill from her father and had sons and a daughter, worked at the Wal Can fish cannery in Quathiaski Cove as long as they let her. When August died he cut Marion out of his will, but Pearl gave her half of what she received. Marion and Robert Tyrrell published *Rumrunner* in 1988, dedicated to "Alma Van der Est a second mother and a friend," who taught Marion to write and fed and supported her during her early years. When I asked Marion about her *Cougar Companions* albums she said, "I'm too old, I can't remember much, I don't want to go back."

A photo can frame just a section of a face or event, corrupt memory and skew meaning. Marion, in creating each slightly different album, organized recollection so the harshness of their lives is replaced by a vision of a life with a mother and the cougars, before August moved

Owen Bay school, Sonora Island, BC, 1935. Back row: Art Van der Est, Pearl Schnarr, Miss Sweetum (teacher), Marion Schnarr, John Van der Est. Front row: Len, Bill and Jim Van der Est.
Van der Est collection

them back to Bute, life split apart and three girls found the road to womanhood rocky. Was this how she let go?

In assembling the archival dossiers and laying images out in suits, I remade their past infused with my own formative engagement with this coast. Pansy's record of their house move is informed by my documentation of Ken MacPherson moving the last floathouse at Refuge Cove in 1988. I mine my childhood memories of Texada Island to construct a time when August smiled, before Zaida died. Here comes baby me crawling across a Blubber Bay lawn toward a cat, a "memory" that really only exists for me as a photo in my mother's family album.

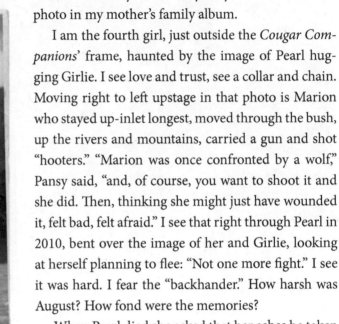

I am the fourth girl, just outside the *Cougar Companions'* frame, haunted by the image of Pearl hugging Girlie. I see love and trust, see a collar and chain. Moving right to left upstage in that photo is Marion who stayed up-inlet longest, moved through the bush, up the rivers and mountains, carried a gun and shot "hooters." "Marion was once confronted by a wolf," Pansy said, "and, of course, you want to shoot it and she did. Then, thinking she might just have wounded it, felt bad, felt afraid." I see that right through Pearl in 2010, bent over the image of her and Girlie, looking at herself planning to flee: "Not one more fight." I see it was hard. I fear the "backhander." How harsh was August? How fond were the memories?

When Pearl died she asked that her ashes be taken back to the site of their Owen Bay cabin. She told Glen that attending the school there, full of other children taught by Alma Van der Est, was the happiest time of her life. At first *Cougar Companions* made me think Leo and Girlie, devoted only to the girls, provided the psychological glue making other aspects of their hard life tolerable after Zaida died. But in Pansy's *Early Days* album I found a happy photo of the girls and their friend Frankie laughing, holding the octopus at

August Schnarr died in 1981 at ninety-five.
Maud Emery collection

Owen Bay. I see cheeky Van der Est boys laughing at Owen Bay school.

I have used the photographs in Marion's theatre of memory to construct and stage, on a magnificent and demanding set, a broader "Cougar Companions." It is a performance of astoundingly rich lives by remarkably strong individuals.

"WE TOOK HIS ASHES UP THERE, WE FIGURED HE WOULD LIKE THAT: HE WAS AN UNRELIGIOUS MAN."

—PANSY SCHNARR FAIR EDDINGTON

Endnotes

1 British Columbia, Ministry of Forests, Lands and Natural Resource Operations publication. From the collection of the University of British Columbia Library Rare Books and Special Collections, Vancouver, Canada.

2 August Schnarr tapes, interview by Joan Skogan and Jan Havelaar, February 15, 1977, #A028 1-3, Campbell River Museum. All of August's comments are from this interview unless otherwise indicated.

3 Judith Williams, *High Slack: Waddington's Gold Road and the Bute Inlet Massacre of 1864* (Vancouver: New Star Books, 1995).

4 These notebooks are now in the Campbell River Museum.

5 This would seem to be the cabin shown as Gus Schnarr's Bakery in photo at the top of page 49.

6 Maud Emery, "Never Believe Them When They Say 'It Can't Be Done,'" *Daily Colonist*, October 2, 1960.

7 Marion Parker and Robert Tyrrell, *Rumrunner: The Life and Times of Johnny Schnarr* (Victoria: Orca Books, 1988).

8 Emery, "Never Believe Them."

9 The term "fonds" originated in French archival practice. In Canada it has officially replaced the misleading term "collection," now only used for document aggregations assembled, but not created, by a collector.

10 Although this photo is in Pearl's *Cougar Companions* album, in the BC Archives and in the "Water Power Investigations" report, the original negative must be missing from the Museum at Campbell River Klinaklini Glacier set.

11 Imbert Orchard interview with Dennis Walker, 1965 (BC Archives); personal communication with Vern Logan, Dennis's grandson.

12 See Dorothy Kennedy and Randy Bouchard, *Sliammon Life, Sliammon Lands* (Vancouver: Talonbooks, 1983).

13 Information from Rankin's wife, Susan, and great-niece Anne Dewar.

14 From a story by Andy Ellingson. Private communication.

15 See Beth Hill, *Upcoast Summers* (Victoria: Horsdal & Schubart, 1985), for Barrow's photos.

16 M.Y. Williams, "Bute Inlet Wax," in *Transactions of the Royal Society of Canada*, vol. 51, series 3 (1957).

17 Kennedy and Bouchard, *Sliammon Life, Sliammon Lands*.

18 The full story is "Raven and the Wind-Maker," told by Homalco elder Noel George Harry, c. 1970s, in Kennedy and Bouchard, *Sliammon Life, Sliammon Lands*.

19 British Columbia, Ministry of Forests, Lands and Natural Resource Operations publication. From the collection of the University of British Columbia Library Rare Books and Special Collections, Vancouver, Canada.

20 Personal communication with John B.H. Edmond.

21 British Columbia, Ministry of Forests, Lands and Natural Resource Operations publication. From the collection of the University of British Columbia Library Rare Books and Special Collections, Vancouver, Canada.

22 British Columbia, Ministry of Forests, Lands and Natural Resource Operations publication. From the collection of the University of British Columbia Library Rare Books and Special Collections, Vancouver, Canada.

23 Don Munday, *The Unknown Mountain* (London: Hodder and Stoughton, 1948). After a number of tries by the Mundays, Fritz Wiessner and William House topped the mountain in 1936.

24 Quoted in Kathryn Bridge, *A Passion for Mountains: The Lives of Don and Phyllis Munday* (Victoria: Rocky Mountain Books, 2006).

25 From Jay Sherwood, ed., *Surveying Central British Columbia: A Photo Journal of Frank Swannell, 1920–28* (Victoria: Royal BC Museum, 2007).

26 Quoted in a 1978 letter by Dorothy McAuley in the Cortes Island Museum and Archives. Dorothy McAuley, a friend of Rasmussen's, was raised on Twin Islands.

27 See Williams, *High Slack*, 79.

28 British Columbia, Ministry of Forests, Lands and Natural Resource Operations publication. From the collection of the University of British Columbia Library Rare Books and Special Collections, Vancouver, Canada.

29 Munday, *The Unknown Mountain*.

30 A small, energetic, agile and fierce critter living in northern deciduous forests, the pine marten (genus *Martes* within the *Mustelinae* sub-family of *Mustelidae*) has a silky brownish pelt with a large bushy tail, and paws with partially retractable claws. Omnivorous relatives of wolverines, mink, ferrets and weasels, they eat squirrels, mice, birds, fish, insects, eggs and occasionally nuts and berries. The 2013 pelt price was $46 to $80.

31 A version of Charlie's diary was made for the *Naming and Claiming: The Creation of Bute Inlet* exhibition, with Sylvia Ives's permission.

32 Charles Blondin, born Jean François Gravelet, was famous for walking a tightrope across Niagara Falls in 1859.

33 Story told to me by Darren Blaney, Homalco Chief.

34 Ulloa, named after the Battle of Ulloa by the Spanish, became known as Twin Islands after the Andrewses' launch *Twin Isles*.

35 Bill Thompson, *Once Upon a Stump* (Powell River: Powell River Heritage Research Association, 1993).

36 Adrian Kershaw and John Spittle, *The Bute Inlet Route: Alfred Waddington's Wagon Road, 1862–1864* (Kelowna: Okanagan College, 1978).

37 Information from a letter Len Parker wrote to Adrian Redford in Lund in 1983 when he and Laurette were living in Victoria.

38 Maud Emery, "Pouncing Pets," *Daily Colonist*, October 23, 1964; Pansy Schnarr tapes, Aural interview # A22, 1-2, Campbell River Museum.

39 From *Cougar Companions*.

40 Pansy Schnarr Eddington tapes, Campbell River Museum.

41 Pansy Schnarr Eddington tapes, Campbell River Museum.

42 "Looking Back," *Musings*, Vol. 2 (July 1991), CRMA.

43 "Looking Back," *Musings*, Vol. 2 (July 1991), CRMA.

44 Emery, "Pouncing Pets."

45 Publisher's description of Susan Howe, *Spontaneous Particulars: The Telepathy of Archives* (New York: New Directions, 2014).

46 Pansy Schnarr Eddington tapes, Campbell River Museum.

47 I have reluctantly edited Pansy's diary (CRMA) but have hopefully left her voice intact.

48 Len Parker "Resume," included with Laurette Parker's letter to the Margrave von Baden and family, September 14, 1987, after Len's death.

49 From Elizabeth Hawkins, *Jack Mould and the Curse of Gold* (Surrey, BC: Hancock House, 1993)

50 Judith Williams, *Dynamite Stories* (Vancouver: New Star Books, 2003).

51 British Columbia, Ministry of Forests, Lands and Natural Resource Operations publication. From the collection of the University of British Columbia Library Rare Books and Special Collections, Vancouver, Canada.

52 Judith Williams, *Clam Gardens: Aboriginal Mariculture on Canada's West Coast* (Vancouver: New Star Books, 2006).

53 From *A Spanish Voyage to Vancouver and the Northwest Coast of America*, trans. Cecil Jane (London: Argonaut, 1930).

54 Whymper's drawings, engraved for his *Illustrated London News* story about the 1864 Homathko events, were later published in *Travels and Adventures in the Territory of Alaska* (London: J. Murray, 1868).

55 See Williams, *High Slack*.

56 Klatsassine, the name of the war chief who allegedly led the attack on the Waddington road crew, can be translated as "nobody knows his name." See Williams, *High Slack*, and Stan Douglas's film *Klatsassin* (2006).

57 There were routes up from Bear River to the Apple River Valley in Loughborough Inlet, and from Bute up the Orford toward the Tuhumming River in Toba.

58 British Columbia, Ministry of Forests, Lands and Natural Resource Operations publication. From the collection of the University of British Columbia Library Rare Books and Special Collections, Vancouver, Canada.

59 British Columbia, Ministry of Forests, Lands and Natural Resource Operations publication. From the collection of the University of British Columbia Library Rare Books and Special Collections, Vancouver, Canada.

60 Parker and Tyrrell, *Rumrunner*.

61 Heather Kellerhals, personal communication.

62 BC Parks Division: Cariboo District, *Tŝ'il?os Provincial Park Master Plan* (Victoria: BC Parks, 1997), 13.

63 Eulachon oil is known for its relatively high docosahexaenoic acid (DHA) content, with a remarkable 1,500 per cent increase after ripening and rendering. DHA repairs and builds material for brain nerve synapses and is involved with replacing the sticky surface of blood cells with a slippery coating to reduce the tendency of the cells to clog the arterial system.

64 Nigel Haggan and Associates, "The Case for Including the Cultural and Spiritual Value of Eulachon in Policy and Decision-Making" (report prepared for Fisheries and Oceans Canada, 2010).

65 Homer G. Barnett, *The Coast Salish of British Columbia* (Portland: University of Oregon Press, 1955).

66 Randy Bouchard and Dorothy Kennedy, private communication.

67 See Richard F. Lee, "Lipids of Zooplankton from Bute Inlet, British Columbia," *Journal of the Fisheries Research Board of Canada*, 31 (2011): 1577–1582. doi 10.1139/f74-198 (www.researchgate.net/publication/237179637).

68 T.C. Jain and T.J. Striha, "Studies Related to Bute Wax: The Identity of Norphytane, Pristane and Bute Hydrocarbon," *Canadian Journal of Chemistry* 47, no. 23 (1969): 4359–4361. Although there has been little recent Canadian study of Bute wax, there are marine oil investigations in Finland. Also see R.F. Lee, W. Hagen, and G. Kattner, "Lipid Storage in Marine Zooplankton," *Marine Ecology Progress Series* 307 (2006): 273–306.

69 Williams, *High Slack*.

70 Richard F. Lee and J.C. Nevenzel, "Wax Esters in the Marine Environment: Origin and Composition of the Wax from Bute Inlet, British Columbia," *Journal of the Fisheries Research Board of Canada*, 36 (1979): 1519–1523.

71 Their optimism is heartening, but the Homalco salmon hatchery at Orford Bay was damaged when the BC Forests Ministry allowed logging directly above a creek feeding into its new fish tanks.

72 From "The Slide," Arne Liseth, Friends of Bute Inlet website, buteinlet.net.

73 Material about the court case in the Schnarr fonds, Campbell River Museum.

74 Quoted in Kennedy and Bouchard, *Sliammon Life, Sliammon Lands*.

75 See *The Man Who Can Fly* (produced by Reel Water Productions for *National Geographic* Channel, 2011), shot in Bute Inlet. Potter died in May 2015.

76 I sent the GPS location to Doris Lundy at the BC Archaeology office for inclusion in their files. Doris sent back its Bordon number, EdSf-3, which now identifies the site.

77 Private communication from Randy Bouchard.

78 P.B. McCall and D.E. Hay, "Distribution of Spawning Eulachon Stocks in the Central Coast of British Columbia as Indicated by Larval Surveys," Department of Fisheries and Oceans Canada, Canadian Stock Assessment Secretariat Document 99/177 (1999), www.dfo-mpo.gc.ca/Library/242316.pdf.

79 Stuart's house in Berkeley Square was later bought by W. Petty Fitzmaurice, 1st Marquess of Lansdowne.

80 From Hawkins, *Jack Mould and the Curse of Gold*, Hancock.

81 Judith Williams, *Two Wolves at the Dawn of Time: Kingcome Inlet Pictographs, 1893–1998* (Vancouver: New Star Books, 2001).

82 Judith Williams, *Two Wolves at the Dawn of Time: Kingcome Inlet Pictographs, 1893–1998* (Vancouver: New Star Books, 2001).

83 Information from Jeanette Taylor interview, 2008, and from private 2018 communication with Darren Blaney, who cites Homalco elder Ambrose Wilson as his source.

84 Although the man in the photograph is identified as "Schnarr," there is a slight possibility it is August's neighbour Dougie Dowler, the owner of the Heriot Bay store.

INDEX